# One [
## Little-know[n
## from World War II
### True Stories of the Greatest Generation
### Alan Best

**One Minute History**

**Little-known and forgotten stories from World War II**

Copyright 2024 (Alan Best)

All rights reserved.

No part of this book may be reproduced, distributed, or transmitted in any form or by any means, including photocopying, recording, or other electronic or mechanical methods, without the prior written permission of the publisher, except in the case of brief quotations embodied in critical reviews and certain other noncommercial uses permitted by copyright law.

For permission requests, email the publisher at AlanBestPublishing@yahoo.com

ISBN:

First Edition

This is a non-fiction work. While every effort has been made to ensure that the information contained in this book is accurate, the author and publisher disclaim any liability in connection with the use of the information.

Cover design: Danielle Allen

To the indomitable spirit of the Greatest Generation, whose unwavering courage and sacrifice forged the path to freedom during the tumultuous years of World War II. This book is dedicated to those who faced unimaginable hardships, stood resolute in the face of adversity, and exemplified the ideals of bravery and resilience. Your legacy endures, reminding us of the profound cost of liberty and the enduring strength of the human spirit.

| | |
|---|---|
| Title page | 1 |
| Disclaimer | 2 |
| Dedication | 3 |
| Contents | 4-8 |
| Quotes | 9 |
| Introduction | 10-11 |
| The Seeds of Conflict: Understanding the Roots of World War II | 12-14 |
| From Aggression to Accountability: The WWII Timeline | 15-16 |
| The Architects of War: Political Leadership | 17-19 |
| Masters of Strategy: The Allied Leadership | 20-24 |
| At the Helm of Conflict: Profiles of Axis Leadership | 25-31 |
| **The European Front: Chronicles of War and Resistance** | **32** |
| Blitzkrieg, the Lightning War | 33-36 |
| Poland under Siege: A Tale of Dual Invasions | 37-40 |
| The Lightning War: Nazi Germany's Western Front | 41-45 |
| Operation Dynamo: The Miracle at Dunkirk | 46-49 |
| The Battle and Fall of France | 50-53 |
| The Battle of Britain: A Battle for Survival | 54-57 |
| Operation Barbarossa: The Invasion that Changed the War | 58-61 |
| Continued Conflict: The Eastern Front and Mediterranean Campaigns | 62-63 |
| D-Day Invasion: The Battle that Changed World War II | 63-66 |
| The Liberation of Paris: A Triumph of Resistance | 67-70 |
| A Bridge Too Far: The Ambitious Failure of Operation Market Garden | 71-74 |
| The Tragic Tale of the Battle of Arnhem | 75-77 |
| The Battle of the Bulge: Hitler's Last Gamble of the Western Front | 78-81 |
| The Battle for Bastogne | 82-84 |
| The Firestorm of Dresden: A City's Destruction and Its Enduring Legacy | 85-87 |
| Rebuilding the Frontlines: Conflicts After Dresden | 88-89 |
| The Fall of Berlin: The Last Stand of the Third Reich | 90=93 |
| V-E Day: The Triumph of Allied Victory and the Dawn of a New Era | 94-97 |
| The Nuremberg Trials: Justice in the Wake of Atrocity | 98-101 |
| **Navigating the Storm: The Battle of the Atlantic** | **102** |
| Shadows Beneath the Waves: U-Boat Campaign Against Britain | 103-107 |
| The Battle of the Atlantic: The Longest Campaign of WWII | 108-112 |
| The Sinking of the Bismarck | 113-116 |
| Arctic Inferno: The Story of Convoy PQ 17 | 117-120 |
| Silent Hunters: The Battle Against U-Boats in the Atlantic | 121-125 |
| Great Losses in the Atlantic Theater | 126-128 |
| **The Mediterranean, Balkans, and Middle East** | **129** |
| Desert Warfare: The Axis in North Africa and Its Impact | 130-135 |
| Battles in North Africa and the Mediterranean | 136-138 |

| | |
|---|---|
| Operation Torch: The Allied Invasion of North Africa | 139-143 |
| Operation Husky: The Invasion of Sicily | 144-148 |
| Operation Avalanche: The Invasion of Italy | 149-151 |
| **The Pacific and Asia** | **152** |
| Japan's Conquests Across the Pacific | 153 |
| Day of Infamy: Japan's Attack on Pearl Harbor | 154-158 |
| Ally Battles with Imperial Japan | 159 |
| The Battles Begin | 160 |
| The Battle of the Coral Sea: Turning the Tide | 161-165 |
| The Battle of Midway: Breaking the Code | 166-169 |
| The Battle of Guadalcanal | 170-174 |
| The Battles Continue | 175-177 |
| The Battle of Leyte Gulf | 178-182 |
| The Battle of Luzon | 183-187 |
| The Battle of Iwo Juma | 188-191 |
| The Battle of Okinawa | 192-196 |
| The Dawn of Atomic Age: Hiroshima and Nagasaki | 197-200 |
| The Japanese Surrender in Tokyo Bay | 201-204 |
| The Japan War Crime Trial | 205-209 |
| **Stories from the Pearl Harbor Attack** | **210** |
| John William Finn | 211-214 |
| Admiral Isaac Kidd | 215-218 |
| George Welch and Kenneth Taylor | 219-222 |
| Doris "Dorie" Miller | 223-226 |
| Ensign Herbert C. Jones | 227-229 |
| Japan's Strategy Behind the Pearl Harbor Attack | 230-234 |
| The Mistakes Japan Made in Attacking Pearl Harbor | 235-238 |
| Hector Bywater and the Great Pacific War | 239-241 |
| The Ghost Plane of Pearl Harbor | 242-244 |
| The Nihan Incident | 245-248 |
| Admiral Joseph Taussig and his Unheeded Advice | 249-251 |
| Hitler's Reaction to the Attack | 252-255 |
| The Pearl Harbor Conspiracy Theories | 256-257 |
| Operation K: The Second Attack on Pearl Harbor | 258-260 |
| Chief Radioman Thomas James Reeves | 261-263 |
| The Deadly Double | 264-266 |
| The Heroism Captain Mervyn Bennion | 267-269 |
| **Stories from D-Day** | **270** |
| The Tragic Prelude to the D-Day Invasion | 271-274 |
| The Crossword Puzzle That Almost Ruined the D-Day Invasion | 275-278 |
| Hitler's Sleep and the D-Day Invasion | 279-281 |
| Erwin Rommel and His Absence on D-Day | 282-285 |
| Silent Wings of D-Day and Beyond | 286-289 |
| General Teddy Roosevelt Jr. | 290-291 |

| | |
|---|---|
| Juan Pujols Garcia and the D-Day Deception | 292-294 |
| US Army Rangers and Pointe du Loc | 295-298 |
| The Mad Piper of D-Day | 299-301 |
| Easy Company | 302-303 |
| The Niland Brothers | 304-309 |
| Operation Fortitude | 310-313 |
| **Military Heroes** | **314** |
| Douglas Bader | 315-318 |
| Nadya Popova and the Night Witches | 319-321 |
| John Basilone- A Marine's Marine | 322-325 |
| The One-Handed Gurkha | 326-328 |
| The Farmer that Became a Legend | 329-332 |
| George Allen Mitchell | 333-336 |
| George Wahlen at Iwo Jima | 337-339 |
| Richard H. Best: Dive Bomber | 340-343 |
| Hollywood Hero and WWII Veteran | 344-345 |
| John F. Kennedy and the PT-109 Incident | 346-348 |
| Major Robert Henry Cain's Heroic Stand | 349-351 |
| The Defiant Hero | 352-355 |
| The Sword and Bagpipes | 356-359 |
| The Remarkable Encounter Between Franz Stigler and Charlie Brown | 360-362 |
| The Flying Tigers | 363-366 |
| Bridge on the River Kwai | 367-370 |
| The Conscientious Objector | 371-373 |
| A Future President's Crash-Landing | 374-376 |
| The Story of Paratrooper Leonard Funk | 377-379 |
| The Dentist That Became a Warrior | 380-382 |
| Soaring Above Prejudice | 383-386 |
| The Japanese Pilot that Bombed Oregon | 387-390 |
| The Kilted Killer | 391-393 |
| The Navigator that Defied Death | 394-396 |
| The Quiet Hero of Iwo Jima | 397-400 |
| The Unkillable Soldier | 401-404 |
| The White Death of the Winter War | 405-407 |
| The Bataan Death March | 408-411 |
| The Angels of Bataan Death | 412-414 |
| Did They Get Off? | 415-416 |
| The Pied Piper of Saipan | 417-418 |
| The Youngest Recipient of the Medal of Honor | 419-420 |
| A German Officer's Courageous Defiance | 421-423 |
| The Great Escape | 424-427 |
| The Heroics of Leo Major | 428-430 |
| Japanese American 442nd Regimental Combat Team | 431-432 |
| The Journey of America's Only Female POW in Europe | 433-436 |

| | |
|---|---|
| Desert Ghosts in Sicily | 437-441 |
| The Heroism of Edward "Butch" O'Hare | 442-444 |
| **Resistance Heroes** | **445** |
| The Formation and Impact of WWII Resistance Groups | 446-448 |
| Sisters From the Dutch Resistance | 449-452 |
| Courage and Resistance in Naples | 453-456 |
| The Girl with Red Hair | 457-460 |
| The Brave Saboteur | 461-463 |
| The Young Heroine of the Soviet Resistance | 464-467 |
| From Resistance Fighter to War Hero | 468-470 |
| Unifier of the French Resistance | 471-472 |
| The Smiling Resistance Fighter | 473-475 |
| The Life and Legacy of Dietrich Bonhoeffer | 476-479 |
| The Courageous Story of the White Rose Group | 480-481 |
| **Holocaust Heroes** | **482** |
| The Forger Who Saved Thousands | 483-486 |
| A Diplomats Courage | 487-489 |
| The Dutch Hero Who Defied the Nazis | 490-491 |
| Saving Hundreds of Jewish Children | 492-495 |
| The British Passport Officer Who Saved Thousands | 496-498 |
| Dancing Ballerina of Auschwitz | 499-501 |
| The Catholic Seminarian Who Saved 3,000 Hungarian Jews | 502-505 |
| The Diplomat Who Saved Thousands of Jewish Lives | 506-508 |
| The Polish Doctors Who Created a Fake Disease | 509-511 |
| The Polish Nurse Who Defied the Nazis | 512-514 |
| Kindertransport and the Lifeline for Jewish Children | 515-519 |
| **Spies** | **520** |
| From Housewife and Mother to Master Spy | 521-523 |
| Homegrown Nazi and Japanese Spies in America | 524-526 |
| How the SOE Derailed the Nazi Nuclear Ambitions | 527-529 |
| The British Man Who Betrayed His Country | 530-531 |
| The German Double Agent Who Betrayed the SOE | 532-535 |
| The Nazi Plan to Infiltrate America with Spies | 536-539 |
| The Story of Double Agents of the Allies and Axis | 540-543 |
| The Betrayal of British MI5 Officer Kim Philby | 544-547 |
| Traitors and Spies within the Vatican | 548-551 |
| **Codebreakers** | **552** |
| Cracking the Enigma Machine and the Nazi Response | 553-556 |
| How British Linguists Fooled the Luftwaffe Pilots | 557-569 |
| Abraham Wald and the Armor Enigma | 560-562 |
| The Navajo Code Talkers | 563-565 |
| The Secret Capture: U-Boat U-110 and the Enigma Prize | 566-569 |
| The Genius Who Broke Enigma | 570-572 |
| Polish Mathematicians and the Enigma Code | 573-576 |

| | |
|---|---|
| The Midway Codebreaker | 577-580 |
| **The Fall of Axis Ambitions** | **581-583** |
| **What If? Alternate Scenarios of World War II** | **584-585** |

Before America entered the war (WWII) I knew we could not win it, but after she entered, I knew we could not lose it.

~Winston Churchill~

I am a soldier. I fight where I am told, and I win where I fight.

~George S. Patton~

Never in the field of human conflict was so much owed by so many to so few.

~Winston Churchill~

World War II, the atomic bomb, the Cold War, made it hard for Americans to continue their optimism.

~Stephen Ambrose~

I would say to the House…I have nothing to offer but blood, toil, tears and sweat…Victory at all costs in spite of all terror, victory however long and hard the road, may be; for without victory, there is no survival.

~Winston Churchill~

December 7, 1941, a date which will live in infamy…no matter how long it may take us to overcome this premeditated invasion, the American people, in their righteous might, will win through to absolute victory.

~President Franklin D. Roosevelt

We shall fight on the beaches. We shall fight on the landing grounds. We shall fight in the fields, and in the streets, we shall never surrender.

~Winston Churchill~

When I was a teenager, I took freedom for granted until I got through the Army and saw what the Nazis had done in Germany. Then I realized that freedom is not automatic, it has a price.

~Ed Tipper~

# Introduction

World War II is one of human history's most significant and transformative events. It reshaped nations, redefined borders, and altered the course of millions of lives. Yet, despite its monumental impact, many stories from this era remain obscured or forgotten, overshadowed by the grand narratives often recounted in textbooks. In this book, *Little Known and Forgotten Stories from World War II*, I seek to illuminate those lesser-known tales, shedding light on the extraordinary experiences of individuals whose contributions and sacrifices have often gone unrecognized.

Tom Brokaw's *The Greatest Generation* introduced the world to a profound appreciation for those who lived through the Great Depression and fought in World War II. Brokaw characterized this generation as one marked by resilience, humility, and an unwavering commitment to duty. These individuals, facing unprecedented challenges, demonstrated a collective strength that helped secure victory and laid the foundation for the modern era. They navigated the complexities of war with a sense of purpose, often placing the needs of others above their own. This generation's legacy is defined not just by their military achievements, but also by their ability to come together in a time of crisis, fostering a spirit of unity and sacrifice.

The Greatest Generation is defined by the values they embodied—selflessness, perseverance, and an enduring belief in the principles of democracy and justice. Their stories, whether of valor on the battlefield or quiet resilience on the home front, resonate with us today, reminding us of the importance of commitment to a cause greater than oneself. As we delve into the lesser-known narratives of World War II, we honor the spirit of this generation by recognizing the myriad ways in which they contributed to the war effort, often in the shadows of more prominent figures.

In my exploration of World War II, I have been deeply moved by my encounters with veterans whose stories have shaped my understanding of this pivotal moment in history. Each meeting has been a window into the past, offering personal insights that textbooks often overlook. These veterans, now in their twilight years, carry with them the weight of their experiences—some harrowing, others heroic, but all profoundly impactful. Their willingness to share these stories, often filled with humor, sorrow, and reflection, has enriched my appreciation for the complexities of war and the resilience of the human spirit.

My passion for history, particularly World War II, has driven me to visit several significant locations that played pivotal roles during the conflict. Standing on the beaches of Okinawa, where fierce battles raged, I felt an overwhelming sense of reverence for the sacrifices made by countless soldiers. In Tokyo, I marveled at the resilience of a city that rebuilt itself from the ashes of destruction. Walking all 62 miles of the trail of the Bataan Death March, I was struck by the sheer brutality endured by those who faced unimaginable adversity yet emerged with stories of courage. Visiting Hiroshima and Nagasaki served as somber reminders of the devastating consequences of war, yet they also highlighted the resilience of humanity in the face of catastrophe. In Singapore, a strategic stronghold during the war, I encountered stories of bravery and betrayal that illustrated the complexities of wartime alliances.

Each location I explored offered a unique perspective on the war, revealing the intricate tapestry of human experiences that often go untold. Through these journeys, I have come to appreciate the depth of history, not merely as a series of events, but as a collection of human narratives filled with emotion, sacrifice, and hope.

As we embark on this journey through the lesser-known stories of World War II, I invite you to join me in honoring the Greatest Generation. Their legacy is not just one of conflict but of the enduring human spirit, shaped by the trials they faced and the triumphs they achieved. By uncovering these forgotten tales, we pay tribute to those who served, ensuring that their sacrifices are remembered and celebrated. The stories within these pages serve as a testament to the resilience of humanity and the enduring power of history to connect us across generations. Through understanding the past, we can better appreciate the present and inspire future generations to uphold the values that define us. Let us remember, reflect, and honor the stories that have shaped our world.

~Alan Best

December 2024

# The Seeds of Conflict: Understanding the Roots of World War II

## Introduction

World War II, which lasted from 1939 to 1945, was one of the most devastating conflicts in human history, resulting in an estimated 60 to 80 million deaths and widespread destruction across Europe and Asia. Understanding the reasons behind this global conflict is crucial for grasping the complexities of international relations and the consequences of political decisions. This story will explore the multifaceted causes of World War II and discuss potential steps that could have been taken to avoid it.

## Background

**The Treaty of Versailles:** The roots of World War II can be traced back to the aftermath of World War I and the Treaty of Versailles signed in 1919. The treaty imposed harsh penalties on Germany, including significant territorial losses, military restrictions, and reparations that crippled its economy. The treaty's punitive nature fostered deep resentment among the German populace, who viewed it as a national humiliation. This sentiment was exploited by Adolf Hitler and the Nazi Party, who promised to overturn the treaty and restore Germany's former glory.

The economic turmoil that followed World War I, particularly the Great Depression of the 1930s, further destabilized Europe. Germany was hit hardest, experiencing hyperinflation and massive unemployment. The economic crisis eroded faith in democratic institutions and led many citizens to support extremist political movements, including the Nazis, who promised economic recovery and national rejuvenation. The global economic downturn also affected other countries, contributing to a climate of instability and desperation that made aggressive foreign policies more appealing.

## The Rise of Totalitarian Regimes

**Adolf Hitler and the Nazi Party:** Adolf Hitler's rise to power in Germany was a direct consequence of the political and economic turmoil of the interwar years. The Nazi Party capitalized on public discontent, promoting a platform of nationalism, militarism, and anti-Semitism. Once in power, Hitler implemented aggressive expansionist policies aimed at acquiring "Lebensraum" (living space) for the German people. His regime's militarization and violation of the Treaty of Versailles set the stage for conflict.

**Fascism in Italy:** In Italy, Benito Mussolini established a fascist regime that sought to restore Italy's imperial past. Mussolini's aggressive foreign policy, including the invasion of Ethiopia in 1935, demonstrated the willingness of totalitarian regimes to use military force to achieve their goals. Italy's alliance with Germany further solidified the Axis powers' ambitions and contributed to the growing tensions in Europe.

**Japanese Militarism:** In Asia, Japan's militaristic government pursued imperial expansion, driven by a desire for resources and regional dominance. The invasion of Manchuria in 1931 and subsequent aggression in China exemplified Japan's ambitions. The Japanese leadership believed that military conquest was essential for securing the nation's future, leading to a series of conflicts that would eventually draw the United States into the war.

## The Failure of International Diplomacy

**League of Nations:** The League of Nations was established after World War I to promote peace and prevent future conflicts. However, it proved ineffective in addressing aggression from totalitarian regimes. The League's inability to respond decisively to Japan's invasion of Manchuria or Italy's aggression in Ethiopia demonstrated its weaknesses. The absence of key powers, such as the United States, further undermined the League's credibility and effectiveness.

**Policy of Appeasement:** In the 1930s, European powers, particularly Britain and France, adopted a policy of appeasement toward Hitler, believing that satisfying his territorial ambitions would prevent another war. This approach culminated in the Munich Agreement of 1938, which allowed Hitler to annex the Sudetenland from Czechoslovakia. The failure to confront Hitler's aggression emboldened him, leading to further territorial expansion and ultimately the invasion of Poland in 1939, which triggered World War II.

## Key Events Leading to War

**The Invasion of Poland:** The immediate cause of World War II was Germany's invasion of Poland on September 1, 1939. This act of aggression prompted Britain and France to declare war on Germany, marking the official beginning of the conflict. The invasion was facilitated by the German-Soviet Non-Aggression Pact, which allowed Hitler to invade Poland without fear of Soviet intervention.

**The Expansion of the Axis Powers:** Following the invasion of Poland, the Axis powers continued their aggressive campaigns. Germany quickly overran much of Western Europe, while Japan expanded its influence in Asia and the Pacific. The failure of the Allies to mount a unified response to these aggressions allowed the Axis powers to gain significant ground early in the war.

## Steps That Could Have Been Taken to Avoid War

**A More Equitable Treaty of Versailles:** One of the most significant factors contributing to World War II was the harshness of the Treaty of Versailles. A more equitable treaty that addressed the legitimate grievances of the German people could have fostered a more stable post-war environment. Instead of imposing punitive reparations, the Allies could have focused on rebuilding Germany's economy and integrating it into the international community.

**Strengthening the League of Nations:** The League of Nations was intended to be a mechanism for resolving international disputes and preventing war. Strengthening the League by ensuring the participation of major powers, including the United States, could have enhanced its effectiveness. Additionally, the League needed the authority to take decisive action against aggressor nations, which would have deterred expansionist policies.

**Early Intervention Against Aggression:** The policy of appeasement allowed Hitler to expand unchecked in the late 1930s. A more assertive stance by Britain and France, including military support for countries threatened by Nazi aggression, could have altered the course of events. For example, a united front against the annexation of Austria or the occupation of Czechoslovakia might have signaled to Hitler that further expansion would not be tolerated.

**Promoting Economic Stability:** Addressing the economic instability that plagued Europe in the interwar years could have mitigated the rise of extremist movements. International cooperation to stabilize economies, promote trade, and provide financial assistance to struggling nations might have reduced the appeal of totalitarian ideologies.

**Fostering International Cooperation:** Encouraging dialogue and cooperation among nations could have helped build trust and reduce tensions. Initiatives aimed at fostering understanding between countries, particularly those with historical grievances, might have created a more conducive environment for peace. Diplomatic efforts to resolve conflicts peacefully, rather than resorting to military solutions, could have prevented the escalation of tensions.

**Conclusion**

The story of why World War II happened is a complex interplay of historical, political, and economic factors. The legacy of World War I, the rise of totalitarian regimes, the failure of international diplomacy, and the aggressive actions of the Axis powers all contributed to the outbreak of the conflict. While it is impossible to predict with certainty what might have prevented the war, a combination of equitable peace treaties, stronger international institutions, early intervention against aggression, and efforts to promote economic stability and cooperation could have altered the course of history.

Understanding these factors is essential not only for comprehending the origins of World War II but also for learning valuable lessons about the importance of diplomacy, cooperation, and the need to address grievances before they escalate into conflict.

# From Aggression to Accountability: The WWII Timeline

**1937**

- **July 7**: The Marco Polo Bridge Incident marks the beginning of the Second Sino-Japanese War as Japan escalates its invasion of China.

**1938**

- **March 12**: Germany annexes Austria (Anschluss).
- **September 30**: The Munich Agreement is signed, allowing Nazi Germany to annex the Sudetenland from Czechoslovakia.

**1939**

- **March 15**: Germany occupies the rest of Czechoslovakia.
- **August 23**: The Molotov-Ribbentrop Pact is signed between Nazi Germany and the Soviet Union, ensuring non-aggression and secret protocols for dividing Eastern Europe.
- **September 1**: Germany invades Poland, marking the official start of World War II in Europe.
- **September 3**: Britain and France declare war on Germany.

**1940**

- **April 9**: Germany invades Denmark and Norway.
- **May 10**: Germany launches its invasion of France, Belgium, the Netherlands, and Luxembourg.
- **June 14**: Paris falls to German forces.
- **June 22**: France signs an armistice with Germany, leading to the establishment of the Vichy regime.
- **July 10**: The Battle of Britain Begins and last through October 1940.
- **September 27**: Germany, Italy, and Japan sign the Tripartite Pact, forming the Axis powers.

**1941**

- **June 22**: Germany invades the Soviet Union in Operation Barbarossa, breaking the non-aggression pact.
- **December 7**: Japan attacks Pearl Harbor, leading to the United States' entry into World War II.
- **December 8**: The U.S. declares war on Japan.
- **December 11**: Germany and Italy declare war on the United States.

**1942**

- **June 4-7**: The Battle of Midway, a turning point in the Pacific theater as U.S. forces defeat the Japanese navy.
- **November 8**: Allied forces land in North Africa (Operation Torch).

**1943**

- **January 14-24**: The Casablanca Conference where Allied leaders (FDR and Churchill) agree on the policy of "unconditional surrender."
- **July 10**: Allied forces land in Sicily.
- **September 3**: Italy surrenders to the Allies; however, fighting continues as Germany occupies northern Italy.

**1944**

- **June 6**: D-Day – Allied forces land on the beaches of Normandy in France, marking the beginning of the liberation of Western Europe.
- **August 25**: Paris is liberated by Allied forces.

**1945**

- **February 4-11**: The Yalta Conference, where Allied leaders discuss post-war reorganization.
- **April 30**: Adolf Hitler commits suicide in his bunker in Berlin.
- **May 7**: Germany surrenders unconditionally to the Allies (V-E Day celebrated on May 8).
- **August 6**: The U.S. drops an atomic bomb on Hiroshima.
- **August 9**: The U.S. drops an atomic bomb on Nagasaki.
- **August 15**: Japan announces its surrender, leading to V-J Day.
- **September 2**: Japan formally surrenders aboard the USS Missouri.

**1946**

- **November 20**: The Nuremberg Trials begin, prosecuting major war criminals for their roles in the Holocaust and other war crimes.

## Allies and Axis Leaders World War II

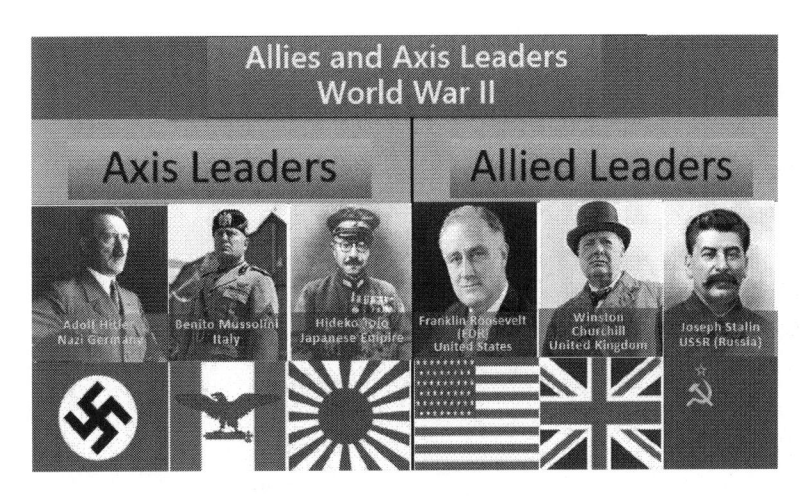

**Axis Leaders:** Adolf Hitler (Nazi Germany), Benito Mussolini (Italy), Hideko Tojo (Japanese Empire)

**Allied Leaders:** Franklin Roosevelt (FDR) (United States), Winston Churchill (United Kingdom), Joseph Stalin (USSR (Russia))

# The Architects of War: Political Leadership

World War II was a conflict of nations and a clash of ideologies, strategies, and personalities. The countries' leaders played pivotal roles in shaping the war's course. This story will explore the key figures from both the Allied and Axis powers, examining their backgrounds, leadership styles, and the impact they had on the war.

**The Allied Leaders**

**Franklin D. Roosevelt (United States):** Franklin Delano Roosevelt (FDR) served as the 32nd President of the United States from 1933 until his death in 1945. He was a central figure in the Allied leadership during World War II. Roosevelt's leadership style was characterized by his ability to communicate effectively with the American public. He often used radio broadcasts known as "fireside chats" to explain his policies and rally support for the war effort.

FDR's foreign policy was initially isolationist, reflecting the American public's reluctance to engage in another European conflict. However, as the war progressed, he recognized the threat posed by the Axis powers and shifted towards a more interventionist stance. Roosevelt played a crucial role in forming the Grand Alliance with Britain and the Soviet Union, emphasizing the need for cooperation among the Allies to defeat the Axis powers. His leadership during key conferences, such as the Atlantic Charter and the Yalta Conference, helped shape post-war plans and strategies.

**Winston Churchill (United Kingdom):** Winston Churchill became the Prime Minister of the United Kingdom in May 1940, during a critical phase of World War II. Known for his indomitable spirit and oratory skills, Churchill rallied the British people during the darkest days of the war. His speeches, filled with determination and resolve, inspired a nation facing the threat of Nazi invasion.

Churchill's leadership was marked by his refusal to consider peace with Hitler. He famously declared, "We shall fight on the beaches," emphasizing his commitment to resist Nazi aggression at all costs. He forged a close relationship with Roosevelt, recognizing the importance of American support in the war effort. Together, they coordinated military strategies and shared intelligence, which proved vital in turning the tide against the Axis powers.

**Joseph Stalin (Soviet Union):** Joseph Stalin was the General Secretary of the Communist Party of the Soviet Union and the country's leader during World War II. Initially, Stalin signed the Molotov-Ribbentrop Pact with Hitler in 1939, a non-aggression treaty that allowed the Soviet Union to annex parts of Eastern Europe. However, this alliance was short-lived, as Hitler launched Operation Barbarossa, invading the Soviet Union in June 1941.

Stalin's leadership style was authoritarian, characterized by purges and repression. However, he proved to be a resilient wartime leader, mobilizing the Soviet Union's vast resources to withstand the German onslaught. The Battle of Stalingrad (1942-1943) marked a turning point in the war, showcasing Stalin's ability to rally his people and military against the Axis forces. His insistence on a second front in Western Europe reflected his strategic vision for defeating Germany.

**Charles de Gaulle (France):** Charles de Gaulle was a French military leader and statesman who played a significant role in the French Resistance during World War II. After France fell to Nazi Germany in 1940, de Gaulle fled to Britain, where he became the leader of the Free French Forces. He famously declared, "France has lost a battle, but France has not lost the war," embodying the spirit of resistance against Nazi occupation.

De Gaulle worked to unify the various factions of the French Resistance and sought recognition from the Allies as the legitimate government of France. His leadership was instrumental in coordinating efforts to liberate France from German occupation. After the war, de Gaulle became the first President of the Fifth Republic, shaping post-war France's political landscape.

**The Axis Leaders**

**Adolf Hitler (Germany):** Adolf Hitler was the Führer of Nazi Germany and the primary architect of World War II. His rise to power was marked by his ability to exploit economic turmoil and nationalistic sentiments in Germany. Hitler's leadership style was characterized by charisma, propaganda, and a ruthless approach to dissent.

Hitler's aggressive expansionist policies, including the annexation of Austria and the invasion of Poland, were driven by his belief in Aryan supremacy and the need for Lebensraum (living space) for the German people. His militaristic ambitions led to the establishment of the Axis alliance with Italy and Japan. Hitler's strategic decisions, including the disastrous invasion of the Soviet Union, ultimately contributed to Germany's defeat.

**Benito Mussolini (Italy):** Benito Mussolini was the Prime Minister of Italy and the founder of Italian Fascism. He came to power in 1922 and sought to create a new Roman Empire through aggressive expansionist policies. Mussolini's leadership was characterized by authoritarianism and a cult of personality, often portraying himself as the embodiment of the Italian nation.

Mussolini aligned Italy with Nazi Germany, believing that a partnership with Hitler would restore Italy's status as a great power. However, his military campaigns, including the invasion of Greece, were largely unsuccessful and revealed the weaknesses of the Italian military. As the war progressed and Italy faced defeats, Mussolini's regime began to crumble, leading to his arrest in 1943.

**Emperor Hirohito (Japan):** Emperor Hirohito was the Emperor of Japan during World War II, serving as a symbolic figurehead of the Japanese state. While he held a position of great reverence, the real power was wielded by military leaders and politicians. Hirohito's role in the war is often debated, as he was seen as both a figure of national unity and a pawn of the militaristic government.

Japan's expansionist policies in Asia, including the invasion of China and the attack on Pearl Harbor, were driven by a desire for resources and regional dominance. Hirohito's approval of military actions was crucial, but he remained largely insulated from the day-to-day decisions of the military. After Japan's defeat, Hirohito was allowed to retain his throne, but his role was redefined as a constitutional monarch, marking a significant shift in Japanese governance.

**Hideki Tojo (Japan):** Hideki Tojo served as the Prime Minister of Japan from 1941 to 1944 and was a key military leader during World War II. A general in the Imperial Japanese Army, Tojo was a staunch advocate for Japan's aggressive expansionist policies. He played a significant role in planning the attack on Pearl Harbor, which brought the United States into the war.

Tojo's leadership was marked by militarism and a commitment to Japan's imperial ambitions. However, as the war turned against Japan, his government faced increasing criticism for military failures. In 1944, Tojo resigned as Prime Minister, and after Japan's surrender in 1945, he was arrested, tried for war crimes, and executed.

**The Interactions Among Leaders:** Allies and Axis powers were complex and often fraught with tension. The Grand Alliance formed by Roosevelt, Churchill, and Stalin was characterized by a shared goal of defeating the Axis powers, despite their differing ideologies and post-war visions. The cooperation among these leaders was crucial in coordinating military strategies and resources.

Conversely, the Axis leaders often struggled to maintain unity. Hitler's ambitions frequently clashed with Mussolini's aspirations, leading to friction between Germany and Italy. The relationship between Japan and Germany was also complicated by differing strategic priorities, particularly in the Pacific theater.

**Conclusion**

The leaders of the Allied and Axis powers played pivotal roles in shaping the course of World War II. Their backgrounds, ideologies, and leadership styles influenced the strategies and decisions made during the conflict. The interplay between these leaders, marked by cooperation and conflict, ultimately determined the outcome of the war and the future of the world.

The legacy of these leaders continues to resonate today, serving as a reminder of the complexities of leadership during times of crisis and the profound impact that individual decisions can have on the course of history.

# Masters of Strategy: The Allied Leadership

# General Dwight Eisenhower

General Dwight D. Eisenhower played a pivotal role as the Supreme Commander of the Allied Expeditionary Forces during World War II, significantly influencing the course of the conflict in Europe. Appointed to this crucial position in 1943, he orchestrated major military operations, including the successful planning and execution of the D-Day invasion at Normandy on June 6, 1944, which marked the beginning of the liberation of Western Europe from Nazi occupation.

Eisenhower's ability to coordinate a diverse coalition of forces from the United States, Britain, and other Allied nations was instrumental in overcoming logistical challenges and ensuring strategic unity among the Allies. His leadership style emphasized collaboration, careful planning, and adaptability, earning him respect and trust from both military leaders and troops.

Eisenhower's successful campaigns contributed to the eventual defeat of Nazi Germany in May 1945, solidifying his legacy as a key architect of Allied victory and paving the way for his later presidency.

# Air Marshal Arthur Harris

Air Marshal Sir Arthur Harris, known as "Bomber Harris," was a prominent British military leader during World War II and the head of the Royal Air Force's Bomber Command from 1942 to 1945. He played a crucial role in developing and executing the strategic bombing campaign against Germany, which aimed to destroy the enemy's industrial capacity and diminish morale through widespread aerial bombardment of cities and infrastructure.

Harris advocated for the use of heavy bombers, particularly the Lancaster, to target key industrial sites and urban centers, leading to significant destruction in cities such as Dresden and Hamburg. His tactics, while controversial due to the high civilian casualties and ethical implications, were seen as necessary to weaken Germany's war effort.

Harris's influence on the bombing strategy and his steadfast commitment to air power was instrumental in shaping the air war in Europe, contributing to the eventual Allied victory, though his legacy remains a subject of debate regarding the moral costs of total war.

# Field Marshall Bernard Montgomery

Field Marshal Bernard Montgomery was a key British commander during World War II, renowned for his leadership and strategic insight, particularly in the North African and European theaters. Rising to prominence as the commander of the Eighth Army, he played a pivotal role in the decisive victory at the Second Battle of El Alamein in late 1942, which marked a turning point in the North African campaign against Axis forces.

Montgomery's meticulous planning and emphasis on preparation helped restore confidence in Allied forces and showcased his ability to coordinate complex offensives. He later led British and Commonwealth troops in the successful invasion of Sicily and the subsequent Italian campaign. In 1944, he commanded the 21st Army Group during the D-Day invasion and the Battle of Normandy, where his leadership contributed to the liberation of Western Europe. Montgomery's insistence on thorough planning and his competitive nature often put him at odds with other Allied commanders, but his contributions were vital to the Allied victory in Europe, establishing him as one of the war's most prominent military figures.

## General George Patton

General George S. Patton was a highly influential and controversial figure in the U.S. Army during World War II, known for his aggressive tactics and charismatic leadership. Commanding the U.S. Third Army, Patton played a crucial role in several key operations, most notably during the liberation of Europe following the D-Day invasion.

His rapid armored advances across France were instrumental in the Allied campaign, particularly in the breakout from Normandy and the subsequent pursuit of German forces. Patton's leadership in the Battle of the Bulge demonstrated his tactical brilliance, as he quickly repositioned his troops to relieve besieged American forces in Bastogne.

His unyielding drive and emphasis on offensive maneuvers earned him a reputation as a formidable commander, though his outspoken nature and controversial statements occasionally created friction with his superiors and allies. Patton's influence was pivotal in the Allied victory in Europe, and he remains a symbol of bold and aggressive military strategy.

## General Omar Bradley

General Omar Bradley was a prominent American commander during World War II, known for his leadership of U.S. ground forces in the European Theater. As the commander of the Twelfth Army Group, he played a crucial role in the planning and execution of major operations, including the D-Day invasion at Normandy and the subsequent liberation of France.

Bradley was respected for his calm demeanor, pragmatic approach, and ability to foster collaboration among diverse Allied forces, which proved essential in coordinating large-scale operations. His leadership during the Battle of the Bulge showcased his strategic acumen as he effectively managed resources to respond to the surprise German offensive. Following the war,

Bradley's influence extended beyond the battlefield; he became a key figure in shaping post-war military policy and served as the first Chairman of the Joint Chiefs of Staff. His contributions to the Allied victory in Europe and his emphasis on the importance of unified command established him as one of the leading military figures of the conflict.

## General Douglas MacArthur

General Douglas MacArthur was a pivotal figure in the Pacific Theater during World War II, known for his bold strategies and charismatic leadership. Initially appointed as the commander of U.S. Army Forces in the Far East, he famously vowed to return after being forced to evacuate from the Philippines in 1942 following the Japanese invasion. MacArthur's return in 1944 marked the beginning of a successful campaign to liberate the Philippines, exemplifying his commitment to his troops and his nation.

His strategy of "island hopping" allowed Allied forces to bypass heavily fortified Japanese positions, capturing strategically important islands to establish bases for further advances. MacArthur's leadership during the post-war occupation of Japan was also significant; he oversaw major reforms that transformed Japan into a democratic nation and fostered economic recovery.

His influence extended beyond military operations, making him a key architect of the post-war order in the Pacific, and he remains a controversial yet iconic figure in American military history.

## General Georgi Zhukov

General Georgi Zhukov was a prominent Soviet military leader whose strategic brilliance and decisive actions significantly influenced the outcome of World War II on the Eastern Front. Known for his aggressive tactics and ability to coordinate large-scale operations, Zhukov played a critical role in several key battles, including the defense of Stalingrad, which marked a turning point in the war against Nazi Germany.

His leadership during the Battle of Kursk in 1943, the largest tank battle in history, and the subsequent offensives that pushed German forces back were instrumental in shifting the momentum in favor of the Soviet Union. Zhukov's successful planning and execution of Operation Bagration in 1944 led to the complete devastation of the German Army Group Centre, further solidifying his reputation as one of the Red Army's most effective commanders.

At the war's conclusion, he was the first to enter Berlin in May 1945, symbolizing the Soviet victory over Nazi Germany. Zhukov's contributions helped secure victory for the Allies and established him as a national hero in the Soviet Union, shaping post-war military doctrine and Soviet military prestige.

## Admiral Chester Nimitz

Admiral Chester W. Nimitz was a key figure in the United States Navy during World War II, serving as the Commander in Chief of the Pacific Fleet. Nimitz played a crucial role in implementing the U.S. "island hopping" strategy to defeat Japan, overseeing major naval battles such as the Battle of Midway, which marked a pivotal turning point in the Pacific Theater.

His ability to coordinate extensive naval operations and his strategic foresight allowed American forces to capture key islands and establish vital air and naval bases, significantly weakening Japanese defenses. Nimitz was known for his calm and measured leadership style, which fostered a strong sense of teamwork among his commanders and crews.

After the war, he continued to influence naval strategy and policy, helping to shape the post-war Navy. Nimitz's contributions were instrumental in securing victory in the Pacific, and he remains a revered figure in American military history.

## General Charles de Gaulle

General Charles de Gaulle was a French military leader and statesman who played a critical role in the resistance against Nazi occupation during World War II. Born in 1890, he became a prominent figure in the Free French Forces, advocating for the continued fight against the Axis powers after the fall of France in 1940. De Gaulle's leadership helped to unite various factions of the French resistance and secure support from the Allies. After the war, he became the founding president of the Fifth Republic in France, emphasizing national sovereignty and a strong, independent France in the post-war world.

These leaders were instrumental in shaping the Allied military strategy and ultimately achieving victory in World War II, each contributing their unique skills and perspectives to the war effort.

## General Theodore Roosevelt Jr.

Theodore Roosevelt Jr. was an American military leader and the son of former President Theodore Roosevelt. Born in 1887, he served as a major general in the U.S. Army during World War II. He is best known for his leadership during the D-Day invasion at Normandy, where he played a critical role in the assault on Utah Beach. His bravery and commitment to his troops were evident as he led from the front despite suffering from health issues. Roosevelt was awarded the Medal of Honor posthumously for his actions during the war, which exemplified his family's legacy of service.

## Admiral William Halsey Jr.

Admiral William Halsey Jr. was a highly regarded commander in the U.S. Navy, known for his aggressive tactics in the Pacific Theater. Born in 1882, Halsey led U.S. naval forces during major battles, including the Battle of Leyte Gulf, which was one of the largest naval battles in history. His bold leadership and emphasis on offensive operations contributed significantly to the success of Allied forces in the Pacific.

## General Henry H. Arnold

General Henry H. "Hap" Arnold was a key leader in the United States Army Air Forces during World War II. Born in 1886, he played a crucial role in developing and expanding American air power, overseeing operations that included strategic bombing campaigns against Germany and Japan. Arnold was instrumental in coordinating Allied air strategies and ensuring air superiority, which was vital for ground operations. His leadership helped to establish the U.S. Air Force as a separate branch of the military after the war.

## General Joseph Stilwell

General Joseph Stilwell was an American military leader known for his significant contributions to the China-Burma-India Theater. Born in 1883, he served as the chief of staff to Chiang Kai-shek and played a key role in coordinating Allied efforts against Japanese forces in the region. Stilwell was known for his relentless pursuit of supply routes and his emphasis on guerrilla warfare tactics. His leadership was critical in maintaining Allied operations in Asia, despite facing numerous challenges.

## General Ivan Konev

General Ivan Konev was a prominent Soviet commander during World War II, recognized for his leadership on the Eastern Front. Born in 1897, he played a pivotal role in major battles, including the Battle of Stalingrad and the liberation of Eastern Europe. Konev commanded the First Ukrainian Front during the final offensives against Germany, contributing significantly to the capture of Berlin. His strategic abilities and emphasis on rapid maneuvering were crucial in the Soviet Union's successes against the Axis powers.

## Field Marshall Claude Auchinleck

Field Marshal Claude Auchinleck was a British commander who played a significant role in the North African Campaign. Born in 1884, he was known for his leadership during the early battles against Axis forces, particularly at the Siege of Tobruk. Auchinleck's strategic planning helped to set the stage for future victories in North Africa, although he faced criticism for some decisions, leading to his eventual replacement.

## General Harry Crerar

General Harry Crerar was a Canadian Army commander who played a crucial role in the Allied campaigns in Europe, particularly during the liberation of the Netherlands. Born in 1888, he commanded the First Canadian Army and was involved in significant operations, including the Battle of Normandy and the Scheldt Campaign. Crerar's leadership was vital in coordinating Canadian forces and contributing to the overall success of Allied operations in Western Europe.

# At the Helm of Conflict: Profiles of Axis Military Leadership

## Oberster SA- Fuhrer Hermann Göring

Hermann Göring was a prominent Nazi leader and one of Adolf Hitler's closest associates. Born in 1893, he served as a fighter pilot during World War I before rising to power in the Nazi Party. Göring became the commander of the Luftwaffe (German Air Force) and played a key role in the early successes of the Blitzkrieg strategy. However, his leadership was marred by disastrous decisions, particularly during the Battle of Britain and later in the war, when he was blamed for the Luftwaffe's failures. He was also heavily involved in the plundering of art and resources in occupied territories and was a key figure in the implementation of the Holocaust. Captured after the war, he was tried at Nuremberg and sentenced to death, committing suicide before his execution.

## SS Commander Heinrich Himmler

Heinrich Himmler was one of the main architects of the Holocaust and a leading figure in the Nazi regime. Born in 1900, he joined the Nazi Party in the early 1920s and rose to become the head of the SS (Schutzstaffel), which was responsible for many of the regime's most heinous crimes. Himmler oversaw the concentration camp system and the implementation of mass extermination policies against Jews and other targeted groups. His obsession with racial purity and loyalty to Hitler made him a key player in the Nazi leadership. As the war turned against Germany, he attempted to negotiate with the Allies but was ultimately rejected. Captured by American forces in 1945, he committed suicide while in custody.

## Field Marshall Erwin Rommel

Erwin Rommel, known as the "Desert Fox," was one of Germany's most respected military leaders during World War II. Born in 1891, he gained fame for his leadership of the Afrika Korps during the North African Campaign, where he showcased his strategic brilliance and innovative tactics. Rommel's ability to conduct rapid maneuvers and supply operations earned him admiration both from his troops and adversaries. However, as the war progressed and German fortunes declined, he faced increasing pressure and responsibility. Rommel was implicated in a conspiracy to assassinate Hitler and, given the choice between execution and suicide, he took his own life in 1944, leaving behind a complex legacy as a skilled commander and a reluctant participant in the Nazi regime.

## Admiral Isoroku Yamamoto

Admiral Isoroku Yamamoto was the commander-in-chief of the Imperial Japanese Navy and a key strategist in Japan's naval operations during World War II. Born in 1884, he was educated in the United States and understood the importance of modern naval warfare. Yamamoto is most famous for planning the attack on Pearl Harbor in December 1941, which aimed to cripple the U.S. Pacific Fleet. His strategy initially succeeded, but he recognized that Japan could not win a prolonged war against the industrial power of the United States. After the pivotal Battle of Midway in June 1942, where Japan suffered significant losses, Yamamoto was killed in 1943 when American forces intercepted and shot down his plane over the Solomon Islands.

## General Tomoyuki Yamashita

General Tomoyuki Yamashita, known as the "Tiger of Malaya," was a prominent Japanese military leader during World War II. Born in 1885, he gained fame for his successful campaign during the Malayan Campaign in 1941, where he rapidly defeated British forces and captured Singapore, a critical British stronghold. His tactics combined speed and surprise, earning him a reputation as a brilliant commander. Following the war, Yamashita was tried for war crimes related to the atrocities committed by Japanese troops in the Philippines, particularly during the Battle of Manila. He was found guilty and executed in 1946, leaving a controversial legacy as a skilled tactician who was also implicated in wartime atrocities.

## General Heinz Guderian

Heinz Guderian was a German general and a pioneer of armored warfare during World War II. Born in 1888, he played a crucial role in developing the concept of Blitzkrieg, or "lightning war," which emphasized rapid, coordinated attacks using tanks and aircraft. Guderian commanded armored divisions during the invasions of Poland and France, achieving significant victories and demonstrating the effectiveness of his tactics. Despite his successes, he often found himself at odds with other senior military leaders and the Nazi high command. Guderian was dismissed in 1945 due to disagreements over strategy but remained influential in post-war military theory. After the war, he wrote extensively on military tactics and strategy, solidifying his legacy as one of the foremost theorists of armored warfare.

## Deputy Fuhrer Rudolf Hess

Rudolf Hess was a prominent Nazi official and Hitler's Deputy Führer. Born in 1894, he joined the Nazi Party early on and became one of Hitler's closest associates. Hess is infamously known for his solo flight to Scotland in 1941, where he sought to negotiate peace with the United Kingdom, believing that his presence could convince British leaders to negotiate a settlement. His mission was a failure, leading to his capture and imprisonment by British authorities. After the war, Hess was tried at the Nuremberg Trials and sentenced to life imprisonment. He spent the remainder of his life in Spandau Prison, where he died in 1987 under controversial circumstances, leaving behind a legacy as a loyal follower of Hitler whose ambitions ultimately led to his downfall.

## Gestapo Chief Reinhard Heydrich

Reinhard Heydrich was one of the main architects of the Holocaust and a high-ranking Nazi official known for his ruthless efficiency. Born in 1904, he served as head of the SS Security Service and played a pivotal role in planning the implementation of the Final Solution. Heydrich was instrumental in the establishment of the Einsatzgruppen (mobile killing units) responsible for mass shootings of Jews and other targeted groups in Eastern Europe. He chaired the Wannsee Conference in 1942, where the logistics of the Holocaust were discussed. Known for his brutal tactics, Heydrich was assassinated in 1942 by Czechoslovak resistance fighters in a plot to undermine Nazi rule. His death led to severe reprisals against the Czech population, showcasing the lengths to which the Nazis would go to maintain control.

## Gestapo Chief Klaus Barbie

Klaus Barbie, known as the "Butcher of Lyon," was a notorious SS officer during World War II, infamous for his brutal tactics in Nazi-occupied France. Born in 1913, he served as the head of the Gestapo in Lyon, where he was responsible for the arrest, torture, and deportation of numerous resistance fighters and Jews.

Barbie's actions contributed significantly to the suffering of the French population under Nazi rule. After the war, he fled to Bolivia, where he lived for decades under a false identity. His past came to light, and he was eventually extradited to France in 1983, where he stood trial for crimes against humanity. Barbie was convicted and sentenced to life in prison, leaving a legacy of terror and a chilling reminder of the brutality of the Nazi regime.

## Field Marshall Wilhelm Keitel

Field Marshal Wilhelm Keitel was a senior military officer in Nazi Germany and served as the Chief of the Oberkommando der Wehrmacht (OKW), the high command of the armed forces. Born in 1882, Keitel was a close confidant of Adolf Hitler and played a significant role in strategic military planning and the execution of operations throughout World War II. He was instrumental in decisions regarding the invasion of the Soviet Union and the implementation of wartime policies. After Germany's defeat, Keitel was captured, tried at the Nuremberg Trials, and executed for war crimes, particularly for his role in the planning and execution of aggressive war and the atrocities committed during the conflict.

## General Fritz Bayerlein

General Fritz Bayerlein was a notable commander in the German Army, particularly recognized for his leadership of the Afrika Korps during the North African Campaign. Born in 1887, Bayerlein demonstrated tactical proficiency and resourcefulness in desert warfare, serving under General Erwin Rommel. He played a key role in the battles of Gazala and El Alamein, where he was responsible for coordinating armored and infantry units. Bayerlein's expertise in mobile warfare contributed to the early successes of German forces in North Africa. After the defeat of Axis powers in the region, he continued to serve in various capacities until the end of the war, ultimately being captured by Allied forces.

## Field Marshall Gerd von Rundstedt

Field Marshal Gerd von Rundstedt was one of Germany's most prominent military leaders during World War II. Born in 1875, he served in both World Wars and was known for his strategic acumen and leadership abilities. Von Rundstedt commanded German forces during key operations, including the invasion of France and the Battle of the Bulge. His approach to warfare emphasized the importance of flexibility and mobility in operations. Despite his successes, he often clashed with Hitler over strategic decisions, particularly regarding defensive tactics. After the war, von Rundstedt was briefly imprisoned but later released. His legacy is marked by his military expertise and the complexities of his relationship with the Nazi regime.

## General Erich von Manstein

General Erich von Manstein was a highly regarded strategist in the German Army, known for his innovative tactics and significant contributions to the success of early German campaigns during World War II. Born in 1887, he played a crucial role in the planning of the invasion of France, where his concept of Blitzkrieg proved effective. Von Manstein also led successful operations on the Eastern Front, including the Battle of Stalingrad, where his strategies were pivotal despite the eventual defeat. His ability to adapt to changing circumstances earned him respect among both allies and adversaries. After the war, von Manstein wrote extensively on military strategy and became influential in post-war military theory.

## General Pietro Badoglio

Pietro Badoglio was an Italian general and politician who played a key role in World War II. Born in 1871, he served in various military capacities, including during World War I. After Mussolini's downfall in 1943, Badoglio became Prime Minister of Italy and led the country through a complicated period of switching sides from the Axis powers to the Allies. He oversaw the armistice with the Allies and attempted to stabilize the internal situation in Italy while facing the challenges of ongoing German occupation. Despite his efforts, Badoglio's leadership was criticized for its ineffectiveness, and he was eventually replaced. After the war, he faced legal challenges but was later acquitted of war crimes.

## Marshall Italo Balbo

Italo Balbo was an Italian marshal and a prominent figure in the Italian Air Force during World War II. Born in 1896, he was known for his leadership in the early years of the war and for his role in the North African Campaign. Balbo gained fame for his aviation exploits, including pioneering transatlantic flights. His military career was marked by his command of air operations in Libya and his efforts to build a strong air force for Italy. However, Balbo's relationship with Mussolini became strained, and he was killed in 1940 by friendly fire while traveling in Libya. His death was a significant loss for the Italian military and underscored the internal conflicts within the Fascist regime.

## General Hideki Tojo

Hideki Tojo was a general in the Imperial Japanese Army and served as Prime Minister of Japan during a significant portion of World War II. Born in 1884, Tojo was a leading figure in Japan's military government and played a crucial role in the decision to attack Pearl Harbor in 1941, which brought the United States into the war. His administration was marked by aggressive expansionist policies and the implementation of brutal military tactics across Asia. As the war turned against Japan, Tojo's influence waned, and he resigned in 1944. After Japan's defeat, he was arrested, tried for war crimes, and executed in 1948, leaving a controversial legacy as a war leader.

## Admiral Kisaburo Yokoyama

Kisaburo Yokoyama was a prominent Japanese admiral during World War II, known for his command of naval operations in the Pacific theater. Born in 1884, he played a critical role in various operations, including the Battle of the Philippine Sea and the defense of the Philippines. Yokoyama was involved in the planning of Japan's naval strategies and worked to coordinate the Imperial Navy's efforts against Allied forces. His leadership was marked by a commitment to naval aviation and the development of aircraft carriers as key components of Japan's maritime strategy. After the war, he was arrested but not tried for war crimes, and he later became a significant figure in Japan's post-war naval reconstruction.

## General Masaharu Homma

General Masaharu Homma was a prominent Japanese military leader known for his command during the invasion of the Philippines in 1941–1942. Born in 1887, he led Japanese forces to a swift victory, culminating in the capture of Manila and the subsequent Bataan Death March, where thousands of American and Filipino prisoners were forced to march under brutal conditions. Homma was initially celebrated for his military successes but later faced scrutiny for his role in the atrocities committed during the occupation. After the war, he was tried for war crimes related to the treatment of prisoners and was executed in 1946, leaving behind a legacy that reflects the complexities of military leadership in wartime.

# The European Front: Chronicles of War and Resistance

# Blitzkrieg: The Lightning War That Reshaped Modern Warfare

## Introduction

In the annals of military history, few strategies have left as profound an impact as Blitzkrieg. This revolutionary tactic, which translates to "Lightning War" in German, reshaped the face of modern warfare and played a pivotal role in the early successes of Nazi Germany during World War II. Blitzkrieg was not merely a military strategy; it was a philosophy of war that emphasized speed, surprise, and overwhelming force to achieve rapid and decisive victories. This approach would come to define the opening stages of World War II and leave an indelible mark on military tactics for generations to come.

## The Birth of Blitzkrieg: From Trenches to Tanks

To understand the genesis of Blitzkrieg, we must first look back to the aftermath of World War I. The Treaty of Versailles, which ended the Great War, imposed severe restrictions on Germany's military capabilities. These limitations, coupled with the bitter memory of trench warfare's brutal stalemates, spurred German military thinkers to innovate and develop new strategies that could overcome numerical and material disadvantages.

The interwar period saw significant advancements in military technology, particularly in the realms of tanks, aircraft, and communication systems. German strategists, keenly aware of these developments, began to envision a new form of warfare that could harness the potential of these technologies to achieve swift and decisive victories.

Key figures emerged in the development of what would become Blitzkrieg tactics. Among them, Heinz Guderian stood out as a visionary who recognized the potential of armored warfare. Guderian advocated for the integration of tanks, motorized infantry, and air support to create a highly mobile and flexible fighting force capable of rapid breakthroughs and encirclements.

## The Anatomy of Blitzkrieg: Speed, Surprise, and Synergy

At its core, Blitzkrieg was built on several key components that worked in concert to overwhelm and incapacitate enemy forces:

**1. Speed and Mobility:** The essence of Blitzkrieg was rapid movement. Fast-moving tanks, known as Panzers, formed the spearhead of the attack, supported by motorized infantry that could keep pace with the advancing armor. This speed was crucial for maintaining the element of surprise and preventing the enemy from organizing an effective defense.

**2. Concentration of Force:** Blitzkrieg tactics emphasized concentrating a large number of forces at a single point to break through enemy defenses. This concentration of force was often applied to a narrow front, creating a breach that could be exploited by following units.

**3. Combined Arms Operations:** The success of Blitzkrieg relied heavily on the coordination between different branches of the military. Tanks, infantry, artillery, and air support worked in tandem to create a synergistic effect that was greater than the sum of its parts.

**4. Air Support:** The Luftwaffe, Germany's air force, played a crucial role in Blitzkrieg operations. Close air support, provided by aircraft such as the Junkers Ju 87 Stuka dive bomber, was used to attack enemy positions, disrupt supply lines, and provide reconnaissance.

**5. Flexible Command Structure:** A decentralized command structure allowed German commanders to make quick decisions on the battlefield, adapting to changing circumstances and exploiting weaknesses in enemy lines.

**6. Psychological Warfare:** The sudden and overwhelming nature of Blitzkrieg attacks was designed to create confusion, panic, and disorganization among enemy troops. This psychological impact often led to quicker surrenders and less resistance.

**Blitzkrieg in Action: The Early Triumphs of World War II**

The true test of Blitzkrieg tactics came with the outbreak of World War II. The invasion of Poland in September 1939 marked the first large-scale application of these strategies. German forces, using a combination of fast-moving infantry, tanks, and air support, quickly penetrated Polish defenses. The speed and coordination of the attack left little time for the Polish military to mount an effective defense, and within weeks, Poland had fallen.

The success in Poland was followed by a series of rapid conquests that shocked the world. In April 1940, German forces swiftly occupied Denmark and Norway, demonstrating the versatility of Blitzkrieg tactics in different terrains. However, it was the invasion of France and the Low Countries in May 1940 that truly showcased the devastating potential of Blitzkrieg.

The German plan for the invasion of France, known as Fall Gelb (Case Yellow), was a masterpiece of strategic deception and tactical brilliance. Instead of attacking through the heavily fortified Maginot Line, German forces executed a daring maneuver through the Ardennes Forest, a region considered impassable by the French military. This surprise move caught the Allies off guard and allowed German armored divisions to break through and rapidly advance toward the English Channel.

The speed and coordination of the German advance were unprecedented. Panzer divisions, supported by dive bombers and motorized infantry, pushed deep into enemy territory, encircling large sections of Allied forces. The result was a stunning victory that saw France, one of the world's major military powers, capitulate in just six weeks.

## The Limits of Lightning: Blitzkrieg Meets Its Match

The early successes of Blitzkrieg created an aura of invincibility around the German military. However, as the war progressed, the limitations of this strategy began to emerge. Operation Barbarossa, the German invasion of the Soviet Union in June 1941, initially saw significant gains as Blitzkrieg's tactics once again proved effective. German forces advanced rapidly, encircling large Soviet armies and capturing vast swathes of territory.

However, the sheer scale of the Soviet Union, combined with its harsh climate and the determination of its defenders, began to expose the weaknesses of Blitzkrieg. The strategy relied heavily on maintaining momentum and exploiting enemy weaknesses, which became increasingly difficult as supply lines stretched, and Soviet resistance stiffened. The onset of the brutal Russian winter further hampered German mobility, bringing the advance to a halt before the gates of Moscow.

As the war progressed, Allied forces began to adapt to and counter Blitzkrieg tactics. Improved communication, better coordination among Allied forces, and the development of their own mobile warfare doctrines reduced the effectiveness of Blitzkrieg in later stages of the war. The tide began to turn against Germany, and by 1943, the initiative had shifted to the Allies.

## Legacy and Impact: The Enduring Influence of Blitzkrieg

Despite its ultimate failure to secure victory for Nazi Germany, Blitzkrieg left an indelible mark on military strategy and tactics. The principles of rapid movement, combined arms operations, and the importance of air support in ground operations continue to influence modern military doctrine.

The success of Blitzkrieg in the early years of World War II demonstrated the importance of mobility and flexibility in warfare. It showed that superior tactics and coordination could overcome numerical and material advantages, a lesson that would be studied and applied by militaries around the world in the decades following the war.

The psychological aspect of Blitzkrieg, with its emphasis on shock and disruption, also had a lasting impact on military thinking. The idea that warfare could be won not just through physical destruction but also through the paralysis of enemy command and control structures became a key component of modern military strategy.

Moreover, the development and application of Blitzkrieg tactics spurred technological advancements in areas such as tank design, aircraft capabilities, and communication systems. The need for fast, reliable, and coordinated military operations drove innovation across multiple fields, many of which had civilian applications in the post-war era.

## Historical Interpretations and Debates

In recent years, historians have engaged in debates about the nature and significance of Blitzkrieg. Some scholars argue that Blitzkrieg was not a coherent doctrine but rather a series of opportunistic strategies that evolved. This revisionist view challenges the traditional narrative of Blitzkrieg as a revolutionary new form of warfare, instead positioning it as an evolution of existing tactics.

The memoirs of German generals like Heinz Guderian have significantly influenced our understanding of Blitzkrieg. These accounts often emphasize the role of armored warfare and strategic mobility, aligning with the theories of military strategists like J.F.C. Fuller and B.H. Liddell-Hart, advocated for the use of armored forces to achieve strategic paralysis.

However, some historians have criticized the mythologization of Blitzkrieg, suggesting that its success was not as inevitable as often portrayed. The risks involved in such rapid operations were significant, and the tactic's effectiveness diminished as the war progressed, particularly on the Eastern Front against the Soviet Union.

**Conclusion: The Lightning War That Illuminated Modern Warfare**

Blitzkrieg, the lightning war that swept across Europe in the early years of World War II, represents a pivotal moment in military history. It was a strategy born out of necessity, shaped by the lessons of the past and the possibilities of emerging technologies. Its success was as much a testament to the innovative thinking of its architects as it was to the skill and coordination of the forces that executed it.

While Blitzkrieg ultimately failed to secure victory for Nazi Germany, its impact on military strategy and tactics has been profound and long-lasting. The principles of speed, surprise, and combined arms operations that defined Blitzkrieg continue to shape military thinking to this day. As we reflect on this revolutionary approach to warfare, we are reminded of the constant evolution of military strategy and the enduring importance of innovation in the face of adversity.

The story of Blitzkrieg serves as a powerful reminder of how technological advancements and strategic thinking can reshape the nature of conflict. It stands as a testament to the impact that bold and innovative ideas can have on the course of history, even as it serves as a cautionary tale about the limitations of any single strategy in the complex and unpredictable theater of war.

**Sources**

Hughes, Thomas. World War II. Encyclopedia Britannica, 2024

Raymond, Limbach. Encyclopedia Britannica, 2024.

Various Sources

# The Dual Invasion of Poland: A Turning Point in World History

## Introduction

In the early hours of September 1, 1939, the world stood on the precipice of a conflict that would reshape global politics for generations to come. As the first rays of dawn broke over the Polish-German border, the thunder of artillery and the roar of aircraft engines shattered the morning calm. Nazi Germany had launched its invasion of Poland, igniting the spark that would engulf the world in the flames of World War II. However, this was only the beginning of Poland's ordeal. Sixteen days later, on September 17, the Soviet Union would join the fray, striking from the east in a coordinated effort that would seal Poland's fate and redraw the map of Eastern Europe.

## The Road to War

The invasion of Poland was the culmination of years of aggressive expansionist policies pursued by Nazi Germany under Adolf Hitler. The seeds of this conflict were sown in the aftermath of World War I, with the Treaty of Versailles imposing harsh penalties on Germany, including significant territorial losses and military restrictions. These terms fostered a sense of humiliation and resentment in Germany, which Hitler expertly exploited to gain political power.

Throughout the 1930s, Hitler pursued an increasingly aggressive foreign policy, withdrawing Germany from the League of Nations and beginning a process of rearmament in direct violation of the Versailles Treaty. The concept of Lebensraum or "living space" became a driving force behind Nazi Germany's expansionist ambitions, particularly towards the East.

The international community's response to these provocations was characterized by a policy of appeasement, exemplified by the Munich Agreement of 1938, which allowed Germany to annex the Sudetenland from Czechoslovakia. This approach, aimed at avoiding another devastating war, ultimately emboldened Hitler and set the stage for further aggression.

## The Danzig Crisis and the Nazi-Soviet Pact

As tensions mounted in Europe, the Free City of Danzig (modern-day Gdańsk) became a focal point of the brewing conflict. Hitler demanded the return of Danzig to Germany, citing the presence of ethnic

Germans and the city's historical ties to Germany. Poland, backed by guarantees from Britain and France, refused to cede Danzig, leading to an escalation of tensions between Germany and Poland.

In a shocking turn of events, on August 23, 1939, Nazi Germany and the Soviet Union signed a non-aggression pact, known as the Molotov-Ribbentrop Pact. This agreement, which stunned the world given the ideological differences between the two regimes, included secret protocols that divided Eastern Europe into German and Soviet spheres of influence. Poland was to be partitioned between the two powers, effectively sealing its fate.

**The German Invasion Begins**

On September 1, 1939, at 4:45 AM, the German battleship Schleswig-Holstein opened fire on the Polish military depot at Westerplatte, marking the official start of the invasion. Simultaneously, German forces poured across the Polish border, employing the revolutionary "Blitzkrieg" or "lightning war" tactics that would come to define the early years of World War II.

The German invasion force was massive, comprising 60 divisions and nearly 1.5 million men. The Luftwaffe quickly established air superiority, destroying much of the Polish air force on the ground within the first few days of the conflict. This left Polish ground forces vulnerable to relentless air attacks and hampered their ability to coordinate an effective defense.

The Polish army, despite being outnumbered and outgunned, fought bravely against the German onslaught. The Battle of Westerplatte became a symbol of Polish resistance, with the garrison holding out for seven days against overwhelming odds before finally surrendering.

**The Soviet Invasion and Poland's Fate**

As Polish forces struggled to contain the German advance from the west, a new threat emerged from the east. On September 17, 1939, Soviet forces crossed the Polish border, catching the already beleaguered Polish military off guard. The Soviet Union justified its actions as a "liberation campaign" to protect Ukrainians and Belarusians living in eastern Poland, but in reality, it was acting under the secret protocols of the Molotov-Ribbentrop Pact.

The Soviet invasion force was massive, numbering between 600,000 to 800,000 troops, supported by thousands of tanks and aircraft. With the bulk of Polish forces engaged in the West, there was little organized resistance to the Soviet advance. Key cities in eastern Poland, such as Lwów (now Lviv, Ukraine), quickly fell to the Red Army.

Caught between two powerful invaders, Poland's fate was sealed. The last major battle of the campaign, the Battle of Kock, ended on October 6, 1939, marking the end of organized Polish resistance. In just over a month, Poland had been conquered and divided between Nazi Germany and the Soviet Union, as per the secret agreement between Hitler and Stalin.

**The Polish Resistance and Underground State**

Despite the swift military defeat, the spirit of Polish resistance remained unbroken. The Polish government-in-exile was established, first in France and later in London, to continue the fight against the occupying powers. Within occupied Poland, a comprehensive underground state was formed, replicating many functions of a sovereign state, including administration, education, and military operations.

The primary resistance force in German-occupied Poland was the Armia Krajowa (AK), or Home Army. Formed in 1942, it became the largest underground resistance movement in Europe, with membership peaking at around 400,000 fighters. The AK was involved in numerous sabotage operations, intelligence gathering, and direct combat actions against German forces.

Key figures emerged in the resistance movement, demonstrating extraordinary courage and resourcefulness. Witold Pilecki voluntarily allowed himself to be captured and sent to Auschwitz to gather intelligence and organize inmate resistance. His reports were crucial in informing the Allies about the atrocities occurring in the camp. Jan Karski, a courier for the Polish government-in-exile, provided detailed reports on the situation in occupied Poland, including the Holocaust, to Allied leaders, significantly raising awareness of Nazi atrocities.

**Global Reactions and Consequences**

The dual invasion of Poland sent shockwaves through the international community. Britain and France, honoring their alliance with Poland, declared war on Germany on September 3, 1939, marking the official start of World War II. However, their military response was limited in the early stages of the conflict, leading to what became known as the "Phoney War" period in Western Europe.

The United States, under President Franklin D. Roosevelt, initially maintained a policy of neutrality. However, the invasion of Poland and subsequent German aggressions led to increased support for the Allies through measures such as the Lend-Lease Act, which provided military aid to countries fighting against the Axis powers.

The invasion of Poland demonstrated the failure of appeasement policies pursued by Western powers in the 1930s. It underscored the need for a more robust international system to prevent aggression and maintain peace. The lessons learned from the invasion and the subsequent war would later influence the formation of the United Nations and the post-war international order.

**The Human Cost and Long-term Impact**

The dual invasion and subsequent occupation of Poland resulted in immense human suffering. Approximately six million Polish citizens, nearly 21.4% of the population, died during the occupation, with half of these victims being ethnic Poles and the other half Polish Jews. The Nazi occupation was particularly brutal, implementing policies aimed at the extermination and displacement of the Polish people, including the infamous Generalplan Ost, which called for the ethnic cleansing and Germanization of Polish territories.

The Jewish population in Poland faced unimaginable horrors. The German invasion brought millions of Jews under Nazi control, leading to the implementation of genocidal policies that would culminate in the Holocaust. Many Jewish refugees attempted to flee to neighboring countries but faced numerous obstacles, including restrictive immigration policies and closed borders.

**Conclusion**

The dual invasion of Poland in 1939 marked a turning point in world history. It exposed the dangers of appeasement, the ruthlessness of totalitarian regimes, and the vulnerability of smaller nations caught between great powers. The swift fall of Poland demonstrated the effectiveness of Germany's Blitzkrieg tactics and the devastating potential of modern warfare.

Yet, amidst the darkness of occupation and oppression, the Polish people's resilience shone through. The Polish resistance movement, one of the largest and most effective in occupied Europe, continued to fight against overwhelming odds, providing crucial intelligence to the Allies and keeping the flame of Polish independence alive.

The invasion of Poland set in motion a chain of events that would reshape the global order. It marked the beginning of World War II, a conflict that would claim millions of lives and redraw the map of Europe and the world. The consequences of this invasion would be felt for decades, influencing Cold War politics, shaping the post-war international system, and leaving an indelible mark on the collective memory of nations.

As we reflect on the dual invasion of Poland, we are reminded of the importance of international cooperation, the dangers of unchecked aggression, and the indomitable spirit of those who resist tyranny. The lessons of 1939 continue to resonate today, serving as a stark reminder of the fragility of peace and the ongoing need for vigilance in the face of threats to freedom and democracy.

**Sources**

Charles River Editors. The Phoney War: The History of the Uneasy Calm along the Western Front at the Start of World War II. Charles River Editors, 2023.

Gilbert, Martin. The Second World War: A Complete History. Holt Paperbacks, 2004.

Various Sources

# The Lightning War: Germany's Blitzkrieg Expansion into the Low Countries

## Introduction

In the early hours of May 10, 1940, the skies over the Low Countries—comprising the Netherlands, Belgium, and Luxembourg—were suddenly filled with the ominous drone of aircraft engines. As dawn broke, German paratroopers descended upon key strategic locations, while armored columns thundered across borders. The Blitzkrieg, or "Lightning War," had begun, marking a pivotal moment in World War II that would reshape the face of modern warfare and alter the course of history.

## The Road to War: Setting the Stage for Blitzkrieg

The seeds of the Blitzkrieg campaign were sown in the aftermath of World War I. The Treaty of Versailles, which ended the Great War, imposed harsh penalties on Germany, including significant territorial losses and military restrictions. These terms fostered a sense of humiliation and resentment in Germany, creating fertile ground for the rise of Adolf Hitler and the Nazi Party.

Throughout the 1930s, Hitler pursued an increasingly aggressive foreign policy, withdrawing Germany from the League of Nations and beginning a process of rearmament in direct violation of the Versailles Treaty. The concept of Lebensraum or "living space" became a driving force behind Nazi Germany's expansionist ambitions, particularly towards the East.

The international community's response to these provocations was characterized by a policy of appeasement, exemplified by the Munich Agreement of 1938, which allowed Germany to annex the Sudetenland from Czechoslovakia. This approach, aimed at avoiding another devastating war, ultimately emboldened Hitler and set the stage for further aggression.

## The Birth of Blitzkrieg: A New Form of Warfare

The concept of Blitzkrieg emerged from the innovative thinking of German military strategists in the interwar period. Seeking to avoid the stalemate of trench warfare that had characterized much of World War I, they developed a strategy that emphasized speed, surprise, and the concentration of forces to achieve quick victories.

Key figures like Heinz Guderian played crucial roles in developing Blitzkrieg tactics. Guderian advocated for the integration of tanks, motorized infantry, and air support to create a highly mobile and flexible fighting force capable of rapid breakthroughs and encirclements.

**The Blitzkrieg strategy involved several key components:**

**1. Speed and Mobility:** Fast-moving tanks, known as Panzers, formed the spearhead of the attack, supported by motorized infantry that could keep pace with the advancing armor.

**2. Concentration of Force:** Blitzkrieg tactics emphasized concentrating a large number of forces at a single point to break through enemy defenses.

**3. Combined Arms Operations:** Tanks, infantry, artillery, and air support worked in tandem to create a synergistic effect that was greater than the sum of its parts.

**4. Air Support:** The Luftwaffe played a crucial role, providing close air support and disrupting enemy communications and supply lines.

**5. Psychological Warfare:** The sudden and overwhelming nature of Blitzkrieg attacks was designed to create confusion, panic, and disorganization among enemy troops.

**The Low Countries: Unprepared for the Storm**

As tensions mounted in Europe, the Low Countries found themselves in a precarious position. Despite their efforts to remain neutral, the Netherlands, Belgium, and Luxembourg were ill-prepared for the coming onslaught.

The Netherlands had mobilized approximately 280,000 men, but they were poorly armed, with only a handful of tanks and outdated aircraft. The Dutch defense strategy heavily relied on the use of water as a defensive barrier, planning to flood certain areas to slow down the German advance. However, this strategy had a critical flaw: it did not effectively integrate with the Belgian defense lines.

Belgium's defenses were more robust, with a fully mobilized army of around 500,000 troops. The primary defensive line was along the Meuse River and the Albert Canal, featuring steep banks and a series of forts, including the formidable Fort Eben-Emael. However, the Belgian strategy was based on the expectation that the main German attack would follow the Schlieffen Plan of World War I, leading to a concentration of forces in central Belgium.

Luxembourg, being a small and neutral country, had minimal military defenses and was quickly overrun by German forces.

**The Lightning Strikes: The Invasion Begins**

On May 10, 1940, the German invasion of the Low Countries began with a series of coordinated attacks. In the Netherlands, German forces used paratroopers to capture key locations, including Rotterdam and The Hague. The speed and coordination of the attack left little time for the Dutch military to mount an effective defense.

In Belgium, the invasion involved intense fighting, including the Battle of Hannut, which was the largest tank battle at the time. The German forces executed a daring maneuver through the Ardennes Forest, a region considered impassable by the French military. This surprise move caught the Allies off guard and allowed German armored divisions to break through and rapidly advance towards the English Channel.

Luxembourg fell within a day due to minimal resistance, providing a route for German forces to bypass the heavily fortified Maginot Line in France.

## The Fall of the Low Countries

The speed and ferocity of the German advance overwhelmed the defenses of the Low Countries. On May 14, the city of Rotterdam was heavily bombed by the Luftwaffe, resulting in significant civilian casualties and widespread destruction. This bombing, coupled with the threat of further attacks on other cities, led to the Dutch surrender on May 15, 1940.

Belgium held out longer, but the rapid German advance through the Ardennes had outflanked their strongest defenses. On May 28, 1940, the Belgian Army, under King Leopold III, surrendered to German forces after being pushed into a small pocket in the northwest of the country.

## The Human Cost and Aftermath

The Blitzkrieg campaign in the Low Countries had profound and far-reaching consequences. The swift German victory led to the occupation of the Netherlands, Belgium, and Luxembourg, which would last until 1944-1945. This occupation had severe consequences, including economic exploitation and the persecution of Jewish populations.

The invasion caused widespread panic among civilians, leading to a massive refugee crisis as millions fled westward to escape the advancing German forces. Personal accounts from the time describe the shock and fear experienced by both soldiers and civilians. The bombing of Rotterdam, in particular, left a lasting scar on the national psyche, symbolizing the brutality of the conflict.

Despite the occupation, resistance movements emerged in the Low Countries, playing crucial roles in gathering intelligence, sabotaging German operations, and assisting Allied forces later in the war.

## International Reactions and Long-term Impact

The rapid fall of the Low Countries and the subsequent invasion of France shocked the world and demonstrated the effectiveness of Germany's new military tactics. The Allies, particularly Britain and France, were forced to reassess their military strategies and defenses. It underscored the need for more mobile and flexible military tactics, leading to changes in Allied military planning and operations.

The events in the Low Countries drew international attention and sympathy, particularly from the United States, which began to increase its support for the Allies through measures like the Lend-Lease Act.

## Conclusion

The Blitzkrieg expansion into the Low Countries was a pivotal moment in World War II, demonstrating the devastating effectiveness of Germany's new military tactics. It reshaped military strategies, influenced political alliances, and had significant humanitarian impacts. The swift fall of the Netherlands, Belgium, and Luxembourg paved the way for the German advance into France and set the stage for the broader European conflict.

While initially successful, the limitations of Blitzkrieg tactics would become apparent as the war progressed, particularly during the invasion of the Soviet Union. Nevertheless, the lessons learned from these early campaigns continue to influence military doctrine and international relations to this day.

The story of the Blitzkrieg in the Low Countries serves as a powerful reminder of the horrors of war, the importance of international cooperation, and the resilience of the human spirit in the face of overwhelming odds. It remains a crucial chapter in the history of World War II, shaping the course of the conflict and the post-war world order.

The occupation of the Low Countries had lasting effects on the region. The economies of these nations were severely disrupted, with industries repurposed to support the German war effort and resources extracted to benefit the Nazi regime. This led to shortages and economic hardship for the local populations. The imposition of Nazi ideology and policies, including anti-Semitic laws, led to the persecution of Jewish communities and other minority groups.

After the liberation of the Low Countries by Allied forces in 1944-1945, these nations faced the daunting task of rebuilding their economies and infrastructure. The war had left significant destruction, and recovery required substantial international aid and cooperation. The experience of occupation and the war led to significant political changes in the Low Countries. There was a shift towards more democratic and socially inclusive policies, as well as a commitment to international cooperation, which eventually contributed to the formation of the European Union.

The invasion and occupation left a lasting legacy on the collective memory and identity of the Low Countries. The events of World War II continue to influence cultural narratives and are commemorated through various memorials and educational programs. The resilience shown by the people of the Low Countries during the occupation, their resistance efforts, and their subsequent recovery serve as a testament to human endurance and the capacity for renewal in the face of adversity.

In the broader context of World War II, the Blitzkrieg campaign in the Low Countries marked a turning point in military strategy and international relations. It demonstrated the vulnerability of smaller nations caught between great powers and the devastating potential of modern warfare. The swift fall of these countries, despite their neutrality and defensive preparations, highlighted the need for stronger international cooperation and collective security arrangements.

The success of the Blitzkrieg tactics in the Low Countries and France led to a period of German dominance in Europe. However, it also set the stage for the eventual Allied counteroffensive. The lessons learned from these early German victories influenced Allied strategy, leading to the development of more effective tactics and technologies that would eventually turn the tide of the war.

In conclusion, the Blitzkrieg expansion into the Low Countries was more than just a military campaign; it was a watershed moment that reshaped the course of World War II and had lasting implications for European and global history. It serves as a stark reminder of the costs of war and the importance of international cooperation in maintaining peace and security. The resilience and eventual recovery of the Low Countries in the aftermath of this devastating invasion stand as a testament to the strength of democratic values and the human spirit in the face of tyranny and oppression.

**Sources**

Hughes, Thomas. World War II. Encyclopedia Britannica, 2024

Cohen, Chaim. Rescue and Resistance: The Story of the Dutch Jews During World War II. University of California Press, 2004.

Various Sources

# Operation Dynamo: The Miracle of Dunkirk

**Introduction**

In the annals of military history, few events capture the imagination quite like the Dunkirk evacuation, codenamed Operation Dynamo. This extraordinary rescue mission, which unfolded on the beaches of northern France in the early days of World War II, stands as a testament to human resilience, ingenuity, and the indomitable spirit of a nation facing its darkest hour. From May 26 to June 4, 1940, the world witnessed an unprecedented military evacuation that would come to be known as the "Miracle of Dunkirk."

**The Road to Dunkirk**

The story of Dunkirk begins with the outbreak of World War II in September 1939. As Nazi Germany unleashed its military might across Europe, the United Kingdom dispatched the British Expeditionary Force (BEF) to aid in the defense of France. For months, an uneasy calm prevailed along the Franco-German border, a period known as the "Phony War." But this calm was shattered in May 1940 when Germany launched its blitzkrieg, or "lightning war," against the Low Countries and France.

The German advance was swift and devastating. Employing a combination of fast-moving tanks, mechanized infantry, and overwhelming air support, the Wehrmacht outflanked the Maginot Line, France's primary defensive fortification, by pushing through the densely forested Ardennes region. This maneuver, which caught the Allies completely off guard, allowed German forces to drive a wedge between the bulk of the Allied armies in Belgium and the French forces south of the Somme River.

By May 19, 1940, the situation for the Allies had become increasingly desperate. General John Gort, commander of the BEF, began considering evacuation as the only viable option to save his forces from encirclement. Faced with the prospect of losing the cream of Britain's professional army, Prime Minister Winston Churchill and his military advisors made the difficult decision to attempt an evacuation.

## Planning the Impossible

The task of organizing this massive undertaking fell to Vice Admiral Bertram Ramsay. Operating from a command center in the tunnels beneath Dover Castle, Ramsay and his team worked tirelessly to cobble together a plan that would come to be known as Operation Dynamo. The name itself was derived from the dynamo room that had once powered the castle's electric generator, a fitting moniker for an operation that would require every ounce of energy and ingenuity the British could muster.

The challenges facing Ramsay were immense. The port facilities at Dunkirk had been heavily damaged by German bombing, and the beaches were too shallow to allow large naval vessels to approach the shore. Moreover, the evacuation would have to be carried out under constant threat of attack from the Luftwaffe, Germany's formidable air force.

## The Miracle Begins

On May 26, 1940, Operation Dynamo was officially launched at 6:57 PM. The initial progress was slow, with only 7,669 men evacuated on the first day. However, as more ships joined the effort and innovative solutions were found to overcome logistical hurdles, the pace of the evacuation quickened.

One of the most crucial innovations came from Captain William Tennant, who had been designated as the "beachmaster" at Dunkirk. Tennant realized that the eastern breakwater, or mole, could be used as an improvised dock, allowing troops to board larger ships directly. This simple yet brilliant idea significantly increased the number of soldiers that could be evacuated each day.

As news of the evacuation spread, the British public rallied to the cause. In one of the most stirring displays of civilian courage in modern history, hundreds of small boats - fishing trawlers, pleasure craft, and even lifeboats - set sail across the English Channel to aid in the rescue effort. These vessels, which came to be known as the "Little Ships," played a vital role in ferrying soldiers from the beaches to the larger naval vessels waiting offshore.

## The Battle for Time

A crucial factor in the success of Operation Dynamo was an unexpected decision by the German high command. On May 24, Adolf Hitler issued a halt order to his panzer divisions, which were poised to overrun Dunkirk. The reasons for this decision remain debated to this day, but it is believed that a combination of factors, including concerns about the terrain around Dunkirk and overconfidence in the Luftwaffe's ability to prevent an evacuation, led to this momentous pause in the German advance.

This halt order provided the Allies with precious time to organize their defenses and accelerate the evacuation. French and British troops fought tenaciously to hold a defensive perimeter around Dunkirk, buying time for their comrades to escape. The Belgian army, though ultimately forced to surrender on May 28, also played a crucial role in slowing the German advance.

## The Evacuation Unfolds

As the evacuation entered its final days, the situation on the beaches became increasingly desperate. The German forces, realizing the opportunity that was slipping away, intensified their attacks. Yet, against all odds, the evacuation continued. The Royal Navy, along with civilian volunteers, made repeated trips across the Channel, often under heavy fire from German artillery and aircraft.

The Royal Air Force, though outnumbered, fought valiantly to provide air cover for the evacuation, engaging in fierce dogfights with the Luftwaffe over the beaches and surrounding waters. Their efforts, while costly, were crucial in preventing the Luftwaffe from completely disrupting the evacuation.

The evacuation reached its peak on May 31, with an astounding 68,014 troops rescued in a single day. However, the operation was not without its setbacks and tragedies. German bombers took a heavy toll on the ships involved in the operation, with several vessels being sunk with significant loss of life. On the beaches, soldiers endured long waits under the constant threat of air attack, with limited food and water.

**The Final Push**

As the evacuation entered its final phase, the focus shifted to rescuing as many French troops as possible. On June 2, the evacuation of the BEF was completed, but the operation continued for two more days to rescue Allied forces. On June 4, 1940, Operation Dynamo officially came to an end.

**Conclusion**

The results of Operation Dynamo far exceeded even the most optimistic initial estimates. Over the course of nine days, 338,226 Allied soldiers were evacuated from Dunkirk, including 198,000 British and 140,000 French troops. This number was far beyond the 45,000 that British military planners had initially hoped to rescue.

However, the success of the evacuation came at a significant cost. Almost all of the BEF's heavy equipment, including tanks, artillery, and vehicles, had to be abandoned on the beaches. The Royal Navy lost six destroyers and over 200 smaller craft during the operation. The RAF, too, suffered heavy losses in its efforts to provide air cover for the evacuation.

In the immediate aftermath of Dunkirk, the mood in Britain was a complex mixture of relief, pride, and apprehension. Winston Churchill, in a speech to the House of Commons, captured this sentiment perfectly when he warned, "We must be very careful not to assign to this deliverance the attributes of a victory. Wars are not won by evacuations."

Yet, despite Churchill's caution, the "Miracle of Dunkirk" quickly became a powerful symbol of British resilience and determination. The successful evacuation preserved a significant portion of Britain's trained military forces, which would prove vital in the continued fight against Nazi Germany. Moreover, the spirit of unity and courage displayed during the operation - which came to be known as the "Dunkirk spirit" - provided a much-needed morale boost to the British public at one of the darkest moments of the war.

The impact of Dunkirk extended far beyond the immediate military situation. It became a defining moment in British national identity, a story of snatching hope from the jaws of defeat that resonated deeply with a nation facing the prospect of invasion and occupation. The image of the "Little Ships" - civilian vessels sailing into danger to rescue their country's soldiers - became an enduring symbol of the home front's contribution to the war effort.

In the broader context of World War II, the Dunkirk evacuation marked a turning point. While it was a tactical retreat, it laid the foundation for Britain's continued resistance and ultimate victory. The preservation of the BEF allowed Britain to defend itself against the threat of invasion and, in time, to build the forces that would return to the continent on D-Day in 1944.

Operation Dynamo, the Miracle of Dunkirk, stands as one of the most remarkable military evacuations in history. It was a moment when the fate of nations hung in the balance, and ordinary people rose to extraordinary challenges. From the soldiers who fought rearguard actions to buy time for their comrades, to the civilian boatmen who braved enemy fire to rescue strangers, to the planners and commanders who organized the impossible, the story of Dunkirk is one of collective heroism and determination. It remains a testament to the power of hope and the indomitable human spirit in the darkest of times, a lesson that continues to inspire and resonate to this day.

**Sources**

Gonzalez, Naomi Cardona. World War II in Europe. Study.com, 2023.

Hart, Bradley W. The Allies of World War II. The National WWII Museum. 2024

Various Sources

# The Battle and Fall of France

## Introduction

As dawn broke on May 10, 1940, an eerie calm hung over the French countryside. The cool spring air carried a sense of foreboding, as if the very land itself could sense the impending storm. For months, the French and British forces had waited, poised behind their defenses, anticipating the German attack that seemed inevitable. This period, known as the "Phoney War," was about to come to an abrupt and violent end.

## The Storm Breaks

The stillness of the morning was shattered by the roar of aircraft engines. German planes filled the skies, their bombs raining down on airfields, communication centers, and defensive positions across France and the Low Countries. The Blitzkrieg, or "Lightning War," had begun.

As the initial shock of the air assault subsided, reports began flooding in from the front lines. German forces were pouring across the borders of the Netherlands, Belgium, and Luxembourg. The speed and ferocity of the attack caught many off guard, despite months of preparation.

One young French soldier, Pierre Dubois, later recalled the chaos of those first hours: "We had trained for months, but nothing could have prepared us for the reality of the German assault. The sky seemed filled with planes, the ground shook with the rumble of tanks. It was as if the very gates of hell had opened before us."

## The Ardennes Gambit

While Allied attention was focused on the expected German thrust through the Low Countries, a far more audacious plan was unfolding in the dense Ardennes Forest. This region, with its rough terrain and thick woods, had been deemed impassable for large military forces by French strategists. It was here that the true masterstroke of the German plan would be revealed.

General Heinz Guderian, the brilliant tactician behind the German armored forces, had seen the potential that others had missed. As his Panzer divisions wound their way through the narrow forest roads, the tension was palpable. Success here could split the Allied forces in two, but a strong defense could bog down the entire German offensive.

On May 13, the German forces emerged from the forest near the town of Sedan. The French defenses, caught completely off guard, crumbled under the combined assault of tanks, infantry, and dive-bombers. By May 15, the Germans had achieved a decisive breakthrough, opening a corridor to the English Channel.

## The Race to the Sea

With the German breakthrough at Sedan, the battle transformed into a desperate race. German armored columns surged westward, while Allied forces scrambled to form a cohesive defense. The speed of the German advance was unprecedented, covering ground that military planners had estimated would take weeks in mere days.

British and French commanders, still operating under pre-war assumptions, struggled to adapt to the fluid situation. Orders and counter-orders flew back and forth, often outdated before they could be implemented. The result was confusion and disarray among the Allied forces.

A British officer, Major John Howard, described the scene: "It was like trying to plug a dam with our bare hands. Every time we thought we had contained the German advance, reports would come in of another breakthrough, another town fallen. The speed of it all was simply overwhelming."

The Allied defensive strategies, which had seemed so solid on paper, were crumbling in the face of the German Blitzkrieg. The Maginot Line, France's pride and supposed bulwark against invasion, was rendered irrelevant as German forces simply bypassed it. The static defenses and rigid command structures that had been the cornerstone of Allied planning proved woefully inadequate against the fast-moving, flexible German tactics.

## Encirclement

By May 20, German forces had reached the English Channel, effectively cutting off the British Expeditionary Force (BEF) and a significant portion of the French army in a pocket around the port of Dunkirk. The situation for the Allies seemed dire, with over 300,000 troops facing the prospect of annihilation or capture.

In London, newly appointed Prime Minister Winston Churchill faced the gravest crisis of his career. The potential loss of Britain's professional army could leave the island nation vulnerable to invasion. It was in this moment of peril that one of the war's most remarkable operations was conceived.

## The Miracle of Dunkirk

Operation Dynamo, the evacuation of Allied forces from Dunkirk, began on May 26. What unfolded over the next nine days would become one of the most stirring episodes of the war. A flotilla of ships, from Royal Navy destroyers to civilian pleasure craft, set out across the English Channel to rescue the stranded troops.

On the beaches of Dunkirk, soldiers waited under constant German air attack. The scene was one of both desperation and determination. Private Arthur Watkins, one of the soldiers awaiting evacuation, later wrote: "We stood in long lines stretching into the sea, the water up to our chests, praying for rescue. The sky was filled with smoke and the thunder of bombs, but still the little ships came, again and again."

The Royal Air Force fought valiantly to provide air cover for the evacuation, engaging in fierce dogfights with the Luftwaffe over the beaches and surrounding waters. Despite being outnumbered, RAF pilots managed to disrupt many German bombing runs, buying precious time for the evacuation efforts.

Against all odds, over 338,000 Allied troops were evacuated from Dunkirk by June 4. While the operation was a logistical triumph, it came at a heavy cost. Most of the BEF's heavy equipment had to be abandoned on the beaches, and the Luftwaffe exacted a heavy toll on the evacuation fleet.

**The Fall of France**

With the bulk of the British forces evacuated and the French army in disarray, the fate of France hung in the balance. The German advance continued relentlessly southward. On June 10, Italy, sensing an opportunity, declared war on France and Britain, further complicating the Allied position.

As German forces approached Paris, the French government faced a terrible dilemma. Prime Minister Paul Reynaud favored continuing the fight, even if it meant retreating to French North Africa. However, many in the government, including the revered World War I hero Marshal Philippe Pétain, argued for an armistice to spare France further destruction.

On June 14, Paris fell, declared an open city to spare it from destruction. The sight of German troops marching down the Champs-Élysées became one of the war's most iconic and heartbreaking images. For many French citizens, the fall of Paris marked the end of hope. Marie Leclerc, a Parisian shopkeeper, described the mood: "It was as if the light had gone out of the world. To see those German soldiers in our beloved city, to hear their boots on our streets... it was a pain beyond words."

The French government, now led by Pétain, sued for peace. On June 22, 1940, France officially surrendered. In a final act of humiliation, the armistice was signed in the same railway carriage where Germany had surrendered in 1918, at Compiègne. The Battle of France was over, lasting just six weeks.

**Aftermath and Reflection**

The swift fall of France sent shockwaves around the world. It demonstrated the devastating effectiveness of the German Blitzkrieg tactics and exposed the inadequacies of Allied strategy and preparation. For the people of France, it marked the beginning of four long years of occupation, hardship, and resistance.

Under the terms of the armistice, Germany occupied three-fifths of France, including Paris and the entire Atlantic coast. The remaining part of the country was left unoccupied but under the control of the Vichy government, a collaborationist regime led by Pétain. This division would have profound implications for France's future and the course of the war.

The battle's outcome reshaped the strategic landscape of World War II. Germany now dominated continental Europe, with only Britain standing against the Nazi regime. The United States, still officially neutral, began to increase its support for Britain, recognizing the growing threat to global security.

For many French citizens, the defeat was a source of deep shame and disillusionment. However, it also sparked the birth of the French Resistance, a movement that would play a crucial role in gathering intelligence, conducting sabotage operations, and maintaining hope for eventual liberation.

The fall of France had significant consequences for the French colonial empire as well. Some colonies, like those in Indochina, fell under Japanese influence, while others, such as those in Africa, became battlegrounds between Vichy forces and those loyal to the Free French movement led by Charles de Gaulle.

As the dust settled on the battlefields of France, the world grappled with the implications of this seismic shift in power. The Battle of France had not only redrawn the map of Europe but had also ushered in a new era of warfare, one where speed, coordination, and adaptability would prove decisive.

## Conclusion

In the years that followed, the lessons of the Battle of France would be studied and debated by military strategists around the world. Its impact would be felt not only in the subsequent campaigns of World War II but in conflicts for generations to come. The failure of static defenses like the Maginot Line led to a reevaluation of military doctrines, emphasizing mobility, air power, and combined arms operations.

In the aftermath of the war, France would undergo significant political and social changes. The experience of defeat and occupation led to a reevaluation of national identity and foreign policy. The Fourth Republic was established, and France embarked on a path of reconstruction and modernization. Perhaps most significantly, the defeat of 1940 played a crucial role in shaping France's post-war relationship with Germany.

## Sources

Gilbert, Martin. The Second World War: A Complete History. Holt Paperbacks, 2004.

Churchill, Sir Winston. The Second World War: A Complete History. Mariner Books, 1986.

Various Sources

# The Battle of Britain: A Triumph of Courage and Technology

**Introduction**

In the summer of 1940, the skies over Britain became the stage for one of the most decisive battles in modern history. The Battle of Britain, fought between July and October of that year, was not merely a clash of air forces; it was a testament to human resilience, technological innovation, and strategic brilliance. As the first major military campaign to be fought entirely in the air, it marked a turning point in World War II and shaped the future of aerial warfare.

Following the fall of France in June 1940, Britain stood alone against the might of Nazi Germany. The English Channel, once a moat of safety, now seemed a narrow barrier against the specter of invasion. Adolf Hitler, flush with victory on the continent, turned his gaze across the water, believing that Britain's defeat was the key to German dominance in Europe. But before any invasion could be launched, the Luftwaffe needed to gain air superiority over the Royal Air Force (RAF). What followed was a battle that would test the limits of both men and machines and ultimately determine the fate of a nation.

**The Gathering Storm**

As dawn broke on July 10, 1940, an eerie calm hung over the English Channel. For months, Britain had braced itself for the inevitable German onslaught. The period known as the "Phoney War" had ended with the swift and brutal conquest of France, leaving the British Isles as the last bastion of resistance in Western Europe.

In the halls of power in London, newly appointed Prime Minister Winston Churchill rallied his nation with words of defiance and determination. "What General Weygand called the Battle of France is over," he had declared to the House of Commons on June 18. "I expect that the Battle of Britain is about to begin." His words would prove prophetic.

Across the Channel, the German high command was finalizing its plans. Operation Sea Lion, the proposed invasion of Britain, hinged on the Luftwaffe's ability to neutralize the RAF and gain control of the skies. Reichsmarschall Hermann Göring, commander-in-chief of the Luftwaffe, was confident of swift victory. "If we beat the RAF," he boasted, "invasion will be like a knife through butter."

## The Opening Salvos

The battle began in earnest with the Kanalkampf, or Channel Battle, as German aircraft launched sustained attacks against British shipping in the English Channel. This phase was intended to draw out the RAF and deplete its resources. The skies over the Channel became a swirling melee of fighters, as Spitfires and Hurricanes clashed with Messerschmitt Bf 109s in a deadly dance of speed and firepower.

One RAF pilot, Flight Lieutenant John Dundas, later recalled the intensity of these early engagements: "It was like nothing we had ever experienced. The sky seemed filled with aircraft, friend, and foe alike. You had to keep your wits about you every second, or you'd be dead before you knew it."

As July gave way to August, the Luftwaffe shifted its focus to RAF airfields and radar stations. This phase, known as Adlerangriff or "Eagle Attack," marked a significant escalation in the battle's intensity. German bombers, escorted by fighters, streamed across the Channel in waves, targeting the vital infrastructure of Britain's air defense system.

## The Dowding System: Britain's Secret Weapon

Unknown to the Germans, Britain possessed a secret weapon that would prove crucial in the coming battle. Air Chief Marshal Sir Hugh Dowding, commander-in-chief of RAF Fighter Command, had overseen the development of an integrated air defense network known as the Dowding System. At its heart was a chain of radar stations along the coast, capable of detecting incoming aircraft at distances of up to 120 miles.

This early warning system, combined with a network of ground observers and a centralized control and command structure, allowed the RAF to efficiently direct its limited resources to meet the German threat. Fighter squadrons could be scrambled with precision, intercepting incoming raids before they reached their targets.

The importance of this system cannot be overstated. As one RAF controller, Betty Webb, later recounted: "We were the eyes and ears of the defense. Without us, our pilots would have been flying blind. Every minute of warning we could give them increased their chances of survival and success."

## The Battle Intensifies

As August wore on, the battle reached a fever pitch. The Luftwaffe launched massive raids against RAF airfields and radar stations, seeking to cripple Britain's air defenses. The strain on RAF pilots was immense, with many flying multiple sorties a day. Exhaustion became as much an enemy as the Luftwaffe.

Squadron Leader Douglas Bader, a legless fighter ace who became one of the iconic figures of the battle, described the relentless pace: "You'd come back from one scramble, land, refuel, rearm, and be off again before you'd even had a chance to catch your breath. But we knew what was at stake. It was a case of fly and fight until you dropped."

The RAF's fighters, particularly the agile Spitfire and the sturdy Hurricane, proved more than a match for their German counterparts. While the Messerschmitt Bf 109 was a formidable opponent, the British aircraft had the advantage of fighting over home territory. Downed RAF pilots could often be back in the air within hours, while Luftwaffe airmen who bailed out over England faced capture.

## The Blitz Begins

A critical turning point came in early September. Frustrated by the RAF's continued resistance, Hitler ordered a change in strategy. On September 7, the Luftwaffe shifted its focus from military targets to London and other major cities. This decision, intended to break British morale, would prove to be a crucial mistake.

The first major raid on London, involving nearly 1,000 aircraft, marked the beginning of the Blitz. For 57 consecutive nights, German bombers pounded the British capital. The civilian population endured terrible hardships but displayed remarkable resilience. The "Blitz spirit" became a byword for British determination in the face of adversity.

A London shopkeeper, Mary Jenkins, recalled those harrowing nights: "We'd hear the sirens and head for the shelters. The noise was terrifying – the drone of the bombers, the crump of bombs, the bark of anti-aircraft guns. But come morning, we'd emerge, dust ourselves off, and carry on. What else could we do?"

While the bombing of cities inflicted significant damage and civilian casualties, it also gave the RAF a much-needed respite. With pressure relieved from its airfields, Fighter Command was able to regroup and repair its battered infrastructure. This strategic error by the Luftwaffe would prove decisive.

## The Tide Turns

As September progressed, it became clear that the Luftwaffe was failing to achieve its objectives. Despite Göring's boasts, the RAF had not been defeated. In fact, British aircraft production was outpacing German losses, while the Luftwaffe was losing irreplaceable experienced pilots over enemy territory.

The climax of the battle came on September 15, a day that would become known as Battle of Britain Day. The Luftwaffe launched two massive raids against London, confident that the RAF was on its last legs. Instead, they met fierce resistance. By day's end, the RAF had shot down 56 German aircraft for the loss of only 28 of its own. The German high command was forced to acknowledge that air superiority over Britain could not be achieved.

Air Vice-Marshal Keith Park, commander of 11 Group RAF, which bore the brunt of the fighting, summed up the day's significance: "Never in the field of air fighting was so much owed by so many to so few." His words echoed those of Churchill, who had earlier paid tribute to the RAF pilots in one of his most famous speeches.

## The Battle Wanes

With the failure of the September 15 raids, the Luftwaffe gradually scaled back its operations. While bombing raids continued, particularly at night, the threat of invasion had passed. On October 12, Hitler officially postponed Operation Sea Lion indefinitely. The Battle of Britain was effectively over.

The cost had been high for both sides. The RAF had lost 544 pilots killed, while the Luftwaffe had lost over 2,500 airmen. But the significance of the victory far outweighed the losses. Britain had stood alone against Nazi Germany and prevailed. The myth of German invincibility had been shattered, and Hitler was forced to turn his attention eastward, towards the Soviet Union.

## Conclusion

The Battle of Britain stands as one of the defining moments of World War II. It was a victory won not just by the skill and courage of RAF pilots, but by the collective effort of an entire nation. From the scientists and engineers who developed radar technology to the ground crews who kept the planes flying, from the observers who spotted incoming raids to the civilians who endured the Blitz, every part of British society contributed to the triumph.

The battle's outcome had far-reaching consequences. It ensured Britain's survival as a base for the eventual Allied invasion of Europe. It marked the first major defeat for Nazi Germany, boosting morale across occupied Europe and demonstrating that resistance was possible. And it established the critical importance of air power in modern warfare, a lesson that would shape military strategy for decades to come.

Perhaps most importantly, the Battle of Britain became a powerful symbol of resistance against tyranny. In the darkest days of the war, when much of Europe lay under Nazi domination, the image of RAF fighters soaring to meet the Luftwaffe offered hope to millions. It showed that courage, determination, and technological innovation could overcome even the most formidable odds.

As we look back on the Battle of Britain, we are reminded of the thin line between victory and defeat in war, and of the profound impact that individual heroism and collective resilience can have on the course of history. The "few" to whom Churchill paid tribute did indeed save the many, and in doing so, they changed the world.

## Sources

Churchill, Sir Winston. The Second World War: A Complete History. Mariner Books, 1986.

Ford, Ken. The Blitz: The British Under Attack/ Osprey Publishing, 2010.

Various Sources

# Operation Barbarossa: The Invasion that Changed the Course of World War II

## Introduction

In the early hours of June 22, 1941, the calm of a summer morning along the Soviet Union's western border was shattered by the roar of engines and the thunder of artillery. Operation Barbarossa, Nazi Germany's massive invasion of the Soviet Union, had begun. This campaign, the largest military operation in history, would reshape the course of World War II and alter the geopolitical landscape of the 20th century.

As dawn broke, more than three million Axis troops surged across an 1,800-mile front, launching a war that would be characterized by its scale, brutality, and far-reaching consequences. Operation Barbarossa was not merely a military campaign; it was the manifestation of Adolf Hitler's ideological crusade against Communism and his quest for Lebensraum, or "living space," for the German people. The invasion would test the limits of human endurance, military strategy, and the capacity for both cruelty and heroism.

## The Road to Barbarossa

The seeds of Operation Barbarossa were sown in the twisted ideology of Nazi Germany and the complex political maneuvering that preceded World War II. Hitler had long viewed the vast expanses of the Soviet Union as the key to Germany's future. In his vision, the fertile lands of Ukraine and the resources of western Russia would provide the German people with the territory and materials needed to build a thousand-year Reich.

Ironically, the path to invasion was paved by an unlikely alliance. In August 1939, Nazi Germany and the Soviet Union shocked the world by signing the Molotov-Ribbentrop Pact, a non-aggression treaty that included secret protocols for dividing Eastern Europe into spheres of influence. This pact allowed Hitler to invade Poland without fear of Soviet intervention, effectively starting World War II.

However, the alliance was always a marriage of convenience, destined to be short-lived. As Germany conquered much of Western Europe in 1940, Hitler began to turn his gaze eastward. On December 18, 1940, he issued Führer Directive 21, ordering the preparation for the invasion of the Soviet Union. The stage was set for one of the most momentous military operations in history.

## The Invasion Begins

As the first light of dawn broke on June 22, 1941, the full might of the German war machine was unleashed. The invasion force was divided into three main army groups: Army Group North, aimed at Leningrad; Army Group Center, driving towards Moscow; and Army Group South, targeting Ukraine and the Caucasus oil fields.

The initial assault was overwhelming. German Panzer divisions, supported by Luftwaffe air strikes, smashed through Soviet defenses. The Blitzkrieg tactics that had proved so effective in Western Europe were now unleashed on a massive scale across the Russian steppes.

A German soldier, Hans Becker, later recalled the early days of the invasion: "We advanced so quickly that we often outran our supply lines. The vast expanse of Russia seemed to swallow us up, yet we kept pushing forward. There was a sense of invincibility among us, a belief that nothing could stop the German army."

The Soviet forces caught off guard despite numerous warnings, reeled under the onslaught. Joseph Stalin, who had dismissed intelligence reports of the impending invasion as British provocations, was initially paralyzed with disbelief. His inaction in the crucial first days of the invasion compounded the disaster.

## The Soviet Response

As the reality of the invasion set in, the Soviet Union began to mobilize its vast resources. Stalin, shaking off his initial shock, addressed the nation on July 3, calling for a patriotic war against the invaders. His speech, beginning with the words "Brothers and sisters," marked a shift in Soviet propaganda, appealing to Russian nationalism rather than Communist ideology.

The Soviet response was characterized by both desperation and determination. As German forces advanced, the Soviets adopted a "scorched earth" policy, destroying anything that could be of use to the invaders. Entire factories were dismantled and shipped east, beyond the Ural Mountains, in a herculean effort to preserve the Soviet Union's industrial capacity.

On the front lines, Soviet soldiers fought with a mixture of fatalism and fierce patriotism. A Soviet infantry officer, Vasily Ivanovich, described the brutal reality of the fighting: "We were often outgunned and outmaneuvered, but we fought for every inch of our motherland. The thought of German boots on Russian soil filled us with a rage that sustained us through the darkest hours."

## The Tide of War

As summer turned to autumn, the German advance began to slow. The vast distances of Russia, poor roads, and increasingly stiff Soviet resistance began to take their toll. The Blitzkrieg, which had been so effective in the war's early stages, began to lose its momentum.

A critical moment came in September 1941 with the Battle of Kiev. The German forces achieved a massive encirclement, capturing over 650,000 Soviet troops. However, this victory came at a cost. The diversion of forces to Kiev delayed the German advance on Moscow, a decision that would have far-reaching consequences.

As the Germans approached Moscow, launching Operation Typhoon in October, they faced not only determined Soviet resistance but also a new enemy: the Russian winter. As temperatures plummeted, the German army found itself woefully unprepared for the harsh conditions. Tanks and vehicles froze, weapons malfunctioned, and soldiers suffered from frostbite and exposure.

A German tank commander, Kurt Meyer, later wrote of the conditions: "The cold was unlike anything we had ever experienced. Our equipment, designed for a swift summer campaign, began to fail us. We watched helplessly as our mighty Panzers were reduced to frozen hulks in the snow."

**The Battle for Moscow**

The battle for Moscow became the crucible in which the fate of Operation Barbarossa would be decided. As German forces approached the Soviet capital, the city was transformed into a fortress. Citizens dug anti-tank ditches and built barricades, while every available soldier was thrown into the defense.

On December 5, 1941, with the Germans within sight of the Kremlin's spires, the Soviets launched a massive counteroffensive. Fresh Siberian divisions, released from the Far East after confirmation that Japan would not attack the Soviet Union, struck the overextended German lines.

The German forces, exhausted and ill-equipped for winter warfare, were driven back. For the first time in the war, the Wehrmacht was forced to retreat. The myth of German invincibility was shattered on the snowy approaches to Moscow.

**The Human Cost**

The Barbarossa Campaign exacted a terrible human toll. Millions of soldiers on both sides were killed, wounded, or captured. But it was the civilian population that suffered the greatest horrors. As the German armies advanced, they were followed by Einsatzgruppen, SS death squads tasked with eliminating those deemed racial or ideological enemies of the Reich.

In occupied territories, civilians faced a grim fate. Many were pressed into forced labor, while others, particularly Jews, faced systematic extermination. The brutality of the occupation fueled a fierce partisan resistance movement, which in turn led to harsh reprisals against the civilian population.

A survivor of the occupation, Maria Petrova, recounted the daily terror: "We lived in constant fear. The Germans could come at any moment, take our food, burn our homes, or worse. Many of us joined the partisans, preferring to die fighting rather than live under Nazi rule."

**The Turning Point**

The failure of Operation Barbarossa to achieve its objectives marked a turning point in World War II. The Soviet Union, despite enormous losses, had survived the initial onslaught. The war in the East devolved into a brutal war of attrition, one that Germany was ill-equipped to win.

The consequences of Barbarossa's failure were far-reaching. It forced Germany to fight a two-front war, dividing its resources and ultimately contributing to its defeat. For the Soviet Union, the victory at Moscow was a turning point, boosting morale and proving that the Nazi war machine could be stopped.

## Conclusion

Operation Barbarossa stands as one of the most significant military campaigns in history. Its failure marked the beginning of the end for Nazi Germany, while the Soviet Union's eventual triumph laid the groundwork for its emergence as a superpower in the post-war world.

The campaign's legacy extends far beyond military history. It shaped the political landscape of the Cold War, influenced military doctrine for generations, and left an indelible mark on the collective memory of the nations involved.

As we reflect on Operation Barbarossa, we are reminded of the enormous human cost of war, the dangers of ideological extremism, and the profound impact that strategic decisions can have on the course of history. The invasion of the Soviet Union was Hitler's greatest gamble, and its failure proved to be the turning point of World War II, setting in motion the events that would lead to the defeat of Nazi Germany and the reshaping of the world order.

The story of Barbarossa is one of monumental battles and sweeping strategies, but it is also a tale of individual courage, suffering, and resilience. From the soldiers who fought in the frozen steppes to the civilians who endured occupation and resistance, the human stories of Barbarossa remind us of the profound impact of war on individuals and societies.

In the end, Operation Barbarossa serves as a powerful reminder of the complexities of war, the limits of military power, and the indomitable spirit of those who fight for their homes and their freedom. Its lessons continue to resonate, offering insights into the nature of conflict and the human capacity for both destruction and heroism.

## Sources

Mawdsley, Evan. Thunder in the East: The Nazi-Soviet War: 1941-1945. Bloomsbury Academic, 2015.

Hart, Sir Basil Liddell. History of the Second World War. Konecky & Konecky, 2007.

Various Sources

# Continued Conflict: The Eastern Front and Mediterranean Campaigns

### Battle of Moscow (October 1941 - January 1942)

The Battle of Moscow began in October 1941, as German forces launched Operation Typhoon, aiming to capture the Soviet capital before winter set in. Initially, the Germans made significant advances, reaching the outskirts of Moscow by late November. However, the Soviet defenders, bolstered by reinforcements from Siberia and a fierce determination to protect their homeland, mounted a counteroffensive on December 5. The harsh winter weather, combined with logistical challenges, took a toll on the poorly equipped German troops. As temperatures plummeted, the Soviets successfully pushed the Germans back, marking a crucial turning point in the Eastern Front and demonstrating the resilience of the Red Army.

### Battle of Stalingrad (August 1942 - February 1943)

The Battle of Stalingrad, fought from August 1942 to February 1943, marked one of the most brutal confrontations of World War II. Hitler aimed to capture the city for its strategic importance and symbolic value, initiating a fierce assault that turned into a protracted battle of attrition. The Soviets, under General Vasily Chuikov, defended the city tenaciously, with combat often occurring in close quarters. By November, the Red Army launched Operation Uranus, encircling the German Sixth Army. The encirclement led to the surrender of over 300,000 German troops in February 1943, a decisive Soviet victory that shifted the tide of the war in favor of the Allies and marked the beginning of a series of Soviet offensives.

### Battle of El Alamein (October - November 1942)

The Second Battle of El Alamein, fought from October 23 to November 11, 1942, was a pivotal confrontation in the North African Campaign. British forces, led by General Bernard Montgomery, launched a counteroffensive against the Axis troops commanded by Field Marshal Erwin Rommel. After a carefully planned artillery barrage, the Allies attacked, successfully pushing back the German and Italian forces. The victory at El Alamein halted the Axis advance toward the Suez Canal and marked a turning point in the North African Campaign, ultimately leading to the retreat of Axis forces from North Africa by May 1943.

## Operation Torch (November 1942)

Operation Torch commenced on November 8, 1942, as Allied forces launched an amphibious invasion of French North Africa. The operation aimed to secure the region and pave the way for further operations in Europe. Landing in Morocco and Algeria, American and British troops faced minimal resistance from Vichy French forces, who were caught off guard. The successful landings marked the first major Allied offensive in the European theater, and within a few months, Axis forces in North Africa were forced to surrender, contributing to the eventual liberation of the region.

## Battle of Kursk (July - August 1943)

The Battle of Kursk, fought from July 5 to August 23, 1943, was the largest tank battle in history and a critical confrontation on the Eastern Front. Following the defeat at Stalingrad, the Germans launched Operation Citadel, aiming to recapture the initiative. However, the Soviets had anticipated the attack and fortified their defenses extensively. The battle saw fierce fighting and massive tank engagements, ultimately resulting in a decisive Soviet victory. The successful defense at Kursk marked the end of German offensive capabilities on the Eastern Front, allowing the Soviets to take the initiative and begin their counteroffensive operations.

## Battle of Sicily (July - August 1943)

The Allied invasion of Sicily, known as Operation Husky, began on July 9, 1943. This significant operation aimed to secure a base for further Allied advances into Italy. American, British, and Canadian forces landed on the island, facing initial resistance from German and Italian troops. However, the Allies quickly gained ground, and by August 17, they had successfully captured the island. The victory in Sicily led to the overthrow of Mussolini and facilitated the subsequent invasion of mainland Italy, marking a turning point in the Italian Campaign.

## Battle of Salerno (September 1943)

The Battle of Salerno began on September 9, 1943, as Allied forces landed on the Italian mainland as part of the Italian Campaign. American and British troops faced stiff German resistance, leading to intense fighting along the beaches. Despite initial setbacks and counterattacks, the Allies managed to establish a beachhead and gradually pushed inland. The battle culminated in the successful establishment of a base for further operations in Italy, paving the way for the Allied advance toward Naples and eventually the liberation of the country.

## Sources

Hughes, Thomas. World War II. Encyclopedia Britannica, 2024

Gilbert, Martin. The Second World War: A Complete History. Holt Paperbacks, 2004.

Various Sources

# D-Day: The Invasion that Changed the Course of the War

**Introduction**

In the predawn hours of June 6, 1944, the largest amphibious invasion in history was poised to begin. Operation Overlord, better known as D-Day, would mark the beginning of the end for Nazi Germany's occupation of Western Europe. As the first light of dawn broke over the English Channel, a vast armada of ships and aircraft prepared to launch an assault that would change the course of World War II and shape the geopolitical landscape for generations to come.

The invasion was the culmination of years of planning, preparation, and sacrifice. It represented not just a military operation, but the hopes and fears of millions across the world who yearned for an end to the tyranny of Nazi rule. As the Allied forces prepared to storm the beaches of Normandy, they carried with them the weight of history and the knowledge that failure was not an option.

**The Road to D-Day**

The roots of Operation Overlord stretched back to the early days of World War II. Following the fall of France in 1940 and the evacuation of Allied forces from Dunkirk, it became clear that a return to the continent was necessary to defeat Nazi Germany. The concept of a cross-Channel invasion to liberate Europe was conceived early in the war, but it would take years of planning and preparation to bring it to fruition.

The entry of the United States into the war in December 1941 accelerated these plans. The Allies, particularly the United States and the United Kingdom, engaged in extensive discussions to agree on a strategy focused on defeating Germany first. At the Tehran Conference in November 1943, Allied leaders Franklin D. Roosevelt, Winston Churchill, and Joseph Stalin made the crucial decision to launch a spring 1944 invasion.

General Dwight D. Eisenhower was appointed as the Supreme Commander of the Allied Expeditionary Force in January 1944, intensifying preparations for the invasion. Under his leadership, the Allies embarked on a massive buildup of forces and resources in the United Kingdom. Millions of men were trained, and thousands of vehicles, ships, and aircraft were constructed in preparation for the assault.

## The Deception Game

A critical component of the D-Day strategy was Operation Fortitude, an elaborate deception plan designed to mislead the German High Command about the location of the invasion. The Allies created a phantom army, led by General George S. Patton, to suggest that the invasion would occur at Pas-de-Calais, rather than Normandy.

This deception involved fake equipment, misleading radio transmissions, and double agents feeding false information to the Germans. The success of this operation would prove crucial in the coming battle, as it kept significant German forces tied down in the wrong location.

## The Eve of Battle

As the invasion date approached, tension mounted among the Allied forces. The original date for the invasion was set for June 5, 1944, but poor weather conditions led to a 24-hour delay. This delay was agonizing for the troops, many of whom had already been briefed on their objectives and were primed for action.

One paratrooper, John Steele, later recalled the atmosphere on the eve of the invasion: "We were all on edge, a mixture of excitement and fear. We knew what was at stake, and we knew many of us wouldn't be coming back. But there was also a sense of purpose, a feeling that we were part of something bigger than ourselves."

On the evening of June 5, General Eisenhower visited the paratroopers of the 101st Airborne Division. In a moment that would be immortalized in photographs, he spoke with the men, offering words of encouragement and sharing the weight of the moment. Later that night, in a decision that would shape the course of history, Eisenhower gave the final order: "Okay, we'll go."

## The Invasion Begins

In the early hours of June 6, the invasion began with airborne operations. Over 13,000 American paratroopers were dropped behind enemy lines to secure key positions and disrupt German defenses. Despite scattered drops and intense enemy fire, the paratroopers managed to achieve many of their objectives, sowing confusion among the German defenders.

As dawn broke, the full might of the Allied invasion force was revealed. A vast armada of over 7,000 naval vessels approached the Normandy coast, carrying approximately 156,000 troops. The ships had to navigate through rough seas and German minefields, adding to the tension of the moment.

At 6:30 AM, the amphibious landings commenced. Allied forces landed on five beaches along a 50-mile stretch of the Normandy coast, codenamed Utah, Omaha, Gold, Juno, and Sword. Each beach presented its own challenges, but it was Omaha Beach that would become synonymous with the brutal reality of the invasion.

## The Battle for the Beaches

The scene that unfolded on Omaha Beach was one of chaos and carnage. The pre-invasion bombardment had failed to neutralize many of the German defenses, and the American troops faced withering fire as they struggled to make their way across the beach. Private Robert Healey, who landed in the first wave at

Omaha, described the scene: "It was hell on earth. The water was red with blood, and the beach was littered with the bodies of my comrades. But we had no choice but to keep moving forward."

Despite the heavy casualties, particularly at Omaha Beach, the Allies succeeded in establishing a beachhead. By the end of the day, approximately 156,000 troops had landed in Normandy. The success of the landings was due in no small part to the bravery and determination of individual soldiers, who fought through fear and exhaustion to secure their objectives.

On the other beaches, the Allies made better progress. At Utah Beach, American forces quickly overcame initial resistance and pushed inland. The British and Canadian forces landing at Gold, Juno, and Sword beaches also made significant gains, despite facing stiff German opposition.

**The Aftermath**

By June 11, the beaches were fully secured, and the Allies had landed over 326,000 troops, 50,000 vehicles, and 100,000 tons of equipment. The successful establishment of a beachhead in Normandy marked a turning point in the war, opening a new front against Nazi Germany and setting the stage for the liberation of Western Europe.

The cost of the invasion was high. Thousands of Allied soldiers lost their lives on D-Day, with many more wounded. Yet their sacrifice paved the way for the eventual defeat of Nazi Germany. By the end of August 1944, the Allies had liberated Paris and were pushing towards the German border.

**Conclusion**

The D-Day invasion stands as one of the most significant military operations in history. Its success was the result of years of planning, the coordination of vast resources, and the courage of thousands of individual soldiers.

The legacy of D-Day extends far beyond the military realm. It demonstrated the power of international cooperation in the face of tyranny and laid the groundwork for the post-war international order.

**Sources**

Eisenhower, Dwight D. Crusade in Europe. Doubleday, 1948.

Ambrose, Stephen E. Citizen Soldiers: The US Army From the Normandy Beaches to the Bulge to the Surrender of Germany. Simon & Schuster, 1997.

Various Sources

**The Liberation of Paris: A Triumph of Resistance and Allied Cooperation**

**Introduction**

In the sweltering heat of August 1944, the city of Paris stood on the brink of a momentous change. For more than four years, the iconic streets of the French capital had echoed with the sound of German jackboots, its grand boulevards overshadowed by Nazi flags. The Liberation of Paris was not just a military operation; it was the culmination of years of resistance, hope, and sacrifice. As Allied forces approached the city, Parisians dared to dream of freedom once more, their spirits buoyed by whispers of approaching liberation carried on clandestine radio waves and passed in hushed conversations.

This pivotal moment in World War II would not only mark the end of the Nazi occupation of Paris but would also reshape the political landscape of France and have far-reaching consequences for the future of Europe. The story of Paris's liberation is one of courage, strategic brilliance, and the indomitable spirit of a people determined to reclaim their city and their freedom.

**The Road to Liberation**

The path to the liberation of Paris began on the beaches of Normandy. On June 6, 1944, Allied forces launched Operation Overlord, the largest amphibious invasion in history. As the Allies pushed inland, establishing a foothold in France, the question of Paris loomed large in strategic discussions. Initially, Allied commanders, including Supreme Commander Dwight D. Eisenhower, were reluctant to divert resources to liberate the city, preferring to bypass it in favor of a direct thrust into Germany.

However, events on the ground would soon force a reconsideration of this strategy. The French Resistance, a diverse and decentralized movement that had been a thorn in the side of the German occupiers for years, began to intensify its activities. Throughout the occupation, the Resistance had engaged in sabotage, intelligence gathering, and acts of defiance both large and small. Now, with Allied forces on French soil, the Resistance saw an opportunity to play a decisive role in liberating their capital.

On August 19, 1944, the powder keg of resistance in Paris finally ignited. Members of the French Forces of the Interior (FFI), the unified Resistance organization, launched an uprising in the city. Police officers who had gone on strike joined the revolt, seizing key buildings and erecting barricades throughout Paris. The sound of gunfire echoed through the streets as Resistance fighters engaged German troops, marking the beginning of a week that would change the course of the war in France.

## The Battle for Paris

As news of the uprising reached Allied headquarters, the strategic calculus shifted dramatically. General Charles de Gaulle, leader of the Free French forces, argued passionately for intervention, warning that failure to act could lead to a bloodbath in Paris and potentially allow communist elements within the Resistance to gain control of the city. Faced with this pressure and the rapidly evolving situation on the ground, Eisenhower made the fateful decision to divert forces to liberate Paris.

On August 22, Eisenhower ordered the French 2nd Armored Division, led by General Philippe Leclerc, to advance on Paris. Alongside them moved the U.S. 4th Infantry Division, providing crucial support to the operation. As these forces approached the city, the situation within Paris grew increasingly tense. Adolf Hitler, in a characteristic display of brutality, had ordered the German commander in Paris, General Dietrich von Choltitz, to destroy the city if it could not be held. "Paris must not fall into the enemy's hand except lying in complete debris," Hitler declared.

Von Choltitz, however, found himself caught between his oath to Hitler and his growing realization of the futility and immorality of such destruction. As Allied forces drew nearer and the Resistance fighters within the city intensified their attacks, von Choltitz hesitated to carry out Hitler's scorched earth policy.

Inside Paris, the atmosphere was electric with a mixture of fear, hope, and determination. One Resistance fighter, Marie Dubois, later recalled the intensity of those days: "We could feel the tide turning. Every street corner became a battlefield, every Parisian a potential soldier. We were fighting not just against the Germans, but for the soul of our city."

On August 24, elements of the French 2nd Armored Division managed to infiltrate the city, reaching the Hôtel de Ville (City Hall) by evening. The sight of French troops entering Paris electrified the population. Parisians poured into the streets, erecting more barricades and joining the fight against the remaining German forces.

The following day, August 25, saw the formal entry of Allied forces into Paris. General Leclerc's division and the U.S. 4th Infantry Division streamed into the city from different directions, greeted by jubilant crowds. Amidst the chaos and celebration, a pivotal moment occurred at the Meurice Hotel, where General von Choltitz had established his headquarters. Recognizing the futility of further resistance and perhaps moved by the historical and cultural significance of Paris, von Choltitz surrendered to French forces.

The formal surrender was signed later that day at the Police Prefecture on the Île de la Cité, marking the official liberation of Paris. As word spread, the city erupted in celebration. The bells of Notre-Dame rang out, joined by church bells across Paris in a cacophony of joy. People danced in the streets, embraced strangers, and wept openly, overwhelmed by the emotions of the moment.

## The Triumph of Liberation

On August 26, General Charles de Gaulle led a triumphant parade down the Champs-Élysées, a powerful symbol of French resilience and the restoration of national pride. Hundreds of thousands of Parisians lined the famous avenue, cheering wildly as de Gaulle and Free French troops marched past. The general's tall figure, striding purposefully down the boulevard, became an iconic image of the liberation, embodying France's determination to reclaim its place on the world stage.

One eyewitness, Pierre Laurent, described the scene: "It was as if the entire city had come alive again. The joy, the sheer exuberance of that moment is impossible to describe. After years of oppression, we were free, and de Gaulle's presence made us believe that France, too, would rise again."

The liberation of Paris came at a cost. Over 1,400 Parisians had died in the fighting, and many more were wounded. Yet, compared to the destruction visited upon other European capitals, Paris had emerged relatively unscathed, its beauty and historical treasures largely preserved.

## Aftermath and Legacy

The immediate aftermath of the liberation was marked by both jubilation and reckoning. While Parisians celebrated their freedom, there was also a dark undercurrent of retribution. Those accused of collaboration with the Nazis faced public humiliation, impromptu trials, and in some cases, execution. Women accused of having relationships with German soldiers had their heads shaved in public, a visible and lasting mark of their perceived betrayal.

Politically, the liberation of Paris gave the newly established Free French government and its leader, Charles de Gaulle, the prestige and authority needed to establish a provisional French Republic. This new government faced the monumental task of rebuilding a nation shattered by war and occupation.

The liberation also set in motion significant social changes. The role played by the Resistance, which included people from all walks of life, challenged pre-war social hierarchies. Women, who had played crucial roles in the Resistance, began to demand greater rights and recognition, leading to their enfranchisement in 1944.

Economically, France faced significant challenges. Years of occupation and exploitation had left the country's infrastructure in tatters and its economy weakened. The Marshall Plan, initiated by the United States in 1948, would prove crucial in rebuilding and modernizing France's economy in the years following the war.

On the international stage, the liberation of Paris and the subsequent re-establishment of French sovereignty helped restore France's position as a major European power. Despite the challenges of the post-war years, including political instability and the painful process of decolonization, France would play a key role in the formation of the European Economic Community, the precursor to the European Union.

## Conclusion

The liberation of Paris stands as a testament to the power of resistance, the importance of allied cooperation, and the indomitable spirit of a people yearning for freedom. It marked not just the end of Nazi occupation in the French capital, but the rebirth of a nation. The events of August 1944 continue to resonate in French national memory, a powerful reminder of the cost of freedom and the triumph of hope over oppression.

As we reflect on the liberation of Paris, we are reminded of the complexities of war and occupation, of heroism and collaboration, of joy and retribution. The story of Paris's liberation is ultimately a human story, filled with acts of extraordinary courage, difficult choices, and the collective will of a people determined to shape their destiny.

The echoes of those August days in 1944 continue to reverberate through history, offering lessons about the fragility of freedom, the power of resistance, and the enduring strength of the human spirit in the face of tyranny. The liberation of Paris remains a powerful symbol of hope, a reminder that even in the darkest of times, the light of liberty can never be fully extinguished.

**Sources**

Ambrose, Stephen E. Citizen Soldiers: The US Army From the Normandy Beaches to the Bulge to the Surrender of Germany. Simon & Schuster, 1997.

Eisenhower, Dwight D. Crusade in Europe. Doubleday, 1948.

Various Sources

# A Bridge Too Far: The Ambitious Failure of Operation Market Garden

**Introduction**

In the late summer of 1944, as Allied forces swept across France in the wake of the successful D-Day landings, a sense of optimism pervaded the Allied high command. The German Wehrmacht seemed on the verge of collapse, and many believed that one final, decisive blow could end the war before Christmas. It was in this atmosphere of hope and urgency that Operation Market Garden was conceived - a daring plan to leapfrog the formidable German defenses and strike at the heart of the Third Reich.

Operation Market Garden, launched on September 17, 1944, was one of the most ambitious military operations of World War II. It combined the largest airborne assault in history with a rapid ground advance, aiming to secure a series of bridges across the Netherlands and create a corridor for Allied forces to bypass the Siegfried Line and thrust into Germany's industrial heartland. However, what began as a bold stroke to end the war quickly devolved into a costly failure, one that would have far-reaching consequences for the course of the conflict and the lives of thousands of soldiers and civilians.

**The Road to Market Garden**

In the wake of the breakout from Normandy, Allied forces found themselves stretched thin across a broad front. Supply lines were strained to the breaking point, and the rapid advance had begun to slow. It was in this context that British Field Marshal Bernard Montgomery proposed a daring plan to maintain the momentum of the Allied offensive.

Montgomery's plan, which would become Operation Market Garden, called for a combined airborne and ground assault to seize a series of bridges over the major rivers and canals of the Netherlands. The operation was divided into two parts: "Market," the airborne component, and "Garden," the ground advance. Three Allied airborne divisions would drop behind enemy lines to capture key bridges, while the British XXX Corps would punch through German lines and relieve the airborne forces, creating a corridor 64 miles long and only a few miles wide - a highway into Germany.

The planning for Market Garden was rushed, with barely a week between its conception and execution. This haste would prove to be a critical factor in the operation's ultimate failure. Intelligence reports warning of the presence of German armored units in the area were largely dismissed, and the logistical challenges of supplying an entire army corps through a narrow corridor were underestimated.

## The Initial Assault

As dawn broke on September 17, the skies over the Netherlands filled with the drone of aircraft engines. More than 1,500 transport planes and 500 gliders carried the 1st Allied Airborne Army - comprising the U.S. 101st and 82nd Airborne Divisions and the British 1st Airborne Division - towards their objectives.

The initial landings were largely successful. The 101st Airborne secured most of its objectives around Eindhoven, while the 82nd captured key bridges around Nijmegen. However, the British 1st Airborne Division, tasked with the most critical and distant objective - the bridge at Arnhem - immediately encountered problems. Only a small force managed to reach the bridge, while the rest of the division was scattered and faced unexpectedly stiff German resistance.

On the ground, XXX Corps began its advance. The narrow road leading north, soon dubbed "Hell's Highway," quickly became a bottleneck. German forces, reacting with unexpected speed and strength, began to attack the corridor from both sides.

## The Battle Unfolds

As the operation progressed, the challenges facing the Allied forces mounted. The British 1st Airborne at Arnhem, led by Major General Roy Urquhart, found themselves vastly outnumbered and outgunned. Contrary to pre-invasion intelligence, they faced elements of the II SS Panzer Corps, including the battle-hardened 9th and 10th SS Panzer Divisions.

One British paratrooper, Private John Shipley, later recalled the intensity of the fighting: "We were surrounded on all sides. The Germans seemed to be everywhere, and we were running low on ammunition and supplies. But we held on, believing that XXX Corps would reach us at any moment."

Meanwhile, the advance of XXX Corps was painfully slow. The single narrow road leading north was vulnerable to German counterattacks, and progress was measured in yards rather than miles. The operation, which had been planned to last only a few days, stretched into a week of intense fighting.

Communication between the airborne forces and the advancing ground troops was poor, exacerbating the already difficult situation. The British 1st Airborne at Arnhem, in particular, found themselves isolated and unable to effectively communicate their dire situation to the forces struggling to reach them.

## The Tide Turns

By September 21, it was becoming clear that Operation Market Garden was in serious trouble. The British forces at Arnhem were clinging to an ever-shrinking perimeter around the bridge, running low on ammunition, food, and medical supplies. Despite heroic efforts, including the crossing of the Waal River by the U.S. 82nd Airborne in canvas boats under heavy fire, the Allied advance was too slow to relieve the beleaguered forces at Arnhem.

On September 25, after nine days of fierce fighting, the remnants of the British 1st Airborne Division were evacuated across the Rhine. Of the nearly 10,000 men who had landed at Arnhem, only about 2,400 made it back to Allied lines. The bridge that had been the operation's primary objective remained in German hands.

## Aftermath and Analysis

The failure of Operation Market Garden had immediate and long-lasting consequences. The hoped-for rapid advance into Germany had been stopped cold, and the war would drag on through the bitter winter of 1944-45. The operation's failure also had a profound impact on the Dutch civilian population. Much of the Netherlands remained under German occupation, leading to the terrible "Hunger Winter" of 1944-45, during which thousands of Dutch civilians died of starvation..

In the years since, historians and military analysts have debated the reasons for Market Garden's failure. Many point to the operation's hasty planning and the dismissal of intelligence reports warning of German armored units in the area. Others criticize the narrow, single-road approach that left the Allied advance vulnerable to counterattacks.

Field Marshal Montgomery, the operation's architect, remained defensive about Market Garden for the rest of his life, arguing that it had been "90% successful." However, many of his contemporaries and subsequent historians have been far more critical. General Dwight D. Eisenhower, the Supreme Allied Commander, later wrote that Market Garden had been "unsuccessful in its primary objective."

## Conclusion

Operation Market Garden stands as a stark reminder of the complexities and unpredictability of war. Despite meticulous planning and the valor of the soldiers involved, the operation failed to achieve its ambitious goals. The bridges that were meant to provide a highway into Germany instead became a symbol of Allied overreach and the resilience of German resistance even in the war's late stages.

Yet, from the ashes of Market Garden emerged valuable lessons. The operation highlighted the importance of accurate intelligence, the dangers of overly optimistic planning, and the critical need for flexibility in the face of changing battlefield conditions. These lessons would be applied in subsequent operations, contributing to the ultimate Allied victory in Europe.

As we reflect on Operation Market Garden, we are reminded of the thin line between victory and defeat in war, and of the profound impact that strategic decisions can have on the lives of soldiers and civilians alike. The "bridge too far" at Arnhem may have remained out of Allied reach, but the sacrifices made in that failed endeavor were not in vain. They contributed to the eventual liberation of Europe and stand as a powerful reminder of the price of freedom.

## Sources

Hart, Sir Basil Liddell. History of the Second World War. Konecky & Konecky, 2007.

Tucker, Spencer C. The Second World War. Patgrave Macmillan, 2003.

Various Sources

# The Tragic Tale of the Battle of Arnhem

## Introduction

In the waning days of summer 1944, as Allied forces swept across France in the wake of the successful D-Day landings, a sense of optimism pervaded the Allied high command. The German Wehrmacht seemed on the verge of collapse, and many believed that one final, decisive blow could end the war before Christmas. It was in this atmosphere of hope and urgency that Operation Market Garden was conceived - a daring plan to leapfrog the formidable German defenses and strike at the heart of the Third Reich.

At the center of this ambitious operation lay the Battle of Arnhem, a desperate struggle for control of the northernmost bridge in a series that would form a corridor into Germany. The battle would become a testament to human courage and resilience, as well as a stark reminder of the unpredictable nature of war. As the events unfolded, the picturesque Dutch city of Arnhem would be transformed into a battleground, its fate intertwined with the lives of thousands of soldiers and civilians caught in the maelstrom of conflict.

## The Grand Design

Operation Market Garden, the brainchild of British Field Marshal Bernard Montgomery, was a bold stroke designed to end the war swiftly. The plan called for the largest airborne assault in history, with three Allied airborne divisions dropping behind enemy lines to secure a series of bridges across the Netherlands. Meanwhile, British XXX Corps would punch through German lines and relieve the airborne forces, creating a 64-mile long corridor - a highway into Germany.

The operation was divided into two parts: "Market," the airborne component, and "Garden," the ground advance. The ultimate prize was the bridge at Arnhem, spanning the Lower Rhine. If captured and held, it would provide the Allies with a gateway into Germany's industrial heartland, potentially bringing the war to a swift conclusion.

As dawn broke on September 17, 1944, the skies over the Netherlands filled with the drone of aircraft engines. More than 1,500 transport planes and 500 gliders carried the 1st Allied Airborne Army towards their objectives. Among them was the British 1st Airborne Division, commanded by Major General Roy Urquhart, tasked with the most critical and distant objective - the bridge at Arnhem.

**The Initial Assault**

As paratroopers descended from the sky, the Dutch countryside erupted into chaos. The initial landings were largely successful, with many units achieving their primary objectives. However, the British 1st Airborne Division immediately encountered problems. Dropped several miles from their objectives due to concerns over anti-aircraft fire, only a small force managed to reach the bridge at Arnhem.

Lieutenant Colonel John Frost, commanding the 2nd Battalion of the 1st Parachute Brigade, led this small group of determined men. They fought their way through German resistance and managed to secure the northern end of the Arnhem bridge. Frost and his men dug in, prepared to hold their position until relieved by the advancing XXX Corps.

One British paratrooper, Private John Shipley, later recalled the intensity of those first hours: "We were surrounded. The Germans seemed to be everywhere, and we were running low on ammunition and supplies. But we held on, believing that XXX Corps would reach us at any moment".

**Unexpected Resistance**

Unknown to the Allied planners, two SS Panzer divisions were refitting in the area around Arnhem. This oversight would prove catastrophic for the operation. As the British paratroopers fought to reach their objectives, they encountered far stiffer resistance than anticipated.

General Wilhelm Bittrich, commander of the II SS Panzer Corps, quickly mobilized his forces to counter the Allied landings. The lightly armed paratroopers found themselves facing the full might of German armored units, a David and Goliath struggle that would define the battle.

Meanwhile, on the ground, XXX Corps began its advance. The narrow road leading north, soon dubbed "Hell's Highway," quickly became a bottleneck. German forces, reacting with unexpected speed and strength, began to attack the corridor from both sides, slowing the Allied advance to a crawl.

**The Bridge Too Far**

As days passed, the situation for the British forces at Arnhem grew increasingly desperate. Lieutenant Colonel Frost and his men at the bridge found themselves isolated and under constant attack. Despite their valiant efforts, they were slowly being overwhelmed by the superior German forces.

Communication between the airborne forces and the advancing ground troops was poor, exacerbating the already difficult situation. Major General Urquhart, attempting to regain control of the scattered division, found himself trapped in a house surrounded by German troops for several crucial days, further complicating the Allied command structure.

By September 21, it was becoming clear that Operation Market Garden was in serious trouble. The British forces at Arnhem were clinging to an ever-shrinking perimeter around the bridge, running low on ammunition, food, and medical supplies. Despite heroic efforts, including the crossing of the Waal River by the U.S. 82nd Airborne in canvas boats under heavy fire, the Allied advance was too slow to relieve the beleaguered forces at Arnhem.

**The Bitter End**

On September 25, after nine days of fierce fighting, the remnants of the British 1st Airborne Division were evacuated across the Rhine. Of the nearly 10,600 men who had landed at Arnhem, only about 2,400 made it back to Allied lines. The bridge that had been the operation's primary objective remained in German hands.

The cost of the battle was staggering. The British 1st Airborne Division had effectively ceased to exist as a fighting force, with 1,485 men killed and 6,525 captured. The Polish 1st Independent Parachute Brigade, which had dropped to reinforce the British, also suffered heavy casualties.

But the toll was not limited to the military. The civilian population of Arnhem and the surrounding areas paid a heavy price. Approximately 453 civilians were killed during the battle, and many more would suffer in the months to come.

**Conclusion**

The Battle of Arnhem stands as a stark reminder of the complexities and unpredictability of war. Despite meticulous planning and the valor of the soldiers involved, the operation failed to achieve its ambitious goals. The bridge that was meant to provide a highway into Germany instead became a symbol of Allied overreach and the resilience of German resistance even in the war's late stages.

The failure at Arnhem had far-reaching consequences. The hoped-for rapid advance into Germany had been stopped cold, and the war would drag on through the bitter winter of 1944-45. For the Dutch civilian population, the aftermath was particularly harsh. Much of the Netherlands remained under German occupation, leading to the terrible "Hunger Winter" of 1944-45, during which thousands of Dutch civilians died of starvation.

Yet, from the ashes of Arnhem emerged valuable lessons. The operation highlighted the importance of accurate intelligence, the dangers of overly optimistic planning, and the critical need for flexibility in the face of changing battlefield conditions.

**Sources**

Ambrose, Stephen E. Citizen Soldiers: The US Army From the Normandy Beaches to the Bulge to the Surrender of Germany. Simon & Schuster, 1997.

Eisenhower, Dwight D. Crusade in Europe. Doubleday, 1948.

# The Battle of the Bulge: Hitler's Last Gamble on the Western Front

**Introduction**

In the frigid forests of the Ardennes, as 1944 drew to a close, the fate of World War II hung in the balance. The Battle of the Bulge, also known as the Ardennes Counteroffensive, would prove to be Nazi Germany's last major offensive on the Western Front. From December 16, 1944, to January 25, 1945, the densely forested regions of Belgium, Luxembourg, and France became the stage for one of the most brutal and decisive battles of the war. This desperate gambit by Adolf Hitler was designed to split the Allied forces, capture the vital port of Antwerp, and potentially force a negotiated peace in the West. What unfolded was a testament to human endurance, strategic brilliance, and the indomitable spirit of soldiers on both sides of the conflict.

**The Road to the Ardennes**

By late 1944, the tide of war had turned decisively against Nazi Germany. The successful D-Day landings on June 6 led to the liberation of France, and Allied forces were advancing into Belgium and Holland, poised along the German border. The Allies were confident, with some leaders predicting that the war might end by Christmas. However, this optimism would soon be shattered by Hitler's audacious plan.

Adolf Hitler, seeing an opportunity to exploit Allied overconfidence, conceived of a massive counteroffensive through the Ardennes region. This area, considered a quiet sector by the Allies, had been the route of the successful German advance in 1940. Now, Hitler hoped to repeat that success, codenamed "Wacht am Rhein" (Watch on the Rhine).

The German strategy relied heavily on surprise and speed. Under the cover of night and strict radio silence, the Germans amassed a force of over 410,000 troops, 1,400 tanks, and significant artillery support. The offensive aimed to split the British and American forces, capture Antwerp, and potentially force a negotiated peace on the Western Front.

**The Storm Breaks**

As dawn broke on December 16, 1944, the calm of the Ardennes was shattered by a massive artillery barrage. The German offensive had begun. The initial assault caught the Allies completely off guard. The area was sparsely defended, with several battle-fatigued divisions sent there for rest and recuperation. The surprise and ferocity of the German attack created chaos among the Allied ranks.

Private Leo B. Woods, serving with the 329th Infantry Regiment, 83rd "Thunderbolt" Division, found himself in the thick of the fighting. "We were north of the main German target," he later recalled, "but we faced fierce counterattacks. For 13 days, I was buried in the snow of the Ardennes Forest, suffering from severe frostbite and shrapnel wounds."

As the German forces advanced, they created a distinctive bulge in the Allied front lines, giving the battle its name. The rapid German advance threatened to split the Allied forces and potentially change the course of the war.

## The Siege of Bastogne

One of the most crucial episodes of the battle centered around the town of Bastogne. This strategic crossroads became a focal point of the German offensive. The 101st Airborne Division, along with elements of other units, found themselves surrounded in Bastogne, holding out against overwhelming odds.

The defense of Bastogne became legendary, epitomized by the response of Brigadier General Anthony McAuliffe to a German demand for surrender. His one-word reply, "Nuts!", became a symbol of American defiance and determination.

Technician 4th Grade Harold Pollard, a radio operator in the 25th Cavalry Reconnaissance Squadron Mechanized of the 4th Armored Division, was part of the force racing to relieve Bastogne. "We made a rapid 150-mile journey to Bastogne, arriving in just 19 hours," Pollard recounted. "The conditions were brutal, but we knew the importance of breaking that siege."

## The Tide Turns

As the battle raged on, several factors began to turn the tide in favor of the Allies. The weather, which had initially favored the German attack by grounding Allied air forces, began to clear. This allowed the Allies to bring their superior air power to bear, attacking German positions and disrupting supply lines.

General Dwight D. Eisenhower, the Supreme Allied Commander, made crucial strategic decisions that would shape the course of the battle. He ordered General George S. Patton's Third Army to pivot north and relieve Bastogne, a maneuver that would prove decisive.

Meanwhile, the German advance began to slow. Logistical issues, particularly a critical shortage of fuel, hampered their progress. The determined resistance of Allied forces, especially at key points like Bastogne, disrupted the German timetable and allowed the Allies to regroup and counterattack.

## The Human Cost

The Battle of the Bulge exacted a terrible toll on both sides. The brutality of the fighting and the harsh winter conditions tested soldiers to their limits. Private First Class John "Jack" Magee of the 423rd Mortar Regiment, 106th Infantry Division, experienced the horror firsthand. Overrun in the initial attack, Magee spent six days alone in the Ardennes Forest before being captured. His subsequent experience as a prisoner of war, including forced labor in a coal mine and a daring escape, underscored the personal ordeals faced by many soldiers.

The civilian population also suffered greatly. The battle led to numerous atrocities, including the infamous Malmedy massacre, where German SS troops executed American prisoners of war. These events added to the already heavy toll of war on the local population.

## The Allied Counteroffensive

By late December, the Allies had regrouped and begun to push back. General Patton's Third Army broke through to Bastogne on December 26, relieving the besieged forces and dealing a significant blow to German morale. The improved weather allowed for increased Allied air support, which played a crucial role in turning the tide of the battle.

As January 1945 began, the German offensive had failed. Hitler's gamble had not paid off, and the Germans were now on the defensive. The Allies launched a determined counteroffensive, slowly but surely pushing the German forces back to their original positions.

## The Aftermath

By January 25, 1945, the Battle of the Bulge was officially over. The German forces had been pushed back to their starting positions, and the bulge in the Allied lines had been eliminated. The cost of the battle was staggering. The Allies suffered over 80,000 casualties, while German losses were estimated at between 80,000 and 100,000.

The failure of the Ardennes offensive marked the beginning of the end for Nazi Germany. The German military had expended its last reserves of men and materiel in the attack, leaving it critically weakened. The Allies, having weathered this last desperate German offensive, were now poised to advance into Germany itself.

## Conclusion

The Battle of the Bulge stands as one of the most significant engagements of World War II. It represented the last throw of the dice for Nazi Germany on the Western Front, a desperate attempt to change the course of a war that was slipping away from them. The battle tested the resolve of the Allied forces and the strategic acumen of their leaders.

The courage and determination displayed by soldiers on both sides, often in appalling conditions, remain a testament to human endurance. From the besieged defenders of Bastogne to the tank crews racing to their relief, from the infantry fighting in the frozen forests to the pilots braving winter skies, the Battle of the Bulge was a crucible that forged countless tales of heroism and sacrifice.

Strategically, the battle underscored the importance of flexibility in military planning and the crucial role of logistics in modern warfare. The Allied ability to rapidly redeploy forces and maintain supply lines proved decisive, as did their air superiority once the weather cleared.

In the end, the Battle of the Bulge not only sealed the fate of Nazi Germany but also demonstrated the strength and resilience of the Allied forces. It paved the way for the final push into Germany and the ultimate victory in Europe. The battle remains a powerful reminder of the cost of war, the value of alliance, and the indomitable human spirit in the face of adversity.

**Sources**

Ambrose, Stephen E. Citizen Soldiers: The US Army From the Normandy Beaches to the Bulge to the Surrender of Germany. Simon & Schuster, 1997.

Eisenhower, Dwight D. Crusade in Europe. Doubleday, 1948.

Various Sources

# The Battle of Bastogne

## Introduction

In the frigid forests of the Ardennes, as 1944 drew to a close, the fate of World War II hung in the balance. The Battle of Bastogne, a critical engagement within the larger Battle of the Bulge, would prove to be a testament to human endurance, strategic brilliance, and the indomitable spirit of soldiers facing overwhelming odds. From December 16, 1944, to January 25, 1945, the picturesque town of Bastogne in Belgium became the epicenter of Hitler's last desperate gambit on the Western Front. This battle, marked by its harsh winter conditions and the tenacity of its defenders, would not only change the course of the war but also etch itself into the annals of military history as a symbol of Allied resilience and determination.

## The Road to Bastogne

As 1944 waned, the Allied forces had pushed the German Wehrmacht back across France, liberating Paris and capturing the vital port of Antwerp. Victory seemed within grasp, with some Allied leaders optimistically predicting the war's end by Christmas. However, Adolf Hitler, in a last-ditch effort to turn the tide, conceived a bold and desperate plan.

On December 16, 1944, the calm of the Ardennes was shattered as the German offensive, codenamed "Operation Watch on the Rhine," began. The Germans aimed to exploit a perceived weak point in the Allied lines, driving through the densely forested Ardennes region to capture the strategic port of Antwerp, potentially splitting the Allied forces and changing the course of the war.

At the heart of this offensive lay the town of Bastogne, a crucial crossroads where seven major roads converged. Its capture was vital for the German advance, as it would facilitate the movement of troops and supplies towards their ultimate objective.

## The Siege Begins

As news of the German offensive reached Allied headquarters, the strategic calculus shifted dramatically. General Dwight D. Eisenhower, the Supreme Allied Commander, quickly grasped the importance of Bastogne. He ordered the 101st Airborne Division, along with elements of the 10th Armored Division, to rush to the town's defense.

By December 20, Bastogne was surrounded by German forces, cutting off the American defenders from reinforcement and resupply. The siege had begun, and the stage was set for one of the most dramatic battles of World War II.

The weather, as if conspiring with the German offensive, turned brutally cold. Temperatures plummeted to as low as -54°F, with about 8 inches of snow blanketing the ground. These harsh conditions not only tested the resolve of the soldiers but also grounded the Allied air forces, denying the defenders crucial air support and resupply.

## A Test of Will

Inside Bastogne, the situation grew increasingly dire. Food, ammunition, and medical supplies dwindled rapidly. The defenders, led by Brigadier General Anthony McAuliffe, the acting commander of the 101st Airborne Division, faced repeated German assaults.

Private John Fitzgerald, one of the besieged soldiers, later recounted the grim reality they faced: "We were hungry, cold, and running low on everything. Two GIs were killed while foraging for food. It was a desperate situation".

Despite the overwhelming odds, the American forces held their ground. Their resilience was epitomized by General McAuliffe's famous response to a German demand for surrender on December 22. His one-word reply, "Nuts!", became a rallying cry for the defenders and a symbol of American defiance.

## The Human Cost

The Battle of Bastogne exacted a terrible toll on both sides. The brutality of the fighting and the harsh winter conditions tested soldiers to their limits. On Christmas Day, amidst the chaos and carnage, a poignant scene unfolded. An American soldier was observed kneeling with a rifle in one hand and a rosary in the other, praying before returning to the battle. This moment, frozen in time, captured the essence of faith and duty in the face of overwhelming adversity.

## The Tide Turns

As the siege wore on, the defenders of Bastogne clung to hope. That hope was realized on December 23 when the weather finally cleared. The blue skies brought with them the welcome sight of Allied aircraft, dropping much-needed supplies to the beleaguered defenders and attacking German positions.

The clearing weather also allowed General George S. Patton's Third Army to launch its relief operation. Patton, known for his aggressive tactics, had pivoted his forces north in a remarkable display of military flexibility. On December 26, elements of the 4th Armored Division broke through the German lines, finally relieving the besieged forces in Bastogne.

Technician 4th Grade Harold Pollard, a radio operator in the 25th Cavalry Reconnaissance Squadron Mechanized of the 4th Armored Division, was part of the force racing to relieve Bastogne. "We made a rapid 150-mile journey to Bastogne, arriving in just 19 hours," Pollard recounted. "The conditions were brutal, but we knew the importance of breaking that siege".

**The Aftermath**

The relief of Bastogne marked a turning point in the Battle of the Bulge. The German offensive, which had initially made significant gains, began to falter. By January 25, 1945, the battle was officially over, with the Germans pushed back to their starting positions.

The cost of the battle was staggering. The Allies suffered over 80,000 casualties during the Battle of the Bulge, with a significant portion of these occurring in and around Bastogne. The German losses were even higher, estimated between 80,000 and 100,000. These losses, particularly in experienced troops and irreplaceable armored units, would haunt the German war effort in the final months of the conflict.

**Conclusion**

The Battle of Bastogne stands as one of the most significant engagements of World War II. It represented the last throw of the dice for Nazi Germany on the Western Front, a desperate attempt to change the course of a war that was slipping away from them. The battle checked the resolve of the Allied forces and the strategic acumen of their leaders.

The courage and determination displayed by the defenders of Bastogne, often in appalling conditions, remain a testament to human endurance. From the besieged soldiers in the town to the tank crews racing to their relief, from the infantry fighting in the frozen forests to the pilots braving winter skies, the Battle of Bastogne forged countless tales of heroism and sacrifice.

Strategically, the battle underscored the importance of flexibility in military planning and the crucial role of logistics in modern warfare. The Allied ability to rapidly redeploy forces and maintain supply lines proved decisive, as did their air superiority once the weather cleared.

In the end, the Battle of Bastogne not only contributed to the defeat of Nazi Germany but also demonstrated the strength and resilience of the Allied forces. It paved the way for the final push into Germany and the ultimate victory in Europe. The battle remains a powerful reminder of the cost of war, the value of alliance, and the indomitable human spirit in the face of adversity.

**Sources**

Ambrose, Stephen E. Citizen Soldiers: The US Army From the Normandy Beaches to the Bulge to the Surrender of Germany. Simon & Schuster, 1997.

Eisenhower, Dwight D. Crusade in Europe. Doubleday, 1948.

Various Sources

# The Firestorm of Dresden: A City's Destruction and Its Enduring Legacy

## Introduction

In the frigid days of February 1945, as World War II entered its final, desperate phase, the ancient city of Dresden stood as a jewel of culture and history amidst the ruins of Nazi Germany. Known as the "Florence on the Elbe" for its baroque splendor and artistic heritage, Dresden had largely escaped the devastation that had befallen other German cities. However, in the span of three days, from February 13 to February 15, this cultural haven would be transformed into a hellscape of fire and destruction, becoming the epicenter of one of the most controversial Allied actions of the war.

The bombing of Dresden, a combined effort by the Royal Air Force (RAF) and the United States Army Air Forces (USAAF), would not only reshape the physical landscape of the city but also ignite a fierce debate about the ethics of strategic bombing that continues to this day. This narrative explores the historical context of Dresden, the details of the bombing raids, the immediate aftermath, and the long-term impact of this pivotal event on the city, Germany, and the international community.

## Dresden Before the Storm

Before World War II, Dresden was a city of immense cultural importance, renowned for its artistic and architectural treasures. The city skyline was dominated by grand structures that drew comparisons to Florence, Italy. The Zwinger Palace, the Semper Opera House, and the Frauenkirche stood as testaments to the Baroque and Rococo architectural styles, attracting visitors from around the world.

Dresden's cultural landscape was further enriched by its vibrant music scene, with composers like Richard Wagner and Carl Maria von Weber having strong ties to the city. The city was not just a repository of physical beauty but a living, breathing center of European culture and art.

However, as the war progressed, Dresden's strategic importance began to overshadow its cultural significance. While not heavily industrialized and lacking major military installations, the city served as a significant transportation hub. Its railways played a crucial role in the movement of troops and supplies for the Third Reich, especially as the Eastern Front became more critical. This strategic positioning, combined with its cultural status, would ultimately make Dresden a target for Allied bombing.

## The Firestorm Descends

On the night of February 13, 1945, the calm of Dresden was shattered as the first wave of RAF bombers appeared in the sky. The initial attack, involving 796 Lancaster bombers and 9 de Havilland Mosquito fighter-bombers, marked the beginning of a devastating assault. The RAF employed a "bomber stream" formation, a tactic designed to overwhelm enemy defenses by concentrating a large number of bombers in a tight formation.

The first raid dropped approximately 2,700 tons of explosives and incendiaries, creating a firestorm that engulfed the city center. The use of incendiary bombs was particularly devastating, as they ignited fires that quickly spread through the city's largely wooden structures.

Victor Gregg, a British prisoner of war held in Dresden during the bombing, provided a harrowing account of the destruction: "The firestorm was so strong that it sucked the air out of the underground shelters, suffocating people before they were burned to death. The heat was so intense that I saw people's bodies reduced to a pile of ashes in seconds".

The USAAF continued the assault with daylight raids on February 14 and 15, involving 527 B-17 Flying Fortress bombers. These raids targeted Dresden's railways, bridges, and transportation facilities to further disrupt German military logistics. The combined effect of these attacks was catastrophic, with large parts of the city reduced to rubble and ash.

## The Immediate Aftermath

As the smoke cleared and the fires died down, the full extent of the destruction became apparent. The bombing had obliterated approximately 15 square kilometers of the city, including about 90% of the historic city center. Iconic landmarks such as the Frauenkirche, the Zwinger Palace, and the Semper Opera House were either destroyed or severely damaged.

The human toll was equally devastating. While exact casualty figures have been debated, recent research suggests that between 22,700 and 25,000 people lost their lives in the bombing. The high number of casualties was attributed to several factors, including the intensity of the firestorm and the presence of refugees fleeing the advancing Soviet army, which had swelled the city's population.

Götz Bergander, who was 18 years old at the time, recalled the chaos and confusion that followed the raids: "There were rumors that the death toll was much higher, that hundreds of thousands had died. The city was in shock, and no one really knew what was happening".

The destruction of infrastructure further complicated rescue and recovery efforts. Essential services such as water, electricity, and transportation were disrupted, and hospitals, overwhelmed by the sheer number of casualties, struggled to provide adequate care to the injured.

## Long-Term Impact and Legacy

The bombing of Dresden had far-reaching consequences that extended well beyond the immediate destruction. For the city itself, the physical and psychological scars persisted for decades, influencing urban development and the collective memory of its citizens. The trauma experienced by survivors was profound, with studies indicating long-lasting psychological effects.

For Germany as a whole, Dresden became a symbol of the destruction wrought by the Allied strategic bombing campaign. It contributed to a narrative of victimhood that some segments of German society adopted post-war, complicating the country's process of coming to terms with its wartime actions.

Internationally, the bombing of Dresden sparked significant debate about the ethics and effectiveness of strategic bombing. It became emblematic of the moral dilemmas associated with targeting civilian populations to achieve military objectives. This controversy has persisted, influencing public opinion and scholarly debate on the use of air power in warfare.

The events in Dresden also led to a reevaluation of military strategies and contributed to the development of international laws aimed at protecting civilians during conflicts. The legacy of Dresden underscores the complex interplay between military necessity and humanitarian considerations in conflict.

**Conclusion**

The destruction of Dresden stands as a stark reminder of the brutal realities of total war. From a city of culture and beauty, it was transformed in three days into a symbol of the devastating power of modern warfare. The controversy surrounding the bombing continues to this day, raising questions about the ethics of strategic bombing and the limits of military necessity.

**Sources**

Gregg, Victor. I Survived the bombing of Dresden and continue to believe it was a war crime. The Guardian, 2013.

Taylor, Frederick. Dresden: Tuesday, February 13, 1945. New York: Harper Collins, 2004

Various Sources

# Rebuilding the Frontlines: Conflicts After Dresden

**Battle of Remagen (March 1945)**

The Battle of Remagen, fought from March 7 to March 25, 1945, was a significant engagement in the final stages of World War II in Europe. American forces captured the Ludendorff Bridge over the Rhine River, a strategic asset that allowed them to establish a foothold in Germany. The bridge, which was critical for German supply lines, had been hastily fortified by the Germans but was still intact when American troops arrived. The capture of the bridge was unexpected, as the Germans had planned to demolish it to prevent Allied access. The quick action of the 9th Armored Division and other units allowed them to seize the bridge before it could be destroyed, enabling thousands of troops and equipment to cross into German territory.

The significance of the Battle of Remagen extended beyond the immediate capture of the bridge. It marked one of the first times Allied forces crossed the Rhine, which had long been considered a formidable natural barrier. The bridgehead established at Remagen facilitated further advances into Germany, contributing to the Allies' rapid progress toward the heart of the Third Reich. However, the German forces regrouped and launched counterattacks to recapture the bridge, resulting in intense fighting. Despite the challenges, the Allies managed to hold their position, ultimately leading to the collapse of German resistance in the region.

**Battle of the Ruhr (March-April 1945)**

The Battle of the Ruhr, fought from March to April 1945, was a critical campaign aimed at capturing the industrial heartland of Germany. Allied forces sought to disrupt German production capabilities and deal a decisive blow to the Nazi war machine. The campaign involved a series of coordinated attacks on major cities, including Essen, Duisburg, and Dortmund, which were vital to German industry. As Allied forces advanced, they encountered fierce resistance from German troops, but the combination of overwhelming air power and coordinated ground assaults allowed the Allies to gradually encircle and capture key locations in the Ruhr area.

The battle culminated in the encirclement of German forces within the Ruhr, effectively cutting off their supply lines and resources. The Allied strategy to target critical industrial sites paid off, as production capabilities were severely hampered. By the end of April, Allied forces had fully captured the Ruhr, leading to the surrender of thousands of German soldiers and further crippling the German war effort. The successful campaign not only weakened Germany's ability to continue fighting but also set the stage for the final push into the heart of the country.

**Battle of Nuremberg (April 1945)**

The Battle of Nuremberg, fought from April 16 to April 20, 1945, was part of the final Allied offensive in Germany. As American forces continued their advance through Bavaria, capturing key cities and towns, Nuremberg became a strategic objective due to its historical significance and infrastructure. The battle began with intense artillery bombardments and air support, followed by ground assaults from the 3rd Infantry Division and other units. The German defenders, although demoralized and outnumbered, fought fiercely to protect the city, employing entrenched positions and urban combat tactics.

Despite the determined resistance, the overwhelming firepower and tactics of the Allied forces eventually led to the capture of Nuremberg. The battle concluded with American troops entering the city on April 20, 1945, marking a significant victory in the final stages of the war. The capture of Nuremberg not only had military significance but also symbolic importance, as it was a center of Nazi propaganda and a site of major party rallies. The fall of the city underscored the rapid decline of Nazi Germany and brought the Allies one step closer to victory in Europe, paving the way for the eventual surrender of German forces just weeks later.

**Battle of Leipzig (April 1945)**

The Battle of Leipzig took place in mid-April 1945 as Allied forces advanced into Germany during the final stages of World War II. After the successful capture of Nuremberg, American troops pushed toward Leipzig, a key city in Saxony. The battle involved fierce fighting as German defenders, though demoralized and increasingly outnumbered, attempted to hold their ground. The Allies, including American and British forces, employed coordinated attacks and combined arms tactics, leveraging artillery and air support to break through German lines. By April 19, Leipzig fell to the Allies, marking a significant victory that further weakened German resistance and opened the way for the continued advance into eastern Germany.

**Sources**

Hart, Sir Basil Liddell. History of the Second World War. Konecky & Konecky, 2007.

Tucker, Spencer C. The Second World War. Patgrave Macmillan, 2003.

Various Sources

# The Fall of Berlin: The Last Stand of the Third Reich

## Introduction

In the frigid spring of 1945, as the Allied forces closed in on Nazi Germany from all sides, the once-mighty Third Reich found itself cornered in its capital, Berlin. The Battle of Berlin, which unfolded from April 16 to May 2, 1945, would mark the final major offensive of World War II in Europe and the death knell of Adolf Hitler's regime. This battle, characterized by its ferocity, desperation, and far-reaching consequences, would not only decide the fate of Germany but also shape the post-war world order.

As Soviet forces, led by the determined Marshal Georgy Zhukov, prepared to launch their final assault on the Nazi capital, the city braced itself for an onslaught of unprecedented scale. Within the concrete depths of the Führerbunker, Adolf Hitler, once the charismatic leader of a regime that had terrorized Europe, now found himself a broken man, clinging to delusions of victory even as his empire crumbled around him.

This story explores the Battle of Berlin in its entirety - from the strategic decisions that led to this climactic confrontation to the human stories of soldiers and civilians caught in the maelstrom of war. It is a tale of military might, political machinations, and human endurance that would bring about the end of the most destructive conflict in human history.

## The Road to Berlin

By early 1945, the writing was on the wall for Nazi Germany. The successful D-Day landings in June 1944 led to the liberation of France, and Allied forces were advancing into Belgium and Holland, poised along the German border. In the east, the Soviet Red Army, having repelled the German invasion at great cost, was now pushing westward with a vengeance.

On January 12, 1945, the Soviet forces began their Vistula-Oder Offensive, a massive operation that would bring them to the gates of Berlin. The German Army, once the terror of Europe, was now a shadow of its former self, depleted by years of grueling warfare and struggling with dwindling resources.

As the Soviets advanced, they left a trail of destruction in their wake. The Red Army, fueled by a desire for revenge against the atrocities committed during the German invasion of the Soviet Union, committed widespread acts of violence against German civilians. This wave of retribution added to the terror and desperation felt by the German population as the war reached their homeland.

**The Final Preparations**

As the Soviet forces closed in on Berlin, both sides made their final preparations for the battle that would decide the fate of the German capital. The Soviet strategy, masterminded by Marshal Georgy Zhukov and Marshal Ivan Konev, involved a massive assault on the city from multiple directions. The Red Army amassed an overwhelming force, with over 2.5 million soldiers, 6,250 tanks, and 7,500 aircraft poised to strike at Berlin.

On the German side, the situation was dire. General Helmuth Weidling, tasked with the defense of Berlin, had to make do with a hodgepodge of regular army units, SS divisions, Hitler Youth, and Volkssturm (people's militia) comprising older men and young boys. The city was hastily fortified, with defensive rings established around Berlin, but the German forces were severely outnumbered and outgunned.

**The Battle Begins**

On April 16, 1945, the silence of the early morning was shattered by a massive Soviet artillery barrage, signaling the beginning of the Battle of Berlin. The initial assault focused on the Seelow Heights, the last major defensive line outside Berlin. Despite fierce German resistance, the sheer weight of the Soviet attack proved overwhelming.

As the Soviet forces broke through the German defenses, they began to encircle Berlin, cutting off the city from potential reinforcements. By April 20, Hitler's 56th birthday, Soviet artillery was shelling the city itself, a bombardment that would continue relentlessly until Berlin's surrender.

**Street-by-Street, House-by-House**

As Soviet troops entered the outskirts of Berlin on April 21, the battle transformed into a brutal urban conflict. The streets of Berlin became a maze of rubble and improvised barricades as German defenders fought desperately to hold back the Soviet advance. The fighting was intense and often hand-to-hand, with both sides suffering heavy casualties.

One Soviet soldier, recounting the ferocity of the urban combat, stated, "We fought for every street, every house, every stairwell, every room. It was a battle of attrition, where victory was measured in meters gained."

The civilian population of Berlin, caught in the crossfire, suffered tremendously. Food and water were scarce, and many civilians took shelter in basements and subway stations to escape the constant bombardment. The fear of Soviet retribution added to the terror, with many Berliners dreading the arrival of the Red Army.

**The Last Days in the Führerbunker**

As the battle raged above ground, a drama of historic proportions unfolding beneath the streets of Berlin. In the Führerbunker, a reinforced concrete bunker complex beneath the Reich Chancellery, Adolf Hitler and his inner circle spent their final days.

The atmosphere in the bunker was one of despair and decadence. Hitler, physically and mentally deteriorating, alternated between rage and despondency as he received reports of the Soviet advance. Despite the hopeless situation, he continued to issue orders for counterattacks with nonexistent units, clinging to the delusion of a final victory.

On April 29, with Soviet forces less than a mile from the bunker, Hitler married his long-time companion, Eva Braun, in a somber ceremony. The next day, on April 30, 1945, Hitler and Eva Braun committed suicide. Their bodies were carried outside, doused in petrol, and burned, as Hitler had instructed, to prevent them from being captured and displayed by the Soviets.

**The Fall of the Reichstag**

As the drama in the Führerbunker reached its climax, Soviet forces were closing in on the Reichstag, the German parliament building that had come to symbolize Nazi power. The battle for the Reichstag was particularly fierce, with German defenders fighting to the last man.

On April 30, the same day Hitler committed suicide, Soviet soldiers finally fought their way into the Reichstag. The iconic image of Soviet soldiers raising the red flag over the Reichstag, captured by photographer Yevgeny Khaldei, would become one of the most famous photographs of World War II, symbolizing the Soviet victory over Nazi Germany.

**The End of the Battle**

With Hitler dead and the Reichstag captured, the remaining German forces in Berlin began to crumble. On May 2, 1945, General Helmuth Weidling, the commander of Berlin's defense, surrendered the city to the Soviet forces. The Battle of Berlin was over, and with it, the Third Reich had fallen.

The cost of the battle had been enormous. It is estimated that the Soviet forces suffered around 80,000 killed and 280,000 wounded, while German military and civilian casualties are believed to be between 150,000 and 300,000. The city itself lay in ruins, with much of its infrastructure destroyed and its population traumatized.

**Conclusion**

The Battle of Berlin marked the final chapter of World War II in Europe and the end of the Third Reich. It was a battle characterized by its intensity, the desperation of the defenders, and the determination of the Soviet forces to capture Hitler's capital. The fall of Berlin not only signified the defeat of Nazi Germany but also set the stage for the post-war division of Germany and the onset of the Cold War.

The battle left an indelible mark on the city and its people. Berlin, once the center of Nazi power, was reduced to rubble, its population traumatized by the brutality of the fighting and the subsequent occupation. The Soviet victory came at a terrible cost, both in terms of lives lost and the atrocities committed against the civilian population.

As the dust settled on the ruins of Berlin, the world order was irrevocably changed. The defeat of Nazi Germany eliminated one of the most brutal regimes in history, but it also marked the rise of the Soviet Union as a global superpower. The division of Berlin between the Western Allies and the Soviet Union would become a potent symbol of the Cold War, with the city serving as a flashpoint for East-West tensions for decades to come.

**Sources**

Millet, Allan R.A. War to be Won: Fighting the Second World War. Harvard University Press, 2000.

Parker, Geoffrey. The Second World War: A Short History. New York: HarperCollins, 2002.

Various Sources

# V-E Day: The Triumph of Allied Victory and the Dawn of a New Era

## Introduction

On May 8, 1945, the world erupted in jubilation as the Allied powers declared Victory in Europe Day, marking the end of World War II in Europe. This momentous occasion, known as V-E Day, signified the culmination of nearly six years of brutal conflict that had reshaped the global landscape. From the streets of London to the ruins of Berlin, from the beaches of Normandy to the steppes of Russia, millions of people united in celebration, relief, and somber reflection on the immense sacrifices made during the war.

V-E Day was not merely a single moment in time, but the culmination of a series of events that unfolded in the final days of the war. It represented the end of Nazi tyranny in Europe, the liberation of occupied territories, and the promise of a new world order. This narrative explores the lead-up to V-E Day, the events of May 7-8, 1945, the varied reactions across different nations, and the immediate aftermath that would shape the post-war world.

## The Final Days of the Third Reich

As April 1945 ended, the once-mighty Nazi war machine was in its death throes. The Allied forces, advancing from both east and west, had penetrated deep into German territory. The Soviet Red Army, driven by a thirst for vengeance after years of brutal occupation, was closing in on Berlin. Meanwhile, American and British forces were making rapid progress from the west, liberating towns and cities as they went.

In the heart of Berlin, Adolf Hitler, the man whose megalomaniacal vision had plunged the world into chaos, faced the collapse of his thousand-year Reich. On April 30, 1945, with Soviet troops just blocks away from his bunker, Hitler took his own life, along with his newly wedded wife, Eva Braun. His death marked the effective end of Nazi resistance, though fighting would continue for several more days.

## The Path to Surrender

With Hitler gone, the remnants of the Nazi leadership scrambled to negotiate an end to the conflict. Grand Admiral Karl Dönitz, Hitler's designated successor, sought to buy time to allow as many German troops as possible to surrender to Western Allied forces rather than to the Soviets, whom they feared would be less merciful.

On May 4, 1945, German forces in northwest Germany, Denmark, and the Netherlands surrendered to British Field Marshal Bernard Montgomery at Lüneburg Heath. This partial surrender was a prelude to the events that would unfold in the coming days.

**May 7, 1945: The Surrender at Reims**

In the early hours of May 7, 1945, in a small red schoolhouse in Reims, France, that served as the headquarters of General Dwight D. Eisenhower, the Supreme Allied Commander, history was made. At 2:41 a.m., General Alfred Jodl, representing the German High Command, signed the instrument of unconditional surrender of all German forces to the Allied Expeditionary Force and the Soviet High Command.

The signing was a solemn affair, witnessed by representatives of the United States, the Soviet Union, Britain, and France. General Walter Bedell Smith, Eisenhower's chief of staff, signed for the Allied Expeditionary Force, while General Ivan Susloparov signed for the Soviet High Command.

As the ink dried on the surrender document, Jodl addressed the assembled officers: "With this signature, the German people and armed forces are for better or worse delivered into the victors' hands." It was a moment of profound historical significance, marking the formal end of Nazi Germany and the Third Reich.

**May 8, 1945: V-E Day Dawns**

While the surrender had been signed on May 7, the Allied leaders had agreed to delay the public announcement to allow Soviet leader Joseph Stalin to stage a separate surrender ceremony in Berlin. Thus, May 8 was designated as Victory in Europe Day.

As dawn broke on May 8, 1945, the world awoke to the news that the war in Europe was officially over. Radio broadcasts crackled with the long-awaited announcement, and newspapers ran bold headlines declaring victory. The day that millions had longed for through years of hardship, sacrifice, and loss had finally arrived.

**Celebrations Across the Allied Nations**

The reactions to the news of Germany's surrender varied across the Allied nations, reflecting the different experiences and sacrifices of each country during the war.

In London, the heart of a nation that had stood defiant against Nazi aggression even in its darkest hour, the celebrations were particularly poignant. As Big Ben struck 3:00 p.m., Prime Minister Winston Churchill addressed the nation, declaring, "We may allow ourselves a brief period of rejoicing, but let us not forget for a moment the toils and efforts that lie ahead." Despite this note of caution, Londoners poured into the streets in their thousands. Trafalgar Square and the area around Buckingham Palace became seas of jubilant humanity, with people singing, dancing, and embracing total strangers.

Eyewitness accounts paint a vivid picture of the scene. One reveler recalled, "It was as if the grey pall of war had suddenly lifted, and color had returned to the world. People were laughing, crying, hugging – it was unlike anything I'd ever seen."

In the United States, the celebrations were more subdued, tempered by the knowledge that the war in the Pacific against Japan was still raging. President Harry S. Truman, addressing the nation from the White House, dedicated the victory to his predecessor, Franklin D. Roosevelt, who had died just weeks earlier. "This is a solemn but glorious hour," Truman declared, reminding Americans that "our victory is only half won."

In New York City, thousands gathered in Times Square, recreating scenes reminiscent of the celebrations at the end of World War I. However, many Americans remained mindful of the continuing conflict in the Pacific and the possibility that their loved ones might soon be redeployed to that theater.

In the Soviet Union, where the human cost of the war had been staggering, V-E Day was celebrated on May 9 due to the time difference. The mood in Moscow was one of immense pride and relief, tinged with the sorrow of millions lost. Red Square became the focal point of celebrations, with fireworks illuminating the night sky over the Kremlin.

In France, the city of Reims, where the surrender had been signed, became a symbol of victory. In Paris, crowds flooded the Champs-Élysées, waving flags of the Allied nations and singing "La Marseillaise." The French celebrations were particularly emotional, given the years of occupation and the struggle of the Resistance.

**The Situation in Germany and Occupied Territories**

While much of the world celebrated, the situation in Germany and the territories it had occupied was far more complex. For many Germans, V-E Day marked not just defeat, but the beginning of a reckoning with the atrocities committed in their name.

In Berlin and other German cities, which had been reduced to rubble by years of Allied bombing and the final Soviet assault, there was little cause for celebration. Civilians emerged from bunkers and shelters to face an uncertain future under Allied occupation. Many were more concerned with basic survival – finding food, water, and shelter amid the devastation.

In the formerly occupied territories, reactions were mixed. While there was joy at liberation, many countries, particularly in Eastern Europe, faced an uncertain future as the Soviet Union began to exert its influence. The end of Nazi occupation did not immediately bring freedom to all.

The full extent of Nazi atrocities was also becoming clear as concentration camps were liberated and survivors told their harrowing stories. The joy of victory was tempered by the shock and horror at the scale of human suffering inflicted by the Nazi regime.

**The Immediate Aftermath**

The celebrations of V-E Day soon gave way to the monumental task of rebuilding a shattered continent. Europe lay in ruins, with millions displaced, economies in tatters, and the specter of famine looming in many regions.

The Allied powers quickly moved to establish control over defeated Germany, dividing it into four occupation zones administered by the United States, Britain, France, and the Soviet Union. Berlin, deep within the Soviet zone, was similarly divided. This division would become a flashpoint in the emerging Cold War.

The Potsdam Conference in July 1945 set the framework for the post-war order in Europe, but also highlighted the growing tensions between the Western Allies and the Soviet Union. The seeds of the Cold War, which would dominate global politics for the next four decades, were sown in the immediate aftermath of V-E Day.

The end of the war also saw the beginning of a process of reckoning and justice. The Nuremberg Trials, which began in November 1945, brought leading Nazi officials to account for war crimes and crimes against humanity, establishing important precedents in international law.

**Conclusion**

V-E Day marked not just the end of World War II in Europe, but the dawn of a new era in global history. It was a day of jubilation, relief, and hope, but also one that carried the weight of millions of lives lost and the responsibility of building a better world from the ashes of conflict.

The varied reactions to V-E Day across different nations reflected the complex tapestry of experiences during the war. From the exuberant celebrations in London to the more subdued observances in the United States, from the pride and sorrow in Moscow to the mix of joy and uncertainty in liberated territories, V-E Day meant different things to different people.

The immediate aftermath of V-E Day set the stage for the modern world. The reconstruction of Europe, the division of Germany, the establishment of the United Nations, and the onset of the Cold War all trace their roots to this pivotal moment in history.

The legacy of V-E Day challenges us to remember the lessons of history, to remain vigilant against the forces of hatred and oppression, and to work tirelessly for a world of peace and justice.

**Sources**

Roberts, Andrew. The Storm of War: A New History of the Second World War. Harper Perennial, 2012.

Holland, James. Normandy '44: D-Day and the Epic 77-Day Battle for France. Atlantic Monthly Press, 2019.

Various Sources

# The Nuremberg Trials: Justice in the Wake of Atrocity

## Introduction

In the aftermath of World War II, as the world grappled with the unprecedented scale of destruction and human suffering, a new chapter in international justice was about to unfold. The Nuremberg Trials, held from November 20, 1945, to October 1, 1946, marked a watershed moment in legal history. These trials, conducted in the symbolic city of Nuremberg, Germany, sought to bring to justice the architects of Nazi atrocities and establish a framework for addressing war crimes and crimes against humanity on an international scale.

The Nuremberg Trials were not merely a legal proceeding; they represented humanity's collective response to the horrors of the Holocaust and the brutality of the Nazi regime. They stood as a testament to the belief that even in the face of unimaginable evil, justice could prevail, and that those responsible for crimes against humanity could be held accountable regardless of their position or power.

This narrative explores the historical context that led to the establishment of the trials, the key figures involved, the structure and proceedings of the tribunals, and the lasting impact of the verdicts on international law and human rights. Through personal accounts, legal analysis, and historical perspective, we will delve into the complexities, challenges, and significance of what has been called "the greatest trial in history."

## The Road to Nuremberg

As World War II drew to a close in 1945, the Allied powers faced the monumental task of addressing the atrocities committed by the Nazi regime. The scale and nature of these crimes were unprecedented, going beyond the scope of traditional warfare and into the realm of systematic genocide and crimes against humanity.

The idea of holding trials for war crimes was not entirely new. Previous conflicts, such as the American Civil War and the Armenian Genocide, had seen attempts to prosecute individuals for war crimes, but these were limited in scope and conducted under the laws of a single nation. The scale and nature of Nazi crimes, however, necessitated a more comprehensive and international approach.

The decision to hold trials, rather than summarily execute Nazi leaders as some had suggested, was driven by several factors. There was a strong desire for justice, not just retribution. The trials would serve as a means to document the extent of Nazi crimes, educate the world about the horrors of the Holocaust, and establish a legal precedent for prosecuting war crimes and crimes against humanity.

On August 8, 1945, representatives of the United States, the United Kingdom, France, and the Soviet Union signed the London Agreement, which established the legal basis for the trials. This agreement created the International Military Tribunal (IMT) and outlined the charges that would be brought against the Nazi leadership: crimes against peace, war crimes, and crimes against humanity.

**The Structure and Proceedings**

The Nuremberg Trials were held in the Palace of Justice in Nuremberg, a city chosen for its symbolic significance as a former site of Nazi rallies and because its courthouse had largely survived the war intact. The trials were a blend of legal traditions, incorporating elements from both common law and civil law systems.

The IMT was composed of eight judges, two from each of the Allied powers. The chief American prosecutor was Associate Justice Robert H. Jackson, who played a pivotal role in shaping the legal proceedings. Other notable prosecutors included Sir Hartley Shawcross from the United Kingdom, François de Menthon from France, and Roman A. Rudenko from the Soviet Union.

Twenty-four major Nazi officials were indicted, although only 21 would stand trial due to suicides and health issues. The defendants included prominent figures such as Hermann Göring, Rudolf Hess, and Joachim von Ribbentrop. They were allowed to choose their own lawyers, and the defense often argued against the retroactive application of laws, claiming the trials were a form of "victor's justice."

The proceedings were marked by several innovative features. A simultaneous translation system was implemented to manage the multilingual nature of the trials. The prosecution made extensive use of documentary evidence, including films of concentration camps, which provided irrefutable proof of the Nazi atrocities.

**Key Moments and Testimonies**

One of the most significant aspects of the trials was the presentation of evidence that revealed the full extent of the Holocaust and other Nazi crimes. The testimony of Rudolf Hoess, the commandant of Auschwitz, was particularly chilling. Hoess provided a firsthand account of the systematic extermination of over two million Jews at Auschwitz, offering irrefutable evidence of the Nazi regime's crimes and the scale of the genocide.

Götz Bergander, who was 18 years old at the time, recalled the impact of Hoess's testimony: "It was as if a veil had been lifted, revealing the true horror of what had happened. The courtroom was stunned into silence."

The trials also introduced the concept of individual responsibility for war crimes, rejecting the defense of following orders as a valid excuse for committing atrocities. This principle would have far-reaching implications for international law.

**Verdicts and Sentences**

On October 1, 1946, after months of testimony and deliberation, the verdicts were delivered. Of the 21 defendants who stood trial, 19 were found guilty. The tribunal handed down 12 death sentences, including those for Hermann Göring, Joachim von Ribbentrop, and Alfred Rosenberg. Seven defendants received prison sentences ranging from 10 years to life imprisonment. Three defendants were acquitted.

The executions were carried out on October 16, 1946, in the gymnasium of the Nuremberg Prison. Göring, however, cheated the hangman's noose by committing suicide the night before his scheduled execution.

The verdicts and sentences reflected the gravity of the crimes committed and aimed to deliver justice for the atrocities of the Nazi regime. They sent a clear message that those in positions of power could be held accountable for their actions, regardless of their status or claims of state sovereignty.

**Legacy and Impact**

The Nuremberg Trials had a profound and lasting impact on international law and human rights. They established several key legal principles that have become foundational in international criminal justice:

1. The rejection of the defense of superior orders, establishing that individuals have a duty to refuse unlawful orders.

2. The establishment of crimes against humanity as a legal category, recognizing that certain acts are criminal regardless of whether they violate domestic law.

3. The principle that individuals have duties under international law that transcend national obligations.

These principles were incorporated into subsequent international legal instruments, including the Genocide Convention (1948), the Universal Declaration of Human Rights (1948), and the Geneva Conventions (1949). The trials also inspired the creation of the International Criminal Court (ICC) and other ad hoc tribunals, such as those for the former Yugoslavia and Rwanda.

However, the Nuremberg Trials were not without criticism. Some argued that they represented "victor's justice," as the victorious Allied powers conducted them and did not address war crimes committed by the Allies. The concept of ex post facto law—punishing individuals for actions that were not explicitly illegal at the time they were committed—was also a point of contention.

Despite these criticisms, the Nuremberg Trials remain a pivotal moment in the development of international criminal law. They demonstrated the feasibility and necessity of international legal mechanisms to address atrocities and reinforced the notion that justice is essential to peace and reconciliation.

**Conclusion**

The Nuremberg Trials stand as a watershed moment in the history of international law and human rights. They represented humanity's response to the unimaginable atrocities of World War II and the Holocaust, establishing the principle that individuals, regardless of their position or the orders they followed, could be held accountable for war crimes and crimes against humanity.

The trials were not perfect, and they faced significant challenges and criticisms. Yet, their legacy is undeniable. They set a precedent for international cooperation in pursuing justice, laid the groundwork for the development of international criminal law, and contributed to the global movement toward accountability for mass atrocities.

The spirit of Nuremberg continues to influence international justice today, from the work of the International Criminal Court to efforts to hold individuals accountable for contemporary war crimes and crimes against humanity. As long as some would commit atrocities, the legacy of Nuremberg remains relevant, challenging us to uphold the principles of justice and human dignity in an often turbulent world.

In the words of Robert H. Jackson, the chief American prosecutor at Nuremberg: "The wrongs which we seek to condemn and punish have been so calculated, so malignant, and so devastating, that civilization cannot tolerate their being ignored, because it cannot survive their being repeated." This sentiment encapsulates the enduring importance of the Nuremberg Trials and their quest for justice in the wake of atrocity.

**Sources**

Gilbert, Martin. The Second World War: A Complete History. Holt Paperbacks, 2004.

Churchill, Sir Winston. The Second World War: A Complete History. Mariner Books, 1986.

Wittman, Rebecca. Beyond Justice: The Auschwitz Trial. Harvard University Press, 2005.

Various Sources

# Navigating the Storm: The Battle of the Atlantic

Cross section view of the U-505

## The Shadow Beneath the Waves: The U-Boat Campaign Against Britain, 1939-1941

### Introduction

As the storm clouds of World War II gathered over Europe in 1939, a silent menace lurked beneath the waves of the Atlantic Ocean. The German U-boat fleet, under the command of Grand Admiral Karl Dönitz, was poised to strike at the heart of Britain's maritime lifelines. This campaign would become one of the most critical and prolonged battles of the war, testing the resolve of both nations and the ingenuity of their naval forces.

The U-boat threat to Britain was not merely a military challenge; it was an existential one. As an island nation, Britain relied heavily on its sea lanes for survival. Food, raw materials, and military supplies all had to cross the treacherous waters of the Atlantic, where German submarines waited in the depths, ready to sever these vital arteries of the British war effort.

This narrative explores the dramatic events of the U-boat campaign against Britain from 1939 to 1941, a period that saw initial German successes, desperate British countermeasures, and the gradual shift in the balance of power beneath the waves. Through the eyes of those who lived through these perilous times, we will witness the courage, ingenuity, and sacrifice that defined this crucial phase of the Battle of the Atlantic.

### The Opening Salvo: September 1939

On September 3, 1939, just hours after Britain declared war on Germany, the tranquility of the North Atlantic was shattered. The British passenger liner SS Athenia, carrying 1,103 passengers, including many Americans, was torpedoed by the German submarine U-30, commanded by Oberleutnant Fritz-Julius Lemp. This attack, which violated standing orders not to target passenger ships, marked the opening salvo of the U-boat campaign and sent shockwaves through the Allied nations.

As news of the Athenia's sinking reached London, the Admiralty sprang into action. The memory of the devastating U-boat campaign of World War I was still fresh, and British naval leaders were determined not to repeat the mistakes of the past. Within days, the convoy system was reactivated, with merchant ships grouped for mutual protection under naval escort.

The first convoy, designated HX-1, sailed from Halifax on September 16, 1939, escorted by Canadian destroyers. As these ships plowed through the grey Atlantic swells, their crews were acutely aware of the danger that lurked beneath the surface. The Battle of the Atlantic had begun in earnest.

## The Wolf Pack Emerges: Early U-boat Tactics

In the early months of the war, German U-boats operated primarily as lone hunters, striking at isolated merchant ships and evading Allied patrols. However, Grand Admiral Dönitz had a grander vision. Drawing on his experiences from World War I, Dönitz developed the "wolf pack" tactic, where groups of U-boats would coordinate their attacks on Allied convoys, overwhelming their defenses through sheer numbers and coordinated assaults.

The effectiveness of this strategy was demonstrated on October 14, 1939, in one of the most audacious U-boat attacks of the war. U-47, commanded by the skilled and daring Günther Prien, penetrated the supposedly impregnable British naval base at Scapa Flow in the Orkney Islands. In the dead of night, Prien navigated the treacherous channels and fired his torpedoes at the battleship HMS Royal Oak. The massive warship, caught completely by surprise, capsized and sank, taking 833 of her crew to the bottom.

The attack on Scapa Flow sent shockwaves through the British Admiralty and demonstrated the boldness and skill of the U-boat commanders. It also highlighted the vulnerability of even the most heavily defended British assets to determined U-boat attacks.

## The "Happy Time": U-boats Ascendant

The fall of France in June 1940 marked a turning point in the U-boat campaign. With access to French Atlantic ports, German submarines could now extend their reach far into the Atlantic, threatening shipping lanes that had previously been considered safe. This geographical advantage, combined with the growing number of U-boats and the refinement of wolf pack tactics, ushered in a period known to German submariners as the "Happy Time".

From mid-1940 to early 1941, U-boats wreaked havoc on Allied shipping. Convoy after convoy came under attack, with merchant ships being sunk at an alarming rate. The British, struggling to protect their vital supply lines, found themselves outmatched by the coordinated U-boat assaults.

Franz Becker, a German U-boat commander, later recalled the mixed emotions of this period: "We were elated by our successes, but there was also a growing awareness of the human cost. Once, after sinking a British tugboat, we had to take the crew aboard due to rough weather. Looking into the eyes of those men, whose lives we had just upended, was a sobering experience".

The toll on British shipping was severe. In 1940 alone, U-boats sank over 1,000 Allied ships, representing millions of tons of vital cargo lost to the depths. The situation became so dire that Winston Churchill later wrote, "The only thing that ever really frightened me during the war was the U-boat peril".

## British Countermeasures: Innovation Under Pressure

As U-boat successes mounted, the British scrambled to develop effective countermeasures. The convoy system, while helpful, was not enough on its own to stem the tide of losses. The Royal Navy and its allies began to implement a series of technological and tactical innovations aimed at turning the tide of the undersea war.

One of the most significant developments was the improvement of ASDIC, an early form of sonar. This technology allowed escort ships to detect submerged U-boats by emitting sound waves and listening for echoes. While ASDIC had limitations, particularly against surfaced submarines, it provided a crucial tool for locating and engaging the elusive U-boats.

The development of radar technology also played a vital role in the battle against the U-boats. Early radar systems allowed surface ships and aircraft to detect submarines on the surface, even in conditions of poor visibility. As the technology improved, with innovations like the cavity magnetron reducing radar wavelengths, the ability to locate U-boats increased dramatically.

Perhaps the most crucial development in the anti-submarine effort was in the realm of intelligence. British codebreakers at Bletchley Park worked tirelessly to crack the German Enigma code, which was used for all U-boat communications. Their eventual success, known as the Ultra secret, would prove to be a game-changer in the Battle of the Atlantic, allowing the Allies to anticipate U-boat movements and redirect convoys away from danger.

Thomas Elmhirst, a member of the Royal Naval Air Service, described the urgency of these efforts: "We knew that every technological advance, every new tactic we developed, could mean the difference between life and death for countless sailors and merchant seamen. The pressure was immense, but so was our determination".

**The Human Cost: Life and Death in the Atlantic**

As the battle raged on, the human toll of the U-boat campaign became increasingly apparent. For the crews of merchant ships and their naval escorts, every voyage across the Atlantic was a journey into potential oblivion. The constant threat of U-boat attack wore on the nerves of even the most seasoned sailors.

Bert Stevens, serving aboard HMS Chester, witnessed the sinking of HMS Falmouth by a U-boat. His account vividly captures the terror of these moments: "One minute the Falmouth was there, the next she was gone, swallowed by the sea. The screams of men in the water, the smell of oil and smoke – it's something you never forget".

For the U-boat crews, life was equally perilous. Crammed into steel tubes beneath the waves, they faced the constant threat of depth charges, aerial attack, and the myriad dangers of the sea itself. Peter Petersen, a German submariner who survived three patrols aboard U-518, spoke of the psychological toll: "The tension was unbearable at times. Every ping of the enemy's sonar could be our death knell. Many of us wondered if we would ever see home again".

The civilian population of Britain also felt the effects of the U-boat campaign. As ships carrying food and other essential supplies were sunk, rationing became a fact of life. Long queues formed outside shops, and the British people were called upon to "dig for victory," turning parks and gardens into vegetable plots to supplement dwindling food stocks.

**The Tide Begins to Turn: Late 1941**

As 1941 progressed, the balance of power in the Battle of the Atlantic began to shift. The cumulative effect of British and Allied countermeasures started to tell, while the entry of the United States into the war in December 1941 would soon bring much-needed resources to the fight against the U-boats.

The formation of the Battle of the Atlantic Committee in March 1941 marked a turning point in the British approach to the U-boat threat. This high-level committee, recognizing the strategic importance of the Atlantic battle, coordinated efforts to increase the production of escort vessels, improve anti-submarine tactics, and prioritize the defeat of the U-boat menace.

By the end of 1941, the "Happy Time" for U-boat crews was drawing to a close. Improved convoy tactics, better technology, and the growing number of escort vessels made successful attacks more difficult and dangerous. The tide had not yet fully turned, but the days of easy U-boat victories were over.

George Wainford, who served on the escort ship HMS Onslaught, reflected on this period: "We began to feel that we were no longer just reacting to the U-boats, but actively hunting them. The addition of air cover, better depth charges, and improved detection equipment gave us a fighting chance. For the first time, we felt we might actually win this battle".

**Conclusion: The Battle Continues**

As 1941 drew to a close, the U-boat campaign against Britain had entered a new phase. The initial German successes had been blunted by determined British resistance and technological innovation. Yet the battle was far from over. The U-boats remained a potent threat, and the waters of the Atlantic would continue to be a battleground for years to come.

The period from 1939 to 1941 had seen the U-boat campaign evolve from individual submarine attacks to coordinated wolf pack assaults, and finally to a complex chess game of technology, tactics, and intelligence. Both sides had learned harsh lessons and paid a heavy price in lives and material.

The courage and resilience displayed by both the Allied sailors who braved the U-boat-infested waters and the German submariners who faced increasingly deadly countermeasures stand as a testament to human endurance in the face of mortal peril. The Battle of the Atlantic would continue to rage, but the experiences of these early years would shape the strategies and tactics that would ultimately lead to Allied victory.

As we reflect on this critical period of World War II, we are reminded of the pivotal role that the battle against the U-boats played in the larger conflict. Britain's survival, the ability to build up forces for the liberation of Europe, and ultimately the outcome of the war itself all hinged on the courage and determination of those who fought the silent, deadly struggle beneath the waves of the Atlantic.

**Sources**

Morison, Samuel Eliot. Victory in the Pacific 1945. History of the United States Naval Operations in World War II. Book Sales, 2001.

Weinberg, Gerhard L. A World at Arms: A Global History of World War II. Cambridge University Press, 1994

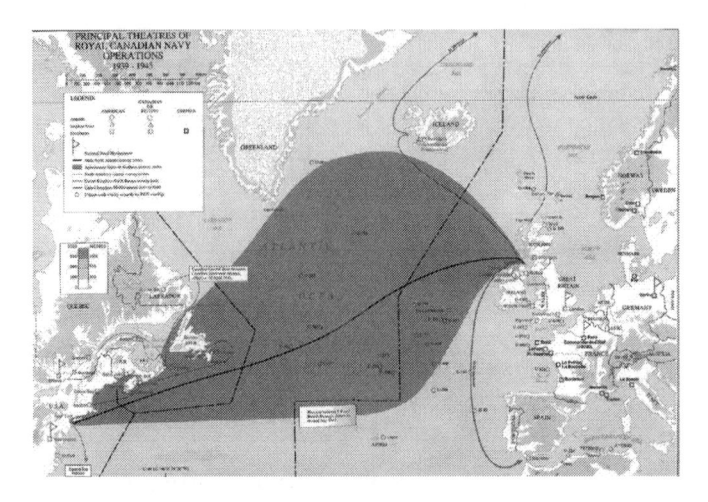

# The Battle of the Atlantic: The Longest Campaign of World War II

Introduction

As the storm clouds of World War II gathered over Europe in September 1939, a silent menace lurked beneath the waves of the Atlantic Ocean. The German U-boat fleet, under the command of Grand Admiral Karl Dönitz, was poised to strike at the heart of Britain's maritime lifelines. This campaign, known as the Battle of the Atlantic, would become the longest continuous military campaign of World War II, spanning from September 3, 1939, to May 8, 1945.

The Battle of the Atlantic was not merely a military contest; it was an existential struggle for Britain and a critical component of the Allied war effort. As an island nation, Britain relied heavily on its sea lanes for survival. Food, raw materials, and military supplies all had to cross the treacherous waters of the Atlantic, where German submarines waited in the depths, ready to sever these vital arteries of the British war effort.

This story explores the dramatic events of the Battle of the Atlantic, from the initial German successes to the eventual Allied triumph. Through the eyes of those who lived through these perilous times, we will witness the courage, ingenuity, and sacrifice that defined this crucial campaign of World War II.

**The Opening Salvo: September 1939**

On September 3, 1939, just hours after Britain declared war on Germany, the tranquility of the North Atlantic was shattered. The British passenger liner SS Athenia, carrying 1,103 passengers, including many Americans, was torpedoed by the German submarine U-30, commanded by Oberleutnant Fritz-Julius Lemp. This attack, which violated standing orders not to target passenger ships, marked the opening salvo of the U-boat campaign and sent shockwaves through the Allied nations.

As news of the Athenia's sinking reached London, the Admiralty sprang into action. The memory of the devastating U-boat campaign of World War I was still fresh, and British naval leaders were determined not to repeat the mistakes of the past. Within days, the convoy system was reactivated, with merchant ships grouped for mutual protection under naval escort.

The first convoy, designated HX-1, sailed from Halifax on September 16, 1939, escorted by Canadian destroyers. As these ships plowed through the grey Atlantic swells, their crews were acutely aware of the danger that lurked beneath the surface. The Battle of the Atlantic had begun in earnest.

## The Wolf Pack Emerges: Early U-boat Tactics

In the early months of the war, German U-boats operated primarily as lone hunters, striking at isolated merchant ships and evading Allied patrols. However, Grand Admiral Dönitz had a grander vision. Drawing on his experiences from World War I, Dönitz developed the "wolf pack" tactic, where groups of U-boats would coordinate their attacks on Allied convoys, overwhelming their defenses through sheer numbers and coordinated assaults.

The effectiveness of this strategy was demonstrated on October 14, 1939, in one of the most audacious U-boat attacks of the war. U-47, commanded by the skilled and daring Günther Prien, penetrated the supposedly impregnable British naval base at Scapa Flow in the Orkney Islands. In the dead of night, Prien navigated the treacherous channels and fired his torpedoes at the battleship HMS Royal Oak. The massive warship, caught completely by surprise, capsized and sank, taking 833 of her crew to the bottom.

The attack on Scapa Flow sent shockwaves through the British Admiralty and demonstrated the boldness and skill of the U-boat commanders. It also highlighted the vulnerability of even the most heavily defended British assets to determined U-boat attacks.

## The "Happy Time": U-boats Ascendant

The fall of France in June 1940 marked a turning point in the U-boat campaign. With access to French Atlantic ports, German submarines could now extend their reach far into the Atlantic, threatening shipping lanes that had previously been considered safe. This geographical advantage, combined with the growing number of U-boats and the refinement of wolf pack tactics, ushered in a period known to German submariners as the "Happy Time."

From mid-1940 to early 1941, U-boats wreaked havoc on Allied shipping. Convoy after convoy came under attack, with merchant ships being sunk at an alarming rate. The British, struggling to protect their vital supply lines, found themselves outmatched by the coordinated U-boat assaults.

Franz Becker, a German U-boat commander, later recalled the mixed emotions of this period: "We were elated by our successes, but there was also a growing awareness of the human cost. Once, after sinking a British tugboat, we had to take the crew aboard due to rough weather. Looking into the eyes of those men, whose lives we had just upended, was a sobering experience."

The toll on British shipping was severe. In 1940 alone, U-boats sank over 1,000 Allied ships, representing millions of tons of vital cargo lost to the depths. The situation became so dire that Winston Churchill later wrote, "The only thing that ever really frightened me during the war was the U-boat peril."

## British Countermeasures: Innovation Under Pressure

As U-boat successes mounted, the British scrambled to develop effective countermeasures. The convoy system, while helpful, was not enough on its own to stem the tide of losses. The Royal Navy and its allies began to implement a series of technological and tactical innovations aimed at turning the tide of the undersea war.

One of the most significant developments was the improvement of ASDIC, an early form of sonar. This technology allowed escort ships to detect submerged U-boats by emitting sound waves and listening for echoes. While ASDIC had limitations, particularly against surfaced submarines, it provided a crucial tool for locating and engaging the elusive U-boats.

The development of radar technology also played a vital role in the battle against the U-boats. Early radar systems allowed surface ships and aircraft to detect submarines on the surface, even in conditions of poor visibility. As technology improved, with innovations like the cavity magnetron reducing radar wavelengths, the ability to locate U-boats increased dramatically.

Perhaps the most crucial development in the anti-submarine effort was in the realm of intelligence. British codebreakers at Bletchley Park worked tirelessly to crack the German Enigma code, which was used for all U-boat communications. Their eventual success, known as the Ultra secret, would prove to be a game-changer in the Battle of the Atlantic, allowing the Allies to anticipate U-boat movements and redirect convoys away from danger.

Thomas Elmhirst, a member of the Royal Naval Air Service, described the urgency of these efforts: "We knew that every technological advance, every new tactic we developed, could mean the difference between life and death for countless sailors and merchant seamen. The pressure was immense, but so was our determination."

**The Human Cost: Life and Death in the Atlantic**

As the battle raged on, the human toll of the U-boat campaign became increasingly apparent. For the crews of merchant ships and their naval escorts, every voyage across the Atlantic was a journey into potential oblivion. The constant threat of U-boat attack wore on the nerves of even the most seasoned sailors.

Bert Stevens, serving aboard HMS Chester, witnessed the sinking of HMS Falmouth by a U-boat. His account vividly captures the terror of these moments: "One minute the Falmouth was there, the next she was gone, swallowed by the sea. The screams of men in the water, the smell of oil and smoke – it's something you never forget."

For the U-boat crews, life was equally perilous. Crammed into steel tubes beneath the waves, they faced the constant threat of depth charges, aerial attack, and the myriad dangers of the sea itself. Peter Petersen, a German submariner who survived three patrols aboard U-518, spoke of the psychological toll: "The tension was unbearable at times. Every ping of the enemy's sonar could be our death knell. Many of us wondered if we would ever see home again."

The civilian population of Britain also felt the effects of the U-boat campaign. As ships carrying food and other essential supplies were sunk, rationing became a fact of life. Long queues formed outside shops, and the British people were called upon to "dig for victory," turning parks and gardens into vegetable plots to supplement dwindling food stocks.

## The Tide Begins to Turn: Late 1941 to Mid-1943

As 1941 progressed, the balance of power in the Battle of the Atlantic began to shift. The cumulative effect of British and Allied countermeasures started to tell, while the entry of the United States into the war in December 1941 would soon bring much-needed resources to the fight against the U-boats.

The formation of the Battle of the Atlantic Committee in March 1941 marked a turning point in the British approach to the U-boat threat. This high-level committee, recognizing the strategic importance of the Atlantic battle, coordinated efforts to increase the production of escort vessels, improve anti-submarine tactics, and prioritize the defeat of the U-boat menace.

By the end of 1941, the "Happy Time" for U-boat crews was drawing to a close. Improved convoy tactics, better technology, and the growing number of escort vessels made successful attacks more difficult and dangerous. The tide had not yet fully turned, but the days of easy U-boat victories were over.

The period from mid-1942 to mid-1943 saw a decisive shift in favor of the Allies. The introduction of long-range aircraft, particularly the B-24 Liberator, closed the "mid-Atlantic gap" where U-boats had previously operated with impunity. Escort carriers provided crucial air cover for convoys, while improved depth charges and the innovative "Hedgehog" anti-submarine mortar increased the lethality of escort ships.

Perhaps most crucially, the breaking of the Enigma code allowed the Allies to route convoys away from U-boat concentrations and direct their forces to where they were most needed. This intelligence advantage, combined with improved tactics and technology, led to a dramatic increase in U-boat losses.

## The Turning of the Tide: May 1943 and Beyond

May 1943 marked a decisive moment in the Battle of the Atlantic. In what became known as "Black May" for the U-boat force, 43 German submarines were sunk in a single month. This devastating loss rate forced Dönitz to temporarily withdraw his U-boats from the North Atlantic, effectively conceding defeat in that crucial arena.

From this point on, the Allies held the upper hand in the Atlantic. While U-boats continued to operate and pose a threat until the end of the war, they were never again able to seriously threaten Allied control of the sea lanes. The Battle of the Atlantic had been won, ensuring the flow of men and materiel that would make possible the D-Day landings and the eventual liberation of Europe.

## Conclusion

The Battle of the Atlantic was a pivotal campaign that shaped the course of World War II. Its outcome determined the ability of the Allies to maintain vital supply lines and project military power across the Atlantic. The technological advancements and strategic decisions made during this battle had far-reaching implications, contributing to the eventual defeat of the Axis powers.

The victory in the Atlantic was not only a testament to the resilience and ingenuity of the Allied forces but also a crucial element in the broader strategy that led to the liberation of Europe and the end of the war. It demonstrated the critical importance of naval power, technological innovation, and intelligence in modern warfare.

**Sources**

Weinberg, Gerhard L. A World at Arms: A Global History of World War II. Cambridge University Press, 1994.

Overy, Richard. Why the Allies Won. W.W. Norton & Company, 1997.

Various Sources

# The Sinking of the Bismarck: A Turning Point in Naval Warfare

## Introduction

In the spring of 1941, as World War II raged across Europe and the Atlantic, one of the most dramatic naval pursuits in history was about to unfold. The German battleship Bismarck, pride of the Kriegsmarine and one of the most formidable warships ever built, was poised to break into the Atlantic to wreak havoc on Allied shipping. What followed was a relentless chase, a fierce battle, and ultimately the sinking of the mighty Bismarck—an event that would have far-reaching consequences for the course of the war and the future of naval warfare itself.

The story of the Bismarck's final mission is one of strategic ambition, technological prowess, and human courage on both sides of the conflict. It encapsulates the high stakes of the Battle of the Atlantic and serves as a microcosm of the larger struggle for control of the seas during World War II. This narrative explores the background of the Bismarck, the events leading up to its fateful mission, the dramatic pursuit by the British Royal Navy, and the aftermath of its sinking, shedding light on how this single engagement helped shape the future of naval combat.

## The Birth of a Titan

The story of the Bismarck begins in the shipyards of Hamburg, Germany. Laid down on July 1, 1936, at the Blohm & Voss shipyard, the Bismarck was a marvel of German engineering and a symbol of Nazi Germany's resurgent naval ambitions. Named after the former German Chancellor Otto von Bismarck, this battleship was designed to outclass its rivals and reassert German power on the high seas.

The Bismarck was a behemoth, measuring 824 feet in length with a beam of 118 feet. Its standard displacement was 41,700 tons, swelling to 50,900 tons when fully loaded. Powered by twelve Wagner high-pressure boilers and three Blohm & Voss geared turbines, the Bismarck could reach speeds of up to 30 knots, an impressive feat for a vessel of its size.

But it was the Bismarck's armament that truly set it apart. Its main battery consisted of eight 15-inch (38 cm) guns mounted in four twin turrets, capable of hurling one-ton shells over 21 miles. This was supplemented by a secondary battery of twelve 5.9-inch guns, sixteen 4.1-inch anti-aircraft guns, and numerous smaller caliber weapons. Protected by armor up to 360mm thick in places, the Bismarck seemed all but invincible.

As the Bismarck underwent sea trials and training exercises, its crew honed their skills, preparing for the day when they would put this floating fortress to the test in actual combat. That day was fast approaching.

**Operation Rheinübung: The Final Mission Begins**

In May 1941, the German high command set in motion Operation Rheinübung (Rhine Exercise), a bold plan to disrupt Allied shipping in the Atlantic. The Bismarck, along with the heavy cruiser Prinz Eugen, was to break out into the Atlantic, evade the British Home Fleet, and wreak havoc on the vital supply convoys between North America and Britain.

On May 18, 1941, under the command of Admiral Günther Lütjens, the Bismarck and Prinz Eugen set sail from Gotenhafen (now Gdynia, Poland). As they moved through the Baltic and into the North Sea, tension mounted among the crew. They knew that the success of their mission could have a significant impact on the course of the war, potentially starving Britain of crucial supplies and turning the tide in Germany's favor.

The British, however, were not caught unawares. Intelligence reports had alerted them to the possibility of a major German naval operation, and the Royal Navy was on high alert. As the Bismarck and Prinz Eugen approached the Denmark Strait between Iceland and Greenland, they were spotted by British reconnaissance aircraft. The hunt was on.

**The Battle of the Denmark Strait**

On May 24, 1941, the Bismarck encountered its first major opposition. The British battlecruiser HMS Hood and the newly commissioned battleship HMS Prince of Wales moved to intercept the German ships. What followed was one of the most famous naval engagements of the war.

At 05:52, the Hood opened fire, followed quickly by the Prince of Wales. The Bismarck returned fire at 05:55, unleashing the full fury of its main batteries. The battle was brief but intense. Just six minutes after the Bismarck opened fire, a shell from its guns penetrated the Hood's thin deck armor, reaching a magazine. The resulting explosion tore the Hood apart, and within minutes, the pride of the Royal Navy sank beneath the waves, taking with it all but three of its crew of 1,419 men.

The loss of the Hood sent shockwaves through the British Admiralty and the nation at large. However, the engagement was not without cost for the Germans. The Prince of Wales, despite being outgunned, managed to score three hits on the Bismarck before being forced to disengage. One of these hits ruptured a fuel tank, causing the Bismarck to leave an oil slick in its wake—a crucial factor in the events to come.

**The Pursuit**

Following the Battle of the Denmark Strait, the Bismarck and Prinz Eugen separated, with the damaged Bismarck making for the French port of Saint-Nazaire for repairs. The British, stung by the loss of the Hood and determined to avenge her, threw every available resource into the pursuit.

For several days, the Bismarck managed to elude its pursuers, aided by poor weather conditions. However, on May 26, a breakthrough came when a Catalina flying boat from RAF Coastal Command spotted the German battleship. This sighting allowed the British to vector in their forces for the kill.

The aircraft carrier HMS Ark Royal launched a strike force of obsolete Swordfish biplanes. In a feat of remarkable airmanship, these slow, fabric-covered aircraft managed to score a critical hit on the Bismarck. A torpedo struck the ship's stern, jamming its rudders and leaving it able only to steam in a large circle.

This damage sealed the Bismarck's fate. Unable to escape or make for port, the mighty battleship was at the mercy of the approaching British fleet.

**The Final Battle**

As dawn broke on May 27, 1941, the Bismarck found itself surrounded by British warships. The battleships HMS King George V and HMS Rodney opened fire at 08:47, joined by the heavy cruisers HMS Norfolk and HMS Dorsetshire.

For nearly two hours, the Bismarck was subjected to a relentless bombardment. Despite being virtually unable to maneuver, the German battleship fought back fiercely. However, the outcome was never in doubt. By 10:15, the Bismarck's main guns had fallen silent, its superstructure a twisted mass of burning metal.

At 10:36, with the ship clearly doomed, the order was given to scuttle the Bismarck. As German sailors opened the sea valves, British torpedoes continued to slam into the stricken vessel. At 10:40, the pride of the Kriegsmarine slipped beneath the waves, taking with it over 2,000 of its crew.

The sinking of the Bismarck was witnessed by survivors from both sides. Peter Petersen, a German submariner who later served on U-518, recalled the psychological impact of the event: "The loss of the Bismarck was a shock to us all. We had believed her to be unsinkable, and her destruction shook our confidence in the invincibility of our navy."

On the British side, George Wainford, serving on the escort ship HMS Onslaught, reflected on the mixed emotions of victory and the cost of war: "When we saw the Bismarck go down, there was a sense of triumph, but also a somber realization of the human toll. The sea was filled with German sailors struggling for survival, and it brought home the grim reality of naval warfare."

**Aftermath and Impact**

The sinking of the Bismarck had immediate and long-lasting consequences for the conduct of naval warfare in World War II and beyond. For the Germans, it marked the end of major surface raider operations in the Atlantic. Hitler, disillusioned by the vulnerability of large battleships, shifted focus towards U-boat warfare, believing submarines would be more effective in disrupting Allied supply lines.

For the Allies, particularly the British, the destruction of the Bismarck was a significant morale boost at a time when the war's outcome was still uncertain. It demonstrated that even the most powerful German warships could be defeated, providing a psychological lift to Allied naval forces.

Strategically, the engagement underscored the growing importance of air power in naval warfare. The critical role played by aircraft from HMS Ark Royal in crippling the Bismarck highlighted the vulnerability of battleships to aerial attack. This event accelerated the shift in naval strategy towards the use of aircraft carriers as the dominant force in naval warfare, a trend that would continue throughout the war and into the postwar era.

The battle also demonstrated the effectiveness of combined arms tactics, where coordination between different branches of the military—naval and air forces—proved crucial in achieving victory. This approach became a cornerstone of Allied naval strategy in subsequent operations.

In the long term, the sinking of the Bismarck influenced naval design and strategy. The vulnerability of battleships to air attacks led to a reevaluation of their role in naval warfare. The emphasis shifted towards more versatile and mobile naval forces, with aircraft carriers taking center stage. This shift was particularly evident in the Pacific Theater, where carrier-based operations became the norm.

**Conclusion**

The sinking of the Bismarck stands as a pivotal moment in naval history, marking both the end of an era and the beginning of a new one. It demonstrated the changing nature of naval warfare in the 20th century, where the dominance of the battleship was giving way to the ascendancy of air power and the aircraft carrier.

The human drama of the Bismarck's final mission—from its initial victory over the Hood to its relentless pursuit and ultimate destruction—captures the intensity and high stakes of the Battle of the Atlantic. It serves as a testament to the courage and determination of sailors on both sides of the conflict, who faced the perils of war at sea with remarkable resilience.

**Sources**

Roberts, Andrew. The Storm of War: A New History of the Second World War. Harper Perennial, 2012.

Millet, Allan R.A. War to be Won: Fighting the Second World War. Harvard University Press, 2000.

# Arctic Inferno: The Tragic Tale of Convoy PQ 17

### Introduction

In the frigid waters of the Arctic Ocean, during the summer of 1942, one of the most devastating naval disasters of World War II was about to unfold. Convoy PQ 17, a vital lifeline of supplies destined for the beleaguered Soviet Union, would soon become a tragic testament to the perils of war at sea and the consequences of strategic misjudgment.

As the convoy set sail from Hvalfjörður, Iceland, on June 27, 1942, none of the sailors aboard the 35 merchant ships could have foreseen the harrowing ordeal that awaited them. Their mission was critical: to deliver essential war materials to the Soviet Union, including tanks, aircraft, and vehicles, all desperately needed to sustain the fight against Nazi Germany on the Eastern Front.

This narrative explores the dramatic events surrounding Convoy PQ 17, from its formation and initial journey to its fateful scattering and the subsequent disaster that unfolded. Through the eyes of those who lived through these perilous times, we will witness the courage, fear, and ultimate sacrifice that defined this crucial episode in the Battle of the Atlantic.

### The Arctic Lifeline

The story of Convoy PQ 17 begins with the strategic necessity of the Arctic convoys. In 1942, the situation on the Eastern Front was dire. The German Wehrmacht had pushed deep into Soviet territory, and the survival of the Soviet Union hung in the balance. The Arctic convoys represented a vital lifeline, delivering much-needed supplies to keep the Soviet war machine operational.

Bill Martin, a seaman and radar operator on a minesweeper accompanying PQ 17, recalled the sense of purpose that drove them: "We knew how important our cargo was. Every tank, every plane we delivered could make the difference between victory and defeat for the Soviets. The danger was ever-present, but so was our determination".

Convoy PQ 17 was the largest and most valuable convoy to attempt the treacherous Murmansk Run. Its 35 merchant ships carried a precious cargo: 3,350 vehicles, 210 aircraft, 430 tanks, and countless other supplies. Protecting this vital shipment was a substantial escort force, including destroyers, cruisers, and even the distant support of the battleship USS Washington and the aircraft carrier HMS Victorious.

**The Journey Begins**

As the convoy departed from Iceland on June 27, 1942, the mood was tense but optimistic. The summer months offered the advantage of perpetual daylight, which the Allies hoped would deter U-boat attacks. However, this same light also made the convoy more visible to German reconnaissance aircraft.

The early days of the journey were marked by the constant vigilance of the escort ships and the nervous anticipation of the merchant crews. The harsh Arctic environment posed its own challenges, with freezing temperatures, fog, and the ever-present threat of ice.

On July 1, 1942, the convoy's worst fears were realized when German forces spotted them. U-boats and reconnaissance aircraft began shadowing the convoy, reporting its position back to German naval command. The stage was set for a confrontation that would test the mettle of every sailor involved.

**The Storm Breaks**

The first wave of German air attacks came on July 2, 1942. The convoy's anti-aircraft guns blazed as Luftwaffe planes dove from the sky, their bombs sending plumes of water skyward. Despite the ferocity of the assault, the convoy's defenses held, and no ships were lost in this initial engagement.

Seaman Second Class Donald Ross Naggatz, aboard the SS Pan Atlantic, described the tension of those moments: "The sky was filled with tracers and the roar of engines. We all knew that one direct hit could send us to the bottom. But somehow, we held on, our guns never falling silent".

As the attacks intensified over the next two days, the convoy continued to push eastward. The escort ships darted back and forth, depth charges booming as they sought to keep the lurking U-boats at bay. But the worst was yet to come.

**The Fatal Decision**

On July 4, 1942, a series of decisions were made that would seal the fate of Convoy PQ 17. Based on intelligence reports suggesting an imminent attack by the German battleship Tirpitz and other surface ships, Admiral Sir Dudley Pound, the First Sea Lord, made the fateful call to scatter the convoy.

At 2111 hours, the order was given for the cruiser force to withdraw westward at high speed. Twelve minutes later, at 2123 hours, the convoy was instructed to disperse and proceed independently to Russian ports. The final order to scatter came at 2136 hours.

The decision sent shockwaves through the convoy. Captain Jack Broome, the convoy's escort commander, later recalled the moment with bitter clarity: "It was as if we had suddenly abandoned a flock of sheep in a wilderness infested with wolves. We were leaving these merchantmen to their fate, and we all knew it".

**The Slaughter Begins**

With the protective escort withdrawn and the convoy scattered, the merchant ships were left desperately vulnerable to attack. The German forces, sensing their opportunity, pounced with savage efficiency.

Over the next five days, from July 5 to July 10, 1942, a relentless assault was unleashed upon the scattered ships of PQ 17. U-boats and aircraft hunted down the isolated vessels one by one. On July 5 alone, twelve merchant ships were sent to the bottom.

Bill Martin's account captures the horror of those days: "It was a slaughter. We could hear the distress calls on the radio, ship after ship reporting attacks. The sea was littered with burning wreckage and men struggling in the freezing water. We were powerless to help, ordered to save ourselves".

The fate of the SS Pan Atlantic, carrying Seaman Naggatz, was typical of many. On July 6, the ship was hit by bombs from a German Ju-88 bomber and sank within minutes. Naggatz and his crewmates found themselves fighting for survival in the icy Arctic waters.

**The Grim Tally**

By the time the remnants of Convoy PQ 17 limped into Arkhangelsk on July 10, 1942, the scale of the disaster was clear. Of the 35 merchant ships that had set out from Iceland, only 11 had survived to deliver their cargo. The human cost was equally devastating, with 153 merchant seamen lost to the unforgiving sea.

The material losses were staggering. Thousands of vehicles, hundreds of tanks and aircraft, and tons of other vital supplies now lay at the bottom of the Arctic Ocean. The impact on the Allied war effort, and particularly on Soviet resistance, was severe.

**Aftermath and Reflection**

The disaster of Convoy PQ 17 sent shockwaves through the Allied high command. Winston Churchill, in a moment of somber reflection, described it as "one of the most melancholy naval episodes in the whole of the war".

The immediate consequence was a temporary suspension of the Arctic convoys, a pause that lasted until September 1942. This delay in the flow of supplies to the Soviet Union came at a critical time, as German forces pushed ever deeper into Soviet territory.

The event prompted a thorough reevaluation of convoy tactics and the importance of maintaining cohesive protection for merchant ships. The decision to scatter the convoy based on the perceived threat from the Tirpitz, which never materialized, became a case study in the dangers of acting on incomplete intelligence.

For the survivors, the memories of PQ 17 would haunt them for years to come. Peter Petersen, a German submariner who later reflected on the events, captured the complex emotions of those involved: "We were elated by our successes, but there was also a growing awareness of the human cost. Looking into the eyes of those men, whose lives we had just upended, was a sobering experience".

**Conclusion**

The tragedy of Convoy PQ 17 stands as a stark reminder of the brutal realities of war at sea. It highlights the immense challenges faced by the Allies in maintaining the vital supply lines that would ultimately contribute to victory in World War II.

The disaster also serves as a poignant lesson in the complexities of military decision-making, the importance of accurate intelligence, and the devastating consequences that can result from strategic misjudgments.

The Arctic convoys would resume, lessons learned from the tragedy applied to future operations. The sacrifice of those lost in Convoy PQ 17 was not in vain, as their story helped shape the strategies that would ultimately lead to Allied victory in the Battle of the Atlantic and, indeed, in World War II itself.

**Sources**

Konstam, Angus. Convoy PQ-17 1942: Disaster in the Arctic. Osprey Publishing

Irving, David. The Destruction of Convoy PQ-17. St, Martin's Press, 1989

Various Sources

# Silent Hunters: The Battle Against U-Boats in the Atlantic

## Introduction

As the storm clouds of World War II gathered over Europe in September 1939, a silent menace lurked beneath the waves of the Atlantic Ocean. The German U-boat fleet, under the command of Grand Admiral Karl Dönitz, was poised to strike at the heart of Britain's maritime lifelines. What followed was the longest continuous military campaign of World War II, spanning from September 3, 1939, to May 8, 1945 - the Battle of the Atlantic.

This epic struggle was not merely a contest between warships; it was an existential battle for the survival of Britain and the success of the Allied war effort. As an island nation, Britain relied heavily on its sea lanes for survival. Food, raw materials, and military supplies all had to cross the treacherous waters of the Atlantic, where German submarines waited in the depths, ready to sever these vital arteries.

Against this threat stood the U-boat hunters - the men and ships of the Allied navies and air forces tasked with protecting the convoys and seeking out the underwater predators. Their story is one of courage, innovation, and perseverance in the face of a formidable enemy.

This story explores the dramatic events of the Battle of the Atlantic, focusing on the efforts of the U-boat hunters. From the early days of the war to the final victory, we will witness the evolution of tactics, technology, and strategy that ultimately turned the tide against the U-boat menace. Through the eyes of those who lived through these perilous times, we will experience the tension, fear, and triumph that defined this crucial campaign of World War II.

## The Early Days: A Deadly Game of Cat and Mouse

The Battle of the Atlantic began in earnest on September 3, 1939, mere hours after Britain declared war on Germany. The tranquility of the North Atlantic was shattered when the German submarine U-30, commanded by Oberleutnant Fritz-Julius Lemp, torpedoed the British passenger liner SS Athenia. This attack, which violated standing orders not to target passenger ships, marked the opening salvo of the U-boat campaign and sent shockwaves through the Allied nations.

As news of the Athenia's sinking reached London, the Admiralty sprang into action. The memory of the devastating U-boat campaign of World War I was still fresh, and British naval leaders were determined not to repeat the mistakes of the past. Within days, the convoy system was reactivated, with merchant ships grouped together for mutual protection under naval escort.

The first convoy, designated HX-1, sailed from Halifax on September 16, 1939, escorted by Canadian destroyers. As these ships plowed through the grey Atlantic swells, their crews were acutely aware of the danger that lurked beneath the surface. The Battle of the Atlantic had begun in earnest.

In these early days, the U-boat hunters faced a daunting task. Their primary weapon against the submarine threat was ASDIC, an early form of sonar. While revolutionary, ASDIC had significant limitations. It struggled in rough seas and had difficulty determining the depth of detected targets. Moreover, the U-boats often attacked on the surface at night, rendering ASDIC ineffective.

Despite these challenges, the convoy system proved its worth. By grouping merchant ships under the protection of naval escorts, the Allies reduced the number of potential targets and concentrated their defensive efforts. However, the U-boats were quick to adapt, developing new tactics to counter the convoy system.

**The Wolf Pack Emerges: A New Threat**

As the war progressed, Grand Admiral Dönitz refined his strategy. Drawing on his experiences from World War I, Dönitz developed the "wolf pack" tactic, where groups of U-boats would coordinate their attacks on Allied convoys, overwhelming their defenses through sheer numbers and coordinated assaults.

The effectiveness of this strategy was demonstrated on October 14, 1939, in one of the most audacious U-boat attacks of the war. U-47, commanded by the skilled and daring Günther Prien, penetrated the supposedly impregnable British naval base at Scapa Flow in the Orkney Islands. In the dead of night, Prien navigated the treacherous channels and fired his torpedoes at the battleship HMS Royal Oak. The massive warship, caught completely by surprise, capsized and sank, taking 833 of her crew to the bottom.

The attack on Scapa Flow sent shockwaves through the British Admiralty and demonstrated the boldness and skill of the U-boat commanders. It also highlighted the vulnerability of even the most heavily defended British assets to determined U-boat attacks.

For the U-boat hunters, this new threat demanded new tactics and technologies. The Western Approaches Tactical Unit (WATU), established in January 1942, played a crucial role in developing these countermeasures. Led by Captain Gilbert Roberts, WATU used wargaming to simulate U-boat attacks and develop tactics such as the "Raspberry" maneuver, which significantly improved the effectiveness of convoy escorts.

**Technological Innovation: The Hunters Gain New Tools**

As the battle intensified, both sides raced to develop new technologies that could tip the balance. For the U-boat hunters, these innovations would prove crucial in turning the tide of the war.

One of the most significant developments was the improvement of radar systems. Early in the war, the British installed radar on their ships, although these initial systems were not particularly effective. However, as the war progressed, radar technology improved significantly. The introduction of the cavity magnetron allowed for the development of more compact and powerful radar systems, greatly enhancing the ability of ships and aircraft to detect surfaced U-boats, even in conditions of poor visibility.

The Leigh Light, introduced in 1942, was another game-changing innovation. This powerful searchlight, mounted on aircraft, allowed Allied pilots to illuminate and attack U-boats at night. This technology was particularly effective in the Bay of Biscay, where U-boats frequently surfaced to recharge their batteries.

Perhaps the most crucial development in the anti-submarine effort was in the realm of intelligence. British codebreakers at Bletchley Park worked tirelessly to crack the German Enigma code, which was used for all U-boat communications. Their eventual success, known as the Ultra secret, would prove to be a game-changer in the Battle of the Atlantic, allowing the Allies to anticipate U-boat movements and redirect convoys away from danger.

**The Human Element: Courage Under Fire**

While technology played a crucial role, the Battle of the Atlantic was ultimately won by the courage and determination of the men who sailed the treacherous waters of the North Atlantic. For the crews of merchant ships and their naval escorts, every voyage was a journey into potential oblivion. The constant threat of U-boat attack wore on the nerves of even the most seasoned sailors.

Elmer Auld, a 98-year-old veteran from Thunder Bay, Ontario, shared his experiences as a U-boat hunter aboard an escort vessel on transatlantic missions. He reflects on the war at sea daily, indicating the profound impact these experiences had on him. His account provides a glimpse into the tension and danger faced by those on the front lines of the Atlantic battle.

Lieutenant Commander Desmond Piers of the Royal Canadian Navy described a harrowing 72-hour ordeal where his convoy was surrounded by U-boats. His account highlights the intense and dangerous nature of these engagements, where the hunters could quickly become the hunted.

For the U-boat crews, life was equally perilous. Crammed into steel tubes beneath the waves, they faced the constant threat of depth charges, aerial attack, and the myriad dangers of the sea itself. Peter Petersen, a German submariner who survived three patrols, spoke of the psychological toll: "The tension was unbearable at times. Every ping of the enemy's sonar could be our death knell. Many of us wondered if we would ever see home again".

**Turning the Tide: The Hunters Become the Hunted**

As 1942 progressed into 1943, the balance of power in the Battle of the Atlantic began to shift. The cumulative effect of Allied countermeasures started to tell, while the entry of the United States into the war brought much-needed resources to the fight against the U-boats.

The introduction of long-range aircraft, particularly the B-24 Liberator, closed the "mid-Atlantic gap" where U-boats had previously operated with impunity. Escort carriers provided crucial air cover for convoys, while improved depth charges and the innovative "Hedgehog" anti-submarine mortar increased the lethality of escort ships.

One of the most significant engagements of this period was the Battle of Convoy ONS 5 in May 1943. This convoy of 42 merchant ships was attacked by a wolf pack of 30 U-boats. Despite the loss of 13 ships, the convoy's escorts managed to sink six U-boats, marking a turning point in the battle as Allied anti-submarine tactics and technology began to take effect.

The tide had decisively turned. In what became known as "Black May" for the U-boat force, 43 German submarines were sunk in a single month. This devastating loss rate forced Dönitz to temporarily withdraw his U-boats from the North Atlantic, effectively conceding defeat in that crucial arena.

**The Final Act: Victory in the Atlantic**

By 1944, the Allies had largely neutralized the U-boat threat through superior technology, tactics, and overwhelming production of ships and aircraft. The introduction of hunter-killer groups, which included escort carriers and destroyers, allowed the Allies to take a more offensive approach, actively seeking out and destroying U-boats.

One of the most dramatic episodes of this final phase was the capture of U-505 on June 4, 1944. A U.S. Navy hunter-killer group, organized around the USS Guadalcanal, successfully captured the U-boat off the coast of West Africa. This was the first time since the War of 1812 that the U.S. Navy had captured an enemy vessel on the high seas. More importantly, it provided the Allies with valuable codebooks and an intact Enigma machine, further aiding in the decryption of German communications.

As the war drew to a close, the once-feared U-boats had become the hunted, with Allied aircraft and warships dominating the Atlantic. The Battle of the Atlantic concluded with the surrender of Germany in May 1945, marking the end of the U-boat threat.

**Conclusion: The Legacy of the U-Boat Hunters**

The victory of the U-boat hunters in the Battle of the Atlantic was a testament to the power of innovation, adaptability, and sheer determination. From the dark days of 1940, when U-boats seemed poised to strangle Britain's lifelines, to the final triumph in 1945, the story of the Atlantic campaign is one of continuous evolution in tactics, technology, and strategy.

The success of the U-boat hunters ensured the survival of Britain, enabled the buildup of Allied forces in Europe, and ultimately contributed significantly to the defeat of Nazi Germany. The lessons learned in this longest of campaigns - the value of intelligence, the importance of technological innovation, and the effectiveness of combined arms operations - would shape naval warfare for generations to come.

In the words of Winston Churchill, who understood better than most the stakes of the Battle of the Atlantic: "The only thing that ever really frightened me during the war was the U-boat peril." Thanks to the efforts of the U-boat hunters, that peril was overcome, and the course of history was forever changed.

**Sources**

Paterson, Laurence. U-Boats in the Mediterranean: 1941-1944. Skyhorse, 2019.

Paterson, Laurence. The U-Boat War: A Global History 1939-45. Osprey Publishing, 2022.

Various Sources

## Great Losses in the Atlantic Theater

**Introduction**

World War II was marked by unprecedented naval warfare, particularly in the Atlantic Theater, where the Battle of the Atlantic raged from 1939 until the defeat of Nazi Germany in 1945. This conflict was characterized by the struggle between the Allied forces and the Axis powers, primarily Germany, as they fought for control of vital shipping routes. The losses incurred during this period were staggering, affecting merchant ships, military vessels, submarines, and countless personnel. This story explores the extent of these losses, highlighting the sacrifices made by those involved in this critical theater of war.

**Overview of Merchant Shipping**

The merchant marine played a crucial role in supporting the Allied war effort by transporting troops, supplies, and equipment across the Atlantic. However, this vital service came at a high cost. The German U-boat campaign aimed to disrupt these supply lines, leading to significant losses among merchant vessels.

**Total Losses**

- **Merchant Ships Sunk**: Approximately **3,500 merchant ships** were lost during the Battle of the Atlantic. This figure includes both Allied and neutral vessels targeted by German U-boats and surface raiders.
- **Civilian Casualties**: The loss of merchant ships resulted in the deaths of around **72,000 Allied seamen**, including merchant mariners and naval personnel. This figure reflects the high casualty rates faced by those serving in the merchant fleets.

**Notable Incidents**

Several notable incidents exemplify the dangers faced by merchant ships during the war:

- **SS Athenia**: The first British ship sunk by a U-boat in the war was the SS Athenia, torpedoed on September 3, 1939, resulting in the deaths of 112 passengers and crew members.

- **Convoy Battles**: Throughout the war, numerous convoy battles occurred, where U-boats would attack groups of merchant ships. For example, during the attack on Convoy SC-7 in October 1940, U-boats sank 20 of the 35 merchant ships involved, leading to significant loss of life.

**Military Ship Losses**

**Overview of Naval Engagements:** The naval forces of the Allies and Axis powers engaged in numerous battles throughout the Atlantic Theater. These engagements resulted in the loss of military vessels, including destroyers, cruisers, and aircraft carriers.

**Total Losses**

- **Warships Sunk**: Approximately **175 warships** were lost by the Allies during the Battle of the Atlantic. This includes destroyers, frigates, and other naval vessels that were either sunk by U-boats or lost in surface engagements.
- **Personnel Casualties**: The losses among naval personnel were also significant, with thousands of sailors losing their lives in the line of duty. The Royal Canadian Navy alone suffered approximately **2,000 casualties** during the conflict.

**Notable Incidents**

Several key naval engagements highlight the dangers faced by military vessels:

- **The Battle of the Barents Sea**: In December 1942, British naval forces engaged German ships in the Barents Sea, resulting in the sinking of several German vessels but also leading to the loss of British ships and personnel.
- **The Sinking of HMS Hood**: The British battlecruiser HMS Hood was sunk by the German battleship Bismarck in May 1941, resulting in the deaths of 1,415 crew members, marking one of the most significant losses for the Royal Navy during the war.

**Submarine Losses**

**Overview of U-Boat Operations:** The German U-boat fleet was a formidable force during the Battle of the Atlantic, employing tactics that caused significant disruption to Allied shipping. However, the U-boat campaign also came at a cost to the German Navy.

**Total Losses**

- **U-Boats Sunk**: Approximately **783 U-boats** were lost during the course of the war. This figure reflects the high attrition rate faced by German submarines as Allied anti-submarine tactics improved.
- **Personnel Casualties**: The loss of U-boats resulted in the deaths of around **30,000 German sailors**. Many of these personnel were lost at sea, with their vessels sunk by Allied warships and aircraft.

**Notable Incidents**

Several incidents illustrate the dangers faced by U-boats:

- **The Sinking of U-47**: The famous U-boat commanded by Günther Prien was sunk in March 1941, resulting in the loss of 45 crew members. Prien had previously gained fame for his daring attack on the British battleship HMS Royal Oak.
- **The Battle of the Atlantic's Turning Point**: By mid-1943, the Allies had developed effective countermeasures, leading to increased U-boat losses. The introduction of long-range aircraft and improved convoy tactics significantly reduced the effectiveness of the U-boat campaign.

## The Human Cost of War

**Overview of Personnel Losses:** The human cost of the Battle of the Atlantic was immense, affecting not only military personnel but also civilians involved in maritime operations.

## Total Personnel Losses

- **Allied Casualties**: The total number of Allied personnel lost during the Battle of the Atlantic is estimated to be around **72,000**, including merchant mariners, naval personnel, and airmen [3].
- **German Casualties**: The German Navy suffered approximately **30,000 casualties** among U-boat crews, reflecting the high risks associated with submarine warfare.

## Notable Stories of Sacrifice

The sacrifices made by individuals during the Battle of the Atlantic are numerous and poignant:

- **The Merchant Mariners**: Many merchant mariners faced perilous conditions, often sailing unarmed ships into dangerous waters. Their bravery and commitment to the war effort were crucial in maintaining supply lines to the Allies.
- **The Royal Canadian Navy**: Canadian sailors played a vital role in escorting convoys and engaging U-boats. Their contributions were marked by significant losses, with many ships sunk and lives lost in the line of duty.

## Conclusion

The Battle of the Atlantic was a defining conflict of World War II, characterized by significant losses among merchant ships, military vessels, submarines, and personnel. The staggering figures—approximately 3,500 merchant ships, 175 warships, and 783 U-boats lost—underscore the high stakes of this theater of war. The sacrifices made by those involved, both military and civilian, highlight the human cost of the struggle for control of the Atlantic.

# The Mediterranean, Balkans, and Middle East

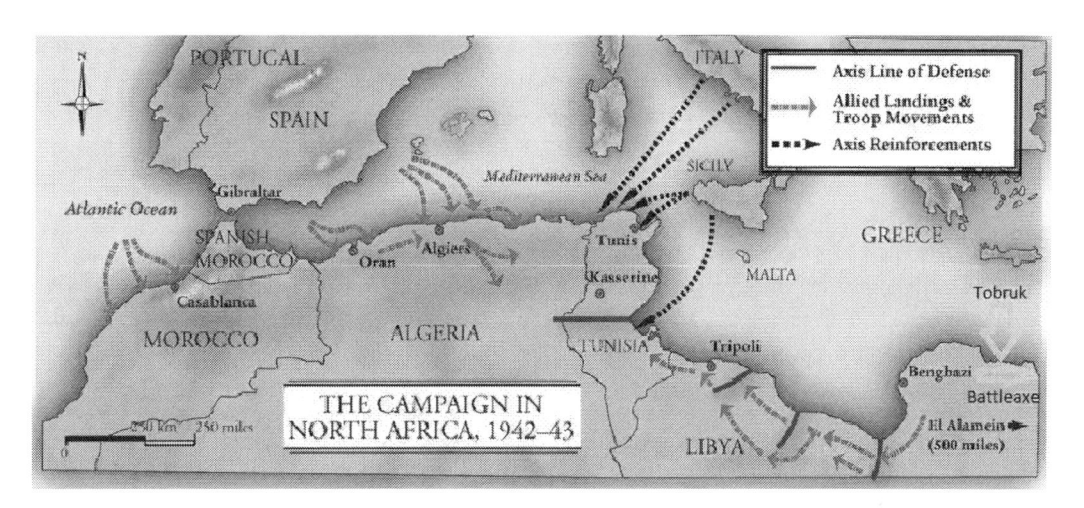

# Desert Warfare: The Axis Powers in North Africa

## Introduction

As the storm clouds of World War II gathered over Europe in 1940, a new theater of war was about to open in the sun-scorched deserts of North Africa. The North African Campaign, spanning from June 10, 1940, to May 13, 1943, would become one of the most dramatic and consequential campaigns of the war, pitting the Axis powers of Germany and Italy against the Allied forces of Britain, the Commonwealth, and later the United States.

This campaign was not merely a sideshow to the larger conflict in Europe; it was a crucial battleground that would shape the course of the war. At stake was control of the Suez Canal, a vital maritime route for the British Empire, and access to the oil-rich Middle East. For the Axis powers, North Africa represented an opportunity to cut off Britain from its colonial resources and secure their own access to these strategic assets.

The North African Campaign would be characterized by sweeping advances and retreats across vast desert expanses, innovative tactics, and the harsh realities of warfare in one of the world's most unforgiving environments. It would see the rise of legendary commanders, test the limits of military logistics, and ultimately play a pivotal role in the eventual Allied victory in World War II.

This story explores the Axis involvement in North Africa, from the initial Italian invasion to the final surrender in Tunisia. Through the eyes of those who fought and led on both sides, we will witness the triumphs and tragedies, the strategic decisions and logistical challenges that defined this crucial campaign. From the tactical brilliance of Erwin Rommel to the grim realities faced by ordinary soldiers in the desert, this is the story of the Axis in North Africa.

## The Opening Gambit: Italy's Desert Ambitions

The North African Campaign began with Italian ambitions to expand their colonial empire. On June 10, 1940, Italy declared war on France and the United Kingdom, setting the stage for conflict in North Africa.

Benito Mussolini, the Italian dictator, saw an opportunity to seize British-held Egypt and the Suez Canal, thereby cementing Italian dominance in the Mediterranean.

On September 13, 1940, Italian forces under the command of Marshal Rodolfo Graziani launched an invasion into Egypt from their colony in Libya. The Italian army, numbering some 200,000 men, advanced about 60 miles into Egypt before halting to establish defensive positions. This cautious approach would prove to be a critical mistake.

The British Western Desert Force, though vastly outnumbered, was better trained and equipped for desert warfare. On December 9, 1940, they launched Operation Compass, a counterattack that would have far-reaching consequences. What was initially planned as a five-day raid turned into a devastating two-month campaign for the Italians.

British and Commonwealth forces, under the command of General Richard O'Connor, routed the Italian 10th Army, pushing them out of Egypt and pursuing them deep into Libya. By February 1941, the Italians had been driven out of Cyrenaica, losing 130,000 men as prisoners and nearly 400 tanks. The port city of Tobruk fell to the Allies on January 22, dealing a severe blow to Italian prestige and their ability to supply forces in North Africa.

This stunning reversal of fortune alarmed Adolf Hitler and the German High Command. The potential loss of Libya would not only be a significant blow to their Axis partner but could also threaten German ambitions in the Balkans and the Middle East. Hitler decided to intervene, setting the stage for the arrival of a commander who would change the face of the desert war: Erwin Rommel.

**Enter the Desert Fox: Rommel and the Afrika Korps**

In February 1941, Lieutenant General Erwin Rommel arrived in Tripoli with the initial units of what would become the legendary Afrika Korps. Rommel, already renowned for his leadership during the invasion of France, was tasked with shoring up the crumbling Italian defenses and preventing a total Axis collapse in North Africa.

Rommel wasted no time in making his presence felt. Disobeying orders to remain on the defensive, he launched a daring counteroffensive on March 24, 1941. This bold move caught the British, who had weakened their desert forces to support operations in Greece, completely off guard.

The Afrika Korps, combined with rebuilt Italian units, drove eastward with stunning speed. By April 10, they had recaptured Cyrenaica and surrounded Tobruk, which was now held by Allied forces. The speed and audacity of Rommel's advance earned him the nickname "The Desert Fox" from both his own troops and his adversaries.

A German soldier, Hermann Franz, captured the excitement of these early days in a letter home: "The Arabs are very fond of us. Our advance is so rapid that we ourselves can hardly believe it. The English are fleeing before us. It is like a huge exercise with live ammunition."

However, Rommel's advance was not without its challenges. The siege of Tobruk, which began on April 10, 1941, would prove to be a thorn in his side. The Allied garrison, primarily consisting of Australian troops, held out tenaciously, tying down significant Axis forces and disrupting their supply lines.

Despite this setback, Rommel's early successes had a profound impact on the campaign. He had restored Axis prestige, pushed the British back to the Egyptian frontier, and demonstrated the effectiveness of mobile, armored warfare in the desert environment. His leadership style, often leading from the front and making rapid, intuitive decisions, inspired his troops and confounded his enemies.

Yet, these early triumphs also sowed the seeds of future problems. Rommel's aggressive style often outpaced his supply lines, a critical vulnerability in the harsh desert environment. His tendency to ignore orders from both his Italian allies and his own high command would lead to strategic overreach and logistical nightmares in the campaigns to come.

**The Pendulum Swings: Battles of 1941-1942**

The year 1941 saw a series of offensives and counteroffensives as both sides struggled for supremacy in the Western Desert. Operation Brevity in May and Operation Battleaxe in June were British attempts to relieve Tobruk and push the Axis forces back. Both operations failed, with Rommel's forces proving adept at defensive tactics and counterattacks.

November 1941 saw the launch of Operation Crusader, a major British offensive. After weeks of hard fighting, the Axis forces were compelled to retreat. The siege of Tobruk was lifted on December 10, 1941, and the Axis were pushed back to El Agheila in Libya. This setback was a blow to Axis morale, but Rommel was far from defeated.

As 1942 dawned, the desert war entered a new phase. Rommel, having received reinforcements and supplies, launched a new offensive on January 21. In a series of swift maneuvers, he recaptured Benghazi and pushed the British back to the Gazala Line, a series of fortified positions west of Tobruk.

The Battle of Gazala, which began on May 26, 1942, was one of the most crucial engagements of the North African Campaign. Rommel's plan was audacious: while the Italian forces pinned down the Allied troops along the Gazala Line, the Afrika Korps would swing around the southern end of the line in a maneuver known as the "Cauldron" battle.

The initial stages of the battle were chaotic, with Rommel's forces nearly encircled and running critically low on supplies. However, the Desert Fox's leadership and the skill of his troops turned the tide. By June 11, the British were in full retreat, and on June 21, Tobruk fell to the Axis forces. The capture of Tobruk, with its valuable supplies and 33,000 prisoners, was perhaps the high-water mark of Axis fortunes in North Africa.

Buoyed by this success, Rommel pushed on into Egypt, reaching El Alamein, a mere 60 miles from Alexandria. Here, however, the Axis advance ground to a halt. Exhausted, overstretched, and critically low on supplies, Rommel's forces could go no further. The First Battle of El Alamein in July 1942 saw the British, under new leadership, stop the Axis advance decisively.

**Logistics: The Achilles Heel of the Axis**

While Rommel's tactical brilliance had brought the Axis to the gates of Egypt, it was logistics that would ultimately prove to be their undoing. The challenges of supplying an army in the North African desert were enormous, and the Axis supply situation was particularly precarious.

The primary supply ports for the Axis forces were Tripoli, Benghazi, and Tobruk. However, these ports had limited capacity and were under constant threat from Allied air and naval forces. Tripoli, the largest port, could only handle about 45,000 tons of supplies a month, far short of what was needed to sustain a major offensive.

Transportation of supplies from the ports to the front lines was another major challenge. There was only one major road, the Via Balbia, running along the North African coast. This made supply convoys vulnerable to Allied air attacks. The lack of a comprehensive rail network further complicated logistics.

Fuel was a constant concern. The German and Italian vehicles, designed for European battlefields, were fuel-hungry and prone to breakdowns in the harsh desert conditions. On average, about a third of Rommel's supply vehicles were out of action due to mechanical problems or lack of spare parts.

The diversity of vehicles used by the Axis forces - a mix of German, Italian, captured British, and even French vehicles - made maintenance and spare parts supply a logistical nightmare. Tires, in particular, wore out quickly on the abrasive desert terrain, and replacements were always in short supply.

Water was another critical issue. Each soldier required at least a gallon of water per day in the desert heat, and this had to be transported from the coast. Food supplies were often inadequate, leading to health problems among the troops. At one point, over 40% of the men in the 15th Panzer Division were suffering from diseases related to poor nutrition.

The Allied control of Malta, strategically located in the middle of the Mediterranean, allowed them to interdict Axis supply convoys effectively. Allied submarines and aircraft operating from Malta sank a significant portion of the supplies destined for North Africa. In the critical month of November 1941, for example, only 29,843 tons of supplies reached Libya out of 79,208 tons sent.

A German quartermaster, reflecting on these challenges, wrote: "The quartermaster in Africa was always in the unfortunate position of having to operate with too little of everything. The problem was not one of economizing, but of making do with totally inadequate resources."

These logistical challenges would prove to be the Achilles heel of the Axis forces in North Africa. No matter how brilliant Rommel's tactics, without adequate supplies, his forces could not sustain their operations or capitalize on their successes.

**The Tide Turns: El Alamein and Operation Torch**

By the autumn of 1942, the strategic situation in North Africa had reached a critical juncture. The Axis forces, though tantalizingly close to Alexandria and the Suez Canal, were exhausted and critically short of supplies. The Allies, on the other hand, had been steadily building up their strength under their new commander, Lieutenant-General Bernard Montgomery.

The Second Battle of El Alamein, which began on October 23, 1942, would prove to be the turning point of the North African Campaign. Montgomery had spent months preparing for this battle, accumulating supplies and training his troops. The British Eighth Army now outnumbered and outgunned Rommel's forces.

The battle began with a massive artillery barrage, followed by infantry attacks to clear paths through the Axis minefields. Despite fierce resistance from the Axis forces, the weight of Allied men and materiel gradually told. By November 4, Rommel's forces were in full retreat.

The defeat at El Alamein was catastrophic for the Axis. They had lost 30,000 men killed or captured, and much of their equipment. More importantly, they had lost the initiative in North Africa. Rommel would later write: "We had neither the men nor the material to withstand attacks of such weight for any length of time."

As Rommel's forces retreated westward, they faced a new threat. On November 8, 1942, Allied forces landed in Morocco and Algeria as part of Operation Torch. This massive amphibious operation, involving American and British troops, opened a second front in North Africa.

The Axis forces now found themselves caught between the British Eighth Army advancing from the east and the new Allied force pushing from the west. Despite this, they managed to inflict a sharp defeat on inexperienced American forces at the Battle of Kasserine Pass in February 1943. This battle, however, proved to be the last major Axis success in North Africa.

**The Final Act: Tunisia and Surrender**

As 1943 began, the Axis position in North Africa was becoming increasingly untenable. Rommel, recognizing the hopelessness of the situation, had argued for a complete withdrawal from North Africa, but Hitler insisted on a policy of "holding at all costs."

The Axis forces retreated into Tunisia, where they prepared for a final stand. Despite facing inevitable defeat, they fought on with remarkable tenacity. The Battle of Medenine on March 6, 1943, saw Rommel launch one last offensive, which was decisively repulsed by the British Eighth Army.

Rommel, suffering from health problems and disillusioned with Hitler's leadership, left North Africa for the last time on March 9, 1943. His departure marked the end of an era in the desert war.

The remaining Axis forces, now under the command of Italian General Giovanni Messe, continued to resist. However, they were steadily pushed back by the combined Allied forces. Tunis fell on May 7, 1943, and on May 13, the last Axis resistance in North Africa came to an end.

The toll of the campaign was staggering. The Allies took 238,000 German and Italian prisoners in the final phase of the campaign alone. The material losses were equally severe, with the Axis losing vast quantities of tanks, aircraft, and other equipment that could not be easily replaced.

**Conclusion**

The defeat of the Axis powers in North Africa was a turning point in World War II. It eliminated the Axis threat to the Suez Canal and the Middle East oil fields, secured the Mediterranean for Allied shipping, and provided a springboard for the invasion of Sicily and Italy.

For the Axis, the North African Campaign was a story of initial success followed by ultimate failure. Rommel's tactical brilliance and the fighting skill of the Afrika Korps had brought them to the brink of victory, but they were ultimately undone by strategic overreach, logistical challenges, and the overwhelming material superiority of the Allies.

In the end, the Axis defeat in North Africa opened the way for the Allied invasion of Europe. The lessons learned and the experience gained in the desert would prove invaluable in the campaigns to come. The North African Campaign, while often overshadowed by events in Europe and the Pacific, played a crucial role in shaping the outcome of World War II and stands as a testament to the courage, endurance, and sacrifice of those who fought there.

**Sources**

Charles River Editors. The Afrika Korps: The History of Nazi Germany's Expeditionary Force in North Africa during World War II. CreateSpace Independent Publishing Platforms, 2017

Spring, Ian. Rommel's Afrika Korps in Colour: Rare German Photographs from the Second World War. Greenhill Books, 2023.

Various Sources

# Battles in North Africa and the Mediterranean

## Fall of Crete

The Fall of Crete, which began on May 20, 1941, marked a significant turning point in World War II, showcasing the effectiveness of airborne warfare. The German invasion, known as Operation Mercury, involved a massive airborne assault that aimed to seize the strategically important island from British and Commonwealth forces. The operation was unprecedented in scale, with thousands of German paratroopers dropping onto the island, facing fierce resistance from Allied troops and the local population. Despite the Allies' efforts to fortify their defenses, the rapid and overwhelming German air assault proved to be a decisive factor.

As the battle progressed, the Allies struggled to maintain their positions. The terrain of Crete complicated defensive efforts, and the initial shock of the airborne invasion left many Allied troops disorganized. German forces, leveraging their air superiority, were able to capture key locations, including Maleme airfield, which became crucial for reinforcements. The fierce fighting led to heavy casualties on both sides, but the Germans ultimately gained the upper hand, forcing the Allies to retreat.

By June 1, 1941, the island was fully under German control, marking a significant victory for the Axis powers. The Fall of Crete had far-reaching implications, as it demonstrated the effectiveness of airborne operations and shifted the balance of power in the Mediterranean. The defeat also prompted the Allies to reevaluate their strategic approach in the region, leading to increased focus on preventing further Axis expansion in North Africa and the Mediterranean.

## Naval and Air Blockade of Axis Forces in Tunisia

The naval and air blockade of Axis forces in Tunisia was a crucial operation during the North African Campaign, aimed at crippling the supply lines of German and Italian troops. As Allied forces advanced into Tunisia following the defeat of Axis forces in Egypt, they sought to cut off the remaining enemy units. The blockade was executed through coordinated efforts between the British Royal Navy and the United States Navy, alongside air support from the Royal Air Force and the United States Army Air Forces. This multi-faceted approach aimed to restrict the movement of Axis reinforcements and supplies, thereby weakening their defensive capabilities.

The blockade intensified in early 1943 as Allied forces prepared for a final assault on the Axis positions in Tunisia. Allied naval forces patrolled the Mediterranean Sea, intercepting supply ships and engaging in skirmishes with Axis naval units. Air power played a critical role, with Allied aircraft targeting supply depots, transport ships, and communications lines, significantly disrupting the logistical capabilities of the Axis forces. The blockade not only diminished the resources available to German and Italian troops but also boosted the morale of Allied forces, knowing that their opponents were increasingly isolated.

By May 1943, the effectiveness of the blockade was evident as Axis forces in Tunisia began to collapse under the pressure of sustained attacks and dwindling supplies. The success of the blockade contributed to the surrender of approximately 250,000 Axis troops, marking a significant victory for the Allies in the North African Campaign. This operation not only solidified Allied control over North Africa but also set the stage for future operations in the Mediterranean and Europe, demonstrating the importance of logistical superiority in modern warfare.

**Battle of Tobruk**

The Battle of Tobruk, fought from April to December 1941, was a pivotal confrontation in the North African Campaign. Tobruk, a strategic port city in Libya, became a focal point for Allied and Axis forces due to its importance as a supply hub. The battle began when Axis forces under General Erwin Rommel launched an offensive to capture the city, which was defended by Australian, British, and other Allied troops. The siege quickly turned into a fierce struggle, with the defenders determined to hold their ground against the advancing German and Italian forces.

Throughout the siege, Tobruk's defenders displayed remarkable resilience, employing a combination of defensive tactics and counterattacks to repel the Axis advances. The Allies utilized the port's fortifications and the surrounding terrain to their advantage, managing to withstand several assaults. The situation was dire, but the Allies received crucial supplies and reinforcements, which allowed them to maintain a foothold in the city. The defense of Tobruk became symbolic of Allied determination in North Africa, earning the city the nickname "The Fortress."

The siege lasted until December 1941, when Allied forces launched a successful counteroffensive, eventually pushing the Axis troops back. The Battle of Tobruk not only prevented Axis control of a key supply point but also bolstered Allied morale in the region. The eventual relief of Tobruk showcased the strength of Allied cooperation and set the stage for further offensives in North Africa, contributing to the eventual defeat of Axis forces in the region.

**Battle of Alamein**

The Battle of Alamein, fought from October 23 to November 11, 1942, was a decisive turning point in the North African Campaign. Located near the Egyptian town of El Alamein, the battle pitted British forces, commanded by General Bernard Montgomery, against the German-Italian Afrika Korps led by General Erwin Rommel. The Allies sought to halt the Axis advance into Egypt, which threatened the Suez Canal and Middle Eastern oil supplies. Montgomery's forces were well-prepared and fortified, having learned from previous engagements with Rommel's troops.

The battle began with an extensive artillery barrage, followed by ground assaults aimed at breaking through Axis lines. The Allies employed a combination of infantry, armored units, and air support to gain the upper hand. Despite fierce resistance, the well-coordinated Allied tactics and superior logistics gradually pushed back the Axis forces. The tenacity of the Allied troops, coupled with the exhaustion of Rommel's forces, marked a critical shift in the momentum of the war in North Africa.

By November 11, 1942, the Axis forces were in retreat, and the victory at Alamein marked a significant turning point for the Allies. The battle not only halted the Axis advance but also boosted Allied morale and showcased the effectiveness of coordinated military strategy. Following Alamein, the Allies began a series of successful offensives that ultimately led to the expulsion of Axis forces from North Africa, setting the stage for future campaigns in Europe.

**Battle of Taranto**

The Battle of Taranto, fought on November 11-12, 1940, was a significant naval engagement during World War II, marking the first major aircraft carrier strike against a naval base. British forces aimed to cripple the Italian Navy, which posed a threat to Allied operations in the Mediterranean. The Royal Navy's aircraft carrier HMS Illustrious launched a surprise attack on the Italian fleet stationed at Taranto, using Swordfish torpedo bombers to target battleships and other vessels in the harbor.

The attack was meticulously planned, with the British forces employing innovative tactics to overcome the defenses of Taranto. Despite facing challenging weather conditions and enemy anti-aircraft fire, the British pilots achieved remarkable success. They managed to sink or severely damage several Italian battleships, including the battleship Conte di Cavour, significantly diminishing Italy's naval power in the Mediterranean. The operation demonstrated the effectiveness of air power in naval warfare and highlighted the vulnerabilities of battleships to aerial attacks.

The Battle of Taranto had far-reaching consequences for naval strategy during the war. It not only weakened the Italian Navy but also prompted a shift in naval doctrine, emphasizing the importance of aircraft carriers over traditional battleships. The success of the British attack at Taranto bolstered Allied morale and showcased the potential of naval aviation, setting the stage for future operations in the Mediterranean Theater.

**Malta Under Siege**

The Siege of Malta, which lasted from 1940 to 1942, was a critical episode in the Mediterranean Campaign of World War II. Malta, a small island nation strategically located between Europe and North Africa, became a key target for Axis forces seeking to disrupt Allied supply lines and establish control over the Mediterranean. The island was heavily bombed by German and Italian forces, enduring relentless air raids aimed at crippling its defenses and undermining its strategic significance.

**Sources**

Atkinson, Rick. An Army at Dawn: The War in North Africa, 1942-1945. Holt Paperbacks, 2007.

Diamond, Jon. First Blood in North Africa: Operation Torch and the US Campaign in Africa in WWII. Stackpole Books, 2017.

Various Sources

# Operation Torch: The Allied Invasion of North Africa

## Introduction

In the dark hours of November 8, 1942, as the world was engulfed in the flames of World War II, a daring and ambitious military operation was about to unfold on the shores of North Africa. Operation Torch, the first major Allied offensive in the European-North African theater, would mark a turning point in the war and set the stage for the eventual liberation of Europe from Axis control.

This operation, born from intense strategic debates and meticulous planning, was more than just a military maneuver. It was a bold statement of Allied resolve, a test of American and British cooperation, and a complex diplomatic dance with Vichy French authorities. Operation Torch would not only shape the course of the North African campaign but would also have far-reaching implications for the entire war effort.

As the invasion fleet sailed towards the North African coast, carrying over 100,000 Allied troops, the fate of the war hung in the balance. The success or failure of Operation Torch would determine whether the Allies could gain a foothold in North Africa, relieve pressure on the beleaguered Soviet Union, and begin to turn the tide against the seemingly unstoppable Axis powers.

This is the story of Operation Torch - a tale of strategic vision, logistical marvels, battlefield heroism, and the complex interplay of military and political forces that would help shape the outcome of World War II.

## The Genesis of Operation Torch

The roots of Operation Torch can be traced back to the Arcadia Conference held in Washington, D.C., in December 1941. As the world reeled from the Japanese attack on Pearl Harbor and the entry of the United States into the war, Allied leaders gathered to chart a course for victory. President Franklin D. Roosevelt and British Prime Minister Winston Churchill, along with their military advisors, debated the best strategy to counter Axis advances and relieve pressure on the embattled Soviet Union.

Initially, American military strategists, led by General George Marshall, advocated for a direct assault on Nazi-occupied Europe through a cross-channel invasion. This plan, known as Operation Bolero, called for a massive buildup of forces in Great Britain. However, Churchill and the British high command, wary of a premature invasion of France, pushed for an alternative strategy. They proposed an invasion of North

Africa, arguing that it would secure the Mediterranean, provide a base for future operations in Southern Europe, and offer American troops valuable combat experience.

The debate was intense, with strong arguments on both sides. General Dwight D. Eisenhower, who would later command Operation Torch, recalled the heated discussions: "The arguments went back and forth, with each side presenting compelling reasons for their preferred strategy. In the end, it was a matter of balancing immediate action against long-term goals."

After months of deliberation and compromise, the Allied leaders agreed on the North African option. The operation, initially codenamed Gymnast, evolved into Operation Torch. This decision would have far-reaching consequences for the course of the war and the shape of the Allied coalition.

**Planning and Preparation**

With the strategic decision made, the Allies embarked on the monumental task of planning and preparing for what would be, at that time, the largest amphibious operation in military history. General Eisenhower was appointed as the supreme commander of the Allied forces for Operation Torch, a role that would test his diplomatic skills as much as his military acumen.

The planning phase was a complex juggling act of military strategy, logistics, and diplomacy. The operation was designed as a three-pronged assault, with simultaneous landings on the Atlantic coast of Morocco and the Mediterranean coast of Algeria. The primary objectives were to secure key ports and airfields at Casablanca, Oran, and Algiers, establishing a foothold for further operations into Tunisia.

Logistically, Operation Torch was a Herculean task. It involved coordinating the movement of over 107,000 troops, 350 warships, and 500 transport ships across vast distances without detection by Axis forces. Admiral Sir Andrew Cunningham, who led the naval component, described the challenge: "Moving such a large force across the Atlantic and through the Strait of Gibraltar was like threading a needle while riding a galloping horse."

The planners had to consider numerous factors: the availability of landing craft, the unpredictable Mediterranean weather, the potential for resistance from Vichy French forces, and the risk of drawing neutral Spain into the conflict. Each decision carried enormous weight, and the margin for error was razor-thin.

Diplomatic efforts played a crucial role in the planning. U.S. diplomat Robert Murphy engaged in secret negotiations with Vichy French officials, including Admiral François Darlan, the Vichy High Commissioner for North Africa. These delicate talks aimed to minimize French resistance

and potentially secure their cooperation. Murphy later wrote, "We were walking a tightrope, trying to gain French support without alerting the Germans to our plans."

As the plans took shape, the Allied forces began to assemble. In Britain, American and British troops trained together, learning the intricacies of amphibious warfare. In the United States, a massive convoy prepared to sail directly to the shores of Morocco. The stage was set for one of the most ambitious military operations of the war.

## The Invasion Begins

In the pre-dawn hours of November 8, 1942, Operation Torch was launched. The invasion force was divided into three task forces, each targeting a specific area of French North Africa:

1. The Western Task Force, commanded by Major General George S. Patton, aimed for Casablanca on the Atlantic coast of Morocco. This force, consisting of 35,000 American troops, including the 3rd Infantry Division and 2nd Armored Division, had sailed directly from the United States.

2. The Center Task Force, led by Major General Lloyd R. Fredendall, targeted Oran in Algeria. It comprised 39,000 U.S. troops, including the 1st Infantry Division, 1st Armored Division, and U.S. Army Rangers.

3. The Eastern Task Force, under the command of British Lieutenant General K.A.N. Anderson, was tasked with capturing Algiers. This force included both British and American troops, with U.S. Major General Charles Ryder leading the American contingent.

As the invasion fleet approached the North African coast, tension among the troops was palpable. Many of the American soldiers had never seen combat, and the uncertainty of the Vichy French response added to the anxiety. John Timothy, a soldier in the 2nd Battalion, later recalled, "As we neared the shore, you could hear a pin drop. We didn't know if we'd be greeted with handshakes or bullets."

The landings were met with varying degrees of resistance. In some areas, Vichy French forces fought fiercely, while in others, they quickly surrendered or even joined the Allies. The Western Task Force faced the stiffest opposition, with heavy fighting around Casablanca. Patton, in his characteristic style, was in the thick of the action, personally directing operations from the front lines.

At Oran, the Center Task Force encountered initial resistance but quickly overcame it. A daring raid by U.S. Army Rangers on the port facilities helped secure the city. In Algiers, the Eastern Task Force benefited from a pro-Allied coup attempt by French resistance fighters, which facilitated their capture of the city.

The naval and air components of Operation Torch played crucial roles in supporting the landings. Allied aircraft provided air cover and struck at French airfields and naval bases. The naval forces engaged French ships that attempted to interfere with the landings, resulting in several naval battles off the coast of Morocco.

Despite the challenges, including rough seas and navigational errors that disrupted landing schedules, the Allied forces achieved their initial objectives within days. By November 10, Casablanca, Oran, and Algiers were under Allied control.

## Diplomatic Maneuvers and Political Fallout

The military success of the initial landings was accompanied by complex political maneuvering. The Allies had hoped to gain the cooperation of Vichy French forces without alienating the Free French forces led by Charles de Gaulle. This delicate balancing act led to one of the most controversial decisions of the operation.

Admiral François Darlan, the Vichy French High Commissioner in North Africa, happened to be in Algiers during the invasion. After initial resistance, Darlan agreed to order a ceasefire and cooperate with the Allies in exchange for being recognized as the political leader of French North Africa. This deal, while expedient in military terms, was politically problematic.

General Eisenhower, weighing the military benefits against the political costs, decided to accept Darlan's offer. He later explained, "We were fighting a war, not running a debating society. The deal with Darlan saved thousands of lives and gave us a foothold in North Africa."

The "Darlan Deal" was met with outrage by many, including the Free French and some Allied political leaders. It seemed to legitimize the Vichy regime and undermined the moral high ground of the Allied cause. Churchill, who had to defend the decision in Parliament, described it as "kissing Himmler's boots," but ultimately supported Eisenhower's decision as a military necessity.

The political fallout from the Darlan affair was significant but short-lived. On December 24, 1942, Darlan was assassinated by a young French monarchist. While this solved the immediate political problem, it also created a power vacuum that the Allies had to address.

**The Race for Tunisia**

With the coastal cities secured, the Allies faced their next challenge: the race for Tunisia. The ultimate success of Operation Torch depended on quickly advancing eastward to link up with British forces under General Bernard Montgomery, who were pursuing Rommel's Afrika Korps across Libya.

However, the Axis powers reacted swiftly to the Allied landings. Hitler, enraged by what he saw as Vichy French betrayal, ordered the occupation of Vichy France and rushed reinforcements to Tunisia. German and Italian troops poured into Tunis and Bizerte, establishing a strong defensive position before the Allies could reach them.

The Allied advance eastward was hampered by logistical challenges, difficult terrain, and increasingly bad weather. The inadequate road and rail network in North Africa strained supply lines, while autumn rains turned dry wadis into muddy quagmires. Despite these obstacles, elements of the British First Army, along with American forces, pushed towards Tunis.

In late November and early December, the Allies launched several attacks aimed at capturing Tunis, but they were repulsed by determined Axis resistance. The fighting was fierce, with both sides suffering heavy casualties. A young American officer, describing the intensity of the combat, wrote home: "The Germans fight like demons. Every inch of ground is contested, and the artillery never stops."

As 1942 drew to a close, it became clear that the hope for a quick victory in Tunisia was fading. The Allies would have to settle in for a longer campaign, building up their forces and preparing for a major offensive in the spring.

**The Aftermath and Impact**

While the immediate goal of capturing Tunisia remained elusive, Operation Torch had achieved significant strategic objectives. The Allies had secured a foothold in North Africa, effectively opening a second front against the Axis powers. This new front forced Hitler to divert significant resources from other theaters, particularly the Eastern Front, where the Soviet Union was bearing the brunt of the Nazi war machine.

The operation also marked a turning point in Allied cooperation. Despite initial tensions and disagreements, American and British forces had worked together effectively, laying the groundwork for future joint operations. For the American forces, Operation Torch provided invaluable combat experience. The lessons learned in North Africa – from the importance of air superiority to the challenges of supply in difficult terrain – would prove crucial in future campaigns in Sicily, Italy, and eventually, Normandy.

**Conclusion**

Operation Torch stands as a pivotal moment in World War II, marking the beginning of the end for Axis power in North Africa and setting the stage for the liberation of Europe. It demonstrated the growing strength and capability of American forces, the effectiveness of Allied cooperation, and the complex interplay between military strategy and political considerations.

The operation was not without its controversies and setbacks, from the Darlan affair to the initial failure to capture Tunisia. Yet, these challenges were ultimately overcome through perseverance, adaptability, and the shared determination of the Allied forces.

In the words of General Eisenhower, speaking after the war, "Operation Torch was more than just a military campaign. It was a testament to what could be achieved when free nations united against tyranny. The lessons we learned and the bonds we forged in North Africa would carry us through to final victory."

**Sources**

Atkinson, Rick. An Army at Dawn: The War in North Africa, 1942-1945. Holt Paperbacks, 2007.

Diamond, Jon. First Blood in North Africa: Operation Torch and the US Campaign in Africa in WWII. Stackpole Books, 2017.

Various Sources

# Operation Husky: The Allied Invasion of Sicily

## Introduction

In the sweltering summer of 1943, as World War II raged across the globe, the Allies embarked on one of the most ambitious and consequential military operations of the conflict. Operation Husky, the invasion of Sicily, would mark a turning point in the war, opening a new front in Europe and setting the stage for the eventual liberation of the continent from Axis control.

This massive amphibious assault, involving over 150,000 troops, 3,000 ships, and 4,000 aircraft, was more than just a military maneuver. It was a bold statement of Allied resolve, a test of inter-Allied cooperation, and a complex dance of strategy, deception, and raw courage. Operation Husky would not only shape the course of the war in the Mediterranean but would also have far-reaching implications for the entire Allied war effort.

As the invasion fleet sailed towards the Sicilian coast on the night of July 9-10, 1943, the fate of the war hung in the balance. The success or failure of Operation Husky would determine whether the Allies could gain a foothold in Europe, knock Italy out of the war, and begin to turn the tide against the seemingly unstoppable Axis powers.

This is the story of Operation Husky - a tale of meticulous planning, daring execution, and the complex interplay of military and political forces that would help shape the outcome of World War II.

## The Genesis of Operation Husky

The roots of Operation Husky can be traced back to the Casablanca Conference held in January 1943. As the Allies celebrated their recent victory in North Africa, U.S. President Franklin D. Roosevelt and British Prime Minister Winston Churchill, along with their military advisors, gathered to chart the next phase of the war against the Axis powers.

The decision to invade Sicily was not without controversy. American military strategists, led by General George Marshall, initially advocated for a direct assault on Nazi-occupied France. However, Churchill and the British high command pushed for an alternative strategy, arguing for an invasion of what Churchill famously called the "soft underbelly of Europe."

The debate was intense, with strong arguments on both sides. General Dwight D. Eisenhower, who would later command the operation, recalled the heated discussions: "The arguments went back and forth, with each side presenting compelling reasons for their preferred strategy. In the end, it was a matter of balancing immediate action against long-term goals."

The decision to target Sicily was ultimately driven by several strategic considerations. First, it would secure Allied control of the Mediterranean Sea lanes, vital for the movement of troops and supplies. Second, it would divert German resources from other fronts, particularly the Eastern Front, where the Soviet Union was bearing the brunt of the Nazi war machine. Finally, a successful invasion of Sicily could potentially knock Italy out of the war, dealing a significant blow to the Axis alliance.

**Planning and Preparation**

With the strategic decision made, the Allies embarked on the monumental task of planning and preparing for what would be, at that time, the largest amphibious operation in military history. General Eisenhower was appointed as the supreme commander of the Allied forces for Operation Husky, a role that would test his diplomatic skills as much as his military acumen.

The planning phase was a complex juggling act of military strategy, logistics, and diplomacy. The operation was designed as a two-pronged assault, with the British Eighth Army under General Bernard Montgomery landing on the southeastern coast, and the U.S. Seventh Army under General George S. Patton landing on the southern coast.

Logistically, Operation Husky was a Herculean task. It involved coordinating the movement of over 150,000 troops, 3,000 ships, and 4,000 aircraft across vast distances. Admiral Sir Andrew Cunningham, who led the naval component, described the challenge: "Moving such a large force across the Mediterranean was like threading a needle while riding a galloping horse."

The planners had to consider numerous factors: the availability of landing craft, the unpredictable Mediterranean weather, the potential for Axis resistance, and the need for air superiority. Each decision carried enormous weight, and the margin for error was razor-thin.

One of the most crucial aspects of the planning was the element of deception. The Allies launched an elaborate ruse known as Operation Mincemeat, which involved planting false documents on a corpse dressed as a British officer. These documents suggested that the Allies were planning to invade Greece and Sardinia, rather than Sicily. This deception operation was remarkably successful, leading the Germans to divert significant forces away from Sicily.

As the plans took shape, the Allied forces began to assemble. In North Africa, American and British troops trained together, learning the intricacies of amphibious warfare. The stage was set for one of the most ambitious military operations of the war.

**The Invasion Begins**

In the pre-dawn hours of July 10, 1943, Operation Husky was launched. The invasion began with airborne assaults by American and British paratroopers, tasked with securing key objectives inland. However, strong winds scattered many of the paratroopers, leading to confusion and disorganization. Despite this setback, the airborne troops managed to cause significant disruption behind enemy lines.

As dawn broke, the main amphibious landings commenced. The invasion force was divided into two main task forces:

1. The Eastern Task Force, led by General Montgomery, aimed for the southeastern coast of Sicily. This force included the British Eighth Army and the 1st Canadian Infantry Division.

2. The Western Task Force, commanded by General Patton, targeted the Gulf of Gela on the southern coast. This force comprised the U.S. Seventh Army.

As the landing craft approached the Sicilian shores, tension among the troops was palpable. Many of the American soldiers had never seen combat, and the uncertainty of the enemy's response added to the anxiety. John Timothy, a soldier in the 2nd Battalion, later recalled, "As we neared the shore, you could hear a pin drop. We didn't know if we'd be greeted with handshakes or bullets."

The initial landings met with varying degrees of resistance. In some areas, particularly those defended by Italian troops, the resistance was light. However, in sectors defended by German forces, the fighting was intense. The Allied forces faced not only enemy fire but also challenging terrain and adverse weather conditions.

Despite these obstacles, the Allies managed to establish beachheads along the coast. By the end of the first day, over 150,000 Allied troops had landed on Sicily, along with significant amounts of equipment and supplies. The success of the landings was due in large part to the effectiveness of the pre-invasion bombardment and the Allied air superiority, which had neutralized many of the Axis defensive positions.

**The Battle for Sicily**

With the beachheads secured, the Allied forces began their push inland. The campaign quickly developed into a race between Montgomery's British Eighth Army advancing north along the eastern coast, and Patton's U.S. Seventh Army driving northwest across the island.

The terrain of Sicily posed significant challenges for the advancing Allied forces. The island's mountainous interior, with its narrow roads and steep valleys, favored the defenders and made rapid movement difficult. The summer heat was also a formidable enemy, with temperatures soaring and water supplies often running low.

One of the most significant engagements of the campaign was the Battle of Gela, where the U.S. 1st Infantry Division faced a determined counterattack by German armor. The fighting was intense, with American troops using bazookas and artillery to halt the German tanks. A U.S. soldier, Dale Jones, later described the battle: "The noise was deafening, and the sky was filled with tracer fire. We were all scared, but we held our ground."

As the campaign progressed, a rivalry developed between Montgomery and Patton, each eager to reach the key port of Messina first. This competition, while sometimes criticized by military historians, did serve to drive the Allied advance forward at a rapid pace.

The Axis forces, under the command of German General Hans-Valentin Hube and Italian General Alfredo Guzzoni, fought a skilled defensive action, gradually falling back while inflicting casualties on the advancing Allies. However, the overwhelming Allied superiority in men and materiel, coupled with their control of the air, made the Axis position increasingly untenable.

One of the most controversial aspects of the campaign was the escape of a significant portion of the Axis forces across the Strait of Messina to mainland Italy. Despite Allied efforts to prevent this evacuation, over 100,000 German and Italian troops, along with much of their equipment, managed to escape. This failure to trap the Axis forces would have consequences for the subsequent Italian campaign.

## The Fall of Mussolini and the End of the Campaign

As the Allied forces advanced across Sicily, the political situation in Italy was rapidly deteriorating. The invasion had shaken the Italian people's faith in Mussolini's regime, and opposition to the war was growing. On July 25, 1943, just over two weeks after the invasion began, Mussolini was deposed by the Fascist Grand Council and arrested on the orders of King Victor Emmanuel III.

The fall of Mussolini was a significant strategic victory for the Allies, as it led to Italy's eventual withdrawal from the Axis alliance. However, it also complicated the military situation on the ground in Sicily, as Italian troops were now uncertain about their role in the conflict.

Despite this political upheaval, the German forces continued to fight tenaciously. The final phase of the campaign centered on the drive towards Messina, the key port that would allow the Axis forces to evacuate to mainland Italy. Both Montgomery and Patton raced to be the first to reach the city.

On August 17, 1943, elements of Patton's Seventh Army entered Messina, just hours ahead of Montgomery's forces. The capture of Messina marked the end of the Sicily campaign, 38 days after the initial landings. The island was now firmly in Allied hands, providing a crucial stepping stone for the invasion of mainland Italy.

## Aftermath and Strategic Significance

The success of Operation Husky had far-reaching consequences for the course of World War II. The invasion achieved several key strategic objectives:

1. It secured Allied control of the Mediterranean Sea lanes, facilitating the movement of troops and supplies.

2. It led to the fall of Mussolini and Italy's eventual withdrawal from the Axis alliance, dealing a significant blow to Hitler's coalition.

3. It forced the Germans to divert significant resources to defend southern Europe, relieving pressure on other fronts, particularly in the Soviet Union.

4. It provided valuable experience in large-scale amphibious operations, which would prove crucial for the Normandy landings the following year.

However, the campaign also had its shortcomings. The failure to trap the Axis forces in Sicily allowed a significant number of experienced troops to escape to fight another day in Italy. Additionally, the rivalry between Allied commanders sometimes led to uncoordinated actions that reduced the overall effectiveness of the operation.

For the soldiers who fought there, the Sicily campaign was a brutal and challenging experience. The intense heat, difficult terrain, and determined enemy resistance tested the limits of their endurance and courage. As one Canadian veteran, reflecting on the campaign years later, said, "Sicily was our baptism of fire. It was where we learned what war really meant."

**Conclusion**

Operation Husky stands as a pivotal moment in World War II, marking the beginning of the end for Axis power in the Mediterranean and setting the stage for the liberation of Europe. It demonstrated the growing strength and capability of Allied forces, the effectiveness of combined operations, and the complex interplay between military strategy and political considerations.

The operation was not without its controversies and setbacks, from the escape of Axis forces to the sometimes problematic command rivalries. Yet, these challenges were ultimately overcome through perseverance, adaptability, and the shared determination of the Allied forces.

In the words of General Eisenhower, speaking after the war, "Operation Husky was more than just a military campaign. It was a testament to what could be achieved when free nations united against tyranny. The lessons we learned and the bonds we forged in Sicily would carry us through to final victory."

**Sources**

Holland, James. Sicily '43: The First Assault on Fortress Europe. Grove Press 2021.

Diamond, Jon. The Invasion of Sicily 1943. Pen and Sword Military, 2017.

Various Sources

# Operation Avalanche: The Invasion of Italy

## Introduction

The invasion of Italy during World War II was a critical campaign that significantly impacted the course of the war in Europe. Following the successful Allied invasion of Sicily in July 1943, the Allies turned their attention to the Italian mainland, launching a series of operations that would ultimately lead to the downfall of Mussolini's regime and the weakening of Axis powers in Europe.

## Background to the Invasion

**Italy's Role in World War II:** Italy entered World War II on June 10, 1940, aligning itself with Nazi Germany as part of the Axis powers. Under the leadership of Benito Mussolini, Italy sought to expand its territory and influence in the Mediterranean and Africa. However, the Italian military faced a series of defeats, particularly in North Africa and Greece, which necessitated German intervention to stabilize the situation.

By 1943, the tide of the war had turned against the Axis. The Allies had successfully invaded North Africa and Sicily, and the Italian military was in disarray. The fall of Mussolini's regime was imminent, and the Allies recognized that an invasion of the Italian mainland could capitalize on this instability.

**Operation Avalanche:** The Allied invasion of Italy, codenamed Operation Avalanche, commenced on September 9, 1943. The operation involved a massive amphibious assault on the Salerno beachhead, approximately 150 miles south of Naples. The Allied forces consisted primarily of the U.S. Fifth Army, commanded by General Mark W. Clark, and British forces under General Bernard Montgomery.

The planning for the invasion was complex and involved coordination between American and British military leaders. The Allies aimed to secure a foothold in Italy, disrupt German supply lines, and ultimately push northward toward Rome.

## The Invasion Begins

**Landings at Salerno:** On the morning of September 9, 1943, Allied forces landed at Salerno. The initial landings were met with fierce resistance from German troops, who had fortified their positions along the coast. The Germans were caught off guard by the scale of the invasion, but they quickly regrouped and launched counterattacks against the beachhead.

General Clark's forces faced significant challenges in the early days of the invasion. The Germans, anticipating an Allied landing, had moved reinforcements to the area, and the Allies found themselves in a precarious situation. The beachhead was vulnerable, and the possibility of being pushed back into the sea loomed large.

The Battle of Salerno was characterized by intense fighting as German forces attempted to encircle the Allied beachhead. The Allies, however, managed to hold their ground, thanks in part to naval support from the U.S. Navy and air cover from the RAF. Over several days, the Allies gradually expanded their foothold, pushing back German forces and securing vital supply lines.

Despite the initial setbacks, the Allies were able to reinforce their positions and bring in additional troops and supplies. The successful establishment of the beachhead at Salerno marked a crucial turning point in the campaign, allowing the Allies to begin their advance into Italy.

**The Italian Campaign**

**Advancing Northward:** Following the successful landings at Salerno, Allied forces began their advance northward. The campaign faced numerous challenges, including difficult terrain, harsh weather conditions, and fierce German resistance. The Allies captured Naples in October 1943, which provided a critical logistical base for further operations.

As the Allies pushed north, they encountered well-prepared German defenses along the Gustav Line, a series of fortifications that stretched across Italy. The most famous of these was the Monte Cassino area, where the Allies faced fierce resistance from German troops entrenched in the mountains.

**The Battle of Monte Cassino:** The Battle of Monte Cassino, fought from January to May 1944, was one of the most brutal and costly battles of the Italian Campaign. The Allies launched multiple assaults on the German positions, but each attempt was met with heavy casualties and limited success. The destruction of the historic Monte Cassino Abbey in February 1944, intended to eliminate a German observation point, became a controversial decision that drew criticism.

After months of fighting, the Allies finally broke through the German defenses at Monte Cassino in May 1944. This victory opened the way for the Allies to advance toward Rome, which was captured on June 4, 1944. The fall of Rome marked a significant milestone in the Italian Campaign and was the first Axis capital to be liberated by the Allies.

**Impact on World War II**

**Strategic Consequences:** The invasion of Italy had far-reaching strategic implications for the Allied war effort. By securing a foothold in Italy, the Allies were able to divert German resources and attention away from the Eastern Front and the impending invasion of France. The Italian Campaign forced the Germans to fight on multiple fronts, stretching their forces thin and contributing to their eventual defeat.

The campaign also provided valuable experience for Allied forces in conducting amphibious operations and urban warfare, lessons that would be applied in the D-Day invasion of Normandy in June 1944.

**Political Ramifications:** The political ramifications of the invasion were significant. The fall of Mussolini's regime in July 1943 and the subsequent armistice with the Allies in September marked a turning point in Italian politics. The new Italian government, led by Marshal Pietro Badoglio, sought to distance itself from the Axis powers and align with the Allies.

However, the situation in Italy remained complex. While the southern regions were under Allied control, northern Italy remained occupied by German forces, leading to a protracted struggle between the Allies and Axis powers. The Italian resistance movement also gained momentum during this period, contributing to the fight against German occupation.

**Human Cost:** The Italian Campaign was marked by significant human cost. Allied forces suffered heavy casualties, with thousands of soldiers killed or wounded in the fighting. The civilian population also endured immense suffering, as cities were bombed, and infrastructure was destroyed. The campaign left a lasting impact on the Italian landscape and its people.

## Conclusion

The invasion of Italy was a pivotal moment in World War II, shaping the course of the conflict in Europe. The successful landings at Salerno and the subsequent advance into Italy demonstrated the effectiveness of Allied cooperation and military strategy. The campaign not only contributed to the eventual defeat of the Axis powers but also altered the political landscape of Italy and Europe as a whole.

## Sources

Gooch, John. Mussolini's War: Fascist Italy from Triumph to Collapse: 1935-1943. Pegasus Books, 2020.

Tregaskis, Richard. Invasion Diary: A Dramatic Firsthand Account of the Allied Invasion of Sicily. Bison Books, 2004.

Various Sources

# The Pacific and Asia

## Japan's Conquests Across the Pacific

During World War II, Japan expanded its empire through military conquests. Here is a chronological list of the countries and territories Japan conquered, starting with China and ending with their surrender in 1945:

1. **China** (First significant invasion began in 1937 during the Second Sino-Japanese War)
2. **Hong Kong** (Captured in December 1941)
3. **Philippines** (Captured in 1942)
4. **Malaya** (Captured in early 1942)
5. **Singapore** (Captured in February 1942)
6. **Burma (Myanmar)** (Captured in 1942)
7. **Thailand** (Joined Japan as an ally in December 1941, effectively controlled by Japan)
8. **Dutch East Indies (Indonesia)** (Captured in mid-1942)
9. **New Guinea** (Captured in 1942)
10. **Guam** (Captured in December 1941)
11. **Wake Island** (Captured in December 1941)
12. **Solomon Islands** (Various islands captured from 1942)
13. **Hong Kong** (Recaptured in 1945)
14. **Korea** (Under Japanese rule since 1910, but continued control during the war)

Japan's conquests were ultimately halted, and they surrendered on August 15, 1945, following the bombings of Hiroshima and Nagasaki and the Soviet declaration of war against Japan.

# Day of Infamy: The Japanese Attack on Pearl Harbor

**Introduction**

In the early hours of December 7, 1941, as the sun began to rise over the tranquil waters of Pearl Harbor, Hawaii, the world stood on the brink of a momentous change. Unbeknownst to the American forces stationed there, a Japanese fleet was approaching from the north, carrying with it the weight of years of mounting tensions and strategic calculations. What would unfold in the next few hours would not only alter the course of World War II but would also reshape the global order for generations to come.

The attack on Pearl Harbor was more than just a military strike; it was the culmination of a complex interplay of imperial ambitions, economic pressures, and the broader context of a world already engulfed in war. This event would thrust the United States into the global conflict, transforming it from a reluctant bystander to a central player in the fight against the Axis powers.

This story explores the lead-up to the attack, the events of that fateful Sunday morning, and the far-reaching consequences that continue to echo through history. Through the eyes of those who lived through these perilous times, we will experience the shock, the courage, and the determination that defined this pivotal moment in world history.

**The Road to War**

The roots of the Pearl Harbor attack can be traced back to the early 20th century, as Japan's rapid industrialization fueled its imperial ambitions. Like the Western powers it sought to emulate, Japan looked to expand its empire to secure resources and markets. This expansionist policy began in earnest with the invasion of Manchuria in 1931, where Japan established the puppet state of Manchukuo.

The United States, adhering to the Stimson Doctrine, refused to recognize territories acquired by force, setting the stage for increasing tensions between the two nations. As Japan continued its aggressive expansion into China, culminating in a full-scale invasion in 1937, the United States responded with economic sanctions. These included the termination of the 1911 Treaty of Commerce and Navigation and restrictions on exports of materials crucial for war, such as oil and steel.

The situation reached a critical point when Japan occupied French Indochina in 1941. In response, the United States froze Japanese assets and imposed a full embargo on oil exports. This action, more than any other, set Japan on a collision course with the United States. Without access to vital resources, particularly oil, Japan's military and industrial machine would grind to a halt.

Japan's alignment with the Axis powers through the Tripartite Pact with Germany and Italy in 1940 further exacerbated tensions. This alliance was seen as a direct threat to U.S. interests in the Pacific and contributed to the perception of an inevitable conflict.

Despite the mounting tensions, diplomatic negotiations continued between Japan and the United States throughout 1941. However, these talks were doomed to failure. Japan was unwilling to withdraw from its occupied territories, and the U.S. insisted on such a withdrawal as a precondition for lifting economic sanctions.

As diplomacy faltered, Japan's military leaders began to consider more drastic options. Admiral Isoroku Yamamoto, the architect of the Pearl Harbor attack, believed that a decisive strike against the U.S. Pacific Fleet would cripple American naval power, allowing Japan to secure resources in Southeast Asia without immediate interference.

**The Plan Unfolds**

The planning for the attack on Pearl Harbor was meticulous and shrouded in secrecy. Admiral Yamamoto, who had studied in the United States and understood the risks of provoking such a powerful nation, believed that a surprise attack was necessary to achieve Japan's strategic goals.

On November 26, 1941, the Japanese First Air Fleet, commanded by Admiral Chuichi Nagumo, departed Japan, moving towards Pearl Harbor. This fleet, consisting of six aircraft carriers along with support ships, traveled across 3,000 miles of ocean under strict radio silence to maintain the element of surprise.

The Japanese plan was audacious. It called for a two-wave attack using aircraft launched from carriers positioned approximately 275 miles north of Oahu. The first wave would target battleships and aircraft carriers, while the second wave would attack other ships and shore facilities. Simultaneously, midget submarines would infiltrate the harbor to cause additional damage and confusion.

As the Japanese fleet sailed towards Hawaii, the tension among the crew was palpable. Many understood the gravity of their mission and the potential consequences. A young Japanese pilot, Zenji Abe, later recalled, "We all knew that if we succeeded, it would mean war with America. But we trusted our leaders and believed in the righteousness of our cause".

**December 7, 1941: A Day of Infamy**

The events of December 7, 1941, unfolded with a terrible swiftness that would forever change the course of history.

At 3:42 AM Hawaiian time, the minesweeper USS Condor spotted what appeared to be a submarine periscope near the entrance to Pearl Harbor. This sighting was the first indication that something was amiss, though its significance would not be fully realized until it was too late.

At 6:10 AM, the first wave of nearly 200 Japanese planes took off from their carriers, their engines roaring in the pre-dawn darkness. As they approached Oahu, the element of surprise remained intact, despite a few close calls.

At 7:02 AM, two Army radar operators on Oahu detected a large formation of aircraft approaching the island. They reported their findings to a lieutenant at the newly established Intercept Center. However, the lieutenant, believing it to be a flight of American B-17 bombers due to arrive that morning, told them not to worry about it. This misinterpretation of the radar data would prove to be a critical missed opportunity to prepare for the impending attack.

At 7:55 AM, the silence of the Sunday morning was shattered as the first Japanese planes descended on Pearl Harbor. Commander Mitsuo Fuchida, leading the attack, sent the now-famous message "Tora! Tora! Tora!" (Tiger! Tiger! Tiger!) back to the fleet, indicating that complete surprise had been achieved.

The scene that unfolded was one of chaos and devastation. Japanese dive bombers and torpedo planes swarmed over the harbor, their bombs and torpedoes finding targets with deadly accuracy. The battleships moored at Ford Island, lined up in neat rows and known as "Battleship Row," bore the brunt of the initial assault.

One of the most devastating moments came at 8:10 AM when a bomb penetrated the forward magazine of the USS Arizona, causing a massive explosion that split the ship in two and killed 1,177 of her crew. The sight of the Arizona's destruction became one of the enduring images of the attack, symbolizing the brutality and shock of that morning.

Amid the chaos, acts of incredible bravery emerged. Doris Miller, an African American mess attendant on the USS West Virginia, manned an anti-aircraft gun despite having no training, shooting down several Japanese planes. His actions that day would make him one of the first heroes of World War II and an important symbol in the fight for civil rights.

The second wave of the attack began at 8:54 AM, focusing on other military targets around Pearl Harbor. By this time, American forces had begun to mount a defense, and the Japanese encountered significantly more anti-aircraft fire.

Throughout the morning, the skies above Pearl Harbor were filled with smoke, the air rent by the sound of explosions and gunfire. On the ground, sailors, soldiers, and civilians scrambled to respond to the unexpected onslaught. Many, like Mess Attendant 2nd Class Telesforo Trinidad, risked their lives to save their comrades, pulling injured sailors from burning and sinking ships.

By 10:00 AM, just over two hours after it began, the attack was over. The Japanese planes returned to their carriers, which then set course back to Japan. In their wake, they left a scene of utter devastation.

**The Aftermath**

As the smoke cleared and the full extent of the damage became apparent, the toll was staggering. Over 2,400 Americans had been killed, with another 1,178 wounded. The attack had sunk or severely damaged 18 ships, including eight battleships, and destroyed or damaged over 300 aircraft.

The human cost was immeasurable. Families were torn apart, promising young lives cut short. The survivors were left to grapple with the shock of the attack and the grim task of recovering the dead and salvaging what they could from the wreckage.

In Washington D.C., the news of the attack was met with disbelief and then grim determination. President Franklin D. Roosevelt, upon hearing the news, knew immediately that this event would fundamentally alter the course of American history. The next day, December 8, he addressed Congress and the nation, delivering his famous "Day of Infamy" speech. His words captured the mood of the nation: "Yesterday, December 7, 1941—a date which will live in infamy—the United States of America was suddenly and deliberately attacked by naval and air forces of the Empire of Japan".

Congress responded swiftly, declaring war on Japan with near unanimity. The United States had entered World War II.

**Long-term Consequences**

The attack on Pearl Harbor had far-reaching consequences that would reshape the global order. For the United States, it marked the end of isolationism and the beginning of its emergence as a global superpower. The nation mobilized for total war, with its vast industrial capacity turned to the production of weapons and supplies for the Allied war effort.

The war in the Pacific, initiated by the Pearl Harbor attack, would be long and brutal. It would see epic naval battles, fierce island-hopping campaigns, and ultimately, the use of atomic weapons against Japan. The conflict would end only with Japan's unconditional surrender in August 1945.

In the aftermath of the war, the relationship between the United States and Japan underwent a remarkable transformation. The post-war American occupation of Japan, led by General Douglas MacArthur, implemented democratic reforms and oversaw the country's economic reconstruction. This period laid the foundation for Japan's emergence as an economic powerhouse and a key American ally in Asia.

The legacy of Pearl Harbor continues to shape American foreign policy and military strategy. The attack underscored the importance of intelligence and preparedness, leading to significant reforms in how the United States gathers and analyzes intelligence. It also cemented the U.S. commitment to maintaining a strong military presence in the Pacific, a stance that continues to influence geopolitics in the region to this day.

**Conclusion**

The attack on Pearl Harbor stands as one of the most consequential events of the 20th century. It catapulted the United States into World War II, setting in motion a chain of events that would reshape the global order. The shock and tragedy of that Sunday morning in December 1941 galvanized the American people, uniting them in a common purpose that would see them through the trials of war and emerge as a leading global power.

The story of Pearl Harbor – from the complex factors that led to the attack, through the chaos and heroism of December 7, to its long-lasting repercussions – remains a powerful reminder of the fragility of peace and the importance of vigilance. It stands as a testament to the resilience of the human spirit and the ability of nations to rise from the ashes of conflict to forge new bonds of friendship and cooperation.

In the words of President Roosevelt, delivered the day after the attack, "No matter how long it may take us to overcome this premeditated invasion, the American people in their righteous might will win through to absolute victory." This prophecy, born in America's darkest hour, would prove true, shaping not only the outcome of World War II but the entire post-war world order.

**Sources**

Prange, Gordon W. At Dawn We Slept: The Untold Story of Pearl Harbor. McGraw-Hill, 1981

Morison, Samuel Eliot. Victory in the Pacific 1945. History of the United States Naval Operations in World War II. Book Sales, 2001.

Various Sources

## Ally Battles with Imperial Japan

Here's a chronological list of significant battles fought between the United States and Japan from the attack on Pearl Harbor in December 1941 until Japan's surrender in August 1945:

1. **Battle of Wake Island** (December 8-23, 1941)
2. **Battle of the Philippines** (December 8, 1941 – May 1942)
   - **Includes the Battles of Bataan and Corregidor**
3. **Battle of the Coral Sea** (May 4-8, 1942)
4. **Battle of Midway** (June 4-7, 1942)
5. **Battle of Guadalcanal** (August 7, 1942 – February 9, 1943)
6. **Battle of the Eastern Solomons** (August 23-25, 1942)
7. **Battle of Santa Cruz Islands** (October 26, 1942)
8. **Battle of Guadalcanal** (Naval Battles) (November 12-15, 1942)
9. **Battle of Tarawa** (November 20-23, 1943)
10. **Battle of Kwajalein** (January 31 – February 3, 1944)
11. **Battle of Eniwetok** (February 17-22, 1944)
12. **Battle of Saipan** (June 15 – July 9, 1944)
13. **Battle of Guam** (July 21 – August 10, 1944)
14. **Battle of Tinian** (July 24 – August 1, 1944)
15. **Battle of Leyte Gulf** (October 23-26, 1944)
16. **Battle of Luzon** (January 9 – August 15, 1945)
17. **Battle of Iwo Jima** (February 19 – March 26, 1945)
18. **Battle of Okinawa** (April 1 – June 22, 1945)

**Japan officially surrendered on August 15, 1945, marking the end of World War II.**

# The Battles Begin

## The Battle of Wake Island

The Battle of Wake Island, fought from December 8 to December 23, 1941, was a crucial early conflict in the Pacific Theater of World War II, following Japan's attack on Pearl Harbor. Japanese forces aimed to capture the strategically located island, which was defended by a small contingent of U.S. Marines and Navy personnel, alongside local civilian contractors.

Despite fierce resistance and a valiant defense, the defenders were ultimately overwhelmed by superior Japanese numbers and resources. After 15 days of intense fighting, Wake Island fell to Japanese forces on December 23, 1941, marking a significant victory for Japan and contributing to its expansion in the Pacific.

## The Battle of the Philippines

The Battle of the Philippines, which unfolded from December 8, 1941, to May 1942, was a critical campaign in the Pacific Theater during World War II, following the attack on Pearl Harbor. Japanese forces launched a swift and coordinated assault on the Philippines, targeting both air and naval bases, as well as ground positions held by U.S. and Filipino troops.

Despite initial resistance, particularly during the defense of Bataan and the stronghold of Corregidor, the American and Filipino defenders faced overwhelming odds, including superior Japanese numbers and resources. By May 1942, after months of fierce fighting and with dwindling supplies, the last organized American resistance on Corregidor fell, leading to the complete conquest of the Philippines by Japan.

This defeat resulted in the capture of thousands of American and Filipino soldiers, many of whom were subjected to the brutal Bataan Death March which marked a significant setback for Allied forces in the Pacific.

## Sources

Spector, Ronald H. Eagle Against the Sun: The American War with Japan. Free Press, 1985.

Toland, John. The Rising Sun: The Decline and Fall of the Japanese Empire, 1936-1945. Random House, 1970.

Various Sources

# The Battle of the Coral Sea: Turning the Tide

## Introduction

In the early months of 1942, as the world was engulfed in the flames of World War II, a pivotal confrontation was brewing in the vast expanse of the Pacific Ocean. The Battle of the Coral Sea, fought from May 4 to May 8, 1942, would mark a turning point in the war against Japan and usher in a new era of naval warfare. This engagement, the first in history where aircraft carriers clashed without the ships themselves coming into direct contact, would not only halt the seemingly unstoppable Japanese advance but also set the stage for future Allied victories in the Pacific.

As the sun rose over the Coral Sea on that fateful May morning, neither the Allied nor the Japanese forces could have fully grasped the significance of the battle that was about to unfold. The outcome would shape the course of the war, influence the fate of nations, and forever change the nature of naval combat. This is the story of courage, strategy, and the thin line between victory and defeat that defined the Battle of the Coral Sea.

## The Road to Confrontation

The roots of the Battle of the Coral Sea can be traced back to the shocking Japanese attack on Pearl Harbor on December 7, 1941. This surprise assault had severely crippled the U.S. Pacific Fleet, allowing Japan to rapidly expand its control over vast swathes of the western Pacific. By May 1942, the Japanese Empire had established a formidable defensive perimeter stretching from the Kuriles in the north to the Solomon Islands in the south, and from the Marshall Islands in the east to Burma in the west.

However, the Japanese military leadership was not content with consolidation. Their ambitious strategy aimed to extend this perimeter further, with plans to capture Port Moresby in New Guinea and Tulagi in the Solomon Islands. Control of Port Moresby was particularly crucial, as it would allow Japan to threaten northern Australia and secure its southern flank. Moreover, these new positions would enable the Japanese to sever the vital Allied supply lines between the United States and Australia, potentially dealing a crippling blow to any future Allied counter-offensives in the Pacific.

The rapid Japanese expansion sent shockwaves through the Allied high command. The fall of Singapore in February 1942 and the subsequent Japanese advances in Southeast Asia and the Pacific heightened the sense of urgency among Allied leaders. Australia, in particular, felt acutely vulnerable, fearing that it might be the next target of Japanese aggression.

In this tense atmosphere, Allied codebreakers achieved a crucial breakthrough. By breaking Japanese naval codes, they uncovered plans for the invasion of Port Moresby and Tulagi. Armed with this vital intelligence, the United States began to prepare a naval response to intercept the Japanese forces.

As both sides marshaled their forces, the stage was set for a confrontation that would alter the course of the Pacific War.

**The Opposing Forces**

As the battle loomed, both the Allied and Japanese forces brought formidable naval power to bear in the Coral Sea.

The Allied forces, under the command of Rear Admiral Frank J. Fletcher, centered around Task Force 17. This force included two fleet carriers: the USS Yorktown and the USS Lexington. These ships, each carrying dozens of aircraft, would form the backbone of the Allied striking power. Supporting these carriers were several cruisers and destroyers, including the heavy cruiser USS Chicago and the destroyers USS Perkins and USS Walke.

The air groups aboard the Allied carriers consisted of F4F Wildcat fighters, which would provide air cover, and SBD Dauntless dive bombers and TBD Devastator torpedo bombers for striking enemy ships. These aircraft, while not always a match for their Japanese counterparts in performance, were flown by skilled and determined pilots.

On the Japanese side, Vice Admiral Shigeyoshi Inoue commanded a powerful force built around the carriers Shōkaku and Zuikaku, both part of the elite First Air Fleet. These modern carriers, veterans of the Pearl Harbor attack, carried complement of the feared A6M Zero fighters, D3A Val dive bombers, and B5N Kate torpedo bombers. The Japanese naval aviators, at this stage of the war, were among the best trained and most experienced in the world.

Supporting the Japanese carriers were numerous cruisers and destroyers, including the heavy cruiser Myōko and the destroyer Arashi. Additionally, the Japanese had a light carrier, Shōhō, which was part of the invasion force headed for Port Moresby.

As these powerful fleets converged on the Coral Sea, the stage was set for a new kind of naval battle, one that would be fought not by guns and torpedoes, but by aircraft launched from carriers hundreds of miles apart.

**The Battle Unfolds**

The Battle of the Coral Sea began on May 3, 1942, when Japanese forces successfully landed and occupied Tulagi in the Solomon Islands. This move was part of their strategy to establish a seaplane base for reconnaissance and air operations. However, their success was short-lived.

On May 4, the USS Yorktown launched a surprise air attack on the Japanese forces at Tulagi. This strike caught the Japanese off guard, sinking several warships and damaging others. It was a clear message that the Allies were ready to contest Japanese expansion in the region.

For the next two days, both the Japanese and American carrier groups maneuvered in the vast expanse of the Coral Sea, each aware of the other's presence but unable to locate their adversary. The tension among the sailors and airmen was palpable. Many had never experienced combat before, and the knowledge that the enemy could appear at any moment kept everyone on edge.

A young pilot aboard the USS Lexington later recalled, "We knew the Japanese were out there somewhere. Every time we took off, we wondered if this would be the mission where we'd finally find them. The waiting was almost worse than the fighting."

The real action began on May 7. In the morning, Japanese aircraft stumbled upon what they believed to be a carrier task force. They launched a full strike, only to discover that their targets were actually the destroyer USS Sims and the fleet oiler USS Neosho. Both ships were sunk, but the mistake had cost the Japanese valuable time and fuel.

Meanwhile, American scout planes had located the Japanese invasion force, including the light carrier Shōhō. In a coordinated attack, dive bombers and torpedo planes from both Yorktown and Lexington descended on the Shōhō. Despite fierce anti-aircraft fire and the efforts of Japanese fighters, the American aviators pressed home their attack. Multiple bomb and torpedo hits sealed the fate of the Shōhō, which sank rapidly with heavy loss of life. As the ship went down, an American pilot radioed back the now-famous message: "Scratch one flattop!"

The sinking of the Shōhō was a significant blow to the Japanese operation, but the main carrier battle was yet to come. Both sides spent a restless night, knowing that the next day would likely bring a decisive engagement.

The morning of May 8 dawned with both forces launching search planes to locate their adversaries. In a quirk of fate, the opposing carrier groups passed each other in the night and were now sailing in opposite directions. This led to a confusing series of events where each side's scout planes found the other almost simultaneously.

The Japanese struck first. At 11:00 AM, a massive wave of 69 aircraft from Shōkaku and Zuikaku arrived over the American carriers. The sky was suddenly filled with diving Val bombers and torpedo-carrying Kates, while Zeros tangled with American Wildcats in swirling dogfights.

The American defenses were fierce, but the Japanese managed to land telling blows. The Yorktown was hit by a bomb that penetrated several decks before exploding, causing significant damage. The Lexington, however, took the brunt of the attack. Two torpedoes tore into her port side, and two bombs struck her flight deck. Despite the damage, both carriers remained operational and continued to launch and recover aircraft.

Even as the Japanese attack was underway, American strike aircraft were winging their way towards the Japanese carriers. When they arrived, they found the Shōkaku and Zuikaku hidden under a heavy overcast. Undeterred, the American pilots pushed through anti-aircraft fire and clouds to press home their attack.

The Shōkaku was hit multiple times by bombs, causing severe damage to her flight deck and starting fires below. The Zuikaku, however, managed to evade the American attacks, emerging unscathed.

As the day wore on, both sides counted their losses and assessed the damage. The Japanese, believing they had sunk two American carriers, decided to withdraw. They were unaware that both Yorktown and Lexington were still afloat.

However, the Lexington's ordeal was not over. The torpedo hits had ruptured her fuel tanks, allowing gasoline vapors to spread throughout the ship. In the afternoon, a series of massive explosions rocked the carrier. Despite heroic damage control efforts, the fires proved uncontrollable. As evening fell, the order was given to abandon ship. In a solemn moment, the mortally wounded Lexington was scuttled by American destroyers to prevent her capture.

**Aftermath and Significance**

As the smoke cleared and the survivors were rescued, both sides sought to assess the outcome of this unprecedented carrier battle. In purely material terms, the battle could be seen as a tactical victory for Japan. They had sunk the fleet carrier Lexington and damaged the Yorktown, while losing only the light carrier Shōhō.

However, the strategic picture told a different story. The Japanese invasion force, deprived of air cover by the battle, was forced to turn back. The planned conquest of Port Moresby had been thwarted, marking the first significant check to Japanese expansion in the Pacific War. Australia, which had feared imminent invasion, could breathe a sigh of relief.

Moreover, the damage inflicted on the Shōkaku and the depletion of Zuikaku's air group meant that neither carrier would be available for the upcoming Battle of Midway. This would prove crucial, as it deprived the Japanese of two of their finest carriers at a critical moment.

The Battle of the Coral Sea had profound implications for the conduct of naval warfare. It demonstrated conclusively that aircraft carriers, not battleships, were now the decisive weapon in fleet engagements. Never again would capital ships clash in traditional line-of-battle formations. The future of naval combat would be dominated by strikes from carrier-based aircraft, often against enemies hundreds of miles away.

For the Allies, particularly the Americans, the battle provided a much-needed morale boost. It proved that the Japanese were not invincible and that American sailors and airmen could go toe-to-toe with the best the enemy had to offer. This newfound confidence would serve them well in the battles to come.

The battle also highlighted the critical importance of intelligence and reconnaissance. Both sides suffered from incomplete or inaccurate information during the engagement, leading to missed opportunities and wasted efforts. Future operations would place an even greater emphasis on gathering and analyzing intelligence to gain a decisive edge.

**Conclusion**

The Battle of the Coral Sea stands as a pivotal moment in World War II and in the history of naval warfare. It marked the end of Japan's unchecked expansion in the Pacific and set the stage for the decisive American victory at Midway just a month later. The courage and skill displayed by sailors and airmen on both sides demonstrated the best qualities of their respective nations, even amid a terrible conflict.

In the words of Admiral Chester Nimitz, Commander in Chief of the U.S. Pacific Fleet, "The Battle of the Coral Sea was a strategic victory for the Allies, but it was a victory that was purchased at a heavy cost." This sentiment captures the bittersweet nature of the engagement – a necessary step on the long road to ultimate victory in the Pacific.

The legacy of the Coral Sea extends far beyond the immediate outcome of the battle. It ushered in a new era of naval warfare; one dominated by aircraft carriers and long-range strikes. The lessons learned in this engagement would shape naval strategy and tactics for generations to come.

As we honor the memory of those who fought and died in the Coral Sea, we recognize their sacrifice as a turning point in the war – the moment when the tide began to turn against Japanese expansion and toward eventual Allied victory in the Pacific.

**Sources**

Spector, Ronald H. Eagle Against the Sun: The American War with Japan. Free Press, 1985.

Toland, John. The Rising Sun: The Decline and Fall of the Japanese Empire, 1936-1945. Random House, 1970.

Various Sources

# The Battle of Midway: Breaking the Code

### Introduction

In the early summer of 1942, as the world was engulfed in the flames of World War II, a pivotal confrontation was brewing in the vast expanse of the Pacific Ocean. The Battle of Midway, fought from June 4 to June 7, 1942, would mark a turning point in the war against Japan and usher in a new era of naval warfare. This engagement, the first in history where aircraft carriers clashed without the ships themselves coming into direct contact, would not only halt the seemingly unstoppable Japanese advance but also set the stage for future Allied victories in the Pacific.

As the sun rose over the Midway Atoll on that fateful June morning, neither the Allied nor the Japanese forces could have fully grasped the significance of the battle that was about to unfold. The outcome would shape the course of the war, influence the fate of nations, and forever change the nature of naval combat. This is the story of courage, strategy, and the thin line between victory and defeat that defined the Battle of Midway.

### The Road to Confrontation

The roots of the Battle of Midway can be traced back to the shocking Japanese attack on Pearl Harbor on December 7, 1941. This surprise assault had severely crippled the U.S. Pacific Fleet, allowing Japan to rapidly expand its control over vast swathes of the western Pacific. By May 1942, the Japanese Empire had established a formidable defensive perimeter stretching from the Kuriles in the north to the Solomon Islands in the south, and from the Marshall Islands in the east to Burma in the west.

However, the Japanese military leadership was not content with consolidation. Their ambitious strategy aimed to extend this perimeter further, with plans to capture Port Moresby in New Guinea and Tulagi in the Solomon Islands. Control of these strategic locations would allow Japan to threaten northern Australia and secure its southern flank. Moreover, these new positions would enable the Japanese to sever the vital Allied supply lines between the United States and Australia, potentially dealing a crippling blow to any future Allied counter-offensives in the Pacific.

The rapid Japanese expansion sent shockwaves through the Allied high command. The fall of Singapore in February 1942 and the subsequent Japanese advances in Southeast Asia and the Pacific had heightened the sense of urgency among Allied leaders. Australia, in particular, felt acutely vulnerable, fearing that it might be the next target of Japanese aggression.

In this tense atmosphere, Allied codebreakers achieved a crucial breakthrough. By breaking Japanese naval codes, they uncovered plans for the invasion of Midway Atoll, a tiny but strategically vital island located approximately 1,300 miles northwest of Hawaii. Armed with this vital intelligence, the United States began to prepare a naval response to intercept the Japanese forces.

**The Stage is Set**

As both sides marshaled their forces, the stage was set for a confrontation that would alter the course of the Pacific War. The Japanese plan, known as Operation MI, was the brainchild of Admiral Isoroku Yamamoto, the architect of the Pearl Harbor attack. Yamamoto's strategy was ambitious and complex, involving multiple battle groups spread across a vast area of the Pacific Ocean.

The primary objective was to lure the American aircraft carriers into a trap and destroy them, thereby neutralizing the U.S. naval power in the Pacific. Yamamoto believed that by attacking Midway, the Americans would be forced to respond, allowing the Japanese to spring their trap. The plan was also a response to the Doolittle Raid on Tokyo, which had exposed vulnerabilities in Japan's defenses and shocked the Japanese leadership.

On the American side, Admiral Chester W. Nimitz, Commander in Chief of the Pacific Fleet, faced a daunting challenge. To counter the Japanese threat, he needed every available flight deck. In a race against time, the USS Yorktown, severely damaged in the Battle of the Coral Sea just a month earlier, was rushed through repairs at Pearl Harbor. Working around the clock, repair crews managed to get the Yorktown battle-ready in just 72 hours, a feat that would prove crucial in the coming engagement.

As the Japanese fleet sailed towards Midway, the tension among the sailors and airmen on both sides was palpable. Many had never experienced combat before, and the knowledge that the fate of the war might hinge on their actions weighed heavily on their minds. A young American pilot, preparing for what would be his first combat mission, later recalled, "We knew the Japanese were out there somewhere. Every time we took off, we wondered if this would be the mission where we'd finally find them. The waiting was almost worse than the fighting".

**The Battle Unfolds**

The Battle of Midway began in earnest on the morning of June 4, 1942. At dawn, Japanese aircraft launched a devastating attack on Midway Atoll, causing significant damage to the island's facilities. However, the American defenders fought back fiercely, and the Japanese failed to neutralize the airfield completely.

As the Japanese planes returned to their carriers to rearm for a second strike, the tide of battle was about to turn dramatically. American scout planes had finally located the Japanese fleet, and waves of U.S. aircraft began their attacks on the enemy carriers.

The initial American attacks were met with disaster. Squadrons of torpedo bombers, flying low and slow, were decimated by Japanese fighters and anti-aircraft fire. Of the 41 Devastator torpedo bombers that participated in the attack, only six returned. However, their sacrifice was not in vain. The Japanese combat air patrol was drawn down to sea level to counter the torpedo threat, leaving the skies above the carriers unprotected.

It was at this crucial moment that fate intervened. As the Japanese carriers were preparing to launch their second strike against Midway, American dive bombers appeared high above them. In a span of just five minutes, three Japanese carriers - Akagi, Kaga, and Soryu - were hit by multiple bombs, transforming them into blazing infernos.

The scene on the Japanese carriers was one of chaos and horror. Lieutenant Yoshio Tomonaga, a Japanese pilot who had just returned from the attack on Midway, described the moment: "I had just landed on the Hiryu when I saw huge columns of black smoke rising from the other carriers. It was a sight I will never forget. In that instant, I knew the tide of battle had turned against us".

The fourth Japanese carrier, Hiryu, managed to launch a counterattack that severely damaged the USS Yorktown. However, this last Japanese strike was a double-edged sword. It revealed Hiryu's position to the Americans, and late in the afternoon, dive bombers from the USS Enterprise found and fatally damaged the last remaining Japanese carrier.

By the end of the day, the Japanese had lost four fleet carriers - the core of their naval strength. The once-mighty First Air Fleet, which had wreaked havoc across the Pacific, from Pearl Harbor to the Indian Ocean, was now reduced to burning wreckage.

**The Aftermath**

As the smoke cleared and the full extent of the Japanese defeat became apparent, the strategic landscape of the Pacific War had been irrevocably altered. The Battle of Midway marked a decisive turning point, shifting the balance of naval power from Japan to the United States.

The loss of four fleet carriers and hundreds of experienced pilots was a blow from which the Japanese navy would never fully recover. Admiral Yamamoto, the architect of the Pearl Harbor attack and the Midway operation, was forced to abandon his ambitious plans for further expansion. From this point on, Japan would be on the defensive for the remainder of the war.

For the United States, the victory at Midway provided a much-needed morale boost. It proved that the Japanese were not invincible and that American sailors and airmen could go toe-to-toe with the best the enemy had to offer. This newfound confidence would serve them well in the battles to come.

The battle also highlighted the critical importance of intelligence and codebreaking in modern warfare. The ability of American cryptanalysts to break Japanese naval codes had given the U.S. fleet a crucial advantage, allowing them to anticipate and counter Japanese plans. This intelligence edge would continue to play a vital role throughout the remainder of the war.

**Legacy and Reflection**

The Battle of Midway stands as a pivotal moment in World War II and in the history of naval warfare. It marked the end of Japan's unchecked expansion in the Pacific and set the stage for the Allied offensive that would eventually bring the war to Japan's doorstep.

The courage displayed by the sailors and airmen on both sides demonstrated the best qualities of their respective nations, even amid a terrible conflict. The American torpedo bomber crews, who flew into the teeth of Japanese defenses knowing their chances of survival were slim, exemplified the spirit of sacrifice that would ultimately lead to Allied victory.

In the words of Admiral Chester Nimitz, "Midway was the most decisive single action in the history of naval warfare." This sentiment captures the profound impact of the battle - a turning point that reshaped the course of World War II and the world we inhabit today.

The legacy of Midway extends far beyond the immediate outcome of the battle. It ushered in a new era of naval warfare, one dominated by aircraft carriers and long-range strikes. The lessons learned in this engagement would shape naval strategy and tactics for generations to come.

As we honor the memory of those who fought and died at Midway, we recognize their sacrifice as a pivotal moment in history - the point at which the tide began to turn against Japanese expansion and toward eventual Allied victory in the Pacific. The Battle of Midway remains a testament to the courage, skill, and determination of those who fought for freedom in the face of seemingly insurmountable odds.

**Sources**

Spector, Ronald H. Eagle Against the Sun: The American War with Japan. Free Press, 1985.

Toland, John. The Rising Sun: The Decline and Fall of the Japanese Empire, 1936-1945. Random House, 1970.

Various Sources

# The Battle of Guadalcanal

## Introduction

In the sweltering summer of 1942, as World War II raged across the globe, a pivotal confrontation was brewing in the vast expanse of the Pacific Ocean. The Battle of Guadalcanal, fought from August 7, 1942, to February 9, 1943, would mark a turning point in the war against Japan and usher in a new era of Allied offensive operations. This campaign, involving fierce fighting on land, sea, and air, would not only halt the seemingly unstoppable Japanese advance but also set the stage for future Allied victories in the Pacific.

As the sun rose over the lush, tropical island of Guadalcanal on that fateful August morning, neither the Allied nor the Japanese forces could have fully grasped the significance of the battle that was about to unfold. The outcome would shape the course of the war, influence the fate of nations, and forever change the nature of combat in the Pacific Theater. This is the story of courage, strategy, and the thin line between victory and defeat that defined the Battle of Guadalcanal.

## The Road to Confrontation

The roots of the Guadalcanal campaign can be traced back to the shocking Japanese attack on Pearl Harbor on December 7, 1941. This surprise assault had severely crippled the U.S. Pacific Fleet, allowing Japan to rapidly expand its control over vast swathes of the western Pacific. By May 1942, the Japanese Empire had established a formidable defensive perimeter stretching from the Kuriles in the north to the Solomon Islands in the south, and from the Marshall Islands in the east to Burma in the west.

However, the Japanese military leadership was not content with consolidation. Their ambitious strategy aimed to extend this perimeter further, threatening Allied supply lines and potentially isolating Australia from American support. It was in this context that the Japanese began constructing an airfield on the island of Guadalcanal in May 1942.

The strategic significance of this airfield was not lost on Allied planners. If completed, it would provide the Japanese with a base to threaten the vital sea lanes between the United States and Australia. Admiral

Ernest J. King, the U.S. Chief of Naval Operations, recognized the danger and pushed for immediate action to neutralize this threat.

The decision to launch an offensive on Guadalcanal was part of a broader strategy to seize the initiative in the Pacific following the strategic Allied victories at the Battles of Coral Sea and Midway. These battles had weakened Japanese naval capabilities, providing the Allies an opportunity to transition from defensive to offensive operations.

As both sides marshaled their forces, the stage was set for a confrontation that would alter the course of the Pacific War.

**The Initial Assault**

In the pre-dawn hours of August 7, 1942, a powerful Allied task force approached the shores of Guadalcanal. The invasion force, primarily composed of the U.S. 1st Marine Division under the command of Major General Alexander Vandegrift, was about to embark on the first major Allied offensive of the Pacific War.

As the sun began to rise, illuminating the lush green coastline of Guadalcanal, the first waves of Marines stormed ashore. The initial landings caught the Japanese defenders completely by surprise. The Marines quickly secured a beachhead and began pushing inland toward their primary objective: the partially completed airfield.

A young Marine, Private Robert Leckie, later recalled the moment of landing: "The beach was silent and empty. We had achieved total surprise. It was almost eerie how smoothly everything was going." However, this initial ease would soon give way to some of the most brutal fighting of the war.

By the end of the first day, the Marines had secured the airfield with minimal resistance. They renamed it Henderson Field, in honor of Major Lofton Henderson, a Marine pilot killed at the Battle of Midway. The capture of this airfield would prove to be crucial in the months of fighting that lay ahead.

**The Japanese Response**

The ease of the initial landing belied the ferocity of the battle to come. The Japanese, stunned by the audacity of the Allied offensive, quickly began to mobilize their forces for a counterattack. Admiral Isoroku Yamamoto, the architect of the Pearl Harbor attack, recognized the strategic importance of Guadalcanal and committed significant resources to its defense.

The first major Japanese counterattack came on August 21, 1942, in what would become known as the Battle of the Tenaru River. In the dead of night, over 900 Japanese troops under the command of Colonel Kiyonao Ichiki launched a frontal assault on the Marine positions. The attack was a disaster for the Japanese. The Marines, well-entrenched and supported by artillery, decimated the attacking force. By dawn, over 700 Japanese lay dead, with the Marines suffering only 44 casualties.

This battle set the tone for much of the land campaign on Guadalcanal. The Japanese, trained in offensive tactics and imbued with a spirit of sacrifice, repeatedly launched frontal assaults against well-prepared American positions. The results were often catastrophic for the Japanese forces.

## The Battle for Henderson Field

As the land battle raged, both sides recognized the critical importance of Henderson Field. For the Americans, it provided a vital base for air operations, allowing them to contest Japanese air and naval superiority. For the Japanese, recapturing the airfield became an obsession, leading to repeated, costly assaults.

The battle for Henderson Field reached its climax in October 1942, during what became known as the Battle for Henderson Field. Japanese forces, now reinforced and under the command of Lieutenant General Harukichi Hyakutake, launched a major offensive to recapture the airfield. The fighting was intense and often hand-to-hand. Marine Corps General Merritt Edson described the ferocity of the combat: "It was a nightmare. The Japanese came at us wave after wave. Their courage was incredible, but so was the determination of our men to hold the line."

Despite repeated assaults, the Marines held their ground. The Japanese attacks, while ferocious, were poorly coordinated and lacked adequate artillery support. By the end of October, the Japanese had suffered over 3,000 casualties in their failed attempts to recapture the airfield, while the Marines had lost around 80 men.

## Naval Battles: The Struggle for Control of the Seas

While the land battle raged on Guadalcanal, an equally crucial struggle was taking place in the waters surrounding the island. Control of the seas was vital for both sides – for the Allies, it meant the ability to resupply and reinforce their troops on Guadalcanal; for the Japanese, it offered the chance to land reinforcements and potentially recapture the island.

This struggle led to a series of naval engagements that would rank among the most ferocious of the war. The Battle of Savo Island on August 9, 1942, saw a Japanese force under Admiral Gunichi Mikawa inflict a devastating defeat on Allied naval forces, sinking four heavy cruisers and killing over 1,000 Allied sailors.

The naval battles continued throughout the campaign, with engagements such as the Battle of Cape Esperance, the Battle of the Santa Cruz Islands, and the Naval Battle of Guadalcanal in November 1942. These battles were characterized by their ferocity and the heavy losses suffered by both sides.

One of the most significant of these engagements was the Naval Battle of Guadalcanal, fought between November 12-15, 1942. This series of engagements saw both sides commit major naval forces in an all-out struggle for control of the seas around Guadalcanal. The battle resulted in heavy losses for both sides, including the death of two American admirals, but ultimately left the U.S. in control of the waters around Guadalcanal.

A U.S. Navy officer, Lieutenant Commander John Monsarrat, described the chaos of night naval combat: "The sea was alive with tracers, shellfire, and explosions. Ships appeared out of nowhere, engaged in furious combat, and disappeared just as quickly. It was like fighting ghosts."

## War in the Air

The air war over Guadalcanal was equally intense. The Japanese made repeated attempts to neutralize Henderson Field through air attacks, while American pilots fought to maintain control of the skies. The air battles over Guadalcanal produced numerous aces on both sides and saw the development of new tactics that would influence air combat for the remainder of the war.

One of the most famous units to emerge from the Guadalcanal campaign was the "Cactus Air Force," named after the Allied codename for Guadalcanal. This ad-hoc air group, composed of Marine, Navy, and Army Air Force pilots, played a crucial role in defending Henderson Field and supporting ground operations.

Major John L. Smith, a Marine Corps ace who served with the Cactus Air Force, later recalled the challenges of air combat over Guadalcanal: "We were always outnumbered, always low on fuel, and often flying patched-up planes. But we knew that if we failed, the men on the ground would pay the price. That kept us going, no matter the odds."

**The Tide Turns**

By December 1942, the strategic situation had shifted decisively in favor of the Allies. The Japanese, having suffered heavy losses in men and materiel, began to realize that the battle for Guadalcanal was lost. On December 31, 1942, Emperor Hirohito personally intervened, ordering the evacuation of all Japanese forces from the island.

The evacuation, codenamed Operation Ke by the Japanese, began in early January 1943. Despite Allied attempts to prevent it, the Japanese managed to evacuate over 10,000 troops from Guadalcanal by February 7, 1943. On February 9, American forces secured the island, marking the official end of the Guadalcanal campaign.

**Aftermath and Significance**

The Battle of Guadalcanal was a turning point in the Pacific War. It marked the first major Allied offensive against Japan and the beginning of a long string of Japanese defeats. The campaign demonstrated the effectiveness of combined arms warfare and the importance of air power in modern combat.

The human cost of the battle was staggering. The United States suffered over 7,000 dead, while Japanese losses were estimated at over 30,000. The campaign also took a heavy toll on both sides' naval forces, with dozens of ships sunk and thousands of sailors lost.

Strategically, the Allied victory at Guadalcanal halted Japanese expansion in the South Pacific and provided a base for future operations against Japanese strongholds. It also forced Japan to shift from an offensive to a defensive strategy for the remainder of the war.

**Conclusion**

The Battle of Guadalcanal stands as a testament to the courage, endurance, and sacrifice of those who fought there. It was a campaign that tested the limits of human endurance, fought in a hostile environment against a determined enemy. The victory came at a great cost but ultimately paved the way for Allied success in the Pacific.

The Battle of Guadalcanal – from its audacious beginnings to its grueling conclusion – remains a powerful reminder of the strategic decisions and individual acts of bravery that shaped the course of

World War II and the world we inhabit today. It stands as a turning point in the Pacific War, the moment when the Allies seized the initiative and began the long, hard road to victory.

**Sources**

Dower, John W. Without Mercy: Race and Power in the Pacific War. Pantheon, 1986.

Toland, John. The Rising Sun: The Decline and Fall of the Japanese Empire, 1936-1945. Random House, 1970.

Various Sources

# The Battles Continue

## The Battle of the Eastern Solomons

The Battle of the Eastern Solomons, fought from August 23 to August 25, 1942, was a significant naval engagement during World War II that served as a follow-up to the Battle of Midway. This battle involved aircraft carriers from both the United States and Japan, with the U.S. forces aiming to disrupt Japanese plans for reinforcing their positions in the Solomon Islands.

The conflict featured intense air combat, resulting in the U.S. sinking the Japanese aircraft carrier Ryujo and damaging the carrier Shokaku, while also losing the USS Enterprise's torpedo squadron during the fighting. Although the U.S. carriers sustained damage, the battle ultimately ended in a strategic victory for the Allies, further weakening Japanese naval capabilities and helping to secure the area around Guadalcanal for future Allied operations.

## The Battle of the Santa Cruz Islands

The Battle of the Santa Cruz Islands, fought on October 26, 1942, was a critical naval engagement in the Pacific Theater during World War II, occurring in the wake of the Guadalcanal campaign. The battle involved U.S. carrier forces, primarily the USS Enterprise and USS Hornet, engaging a Japanese fleet aiming to reinforce their troops on Guadalcanal. Intense air battles ensued, resulting in the U.S. suffering significant losses, including the sinking of the USS Hornet and the damage of the USS Enterprise.

Although the Japanese also lost several aircraft and pilots, the battle was strategically important for Japan as it allowed them to maintain temporary air superiority over Guadalcanal. However, the heavy attrition of experienced pilots ultimately contributed to Japan's declining capability in subsequent engagements, as the Allies continued to build their strength in the Pacific.

## The Battle of Tarawa

The Battle of Tarawa, fought from November 20 to November 23, 1943, was a pivotal amphibious assault by U.S. forces during World War II, aimed at capturing the heavily fortified Japanese-held atoll in the Gilbert Islands. The battle began with a massive naval bombardment intended to soften Japanese defenses, but the landing forces encountered unexpectedly fierce resistance from well-entrenched Japanese troops.

The U.S. Marines faced challenging conditions, including shallow reefs that complicated landing operations and led to significant casualties. After intense fighting, U.S. forces eventually secured the atoll, but the battle resulted in heavy losses, with nearly 1,000 Marines killed and thousands wounded.

Despite the high cost, the successful capture of Tarawa showcased the determination of American forces and marked an important step in the island-hopping campaign, paving the way for further assaults in the Pacific and demonstrating the need for improved strategies in amphibious warfare.

## The Battle of Kwajalein

The Battle of Kwajalein, fought from January 31 to February 3, 1944, was a key operation in the U.S. island-hopping campaign during World War II, targeting the Japanese-held Kwajalein Atoll in the Marshall Islands. The assault began with extensive naval bombardment, followed by a swift invasion by

U.S. forces, including Marines and Army troops. Despite the challenging terrain and determined Japanese resistance, the U.S. forces quickly overwhelmed the defenders, securing key positions on the atoll within a matter of days.

The battle resulted in significant American victories with relatively low casualties compared to previous engagements, and it marked a strategic success by providing the Allies with a critical base for future operations in the Pacific.

The capture of Kwajalein not only advanced U.S. military objectives but also showcased the effectiveness of coordinated amphibious assaults in overcoming fortified defenses.

**The Battle of Eniwetok**

The Battle of Eniwetok, fought from February 17 to February 22, 1944, was a significant U.S. amphibious operation aimed at capturing the strategically important Eniwetok Atoll in the Marshall Islands during World War II. Following a preliminary naval bombardment to weaken Japanese defenses, U.S. Marines and soldiers landed on the atoll, facing stiff resistance from entrenched Japanese forces.

Despite the challenging conditions and fierce fighting, the American forces quickly adapted their tactics, utilizing combined arms and overwhelming firepower to secure the islands of Engebi and Eniwetok. The battle concluded with a decisive victory for the U.S., resulting in the capture of the atoll and the destruction of Japanese defensive positions.

This successful operation not only provided the Allies with a vital base for future operations in the Pacific but also demonstrated the effectiveness of coordinated assaults in overcoming fortified enemy positions, contributing to the broader strategy of island-hopping.

**The Battle of Saipan**

The Battle of Saipan, fought from June 15 to July 9, 1944, was a crucial campaign in the Pacific Theater of World War II, aimed at capturing the strategically significant island of Saipan in the Mariana Islands. U.S. forces launched a massive amphibious assault, facing fierce resistance from well-entrenched Japanese troops, who were determined to defend the island to prevent Allied access to the Philippine Sea.

The battle featured intense ground combat, air support, and naval engagements, resulting in heavy casualties on both sides. Ultimately, U.S. forces secured Saipan after weeks of brutal fighting, leading to the deaths of approximately 30,000 Japanese soldiers and civilians, many of whom chose suicide over capture.

The capture of Saipan provided the Allies with a vital base for launching air raids against the Japanese home islands and marked a significant turning point in the war, as it brought the U.S. within striking distance of Japan and significantly weakened Japanese defenses in the Pacific.

**The Battle of Guam**

The Battle of Guam, fought from July 21 to August 10, 1944, was a key engagement in the Pacific Theater during World War II, aimed at recapturing the island from Japanese occupation. U.S. forces launched a well-coordinated amphibious assault, landing on the western beaches of Guam and quickly encountering fierce resistance from Japanese defenders who were determined to hold their ground.

Despite the difficult terrain and strong fortifications, American troops utilized combined arms tactics and superior naval and air support to push inland. After intense fighting, including notable engagements in the jungles and hills, U.S. forces successfully secured the island, resulting in heavy casualties for the Japanese, with many troops killed or captured.

The victory in Guam not only restored the island to American control but also provided a critical base for future operations in the Pacific, significantly contributing to the ongoing island-hopping campaign and facilitating further advances toward Japan.

**The Battle of Tinian**

The Battle of Tinian, fought from July 24 to August 1, 1944, was a pivotal operation in the U.S. island-hopping campaign during World War II, aimed at capturing Tinian Island in the Mariana Islands. Following a heavy naval bombardment to soften Japanese defenses, U.S. Marines landed on the beaches and encountered fierce resistance from well-entrenched Japanese forces.

Despite challenging conditions, including fortified positions and counterattacks, American troops employed combined arms tactics and overwhelming firepower to systematically secure the island. The battle concluded with a decisive victory for the U.S., resulting in significant Japanese casualties and the capture of Tinian.

This strategic victory was crucial as it provided the Allies with a critical airbase for launching bombing raids against the Japanese home islands, including the eventual atomic bombings of Hiroshima and Nagasaki, marking a significant step in the Pacific campaign and contributing to the overall Allied efforts to defeat Japan.

**Sources**

Dower, John W. Without Mercy: Race and Power in the Pacific War. Pantheon, 1986.

Toland, John. The Rising Sun: The Decline and Fall of the Japanese Empire, 1936-1945. Random House, 1970.

Various Sources

# The Battle of Leyte Gulf

**Introduction**

In the autumn of 1944, as World War II raged across the globe, a pivotal confrontation was brewing in the vast expanse of the Pacific Ocean. The Battle of Leyte Gulf, fought from October 23 to October 26, 1944, would mark a turning point in the war against Japan and usher in a new era of naval warfare. This engagement, the largest naval battle in history, would not only halt the Japanese Navy's ability to conduct large-scale operations but also set the stage for the liberation of the Philippines and the eventual Allied victory in the Pacific.

As the sun rose over the Philippine archipelago on that fateful October morning, neither the Allied nor the Japanese forces could have fully grasped the significance of the battle that was about to unfold. The outcome would shape the course of the war, influence the fate of nations, and forever change the nature of naval combat. This is the story of courage, strategy, and the thin line between victory and defeat that defined the Battle of Leyte Gulf.

**The Road to Confrontation**

The roots of the Leyte Gulf campaign can be traced back to the shocking Japanese attack on Pearl Harbor on December 7, 1941. This surprise assault had severely crippled the U.S. Pacific Fleet, allowing Japan to rapidly expand its control over vast swathes of the western Pacific. By mid-1944, however, the tide had begun to turn. The Allied "island hopping" strategy had successfully pushed Japanese forces out of key positions, and the next major objective was the Philippines.

The strategic importance of the Philippines was immense. For the Japanese, it was a crucial link in their supply chain, connecting their conquests in Southeast Asia to the home islands. For the Allies, liberating the Philippines would not only sever this lifeline but also provide a staging ground for future operations against Japan itself.

The decision to invade the Philippines was not without controversy. Some Allied commanders, including Admiral Ernest J. King and Admiral Chester Nimitz, favored bypassing the Philippines in favor of Formosa (Taiwan). However, General Douglas MacArthur, who had famously declared "I shall return" when forced to leave the Philippines in 1942, insisted on liberating the islands. Ultimately, MacArthur's plan prevailed, and the invasion of Leyte was set in motion.

As both sides marshaled their forces, the stage was set for a confrontation that would alter the course of the Pacific War. The Japanese, recognizing the existential threat to their empire, committed virtually every operational warship to the defense of the Philippines. The resulting plan, codenamed "Sho-Go" (Victory Operation), was a complex, multi-pronged assault designed to catch the Allied invasion force in a deadly vice.

**The Battle Unfolds**

The Battle of Leyte Gulf was not a single engagement, but rather a series of interconnected battles spread across a vast area of the Philippine Sea and surrounding waters. It began on October 23, 1944, as Allied forces under the overall command of General MacArthur began landing on the island of Leyte.

The Japanese response was swift and determined. Admiral Soemu Toyoda, Commander-in-Chief of the Combined Fleet, set in motion a daring plan that divided the Japanese Navy into three main groups:

1. The Northern Force, led by Vice Admiral Jisaburo Ozawa, consisted of Japan's remaining aircraft carriers, now largely devoid of aircraft and intended to serve as a decoy.

2. The Center Force, commanded by Vice Admiral Takeo Kurita, was the main striking arm, featuring the super battleships Yamato and Musashi.

3. The Southern Force, under Vice Admirals Shoji Nishimura and Kiyohide Shima, was tasked with approaching Leyte Gulf from the south.

The American forces, meanwhile, were divided into the Third Fleet under Admiral William "Bull" Halsey, and the Seventh Fleet under Vice Admiral Thomas Kinkaid. What followed was a series of engagements that would test the mettle of sailors and commanders on both sides.

**The Battle of the Sibuyan Sea**

The first major clash came on October 24 in the Sibuyan Sea. American scout planes spotted Kurita's Center Force, and waves of carrier-based aircraft were launched to intercept. The ensuing battle was fierce, with American pilots braving intense anti-aircraft fire to press home their attacks.

The focus of much of the American effort was the super battleship Musashi. Over the day, the massive warship was struck by at least 17 bombs and 19 torpedoes. A young American pilot, Ensign Jack Lawton, later recalled the awesome sight: "She was enormous... I had never seen anything so big in my life. As we came in, her flak was like a sheet of flame. I remember thinking, 'How could anything survive that?'"

Despite the ferocity of the American attacks, the Musashi's crew fought on with incredible determination. Captain Toshihira Inoguchi, the Musashi's commanding officer, calmly directed damage control efforts even as his ship was being torn apart. However, by late afternoon, the accumulation of damage proved too much, and the mighty Musashi capsized and sank, taking with her over 1,000 of her crew.

The loss of the Musashi was a severe blow to the Japanese, but Kurita's force, though battered, continued on towards its objective.

## The Battle of Surigao Strait

As Kurita's force pushed on, the Southern Force under Nishimura and Shima approached Leyte Gulf through the Surigao Strait. Waiting for them was a powerful American force under Rear Admiral Jesse Oldendorf, arrayed in a classic "crossing the T" formation that allowed maximum firepower to be brought to bear on the approaching enemy.

The ensuing battle on the night of October 24-25 was the last battleship-to-battleship engagement in history. The American battleline, including ships that had been sunk at Pearl Harbor and since raised and repaired, exacted a terrible revenge. The Japanese battleship Yamashiro was sunk, along with several other ships. A survivor from the Yamashiro, Petty Officer Hideo Ogawa, later described the horrific scene: "The sea was on fire, and explosions were everywhere. It was like sailing into hell itself."

By dawn, the Southern Force had been all but annihilated, with only a handful of ships managing to escape.

## The Battle off Cape Engaño

While the Southern Force was being destroyed in Surigao Strait, Admiral Halsey's Third Fleet had taken the bait offered by Ozawa's Northern Force. Believing he had a chance to destroy the last of Japan's carrier fleet, Halsey steamed north with the bulk of his forces, leaving the landing beaches at Leyte relatively unprotected.

The resulting Battle off Cape Engaño on October 25 was a one-sided affair. The Japanese carriers, serving as little more than decoys, were overwhelmed by the American attack. Four Japanese carriers were sunk, along with several other ships. However, Ozawa's sacrifice had achieved its purpose, drawing Halsey away from the main battlefield.

## The Battle off Samar

With Halsey's powerful Third Fleet out of position, the stage was set for the most dramatic and consequential engagement of the entire battle. On the morning of October 25, Kurita's Center Force, having survived the Battle of the Sibuyan Sea, emerged from the San Bernardino Strait to find only a small group of American escort carriers and destroyers between them and the vulnerable invasion beaches.

What followed was one of the most heroic stands in naval history. The American force, known as "Taffy 3" and commanded by Rear Admiral Clifton Sprague, was hopelessly outgunned. Their only hope was to fight a delaying action while calling desperately for help.

The ensuing battle was a chaotic melee of smoke, gunfire, and incredible bravery. American destroyers and destroyer escorts made suicidal torpedo runs against Japanese battleships and cruisers. The escort carriers launched every available aircraft, many armed with nothing more than depth charges or machine guns.

Lieutenant Commander Ernest E. Evans, commanding the destroyer USS Johnston, epitomized the American fighting spirit. Despite being vastly outgunned, Evans took his ship directly at the Japanese fleet, scoring torpedo hits on a heavy cruiser before being sunk. For his actions, Evans was posthumously awarded the Medal of Honor.

As the battle raged, the American forces fought with a ferocity that confused the Japanese commanders. Kurita, believing he was facing a much larger force, and concerned about the possibility of air attacks from Halsey's carriers (which were actually far to the north), made the fateful decision to withdraw. It was a decision that likely saved the American invasion force but would haunt Kurita for the rest of his life.

**Aftermath and Significance**

The Battle of Leyte Gulf was a decisive victory for the Allies and had far-reaching consequences for the remainder of the war. The Japanese Navy, which had once dominated the Pacific, was shattered beyond repair. They lost 26 major warships, including four aircraft carriers, three battleships, six heavy cruisers, four light cruisers, and eleven destroyers. Perhaps even more critically, they lost hundreds of irreplaceable trained pilots and sailors.

For the Allies, the victory secured the Philippines and cut off Japan's vital supply lines to Southeast Asia. It provided a base for future operations against Japan and marked the beginning of the end for the Japanese Empire. The introduction of kamikaze tactics during the battle, while causing significant damage to Allied ships, was a sign of Japan's increasing desperation.

The battle also had significant strategic implications. It demonstrated the ascendancy of carrier-based air power over traditional battleship fleets and highlighted the importance of coordinated joint operations. The controversy surrounding Halsey's decision to take the Third Fleet north in pursuit of the Japanese carriers would lead to changes in command structures and communications protocols.

**Conclusion**

The Battle of Leyte Gulf stands as a testament to the courage, skill, and sacrifice of those who fought there. It was a battle that tested the limits of human endurance and ingenuity, fought across a vast expanse of ocean against a determined and capable enemy. The victory came at a great cost but ultimately paved the way for Allied success in the Pacific.

As we reflect on the events of those fateful days in October 1944, we are reminded of the extraordinary sacrifices made by those who fought there. Their legacy lives on in the annals of naval history, a powerful reminder of the human cost of war and the indomitable spirit of those who fight for freedom.

The Battle of Leyte Gulf – from its complex strategic planning to its moments of individual heroism – remains a powerful reminder of the decisions and actions that shaped the course of World War II and the world we inhabit today. It stands as a turning point in the Pacific War, the moment when the Allies seized the initiative and began the long, hard road to final victory.

**Sources**

Miller, Edward S. War Plan Orange: The US Strategy to Defeat Japan, 1897-1945. Annapolis: Naval Institute Press, 1991.

Parsonson, John. The Battle of Midway: Turning the Tide of the Pacific War. New York: HarperCollins, 1994.

Various Sources

# The Liberation of Luzon

## Introduction

In the winter of 1945, as World War II entered its final, desperate phase, a pivotal confrontation was brewing in the Philippine archipelago. The Battle of Luzon, fought from January 9 to August 15, 1945, would mark a turning point in the war against Japan and usher in the final stages of the Pacific campaign. This engagement, one of the largest and longest battles of the Pacific War, would not only liberate the Philippines from Japanese occupation but also set the stage for the eventual Allied victory in World War II.

As the sun rose over the shores of Lingayen Gulf on that fateful January morning, neither the Allied nor the Japanese forces could have fully grasped the significance of the battle that was about to unfold. The outcome would shape the course of the war, influence the fate of nations, and forever change the lives of millions. This is the story of courage, strategy, and the thin line between victory and defeat that defined the Battle of Luzon.

## The Road to Confrontation

The roots of the Luzon campaign can be traced back to the shocking Japanese invasion of the Philippines in December 1941. This assault had forced the retreat of American and Filipino forces, culminating in the infamous Bataan Death March and the fall of Corregidor in May 1942. As he departed the Philippines, General Douglas MacArthur uttered his famous promise: "I shall return." Now, nearly three years later, he was poised to fulfill that vow.

By late 1944, the strategic landscape of the Pacific War had shifted dramatically. The Allied "island hopping" strategy had successfully pushed Japanese forces out of key positions, and the next major objective was the Philippines. The liberation of Luzon, the largest and most populous island in the archipelago, was crucial for several reasons. For the Japanese, it was a vital link in their supply chain, connecting their conquests in Southeast Asia to the home islands. For the Allies, recapturing Luzon would not only sever this lifeline but also provide a staging ground for future operations against Japan itself.

The decision to invade Luzon was not without controversy. Some Allied commanders, including Admiral Ernest J. King and Admiral Chester Nimitz, favored bypassing the Philippines in favor of Formosa (Taiwan). However, MacArthur insisted on liberating the islands, arguing for its strategic importance and the moral obligation to free the Filipino people from Japanese occupation. Ultimately, MacArthur's plan prevailed, and the invasion of Luzon was set in motion.

As both sides marshaled their forces, the stage was set for a confrontation that would alter the course of the Pacific War. The Japanese, recognizing the existential threat to their empire, committed significant resources to the defense of Luzon. General Tomoyuki Yamashita, known as the "Tiger of Malaya" for his earlier conquests, was tasked with defending the island. Yamashita, a skilled tactician, chose to concentrate his forces in the mountainous regions of Luzon, preparing for a protracted defensive battle.

**The Initial Assault**

The Battle of Luzon began in earnest on January 9, 1945, a day designated as "S-Day" by Allied planners. As dawn broke over Lingayen Gulf, a massive Allied armada appeared on the horizon. The invasion force, primarily composed of the U.S. Sixth Army under Lieutenant General Walter Krueger, was one of the largest assembled in the Pacific War.

The scene was one of controlled chaos as landing craft approached the beaches. A young American soldier, Private John Smith, later recalled the moment: "As we neared the shore, the noise was deafening. The big guns of the navy were pounding the beach, and we could see explosions all along the coastline. I remember thinking, 'How could anyone survive that?' But we knew the Japanese were out there, waiting for us."

The initial landings faced less resistance than expected, as Yamashita had chosen to withdraw his forces inland rather than contest the beaches. However, the invasion was not without peril. Japanese kamikaze attacks targeted the Allied ships, causing significant damage and casualties. The USS New Mexico, a battleship providing fire support, was hit by a kamikaze, killing over 30 crew members including its captain.

Despite these attacks, the Allied forces successfully established a beachhead and began to push inland. The vast logistical operation to support the invasion swung into action, with supplies and reinforcements pouring ashore. By the end of the first day, over 68,000 troops had landed on Luzon, with more following in the subsequent days.

**The Drive to Manila**

As the beachhead expanded, Allied forces began their push towards Manila, the capital city and primary objective of the campaign. The advance was led by the XIV Corps, which encountered stiff resistance, particularly around Clark Air Base. The battle for Clark, a vital airfield, lasted until the end of January and was marked by fierce fighting.

A Filipino guerrilla fighter, Maria Santos, who had been resisting the Japanese occupation for years, described the Allied advance: "We had been waiting for this moment for so long. When we saw the American tanks rolling down the roads toward Manila, it was like a dream come true. But we knew the fight was far from over. The Japanese were dug in, and they would not give up easily."

As the Allied forces neared Manila, the situation for civilians in the city became increasingly desperate. The Japanese, following a scorched earth policy, began destroying infrastructure and supplies. Reports of atrocities against the civilian population began to emerge, adding urgency to the Allied advance.

## The Battle for Manila

The battle for Manila began on February 3, 1945, when elements of the 1st Cavalry Division captured a bridge leading into the city. What followed was one of the most brutal urban battles of World War II. The Japanese defenders, under the command of Rear Admiral Sanji Iwabuchi, had fortified the city and were determined to fight to the last man.

The fighting in Manila was characterized by its intensity and the high toll on civilians. The Japanese had turned many of the city's historic buildings into fortresses, including the Manila Hotel and the Legislative Building. Allied forces were forced to clear the city block by block, often engaging in close-quarters combat.

An American officer, Captain David Johnson, described the scene: "It was like fighting in a maze. Every street, every building could hide an enemy sniper or machine gun nest. The noise was constant – gunfire, explosions, the screams of the wounded. And everywhere, the smell of smoke and death. It was hell on earth."

The battle for Manila lasted until March 3, 1945, and resulted in the near-total destruction of the city. Over 100,000 Filipino civilians lost their lives, many at the hands of Japanese troops in what became known as the Manila Massacre. The devastation of Manila was a stark reminder of the human cost of war and the brutality of the Pacific campaign.

## The Mountain Campaign

While the battle for Manila raged, another equally crucial campaign was unfolding in the mountains of northern Luzon. Here, General Yamashita had established his main defensive positions, taking advantage of the rugged terrain to conduct a protracted guerrilla-style defense.

The mountain campaign was a grueling test of endurance for the Allied forces. The terrain was unforgiving, with dense jungles, steep ridges, and a lack of roads making progress slow and costly. Japanese forces had prepared extensive defensive positions, including caves and tunnels that were difficult to neutralize.

A Japanese soldier, Hiroshi Tanaka, who survived the mountain campaign, later wrote: "We were ordered to hold out as long as possible. Our positions were strong, and we had supplies to last for months. But with each passing day, we could hear the American guns getting closer. Many of us knew that we would never see Japan again, but we were determined to fight to the end for our Emperor."

The Allied forces employed a combination of frontal assaults, flanking maneuvers, and extensive use of artillery and air power to slowly wear down the Japanese defenses. Filipino guerrillas played a crucial role in this campaign, providing intelligence and harassing Japanese supply lines.

## The Final Stages

By March 1945, Allied forces had taken control of all strategically important locations on Luzon. However, pockets of Japanese resistance continued to hold out in the mountains. General Yamashita, true to his reputation, conducted a skillful defensive campaign that tied down significant Allied resources.

The fighting in these final stages was often desperate and at close quarters. An American sergeant, Bill Thompson, recalled one such encounter: "We were clearing a series of caves when we came under heavy fire. I saw my buddy take a hit and go down. In that moment, all the training, all the fear, just disappeared. I charged the Japanese position, firing my Thompson submachine gun. It was over in seconds, but it felt like hours. When it was done, I couldn't believe I was still alive."

As the weeks turned into months, the Japanese forces on Luzon were gradually worn down by lack of supplies, disease, and the relentless Allied pressure. Yet, even as news reached them of the atomic bombings of Hiroshima and Nagasaki, many continued to resist.

## Aftermath and Significance

The Battle of Luzon officially ended with the surrender of Japan on August 15, 1945, although isolated pockets of Japanese resistance continued to hold out for some time afterward. The human cost of the battle was staggering. American forces suffered over 47,000 casualties, while Japanese losses were estimated at over 200,000. Filipino civilian casualties were even higher, with some estimates placing the number at over 300,000.

The strategic importance of the Luzon campaign cannot be overstated. It provided the Allies with crucial bases for the planned invasion of Japan and effectively broke the back of Japanese resistance in the Philippines. The battle also demonstrated the effectiveness of combined arms warfare and the crucial role of logistics in modern military operations.

For the Philippines, the liberation of Luzon came at a terrible cost but marked the end of Japanese occupation and the beginning of the road to independence. The destruction wrought by the battle, particularly in Manila, would take years to overcome.

## Conclusion

The Battle of Luzon stands as a testament to the courage, endurance, and sacrifice of those who fought there. It was a campaign that tested the limits of human endurance, fought across a diverse landscape against a determined enemy. The victory came at a great cost but ultimately paved the way for Allied success in the Pacific and the end of World War II.

The liberation of Luzon – from its daring amphibious assault to the grueling mountain campaign – stands as a turning point in the Pacific War. It marked the moment when the Allies seized the initiative in the Philippines, setting the stage for the final acts of World War II and shaping the geopolitical landscape of the post-war world.

## Sources

Miller, Edward S. War Plan Orange: The US Strategy to Defeat Japan, 1897-1945. Annapolis: Naval Institute Press, 1991.

Murphy, Kevin C. Inside the Bataan Death March: Defeat, Travail and Memory. McFarland, 2014.

Various Sources

# The Battle of Iwo Jima

## Introduction

In the winter of 1945, as World War II entered its final, desperate phase, a pivotal confrontation was brewing on a small, volcanic island in the Pacific. The Battle of Iwo Jima, fought from February 19 to March 26, 1945, would mark a turning point in the war against Japan and become one of the most iconic engagements of World War II. This battle, characterized by its ferocity and the valor of those who fought, would not only secure a crucial strategic asset for the Allies but also become a symbol of American determination and sacrifice.

As the sun rose over the sulfurous shores of Iwo Jima on that fateful February morning, neither the Allied nor the Japanese forces could have fully grasped the significance of the battle that was about to unfold. The outcome would shape the course of the war, influence the fate of nations, and forever change the lives of those who fought there. This is the story of courage, strategy, and the thin line between victory and defeat that defined the Battle of Iwo Jima.

## The Road to Confrontation

The roots of the Iwo Jima campaign can be traced back to the broader Allied strategy in the Pacific. By early 1945, the tide of war had turned decisively against Japan. The Allied "island hopping" strategy had successfully pushed Japanese forces out of key positions, and the next major objective was to bring the war to Japan's doorstep.

Iwo Jima, a small volcanic island located approximately halfway between the Mariana Islands and the Japanese mainland, held immense strategic value. Its three airfields were used by the Japanese to launch attacks on American bomber formations and to send fighter planes aloft to intercept American bombers headed for Japan. For the Allies, capturing Iwo Jima would provide a crucial base for fighter escorts to support bombing raids on Japan, as well as an emergency landing strip for damaged B-29s returning from bombing runs.

The decision to invade Iwo Jima was not without controversy. Some Allied commanders questioned whether the potential benefits outweighed the expected costs. However, the strategic importance of the island, coupled with the psychological impact its capture would have, ultimately led to the green light for the operation.

As both sides prepared for the impending battle, the stage was set for one of the bloodiest and most iconic engagements of World War II.

## Japanese Preparations: A Fortress of Stone and Steel

The Japanese, under the command of Lieutenant General Tadamichi Kuribayashi, had turned Iwo Jima into a veritable fortress. Kuribayashi, a capable and innovative commander, had spent months preparing the island's defenses, determined to make the Americans pay a heavy price for every inch of ground.

The Japanese defensive strategy was a departure from previous tactics. Instead of concentrating forces on the beaches to repel the initial landing, Kuribayashi opted for a defense in depth. He ordered the construction of an elaborate system of tunnels, bunkers, and fortified positions that honeycombed the entire island. This network, spanning approximately 11 miles, allowed the Japanese to move troops and supplies undetected and to launch surprise counterattacks.

One Japanese soldier, recalling the preparations, wrote in his diary: "We are digging tunnels like moles. We hope to resist as long as possible."

The natural terrain of Iwo Jima, with its volcanic rock and sulfur springs, was incorporated into the defenses. Artillery and mortar positions were carefully camouflaged, and the black volcanic sand made it difficult for the attackers to detect enemy positions. The formidable Mount Suribachi, a 546-foot dormant volcano at the southern tip of the island, was transformed into a citadel of Japanese resistance.

## The Initial Assault: Into the Jaws of Hell

The Battle of Iwo Jima began on February 19, 1945, with a massive naval bombardment. As shells rained down on the island, the Japanese defenders waited silently in their underground positions. The initial bombardment, while impressive, did little to dent the Japanese defenses.

As the first waves of Marines approached the beaches, an eerie silence fell over the island. Private Robert Leckie, a Marine who would later become a renowned war correspondent, recalled the moment: "The quiet was unearthly. It felt like we were landing on a dead planet."

The calm was shattered as the Japanese opened fire. The beaches erupted in a maelstrom of shellfire, machine gun bursts, and exploding mortars. The black volcanic sand, so different from the coral beaches the Marines had encountered in previous landings, made movement difficult. Tanks and other vehicles bogged down, becoming easy targets for Japanese gunners.

Despite the withering fire, the Marines pushed forward. By the end of the first day, some 30,000 Marines had landed, but the cost was high. The beaches were littered with dead and wounded, and the gains were measured in yards.

## The Battle for Mount Suribachi: Raising the Flag

The first major objective of the American forces was Mount Suribachi. The mountain, honeycombed with Japanese defensive positions, dominated the southern end of the island and provided the defenders with excellent observation posts.

The fight for Suribachi was brutal. Marines inched their way up the slopes, using flamethrowers and grenades to clear out Japanese positions. On February 23, four days after the initial landing, a patrol of Marines reached the summit of Suribachi. In a moment that would become one of the most iconic images of World War II, six Marines raised the American flag atop the mountain.

Joe Rosenthal, an Associated Press photographer, captured the flag-raising in a photograph that would win the Pulitzer Prize and become one of the most reproduced images in history. The sight of the flag flying over Mount Suribachi provided a much-needed morale boost to the Marines fighting on the island.

Corporal Charles Lindberg, one of the Marines who helped raise the first flag on Suribachi (there were actually two flag-raisings that day), later recalled: "We thought that once the flag went up, the battle would be over. But it was really just beginning."

## The Meat Grinder: Fighting in the North

While the capture of Mount Suribachi was a significant achievement, it marked only the beginning of the battle for Iwo Jima. The northern part of the island, where the airfields were located, remained firmly in Japanese hands.

The terrain in the north was even more favorable to the defenders. The Japanese had fortified a series of hills and ridges, turning each into a fortress. The Marines had to fight for each position, often engaging in hand-to-hand combat to clear out the Japanese defenders.

The fighting was incredibly intense and costly. Marine units suffered casualty rates of up to 75%. The Japanese, following Kuribayashi's orders, fought to the death, rarely surrendering. When one position was taken, the Japanese would use their tunnel network to reoccupy it, forcing the Marines to fight for the same ground multiple times.

Sergeant John Basilone, a Medal of Honor recipient from the Guadalcanal campaign, was killed leading his men against a Japanese strongpoint. His last words, according to those who were with him, were "I'll go first. Watch me and I'll show you how to do it."

## The Role of Air Power and Naval Support

Throughout the battle, American air power and naval gunfire played a crucial role. Carrier-based aircraft provided close air support for the Marines on the ground, while battleships and cruisers offshore pounded Japanese positions.

The first American aircraft landed on Iwo Jima on March 4, even as fighting continued around the airfield perimeters. This marked a significant turning point, as it allowed for even more effective air support and demonstrated that the primary objective of the invasion – securing the airfields – was being achieved.

## The Final Days: Kuribayashi's Last Stand

As the battle entered its final weeks, General Kuribayashi and his remaining forces were pushed back to the northern tip of the island. Despite being vastly outnumbered and running low on supplies, the Japanese continued to resist fiercely.

Kuribayashi, who had led the defense of the island with skill and determination, prepared for a final stand. In one of his last radio messages to Tokyo, he said: "We have not eaten or drunk for five days but our fighting spirit is still high. We are going to fight bravely to the last."

On March 26, 1945, after 36 days of brutal combat, Iwo Jima was declared secured. However, pockets of Japanese resistance continued, with the last two Japanese soldiers not surrendering until 1949, four years after the war's end.

**Aftermath and Significance**

The Battle of Iwo Jima was one of the bloodiest in Marine Corps history. Of the 70,000 Marines who fought on Iwo Jima, nearly 7,000 were killed and another 20,000 wounded. Japanese losses were even more staggering, with approximately 18,000 killed out of a garrison of 21,000. Only 216 Japanese soldiers were taken prisoner.

The capture of Iwo Jima provided the Allies with a crucial base for fighter escorts and emergency landings. By the end of the war, thousands of B-29s had made emergency landings on the island, saving countless American lives.

The battle's significance extended beyond its strategic value. It became a symbol of American determination and the valor of the U.S. Marine Corps. The image of the flag raising on Mount Suribachi became an enduring symbol of American victory, inspiring the Marine Corps War Memorial in Arlington, Virginia.

Admiral Chester Nimitz, Commander in Chief of the Pacific Fleet, said of the battle: "Among the Americans who served on Iwo Island, uncommon valor was a common virtue." This quote, inscribed on the Marine Corps War Memorial, encapsulates the courage and sacrifice displayed by those who fought in this grueling battle.

**Conclusion**

The Battle of Iwo Jima stands as a testament to the courage, endurance, and sacrifice of those who fought there. It was a battle that tested the limits of human endurance, fought in a hostile environment against a determined enemy. The victory came at a great cost but ultimately paved the way for the final stages of the war in the Pacific.

**Sources**

Murphy, Kevin C. Inside the Bataan Death March: Defeat, Travail and Memory. McFarland, 2014.

Hama, Larry. The Battle of Iwo Jima: Guerilla Warfare in the Pacific. Rosen Pub Group, 2006.

Various Sources

# The Battle of Okinawa

## Introduction

In the spring of 1945, as World War II entered its final, desperate phase, a pivotal confrontation was brewing on a small island in the Pacific. The Battle of Okinawa, codenamed Operation Iceberg, would mark the last major engagement of World War II and become one of the bloodiest battles in the Pacific Theater. This battle, characterized by its ferocity, massive scale, and tragic civilian toll, would not only secure a crucial strategic asset for the Allies but also become a grim harbinger of what an invasion of the Japanese mainland might entail.

As the sun rose over the shores of Okinawa on Easter Sunday, April 1, 1945, neither the Allied nor the Japanese forces could have fully grasped the significance of the battle that was about to unfold. The outcome would shape the course of the war, influence the fateful decision to use atomic weapons, and forever change the lives of those who fought there and the civilians caught in the crossfire. This is the story of courage, strategy, and the thin line between victory and defeat that defined the Battle of Okinawa.

## The Road to Confrontation

The roots of the Okinawa campaign can be traced back to the broader Allied strategy in the Pacific. By early 1945, the tide of war had turned decisively against Japan. The Allied "island hopping" strategy had successfully pushed Japanese forces out of key positions, and the next major objective was to bring the war to Japan's doorstep.

Okinawa, the largest island in the Ryukyu archipelago, held immense strategic value. Located just 340 miles from the Japanese mainland, its capture would provide the Allies with a crucial base for the planned invasion of Japan. The island's airfields would allow for increased air strikes on the Japanese homeland and serve as a staging ground for the final assault.

The decision to invade Okinawa was not without controversy. Some Allied commanders questioned whether the potential benefits outweighed the expected costs. However, the strategic importance of the island, coupled with the psychological impact its capture would have, ultimately led to the green light for Operation Iceberg.

## Preparations for Battle

As both sides prepared for the impending confrontation, the stage was set for one of the largest amphibious assaults of the Pacific War. The Allied forces, under the overall command of Admiral Chester W. Nimitz, assembled a massive invasion fleet. The ground forces, designated as the U.S. Tenth Army, were led by Lieutenant General Simon Bolivar Buckner Jr. and consisted of both Army and Marine Corps units, including the battle-hardened veterans of the XXIV Corps and the III Amphibious Corps.

On the Japanese side, Lieutenant General Mitsuru Ushijima, commander of the Thirty-Second Army, was tasked with the defense of Okinawa. Ushijima, along with his chief of staff, Lieutenant General Isamu Cho, and chief strategist, Lieutenant Colonel Hiromichi Yahara, devised a defensive strategy that would prove both effective and costly for the invading forces.

Unlike previous island battles where Japanese forces had contested the beaches, Ushijima opted for a defense in depth. He ordered the construction of an elaborate system of tunnels, bunkers, and fortified positions that honeycombed the southern part of the island. This network allowed the Japanese to move troops and supplies undetected and to launch surprise counterattacks.

## The Initial Assault: A Deceptive Calm

The Battle of Okinawa began on April 1, 1945, with a massive naval bombardment. As shells rained down on the island, the Japanese defenders waited silently in their underground positions. The initial bombardment, while impressive, did little to dent the Japanese defenses.

As the first waves of American troops approached the beaches, an eerie silence fell over the island. The landings on the Hagushi beaches on the western coast of Okinawa were met with little resistance, catching many by surprise. By the end of the first day, some 60,000 troops had landed, securing a beachhead and pushing inland.

The ease of the initial landing belied the ferocity of the battle to come. Ushijima's strategy of drawing the Americans inland before engaging them would soon become apparent, and the true nature of the battle would reveal itself in the coming days and weeks.

## The Battle Intensifies: Kamikaze Attacks and the Shuri Line

As the ground forces pushed inland, the supporting naval forces faced a terrifying new threat. On April 6, the Japanese launched the first of ten large-scale kamikaze attacks, known as "kikusuis." These suicide attacks by Japanese pilots caused significant damage to the Allied fleet, sinking and damaging numerous ships and inflicting heavy casualties.

The intensity of these attacks is vividly captured in the account of Donald W. Panek, who served aboard the USS Revenge. He described the relentless nature of the kamikaze assaults and the heavy toll they took on both ships and men. The psychological impact of these attacks was profound, with sailors living in constant fear of the next wave of suicide planes.

On land, the advancing American forces soon encountered fierce resistance as they approached the Shuri Line, a formidable defensive position that stretched across the southern part of the island. The Japanese, entrenched in their network of caves and tunnels, fought with fanatical determination, often to the last man.

The battle for the Shuri Line would become one of the most brutal phases of the Okinawa campaign. American forces faced not only a determined enemy but also challenging terrain and adverse weather conditions. The torrential rains of late May turned the battlefield into a quagmire, further complicating the American advance.

**Civilian Tragedy: Caught in the Crossfire**

One of the most tragic aspects of the Battle of Okinawa was the enormous toll it took on the civilian population. Unlike many other Pacific islands, Okinawa had a large indigenous population of over 300,000 people. These civilians found themselves caught between the advancing Americans and the desperate Japanese defenders.

The stories of civilians like Masako Robbins and Kiku Nakayama provide heart-wrenching insights into the civilian experience of the battle. Robbins, originally sold into a brothel as a child, was drafted as a combat nurse by the Japanese military. She survived being trapped in a collapsed cave due to shelling, only to find herself later in a refugee camp.

Nakayama, who was 16 at the time, recounts the terror of being handed grenades by Japanese soldiers and instructed to use them against American troops. The psychological trauma of these experiences lingered long after the war, a testament to the lasting impact of the battle on the civilian population.

The Japanese military's treatment of civilians was often brutal. Many Okinawans were forced to serve as human shields or were summarily executed on suspicion of spying. Others were encouraged or forced to commit suicide rather than fall into American hands, a tragic result of Japanese propaganda that portrayed the Americans as brutal invaders.

**Acts of Heroism: Hacksaw Ridge and Humanitarian Efforts**

Amidst the carnage and destruction, there were also remarkable acts of heroism and compassion. One of the most famous examples is the story of Desmond Doss, a conscientious objector serving as a medic with the 307th Infantry Regiment. During the battle for the Maeda Escarpment, known as Hacksaw Ridge, Doss single-handedly saved the lives of 75 wounded men, lowering them down a cliff face while under constant enemy fire. For his actions, Doss was awarded the Medal of Honor, the only conscientious objector to receive this honor during World War II.

Another poignant story is that of Morimasa Kaneshiro, a Nisei (second-generation Japanese-American) soldier serving as an interpreter for the U.S. Navy. Kaneshiro played a crucial role in humanitarian efforts during the battle, using his ability to speak Japanese to build trust with civilians hiding in caves. His efforts saved numerous lives, including that of Yoshino Nakasone, a young girl he helped evacuate along with her grandparents.

These stories of individual bravery and compassion stand in stark contrast to the overall brutality of the battle, reminding us of the human capacity for courage and kindness even in the darkest of circumstances.

**The Final Push: Ushijima's Last Stand**

As June arrived, the battle entered its final, desperate phase. The Shuri Line had been breached, and the Japanese forces were pushed back to their final defensive positions in the southern part of the island. General Ushijima, realizing that defeat was inevitable, prepared for a final stand.

The fighting in these last weeks was some of the most intense of the entire campaign. The Japanese, running low on supplies and with no hope of reinforcement, fought with the desperation of men who knew they were doomed. Many chose suicide over surrender, in keeping with the Japanese military code of the time.

On June 18, in a cruel twist of fate, Lieutenant General Buckner was killed by Japanese artillery fire while observing front-line operations, becoming the highest-ranking U.S. military officer killed by enemy fire during World War II. Command of the Tenth Army passed to Marine General Roy Geiger.

As the noose tightened around the remaining Japanese forces, Ushijima and his chief of staff, Cho, decided to commit ritual suicide rather than surrender. On June 22, 1945, they performed seppuku, marking the effective end of organized Japanese resistance on Okinawa.

**Aftermath and Significance**

The Battle of Okinawa officially ended on June 22, 1945, after 82 days of brutal combat. The human cost was staggering. The United States suffered over 49,000 casualties, including more than 12,500 killed. Japanese military losses were even greater, with approximately 110,000 soldiers killed. Most tragically, Okinawan civilian casualties were estimated between 40,000 and 150,000, representing a significant portion of the island's population.

The capture of Okinawa provided the Allies with a crucial base for the planned invasion of Japan. However, the ferocity of the battle and the high casualty rates on both sides gave American military planners pause. The use of kamikaze tactics and the fanatical resistance of the Japanese forces on Okinawa suggested that an invasion of the Japanese home islands would be extremely costly.

This realization played a significant role in the decision to use atomic weapons against Japan. The experience of Okinawa, combined with the desire to avoid a potentially catastrophic invasion, contributed to President Harry S. Truman's decision to use nuclear weapons on Hiroshima and Nagasaki in August 1945.

**Conclusion**

The Battle of Okinawa stands as a testament to the courage, endurance, and sacrifice of those who fought there, as well as the tragic cost of war for civilian populations caught in the crossfire. It was a battle that tested the limits of human endurance, fought in a hostile environment against a determined enemy.

The Battle of Okinawa, with its strategic significance and human drama, remains a powerful reminder of the complexities of war and the indomitable spirit of those who fight. It stands as a turning point in the Pacific War, the moment when the Allies brought the fight to Japan's doorstep, setting the stage for the final acts of World War II and shaping the geopolitical landscape of the post-war world.

**Sources**

Frank, Richard B. Guadalcanal: The Definitive Account of the Landmark Battle. Penguin Books, 1992.

Hama, Larry. The Battle of Guadalcanal: Land and Sea Warfare in the South Pacific. Rosen Pub Group, 2006.

Various Sources

# The Dawn of the Atomic Age: Hiroshima and Nagasaki

## Introduction

In the sweltering summer of 1945, as World War II entered its final, desperate phase, a pivotal moment in human history was about to unfold. The atomic bombings of Hiroshima and Nagasaki on August 6 and 9, 1945, respectively, would not only bring an abrupt end to the most destructive conflict in history but also usher in a new era of global politics and existential fear. These events, characterized by their unprecedented destructive power and long-lasting consequences, would forever change the course of warfare and international relations.

As the sun rose over the Japanese archipelago on those fateful August mornings, neither the Allied forces nor the Japanese people could have fully grasped the significance of what was about to transpire. The outcome would shape the course of the 20th century, influence the fate of nations, and forever change our understanding of the awesome and terrible power of science. This is the story of the dawn of the atomic age, a tale of scientific achievement, military strategy, and the profound human cost of warfare taken to its ultimate extreme.

## The Road to the Atomic Bomb

The roots of the atomic bombings can be traced back to the early 20th century, with the groundbreaking work of scientists like Ernest Rutherford, Niels Bohr, and Albert Einstein. Their research into the nature of the atom laid the foundation for the discovery of nuclear fission in the late 1930s. This scientific breakthrough, coupled with the looming threat of World War II, set the stage for one of the most ambitious and secretive scientific endeavors in history: the Manhattan Project.

As war engulfed Europe and the Pacific, fears that Nazi Germany might develop an atomic bomb spurred the United States into action. In 1939, Albert Einstein, urged by fellow physicist Leo Szilard, wrote a letter to President Franklin D. Roosevelt, warning of the potential for an atomic weapon and the danger of Germany acquiring such technology. This letter set in motion a chain of events that would culminate in the development of the world's first nuclear weapons.

The Manhattan Project, officially established in 1942, brought together some of the greatest scientific minds of the time under the leadership of physicist J. Robert Oppenheimer and the military oversight of General Leslie Groves. Operating in utmost secrecy, teams of scientists and engineers worked tirelessly at various sites across the United States, including Los Alamos, New Mexico, Oak Ridge, Tennessee, and Hanford, Washington.

The scale and complexity of the Manhattan Project were staggering. At its peak, it employed over 130,000 people and cost nearly $2 billion (equivalent to about $23 billion in 2021). The project's goal was clear yet daunting: to harness the power of the atom and create a weapon of unprecedented destructive capability.

As the war in Europe came to an end in May 1945 with the surrender of Nazi Germany, attention turned to the Pacific Theater, where Japan continued to fight fiercely. The Battle of Okinawa, which had concluded in June, offered a grim preview of what an invasion of the Japanese mainland might entail. American military planners estimated that such an invasion could result in up to a million Allied casualties.

It was in this context that newly sworn-in President Harry S. Truman faced one of the most momentous decisions in history. On July 16, 1945, the first atomic bomb was successfully tested in the New Mexico desert in what was codenamed the Trinity test. The awesome power of the explosion left many of the observing scientists awestruck and troubled. J. Robert Oppenheimer, recalling the event years later, quoted a line from the Hindu scripture Bhagavad Gita: "Now I am become Death, the destroyer of worlds".

With the success of the Trinity test, Truman and his advisors were presented with a new option to end the war. The decision to use the atomic bomb was influenced by a complex mix of military strategy, political considerations, and the desire to bring a swift end to the conflict. On July 26, 1945, the United States, along with Great Britain and China, issued the Potsdam Declaration, demanding Japan's unconditional surrender and warning of "prompt and utter destruction" if they refused.

Japan's militarist government, however, chose to ignore this ultimatum. With this rejection, the stage was set for the unleashing of a weapon that would change the world forever.

**The Bombing of Hiroshima**

On the morning of August 6, 1945, the citizens of Hiroshima went about their daily routines, unaware that their city had been chosen as the target for the first atomic bomb used in warfare. At 8:15 AM, a B-29 bomber named Enola Gay, piloted by Colonel Paul W. Tibbets, approached the city at an altitude of 31,000 feet.

As the bomb bay doors opened, a single atomic bomb, codenamed "Little Boy," was released. The uranium-based device, weighing over 9,000 pounds, fell for 43 seconds before detonating approximately 1,900 feet above the city center. The explosion unleashed a blinding flash of light, followed by a massive fireball and shockwave that devastated everything within a mile radius.

The immediate impact was catastrophic. An estimated 80,000 people were killed instantly, with tens of thousands more succumbing to injuries and radiation exposure in the following days and weeks. The bomb obliterated approximately five square miles of the city, reducing it to ashes and rubble.

Survivors of the initial blast, known as hibakusha, described scenes of unimaginable horror. Masako Robbins, a young woman who had been drafted as a combat nurse, recalled being trapped in a collapsed cave due to the shelling. "The quiet was unearthly," she later recounted. "It felt like we were landing on a dead planet".

The devastation was not limited to the immediate blast area. The intense heat from the explosion caused severe burns to those exposed, while the radiation released had both immediate and long-term effects on survivors. Many who appeared uninjured at first began to show symptoms of radiation sickness in the days following the bombing, suffering from nausea, bleeding, and hair loss.

As news of the bombing reached Tokyo, the Japanese government struggled to comprehend the nature of this new weapon. Emperor Hirohito dispatched a team to Hiroshima to investigate, but before they could fully report their findings, a second atomic bomb was on its way to Japan.

## The Bombing of Nagasaki

On August 9, 1945, just three days after the Hiroshima bombing, a second B-29 bomber, named Bockscar and piloted by Major Charles Sweeney, took off with another atomic bomb. The primary target was the city of Kokura, but due to poor visibility, the mission was diverted to the secondary target: Nagasaki.

At 11:02 AM, the plutonium-based bomb, codenamed "Fat Man," was dropped over Nagasaki. The bomb exploded with a force equivalent to 21 kilotons of TNT, approximately 1,650 feet above the city. Unlike the flat terrain of Hiroshima, Nagasaki's hilly topography somewhat contained the blast, but the destruction was still catastrophic.

The immediate death toll in Nagasaki was estimated at 40,000, with the total rising to approximately 70,000 by the end of 1945. The bomb destroyed about 30% of the city, including significant industrial areas and residential neighborhoods.

The human suffering in both cities was immense. Survivors like Kiku Nakayama, who was 16 at the time of the Nagasaki bombing, carried the trauma for decades. Nakayama recalled being handed grenades by Japanese soldiers and instructed to use them against American troops, a chilling reminder of the desperation that gripped Japan in the final days of the war.

## The Decision to Surrender

The dual atomic bombings, combined with the Soviet Union's declaration of war on Japan on August 8, finally broke the resolve of Japan's leadership. On August 15, 1945, Emperor Hirohito announced Japan's surrender in a radio broadcast, marking the end of World War II.

The decision to use atomic weapons remains one of the most controversial in military history. Proponents argue that it saved lives by avoiding a costly invasion of Japan, while critics contend that Japan was already on the brink of surrender and that the bombings were unnecessary and inhumane.

## The Aftermath and Long-term Consequences

The immediate aftermath of the bombings was characterized by chaos and suffering. The cities of Hiroshima and Nagasaki lay in ruins, with survivors struggling to find food, water, and medical assistance. The unprecedented nature of the atomic explosions meant that many victims suffered from radiation sickness, a condition that local doctors were ill-equipped to treat.

The long-term health effects of the bombings have been the subject of extensive study. Survivors faced an increased risk of various cancers, particularly leukemia and thyroid cancer. The psychological trauma of the bombings also left deep scars, with many hibakusha suffering from post-traumatic stress disorder and facing social stigma.

The global impact of the atomic bombings was profound. The demonstration of nuclear weapons' destructive power ushered in the Cold War era, characterized by an arms race between the United States and the Soviet Union. The fear of nuclear annihilation became a constant undercurrent in global politics and popular culture.

The bombings also sparked intense ethical debates about the use of nuclear weapons and the responsibilities of scientists in military research. Many of the scientists involved in the Manhattan Project, including J. Robert Oppenheimer, later expressed regret and moral anguish over their role in developing these weapons of mass destruction.

**Conclusion**

The atomic bombings of Hiroshima and Nagasaki stand as watershed moments in human history, marking both the end of World War II and the beginning of the nuclear age. These events demonstrated the awesome and terrible power of science harnessed for destruction, forever changing the nature of warfare and international relations.

The legacy of Hiroshima and Nagasaki continues to shape our world today, influencing debates on nuclear proliferation, the ethics of warfare, and the pursuit of peace. As we face the challenges of the 21st century, the lessons of the atomic bombings remain as relevant as ever, urging us to consider the consequences of our actions and to strive for a world free from the shadow of nuclear destruction.

**Sources**

Hastings, Sir Max. Retribution: The Battle for Japan, 1944-45. Knopf, 2008.

Miller, Edward S. War Plan Orange: The US Strategy to Defeat Japan, 1897-1945. Annapolis: Naval Institute Press, 1991.

Various Sources

# Japan's Surrender in Tokyo Bay

**Introduction**

In the late summer of 1945, as the world emerged from the most devastating conflict in human history, a pivotal moment was about to unfold in the calm waters of Tokyo Bay. The Japanese surrender to the Allied forces, which took place on September 2, 1945, aboard the USS Missouri, would not only mark the formal end of World War II but also usher in a new era of global politics and international relations. This event, characterized by its solemn pageantry and profound significance, would forever change the course of history for Japan, the United States, and the world at large.

As the sun rose over the waters of Tokyo Bay on that fateful September morning, neither the Allied forces nor the Japanese delegation could have fully grasped the long-term implications of what was about to transpire. The outcome would shape the course of the 20th century, influence the fate of nations, and set the stage for a new world order. This is the story of the Japanese surrender in Tokyo Bay, a tale of military strategy, diplomatic maneuvering, and the profound human cost of war, culminating in a moment that would echo through the ages.

**The Road to Surrender**

The path to Japan's surrender was paved with a series of devastating military defeats and unprecedented destruction. By mid-1945, Japan's once-mighty empire was crumbling. The Imperial Japanese Navy, which had dominated the Pacific at the war's outset, was no longer capable of conducting major operations. Allied forces, spearheaded by the United States, had steadily advanced across the Pacific, reclaiming territory and pushing ever closer to the Japanese home islands.

The turning point came with the atomic bombings of Hiroshima and Nagasaki on August 6 and 9, 1945, respectively. These attacks, which unleashed a destructive power never before seen in warfare, shocked the Japanese leadership and populace alike. The devastation wrought by these new weapons was compounded by the Soviet Union's declaration of war on Japan on August 8, shattering any hope of Soviet mediation to end the conflict on more favorable terms.

Within Japan, a fierce debate raged among the leadership. The Supreme Council for the Direction of the War, also known as the "Big Six," was deeply divided on the issue of surrender. While some, including

Prime Minister Kantaro Suzuki and Foreign Minister Shigenori Togo, saw the futility of continued resistance, others, particularly among the military leadership, advocated fighting to the bitter end.

It was in this context of internal strife and external pressure that Emperor Hirohito made the momentous decision to intervene. In a move unprecedented in Japanese history, the Emperor broke the deadlock within the Supreme Council, urging them to accept the terms of the Potsdam Declaration and sue for peace. His decision was influenced not only by the atomic bombings and Soviet invasion but also by a deep concern for the suffering of the Japanese people and the very survival of the nation.

On August 15, 1945, in a pre-recorded radio broadcast, Emperor Hirohito announced to a stunned nation that Japan would accept the Allied terms of unconditional surrender. This "Jewel Voice Broadcast," as it came to be known, was the first time many Japanese had ever heard their Emperor's voice. The Emperor's words, couched in formal and indirect language, spoke of "enduring the unendurable and suffering what is insufferable" for the sake of peace.

**The Stage is Set**

With Japan's decision to surrender, attention turned to the formal ceremony that would officially end the war. The choice of venue for this historic event fell to the USS Missouri, a powerful Iowa-class battleship that symbolized American military might. The selection of the Missouri was not without significance; the ship was named after President Harry Truman's home state, a fitting choice given Truman's role in the decision to use atomic weapons against Japan.

As preparations for the ceremony began, General Douglas MacArthur, the Supreme Commander for the Allied Powers, took charge of the proceedings. Known for his theatrical flair and keen sense of history, MacArthur orchestrated every detail of the surrender ceremony with meticulous care. From the positioning of the Allied representatives to the timing of the flyover by hundreds of Allied aircraft, nothing was left to chance.

The USS Missouri steamed into Tokyo Bay on August 29, 1945, joining a massive assemblage of Allied warships. The bay, once the launching point for the attack on Pearl Harbor, now bore silent witness to the final act of the Pacific War. As the Missouri dropped anchor, the stage was set for one of the most significant ceremonies in modern history.

**The Surrender Ceremony**

On the morning of September 2, 1945, under a clear sky that seemed to mock the solemnity of the occasion, Allied and Japanese representatives gathered on the deck of the USS Missouri. The ceremony was brief, lasting only 23 minutes, but its impact would resonate for generations.

At precisely 9:02 a.m., General MacArthur stepped forward to open the proceedings. His carefully chosen words set the tone for the event: "We are gathered here, representatives of the major warring powers, to conclude a solemn agreement whereby peace may be restored."

The Japanese delegation, led by Foreign Minister Mamoru Shigemitsu and General Yoshijiro Umezu, presented a stark contrast to the victorious Allies. Dressed in formal morning coats and top hats, they appeared as if attending a state funeral rather than a surrender ceremony. As they approached the table to sign the Instrument of Surrender, the weight of the moment was palpable.

Shigemitsu, representing the civilian government, signed first, his hand trembling slightly as he put pen to paper. General Umezu followed, signing on behalf of the Imperial General Headquarters. With these signatures, Japan formally surrendered to the Allied powers, bringing an end to nearly four years of brutal conflict in the Pacific.

General MacArthur then signed on behalf of the Allied powers, using six pens to complete his signature. In a gesture laden with symbolism, he handed two of these pens to Generals Jonathan Wainwright and Arthur Percival, both of whom had endured years of captivity following the fall of the Philippines and Singapore, respectively. Their presence on the Missouri's deck, standing tall despite their ordeal, served as a powerful reminder of the early defeats that had now been avenged.

As the other Allied representatives stepped forward to add their signatures, the ceremony took on an air of finality. Fleet Admiral Chester Nimitz signed for the United States, followed by representatives from China, the United Kingdom, the Soviet Union, Australia, Canada, France, the Netherlands, and New Zealand. Each signature represented not just a nation, but the countless lives lost and sacrifices made in the long struggle against Japanese aggression.

With the signing complete, General MacArthur delivered his closing remarks, words that would echo through history: "Let us pray that peace be now restored to the world, and that God will preserve it always. These proceedings are closed!"

As if on cue, the sky above Tokyo Bay filled with the roar of engines as hundreds of Allied aircraft flew overhead in a massive show of force. The war was over, but the work of rebuilding a shattered world was just beginning.

**The Aftermath and Long-term Consequences**

The Japanese surrender in Tokyo Bay marked not just the end of World War II, but the beginning of a new era in global politics and international relations. The immediate aftermath saw the occupation of Japan by Allied forces, primarily led by the United States under General MacArthur's command.

This occupation period would prove transformative for Japan. Under MacArthur's guidance, sweeping reforms were implemented, fundamentally altering Japan's political, economic, and social landscape. A new constitution was drafted, renouncing war as a sovereign right and establishing a parliamentary democracy. The Emperor, once considered divine, was reduced to a symbolic figurehead.

The economic reforms implemented during the occupation laid the groundwork for Japan's remarkable post-war recovery. Land reform redistributed property from large landowners to tenant farmers, reshaping rural society. The zaibatsu, powerful family-controlled conglomerates, were broken up, paving the way for a more competitive and dynamic economy.

On the international stage, the end of World War II and Japan's surrender contributed to the establishment of the United Nations, an organization dedicated to preventing future global conflicts. Japan's reintegration into the international community was marked by its admission to the UN in 1956, symbolizing its return as a peaceful nation.

The use of atomic weapons in the final days of the war cast a long shadow over the post-war world. The devastating power of these new weapons sparked a global discourse on nuclear disarmament and arms control, influencing international relations for decades to come.

Perhaps most remarkably, the relationship between Japan and the United States, once bitter enemies, evolved into a strong alliance. This partnership would play a crucial role in shaping the geopolitics of the Cold War and beyond.

**Conclusion**

The Japanese surrender in Tokyo Bay on September 2, 1945, stands as a watershed moment in world history. It marked not only the end of the most destructive conflict humanity had ever known but also the beginning of a new world order. The ceremony aboard the USS Missouri, with its carefully choreographed symbolism and solemn pageantry, provided a fitting conclusion to six years of global warfare.

The legacy of the Japanese surrender continues to shape our world today. It serves as a powerful reminder of the consequences of unchecked aggression, the horrors of total war, and the importance of international cooperation in maintaining peace. As we face the challenges of the 21st century, the lessons of that solemn ceremony in Tokyo Bay remain as relevant as ever, urging us to work tirelessly for a world where such surrenders are no longer necessary.

In the words of General MacArthur, spoken as the ceremony concluded: "Let us pray that peace be now restored to the world, and that God will preserve it always." It is a sentiment that echoes through time, a plea for humanity to learn from its past and to strive for a future where the horrors of war remain firmly in the realm of history.

**Sources**

Thomas, Evan. Road to Surrender: Three Men and the Countdown to the End of World War II. Random House, 2023.

Miller, Edward S. War Plan Orange: The US Strategy to Defeat Japan, 1897-1945. Annapolis: Naval Institute Press, 1991.

Various Sources

# The Japan War Crime Trials

## Introduction

In the aftermath of World War II, as the world grappled with the unprecedented scale of destruction and human suffering, a pivotal chapter in international justice was about to unfold in Tokyo, Japan. The International Military Tribunal for the Far East (IMTFE), commonly known as the Japan War Crime Trials or the Tokyo Trials, would not only seek justice for the atrocities committed during the war but also set the stage for the future of international criminal law. From 1946 to 1948, the world watched as high-ranking Japanese military and political leaders faced charges for their roles in one of the most devastating conflicts in human history.

As the sun rose over Tokyo Bay on April 29, 1946, neither the Allied powers nor the Japanese defendants could have fully grasped the long-term implications of what was about to transpire. The outcome would shape the course of post-war Japan, influence the development of international law, and set precedents for addressing war crimes and crimes against humanity for generations to come. This is the story of the Japan War Crime Trials, a tale of justice, controversy, and the complex process of reconciliation in the wake of global conflict.

## Narrative

### The Road to the Trials

The roots of the Japan War Crime Trials can be traced back to Japan's aggressive expansionist policies in the years leading up to and during World War II. The invasion of Manchuria in 1931 marked the beginning of Japan's campaign to dominate Southeast Asia and the Pacific. This aggression escalated with the invasion of China in 1937, leading to the infamous Nanjing Massacre, where Japanese forces committed widespread atrocities against civilians and prisoners of war.

As World War II progressed, Japan's military actions extended across Asia and the Pacific, resulting in numerous war crimes, including the mistreatment of prisoners of war and the use of chemical and biological warfare. The Allied powers, particularly the United States, became increasingly determined to hold Japanese leaders accountable for these actions.

The legal groundwork for the trials was laid in a series of wartime declarations and agreements. The Potsdam Declaration of July 1945, issued by the Allied leaders, explicitly called for the prosecution of those who had "deceived and misled" the Japanese people into war. This declaration emphasized the need to eliminate militaristic influences in Japan and ensure justice for war crimes, including the inhumane treatment of Allied prisoners.

Following Japan's surrender in August 1945, General Douglas MacArthur was appointed as the Supreme Commander for the Allied Powers (SCAP) and oversaw the occupation of Japan. Under his leadership, the stage was set for the war crime trials that would seek to bring justice to the victims of Japanese aggression and reshape the future of the defeated nation.

**Establishment of the Tribunal**

On January 19, 1946, General MacArthur issued a special proclamation ordering the establishment of the International Military Tribunal for the Far East (IMTFE). The tribunal was modeled after the Nuremberg Trials in Germany, which had begun just months earlier. The IMTFE was tasked with trying Japanese leaders for crimes against peace, conventional war crimes, and crimes against humanity.

The structure of the tribunal reflected its international nature. Judges were appointed from eleven Allied nations: Australia, Canada, China, France, India, the Netherlands, New Zealand, the Philippines, the Soviet Union, the United Kingdom, and the United States. The tribunal's president was Sir William Webb from Australia, who played a crucial role in maintaining the tribunal's focus and ensuring fair trial standards.

The prosecution team was led by chief prosecutor Joseph B. Keenan, appointed by U.S. President Harry S. Truman. Keenan was responsible for coordinating the efforts of the international team of prosecutors from the Allied nations. Their task was monumental: to present evidence of Japan's wartime atrocities and prove the culpability of its leaders in a way that would stand up to international scrutiny.

**The Charges and Defendants**

Twenty-eight high-ranking Japanese military and political leaders were indicted on 55 counts of crimes against peace, war crimes, and crimes against humanity. The charges covered a wide range of offenses, including:

1. Conspiracy to wage aggressive war

2. Waging aggressive war

3. Conventional war crimes, including the mistreatment of prisoners of war

4. Crimes against humanity, such as the mass murder of civilians

Among the most prominent defendants was General Hideki Tojo, who had served as Prime Minister of Japan during much of the war. Tojo faced multiple counts of crimes against peace, war crimes, and crimes against humanity. Other notable defendants included Kōki Hirota, a former Prime Minister and Foreign Minister, and General Iwane Matsui, who was charged for his role in the Nanking Massacre.

The inclusion of "crimes against peace" as a charge was particularly significant, as it established the principle that individuals could be held accountable for planning and initiating wars of aggression, a concept that would have far-reaching implications for international law.

## The Proceedings

The trials began on May 3, 1946, in the War Ministry office in Tokyo, which had been converted into a courtroom for the proceedings. Over the next two and a half years, the tribunal would hear testimony from 419 witnesses and review 4,336 pieces of evidence, including depositions and affidavits from 779 individuals.

The prosecution's case, presented over 192 days, sought to demonstrate the systematic nature of Japan's wartime atrocities and the direct involvement of the accused in planning and executing these crimes. The defense, which took 225 days to present its case, faced the challenging task of countering the overwhelming evidence presented by the prosecution.

Throughout the trials, the proceedings were marked by legal and cultural challenges. The use of multiple languages required extensive translation, slowing the pace of the trials. Additionally, the clash between different legal systems and cultural norms sometimes led to misunderstandings and controversies.

One of the most contentious aspects of the trials was the decision not to indict Emperor Hirohito. This decision, influenced by political considerations to maintain stability in post-war Japan, would remain a point of debate and criticism for years to come.

## Verdicts and Sentences

After months of deliberation, the tribunal reached its verdicts on November 12, 1948. The outcomes were as follows:

- Seven defendants, including General Hideki Tojo and Kōki Hirota, were sentenced to death by hanging for their roles in planning and executing the war.

- Sixteen defendants received life sentences. Some of these individuals were later paroled in the 1950s.

- Two defendants received lesser sentences.

- Charges were dropped against one defendant due to mental unfitness.

The executions of those sentenced to death were carried out at Sugamo Prison in Tokyo on December 23, 1948. These executions marked the end of the trial phase but were far from the end of the trials' impact on Japan and the world.

## Aftermath and Long-Term Impact

The Japan War Crime Trials had profound and far-reaching consequences, both for Japan and for the international community. In Japan, the trials were part of a broader effort to demilitarize and democratize the nation. Under the supervision of the Allied occupation, Japan underwent significant political and social transformations, including the drafting of a new constitution that reduced the emperor's role to a symbolic figurehead and promoted democratic governance.

The trials also played a crucial role in Japan's economic reconstruction. The occupation authorities implemented reforms to dismantle the zaibatsu (large industrial conglomerates) and promote a free-market economy, which contributed to Japan's remarkable post-war economic recovery.

On the international stage, the Tokyo Trials, alongside the Nuremberg Trials, were instrumental in the development of international criminal law. They established precedents for prosecuting war crimes, crimes against humanity, and crimes against peace, which have been incorporated into subsequent international legal frameworks. The concept of individual criminal responsibility for state actions, regardless of official position, became a cornerstone of international justice.

However, the trials were not without criticism. Some viewed them as "victor's justice," arguing that they were biased towards the Allied powers and overlooked potential war crimes committed by the Allies themselves. The immunity granted to certain groups, such as those involved in Unit 731's biological experiments, in exchange for their research data, remains a controversial aspect of the trials.

Despite these criticisms, the legal principles and procedures developed during the Tokyo Trials have had a lasting impact. They have influenced the establishment of modern international criminal courts, such as the International Criminal Court (ICC), which continue to prosecute individuals for serious international crimes.

## Conclusion

The Japan War Crime Trials stand as a watershed moment in the history of international justice. They marked not only the end of World War II in the Pacific but also the beginning of a new era in which individuals could be held accountable for actions taken in the name of the state. The trials grappled with fundamental questions of justice, responsibility, and reconciliation in the aftermath of unprecedented global conflict.

As we reflect on the events of those two and a half years in Tokyo, we are reminded of the complex interplay between justice, politics, and national interests in the international arena. The trials' legacy is evident in the ongoing efforts to uphold international justice and accountability, from the tribunals for the former Yugoslavia and Rwanda to the permanent International Criminal Court.

The transformation of Japan from a militaristic empire to a peaceful, democratic nation in the wake of the trials is perhaps one of their most remarkable outcomes. It demonstrates the potential for change and renewal even in the aftermath of devastating conflict.

Yet, the controversies and criticisms surrounding the trials also serve as a reminder of the challenges inherent in pursuing international justice. They underscore the importance of continually refining and improving our approaches to addressing war crimes and crimes against humanity.

In the end, the Japan War Crime Trials remain a powerful testament to the international community's commitment to justice and the rule of law. They stand as a solemn reminder of the costs of war and the enduring hope for a more peaceful world. As we face the challenges of the 21st century, the lessons of the

Tokyo Trials continue to resonate, urging us to remain vigilant in the pursuit of justice and the prevention of atrocities.

**Sources**

Bass, Gary J. Judgement at Tokyo: World War II on Trial and the Making of Modern Asia. Knopf, 2023.

Totani, Yuma. The Tokyo War Crimes Trial: The Pursuit of Justice in the Wake of World War II. Harvard University Press Asia Center, 2009.

Various Sources

# Stories from the Pearl Harbor Attack

# John William Finn

## Introduction

Among the heroic stories from Pearl Harbor, comes the true tale of John William Finn. His extraordinary acts of bravery during the attack on Pearl Harbor not only earned him the Medal of Honor but also cemented his place as a symbol of American courage and resilience. This narrative explores the life of John Finn, from his humble beginnings to his heroic actions on December 7, 1941, and beyond, painting a picture of a man whose dedication to duty and country left an indelible mark on the nation's history.

## Early Life and Naval Career

John William Finn's journey began on July 23, 1909, in Los Angeles County, California. Born into modest circumstances, Finn's formal education ended after the seventh grade. However, his lack of schooling did not diminish his ambition or his desire to see the world. Driven by a thirst for adventure and a sense of duty, Finn enlisted in the United States Navy in July 1926, just shy of his seventeenth birthday.

Finn's early naval career was marked by a rapid ascension through the ranks, a testament to his work ethic and aptitude. After completing recruit training in San Diego, he served with a ceremonial guard company before attending General Aviation Utilities Training at Naval Station Great Lakes. This training laid the foundation for his expertise in aircraft maintenance and ordnance handling, skills that would prove crucial in the years to come.

By 1935, at the age of 26, Finn had achieved the rank of Chief Petty Officer, an impressive feat in the competitive pre-World War II Navy. His career took him to various naval ships, including the USS Lexington, USS Houston, USS Jason, USS Saratoga, and USS Cincinnati, fulfilling his youthful desire for travel and new experiences.

## The Day That Changed Everything

On the morning of December 7, 1941, Chief Petty Officer John Finn was stationed at Naval Air Station Kaneohe Bay on the island of Oahu, Hawaii. As the Chief Aviation Ordnanceman, he was responsible for a team of twenty men tasked with maintaining the weapons of a squadron of PBY Catalina flying boats.

Little did he know that this ordinary Sunday morning would thrust him into the center of one of the most pivotal moments in American history.

The tranquility of the Hawaiian morning was shattered by the sound of aircraft overhead. Finn, who was at home when the attack began, quickly realized the gravity of the situation. Without hesitation, he drove to his duty station, arriving to find the base under heavy attack by Japanese aircraft.

In the face of chaos and danger, Finn's training and courage came to the fore. He secured a .50-caliber machine gun from one of the planes he maintained and, in an act of extraordinary bravery, mounted it on an instruction stand in an exposed section of the parking ramp. This area was under intense enemy fire, yet Finn manned the gun with complete disregard for his personal safety.

For over two hours, Finn fired at the attacking Japanese planes, his determination unwavering despite sustaining numerous painful wounds. He was hit by shrapnel in his left arm, left foot, chest, and abdomen. His scalp was lacerated, and his right elbow and thumb were damaged. Yet, through it all, Finn continued to operate the machine gun, providing a crucial defense against the onslaught.

Finn's own words best capture the intensity of the moment: "I got that gun and I started shooting at Japanese planes," he recounted in a later interview. "I was out there shooting the Jap planes and just every so often I was a target for some," he added, with characteristic understatement.

Only when explicitly ordered did Finn leave his post to seek medical attention. Even then, his sense of duty remained paramount. After receiving first-aid treatment, he returned to supervise the rearming of returning planes, ensuring that the counterattack could proceed.

**Recognition and the Medal of Honor**

John Finn's extraordinary actions on that fateful day did not go unnoticed. He became the first service member to receive the Medal of Honor during World War II. The citation for his Medal of Honor eloquently captures the essence of his heroism, noting his "extraordinary heroism, distinguished service, and devotion above and beyond the call of duty".

On September 14, 1942, in a ceremony aboard the USS Enterprise at Pearl Harbor, Admiral Chester W. Nimitz presented Finn with the Medal of Honor. This moment not only recognized Finn's individual bravery but also symbolized the resilience and fighting spirit of the entire U.S. Navy in the face of the Pearl Harbor attack.

**Continued Service and Later Life**

John Finn's military career did not end with his heroic actions at Pearl Harbor. He continued to serve in the Navy, transitioning to Limited Duty Officer with the rank of Ensign in 1942. After five years, he chose to revert to his enlisted rank of Chief Petty Officer, eventually rising to the rank of Lieutenant before his retirement in 1956.

Throughout World War II and beyond, Finn served in various capacities, including with Bombing Squadron VB-102 and aboard the USS Hancock. His 30-year naval career was a testament to his unwavering commitment to service and his country.

Upon retirement, Finn settled on a 90-acre ranch in Live Oak Springs, near Pine Valley, California. His dedication to service took on a new form as he and his wife, Alice, became foster parents to five Native American children. This act of kindness fostered a close relationship with the Campo Band of Diegueño Mission Indians, demonstrating Finn's commitment to community and family even in his civilian life.

## Legacy and Final Years

In his later years, John Finn remained an active figure in veteran affairs, making numerous appearances at events honoring veterans and Pearl Harbor survivors. His presence at these events was a living link to one of the most significant moments in American history. In 2009, at the age of 100, Finn stood beside President Barack Obama during a wreath-laying ceremony at Arlington National Cemetery, a poignant reminder of the enduring impact of his generation's sacrifice.

Finn maintained a humble perspective on his actions throughout his life, often downplaying his heroism. "That damned hero stuff is a bunch of crap, I guess," he once remarked in a 2009 interview. "You gotta understand that there's all kinds of heroes, but they never got a chance to be in a hero's position". This modesty, combined with his undeniable courage, only served to enhance his stature as an American hero.

John William Finn passed away on May 27, 2010, at the age of 100, at the Chula Vista Veterans Home in California. He was laid to rest beside his wife at the Campo Indian Reservation's cemetery, a fitting final resting place for a man who had given so much to his country and community.

## Conclusion

John William Finn's life story is a testament to the power of courage, duty, and perseverance. From his humble beginnings to his heroic actions at Pearl Harbor and his continued service throughout World War II, Finn embodied the best qualities of the American military tradition. His bravery in the face of overwhelming odds during the Pearl Harbor attack not only earned him the Medal of Honor but also inspired generations of service members.

Finn's post-retirement years, marked by community involvement and mentorship, demonstrate that the spirit of service that defined his military career continued to guide his actions throughout his life. The naming of the USS John Finn (DDG-113), an Arleigh Burke-class destroyer, in his honor ensures that his story will continue to inspire future generations of sailors and citizens alike.

In the broader context of World War II, Finn's actions during the Pearl Harbor attack represent a microcosm of the American response to that day of infamy. His quick thinking, courage under fire, and unwavering dedication to duty mirror the national resolve that emerged from the ashes of Pearl Harbor. As the United States transitioned from a peacetime footing to become the "Arsenal of Democracy," individuals like John Finn led the way, setting an example of bravery and sacrifice that would characterize the American war effort.

John William Finn's life reminds us of the extraordinary potential that lies within ordinary individuals when faced with extraordinary circumstances. His story is not just one of personal heroism, but a reflection of the values and spirit that have shaped the American experience. As we face the challenges of the future, the legacy of John Finn and his generation continues to serve as a beacon of courage, resilience, and unwavering commitment to duty.

**Sources**

Tully, Anthony. Pearl Harbor: The Real Story. Naval Institute Press, 2006.

Lord, Walter. The Day of Infamy. Open Road Media, 2012.

Various Sources

# Admiral Isaac C. Kidd

**Introduction**

Few stories resonate as deeply as that of Rear Admiral Isaac Campbell Kidd. His extraordinary life, distinguished career, and heroic sacrifice during the attack on Pearl Harbor not only earned him the Medal of Honor but also cemented his place as a symbol of American courage and leadership. This narrative explores the life of Admiral Kidd, from his humble beginnings in Cleveland to his final moments aboard the USS Arizona, painting a picture of a man whose dedication to duty and country left an indelible mark on the nation's history.

**Early Life and Naval Career**

Isaac Campbell Kidd's journey began on March 26, 1884, in Cleveland, Ohio, born to Isaac and Jemima Campbell Kidd. Growing up in a diverse neighborhood of English, Irish, and German immigrants, many of whom worked on the Great Lakes, young Isaac was exposed to a maritime environment that would shape his future. His leadership qualities were evident from an early age, as he was recognized as a leader in both grade school and high school.

Kidd's path to naval service was set when he was recommended for an appointment to the U.S. Naval Academy by former Ohio Senator Marcus Hanna. Entering the academy in 1902, Kidd excelled not only in his studies but also in athletics, becoming the heavyweight boxing champion and playing football. His time at the Naval Academy laid the foundation for a career marked by dedication, courage, and leadership.

Upon graduating in 1906, Kidd was commissioned as an ensign in 1908. His early naval career was characterized by diverse assignments that broadened his experience and honed his skills. He served on the USS Columbia during the Panama Expedition of 1906 and was part of the Great White Fleet's global cruise from 1907 to 1909 aboard the USS New Jersey. These early

experiences exposed Kidd to the complexities of naval operations and international diplomacy, preparing him for the leadership roles he would later assume.

As Kidd's career progressed, he took on increasingly significant roles. During World War I, he was stationed on the USS New Mexico, although he did not see active combat. In the interwar years, Kidd served as an instructor at the U.S. Naval Academy from 1916 to 1917, sharing his knowledge and experience with the next generation of naval officers. His leadership abilities were further recognized as he took on executive roles, serving as the executive officer of the USS Utah and commanding officer of the USS Vega.

**Rise to Command**

Kidd's career reached new heights in 1938 when he was appointed as the commanding officer of the USS Arizona. This prestigious command was a testament to his leadership skills and strategic acumen. His time as the Arizona's captain was marked by a commitment to readiness and training, preparing the ship and its crew for the possibility of conflict in an increasingly tense global environment.

In February 1940, Kidd's exemplary service was rewarded with a promotion to Rear Admiral and appointment as Commander of Battleship Division One. This division, which included the USS Arizona, Nevada, and Pennsylvania, was a crucial component of the U.S. Pacific Fleet. The Arizona served as Kidd's flagship, a reflection of the trust placed in his leadership during a time of escalating global tensions.

As Commander of Battleship Division One, Kidd was known for his attention to detail and his ability to inspire those under his command. He developed a deep knowledge of his crew and their families, earning both respect and a degree of fear among the sailors. This personal approach to leadership fostered a sense of unity and purpose within the division, crucial elements for maintaining readiness in the face of potential conflict.

**The Road to Pearl Harbor**

As Kidd led Battleship Division One through training exercises and operations, the geopolitical situation in the Pacific was deteriorating rapidly. Japan's aggressive expansion in Asia, which had begun with the invasion of Manchuria in 1931 and escalated with the invasion of China in 1937, put it on a collision course with the United States. The U.S. response, which included economic sanctions and an oil embargo in 1940, further heightened tensions.

Throughout 1941, diplomatic efforts to resolve the growing crisis failed. Japan sought recognition of its territorial gains and an end to U.S. sanctions, while the U.S. demanded Japan's withdrawal from China and Indochina. As negotiations broke down, Japan began planning a preemptive strike against the United States, with Pearl Harbor as the primary target.

Unaware of the impending danger, Kidd continued to lead Battleship Division One with diligence and foresight. His focus on readiness and training would prove crucial in the face of the unexpected attack that was to come.

**The Attack on Pearl Harbor**

On the morning of December 7, 1941, the tranquility of Pearl Harbor was shattered by the arrival of Japanese aircraft. The USS Arizona, with Rear Admiral Kidd aboard, was moored at "Battleship Row" and quickly became a primary target for the attackers.

As the first bombs fell, Kidd immediately sprang into action, displaying the leadership and courage that had defined his career. Despite the chaos and danger, he manned the bridge of the Arizona alongside the ship's captain, Franklin Van Valkenburgh, directing the ship's defense. As the Senior Officer Present Afloat, Kidd's leadership was crucial during these initial moments of the attack.

At approximately 8:06 a.m., tragedy struck. A massive armor-piercing bomb penetrated the Arizona's decks, igniting the forward magazines. The resulting explosion was catastrophic, lifting the battleship out of the water and causing it to sink rapidly. In this moment of ultimate crisis, Rear Admiral Kidd was killed when a bomb hit directly on the bridge.

Kidd's death marked him as the first U.S. Navy flag officer to die in World War II and the first to be killed by a foreign enemy in American history. His final moments were characterized by the same courage and devotion to duty that had defined his entire career. In the face of overwhelming odds, Kidd remained at his post, leading his men until the very end.

**Legacy and Remembrance**

The attack on Pearl Harbor resulted in the loss of 1,177 crew members aboard the USS Arizona, nearly half of all U.S. military deaths at Pearl Harbor that day. Among these fallen heroes, Rear Admiral Kidd's sacrifice stood out as a symbol of leadership and courage in the face of adversity.

In recognition of his "conspicuous devotion to duty, extraordinary courage, and complete disregard of his own life," Kidd was posthumously awarded the Medal of Honor. This highest military decoration underscored the significance of his actions and the impact of his leadership during the attack.

Kidd's legacy extends far beyond his final moments at Pearl Harbor. His name lives on through the three U.S. Navy destroyers named in his honor. The first, USS Kidd (DD-661), commissioned in 1943, now serves as a museum ship and national historic landmark in Baton Rouge, Louisiana. The second, USS Kidd (DDG-993), was the lead ship of the Kidd-class destroyers, while the third, USS Kidd (DDG-100), an Arleigh Burke-class guided missile destroyer, was commissioned in 2007. These ships serve as floating memorials to Kidd's bravery and leadership, inspiring new generations of sailors.

In his hometown of Cleveland, Ohio, an Ohio Historical Marker stands outside the Naval Reserve Center near the lakefront, ensuring that Kidd's contributions are remembered in the city where his journey began. At the National Memorial Cemetery of the Pacific in Honolulu, Hawaii, Kidd's name is inscribed on the Wall of the Missing, a solemn reminder of his sacrifice alongside other service members who gave their lives during World War II.

**Conclusion**

Rear Admiral Isaac Campbell Kidd's life and career embody the highest ideals of naval service and leadership. From his early days in Cleveland to his final moments on the bridge of the USS Arizona, Kidd's journey was marked by unwavering dedication, exceptional courage, and a commitment to duty that transcended personal safety.

The attack on Pearl Harbor and the loss of leaders like Admiral Kidd serve as a somber reminder of the costs of war and the importance of vigilance and preparedness. Yet, from this tragedy emerged a renewed sense of national purpose and unity that would carry the United States through World War II and beyond.

Kidd's legacy continues to inspire and educate those who learn about the events of December 7, 1941. His story is not just one of personal heroism, but a reflection of the values and spirit that have shaped the American naval tradition. As we face the challenges of the future, the example set by Admiral Isaac C. Kidd remains a beacon of courage, leadership, and unwavering commitment to duty.

In the words of the Medal of Honor citation, Kidd's "distinguished service, extraordinary courage, and complete disregard of his own life, above and beyond the call of duty" stand as a testament to the best of American character. His sacrifice, along with those of his fellow servicemen, ensured that their loss would not be in vain, but would instead fuel the resolve that led to ultimate victory in World War II and shape the course of history for generations to come.

**Sources**

Prange, Gordon W. At Dawn We Slept: The Untold Story of Pearl Harbor. McGraw-Hill, 1981

Various Sources

# The Extraordinary Tale of George Welch and Kenneth Taylor

## Introduction

In the annals of American military history, few stories shine as brightly as that of George Welch and Kenneth Taylor. Their extraordinary acts of bravery during the attack on Pearl Harbor not only earned them national recognition but also cemented their place as symbols of American courage and resilience. This narrative explores the lives of these two remarkable pilots, from their humble beginnings to their heroic actions on December 7, 1941, and beyond, painting a picture of two men whose dedication to duty and country left an indelible mark on the nation's history.

As the sun rose over the Hawaiian Islands on that fateful December morning, neither Welch nor Taylor could have grasped the significance of what was about to transpire. Their actions in the face of overwhelming odds would not only shape their own destinies but also inspire generations of Americans to come. This is the story of two young pilots who, in the crucible of war, exemplified the best of American character and valor.

## Early Lives and Military Careers

George Schwartz Welch was born in Wilmington, Delaware, his early years marked by a keen interest in aviation that would shape his future. Kenneth Marlar Taylor entered the world on December 23, 1919, in Enid, Oklahoma, his path to the skies beginning in the heartland of America. Both men were drawn to the allure of flight, a passion that would lead them to the Army Air Corps and ultimately to the skies above Pearl Harbor.

Welch's journey took him directly from civilian life to military aviation, while Taylor's path included a brief stint as a pre-law student at the University of Oklahoma before answering the call to serve. Their paths converged at Wheeler Army Airfield in Honolulu, Hawaii, where they were assigned to the 47th Pursuit Squadron. Here, under the watchful eye of General Gordon Austin, they honed their skills in the Curtiss P-40B Warhawk, accumulating hundreds of flight hours and earning positions as flight commanders.

In the days leading up to December 7, 1941, Welch and Taylor found themselves at Haleiwa Field for gunnery practice, a temporary assignment that would prove fateful. On the night of December 6, the two young lieutenants attended a dance at the officers' club at Wheeler Field, followed by an all-night poker game. Little did they know that their evening of leisure would soon give way to a morning that would test their mettle and change their lives forever.

**The Day That Changed Everything**

As dawn broke over Oahu on December 7, 1941, the tranquility of the Hawaiian morning was shattered by the roar of aircraft engines and the thunder of explosions. At approximately 7:51 a.m., Welch and Taylor, still in their tuxedo pants from the previous night's festivities, were jolted awake by the sounds of war.

In a moment that would define their lives, Welch and Taylor sprang into action. Without waiting for orders, Taylor made a crucial phone call to Haleiwa Auxiliary Air Field, instructing ground crews to prepare their P-40 fighters for immediate takeoff. The two pilots then raced to Taylor's Buick, tearing down the road at speeds approaching 100 mph, their determination to reach their aircraft evident in every mile covered.

Arriving at Haleiwa, Welch and Taylor found their planes fueled but not fully armed. Undeterred by this setback and the overwhelming odds they faced, the two lieutenants took to the skies, becoming among the very few American pilots airborne during the initial wave of the Japanese attack.

What followed was a display of courage and skill that would become legendary. Facing an enemy force of 200 to 300 aircraft, Welch and Taylor engaged the Japanese fighters and bombers with a ferocity that belied their youth and relative inexperience. In their first sortie, Welch managed to shoot down two Japanese planes, while Taylor, despite sustaining injuries from enemy fire, was credited with at least two kills of his own.

After expending their ammunition, Welch and Taylor returned to Wheeler Field to rearm, defying orders to remain grounded as the second wave of Japanese planes approached. Their determination to return to the fight exemplified the spirit of resistance that would come to characterize America's response to the attack.

During their second sortie, Welch added two more enemy aircraft to his tally, bringing his total to four confirmed kills. Taylor, pushing through the pain of his injuries, continued to engage the enemy, his actions contributing significantly to the day's defensive efforts.

**Recognition and Aftermath**

In the immediate aftermath of the attack, the bravery of Welch and Taylor did not go unnoticed. Their quick thinking and valor under fire earned them the Distinguished Service Cross, making them the first recipients of this prestigious honor in World War II. The award, second only to the Medal of Honor, recognized their extraordinary heroism in the face of overwhelming odds.

Welch's actions were deemed so exceptional that he was nominated for the Medal of Honor. However, in a twist of fate that speaks to the chaos and confusion of that day, this nomination was reportedly denied because he had taken off without proper authorization from his superiors. Despite this setback, Welch's bravery remained celebrated, a testament to the impact of his actions.

Taylor, in addition to the Distinguished Service Cross, received the Purple Heart for the injuries he sustained during the attack. His wounds, far from deterring him, seemed to fuel his determination to continue the fight against the Axis powers.

## Continued Service and Later Lives

The attack on Pearl Harbor marked the beginning, not the end, of Welch and Taylor's service to their country. Both men continued to fly combat missions in the Pacific Theater, their experiences on December 7 having forged them into seasoned warriors.

George Welch's post-Pearl Harbor career was marked by continued excellence in the air. He flew nearly 350 combat missions, during which he shot down 12 more enemy aircraft, showcasing the skills that had served him so well on that fateful December morning. His combat career was cut short in 1943 due to malaria, which required hospitalization in Sydney, Australia. It was during this recovery period that Welch met his future wife, a testament to the unexpected turns life can take even amid war.

After the war, Welch transitioned to a career as a test pilot for North American Aviation. His daring spirit, evident in his actions at Pearl Harbor, found new expression in the world of experimental aircraft. Welch was involved in several significant aviation milestones, including claims that he broke the sound barrier in an unauthorized flight over the California desert in 1947, preceding Chuck Yeager's officially recognized flight. Tragically, Welch's life was cut short in 1954 when he died while ejecting from a disintegrating F-100 Super Sabre fighter jet during a test flight, a final act of courage in a life defined by pushing the boundaries of flight.

Kenneth Taylor's post-war journey took a different path. After continuing to serve in the South Pacific, where he was credited with downing another Japanese aircraft while flying out of Guadalcanal, Taylor's combat career came to an abrupt end when he suffered a broken leg during an air raid. This setback, however, did not end his military service. Taylor remained in the Air Force, eventually becoming a commander in the Alaska Air National Guard. Over his 27-year active duty career, he rose to the rank of brigadier general, his service recognized with numerous awards including the Legion of Merit and the Air Medal.

After retiring from the military, Taylor embarked on a civilian career as an insurance underwriter, bringing the same dedication and attention to detail to this new field that had characterized his military service. He passed away in Tucson, Arizona, in 2006 at the age of 86, leaving behind a legacy of service and bravery that continues to inspire.

## Conclusion

The story of George Welch and Kenneth Taylor is more than a tale of heroism on a single day. It is a testament to the enduring spirit of service, the power of quick thinking and bravery in the face of overwhelming odds, and the lasting impact that individual actions can have on the course of history.

Their actions on December 7, 1941, stand as a beacon of hope and resistance in one of America's darkest hours. In the chaos and devastation of the Pearl Harbor attack, Welch and Taylor's courage provided a rallying point for a nation suddenly thrust into war. Their continued service throughout World War II and beyond demonstrates the depth of their commitment to their country and the values they fought to defend.

As we reflect on the lives of these two extraordinary men, we are reminded of the sacrifices made by an entire generation in the defense of freedom. Welch and Taylor's story, from their early morning scramble to take off in their P-40 fighters to their distinguished post-war careers, embodies the best of American character – courage, ingenuity, and an unwavering commitment to duty.

In the annals of military history, the names of George Welch and Kenneth Taylor will forever be associated with the valor displayed on December 7, 1941. But their legacy extends far beyond that single day. It lives on in the spirit of service they exemplified throughout their lives, in the advancements in aviation that Welch contributed to, and in the leadership Taylor provided to subsequent generations of airmen.

Their story serves as an enduring reminder of the difference that individual courage and initiative can make, even in the face of seemingly insurmountable odds. As we face the challenges of the future, the example set by Welch and Taylor continues to inspire, urging us to meet adversity with bravery, quick thinking, and an unwavering commitment to our highest ideals.

**Sources**

Prange, Gordon W. At Dawn We Slept: The Untold Story of Pearl Harbor. McGraw-Hill, 1981

Gordon, John S. Pearl Harbor: A History. New York: Simon & Schuster, 2001.

Various Sources

# Doris Miller

### Introduction

Doris "Dorie" Miller and his extraordinary acts of bravery during the attack on Pearl Harbor not only earned him the Navy Cross but also cemented his place as a symbol of African American courage and resilience in the face of adversity. This narrative explores the life of Doris Miller, from his humble beginnings in Waco, Texas, to his heroic actions on December 7, 1941, and beyond, painting a picture of a man whose dedication to duty and country left an indelible mark on the nation's history.

As the sun rose over Pearl Harbor on that fateful December morning, neither Miller nor anyone else could have grasped the significance of what was about to transpire. His actions in the face of overwhelming odds would not only shape his destiny but also inspire generations of Americans to come. This is the story of a young sailor who, in the crucible of war, exemplified the best of American character and valor, challenging racial barriers and paving the way for greater equality in the U.S. military.

### Early Life and Naval Career

Doris Miller's journey began on October 12, 1919, in Waco, Texas. Born to Connery and Henrietta Miller, he was the third of four sons in a family of sharecroppers. The Millers worked a 28-acre farm near Waco, their lives marked by the challenges of tenant farming and the pervasive racial segregation of the era.

Despite these obstacles, young Doris distinguished himself through his physical prowess. He played football at A.J. Moore High School in Waco, earning the nickname "Raging Bull" for his athletic abilities. However, the economic realities of the time forced Miller to drop out of school to help support his family, a common necessity for many African American families in the rural South during this period.

In September 1939, seeking better opportunities and a chance to see the world beyond the cotton fields of Texas, Miller enlisted in the U.S. Navy. At the time, the Navy was one of the few branches of the military that offered African Americans a chance to serve, although they were limited to roles such as mess attendants due to the segregation policies of the era.

Miller's early naval career was shaped by these racial constraints. After completing his training at the Naval Training Center in Norfolk, Virginia, he was assigned to the ammunition ship Pyro (AE-1) before being transferred to the battleship USS West Virginia (BB-48) on January 2, 1940. Despite the limitations placed on African American sailors, Miller's dedication and physical strength did not go unnoticed. He became the ship's heavyweight boxing champion, a testament to the qualities that would serve him well in the coming crisis.

In the months leading up to the attack on Pearl Harbor, Miller's duties primarily involved serving meals and maintaining the officers' quarters. However, his naval experience also included a brief stint at the Secondary Battery Gunnery School aboard the USS Nevada in July 1940, where he received some training in gunnery, though not specifically on anti-aircraft weapons. This limited exposure to combat training would prove crucial in the events to come.

**The Day That Changed Everything**

On the morning of December 7, 1941, Doris Miller woke at 6:00 a.m. to begin his duties aboard the USS West Virginia. By 7:57 a.m., as he was collecting laundry, the tranquility of the Hawaiian morning was shattered by the roar of aircraft engines and the thunder of explosions. The Japanese attack on Pearl Harbor had begun, and Miller's life was about to change forever.

In the chaos that ensued, Miller's actions would become the stuff of legend. As the West Virginia sustained multiple torpedo hits, Miller rushed to his battle station, only to find it had been destroyed by a torpedo blast. Undeterred, he raced to the main deck, where he found the ship's captain, Mervyn Bennion, mortally wounded. Without hesitation, Miller moved to assist his fallen commander, carrying him to a safer location despite the captain's insistence on remaining at his post.

But Miller's most famous act was yet to come. During the attack, he took the initiative to man a .50-caliber anti-aircraft machine gun, a weapon he had no formal training to operate. This was a significant act of bravery, as African American sailors were typically not trained for combat roles due to the racial segregation policies of the time. Nevertheless, Miller operated the gun with remarkable effectiveness, firing at the attacking Japanese aircraft until he ran out of ammunition.

Miller's heroism did not end there. After exhausting the ammunition, he continued to assist his fellow sailors, helping to move wounded men to safety. He was one of the last three men to abandon the sinking USS West Virginia, and even after leaving the ship, he continued to aid in rescue efforts, pulling sailors from the oil-slicked, burning waters.

**Recognition and Aftermath**

In the immediate aftermath of the attack, Miller's actions were initially recognized through word of mouth and reports from the Black press. However, it took several months for the Navy to formally acknowledge his heroism. On May 27, 1942, in a ceremony at Pearl Harbor, Miller was awarded the Navy Cross by Admiral Chester W. Nimitz, making him the first African American to receive this prestigious honor.

The citation for Miller's Navy Cross praised his "distinguished devotion to duty, extraordinary courage, and disregard for his own personal safety" during the attack. This recognition was a historic moment, not only for Miller personally but also as a milestone in the history of racial equality in the U.S. military.

Following the award ceremony, the U.S. Navy utilized Miller's newfound fame to inspire and recruit more African Americans into the military. He was sent on a war bond tour and served as a recruiter, a strategic move by the Navy to leverage his status and encourage enlistment among African Americans. This role was crucial in breaking down racial barriers and promoting the integration of African Americans into the armed forces.

## Continued Service and Sacrifice

Despite his hero status, Miller continued to serve in the Navy with the same dedication he had shown at Pearl Harbor. In 1943, he was promoted to petty officer, ship's cook third class, and assigned to the escort carrier USS Liscome Bay. Tragically, Miller's naval career and life were cut short during the Battle of Makin Island on November 24, 1943. The Liscome Bay was struck by a Japanese torpedo and sank within minutes. Doris Miller was among the 646 men who lost their lives in the attack.

Miller was posthumously awarded the Purple Heart for his service and sacrifice. His death, while a great loss, did not diminish the impact of his heroism. Instead, it further cemented his legacy as a symbol of African American valor and sacrifice in service to the nation.

## Legacy and Remembrance

Doris Miller's legacy extends far beyond his heroic actions at Pearl Harbor and his ultimate sacrifice. His bravery challenged racial stereotypes and played a significant role in the early civil rights movement, highlighting the contributions and capabilities of African Americans in the military.

Today, Doris Miller is remembered through various memorials and honors. His hometown of Waco, Texas, has established the Doris Miller Memorial, a public art installation on the banks of the Brazos River. The memorial features a nine-foot bronze statue of Miller, unveiled in December 2017, serving as a powerful reminder of his courage and sacrifice.

The U.S. Navy has also taken significant steps to honor Miller's memory. In 1973, they commissioned the USS Miller, a Knox-class frigate, named in his honor. More recently, in a historic decision, the Navy announced that a future Ford-class aircraft carrier would be named the USS Doris Miller, marking the first time an aircraft carrier has been named after an enlisted sailor or an African American. This decision represents a profound recognition of Miller's impact on naval history and the ongoing struggle for equality in the armed forces.

Miller's story continues to be an important part of educational curricula and public commemorations, particularly during Black History Month. His life and actions serve as an inspiration for future generations, emphasizing his role in advancing civil rights and equality in the military.

## Conclusion

The story of Doris Miller is more than a tale of heroism on a single day. It is a testament to the enduring spirit of service, the power of courage in the face of overwhelming odds, and the lasting impact that individual actions can have on the course of history.

Miller's actions on December 7, 1941, stand as a beacon of hope and resistance in one of America's darkest hours. In the chaos and devastation of the Pearl Harbor attack, his bravery provided a rallying point for a nation suddenly thrust into war. His continued service throughout World War II, culminating in his ultimate sacrifice, demonstrates the depth of his commitment to his country and the values he fought to defend.

Doris Miller's life serves as an enduring reminder of the difference that individual courage and initiative can make, even in the face of seemingly insurmountable odds. As we face the challenges of the future, his example continues to inspire, urging us to meet adversity with bravery, determination, and an unwavering commitment to our highest ideals. In doing so, we honor not only the memory of Doris Miller but also the countless others who have served and sacrificed in the name of freedom and equality.

**Sources**

O'Neal, Bill. Doris Miller – Hero of Pearl Harbor. Eakin Books, 2007.

Cutrer, Thomas W. Doris Miller, Pearl Harbor, and the Birth of the Civil Rights Movement. Texas A&M University Press, 2017.

Various Sources

# Ensign Herbert C. Jones

## Introduction

Few stories shine as brightly as that of Ensign Herbert Charpiot Jones. His extraordinary acts of bravery during the attack on Pearl Harbor not only earned him the Medal of Honor but also cemented his place as a symbol of American courage and sacrifice. This story explores the life of Herbert C. Jones, from his humble beginnings in Los Angeles to his heroic actions on December 7, 1941, and beyond, painting a picture of a young man whose dedication to duty and country left an indelible mark on the nation's history.

As the sun rose over Pearl Harbor on that fateful December morning, neither Jones nor anyone else could have grasped the significance of what was about to transpire. His actions in the face of overwhelming odds would not only shape his own destiny but also inspire generations of Americans to come. This is the story of a young naval officer who, in the crucible of war, exemplified the best of American character and valor.

## Early Life and Naval Career

Herbert Charpiot Jones' journey began on January 21, 1918, in Los Angeles, California. Born into a family with a strong military tradition, young Herbert was imbued with a sense of patriotism and duty from an early age. His father's military service served as an inspiration, setting the stage for Herbert's own path of service to his country.

Growing up in the sunny climate of California, Jones balanced a love for fun with a deep sense of responsibility. This combination of youthful exuberance and mature dedication would serve him well in his future naval career. At the young age of 17, driven by a desire to serve his nation, Jones enlisted in the United States Naval Reserve on May 14, 1935.

Jones' early naval career was marked by dedication and rapid advancement. He received Midshipmen's training on the drill boat USS Prairie State (IX-15), distinguishing himself as part of the first Midshipmen class to be trained aboard this vessel. His hard work and commitment did not go unnoticed, and in November 1940, Jones was commissioned as an ensign in the United States Navy.

Shortly after his commissioning, Ensign Jones reported for duty aboard the USS California (BB-44), a Tennessee-class battleship stationed at Pearl Harbor. This assignment placed him at the heart of the Pacific Fleet, where he would soon face one of the most pivotal moments in American history. As a junior officer on the USS California, Jones' responsibilities included overseeing ship operations and ensuring the readiness of the crew, particularly in the anti-aircraft battery.

**The Day That Changed Everything**

On the morning of December 7, 1941, Ensign Herbert C. Jones was preparing to relieve the officer-of-the-deck aboard the USS California when the tranquility of the Hawaiian morning was shattered by the roar of aircraft engines and the thunder of explosions. The Japanese attack on Pearl Harbor had begun, and Jones' life was about to change forever.

As the attack unfolded, Jones demonstrated exceptional leadership and courage. When the USS California was hit by torpedoes and bombs, causing severe damage and fires, Jones sprang into action. Despite the chaos and danger, he navigated through the smoke-filled ship to rescue an injured sailor. Temporarily overcome by fumes, Jones quickly regained consciousness and continued his efforts to assist his fellow servicemen.

In a display of remarkable initiative, Jones took command of an anti-aircraft battery that had lost its leader. He ordered the men to fire back at the incoming Japanese planes, demonstrating composure under fire that belied his young age. When the battery ran out of ammunition, Jones organized a volunteer party to manually transport shells from the magazines below decks to the battery.

It was during this heroic effort that tragedy struck. As Jones and his team worked to resupply the anti-aircraft battery, another bomb hit the USS California. The blast mortally wounded Jones, but even in his final moments, his thoughts were for his fellow sailors. His last words, as reported, were, "Leave me alone! I am done for. Get out of here before the magazines go off". These words encapsulate the selflessness and bravery that defined Jones' actions throughout the attack.

**The USS California's Struggle**

The USS California, where Ensign Jones served and ultimately gave his life, played a significant role in the events of December 7, 1941. As the flagship of the Battle Force, the California was moored at berth F-3, somewhat isolated from the other battleships at "Battleship Row" off Ford Island. The ship was in a vulnerable state due to preparations for an inspection, with several manhole covers removed or loosened, leaving it susceptible to flooding.

During the attack, the USS California was hit by two torpedoes on its port side, causing significant damage and flooding. The ship began to list to port, and counterflooding measures were taken to prevent capsizing. Despite these challenges, the crew, including Ensign Jones, manned their battle stations and fought back with .50-caliber machine guns and 5-inch anti-aircraft guns, although they faced an acute shortage of ammunition due to power loss affecting the ammunition hoists.

The California also sustained bomb hits, including one that caused a fire amidships, which was difficult to control due to a lack of water pressure and fire extinguishers. Despite these overwhelming odds, the crew's efforts, including those of Ensign Jones, were commendable. They managed to restore some power and water pressure, allowing the ship to potentially get underway, but a patch of burning oil from Battleship Row forced the crew to abandon ship temporarily.

**Recognition and Legacy**

In the aftermath of the attack, the heroic actions of Ensign Herbert C. Jones did not go unnoticed. For his extraordinary bravery and selfless sacrifice, Jones was posthumously awarded the Medal of Honor, the highest military decoration presented by the United States government. The citation for his Medal of Honor eloquently captures the essence of his heroism, noting his "distinguished devotion to duty, extraordinary courage, and disregard for his safety" during the attack.

Jones' legacy extends far beyond his heroic actions on that fateful day. His story has become a powerful symbol of the courage and sacrifice displayed by American servicemen during the Pearl Harbor attack. Today, Ensign Herbert C. Jones is remembered as a hero whose sacrifice serves as a poignant reminder of the true cost of freedom.

The memory of Ensign Jones continues to inspire future generations of naval officers and sailors. His actions exemplify the core values of the United States Navy: honor, courage, and commitment. By honoring heroes like Herbert C. Jones, we preserve our national memory and identity, celebrating the human capacity for courage in the face of unimaginable challenges.

**Conclusion**

The story of Ensign Herbert C. Jones is more than a tale of heroism on a single day. It is a testament to the enduring spirit of service, the power of courage in the face of overwhelming odds, and the lasting impact that individual actions can have on the course of history.

The name of Herbert C. Jones will forever be associated with the valor displayed on December 7, 1941. But his legacy extends far beyond that single day. It lives on in the ongoing commitment to service and sacrifice that characterizes the United States Navy, in the lessons taught to new generations of sailors, and in the inspiration he continues to provide to all who learn of his story.

**Sources**

Prange, Gordon W. At Dawn We Slept: The Untold Story of Pearl Harbor. McGraw-Hill, 1981

Wohlstetter, Roberta. Pearl Harbor: Warning and Decision. Stanford University Press. 1962.

Various Sources

# Japan's Strategy Behind the Pearl Harbor Attack

**Introduction**

The attack on Pearl Harbor on December 7, 1941, stands as one of the most pivotal moments in modern history, a day that President Franklin D. Roosevelt declared would "live in infamy." This surprise military strike by the Imperial Japanese Navy Air Service against the United States naval base at Pearl Harbor, Hawaii, not only drew America into World War II but also marked a significant turning point in global power dynamics. To understand the full scope of this momentous event, we must delve into the complex web of strategic planning, political maneuvering, and military precision that led to Japan's fateful decision to awaken the "sleeping giant" of the United States.

**Narrative**

**The Seeds of Conflict: Japan's Imperial Ambitions**

The roots of the Pearl Harbor attack can be traced back to Japan's imperial ambitions in the late 19th and early 20th centuries. Following the forced opening of Japan by Western powers in the 1850s, the island nation embarked on a rapid modernization process, transforming itself from a feudal society into a formidable industrial and military power. This transformation was driven by a desire to avoid the fate of other Asian nations that had fallen under Western colonial rule.

By the 1930s, Japan's imperial ambitions had led to aggressive expansion into China. The invasion of Manchuria in 1931 and the outbreak of full-scale war with China in 1937 marked Japan's determination to dominate Asia. These actions, however, put Japan on a collision course with Western powers, particularly the United States, which viewed Japan's expansionism as a threat to its own interests in the Pacific.

**The Road to War: Escalating Tensions**

As Japan's territorial ambitions grew, so did tensions with the United States. The occupation of French Indochina in 1940 was a strategic move by Japan to cut off supplies to China and secure resources for its war efforts. This action prompted a strong response from the United States, which imposed economic sanctions, including an embargo on oil exports to Japan and the freezing of Japanese assets.

These sanctions posed a significant threat to Japan's military capabilities and economic stability. Japan, heavily reliant on imported oil to fuel its military and industrial sectors, found itself in a precarious position. The Japanese leadership faced a difficult choice: either abandon their imperial ambitions and withdraw from China and Indochina, or secure the resources needed to sustain their empire through military action.

## The Architects of Attack: Key Figures in Japan's Strategy

The decision to attack Pearl Harbor was not made lightly, nor was it the work of a single individual. Several key figures played crucial roles in shaping Japan's strategy:

**1. Admiral Isoroku Yamamoto:** As the commander-in-chief of the Japanese Combined Fleet, Yamamoto was the mastermind behind the Pearl Harbor attack. A brilliant strategist, Yamamoto recognized that Japan's only chance of success in a war against the United States lay in a swift, decisive blow that would cripple American naval power in the Pacific.

**2. Prime Minister Hideki Tōjō:** As the head of government, Tōjō was instrumental in the decision to go to war. His militaristic policies and belief in Japan's imperial destiny aligned with the objectives of the Pearl Harbor attack.

**3. Vice Admiral Chuichi Nagumo:** Commander of the First Air Fleet, Nagumo led the task force that carried out the attack. His leadership was crucial in executing the complex operation involving six aircraft carriers and hundreds of planes.

**4. Rear Admiral Ryūnosuke Kusaka:** As Chief of Staff to Nagumo, Kusaka played a vital role in the detailed planning and coordination of the attack, ensuring the smooth execution of the operation.

## Strategic Objectives: Beyond the Smoke and Fire

The attack on Pearl Harbor was not merely a tactical strike but part of a broader strategic vision. Japan's objectives were multifaceted:

**1. Neutralizing the U.S. Pacific Fleet:** The primary goal was to destroy or severely damage the American naval presence in the Pacific, preventing it from interfering with Japan's planned military actions in Southeast Asia. By crippling the fleet, Japan hoped to gain a free hand in the Pacific for at least six months, allowing it to consolidate its gains in resource-rich territories.

**2. Gaining Time for Consolidation:** Japan's leadership believed that a swift and overwhelming victory at Pearl Harbor would demoralize the United States, potentially forcing it to negotiate peace on terms favorable to Japan. This would allow Japan to establish and fortify a defensive perimeter in the Pacific, securing its newly acquired territories.

**3. Demonstrating Military Prowess:** The attack was also intended as a demonstration of Japan's military capabilities, asserting its status as a dominant power in the Pacific and deterring other nations from challenging its expansionist agenda.

## Meticulous Planning: Crafting the Perfect Strike

The planning for the Pearl Harbor attack was a testament to Japanese military precision and ingenuity. Admiral Yamamoto and his staff spent months developing and refining the plan, which involved extensive intelligence gathering and innovative tactics:

**1. Intelligence Gathering:** Japanese spies in Hawaii, such as Takeo Yoshikawa, provided crucial information about the layout of Pearl Harbor, ship movements, and harbor defenses. This intelligence was vital in planning the attack's timing and execution.

**2. Military Exercises:** The Japanese Navy conducted extensive exercises to simulate the conditions at Pearl Harbor. Pilots practiced torpedo bombing runs and dive-bombing techniques, honing their skills for the shallow waters of the harbor.

**3. Technological Innovations:** To overcome the shallow depth of Pearl Harbor, which would normally prevent the use of aerial torpedoes, Japanese engineers developed specially modified torpedoes that could operate effectively in shallow waters.

**4. Maintaining Secrecy:** The Japanese went to great lengths to maintain the element of surprise. The attack fleet departed from Japan on November 26, 1941, maintaining radio silence and taking a circuitous route to avoid detection.

## The Day of Infamy: Execution and Immediate Aftermath

On the morning of December 7, 1941, the Japanese plan was put into action. At 7:48 a.m. Hawaiian time, the first wave of 353 Japanese fighter planes, bombers, and torpedo planes launched their attack on Pearl Harbor. The strike came in two waves, targeting battleships, airfields, and other military installations.

The attack achieved significant tactical success. Eight U.S. Navy battleships were damaged, with four sunk. Additionally, 188 U.S. aircraft were destroyed, and 2,403 Americans were killed, with 1,178 wounded. The Japanese losses were comparatively light, with 29 aircraft and five midget submarines lost, and 64 servicemen killed.

In the immediate aftermath, Japan declared war on the United States and the British Empire on December 8, 1941. The Japanese government sought to justify the attack by claiming that all avenues for peace had been exhausted due to the actions of the United States and the United Kingdom.

## The Strategic Miscalculation: Unintended Consequences

While the attack on Pearl Harbor was a tactical success, it proved to be a strategic blunder of monumental proportions. The Japanese leadership had fundamentally misjudged the American response:

**1. United American Resolve:** Rather than demoralizing the United States, the attack galvanized American public opinion. The nation, which had been divided on the issue of entering the war, was now united in its determination to defeat Japan.

**2. Industrial Mobilization:** The attack spurred a massive mobilization of American industrial and military resources. The United States' vast production capabilities, which Japan had hoped to neutralize, were instead fully activated and directed toward the war effort.

**3. Missed Targets:** Crucially, the attack failed to destroy the Pacific Fleet's aircraft carriers, which were not present at Pearl Harbor on December 7. These carriers would prove instrumental in turning the tide of the war in the Pacific.

**4. Global Conflict:** The attack led to declarations of war not only from the United States but also from the United Kingdom, Australia, Canada, and other Allied nations, expanding the conflict into a truly global war.

## The Aftermath

In the months following Pearl Harbor, Japan achieved a series of rapid victories, capturing territories across Southeast Asia and the Pacific. By mid-1942, Japanese forces had occupied a vast area, including the Philippines, Malaya, Singapore, and the Dutch East Indies. These conquests aligned with Japan's strategy to secure vital resources and establish a defensive perimeter.

However, these initial successes masked fundamental weaknesses in Japan's position. The overextension of Japanese forces and the logistical challenges of maintaining control over such a vast empire strained Japan's military capabilities. Moreover, the United States' entry into the war brought immense industrial and military power to bear against Japan.

The tide of war began to turn against Japan with the Battle of Midway in June 1942, where the U.S. Navy dealt a significant blow to Japanese naval power. This battle, coming just six months after Pearl Harbor, marked the beginning of a long series of American counteroffensives that would gradually push back Japanese advances and ultimately lead to Japan's defeat.

## Conclusion

The Japanese strategy behind the Pearl Harbor attack was a complex interplay of military planning, political calculation, and cultural factors. Driven by imperial ambitions and resource needs, Japan's leadership embarked on a high-stakes gamble that initially seemed to pay off but ultimately led to the nation's downfall.

The attack on Pearl Harbor stands as a stark reminder of the unpredictable nature of war and the dangers of strategic miscalculation. While achieving tactical surprise and initial success, Japan's

actions united its enemies and unleashed a force that it could not hope to match in a prolonged conflict.

Pearl Harbor remains a pivotal moment that reshaped the global order. It marked the end of Japanese imperial ambitions and the rise of the United States as a global superpower. The lessons learned from this event continue to influence military and political thinking to this day, serving as a powerful reminder of the far-reaching consequences of strategic decisions in times of international tension.

## Sources

Wohlstetter, Roberta. Pearl Harbor: Warning and Decision. Stanford University Press. 1962.

Gordon, John S. Pearl Harbor: A History. New York: Simon & Schuster, 2001.

Various Sources

# The Mistakes Japan Made in Attacking Pearl Harbor

## Introduction

The attack on Pearl Harbor on December 7, 1941, was a pivotal moment in World War II, marking the United States' entry into the conflict. The surprise assault by the Imperial Japanese Navy aimed to cripple the U.S. Pacific Fleet and prevent American interference in Japan's plans for territorial expansion in Southeast Asia. However, despite the initial success of the attack, Japan made several critical mistakes that ultimately contributed to its defeat in the war. Admiral Chester W. Nimitz, who would later become the Commander in Chief of the Pacific Fleet, identified three significant miscalculations made by Japan during this operation. This story explores Nimitz's insights into these errors, the context of the attack on Pearl Harbor, and the broader implications for the war in the Pacific.

## Background

**Chester Nimitz: A Naval Leader:** Chester William Nimitz was born on February 24, 1885, in Fredericksburg, Texas. He graduated from the United States Naval Academy in 1905 and quickly established himself as a capable officer. Nimitz served in various capacities during World War I and the interwar years, gaining valuable experience in naval operations and strategy.

By the time of the Pearl Harbor attack, Nimitz had been promoted to the rank of Admiral. In the aftermath of the attack, he was appointed Commander in Chief of the Pacific Fleet, taking charge of the U.S. Navy's efforts to respond to Japanese aggression. Nimitz's leadership would prove crucial in the subsequent battles in the Pacific Theater.

## Narrative:

**The Attack on Pearl Harbor:** On the morning of December 7, 1941, Japan launched a surprise aerial assault on the U.S. naval base at Pearl Harbor in Hawaii. The attack involved two waves of Japanese aircraft, totaling 353 planes, targeting battleships, aircraft, and military installations. The assault destroyed eight battleships, three cruisers, and nearly 200 aircraft, with a loss of more than 2,400 American lives.

While the attack was initially devastating, it left several critical elements of the U.S. Pacific Fleet intact, including aircraft carriers and submarines, which would play a vital role in the U.S. response to Japan's aggression.

**Three Critical Mistakes Made by Japan:**

**Mistake 1: Failure to Target the Aircraft Carriers:** One of the most significant mistakes made by Japan during the Pearl Harbor attack was the failure to destroy the American aircraft carriers stationed in the Pacific. At the time of the attack, three aircraft carriers—USS Enterprise, USS Lexington, and USS Saratoga—were not in the harbor. They were out on missions, which spared them from the destruction that befell the battleships and other vessels at Pearl Harbor.

Admiral Nimitz later emphasized the importance of this oversight, noting that the loss of the carriers would have significantly hampered U.S. naval aviation capabilities in the Pacific. The carriers were the backbone of naval power, capable of launching air strikes and providing air cover for fleet operations. The failure to target these vital assets allowed the United States to recover more quickly from the attack and maintain a strong naval presence.

The Japanese high command had underestimated the strategic value of aircraft carriers in modern naval warfare. While they focused on the battleships, considered the dominant force in naval engagements at the time—they ignored the fact that aircraft carriers would become the primary offensive weapon in the Pacific Theater. This oversight would prove costly in the months following the attack, as U.S. carrier groups would go on to achieve significant victories against Japanese forces.

**Mistake 2: Underestimating American Resolve and Industrial Capacity:** Another significant miscalculation made by Japan was the underestimation of American resolve and industrial capacity. The Japanese leadership believed that a swift and decisive strike on Pearl Harbor would demoralize the American public and government, leading to a negotiated peace that would favor Japanese expansion in Asia. However, this assumption proved to be fundamentally flawed.

Admiral Nimitz recognized the awakening of the American spirit following the attack. The devastation inflicted on Pearl Harbor united the nation, galvanizing public support for the war effort. The rallying cry of "Remember Pearl Harbor" became a powerful motivator, propelling America into a total war mobilization.

In addition to the surge in morale, Japan underestimated the United States' industrial capabilities. The U.S. had a robust industrial base capable of producing war material at an unprecedented scale. Following the attack, American factories rapidly converted to wartime production, cranking out ships, aircraft, and munitions at an astonishing rate.

Nimitz and other U.S. military leaders recognized that the ability to produce war material would play a crucial role in the outcome of the conflict. The American war industry quickly outpaced Japan's production capabilities, leading to overwhelming numbers of ships and aircraft in subsequent battles. This industrial advantage allowed the United States to recover from the losses at Pearl Harbor and launch successful offensives in the Pacific.

The United States was outfitted with repair docks locally to assess and repair damaged ships. If local facilities were not available, the alternative was the slow process of towing disabled ships to the West Coast. The ships were repaired and ready for service in record time.

Nimitz also referenced Japan's overlooking the fuel tanks and fuel farms. If these facilities had been destroyed, the ability to respond as quickly as possible would have been hampered.

**Mistake 3: Ignoring Intelligence and the Risk of Counterattacks**

The third critical mistake made by Japan was the failure to adequately analyze intelligence reports and consider the potential for American counterattacks. Before the attack on Pearl Harbor, U.S. intelligence had intercepted numerous Japanese communications, indicating that Japan was preparing for military action. However, the specifics of the intended target remained elusive.

The Japanese high command, while aware of the potential for American military responses, believed that the attack would be so devastating that it would effectively neutralize any immediate threat. They did not foresee the possibility of a swift American counterattack, nor did they fully appreciate the extent of U.S. intelligence capabilities.

In addition, Admiral Nimitz said that Japan's decision not to launch a robust second-wave attack at Pearl Harbor was a mistake. The initial assault caught the American forces off guard. A well-coordinated second wave targeting critical infrastructure and facilities could have dealt a more devastating blow, Instead, the Japanese withdrew, allowing the United States to swiftly regroup and rebuild its naval capabilities.

In the aftermath of the Pearl Harbor attack, Admiral Nimitz quickly mobilized the remaining forces in the Pacific, including the aircraft carriers that had escaped destruction. The U.S. Navy launched a series of retaliatory strikes against Japanese-held territories, including the Doolittle Raid on Tokyo in April 1942, which served to boost American morale and demonstrate that Japan was not invulnerable.

The failure to account for American intelligence and the likelihood of counterattacks would haunt Japan throughout the war. As U.S. forces regrouped and adapted to the challenges posed by the conflict, the Japanese military found itself increasingly on the defensive.

**The Aftermath of Pearl Harbor:** Following the attack on Pearl Harbor, the United States rapidly shifted from a state of isolation to one of total war. President Franklin D. Roosevelt addressed Congress on December 8, 1941, declaring war on Japan. The attack galvanized public support and led to a massive mobilization of American resources for the war effort.

Admiral Nimitz, appointed Commander in Chief of the Pacific Fleet, faced the daunting task of rebuilding the fleet and preparing for the next phase of the conflict. The lessons learned from the attack informed strategies that would be employed in subsequent battles, including the Coral Sea and Midway.

The impact of Japan's mistakes became increasingly evident as the war progressed. The United States' industrial capacity allowed it to produce ships and aircraft at a staggering pace, outmatching Japan's production capabilities. The tide of war began to turn in favor of the Allies.

Notably, the Battle of Midway in June 1942 marked a significant turning point in the Pacific Theater. U.S. forces, armed with intelligence about Japanese plans, launched a successful counterattack that resulted in the sinking of four Japanese aircraft carriers. This defeat severely weakened Japan's naval capabilities and shifted the balance of power in the Pacific.

Admiral Nimitz played a crucial role in this victory, utilizing the lessons learned from the Pearl Harbor attack to inform his strategic decisions. The mistakes made by Japan during the attack had far-reaching consequences, ultimately leading to its defeat in the war.

**Historical Reassessment:** In the years following World War II, historians have continued to debate the events surrounding the Pearl Harbor attack and the implications of Japan's mistakes. The narratives surrounding intelligence failures, military strategy, and the broader context of the war have been scrutinized and reassessed.

The McCollum Memo has become a focal point in discussions about the U.S. government's knowledge of potential threats and the decisions made in the lead-up to the attack. While some argue that there was an intentional provocation, others maintain that the failure to act on intelligence was due to a lack of coordination and communication among intelligence agencies.

Admiral Nimitz's insights into Japan's mistakes serve as a reminder of the complexities of warfare and the importance of understanding one's adversary. The lessons learned from Pearl Harbor continue to inform military strategy and intelligence practices to this day.

**Commemoration and Remembrance:** Pearl Harbor has become a symbol of resilience and sacrifice in American history. The events of December 7, 1941, are commemorated annually, serving as a reminder of the lives lost and the lessons learned from that fateful day. The USS Arizona Memorial stands as a testament to the bravery of those who fought and died in defense of their country.

**Conclusion:**

The attack on Pearl Harbor was a turning point in world history, marking the United States' entry into World War II and reshaping the geopolitical landscape. Admiral Chester Nimitz's analysis of Japan's critical mistakes—failing to target aircraft carriers, underestimating American resolve and industrial capacity, and ignoring the risk of counterattacks—provides valuable insights into the complexities of military strategy and decision-making.

**Sources**

Potter, Professor E.B. Nimitz. Naval Institute Press, 2008.

Symonds, Craig L. Nimitz at War: Command leadership from Pearl Harbor to Tokyo Bay. Oxford University Press, 2022.

Various Sources

# Hector Bywater and "The Great Pacific War"

## Introduction

Few works of fiction have garnered as much attention for their prescience as Hector Bywater's "The Great Pacific War." Published in 1925, this novel not only captivated readers with its detailed portrayal of a hypothetical conflict between Japan and the United States but also raised questions about its potential influence on actual military strategies leading up to World War II. This narrative explores the life of Hector Bywater, the content and reception of his seminal work, and the intriguing connections between his fictional scenario and the real-world events that unfolded at Pearl Harbor on December 7, 1941. By examining the intersection of speculative fiction and military strategy, we delve into the complex relationship between imagination and reality in shaping the course of history.

## Hector Bywater: The Man Behind the Vision

Hector Charles Bywater was born on October 21, 1884, in London, England, into a middle-class Welsh family. His journey from a young emigrant to the United States to becoming one of the most respected naval analysts of his time is a testament to his keen intellect and passion for maritime affairs. At the age of 19, Bywater began writing naval articles for the New York Herald, marking the beginning of a career that would span journalism, intelligence work, and military analysis.

Bywater's expertise in naval matters caught the attention of Mansfield Cumming, the founder of what would later become MI6. Recruited as a "fixed agent abroad" in Germany, Bywater used his position as a journalist to gather crucial intelligence on German naval preparations in the lead-up to World War I. This experience not only honed his analytical skills but also provided him with invaluable insights into the inner workings of naval strategy and international relations.

Throughout his career, Bywater established himself as a leading authority on naval affairs, writing extensively for major newspapers in London and New York. His ability to blend journalistic acumen with strategic foresight set him apart from his contemporaries, earning him a reputation as a visionary in the field of naval analysis.

**"The Great Pacific War": A Prophetic Tale**

In 1925, Bywater published "The Great Pacific War," a work of speculative fiction that would come to be regarded as eerily prophetic. Set in the early 1930s, the novel depicted a conflict between Japan and the United States, beginning with a surprise Japanese attack on U.S. naval forces in the Pacific. The narrative unfolded with a series of strategic military maneuvers, including the seizure of the Philippines and Guam, and attacks on Hawaii and the U.S. West Coast by Japanese submarines and seaplanes.

Several key predictions in Bywater's novel bore striking similarities to the events that would unfold during World War II:

1. The element of surprise in the initial Japanese attack, although Bywater placed this in Manila Bay rather than Pearl Harbor.

2. The U.S. strategy of island hopping, became a cornerstone of the Allied campaign in the Pacific.

3. The importance of decisive naval battles reflects the prevailing military thought of the time.

However, Bywater's foresight had its limitations. While he included aircraft carriers in his narrative, he did not fully anticipate their pivotal role in naval warfare. He also incorrectly predicted the use of chemical weapons, which did not occur in the actual conflict.

**Reception and Impact**

Upon its release, "The Great Pacific War" garnered significant attention for its detailed and plausible depiction of a potential conflict in the Pacific. The novel was recognized not merely as entertainment but as a serious work of speculative fiction with strategic insights. Bywater's background as a naval intelligence officer and journalist lent credibility to his predictions, resonating with both military professionals and the general public.

The book's influence extended beyond literary circles into military strategy discussions. It was reportedly read by key military figures, including Isoroku Yamamoto, the chief strategist of the Imperial Japanese Navy. The novel was translated into Japanese and became required reading for Japanese naval officers, indicating its significant impact on military thought in Japan.

**Potential Influence on Pearl Harbor Attack Planning**

The connection between Bywater's novel and the actual planning of the Pearl Harbor attack has been a subject of historical analysis and debate. While it is difficult to establish a direct causal link, several historians have argued that "The Great Pacific War" may have influenced Japanese military strategy, particularly the thinking of Admiral Isoroku Yamamoto.

Journalist William H. Honan contended that Bywater's ideas were so influential that they could be seen as having shaped the Pacific War. The novel's depiction of surprise attacks and strategic maneuvers may have reinforced existing military doctrines and strategies within the Japanese Navy.

However, it is crucial to recognize the limitations of Bywater's influence. The concept of a surprise attack was not novel to Japanese military strategy, as evidenced by previous conflicts such as the Russo-Japanese War. Additionally, Bywater did not foresee the importance of aircraft carriers and air power, which were pivotal in the actual attack on Pearl Harbor.

**The Pearl Harbor Attack: From Fiction to Reality**

The planning process for the Japanese attack on Pearl Harbor was a complex endeavor that involved significant strategic considerations. Admiral Yamamoto Isoroku, who was fundamentally opposed to a war with the United States, believed that Japan's best chance in a conflict lay in delivering a crippling first blow to the U.S. Pacific Fleet.

The conceptual origins of such an attack can be traced back to various military studies and exercises conducted by the Japanese Navy in the years leading up to the war. Yamamoto's plan called for a coordinated air assault by several carrier divisions, targeting the U.S. Pacific Fleet at Pearl Harbor.

While Bywater's novel may have contributed to the strategic thinking of Japanese naval leaders, it was not the sole catalyst for the Pearl Harbor attack. The actual planning process involved meticulous preparation, overcoming internal opposition, and adapting to the realities of modern naval warfare.

**Conclusion**

Hector Bywater's "The Great Pacific War" stands as a remarkable example of how fiction can intersect with reality, potentially influencing military strategy and shaping perceptions of international relations. While the novel was not the sole inspiration for the Japanese attack on Pearl Harbor, it likely reinforced existing strategic concepts within the Japanese Navy and contributed to the broader discourse on potential Pacific conflicts.

In the end, the story of Bywater and his novel remains a fascinating chapter in the history of military strategy, illustrating how the power of imagination can sometimes foreshadow the realities of war, and how the written word can echo through time to influence the course of history.

**Sources:**

Zimm, Alan. The Attack on Pearl Harbor: Strategy, Combat, Myths and Deceptions. Casemate Publishers, 2011.

Lord, Walter. Day of Infamy, 60th Anniversary: The Classic Account of the Bombing of Pearl Harbor. Henry Holt and Co., 2001

Various Sources

# The Ghost Plane of Pearl Harbor

**Introduction**

Few stories capture the imagination quite like that of the Ghost Plane incident following the attack on Pearl Harbor. This enigmatic tale, blending elements of fact and folklore, has intrigued historians, aviation enthusiasts, and storytellers for decades. Set against the backdrop of one of the most pivotal moments in World War II, the story of the Ghost Plane serves as a testament to the enduring power of mystery and the human capacity for creating legends in times of crisis. This narrative explores the circumstances surrounding the alleged appearance of a mysterious aircraft in the aftermath of the Pearl Harbor attack, the eyewitness accounts that fueled its legend, and the broader context that allowed such a story to take root in the collective imagination of a nation at war.

**The Pearl Harbor Attack: Setting the Stage**

To understand the context of the Ghost Plane incident, we must first revisit the events of December 7, 1941. On that fateful Sunday morning, the tranquility of Pearl Harbor was shattered by the roar of Japanese aircraft engines. At approximately 7:55 a.m. Hawaiian time, the first wave of 353 Japanese fighters, bombers, and torpedo planes descended upon the unsuspecting U.S. naval base.

The attack, meticulously planned and executed, caught the American forces completely off guard. Within minutes, the peaceful harbor was transformed into a scene of chaos and destruction. Eight U.S. Navy battleships were damaged, with four sunk. The attack also destroyed or damaged over 300 aircraft, killed 2,403 Americans, and wounded 1,178 others.

The initial response from the U.S. forces was hampered by the element of surprise and the effectiveness of the Japanese attack. Many American aircraft were destroyed on the ground before they could be mobilized. However, a few Army P-40 and P-36 pursuit planes managed to get airborne from the small, untargeted airfield at Haleiwa on Oahu's north coast.

These aircraft engaged the Japanese attackers, but their efforts were limited due to the overwhelming number of enemy planes and the surprise nature of the attack. It was in this atmosphere of confusion, shock, and heightened alertness that the stage was set for the emergence of the Ghost Plane legend.

**The Mysterious Sighting**

According to the legend, on December 8, 1942, exactly one year after the Pearl Harbor attack, an unidentified aircraft was detected by radar operators in the United States. The timing and circumstances of this detection immediately raised alarms. The skies were overcast, and it was late in the evening – conditions that did not suggest an imminent attack, yet heightened the sense of unease and mystery surrounding the sighting.

Two American pilots were promptly dispatched to intercept the mysterious aircraft. As they approached, they were struck by an extraordinary sight. The unidentified plane was revealed to be a P-40 Warhawk, a type of aircraft that had not been seen in action since the Pearl Harbor attack a year earlier. But this was no ordinary P-40. The intercepting pilots reported that the aircraft was in a dire state – riddled with bullet holes, missing its landing gear, and seemingly piloted by a lifeless figure slumped over the controls.

In a moment that would cement this incident in the annals of military folklore, the pilots witnessed something truly inexplicable. The seemingly lifeless pilot of the damaged P-40 suddenly raised his head, smiled, and waved at the intercepting pilots. Before they could react or attempt further communication, the mysterious aircraft plummeted to the ground.

**The Aftermath and Investigation**

News of the incident spread quickly among military personnel and civilians alike. American troops swiftly surrounded the crash site, eager to unravel the mystery of the Ghost Plane. However, what they found – or rather, what they didn't find – only deepened the enigma.

Upon reaching the crash site, investigators were baffled to find no trace of the pilot. The wreckage of the P-40 was there, confirming that the incident was not a mere hallucination or false radar reading. Yet, the absence of any human remains or identifiable markings on the plane raised more questions than answers.

Among the wreckage, investigators reportedly discovered a document that appeared to be a diary. This document suggested that the plane had originated from Mindanao, an island in the Philippines over 1,300 miles away from the crash site. This revelation added another layer of impossibility to the already improbable tale. How could a heavily damaged aircraft, without landing gear, have traversed such a vast distance?

**Eyewitness Accounts and Personal Stories**

As news of the Ghost Plane spread, eyewitness accounts began to emerge, each adding to the growing legend. One particularly vivid account came from a radar operator who claimed to have tracked the plane as it approached the U.S. mainland. The operator described the aircraft's movements as erratic, noting that it seemed to be flying without any clear destination or purpose. This unusual behavior further fueled speculation about the plane's origins and the identity of its mysterious pilot. Civilians also reported sightings of the Ghost Plane. One account described the aircraft flying at an impossibly low altitude, its wingtip nearly grazing the ground as it passed over open farmland. This sighting was corroborated by multiple witnesses, lending an air of credibility to the increasingly fantastic tale.

Perhaps the most compelling personal story came from a farmer who claimed to have witnessed the plane's final moments. According to his account, the aircraft appeared to be piloted by a ghostly figure who vanished upon impact. While likely apocryphal, this story became a cornerstone of the local folklore surrounding the Ghost Plane incident.

**The Legend Takes Root**

As the story of the Ghost Plane circulated, it began to take on a life of its own. In the absence of concrete explanations, various theories emerged to account for the mysterious aircraft and its equally enigmatic pilot.

Some speculated that the plane was part of a secret mission from China, while others believed it to be an escape attempt by a lone pilot trying to reach American soil. The more fantastical interpretations suggested supernatural involvement, with the Ghost Plane seen as an omen or a visitation from the spirit world.

The tale found its way into popular culture, appearing in various forms in literature and media. It was notably featured in a short story in the book "Damned to Glory" by Robert Lee Scott, Jr., a P-40 pilot and double flying ace. The story's republication in Reader's Digest further cemented its place in the public imagination.

**Historical Context and Significance**

The Ghost Plane incident, whether fact or fiction, emerged during a time of great uncertainty and heightened emotions in the United States. The nation was still reeling from the shock of the Pearl Harbor attack and had just entered World War II. In this climate of fear, patriotism, and determination, stories of mysterious aircraft and ghostly pilots found fertile ground.

**Conclusion**

The tale of the Ghost Plane, with its blend of mystery, heroism, and the supernatural, continues to captivate imaginations decades after its alleged occurrence. While the veracity of the incident remains unproven, its impact on wartime folklore and its enduring presence in popular culture is undeniable.

**Sources**

Maksel, Rebecca. World War II's Most Famous Ghost Plane. Air and Space Magazine, 2017.

Allen, Thomas B. Remember Pearl Harbor: American and Japanese Survivors Tell Their Stories. National Geographic Kids, 2015.

Various Sources

# The Niihau Incident

## Introduction

In the chaotic hours following the Japanese attack on Pearl Harbor, a lesser-known drama unfolded on the tiny Hawaiian island of Niihau. This remote outpost, isolated from the world and untouched by modern conveniences, became the unlikely stage for a tense confrontation that would have far-reaching consequences for the United States' wartime policies. The Niihau Incident, as it came to be known, is a story of cultural clash, divided loyalties, and unexpected heroism that played out against the backdrop of one of the most significant events in American history. This story explores the events that transpired on Niihau from December 7 to December 13, 1941, weaving together the actions of Japanese pilot Shigenori Nishikaichi, the island's residents, and the complex interplay of duty and identity that defined this unique wartime episode.

## A Fateful Landing

On the morning of December 7, 1941, as the smoke still rose from the devastation at Pearl Harbor, Airman First Class Shigenori Nishikaichi found himself in a precarious situation. His Mitsubishi A6M2 Zero fighter, part of the second wave of the Japanese attack, had been damaged by American anti-aircraft fire. With his fuel tank leaking and return to his carrier impossible, Nishikaichi made a critical decision. Following pre-arranged plans, he set course for Niihau, an island the Japanese mistakenly believed to be uninhabited.

As Nishikaichi's damaged Zero sputtered over Niihau's rugged landscape, the island's residents went about their day, blissfully unaware of the world-changing events unfolding just miles away. Niihau, privately owned by the Robinson family, was a place frozen in time. With no electricity, no telephones, and limited contact with the outside world, its predominantly Native Hawaiian population lived much as their ancestors had for generations.

The peace of the Sunday afternoon was shattered as Nishikaichi's Zero crash-landed in a field. The screech of metal and the pilot's disoriented emergence from the cockpit marked the beginning of a week-long ordeal that would test the loyalties and courage of all involved.

## First Contact

Hawila Kaleohano, a Native Hawaiian resident, was the first to reach the crash site. Approaching the dazed pilot, Kaleohano acted with quick thinking that would prove crucial in the coming days. He relieved Nishikaichi of his pistol and a packet of papers, sensing their potential importance. The pilot, unable to communicate in English or Hawaiian, found himself at the mercy of people he had, just hours earlier, considered enemies.

Initially, the Niihau residents treated Nishikaichi with the hospitality for which Hawaiians are renowned. Unaware of the attack on Pearl Harbor, they saw only a man in need of assistance. The island's isolation, usually a point of pride, became a liability as the residents struggled to understand the significance of their unexpected visitor.

## The Truth Emerges

The veil of ignorance was lifted later that evening when the islanders gathered around a battery-powered radio and heard the shocking news of the Pearl Harbor attack. The atmosphere on Niihau shifted dramatically. Nishikaichi, once a guest, was now seen as a potential threat. The residents decided to hold the pilot until Aylmer Robinson, the island's owner, could arrive on his regular weekly visit to transport Nishikaichi to authorities on Kauai.

However, fate intervened. The U.S. military, reacting to the Pearl Harbor attack, had imposed a ban on inter-island travel. Robinson's expected arrival never came, leaving the Niihau residents to manage an increasingly tense situation on their own.

## A Community Divided

As days passed, the strain began to show. The island's small Japanese population, consisting of three individuals, found themselves caught between loyalty to their adopted home and cultural ties to Japan. Ishimatsu Shintani, a first-generation Japanese immigrant married to a Native Hawaiian, was initially called upon to translate for Nishikaichi. However, visibly disturbed by the situation, Shintani chose not to assist further, leaving the task to the Harada family.

Yoshio and Irene Harada, Hawaiian-born residents of Japanese descent, became key players in the unfolding drama. As they spent more time with Nishikaichi, translating his words and hearing his account of Japan's military might, their loyalties began to waver. The pilot, sensing an opportunity, worked to convince the Haradas to assist him in recovering his papers and weapon.

## The Turning Point

On December 12, five days after Nishikaichi's arrival, the situation reached a boiling point. Yoshio Harada, swayed by Nishikaichi's words and perhaps feeling a pull towards his Japanese heritage, made a fateful decision. In a shocking turn of events, Harada and Nishikaichi

overpowered the guard watching over the pilot's confiscated pistol. Armed and desperate, they began a reign of terror on the small island community.

The duo took several islanders hostage, including Ben Kanahele and his wife, Ella. They demanded the return of Nishikaichi's papers, which were still in Kaleohano's possession. Kaleohano, realizing the gravity of the situation, managed to escape and hide the papers, depriving Nishikaichi of potentially crucial military information.

**The Final Confrontation**

The events of December 13, 1941, would be seared into the memory of Niihau's residents for generations to come. As Nishikaichi and Harada's desperation grew, so did their aggression. In a tense confrontation, Ben Kanahele, a man known for his strength and courage, decided to act. Despite being shot three times by Nishikaichi, Kanahele managed to overpower the pilot. In a moment of extraordinary bravery, Ella Kanahele joined the fray, helping her husband subdue Nishikaichi.

The struggle ended with Nishikaichi's death, but the tragedy was not over. Yoshio Harada, perhaps realizing the full weight of his actions, took his own life. The Niihau Incident, a microcosm of the larger conflict engulfing the world, had come to a bloody end.

**Aftermath and Legacy**

In the days that followed, as military authorities arrived on Niihau to investigate, the full impact of the incident began to emerge. Ben Kanahele, despite his wounds, was hailed as a hero. He would later be awarded the Medal for Merit and the Purple Heart for his actions. Ironically, Ella Kanahele, whose role was equally crucial, received no official recognition, a reflection of the gender norms of the time.

The fate of the other participants varied. Irene Harada was imprisoned until late 1944 for her role in assisting Nishikaichi. Ishimatsu Shintani, despite his initial reluctance to get involved, was sent to an internment camp on the mainland, a fate shared by many Japanese Americans in the wake of Pearl Harbor.

The Niihau Incident had far-reaching consequences beyond the shores of the tiny island. It was cited in official reports and used as evidence to justify the internment of Japanese Americans during World War II. The actions of Yoshio Harada and the initial hesitation of some Japanese residents to oppose Nishikaichi were seen as proof that Japanese Americans might assist Japan if given the opportunity.

This interpretation, while overlooking the heroism of the Kanaheles and the complex nature of identity and loyalty, contributed to a climate of fear and suspicion. The incident became a powerful tool for those arguing for harsh measures against Japanese Americans, overshadowing the fact that the majority of Niihau's residents, including those of Japanese descent, had opposed Nishikaichi's actions.

**Conclusion**

The Niihau Incident stands as a complex and often overlooked chapter in the history of World War II. It is a story that defies simple categorization, challenging our understanding of loyalty, duty, and the impact of cultural identity in times of war. The actions of individuals like Ben and Ella Kanahele demonstrate the potential for heroism in ordinary people faced with extraordinary circumstances. At the same time, the choices made by Yoshio Harada and the consequences faced by Japanese Americans highlight the painful dilemmas and injustices that can arise in the fog of war.

In the end, the legacy of the Niihau Incident extends far beyond the shores of that small Hawaiian island. It stands as a powerful reminder of the unforeseen consequences of war, the strength of the human spirit in the face of adversity, and the enduring importance of understanding and empathy in times of national crisis. As we continue to grapple with issues of identity, loyalty, and national security in our own time, the lessons of Niihau remain as relevant and thought-provoking as ever.

**Sources**

Beekman, Allan. The Niihau Incident: The True Story of the Japanese Fighter Pilot Who, After the Pearl Harbor Attack, Crash-Landed on the Hawaiian Island of Niihau and Terrorized the Residents. Heritage Oress of Pacific, 1982.

Jones, Syd. Before and Beyond the Niihau Zero. CreateSpace Independent Publishing Platform, 2014.

Various Sources

# Admiral Joseph Taussig and his Unheeded Advice

**Introduction**

Few World War II stories are as poignant as that of Admiral Joseph K. Taussig, a man whose foresight could have altered the course of World War II. As storm clouds gathered over the Pacific in the years leading up to 1941, Taussig stood as a lone voice, warning of the impending threat from Imperial Japan. His story is one of prescience and frustration, of duty and dismissal, set against the backdrop of a world hurtling towards conflict. This narrative explores Taussig's life, his warnings, and the fateful decisions that led to one of the most devastating surprise attacks in American history.

**A Naval Legacy**

Joseph Knefler Taussig was born into a world of naval tradition on August 30, 1877, in Dresden, Germany. The son of Rear Admiral Edward D. Taussig, young Joseph seemed destined for a life at sea. His journey began at the U.S. Naval Academy in 1895, where he distinguished himself not only as a scholar but also as an athlete, serving as president of the Naval Academy Athletic Association.

Taussig's early career was marked by action and valor. As a naval cadet aboard the USS New York during the Spanish-American War, he witnessed firsthand the power of naval warfare. His baptism by fire continued during the Philippine Insurrection and the Boxer Rebellion, where he was wounded in action and later awarded the Purple Heart. These experiences shaped Taussig's understanding of conflict and the vital role of naval power in global affairs.

**Rise Through the Ranks**

As Taussig rose through the naval hierarchy, his reputation for both tactical skill and strategic insight grew. His command of the USS Wadsworth during World War I was notable for his famous declaration, "We are ready, now, Sir," in response to a query about readiness for sea duty. This statement would come to epitomize Taussig's approach to naval preparedness – always ready, always vigilant.

In the interwar years, Taussig's career took him to the Naval War College, where he honed his strategic thinking. It was during this period that he began to focus intently on the growing threat in the Pacific. As Japan's imperial ambitions expanded, Taussig saw with clarity the collision course set between the United States and the Empire of Japan.

## The Prophet Speaks

The pivotal moment in Taussig's career came in May 1940, when he testified before the Senate Naval Affairs Committee. With the world already at war in Europe, Taussig turned the committee's attention to the Pacific. His warnings were stark and specific:

"Japan's imperialistic ambitions pose a direct threat to American interests in the Pacific," Taussig declared. "They seek to annex territories including China, the Philippines, and the Dutch East Indies. We must expand our naval capabilities, particularly with Iowa-class and Montana-class battleships, to counter this growing threat".

Taussig went further, predicting not just conflict, but the specific form it might take. "An attack on Pearl Harbor is not just possible, but probable," he warned. "Japan seeks domination of the Far East and will resort to war to achieve its goals. We must establish an impregnable naval base in the Philippines and forge alliances with the English, Dutch, and French to ensure Pacific security".

His testimony was a clear call for action, a plea for preparedness in the face of what he saw as an inevitable conflict.

## The Dismissal

The response to Taussig's warnings was swift – but not in the way he had hoped. His testimony was seen as alarmist, running counter to the prevailing political winds. President Franklin D. Roosevelt, already grappling with the war in Europe and domestic opposition to American involvement in foreign conflicts, was displeased with Taussig's outspoken stance.

The admiral found himself facing potential disciplinary action, saved only by the intervention of Admirals Stark and Nimitz. The political and military leadership, focused on the war in Europe and hopeful of avoiding conflict in the Pacific, chose to dismiss Taussig's warnings as overly pessimistic.

This dismissal was symptomatic of a broader failure to recognize the true nature of the Japanese threat. Despite growing tensions and Japan's aggressive actions in Asia, many in Washington

believed that diplomatic efforts and economic sanctions would be sufficient to curb Japanese ambitions.

## The Fateful Day

On December 7, 1941, Taussig's worst fears were realized. The Japanese attack on Pearl Harbor caught the United States woefully unprepared, despite the warnings that had been sounded. In a cruel twist of fate, Taussig's son, Joseph K. Taussig Jr., was serving as the starboard anti-aircraft battery officer on the USS Nevada during the attack. Despite being severely wounded, the younger Taussig continued to perform his duties, embodying the spirit of readiness his father had long advocated.

As news of the attack spread, the words of Admiral Taussig must have echoed hauntingly in the halls of power in Washington. The very scenario he had warned about – a surprise attack on Pearl Harbor – had come to pass with devastating consequences.

**Aftermath and Reflection**

In the wake of Pearl Harbor, there was a scramble to understand how such an attack could have been possible. Taussig's warnings, once dismissed, were now seen in a new light. The naval expansion he had advocated for was implemented with urgency, but too late to prevent the initial Japanese onslaught.

Taussig himself had retired in 1941, receiving a commendation from the Secretary of the Navy and a promotion to Vice Admiral upon retirement. While he was no longer in active service, his influence continued to be felt as the Navy rapidly expanded to meet the challenges of a two-ocean war.

The legacy of Taussig's warnings extended beyond the immediate aftermath of Pearl Harbor. His emphasis on the importance of intelligence, preparedness, and strategic foresight became key elements of U.S. military doctrine in the post-war era.

**Conclusion**

The story of Admiral Joseph Taussig is a powerful reminder of the importance of heeding expert warnings, even when they run counter to prevailing wisdom. His prescient understanding of the threat posed by Japan, and the tragic dismissal of his warnings, serve as a cautionary tale for military and political leaders.

Taussig's legacy is not one of bitterness or recrimination but of the enduring importance of vigilance and preparedness. The USS Joseph K. Taussig, named in his honor, stands as a testament to his contributions to naval strategy and his unwavering commitment to the defense of his nation.

**Sources**

Wohlstetter, Roberta. Pearl Harbor: Warning and Decision. Stanford University Press. 1962.

Prange, Gordon W. At Dawn We Slept: The Untold Story of Pearl Harbor. McGraw-Hill, 1981

## Hitler's Reaction to the Attack

### Introduction:

On December 7, 1941, the Japanese attack on Pearl Harbor stunned the world, drawing the United States into World War II. While Japan's motives for launching the surprise attack have been extensively studied, the repercussions of this event reverberated far beyond the Pacific. In Europe, Adolf Hitler, the dictator of Nazi Germany, was dealing with his own war on the Eastern Front against the Soviet Union and in North Africa against the British. The attack on Pearl Harbor significantly altered the global dynamics of the war. This story delves into Hitler's reaction to the attack, what he knew in advance, how it impacted his overall strategy, and the reasoning behind his decision to declare war on the United States. It also examines how quickly Hitler's Germany aligned itself with Japan following the U.S. entry into the conflict.

### Background:

**The Axis Powers Before Pearl Harbor:** By the time Japan launched its attack on Pearl Harbor, Nazi Germany and Imperial Japan had already formed a loose alliance as part of the Axis Powers. The Tripartite Pact, signed in September 1940 between Germany, Japan, and Italy, established a formal agreement that these nations would support one another in the event of an attack by a country not already involved in the war. Notably, this agreement was aimed at deterring the United States from entering the war.

However, this alliance was more of a strategic convenience than a deep military partnership. Japan's primary interests lay in the Pacific and Asia, while Germany was focused on Europe. Moreover, communication and cooperation between the two countries were limited due to geographic separation and differing strategic priorities. Hitler admired Japan's militaristic culture and expansionist ambitions, but his focus remained on defeating Britain and the Soviet Union to achieve dominance in Europe.

Hitler and his inner circle had some knowledge of Japan's aggressive plans in the Pacific, but they were not privy to the specific details of the attack on Pearl Harbor. Japan had informed Germany of its intention to go to war with the United States, but there is no evidence to suggest that Hitler knew precisely when or how Japan would strike. The Germans understood that Japanese aggression in the Pacific would inevitably bring the U.S. into the war, but they did not anticipate the exact nature of the attack.

**Narrative:**

**The Attack on Pearl Harbor and Hitler's Initial Reaction:** When news of the Japanese attack on Pearl Harbor reached Hitler, his initial reaction was one of elation. The attack, which crippled the U.S. Pacific Fleet, was seen by Hitler as a significant blow to one of Germany's most formidable potential enemies. He believed that the U.S., now preoccupied with fighting Japan, would be distracted from European affairs, allowing Germany to focus on defeating Britain and the Soviet Union without American interference.

On December 8, 1941, the day after the attack, Hitler expressed his satisfaction with Japan's actions in a meeting with his military advisers. He was particularly pleased because he viewed the U.S. as a future threat to Germany's ambitions in Europe, and now that the U.S. was at war with Japan, Hitler saw an opportunity to neutralize that threat by expanding the conflict. In Hitler's mind, Japan's attack on Pearl Harbor validated his long-held belief that a global conflict was inevitable and that the U.S. would eventually become involved.

However, Hitler was not immediately bound by the Tripartite Pact to declare war on the United States. The pact stipulated that Germany would come to Japan's aid only if Japan was attacked, not if it was the aggressor. This meant that, in theory, Hitler could have refrained from declaring war on the U.S. and focused solely on his campaigns in Europe and the Soviet Union. Despite this, within days of the attack, Hitler made the decision to declare war on the United States.

**Hitler's Strategic Considerations:** Hitler's decision to declare war on the United States was not made lightly, as it had significant strategic implications. In 1941, Germany was already engaged in a brutal war on multiple fronts. The Eastern Front against the Soviet Union had become a quagmire, with the German invasion, Operation Barbarossa, stalling in the face of fierce Soviet resistance and the onset of the harsh Russian winter. In North Africa, the German Afrika Korps, under the command of Erwin Rommel, was locked in a seesaw struggle against British forces.

Despite these challenges, Hitler believed that a declaration of war against the United States would ultimately benefit Germany. Several factors influenced his decision:

**1. Confidence in German Victory in Europe:** Hitler believed that Germany was on the verge of victory in Europe, particularly against Britain and the Soviet Union. He thought that once these enemies were defeated, Germany would be free to turn its attention to the United States. Hitler underestimated the resilience of both Britain and the Soviet Union, assuming that a quick victory on the Eastern Front would allow Germany to shift resources to a potential future conflict with the U.S.

**2. Japanese Assistance Against the Soviet Union:** Hitler hoped that by aligning more closely with Japan, he could persuade the Japanese to attack the Soviet Union from the east, opening up a second front and relieving some of the pressure on German forces in the west. However, this hope was misplaced, as Japan had no intention of engaging the Soviets at that time, having already suffered defeats in earlier border skirmishes with Soviet forces.

**3. Underestimating American Military Strength:** Hitler, like many German military leaders, underestimated the industrial and military capabilities of the United States. Although the U.S. had not yet fully mobilized for war, its vast industrial capacity and resources far exceeded those of Germany. Hitler believed that the U.S. would be too focused on the war in the Pacific to mount a significant challenge in Europe.

**4. Racial Ideology and Anti-American Sentiment:** Hitler's decision was also influenced by his deeply ingrained racial ideology and anti-American sentiment. He saw the United States as a weak, racially mixed society dominated by Jewish influence, and he believed that it would not be able to sustain a prolonged war. Hitler's racial theories clouded his judgment, leading him to underestimate the determination and strength of the American people.

**Hitler's Declaration of War Against the United States:** On December 11, 1941, just four days after the Pearl Harbor attack and three days after the U.S. had declared war on Japan, Adolf Hitler took the fateful step of declaring war on the United States. In a speech to the Reichstag, Hitler formally announced Germany's entry into the war against the U.S., framing his decision as a defensive measure against American aggression. He accused President Franklin D. Roosevelt of systematically undermining Germany through economic sanctions and military aid to Britain and the Soviet Union under the Lend-Lease Act.

Hitler's declaration of war was largely symbolic, as the United States had already committed to supporting the Allied powers. However, it marked the official expansion of World War II into a truly global conflict, pitting the Axis Powers against the full might of the Allied coalition, including the United States, Britain, the Soviet Union, and China.

From a strategic standpoint, Hitler's decision to declare war on the U.S. has been widely criticized by historians as one of his greatest miscalculations. By declaring war, Hitler gave Roosevelt the justification he needed to fully commit American resources to the European theater, where the U.S. would play a decisive role in defeating Nazi Germany.

**The Impact on Hitler's War Strategy:** The entry of the United States into the war had profound consequences for Germany's war strategy. In the short term, the immediate impact was minimal, as the U.S. military was not yet fully mobilized, and American troops would not see significant action in Europe until the invasion of North Africa in November 1942 (Operation Torch). However, the long-term effects of U.S. involvement would be devastating for Germany.

**1. Lend-Lease Aid to the Allies:** With the U.S. now fully committed to the war, the flow of Lend-Lease aid to Britain and the Soviet Union increased dramatically. American industrial might provided the Allies with the tanks, planes, ships, and other war materials they needed to sustain their war efforts. The infusion of American resources helped turn the tide in favor of the Allies, particularly on the Eastern Front, where Soviet forces began to push back against the German invasion.

**2. The Combined Bomber Offensive:** The U.S. entry into the war also allowed for the launch of a massive strategic bombing campaign against Germany. American bombers, along with the British Royal Air Force, targeted German industrial centers, infrastructure, and cities in a sustained effort to cripple the Nazi war machine. The bombing campaign, known as the Combined Bomber Offensive, inflicted significant damage on Germany's ability to produce war materials and maintain its military strength.

**3. The Invasion of Europe:** Perhaps the most significant impact of U.S. involvement was the eventual invasion of Nazi-occupied Europe. The U.S. played a key role in the planning and execution of Operation Overlord, the Allied invasion of Normandy in June 1944. The D-Day landings marked the beginning of the end for Nazi Germany, as Allied forces broke through German defenses and began the liberation of Western Europe.

**Conclusion:**

Adolf Hitler's reaction to the attack on Pearl Harbor was one of initial enthusiasm, believing that Japan's actions would distract the United States and prevent it from interfering in Germany's war in Europe. However, his decision to declare war on the United States just days after the attack would prove to be one of the most significant strategic blunders of World War II. By drawing the U.S. into the conflict, Hitler ensured that Nazi Germany would face the full might of American industrial and military power. The United States' entry into the war hastened Germany's defeat by providing critical support to the Allies and playing a pivotal role in the liberation of Europe.

**Sources**

Kershaw, Ian. Hitler: A Biography. W.W. Norton & Company, 2008.

Ryback, Timothy W. Takeover: Hitler's Final Rise to Power. Knopf, 2008.

Various Sources

# The Pearl Harbor Conspiracy Theories

**Introduction:**

The attack on Pearl Harbor on December 7, 1941, remains one of the most significant events in American history. However, alongside the official narrative, various conspiracy theories have emerged, suggesting that the U.S. government had advance knowledge of the attack or even facilitated it to provoke American entry into World War II. This narrative explores the origins, claims, and counterarguments of these conspiracy theories, shedding light on the enduring fascination with this historical event.

**Background:**

The Japanese attack on Pearl Harbor was a surprise military strike aimed at crippling the U.S. Pacific Fleet. The attack resulted in the deaths of over 2,400 Americans and led to the United States' formal entry into World War II. In the aftermath, questions arose about how such a devastating attack could have caught the U.S. military off guard. These questions laid the groundwork for various conspiracy theories.

One of the earliest and most persistent theories is the "advance-knowledge" theory, which claims that high-ranking officials in the U.S. government knew about the attack in advance but allowed it to happen to galvanize public support for entering the war. This theory has been propagated by several writers and historians, despite being widely discredited by mainstream scholars.

**Narrative:**

**Conspiracy Theories:** The advance-knowledge theory gained traction in the years following the attack, fueled by a combination of circumstantial evidence, misinterpretations, and the natural human tendency to seek explanations for catastrophic events. Proponents of the theory argue that President Franklin D. Roosevelt and his administration had intercepted Japanese communications indicating an imminent attack but chose not to act on this information.

**The McCollum Memo:** One of the key pieces of evidence cited by conspiracy theorists is the "McCollum memo," a document written by Lieutenant Commander Arthur H. McCollum in October 1940. The memo outlined a strategy to provoke Japan into attacking the United States, thereby justifying American entry into the war. Conspiracy theorists argue that this memo is proof of a deliberate plan to incite a Japanese attack.

**Did Churchill Know:** Another frequently cited piece of evidence is the alleged foreknowledge of the attack by British Prime Minister Winston Churchill. Some theorists claim that Churchill knew about the attack and informed Roosevelt, who then chose to withhold the information from military commanders in Hawaii. This claim is based on the close intelligence-sharing relationship between the United States and the United Kingdom during the war.

Despite these claims, most historians reject the advance-knowledge theory, citing several key discrepancies and the lack of credible evidence. For instance, the McCollum memo was a strategic assessment rather than a directive, and there is no evidence that it was ever acted upon. Additionally, intercepted Japanese communications were often vague and did not provide specific details about the timing or location of the attack.

**Back Door to War:** Another prominent conspiracy theory is the "back door to war" theory, which suggests that Roosevelt deliberately provoked Japan into attacking the United States as a means to enter the European theater of World War II. Proponents of this theory argue that Roosevelt's policies, such as the oil embargo on Japan, were designed to push Japan into a corner and force them to strike first.

This theory is also widely disputed by historians, who argue that Roosevelt's actions were consistent with efforts to deter Japanese aggression rather than provoke it. The oil embargo, for example, was a response to Japan's invasion of French Indochina and was intended to pressure Japan to withdraw its forces. Furthermore, there is no concrete evidence to suggest that Roosevelt had any foreknowledge of the specific attack on Pearl Harbor.

The fascination with Pearl Harbor conspiracy theories can be attributed to several factors. First, the sheer scale and impact of the attack make it fertile ground for speculation and alternative explanations. Second, the secrecy and compartmentalization of intelligence operations during the war have led to gaps in the historical record, which conspiracy theorists exploit to support their claims. Finally, the natural human tendency to seek patterns and explanations for traumatic events drives the persistence of these theories.

## Conclusion

The conspiracy theories surrounding the attack on Pearl Harbor highlight the enduring human desire to understand and explain catastrophic events. While the advanced knowledge and back door to war theories offer intriguing narratives, they are not supported by credible evidence and are widely rejected by mainstream historians.

## Sources

Wohlstetter, Roberta. Pearl Harbor: Warning and Decision. Stanford University Press. 1962.

Gordon, John S. Pearl Harbor: A History. New York: Simon & Schuster, 2001.

Various Sources

# Operation K: The Forgotten Second Attack

### Introduction

The attack on Pearl Harbor on December 7, 1941, stands as a defining moment that drew the United States into global conflict. However, less known and often overlooked is the second attack on Pearl Harbor, which occurred just three months later on March 4, 1942. This operation, codenamed "Operation K" by the Japanese, was a bold attempt to assess the damage inflicted by the initial attack and to disrupt ongoing American repair efforts. While not as devastating or well-known as its predecessor, this second strike on Pearl Harbor offers a fascinating glimpse into the strategic thinking of both Japanese and American forces in the early stages of the Pacific War. This story explores the planning, execution, and aftermath of Operation K, shedding light on a little-known chapter of World War II that underscores the ongoing tensions and evolving strategies in the Pacific Theater.

### The Strategic Context

In the wake of the devastating attack on Pearl Harbor on December 7, 1941, the Pacific War had erupted into a full-scale conflict. The Japanese, emboldened by their initial success, sought to capitalize on their advantage and consolidate their gains across the Pacific. Meanwhile, the United States, still reeling from the surprise attack, was scrambling to rebuild its naval power and formulate a strategy to counter Japanese aggression.

It was against this backdrop that the Japanese Imperial Navy conceived Operation K. The mission was twofold: to conduct reconnaissance of Pearl Harbor to assess the damage from the December attack and to disrupt ongoing American repair and salvage operations. The Japanese high command believed that by striking Pearl Harbor again, they could delay the American recovery and buy more time to strengthen their defensive perimeter in the Pacific.

### Planning and Preparation

The architects of Operation K faced significant challenges from the outset. The mission would require long-range aircraft capable of flying from Japan's bases in the Marshall Islands to Hawaii, a distance of over 4,000 miles. To accomplish this feat, the Japanese turned to the Kawanishi H8K "Emily" flying boat, a remarkable aircraft known for its exceptional range and durability.

Initially, the plan called for five H8Ks to participate in the mission. However, due to various constraints, only two were ultimately available for the operation. These aircraft were to fly from the Marshall Islands to a refueling point at the French Frigate Shoals, where they would be met by submarines carrying extra fuel. From there, they would continue to Pearl Harbor to carry out their reconnaissance and bombing mission.

The operation was meticulously planned, with the Japanese relying on a network of submarines to provide weather updates and navigational assistance. One submarine, the I-23, was specifically tasked with monitoring weather conditions near Hawaii and reporting back to the flying boats. However, in a portent of the challenges to come, the I-23 was lost at sea before the operation began, depriving the mission of crucial meteorological intelligence.

**The Mission Unfolds**

On March 4, 1942, the two Kawanishi H8K flying boats took off from the Marshall Islands, each carrying four 250-kilogram bombs. Their flight path took them over vast stretches of open ocean, pushing the limits of their range and the endurance of their crews. As they approached the French Frigate Shoals, the tension mounted. The refueling rendezvous was critical to the success of the mission, and any failure here would doom the operation before it even reached its target.

Despite the loss of the I-23 and the challenges posed by navigating such vast distances, the flying boats successfully met with the refueling submarines. With their tanks topped off, the aircraft set course for Oahu, flying through the night towards their unsuspecting target.

As dawn broke over Hawaii on March 4, the two Japanese flying boats approached Oahu. However, they immediately encountered a significant obstacle: a thick cloud cover obscured their view of Pearl Harbor. Without visual contact with their target and lacking the weather intelligence that the lost I-23 was supposed to provide, the pilots were forced to rely on dead reckoning to locate their objective.

**The Attack**

The poor visibility that hampered the Japanese pilots also worked to their advantage, shielding them from American air defenses. Despite the improvements made to radar and early warning systems following the December 7 attack, the approaching aircraft were not detected until they were relatively close to Oahu.

When American radar operators finally picked up the incoming planes, they quickly scrambled Curtiss P-40 fighters to intercept them. However, the dense cloud cover that had frustrated the Japanese pilots also hindered the American defenders, making it nearly impossible for them to locate and engage the intruders.

In the confusion and poor visibility, the two Japanese flying boats made their bombing runs. One aircraft, unable to locate Pearl Harbor, dropped its bombs into the ocean. The other, believing it had found its target, released its payload. However, instead of striking the vital Ten-Ten Dock as

intended, the bombs fell near Roosevelt High School, north of Honolulu. The explosions shattered windows but caused no significant damage or casualties.

**Aftermath and Significance**

As quickly as they had appeared, the Japanese flying boats disappeared back into the clouds, leaving behind a bewildered and somewhat relieved Pearl Harbor. The attack, if it could be called that, had been a far cry from the devastation wrought on December 7. No ships had been damaged, no facilities destroyed, and remarkably, no lives had been lost.

For the Japanese, Operation K was a disappointment. The mission had failed to achieve its primary objectives of gathering useful intelligence and disrupting American repair efforts. The operation had demonstrated the extreme difficulty of conducting long-range bombing missions with the technology of the time, particularly when faced with adverse weather conditions.

However, the attack was not without significance. For the Americans, it served as a stark reminder that Pearl Harbor remained vulnerable to Japanese attacks, even if those attacks were now more symbolic than destructive. The operation spurred further improvements in air defenses and early warning systems, contributing to the overall strengthening of American military capabilities in the Pacific.

Moreover, Operation K highlighted the shifting nature of the war in the Pacific. The Japanese, who had seemed unstoppable in the wake of Pearl Harbor, were now struggling to maintain their strategic advantage. The limited scale and impact of the March 4 attack stood in stark contrast to the overwhelming force brought to bear on December 7, hinting at the logistical and strategic challenges Japan would face as the war progressed.

For the American public, news of the attack, while not causing the same shock as the December 7 raid, nevertheless raised fears of a potential Japanese invasion of Hawaii. These concerns would influence both military planning and civilian life in Hawaii for the remainder of the war.

**Conclusion**

The second attack on Pearl Harbor, Operation K, stands as a little-known but fascinating episode in the early stages of the Pacific War. While it failed to achieve its military objectives, the operation offers valuable insights into the strategic thinking, technological limitations, and evolving tactics of both Japanese and American forces in the months following the outbreak of war.

Operation K demonstrated the extreme challenges of long-range warfare in the 1940s, showcasing both the remarkable capabilities of aircraft like the Kawanishi H8K and the limitations imposed by navigation, weather, and logistics. It also highlighted the rapid adaptation of American defenses, which, while not perfect, had significantly improved since December 7.

**Sources**

Graff, Cory. The Second Pearl Harbor Attack. The National WWII Museum. 2021.

Prange, Gordon W. At Dawn We Slept: The Untold Story of Pearl Harbor. McGraw-Hill, 1981

# Chief Radioman Thomas James Reeves

## Introduction

Few events in naval history loom as large as the attack on Pearl Harbor on December 7, 1941. Among the many acts of heroism that day, the story of Chief Radioman Thomas James Reeves stands out as a testament to courage, duty, and sacrifice. While initially believed to have served on the USS Arizona, records show that Reeves' valor was demonstrated aboard the USS California. This narrative explores Reeves' background, his actions during the attack, and the lasting legacy of his heroism.

## A Life of Service

Thomas James Reeves was born on December 9, 1895, in Thomaston, Connecticut, to William and Mary A. Reeves, both Irish immigrants. His journey in the United States Navy began on July 20, 1917, when he enlisted in the Naval Reserve as an Electrician Third Class during World War I. After a brief release from duty, Reeves was recalled to active service and transferred to the regular Navy on April 16, 1920. His commitment to naval service was evident in his decision to re-enlist on October 12, 1921, after a short discharge, marking the beginning of a career that would ultimately lead him to the fateful morning of December 7, 1941.

Throughout his naval career, Reeves demonstrated dedication and skill, rising through the ranks to become a Chief Radioman. His expertise in communications would prove crucial in the chaotic moments of the Pearl Harbor attack.

## The Day of Infamy

On the morning of December 7, 1941, Chief Radioman Reeves was aboard the USS California, a Tennessee-class battleship moored at the southernmost berth of Battleship Row in Pearl Harbor. The peaceful Sunday morning was shattered at 7:55 a.m. when the first Japanese bombs fell on the unsuspecting naval base.

As alarms sounded and men rushed to battle stations, the USS California, like other ships in the harbor, became a target of Japanese aircraft. The ship was hit by two bombs and two torpedoes, causing significant damage and starting fires throughout the vessel. Amid this chaos, the ship's mechanized ammunition hoists were put out of commission, severely hampering the crew's ability to defend against the ongoing attack.

## Heroism in the Face of Danger

It was in this moment of crisis that Chief Radioman Reeves demonstrated extraordinary courage. Recognizing the critical need for ammunition at the anti-aircraft guns, Reeves took it upon himself to organize a human chain to manually transport ammunition from the ship's magazines to the gunners above.

In the burning passageways of the USS California, Reeves worked tirelessly, disregarding his safety to ensure that the ship's defenses could continue to fight back against the Japanese onslaught. The heat was intense, and thick smoke filled the air, making each breath a struggle. Yet Reeves persisted, knowing that every round of ammunition he helped deliver could mean the difference between life and death for his fellow sailors and the ship itself.

As the attack continued, Reeves' heroic efforts began to take their toll. The smoke and fire became overwhelming, but still, he pressed on. In a final act of selflessness, Reeves continued to assist in the ammunition transport until he was overcome by smoke and fire. His sacrifice ensured that the USS California's anti-aircraft guns could continue to defend against the attack, potentially saving countless lives.

## The Aftermath and Recognition

The attack on Pearl Harbor left the USS California heavily damaged, and 98 of her crew, including Chief Radioman Reeves, lost their lives. In the days and weeks that followed, as the nation grappled with the shock of the attack and prepared for war, stories of individual heroism began to emerge.

Reeves' actions stood out as a shining example of the bravery and dedication displayed by American servicemen during the attack. For his extraordinary courage and complete disregard for his own life, Chief Radioman Thomas James Reeves was posthumously awarded the Medal of Honor, the highest military decoration presented by the United States government to members of the armed forces.

The citation for Reeves' Medal of Honor reads, in part: "For distinguished conduct in the line of his profession, extraordinary courage and disregard of his safety during the attack on the Fleet in Pearl Harbor, Territory of Hawaii, by Japanese forces on December 7, 1941. Chief Radioman Reeves, stationed in the U.S.S. California, was on duty in the radio room when torpedoes and bombs struck the ship. He remained at his post and rendered valuable service in the repair of the radio installations which were vital to communications."

## Lasting Legacy

The heroism of Thomas James Reeves did not go unnoticed or unremembered. In addition to the Medal of Honor, Reeves was further honored when the Navy named a destroyer escort, the USS Reeves (DE-156), after him. This ship, commissioned in 1943, served as a living memorial to Reeves' sacrifice, carrying his spirit of courage and dedication into further service during World War II.

Today, the memory of Chief Radioman Reeves and his fellow heroes is preserved at the Pearl Harbor National Memorial. While Reeves served on the USS California rather than the USS Arizona, his story is part of the broader narrative of courage and sacrifice that defines the events of December 7, 1941. Visitors to Pearl Harbor can reflect on the bravery of men like Reeves as they view the USS Arizona Memorial and learn about the attack that changed the course of history.

**Conclusion**

The story of Chief Radioman Thomas James Reeves is a powerful reminder of the extraordinary heroism displayed by ordinary Americans in times of crisis. His selfless actions aboard the USS California during the attack on Pearl Harbor exemplify the highest ideals of duty, courage, and sacrifice. While the initial confusion about his service aboard the USS Arizona has been clarified, the essence of Reeves' heroism remains unchanged.

In the words often associated with the Pearl Harbor memorials, "At this shrine to patriotism, may our resolve be as strong as the steel of the ships that once fought here. May it be as lasting as the love we hold for those who served aboard them. May we never forget."

**Sources**

Gordon, John S. Pearl Harbor: A History. New York: Simon & Schuster, 2001.

Prange, Gordon W. At Dawn We Slept: The Untold Story of Pearl Harbor. McGraw-Hill, 1981

Various Sources

## The Deadly Double

**Introduction**

In the wake of the devastating attack on Pearl Harbor on December 7, 1941, a series of mysterious advertisements appeared in American newspapers, captivating public attention and sparking widespread speculation. These enigmatic ads, known as "The Deadly Double," have since become a fascinating footnote in the history of World War II, blending elements of coincidence, conspiracy, and wartime paranoia. This narrative explores the nature of these ads, their impact on the American public, and the various theories that have emerged to explain their existence. Through this exploration, we gain insight into the complex interplay between media, public perception, and national security during one of the most critical periods in American history.

**The Ads Unveiled**

On November 22, 1941, just two weeks before the attack on Pearl Harbor, the New Yorker magazine featured a series of advertisements that would soon become the subject of intense scrutiny and speculation. The main ad, promoting a game called "The Deadly Double," depicted people playing dice in an air raid shelter. The headline read "Achtung, Warning, Alerte!" – a multilingual call to attention that seemed oddly prescient given the events that would soon unfold.

What caught the eye of many readers, both at the time and in the years following the war, were the dice shown in the advertisement. They displayed the numbers 12 and 7 – a combination that would prove to be an eerie coincidence when matched against the date of the Pearl Harbor attack. This seemingly innocuous detail would become the cornerstone of numerous conspiracy theories in the years to come.

**Public Reaction and Speculation**

The impact of these ads on the American public was profound and multifaceted. In the immediate aftermath of the Pearl Harbor attack, as the nation reeled from the shock of sudden war, the ads became a focal point for a populace searching for answers and meaning. The cryptic nature of the advertisements, combined with their timely appearance, led to widespread discussion and debate in both private and public spheres.

Newspapers and radio programs featured analyses and interpretations of the ads, with experts and laypeople alike offering their theories. The ads became a topic of conversation across the country, reflecting the heightened sense of alert and suspicion that permeated American society during the early days of the war. This public fascination with the ads contributed to a climate of vigilance, as citizens became more aware of the potential for hidden messages and propaganda in everyday media.

**Theories and Investigations**

The mysterious nature of "The Deadly Double" ads led to a flurry of theories and investigations. American intelligence officers, recognizing the potential significance of the ads, launched inquiries to determine if they might have been a secret signal to Japanese agents. The numbers on the dice – 12 and 7 – were thought to represent the date of the attack, while other numbers in the ad were speculated to indicate the time, although the actual attack began just before 8 AM.

Ladislas Farago, a prominent military historian, suggested that the ads might have been a covert message designed to alert Japanese operatives in the United States. This theory gained traction in the paranoid atmosphere of wartime America, where the threat of espionage and sabotage loomed large in the public imagination.

However, as investigations progressed, a more mundane explanation began to emerge. It was revealed that the game and the ads were genuine creations of Roger Paul Craig, an entrepreneur looking to capitalize on the popularity of dice games. Craig's widow later confirmed that the ads were merely promotional teasers, their timing an unfortunate coincidence.

**The Role of Wartime Media**

The story of "The Deadly Double" ads highlights the significant role that media played during World War II. In an era before digital communication, newspapers were a primary source of information and a powerful tool for influencing public opinion. The appearance of these mysterious ads underscores the potential for media to shape perceptions and fuel speculation, especially during times of national crisis.

The ads also reflect the broader context of wartime communication strategies. While "The Deadly Double" was ultimately revealed to be an innocent marketing campaign, its impact demonstrates how easily information could be misinterpreted or co-opted for alternative

narratives. This incident serves as a reminder of the power of propaganda and the importance of critical media consumption, lessons that remain relevant in today's information-saturated world.

**Legacy and Continued Fascination**

Despite the debunking of the conspiracy theories surrounding "The Deadly Double" ads, they continue to fascinate historians and the public alike. The incident serves as a case study of how coincidences can be misconstrued as conspiracies, especially in times of heightened national anxiety. It also provides insight into the mindset of Americans in the early days of World War II, revealing the fears, suspicions, and desire for meaning that characterized the era.

The legacy of these ads extends beyond their historical context. They have become a part of Pearl Harbor lore, often cited in discussions about wartime propaganda, media influence, and the nature of coincidence. Their story serves as a cautionary tale about the dangers of reading too much into ambiguous information, while also highlighting the human tendency to seek patterns and meaning in times of chaos and uncertainty.

**Conclusion**

The mysterious ads that appeared in the New Yorker magazine following the Pearl Harbor attack remain a fascinating chapter in the history of World War II. While they were ultimately revealed to be an unfortunate coincidence rather than a deliberate warning or coded message, their impact on the American psyche was significant. The story of "The Deadly Double" ads serves as a poignant reminder of the power of media, the nature of wartime paranoia, and the human desire to find meaning in coincidence.

**Sources**

Wohlstetter, Roberta. Pearl Harbor: Warning and Decision. Stanford University Press. 1962.

The Newspaper Ad Warning. PearlHarbor.org. 2017.

Various Sources

# The Heroism of Mervyn Bennion

## Introduction

In the chronicles of naval history, few stories of individual heroism shine as brightly as that of Captain Mervyn Sharp Bennion during the attack on Pearl Harbor. On December 7, 1941, as Japanese planes unleashed devastation upon the U.S. Pacific Fleet, Captain Bennion's unwavering courage and leadership aboard the USS West Virginia exemplified the highest traditions of the United States Navy. This story explores Bennion's background, his actions during the attack, and the legacy of his sacrifice, offering a glimpse into one of the most pivotal moments of World War II.

## A Life of Service

Mervyn Sharp Bennion's journey to that fateful December morning began far from the shores of Hawaii, in the small farming community of Vernon, Utah. Born on May 5, 1887, Bennion was raised in a family deeply rooted in the Mormon faith, with a heritage tracing back to the early pioneers who settled the Utah Territory. From these humble beginnings, young Mervyn's path led him to the United States Naval Academy, where he graduated third in his class in 1910, setting the stage for a distinguished naval career.

Throughout the interwar years, Bennion honed his skills and leadership abilities across various assignments. From his early days aboard the USS California to his command of destroyer divisions, Bennion's career was marked by a steady ascent through the ranks. His expertise in ordnance and gunnery, developed during World War I at the Washington Navy Yard, would prove invaluable in his future commands.

By June 1941, Captain Bennion had assumed command of the USS West Virginia, a Colorado-class battleship that would soon find itself at the epicenter of one of the most infamous attacks in American history. Little did Bennion know that his years of training and experience would be put to the ultimate test in just a matter of months.

## The Day of Infamy Dawns

On the morning of December 7, 1941, the USS West Virginia lay peacefully moored at berth F-6 on Battleship Row, outboard of the USS Tennessee. The tranquil Sunday atmosphere was shattered at 7:55

a.m. when the first Japanese planes appeared over Pearl Harbor, unleashing a torrent of bombs and torpedoes on the unsuspecting fleet.

As alarms blared and men rushed to battle stations, Captain Bennion quickly took charge, organizing the defense of his ship. The West Virginia's position made her a prime target, and she soon found herself under heavy attack. Despite the chaos unfolding around him, Bennion's calm demeanor and clear commands provided a steadying influence on his crew.

**Wounded but Unbroken**

Amid the onslaught, disaster struck. A bomb hit on the nearby USS Tennessee sent shrapnel flying, and Captain Bennion was struck in the abdomen by a large fragment. The wound was severe, but Bennion's resolve remained unshaken. Despite the excruciating pain, he refused to leave his post on the bridge, insisting that the medical corpsmen attend to other wounded sailors instead.

As the attack intensified, the West Virginia sustained multiple torpedo hits on her port side, causing significant flooding. The ship began to list dangerously, but under Bennion's unwavering leadership, the crew fought valiantly to keep her afloat. Even as fires broke out below the flag bridge, making escape increasingly difficult, Bennion continued to issue orders and direct damage control efforts.

**A Captain's Last Orders**

As the situation on the West Virginia grew dire, Bennion's officers attempted to evacuate him from the bridge. However, true to his sense of duty and leadership, he resolutely refused to abandon his command responsibilities. In a display of extraordinary courage, Bennion had himself tied to a ladder and moved to a safer area on the navigation bridge, away from the thickening smoke.

In his final moments, Captain Bennion demonstrated the selflessness that had characterized his entire career. He instructed his officers to leave him and save themselves if possible. His last thoughts were not of his own peril, but of the safety of his men and the fate of his ship.

**The Legacy of Heroism**

Captain Mervyn Bennion's actions during the attack on Pearl Harbor exemplified the highest ideals of naval service. His unwavering courage in the face of mortal danger, his refusal to abandon his post despite grievous wounds, and his selfless concern for his crew even in his final moments marked him as a true hero.

For his extraordinary bravery and leadership, Captain Bennion was posthumously awarded the Medal of Honor, the highest military decoration presented by the United States government to members of the armed forces. The citation for his Medal of Honor reads, in part: "For conspicuous devotion to duty, extraordinary courage, and complete disregard of his own life, above and beyond the call of duty, during the attack on the Fleet in Pearl Harbor, Territory of Hawaii, by Japanese forces on December 7, 1941".

The legacy of Captain Bennion's heroism extends far beyond that terrible day in December 1941. In 1943, the U.S. Navy commissioned the USS Bennion (DD-662), a Fletcher-class destroyer named in his honor. This ship would go on to earn battle stars for her service in World War II, including participation in the Battle of Okinawa, further cementing Bennion's legacy within the annals of naval history.

**Conclusion**

The story of Captain Mervyn Bennion serves as a powerful reminder of the extraordinary courage and sacrifice displayed by American servicemen during the attack on Pearl Harbor. His unwavering dedication to duty in the face of overwhelming odds exemplifies the best traditions of the United States Navy and stands as a testament to the human capacity for heroism in the direst circumstances.

Today, as visitors to the Pearl Harbor National Memorial gaze upon the waters where the USS West Virginia once stood, they are reminded of the cost of freedom and the indomitable spirit of those who defend it. Captain Mervyn Bennion's legacy lives on, not only in the annals of military history but in the hearts of all who value courage, duty, and selfless service to one's nation.

**Sources**

Martin, Robert J. USS West Virginia. Turner, 1998.

Prange, Gordon W. At Dawn We Slept: The Untold Story of Pearl Harbor. McGraw-Hill, 1981

Various Sources

# Stories from D-Day

# The Tragic Prelude to the D-Day Invasion

**Introduction:**

On June 6, 1944, the Allied forces launched the historic D-Day invasion of Normandy, marking the beginning of the end of Nazi occupation in Western Europe. The success of this massive amphibious assault required extensive planning and preparation, which included numerous rehearsals and training exercises. One such rehearsal was Exercise Tiger, a large-scale training event to simulate the Utah Beach landing. However, what was intended to be a crucial practice run for D-Day ended in tragedy. Exercise Tiger resulted in the deaths of nearly 750 American servicemen, making it one of the most devastating training accidents of World War II. This story examines the events of Exercise Tiger, the factors that led to the disaster, and the impact it had on the D-Day invasion.

**Background:**

**Planning for D-Day:** The D-Day invasion, code-named Operation Overlord, was one of the most complex military operations in history. It involved the coordination of land, sea, and air forces from multiple Allied nations. The success of the invasion hinged on the ability of the Allied forces to land on the beaches of Normandy, secure a foothold, and push inland. To prepare for this massive undertaking, military planners organized a series of training exercises designed to simulate the conditions the soldiers would face during the actual invasion.

One of these exercises was Exercise Tiger, which took place in April 1944 on the coast of southern England. The location chosen for the exercise was Slapton Sands, a stretch of coastline that closely resembled Utah Beach in Normandy, where the American forces would land on D-Day. The goal of Exercise Tiger was to practice the amphibious landings, coordinating the movement of troops, tanks, and supplies from landing craft to the beachhead. It was a crucial part of the overall preparation for D-Day, and the exercise was meant to be as realistic as possible, including live ammunition and simulated enemy attacks.

**Narrative:**

**The Exercise Begins:** Exercise Tiger began on April 22, 1944, with thousands of American soldiers from the 4th Infantry Division and other units taking part. The exercise was designed to span several days, with the troops practicing disembarking from landing ships, securing the beachhead, and moving inland. The planners intended to make the exercise as close to the real invasion as possible, including the use of live fire during certain phases of the operation.

The choice to use live ammunition was controversial, but it was made to ensure that the soldiers were fully prepared for the dangers they would face on D-Day. The decision was also meant to test the effectiveness of the new LCVP (Landing Craft, Vehicle, Personnel), commonly known as "Higgins boats," which would be critical for transporting men and equipment during the actual invasion.

On the night of April 27-28, 1944, the final phase of Exercise Tiger was set to begin. Convoys of landing craft loaded with troops and equipment were to sail through the English Channel, rendezvous with escort ships, and then approach Slapton Sands in a simulated landing. However, a series of miscommunications, coupled with an unforeseen attack by German forces, would turn the exercise into a disaster.

**The German Attack:** As the American convoy sailed through Lyme Bay on the night of April 27, they were unaware that their movements had been detected by German E-boats (fast torpedo boats) based in the French port of Cherbourg. The E-boats, part of the Kriegsmarine, were known for their speed and effectiveness in launching surprise attacks on Allied shipping. Despite the presence of British escort ships, the convoy was vulnerable to attack due to a lack of communication and coordination.

The first sign of trouble came when LST 507, a large landing ship, was hit by a German torpedo. The explosion was devastating, and the ship quickly began to sink. Chaos ensued as the crew and soldiers on board struggled to abandon the ship. Tragically, many men were trapped below deck, unable to escape the flooding compartments. As the night wore on, two more LSTs, LST 531 and LST 289, were also struck by torpedoes. LST 531 sank rapidly, while LST 289 was severely damaged but managed to stay afloat.

The sudden attack left the convoy in disarray. Many of the soldiers and sailors who had been thrown into the cold waters of the English Channel succumbed to hypothermia before they could be rescued. Others drowned while waiting for help that was slow to arrive due to the confusion and miscommunication among the escort ships.

In total, 749 American servicemen were killed during Exercise Tiger, making it one of the deadliest incidents for U.S. forces in the entire war. The majority of the deaths occurred from drowning or hypothermia, as many of the men were unable to don their life jackets properly due to their heavy equipment and the confusion during the attack.

**Miscommunication and Tragedy:** Several factors contributed to the scale of the disaster during Exercise Tiger. One of the most significant issues was a breakdown in communication between the different units involved in the exercise. The convoy's escort ships were not informed of a change in radio frequencies, which meant that when the German attack occurred, the American forces were unable to call for help effectively. This critical mistake left the convoy vulnerable to the E-boats, which were able to strike with little resistance.

Another issue was the lack of adequate safety precautions during the exercise. Although live ammunition was used to simulate real combat conditions, there were insufficient measures in place to ensure the safety of the men participating in the exercise. The chaos and confusion that followed the torpedo strikes were compounded by the fact that many soldiers had not been properly trained in how to respond to such an attack, particularly when it came to escaping from sinking ships or surviving in the frigid waters of the Channel.

Furthermore, the lack of communication extended to the rescue efforts. British and American ships struggled to coordinate their efforts to rescue survivors, and many of the men who were thrown into the water were left stranded for hours before help arrived. The delayed response resulted in a higher death toll than might have been the case if rescue efforts had been more immediate and better organized.

**The Aftermath and the Secrecy Surrounding Exercise Tiger:** In the immediate aftermath of the tragedy, there was a concerted effort by the Allied high command to keep the details of Exercise Tiger a secret. The D-Day invasion was still weeks away, and there were concerns that if the Germans learned of the disaster, they might gain valuable intelligence about the upcoming operation. As a result, survivors were sworn to secrecy, and official reports about the incident were classified.

One of the most significant concerns was the loss of ten officers who had been carrying detailed plans for the D-Day invasion. These officers were aboard the LSTs that were sunk during the attack, and there was an immediate fear that their bodies, along with the invasion plans, might be recovered by the Germans. A frantic search was launched to recover the bodies and ensure that the plans did not fall into enemy hands. Fortunately, all ten bodies were eventually found, and the invasion plans remained secure.

Despite the heavy loss of life, the lessons learned from Exercise Tiger were invaluable for the success of the D-Day invasion. The disaster highlighted the need for better communication, coordination, and safety protocols during amphibious operations. The mistakes made during Exercise Tiger were addressed in the final preparations for D-Day, ensuring that similar errors would not occur during the actual invasion.

**Exercise Tiger's Legacy:** For decades, the events of Exercise Tiger were shrouded in secrecy, and many of the families of those who died were not given full details about the circumstances of their loved ones' deaths. It was not until after the war that the full story of the tragedy began to emerge, and even then, it remained a largely forgotten chapter of World War II history.

In recent years, efforts have been made to commemorate the men who lost their lives during Exercise Tiger. Memorials have been erected at Slapton Sands, and survivors of the exercise have shared their stories in documentaries and books. The tragedy of Exercise Tiger serves as a reminder of the sacrifices made in the lead-up to D-Day and the complexity of preparing for such a monumental operation.

## Conclusion

Exercise Tiger stands as one of the most tragic yet largely unknown prequels to the D-Day invasion. What was meant to be a critical rehearsal for the landing on Utah Beach turned into a disaster due to a combination of miscommunication, inadequate safety measures, and a surprise attack by German E-boats. Nearly 750 American servicemen lost their lives, a staggering loss for a training exercise. However, the lessons learned from this tragedy played a crucial role in ensuring the success of D-Day just weeks later.

## Sources

Small, Ken. The Forgotten Dead: The True Story of Exercise Tiger, the Disastrous Rehearsal for D-Day. Osprey Publishing, 2018.

Lawrence, Wendy. Exercise Tiger: The Forgotten Sacrifice of the Silent Few. Fonthill Media, 2014.

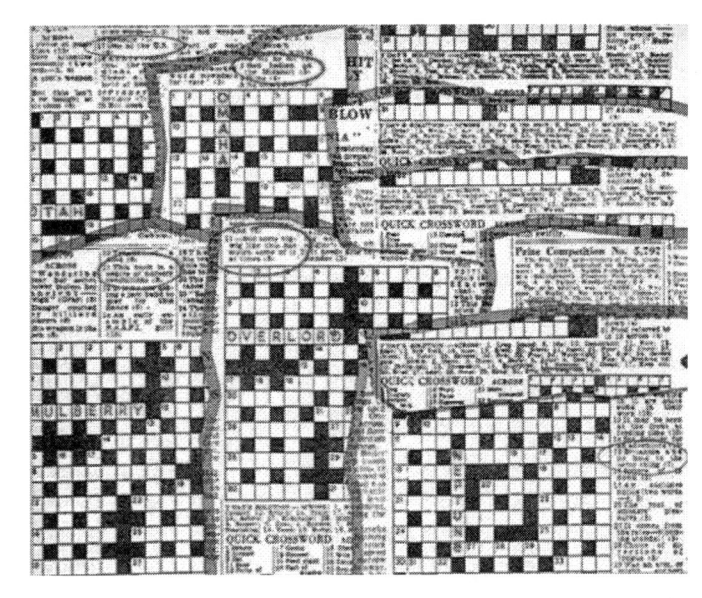

# The Crossword Puzzle That Almost Ruined the D-Day Invasion

## Introduction

The D-Day invasion on June 6, 1944, was one of the most carefully planned and tightly guarded secrets of World War II. Codenamed Operation Overlord, it involved the largest amphibious military assault in history, as the Allied forces stormed the beaches of Normandy to liberate Nazi-occupied France. To ensure the success of this operation, the Allied command went to extraordinary lengths to maintain secrecy, employing deception operations like Operation Bodyguard to mislead the Germans about the location and timing of the invasion. Yet, in an incredible twist, this secrecy was nearly undone by an unexpected and seemingly innocent source: a series of crossword puzzles published in a British newspaper.

This story explores how crucial codenames for the D-Day invasion began appearing in the crossword puzzles of the Daily Telegraph, causing alarm among British intelligence and raising concerns that a breach of security had occurred. Despite the panic, the incident was ultimately a coincidence, but it serves as a fascinating chapter in the history of the D-Day preparations.

## The Importance of Secrecy in Operation Overlord

As the Allies planned the liberation of Europe, they understood that secrecy was paramount. Operation Overlord involved the coordination of hundreds of thousands of troops, ships, and aircraft, with the success of the operation hinging on surprise. The Normandy landings were designed to catch the German forces off-guard, as the bulk of Nazi troops were positioned at Pas de Calais, further north along the French coast, due to an elaborate deception campaign.

The stakes were incredibly high. Any leak of the invasion's details could have led to a disaster for the Allies, with German forces reinforcing their defenses at Normandy. As a result, Allied commanders implemented a strict need-to-know policy, and only a select group of individuals were privy to the full scope of the invasion plan.

In the months leading up to the invasion, codewords like "Overlord", "Utah", "Omaha", "Neptune", and "Mulberry" were used to refer to various aspects of the D-Day operation. These codewords were known only to the highest levels of military and intelligence officers, and any unauthorized mention of them was treated as a severe breach of security.

It was in this climate of intense secrecy that the unexpected appearance of these codewords in a seemingly innocuous crossword puzzle caused an uproar within the British government.

**The Crossword Puzzle Incident**

The story of the crossword puzzle that almost compromised the D-Day invasion begins with the Daily Telegraph, one of Britain's leading newspapers. The paper, like many others during the war, included daily crossword puzzles as a form of entertainment and distraction for the public, who were enduring the hardships of the war.

The compiler of the crossword puzzles for the Daily Telegraph was Leonard Dawe, a schoolteacher, and a well-known puzzle enthusiast. Dawe, who had been creating puzzles for the newspaper since the 1920s, was admired for his clever and challenging clues. He taught at Strand School; a grammar school that had been evacuated from London to the countryside due to the Blitz.

In May 1944, just weeks before the planned Normandy invasion, British intelligence officers began noticing a disturbing pattern in Dawe's crossword puzzles. In the span of several days, key codenames related to the D-Day invasion began appearing as solutions to his puzzles.

- On May 2, 1944, the word "Utah" appeared as a solution in the Daily Telegraph crossword. Utah was the codename for one of the landing beaches where American troops would land.

- On May 22, the word "Omaha" appeared. Omaha was another of the American landing beaches.

- On May 27, "Overlord" appeared in the puzzle. This was the codename for the overall invasion operation.

- On June 1, the word "Neptune" appeared. Operation Neptune referred to the naval phase of the D-Day assault.

- Finally, on June 2, the word "Mulberry" appeared. Mulberry harbors were the portable harbors the Allies planned to use to facilitate the landing of supplies on the beaches after the invasion.

The appearance of these codenames in the crossword puzzles sent shockwaves through MI5, the British counter-intelligence agency responsible for maintaining the security of the D-Day invasion. With the invasion just days away, the coincidence seemed too great to ignore. MI5 officials feared that someone with access to classified information was leaking it through the puzzles, possibly as part of a German espionage operation.

**The Investigation**

In response to the alarming discovery, MI5 immediately launched an investigation into Leonard Dawe and the Daily Telegraph crossword puzzle. Dawe was questioned extensively, and the situation was treated with the utmost seriousness. The fact that so many of the critical codenames appeared in such close succession led investigators to believe that there must have been a deliberate attempt to sabotage the invasion.

MI5 considered several possibilities. Perhaps a German spy had infiltrated the staff of the Daily Telegraph, or maybe someone who knew about the invasion was feeding the information to Dawe without his knowledge. The timing was especially concerning, given how close the invasion was and how crucial secrecy remained.

Dawe, for his part, was completely baffled by the situation. He insisted that the codenames appearing in his puzzles were purely coincidental and that he had no knowledge of their connection to the impending invasion. To MI5's frustration, they could find no evidence that Dawe had any connections to German intelligence or that he had intentionally included the codenames in his puzzles.

Eventually, MI5 broadened its investigation to include Dawe's students at Strand School. Dawe often allowed his students to suggest words for his crossword puzzles, a practice that he enjoyed as a way to engage their minds. It was during interviews with the students that the mystery began to unravel.

**The Innocent Explanation**

The investigation revealed that some of Dawe's students had been interacting with Allied soldiers who were stationed in the area as they prepared for the D-Day invasion. The soldiers, while trying to keep the details of the invasion secret, had occasionally let slip certain codenames in casual conversation with the locals, including the schoolboys. The boys, not understanding the significance of the words, had innocently suggested them to Dawe as crossword solutions.

In other words, the inclusion of the codenames in the crossword puzzles was a coincidence—albeit a highly improbable one. Neither Dawe nor his students had any idea that the words they were using were part of one of the most important military operations of the war. The appearance of the codenames in the puzzles was the result of the schoolboys inadvertently hearing sensitive information from soldiers and later passing those words along without understanding their importance.

Once MI5 realized that there was no deliberate leak or espionage involved, they closed the investigation. While the situation had caused a great deal of alarm, the danger was ultimately averted, and the secrecy of the D-Day invasion remained intact. The invasion went ahead as planned on June 6, 1944, with Allied forces successfully landing on the beaches of Normandy.

**Aftermath and Legacy**

In the years following the war, the story of the Daily Telegraph crossword puzzle incident became something of a legend. While it is often recounted as a near-disaster that could have exposed the D-Day invasion, it is also a testament to the intense secrecy that surrounded Operation Overlord and the efforts of British intelligence to protect the invasion plans.

Leonard Dawe continued to compile crossword puzzles for the Daily Telegraph after the war, though the incident left him somewhat shaken. For many years, the full details of the investigation remained classified, and it wasn't until much later that the public learned the full story of how the crossword puzzle nearly compromised one of the most critical operations of World War II.

Today, the incident is seen as a remarkable example of how even the most carefully guarded secrets can be threatened by the most unexpected sources. The Daily Telegraph crossword puzzle incident is a reminder of the challenges faced by military planners and intelligence agencies during times of war when maintaining secrecy is often a matter of life and death.

**Conclusion**

The appearance of critical D-Day codenames in the Daily Telegraph crossword puzzle in the days leading up to the Normandy invasion is one of the most remarkable coincidences in the history of World War II. What initially appeared to be a significant breach of security was ultimately revealed to be an innocent mistake, the result of schoolboys inadvertently passing along words they had overheard from Allied soldiers.

**Sources**

Rowley, Tom. Who put secret D-Day clues in the 'Telegraph' crossword? Sunday Telegraph, 2014.

Ambrose, Stephen E. D-Day: June 6, 1944: The Climactic Battle of WWII. Simon & Schuster. 2013.

Mayo, Jonathan. D-Day: Minute-by-Minute. Marble Arch Press, 2014.

Various Sources

# Hitler's Sleep and the D-Day Invasion

## Introduction

In the accounts of military history, few events have been as pivotal as the D-Day invasion of June 6, 1944. As Allied forces stormed the beaches of Normandy, a curious drama unfolded within the Nazi high command. At the center of this drama was Adolf Hitler, the Führer of Nazi Germany, whose sleep habits and leadership style would play an unexpected role in shaping the outcome of this momentous day. This story explores the hesitancy of Nazi generals to wake Hitler during the crucial early hours of the invasion, the consequences of this delay, and the broader implications for the German response to Operation Overlord.

## The Eve of Invasion

As the sun set on June 5, 1944, the German high command remained largely unaware of the impending Allied assault. Despite years of anticipation and preparation for an invasion of Western Europe, the Nazi leadership found itself caught off guard by the scale and location of the attack that would unfold in the early hours of June 6.

Field Marshal Erwin Rommel, tasked with defending the Normandy coast, was away from his post, celebrating his wife's birthday. General Friedrich Dollmann, commander of the Seventh Army, was engaged in a planning exercise in Rennes. These absences would prove critical in the confusion that followed.

Meanwhile, in his private quarters at the Berghof, his Bavarian retreat, Adolf Hitler retired for the night. Known for his erratic sleep schedule, Hitler had given strict orders not to be disturbed. This command, born of the Führer's growing paranoia and deteriorating mental state, would have far-reaching consequences in the hours to come.

## The Invasion Begins

At 6:30 AM on June 6, the first Allied troops began landing on the beaches of Normandy. As reports of the invasion trickled in, a sense of disbelief and confusion spread through the German command structure. Field Marshal Gerd von Rundstedt, the top German commander in the West, received initial reports of the landings but was hesitant to act without confirmation.

The German response was hampered by a rigid command structure that required Hitler's personal approval for major decisions. Von Rundstedt, recognizing the need for immediate action, requested the release of two reserve panzer divisions to counter the Allied beachhead. However, these divisions were under the control of the Oberkommando der Wehrmacht (OKW) and could not be deployed without Hitler's explicit authorization.

**The Fateful Decision**

As the invasion unfolded, a crucial decision loomed before Hitler's staff: whether to wake the Führer. This seemingly simple act was fraught with complexity and potential consequences. Hitler's deteriorating mental state and unpredictable reactions had instilled a sense of fear among his subordinates. The strict protocols surrounding his personal schedule further complicated the matter.

General Alfred Jodl, Chief of the Operations Staff of the OKW, was among those who hesitated to disturb Hitler's sleep. Jodl, like many in the high command, was acutely aware of Hitler's volatile temper and the potential repercussions of delivering what might be considered premature or incorrect information.

This hesitancy was compounded by the lingering belief that the Normandy landings might be a diversion. The success of Allied deception operations, particularly Operation Fortitude, had convinced many in the German high command that the main invasion would occur at Pas de Calais. This misconception led to a fatal underestimation of the threat posed by the Normandy landings.

**The Consequences of Delay**

The decision to let Hitler sleep had immediate and far-reaching consequences. As precious hours ticked by, Allied forces consolidated their positions on the Normandy beaches. The delay in German response allowed the invaders to establish a foothold that would prove impossible to dislodge.

When Hitler was finally informed of the invasion later that morning, his initial reaction was one of relief rather than alarm. He believed that the poor weather conditions would favor the German defense and underestimated the capabilities of the Allied forces. This misjudgment further contributed to the lack of urgency in the German response.

The most critical consequence of the delay was the missed opportunity for a decisive counter-attack. By the time Hitler authorized the deployment of panzer divisions, it was too late for them to move under the cover of darkness. Forced to wait until nightfall to avoid destruction by Allied aircraft, which dominated the skies, the German armored units lost the chance to drive wedges between the Allied landing beaches.

**The Broader Context**

The hesitancy to wake Hitler on D-Day was symptomatic of broader issues within the Nazi command structure. The highly centralized decision-making process, with Hitler at its core, had created a paralysis in the face of unexpected events. Field commanders, fearful of acting without explicit orders, often delayed crucial decisions.

This incident also highlighted the deteriorating state of Hitler's leadership. His insistence on personal control over strategic decisions, combined with his increasingly erratic behavior and detachment from reality, had created a command environment ill-suited to respond to the dynamic challenges of modern warfare.

The success of Allied deception operations played a significant role in shaping the German response. Operation Fortitude, which had convinced the Germans that the main invasion would occur at Pas de Calais, contributed to the initial disbelief and hesitation in responding to the Normandy landings. This strategic misdirection amplified the consequences of the delay in waking Hitler.

## The Aftermath

As the day progressed, the full scale of the Allied invasion became apparent. By the end of June 6, over 156,000 Allied troops had landed in France. Within two weeks, that number would swell to 650,000, forming a significant force aimed at advancing towards Berlin.

The delay in German response allowed the Allies to achieve their primary objective: establishing a secure beachhead in Normandy. This foothold would serve as the launching point for the liberation of Western Europe and the eventual defeat of Nazi Germany.

For the German high command, the events of June 6 marked the beginning of a series of strategic failures that would ultimately lead to the collapse of the Third Reich. The hesitancy to wake Hitler on that crucial morning became a symbol of the dysfunction and paralysis that had gripped the Nazi leadership.

## Conclusion

The story of the Nazi generals' hesitancy to wake Hitler on D-Day serves as a powerful illustration of how seemingly small decisions can have monumental consequences in the theater of war. This incident encapsulates the broader failings of the Nazi command structure: an over-reliance on centralized authority, a culture of fear and indecision, and a fatal underestimation of Allied capabilities.

## Sources

Beevor, Antony. D-Day: The Battle for Normandy. Penguin Books, 2010.

Ambrose, Stephen E. D-Day: June 6, 1944: The Climactic Battle of WWII. Simon & Schuster. 2013.

Various Sources

# Erwin Rommel's Role and His Absence During the Invasion

## Introduction

Erwin Rommel, famously known as the Desert Fox, was one of Nazi Germany's most skilled military commanders during World War II. His leadership during the North African Campaign earned him widespread recognition, but his later role in fortifying the Atlantic Wall, the defensive network designed to repel an anticipated Allied invasion of Nazi-occupied France, placed him at the center of one of the most pivotal moments in the war. Ironically, on the morning of June 6, 1944, when the long-awaited D-Day invasion—Operation Overlord—began, Rommel was not at his command post. Instead, he was at home in Herrlingen, Germany, celebrating his wife Lucie-Maria's birthday. story examines Rommel's critical role in preparing France's defenses, the circumstances that led to his absence on D-Day, and the implications of his absence during one of the most significant battles in modern history.

## The Desert Fox

Erwin Rommel's military career had already become the stuff of legend by the time he was tasked with fortifying the Atlantic defenses. Born on November 15, 1891, in Heidenheim, Germany, Rommel rose through the ranks of the German military during World War I and the interwar period. His exceptional strategic acumen and leadership in battle became widely known during the North African Campaign of World War II, where he earned the nickname "Desert Fox" for his cunning tactics and ability to outmaneuver British forces.

By 1943, after the collapse of the Axis forces in North Africa, Rommel was recalled to Europe. Although his reputation remained strong, Rommel was becoming increasingly disillusioned with the Nazi regime and the direction of the war. Nevertheless, he was assigned a critical new task by Adolf Hitler—to oversee the fortification of France's Atlantic coastline, which stretched from the Netherlands to the Spanish border. This defensive line, known as the Atlantic Wall, was intended to prevent the anticipated Allied invasion of Western Europe.

**Rommel's Strategic Vision**

When Rommel assumed command of Army Group B in November 1943, the Atlantic Wall was already in place, but it was far from the impregnable barrier that Nazi propaganda claimed it to be. Stretching over 1,500 miles, the defenses consisted of bunkers, minefields, artillery positions, and beach obstacles. However, much of it was poorly constructed, and large portions of the coastline were inadequately defended.

Rommel immediately recognized the deficiencies in the Atlantic Wall and took swift action to bolster the defenses. His strategy was built on the belief that the Allies would attempt a landing along the coast of France, most likely in the Pas-de-Calais region, the shortest distance between Britain and France. Although Rommel's superior, Field Marshal Gerd von Rundstedt, favored a more flexible defense that would allow for a counterattack after the Allies landed, Rommel believed that the key to victory was stopping the invasion at the beaches. His famous quote, "The first 24 hours of the invasion will be decisive. The fate of Germany depends on the outcome…for the Allies, as well as Germany, it will be the longest day," reflected his understanding of the importance of the initial clash.

Rommel initiated an aggressive building campaign, ordering the construction of millions of mines, beach obstacles, and underwater defenses to hinder the landing of Allied troops and vehicles. He also reinforced bunkers and gun emplacements along the coast and placed mobile artillery units in strategic locations to respond quickly to any Allied landing. In addition, Rommel advocated for the use of Panzer divisions—Germany's armored forces—to be stationed close to the beaches, ready to counterattack as soon as the Allies landed. However, his requests for more Panzer divisions were often met with resistance from Hitler and the Oberkommando der Wehrmacht (OKW), who preferred to keep the tanks in reserve farther inland.

Rommel's efforts made the Atlantic Wall a more formidable obstacle, but internal disagreements within the German high command and limited resources prevented it from becoming the impenetrable barrier Rommel envisioned. Nevertheless, Rommel knew that if the Allies successfully landed, Germany's position in the war would be untenable. As the months passed, he grew increasingly anxious about the possibility of an invasion, which he believed would come during the spring or summer of 1944.

**The D-Day Invasion**

As June 1944 approached, Rommel continued his tireless work to strengthen the defenses along the coast, convinced that the Allies would soon make their move. However, as the month began, Rommel took a brief leave of absence. He had become increasingly frustrated with the lack of reinforcements and the inability of the German high command to resolve disagreements about where to place the Panzer divisions. Believing that the bad weather and rough seas in early June made an Allied landing unlikely in the immediate future, Rommel decided to return to his home in Herrlingen, Germany, to celebrate his wife Lucie's 50th birthday on June 6.

Rommel's departure from his command post in France was a fateful decision. Unbeknownst to him, the Allies had selected June 6 as D-Day, the day they would launch Operation Overlord, the massive amphibious assault that would change the course of the war. In the early hours of June 6, 1944, as Rommel was in Germany, more than 156,000 Allied troops began storming the beaches of Normandy, supported by an armada of 5,000 ships and 11,000 aircraft.

The landings took place across five beaches: Utah, Omaha, Gold, Juno, and Sword, stretching along a 50-mile front. The invasion was preceded by a massive aerial and naval bombardment aimed at softening the German defenses. Despite the overwhelming Allied forces, the Germans were able to mount a fierce resistance, particularly at Omaha Beach, where American forces faced brutal opposition.

Rommel's absence on this critical day is often seen as a stroke of luck for the Allies. He had planned to oversee the defense personally and direct the deployment of reinforcements. Without Rommel's presence, the German forces were slower to react to the landings, and the critical decision of when to deploy the Panzer divisions was delayed. Hitler, who had the final say over the deployment of the Panzer divisions, was initially unconvinced that the Normandy landings were the main Allied assault, believing that they were a diversion from a larger attack that would come at Pas-de-Calais. As a result, the German armored divisions were held in reserve far from the beaches, allowing the Allies to establish a foothold in Normandy.

Rommel did not learn of the invasion until later in the day, and by the time he returned to France, the Allies had already secured significant portions of the beaches. His worst fears had come true—the Atlantic Wall had been breached, and the fate of Nazi Germany was now in jeopardy.

**The Impact of Rommel's Absence**

The delay in the German response to the D-Day invasion proved critical. Without Rommel's immediate presence to coordinate the defense, German forces were unable to mount an effective counterattack. The Panzer divisions, which Rommel had wanted to deploy near the beaches, arrived too late to turn the tide of the battle. The Allied forces, supported by overwhelming naval and air superiority, pushed inland, eventually liberating France and paving the way for the defeat of Nazi Germany.

Rommel's absence on D-Day also highlighted the disunity and inefficiency within the German high command. The disagreements between Rommel, von Rundstedt, and Hitler over how to defend the coast had weakened Germany's ability to respond decisively to the invasion. Rommel's strategy of confronting the Allies at the beaches had merit, but the failure to implement it fully, combined with his absence at the crucial moment, allowed the Allies to gain the upper hand.

**Rommel's Fate**

In the aftermath of D-Day, Rommel continued to play a key role in the defense of France. However, by the summer of 1944, he had become increasingly disillusioned with the Nazi leadership, particularly Hitler. Rommel, who had initially been a loyal supporter of Hitler, began to see the futility of continuing the war. He was also critical of Hitler's refusal to allow a tactical withdrawal from France to more defensible positions in Germany.

Rommel's growing discontent with Hitler's leadership led him to become indirectly involved in the July 20 Plot, a failed assassination attempt on Hitler's life. Although Rommel was not one of the key conspirators, several of the plotters sought his support, and his name was associated with the coup attempt. When the plot failed, Hitler's regime sought to purge those connected to the conspiracy.

On October 14, 1944, Rommel was visited by two German officers who informed him that he had been implicated in the plot. Given his status as a national hero, Rommel was offered a choice: take his own life and receive a state funeral, or face a public trial and execution, which would disgrace his family. Rommel chose the former, and on that day, he committed suicide by taking cyanide. His death was officially announced as the result of wounds sustained in an air raid.

**Conclusion**

Erwin Rommel's absence during the D-Day invasion was one of the most significant factors surrounding the disjointed response from the acting Nazi generals. The internal disagreements about Panzer deployment and the indecisiveness in reacting to the surprise attack location created a disjointed reaction from the Nazis. The fighting was fierce but once their fortifications were breached, they had no choice but to retreat inland.

**Sources**

Beevor, Antony. D-Day: The Battle for Normandy. Penguin Books, 2010.

Ambrose, Stephen E. D-Day: June 6, 1944: The Climactic Battle of WWII. Simon & Schuster. 2013.

Various Sources

# Silent Wings of D-Day and Beyond

## Introduction

When thinking about the Allied forces storming the beaches of Normandy on D-Day, images of tanks, infantry, and paratroopers often come to mind. However, one of the most vital, yet often overlooked, components of the D-Day invasion and other significant Allied operations during World War II was the glider force. Among the most famous of these were the Waco gliders, officially known as the Waco CG-4A. These unpowered aircraft silently carried troops, equipment, and supplies behind enemy lines, playing a crucial role in the success of airborne operations throughout the war. The Waco gliders, flown by brave pilots under the most dangerous conditions, helped to ensure the success of some of the most critical missions of the war, including D-Day, Operation Market Garden, and Operation Varsity. This is the story of the Waco gliders, the men who flew them, and their vital contributions to Allied victory.

## The Need for Gliders

World War II was a conflict that required innovative solutions to overcome unprecedented challenges. One of these challenges was how to quickly insert large numbers of troops and equipment behind enemy lines without the benefit of an airfield. Parachute drops, while useful for infantry, had limitations in terms of the size and weight of equipment that could be transported. The need to land larger forces, including vehicles, artillery, and supplies, without relying on powered aircraft led to the development of military gliders.

Military gliders were designed to be towed by powered aircraft, such as the C-47 Skytrain, and released over a drop zone where they would glide silently to a landing. Unlike paratroopers, who could be scattered over a wide area, gliders could deliver troops and equipment in concentrated locations. Moreover, gliders could transport heavier loads, including jeeps, anti-tank guns, and other crucial equipment that paratroopers could not carry with them.

The Waco CG-4A glider, developed by the Waco Aircraft Company, became the backbone of the U.S. Army's glider force during World War II. It was the most widely used glider in the war, with over 13,900 built. Its simple yet robust design allowed it to carry up to 13 fully equipped troops, or a mix of troops and equipment, including vehicles or artillery. While the glider was unarmed and unarmored, its ability to deliver essential forces behind enemy lines made it an indispensable tool in several major operations.

## Design and Capabilities of the Waco CG-4A

The Waco CG-4A was a high-wing, fabric-covered glider with a wooden and metal frame. It had a wingspan of 83 feet and was 48 feet long. The cockpit, or nose section, could hinge upward, allowing for easy loading and unloading of troops and equipment. This design feature enabled the glider to carry a wide variety of cargo, including jeeps, small artillery pieces, and medical supplies, along with up to 13 soldiers.

The glider was towed into the air by a powered aircraft, typically the C-47 Skytrain, using a 300-foot nylon tow rope. Once released near the designated landing zone, the glider would descend silently to the ground, relying on the skill of the pilot to navigate the descent and land on rough, often improvised landing strips behind enemy lines. The Waco gliders were not equipped with landing gear; instead, they had a skid that allowed for rough landings on grass, dirt, or even plowed fields.

One of the key advantages of the gliders was their ability to land large numbers of troops and equipment in concentrated areas, allowing for rapid consolidation of forces behind enemy lines. However, this came at a cost. Glider landings were extremely dangerous, often resulting in crash landings due to the lack of power and the rough terrain of the landing zones. The glider pilots, who had no way of defending themselves, had to rely on their skill and nerves to bring their aircraft down safely.

## D-Day and the Waco Gliders

The Waco gliders were heavily involved in the D-Day invasion of Normandy on June 6, 1944, as part of the airborne operations that preceded the amphibious landings. Their mission was to deliver troops, equipment, and supplies behind enemy lines to support the paratroopers of the 82nd and 101st Airborne Divisions, who had been dropped earlier that night. The gliders played a key role in securing key objectives such as bridges, crossroads, and causeways, which were critical to the success of the invasion.

On the night of June 5-6, hundreds of Waco gliders were towed across the English Channel, as part of Operation Neptune, the airborne component of the D-Day invasion. Once over Normandy, the gliders were released from their tow planes and descended silently toward their landing zones. Despite facing heavy anti-aircraft fire and the challenges of navigating in the dark, the glider pilots managed to land their aircraft in the designated areas, though many were met with rough landings.

One of the most famous missions involving Waco gliders during D-Day was the capture of the Pegasus Bridge over the Caen Canal by British airborne forces. In the early hours of June 6, a group of six Horsa gliders, a larger variant also used by British forces, landed within yards of the bridge, delivering troops who quickly overwhelmed the German defenders and secured the bridge. Waco gliders, operating in other sectors, helped secure other key objectives, including the town of Sainte-Mère-Église, one of the first towns liberated by the Allies during the invasion.

While the glider landings were not without casualties—many gliders crashed upon landing or were hit by enemy fire—the Waco gliders played a critical role in the success of the airborne operations on D-Day. Their ability to deliver troops and equipment behind enemy lines allowed the paratroopers to consolidate their positions and hold key objectives until the seaborne forces could link up with them.

## Operation Market Garden

Following the success of D-Day, the Waco gliders were called into action again during Operation Market Garden, the largest airborne operation of the war, launched in September 1944. The operation, led by British Field Marshal Bernard Montgomery, aimed to capture key bridges in the Netherlands to create a direct route into Germany, bypassing the heavily defended Siegfried Line.

Market Garden involved a massive airborne assault, with over 35,000 paratroopers and glider-borne troops being dropped behind enemy lines. The Waco gliders were used extensively during the operation to deliver troops, artillery, jeeps, and other equipment to secure the bridges. However, the operation was fraught with difficulties from the start. Poor weather conditions, delays in reinforcements, and unexpectedly strong German resistance turned Market Garden into a costly failure for the Allies.

The Waco gliders performed admirably under the circumstances, delivering vital equipment and reinforcements to the airborne forces. However, many gliders were lost to enemy fire, crash landings, and poor landing conditions. The pilots, who had no way to defend themselves once on the ground, often found themselves in the thick of battle alongside the troops they had delivered.

Despite the overall failure of Market Garden, the glider pilots and the troops they transported demonstrated incredible bravery and resilience. The operation, while a setback, did show the potential of airborne operations on a large scale, and the Waco gliders played a significant role in making it possible.

## Operation Varsity

The Waco gliders had one final, triumphant mission in Operation Varsity, the largest single-day airborne operation of World War II, launched on March 24, 1945. As part of the larger Operation Plunder, which aimed to cross the Rhine River and penetrate deeper into Germany, Varsity involved over 16,000 paratroopers and glider-borne troops.

This time, the Waco gliders were used to great effect, delivering troops and equipment across the Rhine to secure key objectives and pave the way for the ground forces to advance. Unlike Market Garden, Varsity was a resounding success. The airborne forces, including those delivered by the Waco gliders, were able to secure their objectives quickly, and the crossing of the Rhine was achieved with relatively few casualties.

The success of Operation Varsity marked the beginning of the final push into Germany, and the Waco gliders once again played a crucial role in delivering the forces necessary to achieve victory. The glider pilots, who had endured years of dangerous missions, could take pride in knowing that their efforts had contributed to the Allied triumph in Europe.

## The End of an Era

With the end of World War II, the era of the military glider came to a close. Advancements in helicopter technology and powered transport aircraft made gliders obsolete in the post-war years. However, the Waco gliders and the brave men who flew them left an indelible mark on the history of airborne warfare.

The Waco gliders were responsible for delivering tens of thousands of troops and essential equipment into some of the most dangerous battlefields of the war. While they were unarmed and vulnerable, the gliders played a crucial role in the success of airborne operations, from D-Day to the final crossing of the Rhine.

**Conclusion**

The Waco gliders of World War II were an essential, though often underappreciated, part of the Allied victory in Europe. From their role in the D-Day invasion to the daring missions of Operation Market Garden and the final push into Germany during Operation Varsity, these silent aircraft and the brave pilots who flew them helped turn the tide of the war.

**Sources**

Beevor, Antony. D-Day: The Battle for Normandy. Penguin Books, 2010.

Ambrose, Stephen E. D-Day: June 6, 1944: The Climactic Battle of WWII. Simon & Schuster. 2013.

Various Sources

# General Teddy Roosevelt Jr.

## Introduction

The name Teddy Roosevelt is synonymous with American heroism and leadership, and his legacy was carried on by his son, Brigadier General Teddy Roosevelt Jr., who played a pivotal role in one of the most significant military operations of the 20th century – the D-Day landings in Normandy. As the only general officer to personally participate in the initial assault on the beaches of Normandy, Roosevelt's bravery, resilience, and unwavering commitment to his troops have cemented his place in history as a true embodiment of the American spirit.

## Background

Teddy Roosevelt Jr. was born on September 13, 1887, in New York City, the eldest son of the 26th President of the United States, Theodore Roosevelt. Following in his father's footsteps, Teddy Jr. pursued a career in the military, graduating from Harvard University and receiving his commission in the United States Army in 1909.

During World War I, Roosevelt served with distinction, earning the Distinguished Service Cross, the Silver Star, and the Purple Heart for his heroic actions on the battlefield. His leadership, courage, and unwavering determination to achieve victory made him a respected and admired officer, and he quickly rose through the ranks, eventually attaining the rank of brigadier general.

In the interwar years, Roosevelt remained active in the military, serving in various advisory and administrative roles. However, when World War II erupted, he was eager to return to the frontlines and contribute to the Allied effort to defeat the Axis powers.

## Narrative

As the Allied forces prepared for the D-Day invasion of Normandy in June 1944, Roosevelt's wealth of experience and his deep understanding of military strategy made him an invaluable asset. Despite being 56 years old and suffering from various health issues, including a heart condition and arthritis, Roosevelt adamantly insisted on participating in the initial assault on the beaches of Normandy, refusing to sit behind the lines as an observer.

On the morning of June 6, 1944, as the soldiers of the 4th Infantry Division prepared to disembark from their landing crafts and storm the beaches of Utah, Brigadier General Teddy Roosevelt Jr. stood tall, leading his troops into the face of the enemy. Despite the chaos and the heavy German resistance, Roosevelt remained calm and composed, rallying his men and inspiring them to push forward.

As the initial waves of American soldiers struggled to establish a foothold on the beach, Roosevelt, who had landed slightly off-target, found himself in a perilous situation. Surrounded by enemy fire and cut off from his command, he refused to retreat, instead organizing the scattered troops and directing them to secure vital strategic positions.

Roosevelt's unwavering leadership and his willingness to share the dangers of his men had a profound impact on the morale of the troops. Inspired by his bravery and his refusal to abandon them, the soldiers of the 4th Infantry Division fought with renewed vigor, gradually pushing inland and securing the initial objectives.

**Leading from the Front**

Throughout the day, Roosevelt continued to lead from the front, moving from one unit to another, ensuring that his men were well-equipped, motivated, and ready to face the challenges that lay ahead. His presence on the battlefield, his calm demeanor under fire, and his unwavering commitment to his troops were a testament to his exceptional leadership qualities and his deep understanding of the art of war.

As the D-Day operation progressed, Roosevelt's efforts proved crucial to the overall success of the invasion. His ability to adapt to the constantly changing battlefield conditions and his willingness to take personal risks to ensure the safety and well-being of his men earned him the admiration of his fellow officers and the respect of the men he commanded.

**Death**

Tragically, on June 12, 1944, just six days after the initial D-Day landings, Teddy Roosevelt Jr. suffered a heart attack and collapsed while leading his troops in Normandy. Despite the best efforts of the medical personnel, he succumbed to his injuries and passed away at the age of 56.

In recognition of his exceptional service and his ultimate sacrifice, Teddy Roosevelt Jr. was posthumously awarded the Medal of Honor, the highest military decoration in the United States. His citation praised his "coolness and courage in the face of the enemy" and his "personal leadership" in the initial stages of the Normandy campaign.

**Conclusion**

The story of Teddy Roosevelt Jr.'s heroic actions on D-Day and his tragic death in the service of his country serves as a powerful reminder of the extraordinary courage and sacrifice of the men who fought to liberate Europe from the grip of Nazi tyranny. As the only general officer to personally participate in the initial assault on the Normandy beaches, Roosevelt's legacy as a true American hero will forever be etched in the annals of military history.

**Sources**

Jeffers, H Paul. Theodore Roosevelt Jr., The Life of a War Hero. Presidio Press, 2002.

# Juan Pujol Garcia and the D-Day Deception

## Introduction

In the shadowy world of World War II espionage, few figures loom as large as Juan Pujol Garcia, codenamed "Garbo" by his British handlers. His extraordinary journey from a failed chicken farmer to one of the most influential double agents in history is a tale of ingenuity, courage, and unwavering commitment to a cause. This story explores Garcia's background, his pivotal role in Operation Fortitude, and the lasting impact of his deceptions on the success of the D-Day invasion and the ultimate Allied victory in World War II. Through Garcia's story, we gain insight into the power of misinformation in warfare and the profound influence that a single individual can have on the course of history.

## From Humble Beginnings to Master Spy

Juan Pujol Garcia was born on February 14, 1912, in Barcelona, Spain, into a politically liberal family. His early life was marked by a series of unremarkable jobs and a brief, uneventful stint in the Spanish Civil War that left him with a deep-seated loathing for totalitarian regimes. This aversion to fascism would become the driving force behind his later espionage activities.

Garcia's path to becoming a spy was as unconventional as it was determined. After failing to convince the British to recruit him, he took the audacious step of approaching German intelligence, the Abwehr, posing as a pro-Nazi Spanish official willing to spy for them in England. Despite never having set foot in Britain, Garcia managed to convince the Germans of his value, operating from Lisbon and crafting elaborate reports based on information gleaned from public sources such as newsreels, magazines, and tourist guides.

## The Birth of "Garbo"

Garcia's fictitious reports to the Germans were so convincing that they caught the attention of British intelligence, who had intercepted his communications. Recognizing his potential, the British finally recruited him as a double agent in 1942, giving him the codename "Garbo" for his acting abilities. This marked the beginning of one of the most successful deception operations of the war.

Collaborating closely with his British handlers, Garcia developed an intricate network of 27 fictitious sub-agents, each with detailed backstories and personalities. This imaginary network became the conduit for a steady stream of misinformation to the German High Command, carefully crafted to support Allied strategic objectives.

## Operation Fortitude and the D-Day Deception

Garcia's most significant contribution came through his involvement in Operation Fortitude, the elaborate deception plan designed to mislead the Germans about the true location of the Allied invasion of Europe. The operation aimed to convince the German High Command that the main invasion force would land at Pas de Calais, rather than Normandy.

Through a series of over 500 radio messages, Garcia's fictional network provided the Germans with false intelligence that reinforced this belief. He reported on troop movements, supply buildups, and even the presence of a phantom army group led by General George Patton, all designed to keep German attention focused on Calais.

The level of detail in Garcia's reports was astounding. He used his keen understanding of human nature and bureaucracy to create believable scenarios that the Germans eagerly accepted. One of his most audacious moves was to warn the Germans about the impending Normandy invasion just hours before it began, timing the message to arrive too late to be of use. This clever tactic further cemented his credibility with the Germans, who continued to trust his information even after D-Day had commenced.

## The Impact on D-Day and Beyond

The success of Garcia's deception efforts became evident on June 6, 1944, as Allied forces stormed the beaches of Normandy. Thanks in large part to the misinformation provided by Garcia, the German High Command kept significant forces stationed at Pas de Calais, even after the Normandy landings had begun. This strategic misdirection significantly reduced the resistance faced by Allied forces on the beaches and in the crucial days following the initial landings.

Even more remarkably, Garcia's influence extended well beyond D-Day itself. For weeks after the invasion, the Germans remained convinced that the Normandy attack was merely a diversion and that the main Allied thrust would still come at Calais. This belief, fostered by Garcia's continued reports, prevented the Germans from committing their full strength against the Normandy beachhead, giving the Allies crucial time to establish and expand their foothold in France.

## Legacy and Recognition

After the war, fearing potential reprisals from surviving Nazis, Garcia faked his own death and moved to Venezuela, where he lived under an assumed identity for many years. It wasn't until 1984 that his extraordinary contributions were publicly acknowledged when he was awarded an MBE (Member of the Order of the British Empire) by the British government.

Garcia's story has since become the subject of numerous books, documentaries, and even feature films, cementing his place as one of the most fascinating figures in the history of espionage. His work exemplifies the critical role that intelligence and deception play in modern warfare and stands as a testament to the impact that one individual's ingenuity and determination can have on world events.

## Conclusion

Juan Pujol Garcia's journey from a failed businessman to a master of deception is a remarkable tale of personal reinvention and unwavering commitment to a cause. His work as a double agent not only contributed significantly to the success of the D-Day invasion but also saved countless lives by helping to shorten the war.

Garcia's story serves as a powerful reminder of the importance of intelligence and misinformation in warfare. His ability to craft believable narratives and manipulate the perceptions of the enemy highlights the psychological aspects of conflict, demonstrating that battles can be won not just through force of arms, but through clever manipulation of information.

## Sources

Garcia, Juan Pujols, and Nigel West. Operation Garbo: The Personal Story of the Most Successful Spy of World War II. Biteback Publishing.

Talty, Stephan. Agent Garbo: The Brilliant, Eccentric Secret Agent Who Tricked Hitler and Saved D-Day. Mariner Books, 2013.

Various Sources

# The US Army Rangers at Pointe du Hoc

## Introduction

Few operations stand out as vividly as the assault on Pointe du Hoc during the D-Day invasion of June 6, 1944. This daring mission, undertaken by the US Army Rangers, exemplifies the courage, determination, and strategic importance that defined the Allied push into Nazi-occupied Europe. As dawn broke over the English Channel on that fateful day, a group of elite soldiers prepared to scale seemingly insurmountable cliffs in the face of fierce German resistance. Their objective: to neutralize a battery of guns that threatened to decimate the Allied landings on the beaches of Normandy. This story explores the background, preparation, execution, and aftermath of one of the most audacious operations of World War II, highlighting the pivotal role played by the Rangers in the success of Operation Overlord.

## The Strategic Significance of Pointe du Hoc

Pointe du Hoc, a cliff rising 100 feet above the English Channel, stood as a formidable natural fortress between Utah and Omaha beaches. Its strategic importance lay not just in its commanding view of the coastline but in the deadly arsenal it was believed to house. Intelligence reports indicated that the Germans had installed six 155mm guns capable of raining devastation upon Allied forces landing on both beaches. These long-range artillery pieces posed an existential threat to the entire D-Day operation, making their neutralization a top priority for Allied planners.

German engineering had augmented the cliff's natural defenses, transforming Pointe du Hoc into a key stronghold of the Atlantic Wall. Concrete bunkers, gun emplacements, and a network of trenches turned the promontory into a secure fortress. For the Allies, neutralizing this threat was not just a tactical necessity but a symbolic imperative, demonstrating their ability to overcome even the most daunting obstacles in their path to liberate Europe.

## The Rangers: Forged for the Impossible

The task of assaulting Pointe du Hoc fell to the 2nd and 5th Ranger Battalions, led by Lieutenant Colonel James Earl Rudder. These were not ordinary soldiers but elite commandos, trained to undertake the most challenging and dangerous missions. The Rangers' preparation for this operation was as grueling as it was comprehensive, drawing on the expertise of British Commandos and pushing the limits of human endurance.

Their training regimen was a crucible that forged them into a cohesive and lethal fighting force. It included intense physical conditioning, weapons handling, and tactics for stealth and surprise attacks. Recognizing the unique challenges of their mission, the Rangers underwent specialized training in climbing and rappelling, essential skills for scaling the cliffs of Pointe du Hoc. Amphibious assault training prepared them for the beach landings, while live-fire exercises simulated the intense combat conditions they would face.

But perhaps most crucial was the psychological conditioning that steeled their resolve for the trials ahead. Through endurance marches, combat simulations, and exercises designed to build team cohesion, the Rangers were molded into a unit capable of operating under extreme stress and fatigue. This holistic approach to training would prove invaluable in the chaos and carnage of D-Day.

## The Assault Begins

As dawn broke on June 6, 1944, the Rangers faced not only the formidable cliffs and German defenses but also the capricious nature of warfare itself. Rough seas and navigational errors disrupted their carefully laid plans, delaying their landing and causing disarray among the assault force. One landing craft even capsized, a grim reminder of the operation's perils before the first shot was fired.

Sgt. Antonio T. Ruggiero, one of the Rangers involved in the assault, later recounted the harrowing approach to the shore:

"The sea was rough and cold. As we neared the shore, fear gripped me, but I was determined. I prayed not to drown, focusing on my task of firing the grappling hook to scale the cliffs. The weight of our mission pressed upon us all."

Despite these initial setbacks, the Rangers landed at the base of Pointe du Hoc around 7:00 AM. The delay had allowed the German defenders to regroup, and as the Rangers began their ascent, they were met with a hail of machine-gun fire and grenades. Using rocket-propelled grappling hooks, ropes, and ladders, they began the perilous climb up the 100-foot cliffs.

Lt. James Eikner vividly described the chaos of those first moments:

"I was the last man off my boat, bullets whizzing past me. As I climbed, an explosion knocked me unconscious. I came to, buried up to my waist in debris, frantically digging for my weapon. The noise, the fear, the determination – it was all overwhelming."

## The Fight at the Top

Upon reaching the summit, the Rangers faced a shocking discovery: the main artillery guns were not in their expected positions. This unexpected development could have spelled disaster for the mission, but the Rangers' training and adaptability came to the fore. Quickly regrouping, they began a systematic search of the area, eventually locating several guns hidden in an orchard nearby.

Sgt. Leonard G. Lomell, who played a crucial role in finding and disabling the guns, later recalled:

"I was shot as soon as I got off the landing craft, but somehow I made it up the cliff. When we realized the guns weren't where they were supposed to be, we knew we had to find them. It was a race against time, knowing every second those guns remained operational, our comrades on the beaches were in danger."

Using thermite grenades, the Rangers destroyed the guns, accomplishing their primary objective and significantly reducing the threat to the landing forces on Utah and Omaha beaches. However, their mission was far from over. For the next two days, the Rangers would hold their position against fierce German counterattacks, their numbers dwindling but their resolve unshaken.

**Holding the Line**

The aftermath of the initial assault was a testament to the Rangers' tenacity and sacrifice. Of the 225 men who began the mission, only about 90 were still able to fight by the end of D-Day. Yet, they held their ground, repelling German attempts to retake the position.

**Capt. John Raaen, Jr. painted a grim picture of the battlefield:**

"The beach was a scene from hell. Dead and wounded men everywhere, the constant roar of gunfire and explosions. But we couldn't dwell on it. We had a job to do, and by God, we were going to do it."

For two days, the Rangers at Pointe du Hoc fought on, their numbers dwindling but their grip on the strategic position unyielding. Relief finally arrived on June 8, marking the end of one of the most remarkable stands in military history.

**Legacy and Impact**

The Rangers' actions at Pointe du Hoc were pivotal to the success of the D-Day landings. By neutralizing the artillery threat and securing this strategic position, they contributed significantly to the establishment of the Allied beachhead in Normandy. Their bravery and sacrifice became a symbol of the determination and skill of the Allied forces, inspiring troops across the invasion front.

The impact of their actions extended far beyond the immediate tactical gains. The success at Pointe du Hoc played a crucial role in the broader strategy of Operation Overlord, helping to secure the foothold that would ultimately lead to the liberation of Western Europe and the defeat of Nazi Germany.

**Conclusion**

The assault on Pointe du Hoc stands as a testament to the extraordinary courage, skill, and determination of the US Army Rangers. In the face of daunting odds and fierce resistance, these elite soldiers accomplished a mission that many had deemed impossible. Their actions on those windswept cliffs not only secured a crucial military objective but also embodied the spirit of sacrifice and resolve that characterized the Allied effort on D-Day.

The Rangers' assault on Pointe du Hoc remains a powerful reminder of what can be achieved when skill, courage, and determination are brought to bear against seemingly insurmountable odds. It stands as an enduring symbol of the price of freedom and the heights of human valor.

**Sources**

Sterne, Gary. The Cover-Up at Omaha Beach; D-Day, the US Rangers, and the Untold Story of Maisy Battery. Skyhorse, 2016.

Brinkley, Douglas. The Boys of Pointe du Hoc; Ronald Reagan, D-Day, and the US Army 2nd Ranger Battalion. William Morrow, 2005.

Various Sources

# The Mad Piper of D-Day

## Introduction

In the strange but true of World War II, few capture the imagination quite like that of Bill Millin, the "Mad Piper" of D-Day. As Allied forces stormed the beaches of Normandy on June 6, 1944, one man marched through the chaos armed not with a rifle, but with bagpipes. This narrative explores the extraordinary life and actions of Bill Millin, from his early days in Scotland to his iconic role during the D-Day landings and the lasting legacy he left behind. Through Millin's story, we gain insight into the power of tradition, courage, and the unexpected ways in which individuals can impact the course of history.

## A Piper's Journey

William "Bill" Millin's story begins far from the beaches of Normandy. Born on July 14, 1922, in Regina, Saskatchewan, Canada, to Scottish parents, Millin's connection to his heritage would shape the course of his life. When he was just three years old, his family returned to Scotland, settling in the Shettleston area of Glasgow. It was here, amidst the rich cultural traditions of Scotland, that young Bill first encountered the instrument that would one day make him famous.

At the age of 12, Millin took up the bagpipes, an instrument deeply ingrained in Scottish military tradition. This early passion would prove fateful, as it set him on a path that would intersect with one of the most significant military operations in history. By 17, Millin had joined the Territorial Army in Fort William, playing in the pipe bands of the Highland Light Infantry and the Queen's Own Cameron Highlanders.

As war clouds gathered over Europe, Millin, like many young men of his generation, volunteered for military service. His training took him to Achnacarry, Scotland, where he honed his skills alongside troops from various Allied nations. It was during this time that Millin's life took a pivotal turn. His musical talents caught the attention of Simon Fraser, the 15th Lord Lovat, who would later command the 1st Special Service Brigade. Impressed by Millin's piping abilities, Lord Lovat appointed him as his piper.

## The Eve of Invasion

As D-Day approached, the Allied high command issued an order that would have profound implications for Millin's role in the invasion. British Army regulations restricted the use of bagpipes to rear areas, deeming them too hazardous for front-line combat. However, Lord Lovat, with his deep respect for Scottish military traditions, had other ideas.

On the eve of the invasion, as the troops prepared for the most ambitious amphibious assault in history, Lord Lovat approached Millin with an extraordinary request. He ordered Millin to play his bagpipes as they landed on the beaches of Normandy, in defiance of official regulations. This decision would not only shape Millin's fate but would also create one of the most enduring images of the D-Day landings.

## D-Day: The Mad Piper in Action

As dawn broke on June 6, 1944, Bill Millin found himself aboard a landing craft bound for Sword Beach. The sea was rough, and like many of his comrades, Millin battled seasickness. Yet, as they approached the shore, a sense of purpose overtook him. In his own words:

"As we approached the beach, I could see the bodies of the fallen floating in the water. The noise was deafening - explosions, gunfire, the cries of men. But Lord Lovat had given me a job to do, and I was determined to do it."

As the ramp of the landing craft dropped, Millin waded into the surf, his bagpipes held high above the water. And then, amidst the chaos and carnage of the invasion, the stirring notes of "Highland Laddie" rang out across Sword Beach. The sight and sound of a kilted piper marching up and down the beach, playing traditional Scottish tunes, was so surreal that many soldiers initially thought they were hallucinating.

Millin's courage under fire was remarkable. As he marched along the water's edge, bullets whizzed past him, cutting down men on all sides. Yet he continued to play, moving up and down the beach as Lord Lovat had instructed. When asked later why he thought he had survived when so many others fell, Millin recounted a conversation with captured German snipers. They told him they hadn't shot him because they thought he was insane.

As the day wore on, Millin continued to play, his music a constant presence amidst the din of battle. He led the troops inland, piping them across Pegasus Bridge, a crucial objective secured earlier that morning by British glider troops. His tunes included "The Road to the Isles" and "Blue Bonnets Over the Border," each note a defiant challenge to the enemy and a rallying cry for his fellow soldiers.

One of Millin's fellow commandos, recognizing the extraordinary nature of the piper's actions, shouted over the noise of battle, "That's the only time I'll ever admit to being pleased to hear the bagpipes!" This sentiment was echoed by many others who found unexpected comfort in the familiar strains of Millin's music amidst the chaos of war.

## The Aftermath and Legacy

Bill Millin survived D-Day and continued to serve with the 1st Special Service Brigade through subsequent operations in the Netherlands and Germany. After the war, he worked briefly on Lord Lovat's estate before training as a psychiatric nurse, a career he pursued until his retirement in 1988.

However, Millin's D-Day exploits ensured that he would never be forgotten. His actions were immortalized in the 1962 film "The Longest Day," where he was portrayed by Pipe Major Leslie de Laspee, the official piper to the Queen Mother. This cinematic representation helped cement Millin's status as a cultural icon and a symbol of Allied courage and determination.

In the years following the war, Millin became a regular figure at D-Day commemorations, often returning to Normandy to play his pipes in memory of fallen comrades. His bravery was officially recognized in 2009 when the French government awarded him the Légion d'honneur for gallantry.

The legacy of the "Mad Piper" extends beyond official honors and Hollywood portrayals. Millin's bagpipes, the instruments that played such a crucial role in his D-Day story, have been preserved for posterity. One set is displayed at the Pegasus Bridge Museum in Normandy, while another resides in the Dawlish Museum in Devon, England, where Millin spent his later years.

Perhaps the most touching tribute to Millin's legacy came in 2013, nearly three years after his death, when a life-sized bronze statue of him was unveiled near Sword Beach. The statue, funded by a four-year campaign by the D-Day Piper Bill Millin Association, stands as a permanent reminder of his extraordinary courage and the power of music to inspire even in the darkest of times.

**Conclusion**

Bill Millin's D-Day experience stands as a testament to the enduring power of tradition, courage, and the human spirit. In the face of overwhelming odds and unspeakable danger, Millin's music provided a thread of continuity and hope, linking the soldiers on the beaches of Normandy to the homes and heritage they were fighting to protect.

The story of the "Mad Piper" reminds us that in times of great crisis, inspiration can come from unexpected sources. Millin's bagpipes, as incongruous as they might have seemed on that bloody beach, became a symbol of defiance and determination, their music a soundtrack to one of the most pivotal moments in modern history.

**Sources**

Moran, Ian. The Lone Piper: The Story of Bill Millin, Lord Lovat's D-Day Piper. Independently published, 2019

Haskew, Michael E. Piper Bill on the D-Day Beach. WarfareHistoryNetwork.com, 2010

Various Sources

# Easy Company

## Introduction

In the stories of military history, few units have captured the imagination quite like Easy Company, 2nd Battalion, 506th Parachute Infantry Regiment of the 101st Airborne Division. Their journey from the training grounds of Camp Toccoa to the beaches of Normandy and beyond is a testament to the courage, resilience, and brotherhood forged in the crucible of war. This story explores Easy Company's formation, their pivotal role in the D-Day invasion, and their subsequent contributions to the Allied victory in World War II. Through the experiences of individual soldiers and the collective actions of the unit, we gain insight into the extraordinary challenges faced by these "Screaming Eagles" and the lasting impact of their sacrifices.

## Forging the Eagles: The Formation of Easy Company

The story of Easy Company begins in 1942 at Camp Toccoa, Georgia, where the 506th Parachute Infantry Regiment was formed as an experimental airborne unit within the United States Army. Under the command of Colonel Robert Sink, the regiment aimed to create an elite force capable of undertaking the most challenging missions. Easy Company, initially led by 1st Lieutenant Herbert Sobel, would become one of the most renowned units of the war.

The training at Camp Toccoa was notoriously grueling, designed to push the men to their physical and mental limits. Richard Winters, who would later command Easy Company, recalled:

"Three miles up, three miles down. That was Currahee Mountain. We ran it so many times, I lost count. But every step, every drop of sweat, was preparing us for what lay ahead."

The rigorous regimen included running Currahee Mountain, a six-mile round trip, in under 50 minutes, alongside intense obstacle courses, calisthenics, and night marches. This punishing routine, coupled with Sobel's demanding leadership style, forged a tight-knit unit bound by shared hardship and a determination to excel.

## Airborne Training and Deployment

Following their initial training, Easy Company moved to Fort Benning for parachute training. Here, they earned their coveted jump wings, completing five parachute jumps and honing the skills that would prove crucial on D-Day. The company then underwent advanced field training at Camp Mackall and participated in the Tennessee Maneuvers, further refining their tactical abilities.

In September 1943, Easy Company deployed to Aldbourne, England, where they continued to train rigorously for the impending invasion of Europe. The spring of 1944 saw them participate in Operation Eagle, a large-scale night jump involving 15,000 paratroopers, serving as the final dress rehearsal for D-Day.

**The Eve of Invasion**

As June 5, 1944, dawned, the men of Easy Company prepared for the most significant operation of their lives. The atmosphere was tense, a mix of excitement, fear, and determination. Donald Malarkey, one of the company's veterans, later recounted:

"We knew this was it. Everything we'd trained for, everything we'd been through, it all came down to this moment. We were scared, sure, but we were ready."

The soldiers blackened their faces, checked their equipment, and boarded the C-47 aircraft that would carry them into history. As they took off from RAF Upottery in Devon, England, many wondered if they would ever see their comrades again.

**D-Day: Chaos and Courage**

In the early hours of June 6, 1944, Easy Company parachuted into Normandy as part of Operation Overlord. The drop was chaotic, with heavy anti-aircraft fire and poor weather conditions scattering the paratroopers across the countryside. Many missed their designated drop zones, landing in flooded fields or dangerously close to German positions.

Carwood Lipton, who would later become a first sergeant, described the scene:

"It was like jumping into hell. The sky was lit up with tracers and explosions. Men were scattered everywhere. But we had a job to do, and by God, we were going to do it."

Despite the confusion, the rigorous training of Easy Company proved invaluable. Soldiers like Bill Guarnere, Joe Toye, and Don Malarkey managed to regroup near Sainte-Mère-Église, while others like Earl McClung and Paul Rogers found themselves isolated but determined to reach their objectives.

**The Brécourt Manor Assault**

One of Easy Company's most significant actions on D-Day was the assault on Brécourt Manor. Led by Lieutenant Richard Winters, who had assumed command after the death of the original company commander, a small group of men attacked and destroyed a battery of German 105mm cannons that were firing on Utah Beach.

**Winters later described the action**

"We had about twelve men against a superior enemy force. But we had the element of surprise, and we had the training. Every man knew his job, and we executed the assault perfectly."

This operation, which significantly reduced the threat to the landing forces, exemplified the tactical prowess and courage of Easy Company. It would later be studied at West Point as an example of small-unit actions.

**Beyond D-Day: Securing the Beachhead**

In the days and weeks following D-Day, Easy Company played a crucial role in securing and expanding the Allied beachhead. They were involved in capturing and holding strategic positions, securing roads and bridges to facilitate the movement of Allied forces deeper into France.

One of their most notable engagements was the Battle of Carentan, a crucial operation to link the Utah and Omaha beachheads. Easy Company's involvement in capturing the heavily defended town was instrumental in solidifying the Allied position in Normandy.

Albert Blithe, whose experiences during this period were later dramatized, faced and overcame intense fear during these engagements. His story of personal courage became emblematic of the challenges faced by many soldiers in the aftermath of the invasion.

**The Long Road to Victory**

Easy Company's contributions extended far beyond the Normandy campaign. They participated in Operation Market Garden, played a crucial role in defending Bastogne during the Battle of the Bulge, and were among the first units to reach Hitler's Eagle's Nest in Berchtesgaden.

Throughout these campaigns, the bonds forged at Toccoa and strengthened on D-Day continued to define Easy Company. Lewis Nixon, despite struggling with personal demons, remained a key intelligence officer. Ronald Speirs, who joined the company later in the war, became known for his fearless leadership during the Battle of the Bulge.

Bradford Freeman, who would become the last surviving member of Easy Company, summed up their journey:

"We weren't heroes. We were just doing our job. But we did it together, and that made all the difference."

**Legacy and Impact**

The legacy of Easy Company extends far beyond their wartime achievements. Their story, immortalized in Stephen Ambrose's book "Band of Brothers" and the subsequent HBO miniseries, has inspired generations and brought renewed attention to the sacrifices of the World War II generation.

The individual stories of men like Richard Winters, whose leadership was pivotal throughout the war, and Carwood Lipton, who rose from private to first sergeant, continue to be studied for their examples of courage and leadership under fire.

**Conclusion**

The story of Easy Company, from their formation at Camp Toccoa to their pivotal role on D-Day and beyond, is a testament to the power of rigorous training, strong leadership, and unbreakable bonds forged in adversity. Their experiences on the beaches and hedgerows of Normandy, and in the subsequent campaigns across Europe, exemplify the courage and sacrifice of an entire generation.

The enduring fascination with Easy Company's story serves not only as a tribute to their specific achievements but as a lens through which we can understand the broader experiences of soldiers in World War II. Their legacy continues to inspire, educate, and remind us of the true cost of freedom and the extraordinary feats that ordinary individuals can accomplish when united by a common purpose and unwavering determination.

**Sources**

Ambrose, Stephen E. Band of Brothers: E Company, 506th Regiment, 101st Airborne from Normandy to Hitler's Eagles Nest, Simon & Schuster, 1992.

Ambrose, Stephen E. D-Day: June 6, 1944: The Climactic Battle of WWII. Simon & Schuster. 2013.

Various Sources

# The Niland Brothers

**Introduction**

In the journals of World War II, few stories capture the essence of sacrifice and family tragedy quite like that of the Niland brothers. Edward, Preston, Robert, and Frederick "Fritz" Niland, four siblings from Tonawanda, New York, found themselves at the heart of one of history's greatest conflicts. Their story, marked by heroism, loss, and unexpected twists of fate, would later inspire Steven Spielberg's acclaimed film "Saving Private Ryan." This story explores the Niland brothers' background, their experiences during World War II, particularly surrounding D-Day, and the lasting impact of their service on military policy and popular culture. Through their story, we gain insight into the profound personal costs of war and the enduring legacy of those who serve.

**Roots in Tonawanda**

The Niland brothers were born to Mr. and Mrs. Michael C. Niland in Tonawanda, a suburb of Buffalo, New York. Growing up in a close-knit family of German descent, the brothers were raised with a strong sense of duty and patriotism that would later influence their decision to serve their country. Their upbringing in this small, tight-knit community laid the foundation for the bonds that would sustain them through the trials to come.

Education played a significant role in the brothers' early lives. Edward, Robert, and Fritz attended Canisius University, a private Jesuit college in Buffalo, while Preston pursued his studies at the University at Buffalo. This commitment to education reflected the values instilled in them by their family and community, values that would serve them well in their future military careers.

**Answering the Call to Service**

As the United States entered World War II, the Niland brothers, like many young men of their generation, felt compelled to serve. Their enlistment came in the wake of the tragic loss of the Sullivan brothers, five siblings who perished when their ship was sunk during the Battle of Guadalcanal. This event led to a significant change in military policy, with efforts made to separate siblings in service to prevent similar losses.

Each of the Niland brothers found his path in the military:

- Edward, the eldest, became a pilot in the U.S. Army Air Forces.

- Preston was commissioned into the infantry, joining the 22nd Infantry Regiment of the 4th Infantry Division.

- Robert and Fritz both became paratroopers, with Robert joining the 505th Parachute Infantry Regiment of the 82nd Airborne Division, and Fritz serving with the 501st Parachute Infantry Regiment of the 101st Airborne Division.

Their separation into different units was a deliberate strategy to protect families from losing multiple members in combat, a policy that would play a crucial role in their story.

**D-Day and Its Aftermath**

The Niland brothers' war experiences reached their climax during the D-Day invasion and its immediate aftermath. On June 6, 1944, as Allied forces stormed the beaches of Normandy, the fates of the Niland brothers began to unfold in dramatic fashion.

Robert Niland, serving with the 505th Parachute Infantry Regiment, made the ultimate sacrifice on D-Day itself. In a display of extraordinary courage, he volunteered to stay behind with two other soldiers to hold off a German advance, allowing his company to retreat. Robert was killed while manning his machine gun, his actions embodying the selflessness that characterized so many soldiers on that fateful day.

The following day, June 7, 1944, brought more tragedy to the Niland family. Preston Niland, part of the 22nd Infantry Regiment, had survived the initial storming of Utah Beach. However, during an attempt to capture a strategic position near the Crisbecq Battery, Preston was mortally wounded. His death, coming so soon after Robert's, dealt a devastating blow to the family.

Fritz Niland, meanwhile, had parachuted into Normandy with the 101st Airborne Division. As he fought through the early days of the campaign, earning a Bronze Star for his service, Fritz was unaware of the fate that had befallen his brothers.

**The Sole Survivor**

The story of the Niland brothers took another dramatic turn with the application of the "Sole Survivor Policy." This directive, established in the wake of the Sullivan brothers' tragedy, aimed to protect families from losing all their sons to the war.

With Robert and Preston confirmed dead, and Edward presumed killed after his plane was shot down over Burma, Fritz Niland became the focus of this policy. Father Francis L. Sampson, the chaplain of Fritz's regiment, played a crucial role in this process. Upon learning of the deaths of Fritz's brothers, Father Sampson located him and initiated the paperwork necessary to have him sent home.

Fritz Niland's return to the United States under the Sole Survivor Policy was a bittersweet moment. While it spared the Niland family further loss, it also meant leaving behind the comrades with whom he had trained and fought. For the remainder of the war, Fritz served as a military police officer, his combat days behind him.

## An Unexpected Twist

The Niland family's story, already marked by tragedy and the bittersweet relief of Fritz's return, had one more surprising chapter. Edward Niland, previously presumed dead, was found alive. On May 16, 1944, Edward's B-25 Mitchell bomber had been shot down over Burma, leading to his capture by Japanese forces. For nearly a year, he endured the harsh conditions of a prisoner of war camp, until his liberation on May 4, 1945.

Edward's survival brought a measure of solace to a family that had already endured so much loss. His return home was a reminder of the unpredictable nature of war and the resilience of the human spirit.

## Legacy and Cultural Impact

The story of the Niland brothers, with its themes of sacrifice, family, and the arbitrary nature of survival in war, captured the imagination of many. It served as the inspiration for Steven Spielberg's 1998 film "Saving Private Ryan," which brought their story to a global audience.

While the film takes creative liberties with the details, it captures the essence of the Niland brothers' experience. The movie's depiction of a perilous mission to save the last surviving son of a family resonated deeply with viewers, highlighting the human cost of war and the lengths to which soldiers would go to honor the sacrifices of their fallen comrades.

The legacy of the Niland brothers extends beyond popular culture. Their story has become a powerful reminder of the sacrifices made by military families during World War II. The brothers are commemorated at the Normandy American Cemetery in France, where Robert and Preston lie buried alongside thousands of other American soldiers who gave their lives during the war.

Moreover, the Niland brothers' experience had a lasting impact on military policy. The application of the Sole Survivor Policy in Fritz's case underscored the importance of preserving family lines and preventing the complete loss of a generation within a family due to war.

## Conclusion

The story of the Niland brothers stands as a testament to the profound personal costs of war and the enduring bonds of family. From the streets of Tonawanda to the beaches of Normandy and the jungles of Burma, their journey encompasses the full spectrum of the World War II experience – heroism, sacrifice, loss, survival, and unexpected homecomings.

## Sources

Beevor, Antony. D-Day: The Battle for Normandy. Penguin Books, 2010.

Ambrose, Stephen E. D-Day: June 6, 1944: The Climactic Battle of WWII. Simon & Schuster. 2013.

Various Sources

# Operation Fortitude

## Introduction

Few operations have been as audacious, ingenious, and consequential as Operation Fortitude. This masterful deception plan, conceived and executed by the Allies during World War II, played a pivotal role in the success of the D-Day landings and, by extension, the liberation of Europe. Operation Fortitude was not merely a single act of misdirection but a complex, multi-faceted strategy that combined elements of psychological warfare, espionage, and theatrical stagecraft on an unprecedented scale. This story explores the conception, execution, and impact of Operation Fortitude, shedding light on the key figures, innovative tactics, and lesser-known aspects of one of the most successful military deceptions in history.

## The Genesis of Deception

As the tide of World War II began to turn in favor of the Allies, the need for a decisive blow against Nazi Germany became increasingly apparent. The planned invasion of occupied Europe, which would become known as Operation Overlord, was to be the largest amphibious assault in military history. However, its success hinged on achieving the element of surprise – a daunting task given the vigilance of German forces along the Atlantic Wall.

It was in this context that Operation Fortitude was born. Conceived in late 1943 as part of the broader Operation Bodyguard, Fortitude was designed to mislead the German High Command about the location and timing of the Allied invasion. The operation was divided into two main components: Fortitude North, which suggested an invasion of Norway, and Fortitude South, which aimed to convince the Germans that the main Allied thrust would come at the Pas-de-Calais, rather than the actual target of Normandy.

The planning of this elaborate deception fell to a group of brilliant minds within the London Controlling Section (LCS), a secret organization tasked with coordinating Allied deception efforts. Key figures such as John Bevan, the head of the LCS, and Noel Wild, who developed the initial plans, laid the groundwork for what would become one of the most successful military deceptions in history.

## Crafting the Illusion

The execution of Operation Fortitude relied on a multi-pronged approach that combined physical deception, false intelligence, and psychological manipulation. One of the most visually striking elements of the operation was the creation of a phantom army – the First United States Army Group (FUSAG). This fictitious force, supposedly led by General George S. Patton, was "stationed" in southeast England, poised to strike at the Pas-de-Calais.

To bring this ghost army to life, the Allies employed an array of dummy equipment that would have made any Hollywood prop master proud. Inflatable tanks, plywood aircraft, and canvas-covered trucks were strategically placed to create the illusion of massive military buildups. The involvement of technicians from Shepperton Studios, a prominent British film studio, in crafting these decoys highlights the operation's blend of military strategy and cinematic artistry.

The visual deception was complemented by an elaborate scheme of false radio traffic. Fixed and mobile units across southeast England generated a constant stream of fake communications, simulating the chatter of a large army preparing for invasion. This audio illusion was crucial in reinforcing the physical deception and convincing German intelligence of the authenticity of the phantom army.

## The Human Element: Double Agents and Misfits

At the heart of Operation Fortitude lay a network of double agents whose contributions were instrumental to its success. Perhaps the most famous of these was Juan Pujol García, codenamed "Garbo." A Spanish chicken farmer turned master spy, García fed a steady stream of misinformation to his German handlers, building a network of fictitious sub-agents that became a cornerstone of the Allied deception effort.

The cast of characters involved in Fortitude reads like a roster of unlikely heroes. From a convicted safecracker to a flamboyant Serbian lawyer, these unconventional spies brought their unique skills and eccentricities to bear in the service of Allied victory. Their diverse backgrounds and talents contributed to the operation's effectiveness in ways that traditional military planning could never have anticipated.

One particularly colorful figure was Nathalie "Lily" Sergueiew, codenamed "Treasure." Her obsession with her dog, Babs, which she believed had been killed by the British, nearly jeopardized the entire operation. Such human elements added layers of complexity and unpredictability to Fortitude, making the deception all the more convincing to the Germans, who could scarcely imagine such details being fabricated.

## D-Day and Beyond: The Impact of Fortitude

As dawn broke over the beaches of Normandy on June 6, 1944, the true test of Operation Fortitude began. The success of the deception became immediately apparent as Allied forces encountered less resistance than anticipated. The German High Command, convinced that the Normandy landings were merely a diversion, held back significant forces in anticipation of the "real" invasion at Pas-de-Calais.

Even after the scale of the Normandy landings became clear, the ghost of Fortitude continued to haunt German strategic thinking. For weeks after D-Day, substantial German forces remained tied down in the Pas-de-Calais region, awaiting an invasion that would never come. This delay in reinforcements proved crucial, allowing the Allies to establish and expand their beachhead in Normandy.

The effectiveness of Operation Fortitude is perhaps best summed up by the words of a German prisoner of war, who remarked, "We knew you were coming, but we didn't know where. It was very clever." This sentiment encapsulates the strategic genius of Fortitude – it played on what the Germans already believed, reinforcing their preconceptions rather than trying to create entirely new ones.

## The Unsung Heroes

While figures like Patton and García have become synonymous with Operation Fortitude, the success of the deception relied on the efforts of countless unsung heroes. Colonel David Strangeways, for instance, played a crucial role in refining the original Fortitude plan, making it more realistic and convincing to the Germans. Similarly, Thomas Argyle "Tar" Robertson, as the chief of MI5's counterespionage branch, managed the complex network of double agents that formed the human intelligence backbone of the operation.

The contributions of these individuals, often working in the shadows, underscore the collaborative nature of Operation Fortitude. It was not the work of a single brilliant strategist but the combined effort of military planners, intelligence officers, actors, filmmakers, and ordinary soldiers, all playing their parts in a grand performance designed to fool the enemy.

## Legacy and Lessons

The success of Operation Fortitude offers enduring lessons in the art of military deception. It demonstrates the power of playing to an enemy's preconceptions, the importance of coordinating multiple streams of false information, and the value of unconventional thinking in warfare. The operation's use of visual, auditory, and human intelligence elements in concert created a deception so convincing that it influenced German strategy long after the truth should have been apparent.

Moreover, Fortitude's legacy extends beyond its immediate military impact. It has inspired countless books, films, and studies, capturing the imagination of military historians and the general public alike. The operation stands as a testament to the idea that in warfare, the battle of wits can be as decisive as the clash of arms.

## Conclusion

Operation Fortitude stands as one of the most remarkable military deceptions in history, a triumph of strategic planning, creative thinking, and coordinated execution. Its success was instrumental in the Allied victory on D-Day and, by extension, the liberation of Europe from Nazi tyranny. The operation's blend of high-stakes espionage, theatrical illusion, and psychological warfare demonstrates the power of deception as a force multiplier in military strategy.

## Sources

Beyer, Rick. The Ghost Army of World War II. How One Top-Secret Unit Deceived the Enemy with Inflatable Tanks, Sound Effects, and Other Audacious Fakery. Princeton Architectural Press, 2023.

Souter, Gerry. The Ghost Army: Conning the Third Reich. Arcturus, 2019.

# Military Heroes

# Douglas Bader

**Introduction**

In the realm of World War II heroes, few stories are as compelling and inspiring as that of Douglas Bader. His journey from a talented young pilot to a double amputee, and then to one of the most celebrated fighter aces of the Royal Air Force (RAF), is a testament to the power of human determination and resilience. This story explores Bader's extraordinary life, focusing on his remarkable achievement of flying with two prosthetic legs during World War II, while delving into his character's complexities and the controversies surrounding his career.

**Early Life and Career**

Douglas Robert Steuart Bader was born on February 21, 1910, in St John's Wood, London. His early years were marked by separation from his parents and a somewhat tumultuous upbringing. After his father died in 1922, Bader was raised in the rectory of Sprotbrough, near Doncaster, Yorkshire, by his mother and stepfather. Despite the lack of strong parental guidance, young Douglas excelled in sports, particularly rugby, cricket, and boxing, during his time at St Edward's School, Oxford.

Bader's introduction to aviation came through his uncle, Flight Lieutenant Cyril Burge, an adjutant at the Royal Air Force College Cranwell. This connection sparked Bader's interest in flying and set him on the path to joining the RAF. In 1928, he won a scholarship to Cranwell, where he quickly gained a reputation as a skilled and daring pilot, known for his aerobatic prowess.

**The Accident That Changed Everything**

On December 14, 1931, Bader's life took a dramatic turn. While attempting a low-altitude aerobatic maneuver in a Bristol Bulldog aircraft, his wing clipped the ground, resulting in a catastrophic crash. The accident led to the amputation of both his legs—one above the knee and the other below. In his characteristic understated manner, Bader noted in his logbook, "crashed slow-rolling near ground. Bad show."

The road to recovery was arduous and challenging. Bader's rehabilitation involved learning to use artificial legs, a process that tested both his physical and mental resilience. His determination was evident as he quickly adapted to his new circumstances. By 1932, he was driving a specially modified car, playing golf, and even dancing.

## The Fight to Fly Again

Bader's unwavering determination to return to flying became the defining struggle of his early career. Initially decommissioned by the RAF, who believed his disability would prevent him from serving effectively, Bader made several attempts to rejoin as the threat of war loomed over Europe in the late 1930s.

His persistence paid off when Air Vice Marshal Frederick Halahan, a friend from his RAF Cranwell training days, intervened on his behalf. In 1939, as World War II began, Bader was finally given the opportunity to prove himself. He passed a refresher course, demonstrating his flying skills by turning a bi-plane upside down at 600 feet, defying the expectations of many.

## Technical Challenges and Adaptations

Flying with prosthetic legs presented unique technical challenges that Bader overcame through a combination of personal adaptation and the inherent design of the aircraft he flew. The Hurricane and Spitfire, Bader's primary aircraft during the war, had relatively simple foot controls that he could operate with his prosthetic legs without requiring modifications.

The aircraft featured two pedals to control the rudder, which Bader could manage effectively. Importantly, these planes used hand-operated air brakes instead of toe braking, which might have posed a challenge for Bader. This system involved a hand lever to activate the brakes, with the rudder pedals used for differential braking, a setup that suited Bader's capabilities.

Interestingly, Bader's prosthetic legs provided an unexpected advantage in aerial combat. They allowed him to withstand higher G-forces without losing consciousness, a critical factor in dogfights. This unique ability, combined with his exceptional skill and determination, made Bader a formidable opponent in the skies.

## World War II: The Ace Returns

Bader's return to active service was marked by his rapid rise through the ranks. He quickly became one of the most celebrated flying aces of World War II, credited with 22 aerial victories, four shared victories, six probables, one shared probable, and 11 enemy aircraft damaged. His combat career began during the Battle of France in 1940, where he scored his initial victories over Dunkirk.

It was during the Battle of Britain that Bader's leadership and combat skills truly shone. He took command of No. 242 Squadron, which had suffered heavy losses in France. Under his determined leadership, the squadron's morale and operational effectiveness improved dramatically. On August 30, 1940, the squadron achieved a remarkable feat by shooting down 10 enemy aircraft in a single day.

Bader's aggressive flying style and ability to inspire his fellow pilots made him a key figure in the RAF's defense against the German Luftwaffe. However, his advocacy for the controversial "Big Wing" tactic, which involved deploying large formations of aircraft to confront enemy bomber formations, sparked debate within the RAF. While initially seen as successful due to high claims of enemy aircraft shot down, post-war analysis revealed significant overclaiming, with ratios as high as 7:1.

## Capture and Imprisonment

Bader's combat career was interrupted in August 1941 when he was forced to bail out over German-occupied France after a dogfight. His capture marked the beginning of a series of remarkable events during his time as a prisoner of war (POW). Bader's indomitable spirit and repeated escape attempts became legendary.

His first escape attempt occurred shortly after his capture, using a rope made of bed sheets to climb out of a hospital window. Although quickly recaptured, Bader continued to make life difficult for his captors, earning a reputation as a "plain, bloody nuisance." His determination to escape did not wane, even as he was transferred to various POW camps, including the infamous Colditz Castle.

## First-hand accounts and Personal Interactions

Bader's complex personality left a lasting impression on those who interacted with him. While admired for his skills and determination, he was also known for his arrogance and difficult nature. One of his fellow pilots described him as "the most pompous chap" they had ever met, highlighting the mixed feelings many had about his character.

Alex Ross, Bader's aide during his time as a prisoner at Colditz Castle, provided a vivid first-hand account of Bader's demanding nature. Ross described the experience of serving Bader as challenging, emphasizing Bader's domineering and sometimes rude behavior. This account offers insight into the complexities of Bader's personality, revealing a man who was both inspiring and challenging to those around him.

## Post-War Life and Legacy

After the war, Bader continued to make significant contributions to aviation and advocacy for the disabled. He rejoined the RAF briefly before leaving in March 1946, recognizing that his prosthetic legs would limit his ability to serve in hot climates. He then joined Shell, where he flew the company's aircraft across Europe, the Middle East, and the Far East, eventually becoming the Managing Director of Shell Aircraft Ltd.

Bader's fame was further cemented by Paul Brickhill's biography "Reach for the Sky" in 1954 and its subsequent film adaptation. He became a passionate advocate for individuals with disabilities, devoting much of his time to encouraging and inspiring amputees. His message was one of resilience and determination, famously advising people to "never, never let them persuade you that things are too difficult or impossible."

In recognition of his service to the disabled, Bader was appointed Commander of the Order of the British Empire (CBE) in 1956 and was knighted in 1976. However, the physical toll of walking on artificial legs for over 50 years placed extra stress on his heart, leading to his sudden death in 1982 at the age of 72.

## Conclusion

Douglas Bader's life story is one of extraordinary triumph over adversity. His achievement of flying with two prosthetic legs during World War II stands as a testament to human resilience and determination. From the devastating accident that could have ended his flying career to becoming one of the most celebrated fighter aces of the war, Bader's journey inspired a generation and continues to captivate audiences today.

However, Bader's legacy is not without complexity. His controversial tactics, outspoken nature, and sometimes difficult personality add depth to the narrative of his life. These aspects serve to humanize a figure often portrayed in heroic terms, reminding us that even the most extraordinary individuals are multifaceted.

**Sources**

Brickhill, Paul. Reach for the Sky: The Story of Douglas Bader, the Legless Ace of the Battle of Britain. Naval Institute Press, 2001.

Charles River Editors. Douglas Bader: The Life and Legacy of One of the Royal Air Force's Most Famous Fighter Aces.

# Nadya Popova and the Night Witches

## Introduction

In the chronicles of World War II, few stories capture the imagination quite like that of the Night Witches, an all-female Soviet air unit that struck fear into the hearts of German forces. At the center of this remarkable tale stands Nadezhda "Nadya" Vasilyevna Popova, a young woman whose journey from aspiring actress to decorated combat pilot embodies the courage, resilience, and determination that defined this extraordinary group of aviators. This story explores the formation of the Night Witches, their daring tactics, and the indelible mark they left on military history, with a particular focus on Nadya Popova's pivotal role and experiences.

## A Wild Spirit Takes Flight

Nadezhda Vasilyevna Popova was born on December 17, 1921, in Shabanovka, a small village in the Orel Oblast of the Russian SFSR. Growing up near the Donetsk coal fields in Ukraine, young Nadya was far removed from the world of aviation that would come to define her life. As a child, she was drawn to the arts, harboring dreams of becoming an actress or a doctor, her wild spirit finding expression in music, dance, and theater.

Fate intervened in the form of a small aircraft that landed near her village when Popova was just 15 years old. This chance encounter ignited a passion for flight that would alter the course of her life. Against her parents' wishes, she enrolled in a gliding school, making her first parachute jump and solo flight at the tender age of 16. Popova's determination was evident from the start; by 18, she had not only obtained her flying license but had also become a flight instructor.

Popova's early life was marked by a thirst for adventure and freedom. As The Economist noted, she was a "wild spirit, easily bored" who loved to tango, foxtrot, and sing along to jazz. Little did she know that this spirited nature would serve her well in the crucible of war that lay ahead.

## The Birth of the Night Witches

As Nazi Germany launched its invasion of the Soviet Union in June 1941, the country found itself in dire need of every able-bodied citizen to contribute to the war effort. It was in this context that Marina Raskova, a celebrated Soviet aviator often referred to as the "Soviet Amelia Earhart," saw an opportunity to harness the untapped potential of Soviet women.

Raskova had been inundated with letters from women across the Soviet Union, eager to defend their homeland. Many were motivated by personal losses and a burning desire to take the fight to the enemy. Recognizing the urgency of the situation, Raskova petitioned Joseph Stalin to allow women to fly in combat roles.

On October 8, 1941, Stalin approved the formation of three all-female air regiments, a decision that was unprecedented at the time. Among these was the 588th Night Bomber Regiment, which would earn the fearsome nickname "Night Witches" from their German adversaries.

For Nadya Popova, this was the opportunity she had been waiting for. Despite initial resistance from the Soviet military, which had previously barred women from combat roles, Popova's determination and skill earned her a place in the 588th Night Bomber Regiment.

## Training for the Impossible

The women selected for the Night Witches underwent an intense and compressed training program at the Engels Military Aviation School near Stalingrad. What typically took years to learn was condensed into months, as pilots, navigators, mechanics, and ground crew members were prepared for the challenges that lay ahead.

Popova, with her prior flying experience, quickly distinguished herself. The rigorous training honed her skills and prepared her for the unique challenges of night bombing missions. The regiment was equipped with Polikarpov Po-2 biplanes, outdated aircraft primarily used for training and crop-dusting. These wooden planes, slow and vulnerable, would become the unlikely chariots of the Night Witches' daring raids.

## Into the Night Sky

On June 28, 1942, the Night Witches took to the skies for their first combat mission, targeting the headquarters of the invading Nazi forces. Nadya Popova was among the pilots who would soon become the stuff of legend, striking fear into the hearts of the German military.

The tactics employed by the Night Witches were as ingenious as they were daring. Flying in formations of three, two planes would act as decoys, drawing enemy fire, while the third would glide silently to its target, engines off, to drop its payload. This stealth approach, combined with the whooshing sound of their wooden planes, gave rise to their fearsome nickname.

Popova's courage and skill quickly became apparent. She flew an astounding 852 missions over the course of the war, a number that dwarfed the average of 30 missions flown by British bomber crews. Her record of 18 sorties in a single night stands as a testament to her endurance and dedication.

In one harrowing account, Popova reflected on the challenges they faced: "We flew in sequence, one after another, and the Germans lined up all their searchlights to pick us out, and then the anti-aircraft guns joined in. It was like flying through a curtain of fire." Despite the dangers, Popova and her comrades pressed on, their determination unwavering.

**Overcoming Adversity**

The Night Witches faced not only the threat of enemy fire but also skepticism and harassment from their male counterparts. They operated with minimal resources, using outdated equipment and hand-me-down uniforms. The harsh Soviet winters added to their difficulties, as the open-cockpit planes offered little protection from the elements.

Yet, it was perhaps these very challenges that forged the Night Witches into one of the most effective units in the Soviet Air Force. They adapted to their circumstances, using rudimentary tools like maps, compasses, and stopwatches for navigation in the absence of advanced technology.

Popova herself was shot down several times but managed to survive without serious injury. Her resilience was evident in her unwavering commitment to the mission, even in the face of personal loss and constant danger. "When the wind was strong, it would toss the plane like a cork in a raging river," Popova once recalled. "In winter, when you'd look out to see your target better, you got frostbite, our feet froze in our boots, but we carried on flying."

**Legacy of the Night Witches**

By the end of the war, the Night Witches had flown over 30,000 missions and dropped approximately 23,000 tons of bombs on German positions. Their impact on the war effort was significant, disrupting German operations and instilling fear among enemy troops.

Nadya Popova's contributions were recognized with numerous awards, including the title Hero of the Soviet Union, the Order of Lenin, and multiple Orders of the Patriotic War. Her story, along with those of her fellow Night Witches, became a powerful narrative of courage and determination.

**Conclusion**

The story of Nadya Popova and the Night Witches is one of extraordinary courage, innovation, and perseverance. From the fields of Ukraine to the skies over Nazi-occupied Europe, Popova's journey embodies the spirit of a generation of Soviet women who answered their nation's call in its darkest hour.

**Sources**

Night Witches: The Amazing Story of Russia's Women Pilots of World War II. Academy Chicago Publishers, 1990.

Ennis, Garth. The Night Witches. Dead Reckoning, 2019

Various Sources

# John Basilone: A Marine's Marine

## Introduction

In the shrine of American military heroes, few names shine as brightly as that of John Basilone. A United States Marine Corps Gunnery Sergeant, Basilone's extraordinary courage and leadership during World War II earned him the nation's highest military honors and a place in the annals of Marine Corps history. This story explores Basilone's journey from a young man in Raritan, New Jersey, to a legendary figure whose actions at Guadalcanal and Iwo Jima continue to inspire generations of Marines and civilians alike. Through his life story, we gain insight into the character of a man who embodied the core values of the Marine Corps - honor, courage, and commitment - and whose legacy endures as a testament to the indomitable spirit of the American serviceman.

## Early Life and Military Beginnings

John Basilone was born on November 4, 1916, in Buffalo, New York, to Salvatore and Dora Basilone, Italian immigrants who instilled in their children a strong work ethic and sense of patriotism. As one of ten children, Basilone grew up in Raritan, New Jersey, where he learned the values of family, community, and hard work. His early years, shaped by the challenges of the Great Depression, forged in him a resilience that would serve him well in the trials to come.

After completing his education at St. Bernard Parochial School, Basilone worked as a caddy and later as a truck driver, developing the physical stamina and determination that would become hallmarks of his military career. Inspired by tales of World War I veterans and driven by a desire for adventure, Basilone enlisted in the United States Army in 1934 at the age of 18.

His initial military service took him to the Philippines, where he served for more than two years. This experience provided Basilone with valuable exposure to military life and honed his skills as a soldier. After leaving the Army in 1939, Basilone's thirst for action led him to re-enlist, this

time in the United States Marine Corps on June 3, 1940. His decision to join the Marines was motivated by a desire to see combat, particularly in the Pacific, where tensions were escalating.

Basilone's training in the Marine Corps was rigorous and comprehensive. He trained at key installations including the Marine Barracks in Quantico, Virginia, and Parris Island, South Carolina, known for their intensive preparation programs. This training was instrumental in developing Basilone's skills as a machine gunner, a role in which he would later excel. Before his deployment to the Pacific, Basilone also served at Guantánamo Bay, Cuba, further broadening his military experience.

## Heroism at Guadalcanal

The true test of Basilone's mettle came during the Battle of Guadalcanal, a critical campaign in the Pacific Theater of World War II. In August 1942, as the United States sought to halt Japanese expansion by seizing control of a strategic airfield on Guadalcanal, Basilone found himself at the heart of one of the war's fiercest engagements.

On the night of October 24, 1942, Basilone's moment of extraordinary valor arrived. As Japanese forces launched a determined assault to retake Henderson Field, Basilone, in charge of four machine gun positions and a dozen men, faced an overwhelming enemy force. The battle was intense, with the Japanese throwing everything they had at the American defenders in a bid to reclaim the vital airstrip.

Throughout the night, Basilone's leadership and courage were put to the ultimate test. As casualties mounted and two of his machine guns were knocked out of action, Basilone demonstrated remarkable skill and composure. In the darkness, he repaired one of the disabled guns by 'touch' alone, a feat that allowed his unit to maintain its defensive fire. Basilone's expertise with the machine gun was so pronounced that his men focused on loading while he moved between positions, maximizing their firepower against the relentless Japanese assault.

As the battle raged on and ammunition ran low, Basilone undertook a perilous journey through enemy-held territory to resupply his unit. Dodging enemy fire, he returned with the desperately needed ammunition, enabling his men to continue their defense. By sunrise, the Japanese attack had been repelled, with 38 enemy soldiers lying dead around Basilone's positions alone.

Basilone's actions that night were instrumental in turning the tide of the battle and, by extension, the campaign on Guadalcanal. His extraordinary bravery and leadership under fire earned him the Congressional Medal of Honor, the nation's highest military decoration. The citation for his Medal of Honor vividly describes his "extraordinary heroism and conspicuous gallantry in action," highlighting how his "courageous stand against annihilation" and "grim determination in the face of almost certain death" contributed significantly to the American victory.

## War Bond Tour and Return to Combat

Following his heroic actions at Guadalcanal, Basilone was brought back to the United States to participate in a war bond tour. As a Medal of Honor recipient, Basilone's status as a war hero made him an ideal figure for this campaign. His appearances across the country drew large crowds and were instrumental in raising millions of dollars for the war effort. The tour also served to boost public morale, as Basilone's stories of bravery and sacrifice resonated deeply with the American public.

Despite the accolades and relative safety of his stateside duties, Basilone felt uncomfortable with his newfound celebrity status. He longed to return to combat, feeling that his place was with his fellow Marines on the front lines. In a move that spoke volumes about his character, Basilone requested to return to active duty, a request that was eventually granted.

## The Final Battle: Iwo Jima

Basilone's return to combat saw him assigned to the 5th Marine Division, which was preparing for the invasion of Iwo Jima, a strategically significant island in the Pacific theater. On February 19, 1945, as the Battle of Iwo Jima commenced, Basilone once again demonstrated the extraordinary leadership and bravery that had become his hallmark.

Landing with his unit on the beaches of Iwo Jima under heavy enemy fire, Basilone immediately took charge, leading his men off the beach and into the fight. His tactical acumen and courage were evident as he single-handedly destroyed a Japanese blockhouse that was impeding the American advance. This action was crucial in breaking through the enemy's defensive line.

In another display of heroism, Basilone played a vital role in guiding a tank through a minefield, further aiding the Marine advance. His actions in the opening hours of the battle were instrumental in establishing a foothold on the heavily defended island.

Tragically, within hours of landing, Basilone was killed by small arms fire. His death was a significant loss to his unit and the Marine Corps, but his final acts of bravery once again contributed to the success of a critical operation. For his valor at Iwo Jima, John Basilone was posthumously awarded the Navy Cross, making him the only enlisted Marine to receive both the Medal of Honor and the Navy Cross in World War II.

## Legacy and Remembrance

John Basilone's legacy extends far beyond his heroic actions on the battlefields of Guadalcanal and Iwo Jima. His life and service have become an enduring symbol of Marine Corps values and American heroism. The impact of his sacrifice and bravery continues to be felt and honored in numerous ways.

In his hometown of Raritan, New Jersey, a statue of Basilone stands as a focal point for annual commemorative events, including the John Basilone Memorial Parade. This parade, one of the longest-running in the United States dedicated to a single war hero, not only honors Basilone but serves as a tribute to all veterans.

The United States military has also ensured that Basilone's name lives on. The USS Basilone (DD-824), a Gearing-class destroyer, was named in his honor, serving as a floating memorial to his courage and sacrifice. Across the country, various memorials, plaques, and dedications in

military museums pay tribute to Basilone's contributions, serving as educational tools and places of reflection.

Basilone's story has transcended military circles to become part of American popular culture. His life and heroics have been depicted in various forms of media, including the HBO miniseries "The Pacific," which brought his story to a new generation. These portrayals have helped to keep Basilone's memory alive, inspiring countless individuals with his tale of bravery and selflessness.

Perhaps most importantly, Basilone's legacy lives on in the Marine Corps itself. His story is taught to new recruits and seasoned Marines alike, serving as an example of the highest ideals of the Corps. The John Basilone Award for Courage and Commitment is presented annually to an enlisted Marine who demonstrates the values exemplified by Basilone throughout his service.

## Conclusion

John Basilone's life story is one of extraordinary courage, unwavering dedication, and ultimate sacrifice. From his humble beginnings in New Jersey to his heroic actions on the battlefields of the Pacific, Basilone embodied the best qualities of the United States Marine Corps. His bravery at Guadalcanal, his humility during the war bond tour, and his final acts of heroism at Iwo Jima paint a picture of a man who lived and died by the principles of duty, honor, and country.

Basilone's legacy serves as a powerful reminder of the sacrifices made by the "Greatest Generation" during World War II. His story continues to inspire not only Marines but all who hear it, challenging us to live up to the ideals of courage and selflessness that he exemplified. In John Basilone, we see not just a war hero, but a symbol of the indomitable American spirit - a man who, when faced with the ultimate test, rose to meet it with extraordinary valor.

## Sources

Proser, Jim. I'm Staying with My Boys: The Heroic Life of SGT. John Basilone, USMC. St. Martin's Griffin, 2010.

Tatum, Chuck. Red Blood, Black Sand: Fighting Alongside John Basilone from Boot Camp to Iwo Jima. Dutton Caliber, 2013.

# The One-Handed Gurkha

## Introduction

In the chronicles of military history, few stories resonate as deeply as that of Lachhiman Gurung, a Nepalese-British Gurkha soldier whose heroics during World War II turned him into a legend. Despite severe injuries, including the loss of his right hand, Gurung's unwavering bravery and determination earned him the Victoria Cross, the highest military honor for gallantry in the face of the enemy awarded to British and Commonwealth forces. His story is one of indomitable spirit, courage against overwhelming odds, and the unbreakable will to protect his comrades.

## Strong Values

Lachhiman Gurung was born on December 30, 1917, in the remote village of Dahakhani, in the Tanahu District of Nepal. From a young age, he was imbued with the values of courage, loyalty, and service—qualities that would define his military career. In 1940, at the age of 22, Gurung enlisted in the British Indian Army as a rifleman in the 4th Battalion, 8th Gurkha Rifles, a regiment known for its fearsome warriors and storied history.

The Gurkhas, Nepalese soldiers serving in the British Army, were renowned for their fierce combat skills, loyalty, and fearlessness. With their signature curved knives, known as khukuris, and a deep-seated warrior tradition, Gurkhas had long been integral to British military efforts. By the time of World War II, their reputation was well established, and Lachhiman Gurung was about to add his name to the list of legendary Gurkha warriors.

## The Battle of Taungdaw

In May 1945, as the war in the Pacific raged on, Gurung and his comrades were stationed in Burma (now Myanmar), where the British Army was engaged in a brutal campaign against Japanese forces. The Battle of Taungdaw, a key confrontation in this campaign, would become the setting for Gurung's extraordinary act of bravery.

On the night of May 12, 1945, Gurung's company was defending a vital position against a determined Japanese assault. The enemy had encircled the British position and began launching wave after wave of attacks. Armed with grenades, rifles, and bayonets, the Japanese soldiers were relentless in their efforts to overrun the Gurkhas.

As the battle intensified, Gurung found himself in a forward trench with two fellow soldiers. The Japanese, realizing the strategic importance of their position, concentrated their attacks on the trench, hurling a barrage of grenades into it. In quick succession, two grenades landed close to Gurung. Without hesitation, he grabbed the first grenade and threw it back at the enemy, where it exploded harmlessly. However, as he reached for the second grenade, it detonated in his right hand.

The explosion was devastating. Gurung lost his right hand and suffered severe injuries to his face, body, and right leg. Despite the excruciating pain and the loss of his dominant hand, Gurung refused to abandon his post. He realized that if he fell, the Japanese would break through and likely kill or capture his comrades.

**Defying the Odds**

Gurung's injuries were severe enough to incapacitate any ordinary soldier, but he was no ordinary soldier. With his left hand, he continued to load and fire his bolt-action rifle, picking off Japanese soldiers as they advanced. Over the next four hours, Gurung single-handedly held off the enemy, killing over 30 Japanese soldiers and preventing them from overrunning his position.

His actions were nothing short of miraculous. Wounded, outnumbered, and fighting with only one hand, Gurung's determination to protect his comrades drove him to push through unimaginable pain and exhaustion. His trench became a symbol of defiance, and his bravery inspired his fellow soldiers to hold the line until reinforcements arrived.

By dawn, the Japanese assault had been repelled, largely due to Gurung's heroism. The British forces were able to hold their position and eventually push the Japanese back, securing a crucial victory in the Burma campaign.

**Recognition and Legacy**

For his extraordinary bravery and determination in the face of overwhelming odds, Lachhiman Gurung was awarded the Victoria Cross on December 19, 1945. The citation for his award highlighted his "superb gallantry and devotion to duty" and noted that his actions had saved the lives of his comrades and played a crucial role in the successful defense of the position.

Gurung's heroics did not go unnoticed by his peers, his commanding officers, or the British public. He became a symbol of the Gurkhas' valor and an enduring example of the extraordinary feats of bravery that can emerge in the most dire of circumstances. His Victoria Cross was a testament not only to his courage but also to the indomitable spirit of the Gurkhas as a whole.

After the war, Gurung returned to Nepal but eventually moved to the United Kingdom, where he lived out the rest of his life. Despite the loss of his hand and the lasting impact of his injuries, Gurung remained humble about his wartime service. He continued to serve as a source of inspiration for many, attending veterans' events and sharing his story with younger generations.

**Conclusion**

Lachhiman Gurung's story is one of incredible bravery, resilience, and an unyielding sense of duty. His actions during the Battle of Taungdaw exemplify the highest standards of military service and human courage. In the face of overwhelming odds and severe injury, Gurung's determination to protect his comrades and hold his position transformed him from an ordinary soldier into a legend.

**Sources**

Parker, John. The Gurkhas: The Inside Story of the Worlds Most Feared Soldiers. Headline Book Pub., 1999

Atkins, Robert. The Gurkha Diaries of Robert Atkins MC; India and Malaya 1944-1958. Pen and Sword Military, 2021.

Various Sources

# The Farmer Who Became a Legend

## Introduction

In the storied archives of military heroes, few names shine as brightly as that of Charles Hazlitt Upham. A New Zealand farmer turned soldier, Upham's extraordinary courage during World War II earned him the rare distinction of being awarded the Victoria Cross twice - the only combat soldier in history to receive this honor. His story is not just one of battlefield heroics, but a testament to the indomitable human spirit, unwavering leadership, and profound humility. This narrative explores Upham's journey from the peaceful farmlands of New Zealand to the brutal battlefields of Crete and North Africa, and his life beyond the war, painting a portrait of a man whose legacy continues to inspire generations.

## From Farm to Frontline

Charles Hazlitt Upham was born on September 21, 1908, in Christchurch, New Zealand, to John Hazlitt Upham, a lawyer, and Agatha Mary Coates. Growing up as one of three children, young Charles was shaped by the values of hard work and resilience that would define his later years. His education at Waihi School and later at the prestigious Christ's College in Christchurch laid the foundation for his disciplined approach to life.

Upham's connection to the land was forged early. After earning a diploma in agriculture from Canterbury Agricultural College (now Lincoln University) in 1930, he embarked on a career that saw him working on several farms in North Canterbury. The rugged terrain of the Hurunui District, where he engaged in mustering and shepherding, honed his physical strength and endurance - qualities that would serve him well in the crucible of war.

As storm clouds gathered over Europe in 1939, Upham, like many of his countrymen, felt the call to duty. He enlisted in the Second New Zealand Expeditionary Force, joining the 20th Battalion at Burnham Camp. His natural leadership qualities quickly became apparent, and he rose through the ranks, becoming a sergeant before attending Officer Cadet Training. By August 1940, Upham had been commissioned as a second lieutenant, his journey from farmer to soldier complete.

## The Hero of Crete

It was on the sun-baked island of Crete in May 1941 that Charles Upham would first etch his name into the annals of military history. As the German airborne assault on the island unfolded, Upham, despite suffering from dysentery, led his platoon with a ferocity and tactical acumen that would become his hallmark.

On the night of May 21, with the fate of Maleme Airfield hanging in the balance, Upham's actions bordered on the superhuman. Moving through the darkness with lethal efficiency, he single-handedly destroyed four enemy machine-gun posts with hand grenades. His utter disregard for personal safety was evident as he darted from position to position, inspiring his men to fight on against overwhelming odds.

One of Upham's comrades later recounted a particularly daring episode: "We watched in awe as Charlie, wounded and bleeding, crawled towards two German soldiers. He played dead until they approached, then sprang up, killing them both. It was like something out of a movie, but this was real, and Charlie was living it."

Throughout the battle, Upham's leadership was pivotal. He rescued wounded comrades under heavy fire, led isolated groups of men back to safety, and continually put himself in harm's way to protect his soldiers and achieve their objectives. His actions were instrumental in preventing the New Zealand rear-guard from being cut off during the eventual evacuation from Crete.

For his extraordinary heroism on Crete, Upham was awarded his first Victoria Cross. The citation spoke of his "outstanding gallantry and leadership" and "complete indifference to danger" - qualities that would define his entire military career.

## El Alamein: Courage Under Fire

If Crete had revealed Upham's exceptional bravery, the First Battle of El Alamein in July 1942 would cement his status as a legend. Now a captain commanding a company, Upham once again found himself at the heart of fierce combat.

During the breakout at Minqar Qaim, Upham led his men in close-quarter combat, attacking German positions with a ferocity that left even seasoned veterans in awe. Despite being wounded by shrapnel from his own grenades, he pressed on, his determination unshakeable.

At Ruweisat Ridge, Upham's actions transcended conventional notions of bravery. Under heavy fire, he conducted a lone reconnaissance mission, gathering crucial intelligence for his battalion. In the subsequent assault on German positions, Upham, already wounded in the arm, led a fierce attack that saw him destroy a German tank and several guns with grenades.

A fellow officer described the scene: "Charlie was like a man possessed. Despite the blood pouring from his arm, he kept advancing, hurling grenades and firing his weapon. The Germans didn't know what hit them. It was as if he was everywhere at once."

Even as he suffered from severe blood loss, Upham refused to leave his men. He continued to command his company until he was physically incapacitated by further injuries. His leadership and personal courage were instrumental in capturing the objective, turning the tide of the battle.

For his actions at El Alamein, Upham was awarded a Bar to his Victoria Cross - in effect, a second VC. The recommendation was initially met with skepticism due to the award's rarity, but as his commanding officer, Major General Sir Howard Kippenberger, noted, Upham had "earned the VC several times over."

**Captivity and Defiance**

Upham's capture following the battle at El Alamein marked the beginning of a new chapter in his wartime saga. Even as a prisoner of war, his indomitable spirit remained unbroken. He made several daring escape attempts, including a brazen effort to scale barbed-wire fences in broad daylight.

His persistent attempts at escape led to his transfer to the infamous Colditz Castle, a maximum-security prison reserved for the most troublesome Allied officers. Yet even here, Upham's thoughts were always on returning to the fight. A fellow prisoner recalled, "Charlie never gave up. He was always planning, always looking for a way out. His spirit was an inspiration to us all."

Upham's ordeal as a prisoner of war ended in April 1945 when U.S. forces liberated Colditz. As he emerged from captivity, the legend of his exploits had already begun to spread, both at home in New Zealand and among Allied forces.

**The Reluctant Hero**

With the war's end, Charles Upham returned to New Zealand, where he faced a challenge perhaps more daunting than any he had encountered on the battlefield: fame. The quiet farmer from Canterbury now found himself hailed as a national hero, his exploits the stuff of legend.

True to his character, Upham shunned the limelight. When the people of Canterbury raised £10,000 to buy him a farm - a considerable sum at the time - he declined, insisting the money be used for scholarships for children of ex-servicemen. This act of selflessness only served to enhance his reputation.

Upham's post-war life was marked by the same quiet determination that had characterized his military service. He returned to farming, settling into a life of hard work and devotion to his family. He married Molly McTamney in 1945, and together they raised three daughters.

Despite his preference for a quiet life, Upham remained committed to his fellow veterans. He became a vocal advocate for veterans' rights and welfare, using his status to ensure that those who had served alongside him received the support and recognition they deserved.

A fellow veteran once remarked, "Charlie never forgot us. He could have basked in glory, but instead, he fought for us, just as he had in the war. That's the kind of man he was."

**Legacy and Impact**

Charles Upham's impact extends far beyond his military achievements. In New Zealand, he is revered not just as a war hero, but as an embodiment of the nation's values: courage, humility, and a deep sense of duty.

His legacy is preserved in numerous ways. Statues stand in his honor in Amberley and at Christ's College in Christchurch. The Charles Upham School in Christchurch bears his name, ensuring that future generations learn of his courage and character. His portrait graced the New Zealand $20 note from 1990 to 1999, a testament to his national importance.

Upham's story continues to inspire military personnel around the world. His name is invoked in training and leadership courses, his actions studied as examples of exceptional bravery and tactical skill.

**Conclusion**

Charles Hazlitt Upham's life story reads like an epic tale of heroism, yet it is grounded in the quiet determination of a man who saw himself as nothing more than a farmer doing his duty. From the battlefields of Crete and North Africa to his post-war life in New Zealand, Upham exemplified the virtues of courage, leadership, and humility.

His extraordinary acts of bravery during World War II, recognized by the award of two Victoria Crosses, set him apart as one of the most decorated soldiers in Commonwealth history. Yet it was his actions after the war - his dedication to his fellow veterans, his refusal to capitalize on his fame, and his commitment to a quiet life - that truly cemented his status as a national icon.

**Sources**

Crawford, A.A.B. Charles Hazlitt Upham. The Encyclopedia of New Zealand. 2000.

National Army Museum of New Zealand. Charles Upham: New Zealand's Greatest War Hero.

Various Sources

# George Allan Mitchell at Monte Cassino

## Introduction

Throughout military history, few stories capture the essence of individual bravery and sacrifice like George Allan Mitchell's. A young private from London, Mitchell's actions during the Battle of Monte Cassino in World War II exemplify the extraordinary courage that can emerge in the crucible of war. This story explores Mitchell's journey from his early life in London to his fateful night on the Damiano Ridge, where his unwavering bravery and leadership in the face of overwhelming odds would earn him the highest military honor and a place in the pantheon of war heroes.

## Early Life and Background

George Allan Mitchell was born on August 30, 1911, in Highgate, London, to Edward Joseph and Florence Emma Mitchell. Growing up in the bustling metropolis of London in the early 20th century, young George was shaped by the post-World War I environment and the economic challenges of the time. His formative years were spent at Farmer Lane Boys' School in Leyton, then part of Essex but now in the London Borough of Waltham Forest in east London.

Mitchell's character was further molded by his involvement in the local Scouting movement in Leyton. This early exposure to outdoor skills, teamwork, and leadership would prove invaluable in his future military career. The values instilled by Scouting - loyalty, courage, and service to others - resonated deeply with Mitchell, laying the foundation for the extraordinary bravery he would later display on the battlefield.

As Mitchell came of age, the world was once again plunging into conflict. The outbreak of World War II in 1939 saw millions of young men across Britain answering the call to arms. Among them was George Allan Mitchell, who joined the ranks of the 1st Battalion, London Scottish (Gordon Highlanders).

## The London Scottish in World War II

The London Scottish, originally a reserve infantry regiment, had become part of the Gordon Highlanders in 1937. As war engulfed Europe, the regiment raised three battalions, with two serving overseas.

Mitchell's unit, the 1st Battalion, was assigned to the 168th (London) Infantry Brigade, part of the 56th (London) Infantry Division, affectionately known as "The Black Cats."

The battalion's wartime journey would take them far from the streets of London, through the deserts of North Africa and into the rugged terrain of Italy. Each campaign hardened the men of the London Scottish, forging them into a formidable fighting unit. Little did Mitchell know that his greatest test, and his date with destiny, awaited him in the shadow of an ancient monastery.

## The Battle of Monte Cassino

By January 1944, the Allied advance up the Italian peninsula had ground to a halt at the Gustav Line, a formidable series of German defensive positions anchored by the town of Cassino and the imposing Monte Cassino monastery. The battle that would unfold here over the next four months would become one of the most brutal and controversial of the entire war.

The monastery of Monte Cassino, perched atop a commanding hill, overlooked the Liri Valley - the gateway to Rome. Its strategic importance was clear to both sides. For the Allies, breaking through here was crucial to their advance on the Italian capital. For the Germans, holding this position was vital to their strategy of delaying the Allied forces.

On the night of January 23rd, 1944, Private George Allan Mitchell and his comrades in the 1st Battalion, London Scottish, found themselves tasked with a local attack to regain control of a portion of the main Damiano ridge. The importance of their mission was clear, but the challenges they faced were daunting.

## Mitchell's Moment of Truth

As the attack commenced, chaos quickly ensued. The company commander and the only other officer were wounded early in the assault, leaving the men without clear leadership. A section of the company, including Mitchell, was ordered to flank enemy machine guns that were impeding their advance. Fate intervened again when the platoon commander was killed, and with no platoon sergeant available, the section was left to act independently.

It was in this moment of crisis that George Allan Mitchell's true character shone through. Carrying a 2-inch mortar, Mitchell made a split-second decision that would alter the course of the battle and seal his place in history. Dropping the mortar, he charged alone through a hail of machine gun fire, armed only with his rifle and bayonet.

A fellow soldier, Private Thomas Kilpatrick, later recounted the scene: "It was like watching a man possessed. Mitchell just took off, running straight at the German position. We all thought he was done for, but somehow he made it through that wall of lead."

Mitchell's fearless charge caught the German defenders off guard. In a feat of extraordinary courage, he single-handedly silenced the enemy machine gun, killing its crew and clearing the way for his platoon to advance. But Mitchell's heroics were far from over.

As the platoon pushed forward, they encountered more entrenched German positions. Once again, Mitchell took the initiative. Leading from the front, he charged the enemy lines, firing his rifle from the hip and inspiring his comrades to follow. His fearless assault resulted in the capture of the position, with six Germans killed and twelve taken prisoner.

Sergeant William MacLeod, who witnessed Mitchell's actions, later said, "I've never seen anything like it. Mitchell was everywhere at once, shouting encouragement, rallying the men, and taking on the Germans single-handedly. He was a one-man army that night."

**The Final Assault**

With ammunition running low and the enemy still holding the high ground, Mitchell led one final, desperate charge up a steep hillside under heavy fire. His unwavering courage in the face of overwhelming odds inspired his fellow soldiers to feats of bravery they never thought possible. Against all odds, they forced the remaining German defenders to surrender.

It was in the aftermath of this triumphant moment that tragedy struck. As the British soldiers were securing their hard-won position, a German soldier who had previously surrendered managed to grab a rifle. In a final act of defiance, he fired a single shot, fatally wounding George Allan Mitchell.

Captain James Hendry, who arrived on the scene shortly after, described the somber moment: "There was Mitchell, mortally wounded but still trying to give orders, still thinking of his men and the mission. His last words were, 'Did we take the position, sir?' When I told him we had, he smiled and said, 'Good. It was worth it then.' That's the kind of man he was."

**Legacy and Recognition**

George Allan Mitchell's extraordinary actions on that January night at Monte Cassino came at the ultimate cost, but his sacrifice was not in vain. The position he and his comrades captured proved crucial in the subsequent Allied advance. More importantly, his selfless courage and leadership under fire became a rallying point for the entire battalion, inspiring countless acts of bravery in the difficult days that followed.

In recognition of his "courage and devotion to duty of the very highest order," Mitchell was posthumously awarded the Victoria Cross, Britain's highest military honor for gallantry in the face of the enemy. King George VI personally presented the medal to Mitchell's family in a solemn ceremony that underscored the nation's gratitude for his sacrifice.

Today, Mitchell's Victoria Cross is displayed at the London Scottish Regimental Museum, a tangible reminder of one man's extraordinary courage. But perhaps the true measure of Mitchell's legacy lies in the impact he had on those who served with him. For years after the war, veterans of the London Scottish would speak of "Mitchell's charge" with a mixture of awe and reverence, his actions serving as a benchmark for bravery and selfless service.

**Conclusion**

The story of George Allan Mitchell is more than just a tale of individual heroism. It is a testament to the extraordinary potential that lies within ordinary individuals when faced with extraordinary circumstances. From his humble beginnings in London to his final, fateful charge on the slopes of Monte Cassino, Mitchell's life embodies the values of courage, sacrifice, and duty that defined his generation.

In the end, George Allan Mitchell's story stands as a powerful reminder that true heroism is not about seeking glory or recognition, but about rising to the occasion when duty calls, no matter the cost. His sacrifice on that cold January night in 1944 ensures that his name will forever be remembered among the bravest of the brave, a shining example of the indomitable human spirit in the face of overwhelming odds.

**Sources**

Mitchell, Stewart. Fighting Through to Anzio: The Gordon Highlanders in the Second World War. Pen and Sword Military, 2023.

Lloyd, Mark. The London Scottish in the Great War. Pen and Sword Military, 2007

Various Sources

# George Wahlen at Iwo Jima

### Introduction

In the records of military history, few stories capture the essence of bravery and selflessness quite like that of George Edward Wahlen. A young man from Ogden, Utah, Wahlen's journey from aircraft mechanic to decorated war hero embodies the spirit of sacrifice that defined the Greatest Generation. This story explores Wahlen's path to becoming a Navy corpsman, his extraordinary actions during the Battle of Iwo Jima, and the lasting impact of his heroism. Through his story, we gain insight into the brutal realities of war, the bonds forged in combat, and the profound difference one individual can make in the face of overwhelming odds.

### From Mechanic to Medic

George Edward Wahlen was born on August 8, 1924, in Ogden, Utah, to Albert George Wahlen and Doris Lythgoe Wahlen. Growing up in the shadow of the Great Depression, young George developed a strong work ethic and a fascination with aircraft mechanics. This interest led him to train as an aircraft mechanic at Hill Field near Layton, Utah, where he quickly rose to lead a team of five mechanics as a crew chief for the United States Army Air Corps.

As World War II engulfed the globe, Wahlen felt the call to serve his country. In June 1943, at the age of 17, he enlisted in the U.S. Naval Reserve as a seaman apprentice at the Navy Recruiting Station in Salt Lake City. His initial hope was to work on aircraft, leveraging his mechanical skills. However, fate had other plans for the young Utahn.

The Navy and Marine Corps faced a critical shortage of medical personnel, and Wahlen's path was redirected towards becoming a hospital corpsman. This twist of fate would ultimately place him in a position to save countless lives and earn the nation's highest military honor.

Wahlen's training was intense and comprehensive. He completed his basic training at the Naval Training Station in San Diego, California, before advancing to the Naval Hospital Corpsman School. His dedication and aptitude were evident from the start, leading to rapid promotions. By December 1, 1943, Wahlen had advanced to pharmacist's mate third class and was assigned to the Field Medical Service School at Camp Elliott, California, for further field training.

In February 1944, Wahlen joined the 2nd Battalion, 26th Marines, 5th Marine Division at Camp Pendleton, California. This assignment marked the beginning of his transition from a mechanic to a combat medic, setting the stage for the extraordinary events that would unfold on a small, volcanic island in the Pacific.

## The Battle of Iwo Jima

On February 19, 1945, Wahlen found himself part of one of the most significant and brutal campaigns of World War II - the Battle of Iwo Jima. As part of Operation Detachment, Wahlen and his fellow Marines faced the daunting task of capturing this heavily fortified island, which was crucial for the Allied advance towards Japan.

The landing on Iwo Jima was a scene of chaos and carnage. As waves of Marines stormed the beach, they were met with a hail of fire from well-entrenched Japanese defenders. It was in this maelstrom of violence that Pharmacist's Mate Second Class George Wahlen's true mettle would be tested.

From the moment his boots hit the volcanic sand, Wahlen was in constant motion, rushing from one wounded Marine to another. His hands moved with practiced efficiency, applying tourniquets, administering morphine, and dragging injured men to whatever scant cover could be found on the exposed beach.

A fellow Marine, Private First-Class James Buchanan, later recounted, "I saw Wahlen running across that beach like a man possessed. Bullets were kicking up sand all around him, but he never hesitated. He just kept going from one wounded guy to the next, completely focused on saving lives."

As the battle raged on, Wahlen's courage and dedication became legendary among the men of his unit. On March 2, 1945, during a fierce firefight, Wahlen was struck by enemy fire. Despite his wounds, he refused evacuation, choosing instead to remain on the front lines to care for his fellow Marines.

One of the most extraordinary episodes of Wahlen's heroism occurred on March 3. Severely wounded for a second time, Wahlen again refused to leave his post. Instead, he crawled through a barrage of enemy fire to reach a wounded Marine lying exposed in a fire-swept area. With complete disregard for his safety, Wahlen dragged the injured man to safety, undoubtedly saving his life.

Corporal Thomas Reilly, who witnessed this act, later said, "I couldn't believe my eyes. Here was Wahlen, already wounded and barely able to move, crawling out there under heavy fire. We all thought he was done for, but somehow, he made it back with that wounded Marine. It was the bravest thing I've ever seen."

Even after being wounded for a third time on March 4, Wahlen's invincible spirit refused to yield. He continued to treat the wounded and direct their evacuation. It was only after his third wound, when he was physically unable to walk, that Wahlen finally allowed himself to be evacuated.

## Legacy of Valor

George Wahlen's extraordinary actions during the Battle of Iwo Jima did not go unnoticed. For his "conspicuous gallantry and intrepidity at the risk of his life above and beyond the call of duty," Wahlen was awarded the Medal of Honor, the nation's highest military decoration. The citation for his Medal of

Honor vividly describes his "outstanding fortitude and courage" and how his "heroic spirit of self-sacrifice in the face of overwhelming enemy fire" saved many lives.

After the war, Wahlen returned to civilian life, but his commitment to service never wavered. He continued to contribute to his community and country in various capacities, embodying the quiet heroism of many veterans who return to civilian life and continue to impact their communities positively.

Wahlen's story remained largely untold for over 60 years, a testament to his humble nature despite his significant contributions. His passing in 2009 in Salt Lake City, Utah, was marked by an outpouring of respect and admiration from his family, community, and fellow veterans.

Today, George Wahlen's legacy lives on, not only through his military honors but also through the memories and stories shared by those who knew him. His life serves as a powerful reminder of the sacrifices made by the "Greatest Generation" during World War II and the enduring impact of individual courage in the face of overwhelming odds.

## Conclusion

The story of George Edward Wahlen is more than just a tale of battlefield heroics. It is a testament to the extraordinary potential that lies within ordinary individuals when faced with extraordinary circumstances. From his humble beginnings in Ogden, Utah, to the blood-soaked beaches of Iwo Jima, Wahlen's journey embodies the values of courage, sacrifice, and unwavering commitment to duty that defined his generation.

In the end, George Wahlen's story stands as a powerful reminder that true heroism is not about seeking glory or recognition, but about rising to the occasion when duty calls, no matter the cost. His selfless actions on Iwo Jima ensure that his name will forever be remembered among the bravest of the brave, a shining example of the indomitable human spirit in the face of overwhelming odds.

## Sources

Toyn, Gary W. The Quiet Hero: The Untold Medal of Honor Story of George E. Wahlen at the Battle for Iwo Jima. American Legacy Media, 2006.

Hama, Larry. The Battle of Iwo Jima: Guerilla Warfare in the Pacific. Rosen Pub Group, 2006.

Various Sources

# Richard H. Best: Dive Bomber

## Introduction

In the chronicles of naval warfare, few battles have had as profound an impact on the course of history as the Battle of Midway. At the heart of this pivotal engagement was a young naval aviator whose courage, skill, and split-second decision-making would help turn the tide of World War II in the Pacific. This is the story of Richard Halsey Best, a dive bomber pilot whose actions on June 4, 1942, would forever alter the balance of power in the Pacific Theater and cement his place in the pantheon of American military heroes.

## From New Jersey to Annapolis: The Making of a Naval Aviator

Richard Halsey Best was born on March 24, 1910, in Bayonne, New Jersey. Growing up in the aftermath of World War I, young Richard was captivated by the tales of aerial combat that filtered back from the Western Front. These stories of daring pilots dueling in the skies over Europe ignited a passion for aviation that would shape the course of his life.

Best's path to becoming a naval aviator began with his acceptance to the United States Naval Academy in 1928. His time at Annapolis was marked by academic excellence, and he graduated with honors in 1932, earning a commission as an officer in the U.S. Navy. This achievement was just the first step in a career that would see him rise to the challenge of defending his nation in its darkest hour.

Following his graduation, Best's early naval career followed a traditional path. He spent two years aboard the light cruiser USS Richmond (CL-9), gaining valuable experience in naval operations and leadership. However, the call of the sky proved irresistible, and Best soon

transitioned to aviation, a move that would define his military career and ultimately place him at the center of one of the most decisive naval battles in history.

## The Road to Midway

As the clouds of war gathered over the Pacific, Best found himself assigned to Bombing Squadron 6 (VB-6) aboard the USS Enterprise. The attack on Pearl Harbor on December 7, 1941, thrust the United States into World War II, and Best, like many of his fellow aviators, was eager to strike back at the Japanese forces that had dealt such a devastating blow to the American fleet.

The months following Pearl Harbor were a time of intense training and preparation for Best and his squadron. The Navy was determined to avenge the attack and halt the Japanese advance across the Pacific. Little did Best know that he would soon play a crucial role in a battle that would change the course of the war.

**June 4, 1942: A Date with Destiny**

The morning of June 4, 1942, dawned with a sense of anticipation and tension aboard the USS Enterprise. Intelligence reports had indicated that a large Japanese fleet, including four aircraft carriers, was approaching Midway Atoll. The stage was set for a decisive engagement that would determine control of the central Pacific.

As the air group commander prepared to launch the strike against the Japanese fleet, Best and his fellow pilots of VB-6 readied their SBD Dauntless dive bombers for what they knew would be a perilous mission. The gravity of the moment was not lost on Best, who understood that the fate of the Pacific campaign might well rest on the outcome of this single attack.

At 09:55, after a long and harrowing flight, Best and his squadron finally spotted the Japanese fleet through breaks in the cloud cover. What followed was a scene of controlled chaos as the American dive bombers began their attack runs.

In the heat of battle, confusion reigned as all 31 remaining Dauntlesses moved to attack the Japanese carrier Kaga. Best, realizing the error, made a split-second decision that would prove crucial. With only two wingmen following his lead, he broke away from the main group and set his sights on the Japanese flagship, Akagi.

Lieutenant Norman "Dusty" Kleiss, another dive bomber pilot who participated in the attack, later recounted the intensity of the moment: "We were diving through a hail of anti-aircraft fire, watching tracers streak past our wings. But all I could think about was putting my bomb right on target. That's what we had trained for, and that's what we had to do."

At 10:26 am, Best and his two wingmen began their near-vertical dive on Akagi. As they plummeted towards the carrier, Best's focus narrowed to the bombsight in front of him. With practiced precision, he released his 1,000-pound bomb at the perfect moment. His aim was true, and the bomb penetrated Akagi's flight deck, exploding in the upper hangar and igniting a conflagration that would ultimately doom the carrier.

Best's gunner, James Francis Murray, described the scene as they pulled out of their dive: "I saw the flash of our bomb as it struck Akagi amidships. The explosion was massive, and I knew we had scored a critical hit. It was a moment of triumph in the midst of chaos."

But Best's day was far from over. Later that afternoon, he participated in a second strike against the last remaining Japanese carrier, Hiryu. Once again, his bomb found its mark, contributing to the sinking of the fourth and final Japanese carrier of the day.

**The Price of Victory**

As Best landed on the Enterprise after the second strike, he was elated by the success of the mission but unaware of the personal cost he had paid. Shortly after touching down, he began coughing up blood, a result of inhaling caustic soda fumes from a faulty oxygen rebreather during the intense combat.

This injury, which activated a latent tuberculosis infection, would mark the end of Best's flying career. Despite the personal toll, his actions on June 4, 1942, had helped change the course of the war in the Pacific. The destruction of four Japanese aircraft carriers in a single day had dealt a blow from which the Imperial Japanese Navy would never fully recover.

**Legacy and Reflection**

For his extraordinary bravery and skill during the Battle of Midway, Richard H. Best was awarded the Navy Cross and the Distinguished Flying Cross. The citations spoke of his "extreme disregard for his safety" and his significant contribution to the success of U.S. forces.

Despite being medically retired from the Navy in 1944 due to his tuberculosis, Best's contributions to the war effort continued in civilian life. He worked at the Rand Corporation on defense-related projects, quietly continuing to serve his country long after he had hung up his flight suit.

In later years, as historians began to fully appreciate the significance of the Battle of Midway, Best's role in the victory received renewed attention. His decision to break away from the main attack on Kaga to strike at Akagi was recognized as a pivotal moment that had helped tip the scales in favor of the United States.

**Conclusion**

Richard Halsey Best's story is one of courage, skill, and sacrifice. His actions during the Battle of Midway exemplify the best traditions of the U.S. Navy and stand as a testament to the impact that one individual can have in shaping the course of history. From his early days as a young man inspired by tales of aerial combat to his crucial role in one of the most decisive naval battles of World War II, Best's journey is a powerful reminder of the human element in warfare.

The legacy of Richard H. Best and his fellow aviators at Midway extends far beyond the immediate tactical victory. Their actions shifted the strategic balance in the Pacific, marking a turning point in World War II and altering the course of global history.

**Sources**

Symonds, Craig L. The Battle of Midway. Oxford University Press, 2013.

Hourly History. Battle of Midway – World War II: A History from Beginning to End. Independently published, 2018.

Naval History and Heritage Command. Lieutenant Richard H. Best. NHHC, 2020.

# Hollywood Hero and WWII Veteran

**Introduction:**

James Maitland Stewart, known to the world as Jimmy Stewart, was a beloved Hollywood actor whose career spanned over five decades. However, Stewart's legacy extends far beyond his film career. During World War II, he served with distinction in the United States Army Air Forces, where he earned acclaim for his bravery and leadership. His wartime heroics, however, came at a personal cost, as he grappled with depression and PTSD in the years following the war. This story explores Stewart's remarkable military service, his post-war struggles, and how his experiences shaped his legacy both as a public figure and a veteran.

**Mr. Stewart Goes to War**

James Stewart was born on May 20, 1908, in Indiana, Pennsylvania. Before World War II, Stewart was a prominent actor known for his roles in films such as Mr. Smith Goes to Washington and It's a Wonderful Life. His acting career was marked by his distinctive voice and everyman appeal, which won him widespread acclaim and a devoted fan base.

When World War II erupted, Stewart, like many Americans, felt a strong sense of duty. Despite his fame, he chose to enlist in the military, foregoing his career to serve his country. His decision to join the Army Air Forces was influenced by a desire to contribute meaningfully to the war effort and a deep-seated patriotism.

**Military Service**

In March 1941, Jimmy Stewart was commissioned as a second lieutenant in the Army Air Forces. He quickly rose through the ranks, demonstrating exceptional skill and leadership. Stewart's service record is distinguished by his involvement in numerous combat missions over Europe, where he flew as a pilot and squadron leader.

Stewart initially served as a bomber pilot, flying B-17 Flying Fortress missions. His leadership and bravery were evident during numerous high-risk missions. He was promoted to the rank of colonel, leading the 703rd Bomb Squadron and later the 453rd Bomb Group. Under his command, his units achieved significant success, and he was awarded several decorations for his valor, including the Distinguished Flying Cross and the Air Medal with three oak leaf clusters.

One notable mission was Operation Argument, also known as the Big Week, during which Stewart and his squadron played a crucial role in the bombing campaign aimed at crippling German industrial production. Stewart's performance during these missions was exemplary, and his ability to inspire and lead his men earned him widespread respect.

**Post-War Struggles**

Despite his heroism and success, Stewart's return to civilian life was marked by significant personal challenges. The psychological impact of his combat experiences became evident in the post-war years. Stewart struggled with depression and PTSD, symptoms that were not widely recognized or understood at the time.

His struggles with mental health were compounded by the stress of transitioning from a war hero to a civilian career. Stewart's post-war life included periods of anxiety and emotional distress, which he later admitted affected both his personal and professional life. Despite these challenges, Stewart sought to manage his condition through therapy and support from family and friends.

Stewart's struggles were a significant aspect of his post-war life, but he also continued to find success in Hollywood. His resilience and ability to cope with his psychological scars were reflected in his continued acting career, where he returned to the screen in films such as The Philadelphia Story and Rear Window. Stewart's enduring popularity and success were in part a testament to his strength and determination in the face of adversity.

**Legacy and Impact**

Jimmy Stewart's legacy as a World War II hero is intertwined with his contributions to American cinema and his personal battles with mental health. His service record remains a powerful reminder of the sacrifices made by those who served during the war. Stewart's post-war struggles with PTSD and depression also highlight the often-overlooked challenges faced by veterans returning to civilian life.

**Conclusion**

Jimmy Stewart's wartime service and post-war struggles provide a nuanced view of his character and contributions. His bravery and leadership during World War II were pivotal in the success of many missions, and his service record is a testament to his commitment and valor.

**Sources**

Eliot, Marc. Jimmy Stewart: A Biography. Crown, 2007.

Smith, Starr. Jimmy Stewart: Bomber Pilot. Zenith Press, 2006

Various Sources

# John F. Kennedy and PT-109 Incident

**Introduction:**

Before John F. Kennedy became the 35th President of the United States, he was a young naval officer thrust into the horrors of World War II. One of the most defining moments of his life, and one that would shape his character and legacy, occurred in the early hours of August 2, 1943, when the patrol torpedo boat he commanded, PT-109, was struck by a Japanese destroyer in the Solomon Islands. His actions during and after this catastrophic event not only saved the lives of his crew but also showcased Kennedy's remarkable leadership, resilience, and courage under fire. The story of PT-109 would follow Kennedy throughout his political career, casting him as a war hero and further cementing his legacy in American history.

**Early Life and Naval Service**

John Fitzgerald Kennedy, born on May 29, 1917, into a wealthy and politically prominent family, was a man destined for greatness. Despite suffering from chronic health issues, Kennedy led an active and ambitious life. Educated at Harvard University, where he earned a degree in international relations, he became increasingly interested in the state of global affairs as World War II loomed on the horizon. With his father's connections—Joseph P. Kennedy, Sr., was then U.S. Ambassador to the United Kingdom—young John had ample exposure to the complexities of diplomacy and geopolitics.

In 1941, after the United States entered World War II, Kennedy joined the Navy. Initially assigned to intelligence and staff positions due to his health issues, Kennedy was determined to serve in a combat role. After pulling some strings, he transferred to the Motor Torpedo Boat Squadron and was eventually assigned command of PT-109, a Patrol Torpedo boat. PT boats were small, fast, and highly maneuverable vessels used primarily for attacking larger ships with torpedoes. Although Kennedy lacked naval experience, his leadership qualities and sense of duty earned him respect among his crew.

PT-109 and the Solomon Islands Campaign: The Solomon Islands Campaign was a key aspect of the Allied strategy in the Pacific, aimed at halting Japanese advances and securing a path to Japan. In 1943, this region was a hotbed of intense naval and air battles. The Japanese, determined to maintain their control over the South Pacific, often used the waters around the Solomon Islands to transport supplies and troops, especially along the "Tokyo Express" route, which was vital for their logistics.

Kennedy's PT-109 was stationed in this volatile region, where the primary mission was to intercept and destroy Japanese supply ships. PT boats were particularly effective in these night operations, using their speed and agility to navigate shallow waters and launch surprise torpedo attacks. The boats typically operated under cover of darkness to avoid detection by enemy aircraft and ships.

## The Collision with Amagiri

On the night of August 1, 1943, PT-109, along with other PT boats, was sent to intercept a convoy of Japanese destroyers transporting troops to the island of Kolombangara. It was a dangerous mission, as the Japanese vessels were heavily armed and patrolled the waters with vigilance. The night was particularly dark, and the PT boats relied on their lookouts to spot enemy ships. However, the waters were calm, and the darkness provided little visibility.

At around 2:00 a.m. on August 2, while lying in wait, PT-109 was suddenly rammed by the Japanese destroyer Amagiri. The destroyer, traveling at high speed, struck the PT boat with devastating force, splitting it in half. The impact immediately killed two of Kennedy's crew members, while the remaining 11 were thrown into the water. PT-109 quickly became engulfed in flames, and within moments, the survivors were left clinging to the wreckage in the middle of enemy-controlled waters.

## Kennedy's Heroism

Despite being injured during the collision, Kennedy quickly took charge of the situation. Recognizing the immediate danger of being discovered by the Japanese or drifting too far from friendly forces, Kennedy made a bold decision to lead his crew to safety. Spotting a small, uninhabited island roughly 3.5 miles away, Kennedy directed his crew to swim for it. His leadership and physical endurance were tested as he swam tirelessly, towing an injured crew member, Patrick McMahon, by gripping McMahon's life jacket strap between his teeth while swimming through the treacherous waters.

After hours of grueling effort, the crew reached the island of Plum Pudding (now known as Kennedy Island). Exhausted and dehydrated, they had no food, water, or way of signaling for help. Over the next several days, Kennedy made multiple swims to nearby islands in search of help, often at night and through shark-infested waters. His perseverance and unwavering determination were vital in keeping the morale of his crew intact.

Finally, on August 4, Kennedy encountered two native islanders, Biuku Gasa and Eroni Kumana, who were part of the Allied coastwatcher network. In a stroke of ingenuity, Kennedy carved a rescue message on a coconut shell, which read, "NAURO ISL… COMMANDER… NATIVE KNOWS POSIT… HE CAN PILOT… 11 ALIVE… NEED SMALL BOAT… KENNEDY." The islanders paddled 35 miles in a canoe to deliver the message to Allied forces.

On August 8, after six days of being stranded, PT-109's survivors were finally rescued by an American PT boat. Kennedy and his crew were brought back to safety, and the young officer's heroism became a powerful story of survival and leadership.

## The Aftermath and Recognition

Kennedy's actions during the PT-109 incident earned him widespread recognition and praise. He was awarded the Navy and Marine Corps Medal, the highest non-combat decoration awarded for heroism, as well as the Purple Heart for the injuries he sustained. His bravery in leading his men to safety, despite his own injuries and the overwhelming odds, cemented his reputation as a war hero.

Although Kennedy later downplayed his heroics, the story of PT-109 followed him throughout his political career. In 1946, when he ran for Congress, his campaign frequently referenced his wartime service. The story of PT-109 became a central theme in his 1960 presidential campaign, contributing to the image of Kennedy as a young, courageous leader ready to take on the challenges of the Cold War. The carved coconut shell that Kennedy used to send his rescue message remained one of his most cherished possessions and was prominently displayed on his desk in the Oval Office.

## The Legacy of PT-109

The story of PT-109 became legendary, not only because it highlighted John F. Kennedy's courage but also because it encapsulated the spirit of sacrifice and resilience that defined the American experience during World War II. For many, Kennedy's actions embodied the qualities of leadership, bravery, and a deep commitment to his comrades.

In 1963, just months before his assassination, a feature film titled 'PT-109' was released, dramatizing Kennedy's wartime experiences. The film helped solidify the story's place in popular culture and further immortalized Kennedy as a heroic figure.

The island where Kennedy and his crew sought refuge was later renamed Kennedy Island in his honor, and the PT-109 story continues to inspire generations of Americans. To this day, PT-109 remains a symbol of the determination and heroism that defined both Kennedy's life and the broader American effort in World War II.

## Conclusion

John F. Kennedy's experience on PT-109 was more than just a tale of survival; it was a defining moment that revealed his innate leadership and courage. His actions during those six harrowing days in the Pacific would resonate throughout his political career and become an indelible part of his legacy as an American hero.

Sources

Dallek, Robert. An Unfinished Life: John F. Kennedy, 1917 – 1963. Back Bay Books, 2004.

Logevall, Fredrik. JFK: Coming of Age in the American Century, 1917-1956. Random House, 2020.

Various Sources

# Major Robert Henry Cain's Heroic Stand

## Introduction

In the records of military history, few stories capture the essence of individual bravery and leadership quite like that of Major Robert Henry Cain. During the Battle of Arnhem, a crucial component of Operation Market Garden in World War II, Cain's extraordinary courage and unwavering determination in the face of overwhelming odds would earn him the Victoria Cross and cement his place in the pantheon of war heroes. This story explores Cain's journey from his early life to his fateful days on the battlefields of Arnhem, where his actions would change the course of the battle and inspire generations to come.

## From Shanghai to the Battlefield

Robert Henry Cain's path to becoming a war hero began far from the battlefields of Europe. Born on January 2, 1909, in Shanghai, China, to Manx parents, young Robert's early years were marked by a blend of Eastern and Western influences. His family's return to the Isle of Man during his childhood would prove significant, as Cain would later become the first and only native of the island to receive the Victoria Cross.

Educated at King William's College on the Isle of Man, Cain developed the resilience and adaptability that would serve him well in his future military career. In 1928, he joined the Honourable Artillery Company, a unit of the British Territorial Army, balancing his military service with a civilian career at Royal Dutch Shell that took him to Thailand and Malaya.

The outbreak of World War II in 1939 marked a turning point in Cain's life. Commissioned as a second lieutenant in the Royal Northumberland Fusiliers in April 1940, he quickly distinguished himself as a capable leader. By 1942, Cain had transferred to the 2nd Battalion of the South Staffordshire Regiment, part of the 1st Airlanding Brigade within the 1st Airborne Division. His leadership skills were recognized with a temporary promotion to major in April 1943, a rank he would hold with distinction during the events that would define his military career.

## The Battle of Arnhem: A Test of Will

Operation Market Garden, launched on September 17, 1944, was one of the most ambitious Allied operations of World War II. Its goal was to secure a series of bridges in the Netherlands, creating a corridor for a rapid Allied advance into Germany. The Battle of Arnhem, where Major Cain would play a pivotal role, was the operation's most challenging component.

As commander of B Company, 2nd Battalion, South Staffordshire Regiment, Cain and his men were tasked with securing the crucial bridge over the Lower Rhine at Arnhem. However, from the moment they landed, Cain's unit faced intense opposition from unexpectedly strong German forces, including elements of the II SS Panzer Corps.

The situation quickly deteriorated as the Allied forces found themselves outgunned and cut off from reinforcements. It was in this desperate scenario that Major Cain's extraordinary leadership and courage came to the fore. On September 19, with his company isolated from the rest of the division, Cain faced the daunting task of holding the line against German armor with limited anti-tank weapons.

Bob Quayle, a fellow veteran from the Isle of Man, later described Cain as an "inspirational leader" whose actions were pivotal in the battle. "His men would follow him anywhere," Quayle recalled. "In the chaos of battle, Cain's calm determination and personal bravery were a beacon for all of us."

## The Tiger and the PIAT

September 20 would prove to be a defining day in Cain's heroic stand. As a German Tiger tank approached his position, Cain armed himself with a PIAT (Projector, Infantry, Anti-Tank) and waited until the behemoth was a mere 20 yards away. Despite the overwhelming odds and the immense danger, Cain engaged the tank with a level of courage that bordered on the superhuman.

A fellow soldier, who witnessed the encounter, later recounted: "Major Cain stood there, seemingly oblivious to the danger, firing round after round at the Tiger. Even when debris from near misses injured him, he refused to take cover. His determination was unlike anything I'd ever seen."

Cain's relentless assault eventually disabled the Tiger, but this was just the beginning of his one-man war against German armor. Throughout the battle, he destroyed or disabled several tanks and self-propelled guns, including four of the dreaded Tiger tanks. His actions were instrumental in holding the line and preventing a German breakthrough that could have spelled disaster for the Allied forces.

## Inspiration in the Face of Adversity

As the battle raged on, Cain's physical condition deteriorated. He suffered from temporary blindness and burst eardrums due to constant explosions and combat. Yet, even in this state, he refused to leave the battlefield. When PIAT ammunition ran out, Cain adapted, using a two-inch mortar to continue his assault on enemy positions.

One of his men later described the scene: "There was Major Cain, half-blind and barely able to hear, still directing fire and encouraging us. He seemed to be everywhere at once, always where the fighting was thickest. His courage was infectious, and it kept us going when all seemed lost."

Cain's leadership extended beyond his combat prowess. In the lulls between engagements, he moved among his men, boosting morale with his unwavering optimism and determination. His ability to inspire others in the face of overwhelming odds was perhaps his greatest contribution to the battle.

## The Aftermath and Recognition

Despite the heroic efforts of Cain and his fellow soldiers, the Battle of Arnhem ultimately ended in defeat for the Allied forces. The bridge was not held, and Operation Market Garden failed to achieve its ambitious objectives. However, the courage displayed by men like Major Cain ensured that the defeat was not in vain.

For his extraordinary bravery and leadership during the battle, Major Robert Henry Cain was awarded the Victoria Cross, the highest military decoration for valor in the British armed forces. The citation for his award spoke of his "superb gallantry," "outstanding courage and leadership," and "magnificent example to all ranks."

## Conclusion

Major Robert Henry Cain's heroic stand at the Battle of Arnhem is a testament to the impact one individual can have in the face of overwhelming odds. His journey from a young man born in Shanghai to a decorated war hero on the battlefields of Europe embodies the spirit of courage and sacrifice that defined the Greatest Generation.

Cain's legacy extends far beyond his military achievements. After the war, he returned to civilian life, working in the oil industry and living a quiet life away from the public eye. Yet the impact of his actions at Arnhem continued to inspire generations of soldiers and civilians alike.

The story of Major Robert Henry Cain serves as a powerful reminder of the human element in warfare. It challenges us to consider the depths of courage that individuals can summon in the most desperate of circumstances. In an era that often seeks heroes, Cain's life offers a timeless example of heroism in its truest form - not in the pursuit of glory, but in the unwavering commitment to duty, comrades, and country.

## Sources

Beevor, Antony. The Battle of Arnhem: The Deadliest Airborne Operation of World War II. Penguin Books, 2019.

Kershaw, Robert J. It Never Snows in September: The German View of Market-Garden and the Battle of Arnhem, September 1944. Goodall Publications, 2008.

Wikipedia. Robert Henry Cain.

Various Sources

# The Defiant Hero

## Introduction

In the stories of World War II, few stories capture the essence of moral courage and unwavering leadership quite like that of Master Sergeant Roddie Edmonds. Born in the heart of Tennessee, Edmonds' journey from a small-town upbringing to becoming a pivotal figure in one of history's darkest chapters is a testament to the power of individual conviction in the face of overwhelming evil. This narrative explores Edmonds' life, his fateful stand against Nazi oppression, and the enduring legacy of his heroism that continues to inspire generations.

## From Knoxville to the Battlefields of Europe

Roddie Edmonds' story begins in South Knoxville, Tennessee, where he was born on August 20, 1919. Raised in a devout Methodist family, young Roddie was one of four brothers, growing up in a close-knit community that valued faith, education, and service. These early influences would shape the character of the man who would later stand firm against the tide of Nazi tyranny.

Edmonds' formative years were typical of many young Americans of his generation. He graduated from Knoxville High School in 1938, just as the clouds of war were gathering over Europe. Little did he know that the values instilled in him during these early years would soon be put to the ultimate test on the battlefields of a world at war.

In 1941, with the United States on the brink of entering World War II, Roddie Edmonds made a decision that would alter the course of his life and the lives of hundreds of others. He enlisted in the U.S. Army, driven by a sense of duty to his country and a desire to make a difference in the world. This decision set him on a path that would lead to one of the most remarkable acts of moral courage in the history of warfare.

## The Road to Captivity

As Edmonds trained and rose through the ranks, the war in Europe raged on. By December 1944, now a Master Sergeant in the 106th Infantry Division, 422nd Infantry Regiment, Edmonds found himself deployed to the European Theater. The timing of his arrival was critical, as the Allied forces were preparing for what they hoped would be the final push into Germany.

However, fate had other plans. Just days after Edmonds and his unit arrived in Europe, the German Army launched a massive counteroffensive that would come to be known as the Battle of the Bulge. On December 19, 1944, Edmonds and his fellow soldiers found themselves surrounded by German forces. Despite their valiant efforts, they were outgunned and eventually captured, along with approximately 20,000 other American soldiers.

What followed was a harrowing journey into the heart of Nazi-occupied territory. Edmonds and his fellow prisoners were forced to march about 50 kilometers in freezing conditions to the Gerolstein railway station. Many soldiers died during this grueling trek, succumbing to the harsh weather and brutal treatment by their captors. At the station, they were crammed into boxcars, with about seventy men per car, and transported without food or water to Stalag IX-B, a prisoner-of-war camp at Bad Orb, Germany.

**A Leader Among Prisoners**

After enduring about a month at Stalag IX-B, Edmonds and other non-commissioned officers were transferred to Stalag IX-A, near Ziegenhain, Germany. It was here, in this bleak and desperate place, that Roddie Edmonds would face the defining moment of his life.

As the highest-ranking non-commissioned officer among the American POWs, Edmonds found himself responsible for the welfare of 1,292 fellow soldiers. The conditions in the camp were harsh, with inadequate food, poor sanitation, and the constant threat of violence from their Nazi captors. Yet, even in these dire circumstances, Edmonds' leadership shone through, as he worked tirelessly to maintain morale and ensure the survival of his men.

**The Moment of Truth**

On January 27, 1945, the German commandant of Stalag IX-A issued an order that would test Edmonds' courage and moral fiber to their limits. The commandant demanded that all Jewish American soldiers identify themselves and step forward the following morning. This was a common tactic used by the Nazis to isolate Jewish prisoners for harsher treatment or execution.

Edmonds, recognizing the grave danger this posed to his Jewish comrades, made a decision that would echo through history. He ordered all 1,275 American soldiers under his command to stand together in formation the next morning. When the German commandant arrived, expecting to see only the Jewish soldiers, he was confronted instead by a sea of American uniforms.

Furious, the commandant approached Edmonds, demanding to know why his order had been disobeyed. Edmonds, standing tall and unwavering, uttered the words that would define his legacy: "We are all Jews here".

The commandant, enraged by this act of defiance, pressed his pistol against Edmonds' forehead, threatening to shoot him on the spot if he did not identify the Jewish soldiers. Edmonds, showing remarkable composure in the face of death, calmly replied, "According to the Geneva Convention, we only have to give our name, rank, and serial number. If you shoot me, you will have to shoot all of us, and after the war, you will be tried for war crimes."

This extraordinary display of courage and quick thinking forced the commandant to back down. Edmonds' act of defiance saved the lives of approximately 200 Jewish American soldiers who would have otherwise faced certain death.

**The Silent Hero**

Despite the magnitude of his actions, Roddie Edmonds never spoke of his heroism after the war. He returned home to Tennessee, where he worked as a salesman in mobile homes and cable television. He married, raised a family, and lived a quiet life, carrying the weight of his wartime experiences in silence.

It wasn't until after Edmonds' death in 1985 that the full extent of his bravery came to light. His son, Chris Edmonds, discovered his father's story while researching his past, uncovering a legacy of heroism that had remained hidden for decades.

**A Legacy Honored**

As Roddie Edmonds' story emerged, it captured the attention of the world. In 2015, Yad Vashem, Israel's official memorial to the victims of the Holocaust, recognized Edmonds as "Righteous Among the Nations," an honor given to non-Jews who risked their lives to save Jews during the Holocaust. Edmonds became the first American soldier and only one of five Americans to receive this prestigious recognition.

The recognition ceremony, held on January 27, 2016, at the Israeli embassy in Washington, D.C., saw President Barack Obama praising Edmonds for his actions "above and beyond the call of duty". This international acknowledgment brought Edmonds' story to a global audience, inspiring people around the world with his example of moral courage and leadership.

**Conclusion**

Master Sergeant Roddie Edmonds' story is a powerful reminder of the impact one individual can have in the face of overwhelming evil. His unwavering courage, quick thinking, and deep sense of moral responsibility saved the lives of hundreds and stood as a beacon of hope in one of history's darkest hours.

Edmonds' legacy extends far beyond his wartime heroics. His story continues to inspire new generations, teaching valuable lessons about moral courage, leadership, and the importance of standing up for what is right, even in the most dire circumstances.

In a world that often seems divided, Roddie Edmonds' declaration, "We are all Jews here," resonates as a powerful statement of unity and shared humanity. It reminds us that in the face of hatred and discrimination, we have the power to stand together, to protect the vulnerable, and to uphold the values of human dignity and equality.

**Sources**

Ambrose, Stephen E. Citizen Soldiers: The US Army From the Normandy Beaches to the Bulge to the Surrender of Germany. Simon & Schuster, 1997.

Eisenhower, Dwight D. Crusade in Europe. Doubleday, 1948.

Jewish Virtual Library. Roddie Edmonds. 2019

Various Sources

# The Sword and the Bagpipes

## Introduction

In military history, few figures stand out as vividly as Lieutenant Colonel John Malcolm Thorpe Fleming Churchill, better known as "Mad Jack" Churchill. His exploits during World War II read like the pages of an adventure novel, yet they are firmly rooted in historical fact. This is the story of a man who charged into battle with a longbow, a Scottish broadsword, and bagpipes, defying the conventions of modern warfare and leaving an indelible mark on history.

## A Warrior is Born

John Malcolm Thorpe Fleming Churchill's journey to becoming a legend began far from the battlefields of Europe. Born on September 16, 1906, in Colombo, British Ceylon (now Sri Lanka), young Jack was the son of Alec Fleming Churchill, a District Engineer in the Ceylon Civil Service. His early years were marked by frequent moves, including a significant period in British Hong Kong, where his father served as Director of Public Works and a member of the Executive Council.

Churchill's education at King William's College on the Isle of Man laid the foundation for his future exploits. The school's rigorous academic and physical training fostered the adventurous spirit and resilience that would later define his military career. It was here that the seeds of "Mad Jack" were first sown, nurtured by an environment that valued both intellectual prowess and physical courage.

## From Sandhurst to Burma: The Making of an Unconventional Soldier

Churchill's path to military service led him to the Royal Military College, Sandhurst, where he graduated in 1926. Commissioned into the Manchester Regiment, his first posting was to Burma, an assignment that would prove formative in shaping his approach to warfare. The jungles of Burma provided the perfect backdrop for Churchill to develop his taste for adventure and unconventional tactics.

It was during this period that Churchill began to cultivate the eccentricities that would later make him famous. He could often be seen riding his motorcycle across challenging terrains, displaying a fearlessness that would become his trademark. However, the peacetime army proved too tame for Churchill's adventurous spirit. In 1936, he left active service to pursue a diverse range of interests, including working as a newspaper editor in Nairobi and even trying his hand as a male model.

## A Renaissance Man Goes to War

As the storm clouds of World War II gathered over Europe, Churchill's eclectic set of skills would find an unexpected arena. An accomplished archer, he had represented Great Britain at the World Archery Championships in Oslo in 1939, placing 26th. His prowess with the bagpipes was equally notable, earning him second place in a military piping competition at the Aldershot Tattoo in 1938.

With the outbreak of war in 1939, Churchill rejoined the army, eager to put his unique blend of traditional skills and modern military training to the test. It was in the theater of World War II that "Mad Jack" Churchill would truly be born.

## The Longbow at Dunkirk

Churchill's wartime exploits began in earnest during the retreat to Dunkirk in May 1940. As the British Expeditionary Force fought a desperate rearguard action against the advancing German army, Churchill distinguished himself in a manner that would set the tone for his entire wartime career.

Armed with his longbow, Churchill is credited with making the last recorded longbow kill in wartime. In the chaos of battle, he shot and killed a German soldier with an arrow, a feat that seemed to belong more to the age of Agincourt than the era of Blitzkrieg. This act not only demonstrated Churchill's exceptional skill with archaic weapons but also his unwavering courage in the face of overwhelming odds.

## The Sword of Vågsøy

Churchill's most famous exploit came during Operation Archery, a commando raid on the German garrison at Vågsøy, Norway, on December 27, 1941. As the landing craft approached the shore, Churchill stood at the fore, playing "The March of the Cameron Men" on his bagpipes. The sound of the pipes echoing across the water must have been a surreal experience for both his fellow commandos and the German defenders.

Upon landing, Churchill threw a grenade and charged into battle wielding his Scottish broadsword. Amid gunfire and explosions, the sight of a British officer running into combat with a sword must have been both inspiring to his men and terrifying to the enemy. Churchill's actions during this raid earned him the Military Cross for bravery, a testament to his exceptional courage and leadership.

## Capturing 42 with a Sword

The Italian campaign of 1943 provided Churchill with yet another opportunity to demonstrate his unique approach to warfare. During the Allied invasion of Sicily, Churchill led his troops with his trademark sword and bagpipes. In one particularly audacious incident, he managed to capture 42 German soldiers with the help of only one corporal.

Armed with just his broadsword, Churchill surprised the German unit. With a combination of bravado and quick thinking, he disarmed the prisoners by removing the bolts from their rifles. He then had them carry their wounded comrades back to the British lines. This incident not only showcased Churchill's tactical acumen but also his ability to use psychological warfare to his advantage.

## The Yugoslav Campaign and Capture

Churchill's wartime adventures continued in Yugoslavia, where he supported Josip Broz Tito's Partisans in their fight against the German occupation. In 1944, during an assault on the island of Brač, Churchill once again led from the front, charging against a well-defended German position.

Despite being heavily outnumbered, Churchill played his bagpipes as he led the charge, the haunting melody of "Will Ye No Come Back Again" echoing across the battlefield. The attack was initially successful, but the Allied forces were eventually pushed back. Churchill, knocked unconscious by a German grenade, was captured and sent to the infamous Sachsenhausen concentration camp.

## Escape and the End of the War

Churchill's never-say-die spirit could not be contained even by the walls of Sachsenhausen. In September 1944, he and an RAF officer managed to escape the camp. Their freedom was short-lived, however, as they were recaptured near the Baltic coast and returned to the camp.

Undeterred, Churchill escaped again in April 1945 as the German Reich crumbled around him. He managed to link up with American forces, but his war was not yet over. Churchill was eager to continue fighting in the Pacific theater, famously lamenting, "If it wasn't for those damn Yanks, we could have kept the war going another 10 years!"

## The Man Behind the Legend

Throughout his wartime exploits, Churchill's eccentric behavior and unconventional tactics earned him the nickname "Mad Jack" from his fellow soldiers. Yet, behind the larger-than-life persona was a man of extraordinary courage, leadership, and tactical skill. His ability to inspire his troops and strike fear into the enemy with nothing more than a sword and bagpipes spoke to a deeper understanding of the psychological aspects of warfare.

Churchill's famous quote, "Any officer who goes into action without his sword is improperly dressed," was not mere bravado. It reflected his belief in the power of tradition and the importance of leading by example. In an age of mechanized warfare, Churchill's adherence to ancient weapons and tactics served as a powerful reminder of the human element in combat.

## Conclusion

The story of "Mad Jack" Churchill is more than just a tale of wartime heroics. It is a testament to the enduring power of individual courage and the impact that one person can have in shaping the course of history. Churchill's exploits during World War II challenged conventional wisdom about modern warfare and demonstrated that there was still a place for traditional martial skills on the 20th-century battlefield.

In the years following the war, Churchill continued to seek adventure, training as a parachutist and later serving in Palestine. He retired from the army in 1959 and passed away in 1996, leaving behind a legacy that continues to inspire and amaze.

The tale of "Mad Jack" Churchill serves as a reminder that even in the darkest times, there is room for individuality, courage, and even a touch of madness. His story continues to captivate audiences, not just for its sheer audacity, but for what it reveals about the human spirit in times of conflict. In an era of increasingly impersonal warfare, Churchill's legacy stands as a testament to the enduring importance of personal bravery and leadership in the face of overwhelming odds.

**Sources**

Blackie, Benjamin. There's No Place Like War: The Unstoppable Warpath of the Unkillable Jack Churchill. Benjamin Blackie, 2024.

Eisenhower, Dwight D. Crusade in Europe. Doubleday, 1948.

Brown, Henry. Jack Churchill "Unlimited Boldness", Oxon Publishing Ltd. 2015.

Various Sources

# The Remarkable Encounter of Franz Stigler and Charlie Brown

## Introduction

Few stories capture the essence of humanity amidst the brutality of war, like the encounter between Franz Stigler and Charlie Brown. On December 20, 1943, as the skies over Europe raged with conflict, these two men—one a German fighter ace, the other an American bomber pilot—found themselves at the heart of an extraordinary moment that would challenge the very nature of warfare and leave an indelible mark on both their lives. This is a tale of courage, compassion, and the enduring power of human decency in the face of overwhelming odds.

## The Paths to Collision

Franz Stigler's journey to that fateful December day began in the skies over Bavaria. Born on August 21, 1915, in Regensburg, Germany, Stigler's passion for flight was ignited early by his father, a World War I pilot. By the age of 12, young Franz was already soaring in gliders, his heart set on following in his father's footsteps. As war clouds gathered over Europe, Stigler's path led him to the Luftwaffe in 1940, where he quickly distinguished himself as a skilled pilot and instructor.

Across the Atlantic, Charlie Brown's story began in the rolling hills of West Virginia. Raised on a farm, Brown embodied the quintessential American work ethic, milking cows before school and working as a janitor to make ends meet. His journey to the skies was driven by a sense of duty to his country, leading him to join the National Guard and eventually transition to the U.S. Army Air Forces.

As the war intensified, these two men found themselves on a collision course that would test their training, their courage, and ultimately, their humanity.

## The Mission That Changed Everything

On December 20, 1943, the skies over Bremen, Germany, were alive with the drone of engines and the staccato of gunfire. Second Lieutenant Charlie Brown, at the controls of a B-17 Flying Fortress named "Ye Olde Pub," was on only his second combat mission. The objective was clear: bomb a German aircraft factory, a vital cog in the Nazi war machine.

As "Ye Olde Pub" approached its target, the calm of the mission quickly dissolved into chaos. German anti-aircraft fire and waves of fighter attacks tore into the bomber, leaving it severely damaged. The aircraft's nose was shattered, and a gunner lay seriously wounded. With two engines faltering and the plane struggling to maintain altitude, Brown faced the grim reality that their chances of survival were dwindling by the second.

Meanwhile, on the ground at a nearby airfield, Franz Stigler was refueling and rearming his Messerschmitt Bf 109. With 27 victories to his name, Stigler was just one kill away from earning the coveted Knight's Cross. As he prepared to take off, the sight of a lone, struggling B-17 caught his attention. It was an opportunity that any ambitious fighter pilot would seize without hesitation.

## A Moment of Truth

As Stigler's Bf 109 closed in on the crippled bomber, he expected to find an easy target. Instead, what he saw through his gunsight would challenge everything he had been taught about war. The B-17 was in tatters, its gunners either dead or wounded, its fuselage riddled with holes. Stigler could see directly into the shattered nose of the bomber, where the frightened eyes of the American airmen met his own.

In that moment, Stigler was transported back to a conversation with his commanding officer, Gustav Rödel, who had once told him, "If I ever see or hear of you shooting at a man in a parachute, I will shoot you myself... You follow the rules of war for you, not for your enemy. You fight by rules to keep your humanity".

Faced with this test of his humanity, Stigler made a decision that would haunt and define him for the rest of his life. Instead of opening fire, he positioned his fighter alongside the stricken B-17. Brown, still at the controls, watched in disbelief as the German pilot gestured towards him, urging him to land or divert to Sweden.

"I didn't have the heart to finish off those brave men," Stigler would later recall. "They were trying desperately to get home and I was going to let them do it".

## The Escort of Enemies

What followed was one of the most extraordinary acts of chivalry in the history of aerial warfare. Stigler, risking court-martial or worse, escorted the damaged B-17 out of German airspace, ensuring it was not targeted by anti-aircraft guns. For Brown and his crew, the presence of the German fighter was a source of bewilderment and, ultimately, salvation.

Stigler gave Brown a final salute as they approached the North Sea before peeling away and returning to base. The American bomber, against all odds, managed to limp back to England, where it crash-landed, its crew battered but alive.

## The Weight of Silence

In the immediate aftermath of the incident, both Stigler and Brown were forced to keep their encounter a secret. For Stigler, revealing his act of mercy would have meant certain execution for treason. For Brown, the story of a chivalrous enemy pilot seemed too fantastical to be believed.

The years that followed saw both men grappling with the memory of that day. Brown, haunted by the image of the German pilot who spared his life, began a quest to find the man who had shown such extraordinary compassion. Stigler, who emigrated to Canada after the war, carried the weight of his secret, wondering if his act of mercy had been witnessed or appreciated.

**A Reunion of Former Enemies**

It wasn't until 1990, nearly half a century after their encounter, that Brown's tireless search finally bore fruit. Through a notice in a newsletter for former German fighter pilots, Brown found Stigler living in Canada. Their reunion was a powerful testament to the enduring impact of that moment in 1943.

Upon meeting, Stigler embraced Brown, exclaiming, "I love you, Charlie." The two men, once mortal enemies, forged a friendship that would last for the remainder of their lives. They shared their story with the world, offering a powerful narrative of compassion and humanity amidst the horrors of war.

**Conclusion**

The encounter between Franz Stigler and Charlie Brown stands as a beacon of hope and humanity in one of history's darkest chapters. Their story reminds us that even in war's brutality, the capacity for compassion and moral courage can prevail.

The legacy of Stigler and Brown's encounter extends far beyond their personal reconciliation. It serves as a powerful reminder that beneath the uniforms and behind the weapons, our shared humanity remains our strongest bond. In a world still plagued by conflict, their story offers a glimpse of the transformative power of compassion and the enduring strength of the human spirit.

Sources

Bowman, Martin W. RAF Fighter Pilots in WWII. Pen and Sword Military, 2015.

Calwell, Becky. The Charlie Brown and Franz Stigler Incident. West Virginia Encyclopedia, 2024.

Various Sources

# The Flying Tigers

## Introduction

Very few units have captured the imagination and admiration of the public quite like the American Volunteer Group (AVG), famously known as the Flying Tigers. Their story is one of courage, innovation, and international cooperation set against the backdrop of one of history's most devastating conflicts. As the storm clouds of World War II gathered over Asia, this group of American volunteers would play a pivotal role in stemming the tide of Japanese aggression and forging a bond between the United States and China that would endure for generations.

## Political and Military Context

The formation of the Flying Tigers was a direct response to the geopolitical turmoil of the late 1930s and early 1940s. Japan's aggressive expansion in Asia, particularly its invasion of China in 1937, posed a significant threat not only to China but also to Western interests in the region. The United States, while officially neutral, grew increasingly concerned about Japan's growing power and its potential to threaten American territories and interests in the Pacific.

President Franklin D. Roosevelt, acutely aware of the precarious situation, sought ways to support China without directly entering the conflict. This delicate balancing act would lead to one of the most unique military arrangements of the war: the creation of a volunteer group of American pilots to fight for China.

## Claire Lee Chennault: The Architect of the AVG

At the heart of this endeavor was Claire Lee Chennault, a retired U.S. Army Air Corps officer whose vision and determination would shape the Flying Tigers. Born in Commerce, Texas, in 1893, Chennault had pursued a career in education before joining the military during World War I. His passion for aviation and innovative tactics often put him at odds with the prevailing military doctrine, leading to his retirement in 1937.

Chennault's retirement, however, was short-lived. Recruited by the Chinese government to serve as an aviation adviser, he found himself at the forefront of China's desperate struggle against Japanese aggression. Assessing the dire state of the Chinese Air Force, Chennault recognized the need for a well-trained, well-equipped air unit to counter the Japanese threat.

**Formation and Recruitment**

In 1940, with the support of Chinese leader Chiang Kai-shek, Chennault returned to the United States to secure military aid for China. His efforts, combined with the Roosevelt administration's desire to support China covertly, led to a unique arrangement. American pilots and ground crew would be recruited to resign from U.S. military service and join a private military contractor, the Central Aircraft Manufacturing Company (CAMCO), effectively becoming mercenaries in the service of China.

The recruitment process was marked by both secrecy and financial incentive. Pilots were offered salaries significantly higher than their military pay, along with bonuses for confirmed enemy aircraft destroyed. The group consisted of 100 pilots and about 200 ground crew and support personnel, drawn from the U.S. Army Air Corps, Navy, and Marine Corps.

**Training and Preparation**

The AVG began arriving in China in April 1941, with their initial training taking place at a British airfield in Burma. Chennault's training regimen was intense and focused on the specific challenges they would face against Japanese forces. He introduced a new air combat doctrine based on his observations of Japanese tactics and the capabilities of the AVG's Curtiss P-40 Warhawk fighters.

Chennault emphasized a "dive-and-zoom" technique, which involved attacking from an altitude advantage and avoiding turning fights with the more maneuverable Japanese fighters. This approach was contrary to the tactics taught in U.S. service and required pilots to unlearn previous training.

The distinctive shark-mouth nose art on their P-40s, which would become iconic, was inspired by photographs of British RAF planes in North Africa. This fearsome appearance, combined with their fighting prowess, would soon earn them the nickname "Flying Tigers."

**Combat Operations and Achievements**

The Flying Tigers' baptism of fire came on December 20, 1941, just days after the attack on Pearl Harbor. In their first engagement, they intercepted a Japanese bombing raid on Kunming, shooting down nine out of ten Japanese bombers. This success marked the first American victory of World War II and set the tone for the AVG's future operations.

Throughout their brief but intense period of service, the Flying Tigers achieved a remarkable combat record. They were credited with destroying 296 enemy aircraft while losing only 14 pilots in combat. Their efforts were instrumental in defending critical areas and supply lines, including the vital Burma Road.

One of their most significant engagements was the defense of Rangoon, Burma, from December 1941 to February 1942. The Flying Tigers played a crucial role in protecting the city from Japanese air raids, significantly delaying Japanese advances in the region and allowing Allied forces to regroup and strengthen their positions.

The Battle of the Salween River Gorge in May 1942 further demonstrated the AVG's effectiveness. Their aggressive air attacks on Japanese ground forces and supply lines helped prevent the capture of critical Chinese territory, showcasing the strategic impact of air power in the theater.

**Personal Accounts and Experiences**

The experiences of AVG members provide a vivid picture of the challenges and triumphs they faced. While specific quotes from AVG members are not available in the provided research, accounts from veterans like Harry Moyer and Melvin McMullen have highlighted the deep bonds formed between American pilots and the Chinese people. These personal narratives emphasize the camaraderie and mutual support that developed during the war, underscoring the human element of this international cooperation.

The pilots often spoke of the intense combat, the thrill of flying the P-40s, and the satisfaction of achieving victories against a formidable enemy. Their stories also reflect the hardships they endured, from the challenging living conditions to the constant threat of combat in a foreign land.

**Legacy and Impact**

The legacy of the Flying Tigers extends far beyond their military achievements. Their success against numerically superior Japanese forces provided a much-needed morale boost to both the Chinese and American public at a time when the Allies were facing setbacks on multiple fronts. The AVG became a symbol of hope and resistance, their exploits widely publicized and celebrated.

Strategically, the Flying Tigers' operations had a significant impact on the China-Burma-India theater. They helped maintain critical supply lines, disrupted Japanese plans, and forced Japan to divert resources and attention away from other fronts. Their presence laid the groundwork for future U.S. air operations in the region and contributed to the eventual Allied victory in the theater.

The AVG was officially disbanded on July 4, 1942, and absorbed into the U.S. Army Air Forces as the 23rd Fighter Group. Many of the original AVG members returned to their previous military branches, while others continued to serve in China. The lessons learned from their operations influenced future air combat strategies and tactics.

Perhaps most importantly, the Flying Tigers left an enduring impact on U.S.-China relations. Their story became a powerful symbol of cooperation and shared sacrifice between the two nations. Even today, the legacy of the Flying Tigers is invoked in discussions about U.S.-China relations, serving as a reminder of the potential for positive collaboration in the face of common challenges.

**Conclusion**

The story of the Flying Tigers is a testament to the power of individual courage, innovative leadership, and international cooperation. In a time of global conflict, this small group of volunteers made a significant impact that far outweighed their numbers. Their legacy continues to inspire, reminding us of the potential for individuals to shape the course of history and the enduring bonds that can be forged between nations in times of adversity.

**Sources**

Kleiner, Sam. The Flying Tigers: The Untold Story of the American Pilots Who Waged a Secret War Against Japan. Penguin Books, 2019.

Ford, Daniel. Flying Tigers: Claire Chennault and His American Volunteers, 1941-1942. Warbird Books, 2016.

Various Sources

# Bridge on the River Kwai

### Introduction

The construction of the Burma Railway during World War II is a harrowing tale of human suffering, resilience, and the tragic consequences of war. Built by the Japanese Imperial Army to support their campaign in the Asian theater, the railway stands as a testament to the appalling conditions faced by the laborers who toiled under brutal circumstances. This story is further immortalized in popular culture through the film "The Bridge on the River Kwai", directed by David Lean and released in 1957. While the movie captures the essence of the experiences of those involved, it embellishes and dramatizes certain elements for cinematic effect. This story explores the history of the Burma Railway, the experiences of its workers, and how accurately the film reflects these events.

### Historical Context

The Burma Railway, also known as the Death Railway, was constructed during World War II by the Japanese military between 1942 and 1943. Following the fall of Singapore in 1942, the Japanese sought to secure a supply route from Thailand to British-held Burma (now Myanmar) to support their military operations in the region. The railway would facilitate the movement of troops and supplies, providing a strategic advantage in the ongoing conflict against the Allies.

To construct the railway, the Japanese military relied on forced labor, utilizing Allied prisoners of war (POWs) as well as local laborers from various countries, including Malaya, Thailand, and Burma. The project was characterized by extreme conditions, inadequate supplies, and relentless brutality, leading to significant loss of life.

### The Conditions of Construction

The railway stretched over 415 kilometers (approximately 258 miles) through challenging terrain, including dense jungles, mountains, and swamps. Laborers faced a multitude of hardships, including malnutrition, disease, and harsh treatment from their captors. Working long hours under the oppressive sun and in treacherous conditions, many succumbed to illnesses such as cholera, dysentery, and malaria. The Japanese military enforced strict discipline, and any sign of disobedience was met with brutal punishment.

The construction of the railway began in earnest in October 1942, with a workforce that would eventually number in the hundreds of thousands. Estimates suggest that approximately 90,000 forced laborers and around 30,000 Allied POWs worked on the project. The death toll was staggering, with estimates of around 12,000 to 16,000 laborers and POWs dying during the construction.

**The Construction Begins**

As the railway project commenced, the Japanese military implemented a ruthless regime to maximize productivity. Laborers were subjected to constant harassment, inadequate food rations, and insufficient medical care. The combination of grueling work, poor nutrition, and unsanitary conditions resulted in a high mortality rate.

Prisoners of war, including British, Australian, Dutch, and American troops, were transported to the railway site under inhumane conditions. Many arrived weakened and malnourished after months of captivity. Once at the construction site, they were organized into work gangs, tasked with various aspects of the railway's construction, including digging tunnels, laying tracks, and building bridges.

One of the most notorious segments of the railway was the section that crossed the River Kwai, where the famous bridge was constructed. The construction of this bridge became emblematic of the suffering endured by the workers, as it involved significant engineering challenges and required extensive labor.

**Suffering and Resilience**

The construction of the Burma Railway became synonymous with suffering and sacrifice. Laborers faced daily brutality, including beatings, executions, and psychological torment. The Japanese guards often resorted to extreme measures to maintain control, employing fear tactics to suppress dissent and encourage compliance.

Despite the dire conditions, some laborers displayed remarkable resilience. Efforts to provide medical care, share food, and support one another emerged among the POWs. The spirit of camaraderie and solidarity became a crucial source of strength for those enduring the hardships of life on the railway.

Reports of atrocities committed by the Japanese military began to surface, drawing the attention of the outside world. Humanitarian organizations and journalists attempted to document the suffering endured by the laborers, but information was limited due to the wartime environment.

**The Completion of the Railway**

The Burma Railway was completed in October 1943, but the cost of construction was staggering. The suffering endured by the laborers and POWs would leave lasting scars, both physically and emotionally. Many survivors returned home with profound trauma, struggling to reintegrate into civilian life after experiencing the horrors of war.

The railway itself served its intended purpose during the war, facilitating the movement of troops and supplies for the Japanese military. However, as the tide of the war began to turn against Japan, the railway's strategic importance diminished. Allied forces launched successful campaigns in the Pacific and began to reclaim territory, further isolating Japanese forces in the region.

The legacy of the Burma Railway remains a poignant reminder of the atrocities committed during wartime. The plight of the laborers and POWs has been memorialized in various forms, including literature, documentaries, and memorials. The railway's construction and the suffering endured by its workers have become symbols of resilience and the human spirit's capacity to endure even the most harrowing circumstances.

In 1988, a memorial was established at the Hellfire Pass, a significant site along the railway that symbolizes the suffering of those who labored there. The site serves as a place of reflection and remembrance, honoring the memory of the thousands who lost their lives during construction.

**The Film's Depiction:**

"The Bridge on the River Kwai". directed by David Lean and released in 1957, is a cinematic adaptation of the experiences surrounding the construction of the Burma Railway. The film follows a group of British POWs forced to build a bridge for their Japanese captors, highlighting the themes of duty, honor, and the futility of war.

While the film is lauded for its performances, cinematography, and music, it takes significant liberties with historical accuracy. The character of Colonel Nicholson, portrayed by Alec Guinness, is a fictional representation of the British officer's experience, and the narrative diverges from the actual events of the railway's construction.

One of the film's central themes is the complex relationship between the POWs and their captors. The film's depiction of the bridge's construction as a matter of pride for Colonel Nicholson, who becomes obsessed with the quality of the work, contrasts with the grim reality faced by the actual laborers. The construction was marked by suffering and brutality, with little regard for the well-being of the workers.

**Critical Reception and Impact**

Despite its historical inaccuracies, "The Bridge on the River Kwai" received critical acclaim and won several Academy Awards, including Best Picture. The film's portrayal of the psychological conflict experienced by the characters resonated with audiences, leading to discussions about the complexities of war and human nature.

However, the film's romanticized depiction of the Burma Railway has drawn criticism from historians and survivors. Many argue that it oversimplifies the experiences of POWs and laborers, glossing over the brutal realities they faced. The film's narrative choices, while compelling, may obscure the true suffering endured by those involved in the construction of the railway.

**Commemoration and Remembrance**

The story of the Burma Railway and the sacrifices made by those who labored on it serve as a powerful reminder of the horrors of war. Memorials have been established to honor the memory of the laborers and POWs who endured unimaginable suffering. The Kanchanaburi War Cemetery in Thailand is one such site, where the remains of many who perished during the construction are interred.

The legacy of the Burma Railway has also inspired numerous books and documentaries, ensuring that the stories of those who endured the hardships are not forgotten. The accounts of survivors, their resilience, and the lessons learned from their experiences continue to resonate with those who seek to understand the impact of war on individuals and societies.

**Conclusion**

The story of the Burma Railway and its construction during World War II is a poignant reminder of the sacrifices made by individuals in the pursuit of survival and dignity. While "The Bridge on the River Kwai" offers a compelling narrative and powerful themes, it diverges from the harsh realities faced by the laborers and POWs who toiled under brutal conditions. The railway legacy is a testament to the human spirit's resilience and the importance of remembering the lessons learned from history.

**Sources**

Twigg, Reg. Survivor on the River Kwai: The Incredible Story of Life on the Burma Railway. Penguin Books, 2014.

Charles, H Robert. Last Man Out: Surviving the Burma-Thailand Death Railway: A Memoir. Eakin Press, 1988.

Various Sources.

# The Conscientious Objector

## Introduction

During World War II, countless soldiers earned the title of hero for their bravery and sacrifice. Yet few stories are as extraordinary and inspiring as Desmond Doss, a conscientious objector who, without carrying a weapon, became one of the most decorated soldiers of the war. Desmond Doss served as a combat medic in the U.S. Army and is best known for his incredible actions during the Battle of Okinawa, where he single-handedly saved the lives of at least 75 men under intense enemy fire. This story delves into Desmond Doss's life, his conscientious objector beliefs, and the heroics that earned him the Medal of Honor—the first time it was awarded to a soldier who refused to bear arms.

## Early Life and Beliefs

Desmond Thomas Doss was born on February 7, 1919, in Lynchburg, Virginia, to a deeply religious Seventh-day Adventist family. His faith played a significant role in shaping his life and values. From a young age, Doss was taught the importance of the Sixth Commandment, "Thou shalt not kill," which would become the cornerstone of his philosophy. This belief in the sanctity of life, combined with his faith's adherence to non-violence, led Doss to refuse to carry or use a weapon.

Despite his strong convictions, Doss felt a deep sense of duty to serve his country during World War II. When the U.S. entered the war in 1941 following the attack on Pearl Harbor, Doss enlisted in the United States Army as a combat medic. He believed that, even in war, he could save lives rather than take them. However, his refusal to carry a weapon would make him a target of ridicule and skepticism within the military.

## Challenges as a Conscientious Objector

Doss was assigned to the 77th Infantry Division upon joining the Army. From the outset, his fellow soldiers and commanding officers were suspicious of his conscientious objector status. Many saw him as a coward for refusing to carry a rifle, and they questioned his commitment to the war effort. Doss was often ridiculed, harassed, and bullied by his comrades, who believed that a man unwilling to fight was a liability on the battlefield.

Doss's refusal to work on the Sabbath, a holy day for Seventh-day Adventists, only added to the tension. He remained steadfast in his faith, which led to frequent conflicts with both his peers and superiors. Some soldiers even threatened him, believing that his presence on the battlefield would put them in danger. Despite these challenges, Doss never wavered in his beliefs. He was determined to prove that one could serve their country with honor and valor without compromising their principles.

Doss's role as a medic offered him the opportunity to do what he felt called to do—save lives. As a combat medic, he would not be required to carry a weapon, allowing him to stay true to his religious beliefs. Yet, even with this compromise, the road ahead for Doss would be far from easy.

## The Battle of Okinawa: A Defining Moment

The Battle of Okinawa, one of the bloodiest battles of World War II, began in April 1945 and lasted for nearly three months. The U.S. aimed to capture the island of Okinawa, which was strategically located just 350 miles from mainland Japan. Okinawa was seen as a crucial steppingstone for a possible invasion of Japan, and the Japanese defenders were determined to resist the American forces at all costs.

Doss's unit was tasked with capturing a cliff known as Hacksaw Ridge, a heavily fortified Japanese position. The ridge, with its sheer vertical face, proved to be a nearly insurmountable obstacle for the American troops, and the Japanese forces defended it fiercely with machine guns, artillery, and snipers. The battle for Hacksaw Ridge was one of the most brutal engagements of the entire Pacific campaign.

On May 5, 1945, Doss's unit launched an assault on the ridge. As soon as they reached the top, they were met with withering fire from the Japanese defenders. The assault quickly devolved into chaos, with dozens of American soldiers being cut down by enemy fire. The situation was so dire that the U.S. forces were forced to retreat, leaving behind many wounded men stranded on the battlefield.

It was in this moment of desperation that Desmond Doss performed the actions that would define his legacy. Refusing to retreat with the rest of his unit, Doss stayed behind on top of Hacksaw Ridge to tend to the wounded. Unarmed and alone, he began a daring rescue mission that would last for hours. Despite the intense enemy fire raining down on him, Doss crawled from soldier to soldier, administering first aid and dragging them to safety.

One by one, Doss lowered the wounded soldiers down the cliff using a makeshift rope sling. Each time he saved a man, Doss prayed, "Lord, please help me get one more." His faith and determination pushed him to continue his rescue efforts, even as exhaustion and danger mounted. Over several hours, Doss saved the lives of at least 75 men, pulling them from the jaws of death and bringing them to safety below the ridge.

## Doss's Continued Bravery

The rescue at Hacksaw Ridge was not the only instance of Doss's heroism during the Battle of Okinawa. On several other occasions, he displayed extraordinary bravery and selflessness in the face of enemy fire. Just days after the rescue at Hacksaw Ridge, Doss was seriously wounded when he was hit by shrapnel from a grenade while trying to aid a wounded soldier. Despite his injuries, he continued to tend to the wounded before finally allowing himself to be evacuated.

Even after being wounded, Doss's heroism did not end. While being carried on a stretcher to a field hospital, Doss spotted another soldier who was more critically injured than himself. Without hesitation, he rolled off the stretcher and insisted that the other soldier be taken first. Doss later suffered a fractured arm when he was hit by sniper fire, but he fashioned a splint from a rifle and crawled 300 yards to safety.

**The Medal of Honor and Recognition**

For his heroics on Okinawa, Desmond Doss became the first conscientious objector in U.S. history to be awarded the Medal of Honor, the nation's highest military decoration for valor. On October 12, 1945, Doss received the medal from President Harry S. Truman in a ceremony at the White House. Truman reportedly told Doss, "You really deserve this. I consider this a greater honor than being president."

The citation for Doss's Medal of Honor highlighted his extraordinary bravery and selflessness, stating: "Through his outstanding bravery and unflinching determination in the face of desperately dangerous conditions, Private First Class Doss saved the lives of many soldiers. His name became a symbol throughout the 77th Infantry Division for outstanding gallantry far above and beyond the call of duty."

In addition to the Medal of Honor, Doss was awarded the Bronze Star Medal for valor, two Purple Hearts, and several other commendations for his service during the war.

**Life After the War**

After the war, Desmond Doss returned to civilian life in the United States. Despite the recognition he received for his heroism, Doss remained a humble and soft-spoken man. He suffered from lingering health issues because of his war injuries, including tuberculosis, which led to the removal of one lung and five ribs. Nevertheless, Doss continued to live a quiet life with his wife, Dorothy, and their son.

**Conclusion**

Desmond Doss's story is one of the most remarkable tales of heroism to emerge from World War II. As a conscientious objector, Doss faced immense challenges and ridicule from his fellow soldiers, but his unwavering faith and commitment to saving lives ultimately earned him the respect of his peers and the highest military honors. His actions during the Battle of Okinawa, where he single-handedly saved the lives of 75 men, exemplify the true meaning of courage and selflessness.

**Sources**

Doss, Frances. Desmond Doss: Conscientious Objector. Pacific Press, 2005.

Herndon, Booten. Hero of Hacksaw Ridge. Remnant Publications, 2016

# A Future Presidents Crash Landing

### Introduction

George H.W. Bush, the 41st President of the United States, is often remembered for his political career and leadership during pivotal moments in American history. However, his story began in a very different arena: as a young pilot in the U.S. Navy during World War II. Bush's experiences as a naval aviator, particularly his harrowing crash landing and subsequent rescue in the Pacific Theater, reveal a tale of bravery and resilience. This story explores the early life of George H.W. Bush, his service during the war, the dramatic events of his crash, and the broader significance of his experiences during this tumultuous time in history.

### Setting and Early Life

George Herbert Walker Bush was born on June 12, 1924, in Milton, Massachusetts. He grew up in a well-to-do family; his father, Prescott Bush, was a successful banker and later a U.S. Senator from Connecticut. George's upbringing instilled in him strong values of service and leadership. He was educated at Phillips Academy in Andover, Massachusetts, where he excelled academically and athletically.

When World War II began, Bush was just a teenager. Eager to serve his country, he enlisted in the U.S. Navy on his 18th birthday, becoming the youngest naval aviator at the time. His sense of duty and patriotism drove him to join the fight against the Axis powers, marking the beginning of his military career.

### Training as a Naval Aviator

Bush underwent rigorous training as a naval aviator, learning the skills necessary to pilot torpedo bombers. He was assigned to Torpedo Squadron 51 (VT-51) aboard the aircraft carrier USS San Jacinto (CVL-30). As a pilot, Bush demonstrated exceptional skill and determination, quickly earning the respect of his fellow aviators.

By 1944, Bush was stationed in the Pacific Theater, where he participated in several crucial missions against Japanese forces. The Pacific was characterized by intense naval battles and aerial combat, as the Allies sought to reclaim territory from the Japanese Empire.

## The Mission to Chichijima

On September 2, 1944, Bush and his crew were assigned a bombing mission targeting the Japanese-held island of Chichijima, part of the Ogasawara Islands. The mission was a critical part of the broader strategy to weaken Japanese defenses and secure the surrounding waters for future Allied operations.

Bush flew a Grumman TBM Avenger, a torpedo bomber known for its durability and effectiveness in combat. The mission was fraught with danger, as the crew faced the possibility of enemy anti-aircraft fire and the challenge of navigating the vast Pacific. Despite the risks, Bush and his fellow pilots were determined to carry out their orders.

As they approached the target, the formation of aircraft encountered heavy anti-aircraft fire from Japanese defenses. Bush recalled the intensity of the flak, which filled the sky with bursts of smoke and shrapnel. The pilots executed their bombing runs, aiming to strike key military installations on the island.

## The Crash Landing

During the mission, Bush's aircraft was hit by enemy fire, sustaining significant damage. The impact forced him to make a decision: attempt to complete the mission or prioritize the safety of his crew. Despite the damage and the chaos surrounding him, Bush remained focused and determined.

As the situation deteriorated, Bush realized that he could no longer maintain control of the aircraft. With no other options, he made the courageous decision to bail out. He and his crew prepared to eject from the plane, and Bush managed to escape just moments before the aircraft crashed into the ocean.

As he descended into the water, Bush activated his life raft and began to survey his surroundings. He was now in the vast expanse of the Pacific Ocean, alone and vulnerable. The immediate danger of enemy fire had passed, but the uncertainty of his fate loomed large.

## Surviving in Hostile Waters

After hitting the water, Bush quickly inflated his life raft and climbed aboard. He was aware that the waters were not only treacherous but also potentially hostile. The Japanese forces on Chichijima were known to be aggressive, and he would need to evade capture at all costs.

Though he was alone, Bush remained calm and focused on survival. He used his training to stay afloat and protect himself from the elements. The sun beat down on him, and he knew that dehydration and exposure could pose significant threats. As he floated in the ocean, he hoped for rescue and scanned the horizon for any sign of friendly forces.

For hours, Bush waited in the water, grappling with the uncertainty of his situation. He recalled the thoughts racing through his mind, wondering if he would be rescued or if his fate was sealed. The vastness of the ocean seemed daunting, but his determination to survive remained strong.

## The Arrival of Rescue

After several hours adrift, Bush's luck would change. A U.S. Navy search-and-rescue aircraft, responding to the mission's distress signals, spotted him in the water. The crew of the plane quickly directed a nearby ship to his location, and soon, a rescue boat was dispatched to retrieve him.

As the boat approached, Bush felt a wave of relief washing over him. The sight of fellow American sailors was a welcome sight after the harrowing ordeal he had just experienced. They pulled him aboard, providing immediate care and reassurance.

Bush's rescue was a testament to the bravery and dedication of the men and women in the U.S. Navy. The search-and-rescue operations were vital in ensuring the safety of pilots like Bush, who faced constant danger in the Pacific Theater.

## Return to Duty

Following his rescue, Bush was returned to the USS San Jacinto, where he was debriefed about the mission and the events leading to his crash. His experience only strengthened his resolve to continue serving in the Navy. He received medical attention and was quickly cleared to return to flying duties, demonstrating his commitment to his fellow aviators and the mission at hand.

Bush would go on to complete several more combat missions in the Pacific, earning the respect and admiration of his peers. His bravery and resilience during the crash and subsequent rescue exemplified the spirit of the American military during World War II.

## Recognition and Legacy

George H.W. Bush's experiences as a naval aviator during World War II would leave a lasting impact on his life. After the war, he returned to the United States and eventually transitioned into a successful career in business and politics. His service as a pilot instilled in him a sense of duty and leadership that would characterize his public life.

Bush's experiences, along with those of other World War II veterans, have been documented in various forms, including books, films, and interviews. These accounts have become an essential part of preserving the history of the war and ensuring that the sacrifices made by those who served are not forgotten.

## Conclusion

The story of George H.W. Bush's crash landing and rescue during World War II is a powerful testament to the courage and resilience of a young man facing the trials of war. His journey from a naval aviator to the presidency illustrates the profound impact of service and the enduring values of bravery, leadership, and commitment to one's country.

## Sources

Hourly History. George H.W. Bush: A Life from Beginning to End. Independently published, 2024.

Meacham, Jon. Destiny and Power: The American Odyssey of George Herbert Walker Bush. Random House, 2015.

Various Sources

# The Story of Paratrooper Leonard Funk

## Introduction

In the chronicles of World War II, there are countless stories of individual acts of heroism and bravery. Among the most extraordinary is that of Leonard A. Funk Jr., a paratrooper in the 82nd Airborne Division, who earned the Medal of Honor for his valor during the Battle of Holzheim, a village near Neuss, Germany. Funk's actions on January 29, 1945, during the final stages of the war in Europe, have become legendary. His remarkable ability to maintain composure under intense pressure and to single-handedly confront a large group of German soldiers during a critical moment of combat cemented his place in military history. This story recounts Leonard Funk's life, his heroic deeds during the battle of Holzheim, and the legacy of his courage.

## Early Life and Military Service

Leonard Funk Jr. was born on August 27, 1916, in Pittsburgh, Pennsylvania. Raised in a working-class family, Funk grew up during the Great Depression, which instilled in him a strong sense of responsibility and resilience. He worked various jobs to help support his family, but as tensions in Europe and the Pacific escalated in the late 1930s, Funk, like many young men of his generation, felt a call to serve his country.

In June 1941, Funk enlisted in the U.S. Army, a few months before the attack on Pearl Harbor that propelled the United States into World War II. He volunteered for the paratroopers, drawn by the challenge and sense of camaraderie that came with being part of an elite airborne unit. After completing rigorous paratrooper training at Fort Benning, Georgia, Funk was assigned to the 82nd Airborne Division, one of the most distinguished airborne divisions in the U.S. military.

By the time Funk arrived in Europe, he had already participated in some of the most significant battles of the war, including the D-Day invasion of Normandy and Operation Market Garden in the Netherlands. His experiences on the battlefield prepared him for the challenges ahead, but nothing could have prepared him for the intense combat he would face during the battle of Holzheim.

## The Battle of Holzheim

In January 1945, the Allies were pushing deeper into German territory, seeking to bring a swift end to the war in Europe. As part of this effort, the 82nd Airborne Division was tasked with securing key strategic points and liberating towns and villages in the Rhineland region. The village of Holzheim, located near Neuss, became one of the critical battlegrounds in this campaign.

On January 29, 1945, Funk and his unit were engaged in intense combat as they advanced toward Holzheim. The German forces in the area, though weakened by months of relentless fighting, were still putting up stiff resistance. The situation was chaotic, with the 82nd Airborne facing sporadic gunfire, artillery shelling, and pockets of well-defended German positions.

During the advance, Funk's company was assigned the task of clearing a building in Holzheim that had been reported to house enemy soldiers. After a firefight, Funk and his comrades managed to capture the building, along with approximately 80 German soldiers. At this point, the situation seemed to be under control, with the German prisoners disarmed and secured by a small group of American soldiers under Funk's command.

## Funk's Heroic Actions

However, the calm was short-lived. As Funk and his men regrouped, an unexpected turn of events occurred. While Funk was outside the building, an estimated 40 additional German soldiers, who had been hiding in the vicinity, launched a counterattack and overpowered the American guards inside. The German soldiers reclaimed their weapons and surrounded the American troops, turning the situation into a standoff.

When Funk re-entered the building, he was immediately confronted by the sight of German soldiers pointing their rifles at his men. The German officer in charge, armed with a machine pistol, attempted to force Funk to surrender. The situation was dire—outnumbered, outgunned, and with his men held at gunpoint, Funk appeared to have little choice but to comply.

But Funk's response to the demand for surrender was nothing short of remarkable. Instead of raising his hands in submission, he pretended to comply momentarily and then, in a lightning-fast move, raised his Thompson submachine gun and opened fire on the German officer and the surrounding soldiers. In the confusion that followed, Funk unleashed a barrage of gunfire, quickly killing or wounding several of the enemy soldiers.

His bold and unexpected counterattack stunned the Germans, and Funk continued firing until the remaining enemy soldiers were either killed, wounded, or forced to surrender once again. Incredibly, Funk had single-handedly turned the tide of the engagement. His actions allowed his men to regain control of the situation, and the German counterattack was decisively crushed.

In total, Funk and his men recaptured around 40 German prisoners in addition to the original group of 80. Not a single American soldier was killed during the engagement, thanks to Funk's boldness and quick thinking.

## Recognition and Legacy

For his actions during the battle of Holzheim, Leonard Funk was awarded the Medal of Honor, the highest military decoration in the United States, on September 5, 1945. The citation for his Medal of Honor highlighted his "boldness and courage," as well as his ability to maintain composure and take decisive action under intense pressure. Funk's heroism was seen as an embodiment of the values of the U.S. Army and the paratroopers, who were known for their resilience and willingness to fight against overwhelming odds.

## Funk's Medal of Honor citation read, in part

"His quick thinking, indomitable courage, and incredible audacity in the face of apparently insurmountable odds enabled him to personally neutralize a superior enemy force and save the lives of many of his comrades."

In addition to the Medal of Honor, Funk received numerous other awards and commendations throughout his military career, including the Bronze Star and the Purple Heart. His actions at Holzheim became legendary within the 82nd Airborne Division and were celebrated throughout the U.S. military.

Funk's heroism also resonated with the American public, who saw in him the qualities that had defined the "Greatest Generation"—bravery, selflessness, and a commitment to duty. He returned to the United States after the war and lived a quiet life, never seeking fame or recognition for his wartime exploits. He remained modest about his achievements, always attributing his success to the support of his fellow soldiers.

Leonard Funk passed away on November 20, 1992, at the age of 76, but his legacy as one of the most decorated paratroopers in U.S. military history endures.

## The Importance of the Battle of Holzheim

The Battle of Holzheim, while a relatively small engagement in the larger context of World War II, held significant strategic importance. As part of the broader Allied offensive into Germany, the battle helped pave the way for the eventual defeat of Nazi Germany. By securing key locations like Holzheim, the Allies were able to maintain their momentum and push deeper into German territory.

## Conclusion

Leonard Funk's heroism during the battle of Holzheim stands as a testament to the courage and tenacity of the soldiers who fought in World War II. His actions on January 29, 1945, when he single-handedly faced down a large group of enemy soldiers and refused to surrender, embody the highest ideals of bravery and leadership.

## Sources

Ambrose, Stephen E. Citizen Soldiers: The US Army From the Normandy Beaches to the Bulge to the Surrender of Germany. Simon & Schuster, 1997.

Eisenhower, Dwight D. Crusade in Europe. Doubleday, 1948.

Various Sources

# The Dentist Who Became a Warrior

## Introduction

Doctor Benjamin Salomon's extraordinary actions during the Battle of Saipan in World War II stand as a testament to the depths of human courage and the unwavering commitment to duty in the face of overwhelming odds. This is the tale of a dentist who became a warrior, sacrificing everything to save the lives of his fellow soldiers and etching his name into the pantheon of American heroes.

## From Dentist's Chair to Battlefield

Benjamin Lewis Salomon's journey to becoming a war hero began far from the battlefields of the Pacific. Born on September 1, 1914, in Milwaukee, Wisconsin, young Benjamin grew up in a Jewish family that instilled in him the values of service and dedication. His early years were marked by achievement, earning the rank of Eagle Scout and excelling in his studies at Shorewood High School.

Salomon's path led him to the University of Southern California, where he graduated from the School of Dentistry in 1937. As he settled into his dental practice, the world around him was plunging into the chaos of World War II. In 1940, with the implementation of the Selective Service Act, Salomon was drafted into the United States Army, trading his dental tools for the life of an infantry private in the 102nd Infantry Regiment.

His leadership qualities quickly shone through, and within a year, Salomon was promoted to sergeant, taking charge of a machine gun section. This experience would prove invaluable in the crucible of combat that lay ahead. In 1942, recognizing his dental expertise, the Army commissioned Salomon as a first lieutenant in the Dental Corps. By May 1943, he was serving as the regimental dental officer for the 105th Infantry Regiment, part of the 27th Infantry Division.

## The Battle of Saipan: A Turning Point

The summer of 1944 saw the Allied forces pushing ever closer to the Japanese homeland. The Mariana Islands, with Saipan as their crown jewel, stood as a critical steppingstone. Capturing Saipan would provide the Allies with a crucial base for launching B-29 bomber strikes against Japan's main islands, bringing the war to the enemy's doorstep.

On June 15, 1944, the American forces launched a massive amphibious assault on Saipan. Among the troops was Captain Benjamin Salomon, serving with the 105th Infantry Regiment. As the battle raged,

Salomon found himself thrust into a role far removed from his dental duties. With the 2nd Battalion's surgeon wounded, Salomon volunteered to take his place, setting up an aid station just 50 yards behind the front lines.

## The Banzai Attack and Salomon's Stand

The morning of July 7, 1944, dawned with an apocalyptic fury. The Japanese forces, in a desperate bid to break the American lines, launched a massive banzai attack. An estimated 3,000 to 5,000 Japanese soldiers hurled themselves against the American positions in a wave of suicidal determination.

As the front lines buckled under the onslaught, Salomon's aid station was quickly overwhelmed. Wounded American soldiers poured in, seeking treatment and refuge. Salomon worked tirelessly, tending to the injured even as the sounds of battle drew ever closer. Suddenly, the unthinkable happened – Japanese soldiers began entering the aid station, bayoneting the wounded Americans.

In that moment, Doctor Benjamin Salomon transformed from a healer into a warrior. Without hesitation, he engaged the first Japanese soldier, killing him as he attempted to bayonet a wounded American. More enemy soldiers poured in, and Salomon met them with a ferocity that belied his medical background. Using a combination of rifle fire, bayonet thrusts, and hand-to-hand combat, he single-handedly held back the Japanese assault.

Realizing the dire situation, Salomon ordered the evacuation of the wounded. As his patients were carried to safety, he made a decision that would cost him his life but save countless others. Salomon took up position behind a machine gun whose crew had been killed, using it to cover the retreat of his comrades.

What followed was a display of heroism that defies imagination. Salomon held his ground against wave after wave of Japanese attackers. Even as bullets tore into his body and bayonets pierced his flesh, he continued to fire, determined to buy time for the wounded to escape and for reinforcements to arrive.

## The Aftermath and Legacy

When American forces finally retook the position, they found a scene of carnage that told the tale of Salomon's last stand. The bodies of 98 Japanese soldiers lay strewn before his position. Salomon's own body, bearing 76 bullet wounds and multiple bayonet injuries, was slumped over the machine gun, a testament to his unyielding determination to protect his fellow soldiers to his last breath.

Despite the clear heroism of his actions, recognition for Salomon's sacrifice was long in coming. His status as a medical officer and concerns over potential violations of the Geneva Convention's restrictions on medical personnel bearing arms initially prevented him from receiving the Medal of Honor.

It would take nearly six decades for Salomon's extraordinary bravery to receive its due recognition. On May 1, 2002, in a White House Rose Garden ceremony, Doctor Benjamin Salomon was posthumously awarded the Medal of Honor, the nation's highest military decoration. His citation reads, in part, "Captain Salomon's extraordinary heroism and devotion to duty are in keeping with the highest traditions of military service and reflect great credit upon himself, his unit, and the United States Army."

## Conclusion

The story of Doctor Benjamin Salomon is more than just a tale of battlefield heroics. It is a testament to the depths of human courage, the strength of character, and the unwavering commitment to duty that can emerge in the most desperate of circumstances. Salomon's journey from a dentist's office in California to the blood-soaked hills of Saipan serves as a powerful reminder of the sacrifices made by the "Greatest Generation" in defense of freedom.

The legacy of Doctor Benjamin Salomon continues to inspire new generations of soldiers and civilians alike. His selfless sacrifice stands as a beacon of hope and a reminder of the potential for greatness that resides within each of us. In a world often divided by conflict, Salomon's story unites us in admiration for the highest ideals of human courage and self-sacrifice.

## Sources

Hallas, James H. Saipan: The Battle that Doomed Japan in World War II. Stackpole Books, 2019.

Bowers, Colonel William T. (Retired). Ben Salomon. Office of Medical History, 2002.

Various Sources

# Soaring Above Prejudice

### Introduction

Very few stories capture the essence of courage, perseverance, and triumph over adversity quite like that of Benjamin O. Davis Jr. and the Tuskegee Airmen. Their journey from a controversial "experiment" to becoming one of the most respected fighter groups of World War II is a testament to the indomitable human spirit and the power of determination in the face of systemic racism. This narrative explores the formation of the Tuskegee Airmen, the pivotal role of Benjamin O. Davis Jr. in their success, and the lasting impact their achievements had on the course of American history.

### The Making of a Leader: Benjamin O. Davis Jr.'s Early Years

Benjamin Oliver Davis Jr.'s path to becoming a trailblazing military leader began on December 18, 1912, in Washington, D.C. Born into a family with a strong military tradition, Davis was destined for greatness from an early age. His father, Benjamin O. Davis Sr., would later become the first African American to reach the rank of brigadier general in the U.S. Army, setting a powerful example for his son.

Growing up in a military household, young Benjamin was exposed to both the pride of service and the harsh realities of racial discrimination that permeated American society and its armed forces. These early experiences would shape his character and fuel his determination to excel in a world that often sought to limit his potential.

Davis's journey to military leadership was marked by significant challenges from the outset. In 1932, he received an appointment to the United States Military Academy at West Point, becoming only the fourth African American to attend the prestigious institution. His time at the academy was a crucible of endurance and resilience. For four years, Davis faced relentless racial

discrimination, subjected to a "silencing" by his fellow cadets who only spoke to him for official reasons. He lived and dined alone, a solitary figure in a sea of white faces.

Despite these immense challenges, Davis's unwavering determination shone through. He graduated in 1936, ranking 35th in a class of 276, a remarkable achievement given the hostile environment he had to navigate. This early display of fortitude and excellence would become hallmarks of his leadership style in the years to come.

## The Birth of the Tuskegee Airmen: A Controversial Experiment

As World War II loomed on the horizon, the U.S. military faced increasing pressure to integrate its ranks. Civil rights organizations and the Black press pushed for the inclusion of African Americans in all branches of service, including the Army Air Corps. In response to this pressure and the growing need for manpower, the military reluctantly agreed to create an all-Black flying unit.

On January 16, 1941, the 99th Pursuit Squadron was authorized, marking the birth of what would become known as the Tuskegee Airmen. The program was based at the Tuskegee Institute in Alabama, a historically Black college chosen for its existing facilities and favorable flying conditions. This decision, while pragmatic, also reflected the deeply entrenched segregation of the time.

The formation of the Tuskegee Airmen was met with skepticism and outright opposition from many quarters. Racist beliefs about the capabilities of Black individuals were widespread, and many in the military establishment doubted the program's potential for success. However, for aspiring Black aviators like Benjamin O. Davis Jr., it represented a long-awaited opportunity to serve their country and prove their worth.

## Davis Takes Command: Shaping the Tuskegee Airmen

Benjamin O. Davis Jr.'s appointment as commander of the 99th Fighter Squadron in 1942 was a pivotal moment for both his career and the future of the Tuskegee Airmen. Fresh from his experiences at West Point and subsequent military assignments, Davis brought a unique blend of resilience, discipline, and leadership to his new role.

Under Davis's command, the Tuskegee Airmen underwent rigorous training, often facing harsher standards than their white counterparts. Davis instilled in his men a sense of pride and professionalism, knowing that their performance would be scrutinized at every turn. His leadership philosophy was clear: excellence was not just an aspiration but a necessity for survival and success.

As the 99th Fighter Squadron prepared for deployment, Davis fought tirelessly against attempts to sideline or disband the unit. His advocacy extended beyond the military, as he worked to change perceptions and policies that limited opportunities for Black servicemen. Davis's unwavering commitment to his men and their mission would prove instrumental in the successes that lay ahead.

## Into the Fray: Combat Achievements and Challenges

In 1943, the Tuskegee Airmen finally got their chance to prove themselves in combat. Deployed to North Africa and later to Italy, they entered the war with a dual mission: to defeat the enemy abroad and to combat racism at home. The 332nd Fighter Group, which included the 99th Squadron and was commanded by Davis, quickly distinguished itself in the skies over Europe.

Flying P-40, P-47, and later P-51 Mustangs with distinctive red tails, the Tuskegee Airmen earned a reputation for skill and bravery. They flew over 15,000 sorties and were credited with shooting down 112 enemy aircraft. Their most notable achievement came in their role as bomber escorts, where they maintained an impressive record of protecting Allied bombers from enemy fighters.

One of the Tuskegee Airmen, recalling their combat experiences, stated: "We knew we had to be better than the best. We had to dispel all doubts. We had to work harder, be more disciplined, and be better pilots. We had to do everything we could to prove we were as good as anyone else."

Despite their successes, the Tuskegee Airmen continued to face discrimination both on and off the battlefield. They were often given inferior equipment and faced skepticism from fellow servicemen and superior officers. However, under Davis's leadership, they persevered, letting their performance speak for itself.

## Beyond the Battlefield: The Fight for Equality Continues

The achievements of the Tuskegee Airmen extended far beyond their combat record. Their success challenged prevailing racist attitudes and played a crucial role in the eventual desegregation of the U.S. military. In 1948, President Harry Truman signed Executive Order 9981, officially ending segregation in the armed forces. This landmark decision was, in no small part, influenced by the exemplary service of the Tuskegee Airmen.

Benjamin O. Davis Jr.'s career continued to soar after the war. He became the first African American general in the U.S. Air Force and played a key role in implementing the military's desegregation policies. His journey from a lone Black cadet at West Point to a four-star general symbolized the progress made and the battles still to be fought in the quest for racial equality.

The legacy of the Tuskegee Airmen and Benjamin O. Davis Jr. continues to inspire new generations. Their story is a powerful reminder of the importance of perseverance in the face of adversity and the impact that individuals can have in challenging and changing systemic injustice.

## Conclusion

The story of Benjamin O. Davis Jr. and the Tuskegee Airmen is more than just a tale of military achievement. It is a testament to the power of courage, determination, and excellence in overcoming deeply entrenched prejudice and discrimination. Their success in the skies over Europe not only contributed to the Allied victory in World War II but also struck a powerful blow against racial segregation at home.

Benjamin O. Davis Jr.'s leadership of the Tuskegee Airmen stands as a shining example of what can be achieved when individuals are allowed to excel, regardless of their race or background. Their story challenges us to confront our own biases and to work towards a more inclusive and just society.

In the end, the legacy of the Tuskegee Airmen and Benjamin O. Davis Jr. is not just about the battles they fought in the air, but about the barriers they broke on the ground.

## Sources

Davis, Benjamin O Jr. Benjamin O. Davis Jr.: American: An Autobiography. Smithsonian Institute Scholarly Press, 2000.

Handleman, Philip. Soaring to Glory: A Tuskegee Airman's Firsthand Account of World War II. Regnery History, 2021.

# The Japanese Pilot Who Bombed Oregon

## Introduction

Nobuo Fujita, a Japanese pilot during World War II, holds a unique and largely forgotten place in history as the only person to have successfully bombed the continental United States during the war. His mission was part of a daring Japanese effort to bring the war to American soil, specifically targeting the forests of Oregon in hopes of starting massive wildfires. While his mission did not cause the devastation the Japanese had intended, Fujita's story took an unexpected turn decades later when he returned to the very place he had bombed. His journey of reconciliation and peace with the town of Brookings, Oregon, would transform him from a wartime enemy into a symbol of forgiveness and goodwill. Fujita's tale is remarkable in that it shows how individuals can transcend war violence to create lasting bonds of friendship.

## Early Life and Military Career

Nobuo Fujita was born in 1911 in the coastal town of Tamano in Okayama Prefecture, Japan. He grew up in a country experiencing rapid militarization and nationalism, spurred by Japan's imperial ambitions in Asia and the Pacific. Like many young men of his generation, Fujita was deeply influenced by these nationalistic ideals and pursued a military career.

Fujita joined the Imperial Japanese Navy as a young man, where he trained as a pilot and developed a strong sense of duty and loyalty to Japan's military cause. He quickly proved himself as a skilled and capable aviator, specializing in reconnaissance and bombing missions. By the time World War II began, Fujita was an experienced pilot, and he was eager to contribute to Japan's war efforts, particularly as the conflict in the Pacific escalated after Japan attacked Pearl Harbor in December 1941.

## The Plan to Bomb the U.S. Mainland

After the successful surprise attack on Pearl Harbor, Japan sought to further extend its reach by attacking the United States directly on its mainland. While Japan's military leaders understood that large-scale invasions of the U.S. mainland were impossible due to the vast distance across the Pacific Ocean, they explored ways to demoralize the American public and disrupt the war effort. One of these strategies was to create panic and divert resources by starting massive wildfires in the forests of the Pacific Northwest.

The plan was bold and innovative. The Japanese military envisioned using specially designed aircraft to drop incendiary bombs on the dense forests of Oregon and California, hoping that the fires would spread uncontrollably and strain American resources, which were already focused on the war effort. Additionally, the psychological impact of an attack on the American mainland could not be underestimated. Japan believed such an attack could shake the American public's confidence in their safety and lead to panic.

**The I-25 Submarine and Fujita's Mission**

To carry out this daring plan, the Japanese Navy turned to its fleet of long-range submarines. The I-25 submarine was equipped with a small, foldable Yokosuka E14Y seaplane, a reconnaissance aircraft that could be launched from the deck of the submarine. This plane, small and agile, would be used to carry the incendiary bombs over the forests of Oregon.

Nobuo Fujita was chosen to pilot the seaplane for this mission. He was joined by his observer, Shoji Okuda. On September 9, 1942, after traveling across the Pacific Ocean undetected, the I-25 surfaced off the coast of southern Oregon, near Cape Blanco. In the early morning hours, the crew of the I-25 quickly assembled the seaplane on the submarine's deck, and Fujita and Okuda prepared for takeoff. The plane was armed with two incendiary bombs, each weighing 168 pounds, designed to ignite massive fires upon detonation.

Once the plane was launched, Fujita flew inland, heading toward the forests of the Siskiyou National Forest, near the town of Brookings, Oregon. The area was known for its dense and dry forested landscape, making it an ideal target for the firebombing mission. Fujita climbed to about 8,000 feet, flying undetected over the Pacific Northwest, and dropped the bombs in the forest below.

**The Aftermath of the Bombing**

Despite the careful planning and execution of the mission, nature ultimately thwarted the Japanese plan. Although the bombs detonated as intended, recent rain in the region had dampened the forests, and the fires failed to spread. Local forest rangers quickly responded to the small fires that had broken out, and they were able to contain them before they could cause any significant damage.

The attack, which became known as the "Lookout Air Raid," did not achieve the devastation that the Japanese had hoped for. Nevertheless, it was a significant event as it marked the only time during World War II that the continental United States was bombed by an enemy aircraft. While the attack did not lead to widespread panic, it did raise concerns along the West Coast about the vulnerability of American soil to Japanese attacks. The U.S. government, however, chose not to publicize the incident widely, likely to prevent fear and to maintain focus on the war effort.

Fujita, undeterred by the failure of the first attack, returned for a second bombing mission on September 29, 1942. Once again, he launched from the I-25 submarine, dropping incendiary bombs on a different part of the Siskiyou National Forest. As with the first attempt, the bombs failed to cause any significant damage, and the fires were quickly contained. After the second mission, the I-25 submarine returned to Japan, and Fujita resumed other military duties for the remainder of the war.

**Fujita's Life After the War**

Following Japan's defeat in World War II in 1945, Nobuo Fujita returned to Japan, where he struggled with the challenges of post-war life. Like many veterans, he faced the psychological toll of the war and the defeat of his country. In the years following the war, Fujita did not speak much about his role in bombing Oregon, and his life became one of quiet obscurity.

Fujita took up a career as a businessman, opening a hardware store and raising a family. He was deeply affected by the devastation Japan had experienced during the war, particularly the bombings of Hiroshima and Nagasaki, and he became increasingly interested in reconciliation and peace. Although he had once been a loyal pilot carrying out military orders, he now sought to move beyond the conflict and focus on healing the wounds left by the war.

**A Journey of Reconciliation**

In 1962, two decades after Fujita's bombing missions, an unexpected invitation arrived from the town of Brookings, Oregon. The residents of Brookings had learned about the bombing and decided to reach out to Fujita as part of a goodwill gesture. The town invited him to visit as an act of reconciliation, symbolizing a desire to move beyond the past and build a bridge of friendship between former enemies.

Fujita was initially hesitant to accept the invitation. He worried that the people of Brookings might hold resentment against him for bombing their forests, even though the damage had been minimal. Nevertheless, after some reflection and encouragement from his family, Fujita decided to make the journey. In 1962, he traveled to Brookings with his daughter, unsure of what to expect.

To Fujita's surprise, the people of Brookings welcomed him with open arms. Instead of hostility or anger, they greeted him with kindness and understanding. Fujita was deeply moved by the gesture, and he realized that this visit could help bring closure to a painful chapter of his life. As a sign of his sincerity and desire for peace, Fujita brought with him a treasured family heirloom—a 400-year-old samurai sword that had been passed down through generations of his family.

In an emotional ceremony, Fujita presented the sword to the town of Brookings as a symbol of peace and reconciliation. The sword, which held deep cultural and personal significance, was an extraordinary gift, representing Fujita's commitment to mending the past and forging a new relationship with the people of Brookings. The town accepted the sword, and it remains on display in the Brookings Library to this day as a reminder of the power of forgiveness and the bonds of friendship that can be forged even after the war.

**The Legacy of Nobuo Fujita**

Fujita's visit to Brookings marked the beginning of a lasting friendship between him and the town he once bombed. Over the years, Fujita returned to Brookings several times, and each visit deepened the connection between him and the community. The people of Brookings saw Fujita not as a former enemy, but as a man seeking to make peace with his past.

In 1992, on the 50th anniversary of the bombing, Fujita made his final visit to Brookings. By this time, he had become an honorary citizen of the town, and his story was celebrated as an example of reconciliation and healing. During his last visit, Fujita planted a tree at the site of the bombing as a symbol of peace, growth, and renewal.

Nobuo Fujita passed away in 1997, but his legacy of peace and reconciliation endures. His samurai sword remains in Brookings as a symbol of the friendship between Japan and the United States, and the town continues to honor his memory through annual ceremonies and events that celebrate the power of forgiveness.

**Conclusion**

Nobuo Fujita's story is a powerful reminder that even in the aftermath of war, individuals can seek forgiveness and forge new bonds of friendship. While his mission to bomb Oregon during World War II was part of Japan's effort to bring the conflict to American soil, it ultimately failed to achieve its intended goals. However, Fujita's later journey of reconciliation with the town of Brookings transformed him from a wartime enemy into a symbol of peace and goodwill.

**Sources**

Nobleman, Marc Tyler. Thirty Minutes Over Oregon: A Japanese Pilots World War II Story. Clarion Books, 2018.

Morison, Samuel Eliot. Victory in the Pacific 1945. History of the United States Naval Operations in World War II. Book Sales, 2001.

Various Sources

# The Kilted Killer

**Introduction**

Sir Tommy Macpherson, known as the "Kilted Killer," is a name that resonates with courage and boldness. His life story reads like a Hollywood script, filled with daring escapes, audacious missions, and an indomitable spirit that earned him the nickname "The Kilted Killer." From the highlands of Scotland to the occupied territories of France, Macpherson's journey is a testament to the power of courage, ingenuity, and an unwavering commitment to duty. This is the tale of a man who not only survived the trials of World War II but emerged as one of Britain's most decorated soldiers, leaving an indelible mark on the pages of history.

**A Highland Lad: The Early Years**

Tommy Macpherson's story begins in the heart of Scotland, where the rugged landscape and rich traditions would shape the man he was to become. Born on October 4, 1920, in Edinburgh, Tommy was the youngest of seven children in a prominent family. His father, Sir Thomas Stewart Macpherson, was a distinguished figure, while his mother, Helen, came from a line of respected clergy. The Macpherson clan's roots ran deep in the Scottish Highlands, originating from Newtonmore, instilling in young Tommy a profound sense of heritage and duty.

From an early age, it was clear that Tommy was destined for greatness. His education at Edinburgh Academy prep school and later at Cargilfield in Barnton laid the foundation for a brilliant academic career. At 14, he entered Fettes College, where he first donned a military uniform as part of the Officers' Training Corps, foreshadowing the path that would define his life.

Tommy's intellectual prowess found its full expression at Trinity College, Oxford. Here, he not only excelled academically, earning a first-class degree in Philosophy, Politics, and Economics, but also distinguished himself as a formidable athlete. Representing the university in rugby, hockey, and athletics, Tommy demonstrated the physical prowess and competitive spirit that would serve him well in the trials to come.

## From Scholar to Soldier: The Call to Arms

As the storm clouds of World War II gathered over Europe, Tommy Macpherson answered the call to serve. In 1939, he was commissioned into the Queen's Own Cameron Highlanders Territorial Army, marking the beginning of a military career that would become the stuff of legend.

Macpherson's early military service saw him join the elite No. 11 (Scottish) Commando, a unit known for its daring operations. It was here that he first embraced the distinctive Highland battle dress, including the kilt, which would become his trademark and a powerful psychological weapon in the years to come.

## Captured but Unbroken: A Tale of Perseverance

In 1941, Macpherson's mettle was put to the test during Operation Flipper, a high-stakes mission aimed at raiding the headquarters of the infamous German Field Marshal Erwin Rommel. The operation faced severe challenges from the outset, and Macpherson, along with his team, found themselves in the clutches of Italian forces.

For many, capture would have meant the end of the war. For Tommy Macpherson, it was merely the beginning of a new chapter in his saga of defiance. Despite the harsh conditions of prisoner-of-war camps, first under Italian and then German control, Macpherson's spirit remained unbroken. He made several daring attempts to escape, each one bringing him closer to freedom.

In 1943, Macpherson's persistence finally paid off. In a feat worthy of the greatest escape artists, he managed to break free from a German POW camp and make his way back to the United Kingdom. This escape not only demonstrated Macpherson's resourcefulness and determination but also set the stage for the next phase of his wartime career – one that would etch his name in military history.

## The Kilted Killer: Macpherson's Guerrilla War

Upon his return to Britain, Macpherson's unique blend of skills, experience, and courage made him the perfect candidate for one of the war's most daring initiatives: Operation Jedburgh. This clandestine operation involved parachuting small teams of highly trained operatives into occupied Europe to conduct guerrilla warfare and sabotage against Nazi forces.

In June 1944, Macpherson, now leading Team Quinine, parachuted into the heart of occupied France. It was here that the legend of the "Kilted Killer" was born. Clad in his full Highland battle dress, including the distinctive tartan kilt, Macpherson cut a striking figure among the French Resistance fighters he was tasked with leading.

His choice of attire was far from mere eccentricity. The kilt served as a powerful symbol of defiance against the Nazi occupiers and a rallying point for the resistance. As one French fighter reportedly remarked, "With a man in a skirt leading us, how could we not believe in victory?"

Macpherson's exploits in France read like chapters from an adventure novel. He led daring raids against German installations, sabotaged vital infrastructure, and disrupted enemy movements with a combination of military precision and theatrical flair. His audacity knew no bounds – he was known to drive through occupied territories in a car brazenly adorned with a Union Flag, a act of defiance that both inspired his allies and infuriated his enemies.

The impact of Macpherson's operations was so significant that the Germans placed a bounty of 300,000 francs on his head. Yet, this only seemed to embolden the "Kilted Killer," who continued to outmaneuver and outfight his pursuers at every turn.

## The Art of War: Macpherson's Greatest Triumph

Perhaps Macpherson's most remarkable achievement came not through force of arms, but through the power of persuasion. In a feat that would have seemed impossible, he managed to negotiate the surrender of an entire German division without firing a single shot.

Facing Major General Botho Henning Elster and his force of 23,000 troops, Macpherson drew upon every ounce of his courage, wit, and sheer bravado. Dressed in his full Highland regalia, he bluffed his way through negotiations, convincing the German commander that he was surrounded by a vastly superior Allied force.

In reality, Macpherson had only a handful of resistance fighters at his disposal. Yet, through a combination of psychological warfare and masterful negotiation, he achieved what entire armies had failed to do. The sight of 23,000 German soldiers surrendering to a man in a kilt became one of the war's most iconic moments, cementing Macpherson's reputation as a master strategist.

## A Legacy of Valor

Tommy Macpherson's wartime exploits earned him a chest full of medals and a place in military history. He was awarded the Military Cross three times, received the Croix de Guerre on three occasions, and was honored with the Légion d'honneur, among numerous other accolades. Each decoration told a story of bravery, ingenuity, and an unwavering commitment to the cause of freedom.

## Conclusion

The story of Tommy Macpherson is more than just a tale of wartime heroics. It is a testament to the power of individual courage, the importance of quick thinking, and the impact that one person can have in the face of overwhelming odds. From the highlands of Scotland to the battlefields of Europe, Macpherson's journey embodies the spirit of resistance and the triumph of the human spirit.

## Sources

Macpherson Sir Tommy. Behind Enemy Lines: The Autobiography of Britain's Most Decorated Living War Hero. Mainstream Publishing, 2012.

Gilbert, Martin. The Second World War: A Complete History. Holt Paperbacks, 2004.

# The Navigator Who Defied Death

## Introduction

The Second World War was a time of immense courage, sacrifice, and resilience, particularly among the airmen who faced relentless enemy fire in the skies of Europe and beyond. A remarkable story of survival and bravery is that of Ivan Chisov, a Soviet navigator officer aboard an Ilyushin IL-4 bomber. His tale of survival after falling from an unimaginable height without a parachute not only showcases the resilience of the human spirit but also provides a unique window into the brutal realities of the Eastern Front. This is the story of a man who fell from the sky and lived to tell the tale, a testament to human endurance in the face of overwhelming odds.

## A Navigator's Call to Duty

Ivan Mikhailovich Chisov was born in 1916 in Bogdanovka, Poltava Raion, then part of the Russian Empire. Like many of his generation, Chisov's life would be forever altered by the tumultuous events of the 20th century. As the storm clouds of World War II gathered over Europe, Chisov answered the call to serve his country, joining the Soviet Air Force in 1941.

The Eastern Front of World War II was a theater of unparalleled brutality and scale. The conflict between Nazi Germany and the Soviet Union would claim tens of millions of lives and shape the course of the 20th century. It was against this backdrop of epic struggle that Chisov would carve his place in history.

As a navigator in the 98th Long-range Aviation Regiment, Chisov's role was crucial. Flying in the Ilyushin Il-4, a medium bomber that was a workhorse of the Soviet air campaign, Chisov and his comrades struck deep into enemy territory, disrupting German supply lines and supporting the massive ground war raging below.

## A Mission Gone Awry

On a frigid January day in 1942, as the war entered its third year, Chisov's bomber took to the skies on yet another perilous mission. The air war over the Eastern Front was reaching a fever pitch, with both sides committing ever-increasing resources to gain supremacy in the skies.

As Chisov's Il-4 bomber droned through the winter sky, disaster struck. A group of German Messerschmitt Bf 109 fighters, the feared workhorses of the Luftwaffe, swooped down on the Soviet formation. In the ensuing chaos of machine gun fire and explosions, Chisov's aircraft was hit.

With their bomber critically damaged and losing altitude rapidly, the order was given to bail out. At an altitude of approximately 7,000 meters (23,000 feet), Chisov leapt into the frigid air. It was at this moment that he made a decision that would alter the course of his life.

## The Long Fall

Aware that German pilots sometimes targeted parachuting airmen – a practice considered a war crime but nonetheless reported on both sides – Chisov made the split-second decision not to open his parachute immediately. His plan was to free-fall to a lower altitude, below the ongoing air battle, before deploying his chute.

However, the extreme cold and thin air at such a high altitude quickly took their toll. As he plummeted through the sky at speeds estimated between 190 and 240 kilometers per hour (120 to 150 mph), Chisov lost consciousness. Unable to pull his ripcord, he continued his headlong plunge towards the earth.

As the ground rushed up to meet him, fate intervened in the form of a snow-covered slope. Chisov's unconscious body struck the edge of a snowy ravine, the impact partially cushioned by the deep snow. The angle of the slope caused him to slide and roll, further dissipating the enormous energy of his fall.

## A Miraculous Discovery

On the ground, a group of Soviet cavalrymen who had witnessed the aerial battle rushed to the site where they had seen a body fall. What they found defied belief. There, lying in the snow, still strapped into his unopened parachute, was Ivan Chisov – alive.

The injuries Chisov sustained were severe: a broken pelvis, spinal injuries, and numerous other traumas that would have killed most men. Yet, against all odds, he had survived a fall from a height that should have been unsurvivable.

Chisov was immediately rushed for medical treatment, his survival hanging by a thread. For a month, he remained in critical condition, his life balanced on a knife's edge. Yet, true to the resilience that had allowed him to survive the fall, Chisov fought back from the brink.

## Recovery and Return to Duty

In a testament to both the quality of care he received and his spirit to survive, Chisov made a remarkable recovery. Just three months after his brush with death, he was cleared to fly again. However, recognizing the extraordinary nature of his experience, his superiors decided not to return him to combat duty. Instead, Chisov was assigned as a navigational trainer, passing on his hard-won knowledge to the next generation of Soviet airmen.

Throughout the remainder of the war, Chisov continued to serve, eventually flying over 70 combat missions. His experience and dedication made him an invaluable asset to the Soviet war effort, contributing to the eventual victory over Nazi Germany.

## A Life of Service

After the war, Chisov's commitment to serving his country did not waver. He pursued further education, graduating from the Military-Political Academy, an institution that trained military personnel in political and ideological education.

Upon leaving active military service in 1960, Chisov transitioned to a role as a propagandist for the Central House of the Soviet Army. In this capacity, he continued to serve, sharing his experiences and promoting the values and achievements of the Soviet military.

Throughout his life, Chisov's extraordinary act of survival and subsequent service were recognized with numerous honors. He was awarded the prestigious Order of the Red Banner, the Order of the Patriotic War 1st class, and various other medals commemorating the defense of key Soviet cities and the victory over Germany.

## Conclusion

The story of Ivan Mikhailovich Chisov is more than just a tale of miraculous survival. It is a testament to the resilience of the human spirit, the fortitude of those who served in World War II, and the often-thin line between life and death in wartime.

Chisov's experience – from his harrowing fall to his recovery and continued service – encapsulates the broader narrative of the Soviet war effort: determination in the face of overwhelming odds, the will to survive, and the commitment to continue fighting despite unimaginable hardships.

## Sources

Sheppard, Alexander L. The Greatest Battles of World War II: Independently published, 2023.

Reshetnikov, Vasily. Bomber Pilot on the Eastern Front: 307 Missions Behind Enemy Lines. Pen and Sword Military, 2008.

Various Sources

# The Quiet Hero of Iwo Jima

## Introduction

John Bradley, a quiet and humble man from small-town Wisconsin, became one of the most iconic figures of World War II. A Navy corpsman by training, Bradley was not a traditional combat soldier, yet his heroism and dedication to his fellow Marines in the Battle of Iwo Jima saved countless lives.

His journey from a small-town Wisconsin boy to a key figure in one of the most iconic moments of the war is a testament to the extraordinary circumstances that ordinary men found themselves in during those tumultuous years. This is the tale of a man who went to war to heal, but found himself at the center of a moment that would define American resolve for generations to come.

## From Funeral Home to Frontlines

John Henry Bradley's path to becoming a war hero began far from the black sands of Iwo Jima. Born on July 10, 1923, in Antigo, Wisconsin, "Jack" Bradley was the second of five children in a modest Irish Catholic family. Growing up in Appleton, Wisconsin, young John was far more interested in the somber business of funerals than the glory of war. As a teenager, he completed an 18-month apprenticeship with a local funeral director, laying the groundwork for what he believed would be his life's calling.

However, the winds of war were blowing, and like many young men of his generation, Bradley found himself swept up in the global conflict. On January 13, 1943, at the age of 19, he enlisted in the United States Navy. His father, hoping to keep his son away from the brutal ground combat that defined much of World War II, had suggested the Navy as a safer alternative. Little did they know that this decision would lead John Bradley into one of the war's most ferocious battles.

## Training for War

Bradley's journey from civilian to combat medic was a rigorous one. After completing his basic training at the Farragut Naval Training Station in Idaho, he was assigned to the Hospital Corps School at the same facility. Here, Bradley honed the medical skills that would later save countless lives on the battlefield.

His training didn't stop there. In January 1944, Bradley was transferred to the Fleet Marine Force and sent to a field medical service school at a Marine Corps base. This specialized training prepared him for the unique challenges of providing medical care in the heat of combat. By the time he was assigned to the 5th Marine Division, specifically to Easy Company, 2nd Battalion, 28th Marine Regiment, Bradley was as ready as any man could be for the hell that awaited them in the Pacific.

## The Black Sand of Iwo Jima

On February 19, 1945, John Bradley landed on Iwo Jima with the ninth wave of Marines. The scene that greeted him was one of unimaginable chaos and carnage. The black volcanic sand of the beach made movement difficult, and the air was filled with the deafening sounds of gunfire and explosions.

As a Navy Corpsman, Bradley's role was critical. During the brutal fighting, he was responsible for providing immediate medical care to wounded Marines, often under heavy enemy fire. His bravery and dedication to his fellow servicemen would soon be put to the ultimate test.

On February 21, just two days into the battle, Bradley performed an act of extraordinary heroism that would earn him the Navy Cross, one of the highest honors for valor in combat. Under intense enemy fire, he braved open ground to administer plasma to a wounded Marine. Not content with merely treating the soldier, Bradley used his own body as a shield to protect the injured man from further harm. When the plasma was depleted, he carried the Marine to safety, risking his own life in the process.

## The Flag Raising: Myth and Reality

It was on February 23, 1945, that John Bradley would become part of one of the most iconic images in American history – or so it was believed for many years. The raising of the American flag on Mount Suribachi, captured in a photograph by Joe Rosenthal, became an instant symbol of American determination and victory.

For decades, Bradley was identified as one of the six men raising the flag in that famous photograph. However, the truth was more complex. Bradley had indeed participated in a flag-raising on Mount Suribachi, but it was the first, lesser-known raising earlier that day. The famous photograph captured a second, larger flag being raised, in which Bradley was not actually present.

This misidentification, only corrected in 2016 after extensive research and investigation, does nothing to diminish Bradley's heroism. He was there, on that volcanic peak, raising the Stars and Stripes in defiance of the enemy and in honor of his fallen comrades. The fact that he was not in the famous photograph is a mere footnote to his true acts of bravery.

## The Cost of Courage

The Battle of Iwo Jima raged on, and John Bradley continued to serve with distinction. However, war exacts a heavy toll on even the bravest of men. On March 12, 1945, Bradley's war came to an abrupt end when he was wounded by shrapnel from an enemy mortar round.

Despite his injuries, Bradley's instinct to help others remained strong. Before allowing himself to be evacuated, he assisted another wounded Marine to an aid station. This final act of selflessness in the field earned him the Purple Heart, adding to his already impressive list of commendations.

Bradley's journey took him from the blood-soaked beaches of Iwo Jima to hospitals in Guam, Hawaii, and finally to Oakland, California. As he recovered from his physical wounds, the psychological impact of what he had experienced began to set in – a burden he would carry for the rest of his life.

## A Quiet Hero's Return

When John Bradley returned to Antigo, Wisconsin, he did so not as a celebrated war hero, but as a man seeking peace and normalcy. He married his high school sweetheart, Betty Van Gorp, and together they raised eight children. True to his pre-war aspirations, Bradley opened a funeral home, becoming a respected member of his community.

Despite the fame that came with his association with the flag-raising photograph, Bradley remained notably reticent about his wartime experiences. He rarely spoke of Iwo Jima, the flag-raising, or his Navy Cross. When asked about the war, he would often deflect, saying simply, "The real heroes of Iwo Jima are the guys who didn't come back".

This silence speaks volumes about the impact of war on those who fight it. For Bradley, like many veterans, the memories of what he had seen and done were too painful to revisit. His son, James Bradley, would later write in "Flags of Our Fathers" that his father had nightmares about the war for years after his return.

## Legacy and Reflection

John Bradley's story is more than just a tale of wartime heroics. It is a complex narrative about the nature of heroism, the cost of war, and the power of media in shaping public perception. The misidentification in the famous photograph, while unintentional, raises questions about the nature of memory and the way we construct our national myths.

Despite the confusion surrounding the flag-raising photograph, Bradley's heroism remains unquestioned. His Navy Cross citation speaks of a man who repeatedly risked his life to save others, embodying the highest ideals of his calling as a corpsman.

In his later years, Bradley focused on his family and his community, finding purpose in the quiet heroism of everyday life. He passed away on January 11, 1994, leaving behind a legacy that continues to inspire and provoke thought about the true nature of heroism.

## Conclusion

The story of John Bradley is a reminder of the complexities of war and heroism. From a young man dreaming of running a funeral home to a battle-hardened corpsman on the black sands of Iwo Jima,

Bradley's journey embodies the experiences of countless young Americans thrust into the crucible of World War II.

His tale challenges us to look beyond the iconic images and simple narratives of war. It reminds us that true heroism often lies not in grand gestures captured on film, but in the quiet, determined acts of bravery performed out of sight – in Bradley's case, in the selfless care for wounded comrades amidst the chaos of battle.

In the end, John Bradley's legacy is not defined by a single photograph or moment, but by a lifetime of service – to his country in war, and to his community in peace. His story continues to resonate, challenging us to look beyond the surface of heroism and to consider the profound human experiences that lie beneath our national myths and memories.

**Sources**

Bradley, James. Flags of Our Fathers. Bantam, 2006.

Hama, Larry. The Battle of Iwo Jima: Guerilla Warfare in the Pacific. Rosen Pub Group, 2006.

# The Unkillable Soldier

## Introduction

Sir Adrian John Carton de Wiart is often referred to as the "unkillable soldier" a moniker that aptly reflects his extraordinary resilience, remarkable life, and indomitable spirit. His life reads like a work of fiction, filled with daring escapes, countless injuries, and an indomitable spirit that carried him through three major wars. From the dusty plains of South Africa to the corridors of power in wartime London, Carton de Wiart's journey is a testament to the resilience of the human spirit and the extraordinary circumstances that ordinary men can find themselves in during times of conflict. This is the tale of a man who seemed to embody the very essence of soldiering, whose life was so remarkable that it challenged our understanding of what is possible in the face of adversity.

## A Privileged Beginning

Adrian John Carton de Wiart's story begins far from the battlefields where he would make his name. Born on May 5, 1880, in Brussels, Belgium, he entered the world as part of an aristocratic family. His father, Leon Constant Ghislain Carton de Wiart, was a respected Belgian lawyer, while his mother hailed from Ireland, setting the stage for a life that would straddle multiple cultures and continents.

Tragedy struck early when Carton de Wiart's mother passed away when he was just six years old. This loss prompted his father to relocate the family to Cairo, Egypt, where he practiced international law. Young Adrian's formative years were thus split between the cosmopolitan atmosphere of Cairo and the traditional environs of England, where he attended The Oratory School near Birmingham, a choice reflecting his family's devout Roman Catholic faith.

## From Oxford to the Battlefield

As a young man, Carton de Wiart found himself at Balliol College, Oxford, seemingly destined for a life of academic pursuit and gentlemanly pursuits. However, the call of adventure proved too strong to resist. With the outbreak of the Second Boer War in 1899, he made a decision that would alter the course of his life forever.

Driven by a belief that "war was in his blood," Carton de Wiart abandoned his studies and set out for South Africa. His eagerness to join the fray was such that he resorted to subterfuge, faking both his identity and age to enlist as a volunteer in the British Army. This act of deception marked the beginning of a military career that would span over four decades and three major conflicts.

**Baptism by Fire: The Boer War**

Carton de Wiart's first taste of combat came swiftly and brutally. During his service in South Africa, he was shot twice – in the stomach and groin – injuries that would have ended the military aspirations of many. For Carton de Wiart, however, they were merely the opening salvo in what would become a lifelong dance with death.

After a brief recovery in England, he returned to South Africa in 1901, his appetite for combat undiminished. His bravery and leadership potential were recognized with a promotion to corporal, though his independent streak soon manifested in an act of insubordination that saw him demoted. Undeterred, he secured a commission as a second lieutenant in the 4th Dragoon Guards, setting the stage for further adventures.

**From India to Somaliland: The Making of a Legend**

The years following the Boer War saw Carton de Wiart transferred to India with the 4th Dragoon Guards. Here, in the relative peace of colonial service, he indulged his passions for sport, particularly shooting and pig-sticking. Yet the thrill of combat continued to call to him.

His opportunity came in British Somaliland, where he joined the Somaliland Camel Corps to fight against Mohammed bin Abdullah, known as the "Mad Mullah." It was during an attack on an enemy fort that Carton de Wiart suffered an injury that would become part of his legend – a shot to the face that cost him his left eye. This wound, which would have ended many military careers, merely added to Carton de Wiart's growing reputation for indestructibility.

**World War I: The Hell of Combat**

When World War I erupted in 1914, Carton de Wiart was ready. His experiences in the Boer War and Somaliland had prepared him for the brutality of modern warfare, but nothing could have fully readied him for the meat grinder of the Western Front.

Throughout the war, Carton de Wiart's bravery and leadership were on full display. He was wounded multiple times, each injury seeming to only fuel his determination. In addition to his lost eye, he was shot in the head, stomach, ankle, leg, hip, and ear. Perhaps most famously, he bit off his own fingers when a doctor refused to amputate them after they were severely damaged.

His actions during the Battle of the Somme in 1916 earned him the Victoria Cross, Britain's highest military honor. The citation for his award speaks volumes about his character: "For most conspicuous bravery, coolness and determination during severe operations of a prolonged nature... His gallantry was inspiring to all."

Carton de Wiart's own reflections on his injuries reveal his extraordinary perspective. He famously remarked, "People imagine the loss of a hand to be far more serious than the loss of an eye, but having tried both I can say sincerely that it is not my experience." This matter-of-fact approach to what most would consider devastating injuries became a hallmark of his legend.

## Between the Wars: Diplomacy and Adventure

The interwar years did little to dim Carton de Wiart's appetite for action. He was appointed to command the British Military Mission to Poland during the Polish-Soviet War, a role that saw him awarded the Virtuti Militari, Poland's highest military decoration.

His aristocratic background and military reputation made him a valuable asset in diplomatic circles. He moved effortlessly between military duties and diplomatic roles, his experiences and connections allowing him to influence European politics at a crucial time.

Despite his injuries, Carton de Wiart maintained an active lifestyle, indulging his love for sports and adventure. His resilience and zest for life in the face of physical adversity only added to his growing legend.

## World War II: The Unkillable Soldier Returns

When World War II broke out, Carton de Wiart, now in his sixties, was once again ready to serve. He was appointed to lead the British Military Mission to Poland, a mission cut short by the rapid German invasion in 1939. His escape from Warsaw as the Nazis advanced was characteristic of his career – marked by danger, close calls, and ultimate survival.

Perhaps the most extraordinary chapter of Carton de Wiart's World War II service came in 1941. While en route to Yugoslavia on a diplomatic mission, his plane crashed in the Mediterranean off the coast of Italian-controlled Libya. Carton de Wiart, at the age of 61, survived the crash, swam to shore, and was promptly captured by Italian forces.

His time as a prisoner of war was marked by repeated escape attempts, including a remarkable seven-month effort to dig a tunnel. On one occasion, he managed to evade recapture for eight days – no small feat for a one-eyed, one-handed man in his sixties who couldn't speak Italian.

Carton de Wiart's captivity ended in 1943 when the Italians released him to conduct secret negotiations for their surrender. This diplomatic mission was a testament to the respect he commanded, even among his enemies.

## Final Act: China and Retirement

The final act of Carton de Wiart's military career saw him appointed as Winston Churchill's personal representative to Chiang Kai-shek in China. From 1943 to 1946, he played a crucial role in maintaining the alliance between Britain and Nationalist China, bringing his unique blend of military experience and diplomatic skill to bear in this complex theater of war.

After the war, Carton de Wiart finally retired to County Cork, Ireland. Here, he indulged his passion for fishing and lived out his days in relative peace – a stark contrast to the tumultuous life he had led. He passed away in 1963 at the age of 83, leaving behind a legacy that would inspire generations.

## Conclusion

The life of Adrian Carton de Wiart reads like a work of fiction, yet every extraordinary detail is true. From his early days as a young volunteer in the Boer War to his final service in China, Carton de Wiart embodied the spirit of the soldier – brave, resilient, and ever-ready to serve.

His physical resilience – surviving injuries that would have killed or incapacitated most men – is matched only by his mental fortitude. Carton de Wiart's ability to face adversity with a wry smile and an unbreakable spirit made him a legend in his own time and continues to inspire to this day.

Winston Churchill, who knew a thing or two about courage and character, described Carton de Wiart as "a model of chivalry and honour." This simple yet profound assessment captures the essence of a man who, despite the brutality of the conflicts he fought in, never lost his sense of duty or his fundamental humanity.

**Sources**

Carton de Wiart, Sir Adrian. Happy Odyssey. Pen and Sword Military, 2007.

Ogden, Alan. The Life and Times of Lieutenant General Adrian Carton de Wiart: Soldier and Diplomat. Bloomsbury Academic, 2023.

Various Sources

# The White Death of the Winter War

## Introduction

In the annals of military history, there are few figures as legendary and fearsome as Simo Häyhä, a Finnish sniper who became known as "The White Death" during the Winter War between Finland and the Soviet Union. Häyhä's feats on the battlefield, conducted in the frozen forests of Finland between 1939 and 1940, are the stuff of legend. Armed with a simple bolt-action rifle, dressed in white camouflage, and using minimal equipment, Häyhä was credited with over 500 confirmed kills of Soviet soldiers in just 100 days. His ability to operate in brutal winter conditions and his unmatched marksmanship earned him a mythical status, making him one of the most effective snipers in history. This is the story of Simo Häyhä, the man known as the "White Death."

## The Beginning

The Winter War was fought between Finland and the Soviet Union from November 30, 1939, to March 13, 1940. The conflict was a direct result of the Soviet Union's desire to secure its western border by demanding territorial concessions from Finland, particularly in the Karelian Isthmus, a region close to Leningrad (now St. Petersburg). When the Finns refused Soviet demands, the Red Army launched an invasion, expecting a quick and decisive victory. However, the Soviet Union underestimated Finland's resilience and the harshness of the winter conditions, which favored the Finnish defenders.

The Finnish Army was vastly outnumbered and outgunned, with the Soviets deploying hundreds of thousands of soldiers, tanks, and aircraft. In contrast, Finland had a small and poorly equipped army. Despite these disadvantages, the Finns employed guerrilla tactics and used their intimate knowledge of the terrain to hold back the Soviet advance. The battlefields of the Winter War were characterized by thick forests, deep snow, and subzero temperatures, creating a brutal environment for both sides.

## Simo's Early Life

Simo Häyhä was born on December 17, 1905, in the small village of Rautjärvi in southern Finland, close to the Russian border. Growing up in a rural farming family, Häyhä developed a love for the outdoors from an early age. Hunting and shooting were a way of life in the Finnish countryside, and Häyhä became an excellent marksman while hunting small game in the forests near his home.

At the age of 17, Häyhä joined the Finnish Civil Guard, a paramilitary organization that provided military training to civilians. It was here that he honed his skills with a rifle, practicing regularly in marksmanship competitions. His weapon of choice was a bolt-action M/28-30 rifle, a Finnish variant of the Russian Mosin-Nagant rifle. Häyhä preferred the M/28-30 for its reliability and accuracy, and it would become his trusted companion during the Winter War.

**The White Death in Action**

When the Soviet Union invaded Finland in November 1939, Häyhä was called to serve in the Finnish Army's 6th Company, Infantry Regiment 34. His unit was stationed in the Karelian Isthmus, the primary battleground of the Winter War. As Soviet forces pushed into Finnish territory, Häyhä quickly distinguished himself as a highly skilled sniper.

Operating in temperatures as low as -40°C (-40°F), Häyhä's ability to remain concealed and patient for long periods was critical to his success. He wore white camouflage to blend in with the snowy landscape, earning him the nickname "The White Death" from Soviet soldiers who came to fear him. Unlike many snipers of his time, Häyhä preferred to use iron sights rather than a telescopic scope. He believed that scopes could fog up in the cold, reflect sunlight, or force the shooter to raise their head higher, potentially revealing their position. His decision to rely on iron sights made him even more impressive as a marksman.

Häyhä's tactics were simple but effective. He would find a position with good cover, often building small snowbanks to shield himself from enemy fire. He packed snow in front of his rifle to prevent muzzle flash from revealing his position, and he kept snow in his mouth to avoid his breath being visible in the freezing air. From these hidden vantage points, Häyhä would patiently wait for Soviet soldiers to appear, picking them off one by one.

During the Winter War, Häyhä was credited with 505 confirmed kills, all with his bolt-action rifle. In addition to his sniping skills, Häyhä also fought as a soldier, using a Suomi KP/-31 submachine gun in close combat situations. In total, he was credited with over 700 enemy kills during the war. His kill count, achieved over just a few months, remains one of the highest for any sniper in history.

**The Soviet Response**

As news of Häyhä's exploits spread, he became a key target for the Soviet military. The Red Army sent counter-snipers to eliminate him, but none succeeded. Artillery strikes were even ordered on his suspected positions in an attempt to kill him, but Häyhä continued to evade death, further enhancing his reputation as an elusive and deadly opponent.

The psychological impact of Häyhä's sniping was immense. Soviet soldiers reportedly feared venturing into areas where "The White Death" was known to operate. His ability to kill with such precision and efficiency demoralized Soviet troops and contributed to the Soviet military's struggles during the Winter War.

Despite their best efforts, the Soviets were unable to stop Häyhä's reign of terror until March 6, 1940, just days before the Winter War ended. During a battle in the forests near the village of Uytniemi, Häyhä was shot in the face by a Soviet soldier. The bullet entered his left jaw and exited through his right cheek, leaving him gravely wounded. Häyhä was found unconscious on the battlefield by his comrades and was rushed to a field hospital.

**Recovery and Legacy**

Häyhä's injury was severe, and he remained in a coma for several days. He eventually regained consciousness on March 13, 1940—the same day the Winter War officially ended with the signing of the Moscow Peace Treaty. Despite his injuries, Häyhä made a remarkable recovery, though he would bear the scars of his wound for the rest of his life. His jaw was reconstructed, and though his facial appearance was altered, he survived and continued to live a long and peaceful life.

Häyhä's exploits during the Winter War earned him numerous honors, including the Cross of Liberty, first and second class, and the Medal of Liberty. He was promoted from corporal to second lieutenant by the end of the war, a rare distinction for a non-commissioned officer in the Finnish Army.

After the war, Häyhä returned to his quiet life as a farmer in his home village of Rautjärvi. Despite his legendary status, Häyhä remained humble about his accomplishments. He rarely spoke about his experiences during the war and did not seek attention or fame. When asked how he became such an effective sniper, Häyhä's response was simple: "Practice."

Simo Häyhä passed away on April 1, 2002, at the age of 96. In Finland, he is remembered as a national hero, and his legacy as one of the most lethal snipers in history remains intact. His story continues to inspire snipers and military personnel around the world, particularly for his skill, discipline, and endurance in some of the harshest conditions imaginable.

**Conclusion**

Simo Häyhä's achievements as a sniper during the Winter War are unparalleled in military history. His ability to adapt to the harsh conditions of the Finnish winter, his mastery of marksmanship, and his unmatched patience made him one of the deadliest soldiers on the battlefield. Known as "The White Death," Häyhä's fearsome reputation spread far beyond the front lines, leaving a lasting impact on the soldiers who faced him and on the history of warfare.

**Sources**

Captivating History. The Eastern Front: A Captivating Guide to Soviet Union in World War 2, the Winter War, Siege of Leningrad, Operation Barbarossa, and the Battle of Stalingrad. Captivating, 2020.

Larsen, Andrea. Simo Hayha, White Death: The Incredible true story of the deadliest sniper ever. Independently published, 2022.

Various Sources

# The Bataan Death March

**Introduction:**

The Bataan Death March stands as one of the darkest chapters of World War II, particularly in the Pacific Theater. After the fall of the Bataan Peninsula in the Philippines to Japanese forces in April 1942, tens of thousands of American and Filipino soldiers were forced to march over 60 miles under brutal conditions, with thousands dying from exhaustion, starvation, disease, and outright murder by their captors. The march was a stark illustration of the cruelty and horror that many soldiers endured during the war and would become a rallying point for the United States' resolve to win the war in the Pacific. This is the story of the Bataan Death March, a tale of suffering, death, and survival, and how it became a symbol of both the brutality of war and the resilience of the human spirit.

**The Road to Bataan: A Strategic Miscalculation**

The roots of the Bataan Death March can be traced back to the complex web of colonial history and military strategy that defined the Philippines in the early 20th century. Once a Spanish colony, the Philippines had come under American control following the Spanish-American War of 1898. Despite Filipino aspirations for independence, the archipelago remained a crucial piece in America's Pacific strategy, particularly as tensions with Japan began to simmer.

In the years leading up to World War II, American military planners had developed War Plan Orange, a strategy that envisioned a defensive stand in the Philippines in the event of Japanese aggression. The plan called for a withdrawal to the Bataan Peninsula, where forces would hold out until reinforcements could arrive. However, the global nature of World War II forced a shift to Rainbow V, a plan that prioritized the defeat of Germany over operations in the Pacific.

This strategic pivot would have dire consequences for the defenders of the Philippines. When Japanese forces launched their invasion on December 22, 1941, just weeks after the attack on Pearl Harbor, the American and Filipino troops found themselves woefully unprepared. General

Douglas MacArthur, commanding the Allied forces, initially attempted a forward defense but was quickly forced to revert to the Bataan strategy.

## The Battle of Bataan: A Desperate Stand

As allied forces retreated to the Bataan Peninsula, they faced an enemy that was not only numerically superior but also better equipped and supplied. The defenders, a mix of American soldiers and Filipino troops, many of whom were poorly trained and equipped, fought valiantly against overwhelming odds. Their situation was made even more desperate by severe shortages of food, medicine, and ammunition.

For months, the defenders of Bataan held out, their resistance becoming a symbol of Allied determination in the face of Japanese expansion. However, with each passing day, their situation grew more dire. Disease ran rampant through their ranks, with malaria, dysentery, and other tropical ailments weakening the already malnourished troops. By April 1942, it had become clear that the situation was untenable.

On April 9, 1942, Major General Edward P. King made the agonizing decision to surrender. Approximately 75,000 Filipino and American troops laid down their arms, becoming prisoners of the Japanese Empire. Little did they know that their ordeal was far from over.

## The March Begins: A Journey into Hell

The Japanese forces, led by Lieutenant General Homma Masaharu, were unprepared for the large number of prisoners that now fell under their responsibility. Their cultural disdain for surrender, combined with logistical unpreparedness, set the stage for one of the war's most notorious atrocities.

The march began in the town of Mariveles, at the southern tip of the Bataan Peninsula. The prisoners, already weakened by months of fighting and malnutrition, were forced to march approximately 65 miles north to San Fernando. From there, they were to be transported by rail to Camp O'Donnell, their final destination.

The conditions of the march were beyond brutal. Under the scorching Philippine sun, prisoners were forced to march for days with little to no food or water. Those who fell behind or stumbled were often beaten, bayoneted, or shot. The road became littered with the bodies of those who could not continue.

Lester Tenney, a tank commander with the 192nd Tank Battalion, later recalled the horrors he witnessed: "It wasn't a march, it was a trudge. We were beaten for no reason at all. Men were bayoneted for falling down. I saw men shot for trying to get a drink of water from the artesian wells".

The cruelty of the Japanese guards seemed to know no bounds. Prisoners were subjected to what became known as the "sun treatment," forced to sit in the sweltering heat without head covering. Many succumbed to heat stroke and dehydration. Others, driven mad by thirst, drank from muddy puddles, only to fall victim to dysentery.

## The Boxcar Horror: From San Fernando to Capas

Upon reaching San Fernando, the prisoners thought their ordeal might be nearing its end. Instead, they faced a new horror. Crammed into stifling boxcars, sometimes a hundred men to a car designed for forty, they endured a nightmarish journey to the town of Capas. Many died from suffocation or heat exhaustion during this leg of the journey.

Paul Kerchum, another survivor, described the boxcar experience in harrowing detail: "The heat was unbearable, and the stench of urine and feces was overpowering. Men were going mad with thirst, some drinking their own urine in desperation".

## The Final Stretch: Capas to Camp O'Donnell

From Capas, the surviving prisoners were forced to march an additional 9 miles to Camp O'Donnell. For many, these final miles proved too much. Bodies lined the route, a grim testament to the brutality of the march.

The exact number of casualties during the Bataan Death March is difficult to determine, but estimates suggest that between 5,000 to 18,000 Filipino soldiers and 500 to 650 American soldiers died during the march itself. Thousands more would perish in the camps that awaited them.

Despite the unimaginable hardships, many prisoners found the strength to endure. Acts of courage and compassion punctuated the darkness of the march. Prisoners supported one another, sharing what little food and water they had, carrying those too weak to walk.

Marine Pfc. Irvin Scott recalled a rare moment of humanity from a Japanese guard who secretly provided him with food and medicine, an act that likely saved his life. Such moments of kindness, however fleeting, provided a glimmer of hope in despair.

## The Aftermath: Justice and Remembrance

The Bataan Death March, once its full horror became known, galvanized American resolve in the Pacific War. It became a rallying cry, a symbol of the brutality of the enemy and the sacrifices required for victory.

After the war, those responsible for the atrocities faced justice. Lieutenant General Homma Masaharu, the commander of the Japanese forces in the Philippines, was tried and executed for war crimes, specifically for his role in the Bataan Death March.

Today, the Bataan Death March is commemorated through various memorials and events. The Bataan Memorial Death March, an annual event held at the White Sands Missile Range in New Mexico, challenges participants to complete a marathon-length course, honoring the memory of those who endured the original march. In the Philippines, sites like the Capas National Shrine and the Mount Samat National Shrine stand as solemn reminders of the sacrifices made.

## Conclusion

The Bataan Death March stands as one of the most tragic episodes of World War II, a stark reminder of the depths of human cruelty and the heights of human resilience. It is a story of strategic miscalculations, of unpreparedness in the face of aggression, and of the terrible price paid by those caught in the maelstrom of war.

Yet, it is also a story of survival against impossible odds, of small acts of kindness in the face of overwhelming brutality, and of the indomitable human spirit. The survivors of the march, through their courage and their willingness to bear witness, ensure that this chapter of history is not forgotten.

In the words of many survivors, the real heroes of Bataan were those who did not return. Their sacrifice, and the endurance of those who survived, continue to inspire and educate, serving as a powerful testament to the resilience of the human spirit in the face of unimaginable adversity.

**Sources**

Godfrey, Chad, The Bataan Death March: A Soldier's Personal Story of Survival and Captivity under the Japanese. Frontline Books, 2024.

Murphy, Kevin C. Inside the Bataan March: Defeat, Travail, and Memory. McFarland, 2014.

# The Angels of Bataan

## Introduction

In one of the darkest chapters of World War II, the Bataan Death March stands as a brutal symbol of the horrors faced by American and Filipino soldiers after the fall of the Philippines to Japanese forces in 1942. Amid the brutality and suffering, a group of brave and determined women, known as the "Angels of Bataan," risked their lives to care for the sick and wounded soldiers. These military nurses provided not only medical care but also hope and comfort in the direst of circumstances. Their story of courage and compassion remains one of the most inspiring accounts of heroism during World War II.

## The Fall of Bataan and the Death March

After the Japanese attack on Pearl Harbor on December 7, 1941, the Philippines became a critical battleground in the Pacific theater. American and Filipino forces, led by General Douglas MacArthur, were forced to retreat to the Bataan Peninsula following the rapid Japanese advance. Despite their valiant efforts, the combined forces were ill-equipped and outnumbered. After months of fighting under increasingly desperate conditions, the defenders of Bataan surrendered on April 9, 1942.

What followed was the infamous Bataan Death March, during which approximately 76,000 American and Filipino soldiers were forced to march over 60 miles to prisoner of war (POW) camps. Under the scorching sun, without adequate food, water, or medical care, thousands died from exhaustion, dehydration, disease, or were executed by their Japanese captors.

## The Role of the Nurses

Amid this devastation, a group of 77 American nurses, along with Filipino nurses, earned the title "Angels of Bataan" for their tireless efforts to care for the sick and wounded soldiers. These women were part of the U.S. Army Nurse Corps and Navy Nurse Corps stationed in the Philippines when the war broke out. Despite being offered the chance to evacuate, most of the nurses chose to stay behind to care for the soldiers, knowing the great danger they faced.

During the siege of Bataan, the nurses worked at field hospitals and makeshift medical facilities, enduring constant bombardment, inadequate supplies, and the growing threat of capture. When Bataan fell, the nurses were forced to retreat to Corregidor, a fortified island in Manila Bay, where they continued their medical duties under constant attack. Conditions on Corregidor were dire, with the nurses and patients sheltering in underground tunnels to avoid Japanese shelling.

## Life in the POW Camps

After Corregidor fell to the Japanese on May 6, 1942, the nurses were taken as prisoners of war and interned in POW camps, along with the soldiers they had cared for. The largest of these camps was Santo Tomas Internment Camp in Manila, where the nurses spent three years in captivity.

Life in the camp was harsh, with limited food, poor sanitation, and the constant threat of disease. Despite the challenges, the nurses continued to care for their fellow prisoners, often using their resourcefulness and creativity to make up for the lack of medical supplies. They treated wounds, administered medicine, and provided emotional support, becoming beacons of hope for the soldiers who suffered alongside them.

The nurses faced tremendous physical and emotional challenges, as their own health deteriorated due to malnutrition, disease, and the mental strain of captivity. Still, they refused to give up their duties. They worked in shifts, caring for the sick and injured, while also trying to maintain morale within the camp. Their compassion and dedication earned them the enduring respect and gratitude of the soldiers, who referred to them as their "angels."

## Acts of Heroism

The nurses demonstrated incredible bravery during their time in the camps. With meager resources, they found ways to treat patients suffering from malnutrition, dysentery, malaria, and other diseases that ravaged the camp. They boiled water, created makeshift bandages from available materials, and scavenged for anything that could be used to ease the suffering of their patients.

One notable act of courage involved Navy nurse Josephine Nesbit, who acted as the senior officer among the nurses in the camps. Despite the dire conditions, Nesbit maintained strict discipline among the nurses and ensured that medical duties were carried out efficiently. She and the other nurses kept detailed records of patients, ensured that each man received some level of care, and even held meetings to share knowledge about available treatments.

Another act of heroism came from Army nurse Lieutenant Frances Nash, who repeatedly risked her life to sneak into different parts of the camp to procure extra supplies and food for her fellow nurses and the wounded. Nash, along with many of her colleagues, became a symbol of resilience, inspiring both the soldiers and other prisoners to hold on to hope.

## Liberation

After three years in captivity, the "Angels of Bataan" were finally liberated by U.S. forces in February 1945 when General MacArthur returned to the Philippines to reclaim the islands. Despite the extreme hardships they had endured, nearly all of the nurses survived, a testament to their physical and mental strength, as well as their unwavering dedication to their duties.

Upon their return to the United States, the nurses were celebrated as national heroes. They were awarded medals and honors, and their contributions were recognized by both the military and the public. However, like many veterans of the war, they struggled to share their experiences and integrate back into civilian life. Many of the nurses continued their careers in the military, while others returned to their roles as civilian nurses, carrying with them the lifelong impact of their wartime experiences.

## Legacy

The legacy of the "Angels of Bataan" is one of compassion, resilience, and unwavering duty. Their heroic efforts not only saved lives but also provided a sense of dignity and hope to the soldiers they cared for during one of the darkest times in American military history. The nurses' selflessness and bravery under the harshest conditions exemplified the critical role women played during World War II, both on the battlefield and behind the lines.

In the years following the war, the story of the "Angels of Bataan" became a symbol of the broader contributions of women in the military. Their story inspired books, documentaries, and tributes, ensuring that their courage would not be forgotten. In 1983, a monument was erected in Manila to honor the Army and Navy nurses who served in the Philippines during World War II.

## Conclusion

The "Angels of Bataan" were not just nurses; they were heroes who displayed extraordinary courage and compassion during one of the darkest periods of World War II. Their selfless acts in the face of unimaginable adversity saved countless lives and provided a flicker of hope to those trapped in the horror of the Bataan Death March and the ensuing years of captivity. Their legacy serves as a lasting testament to the power of humanity, even in the most inhumane of conditions. The story of these brave women continues to inspire, reminding us of the critical role that compassion, strength, and dedication play in the fight for survival and dignity.

## Sources

Godfrey, Chad, The Bataan Death March: A Soldier's Personal Story of Survival and Captivity under the Japanese. Frontline Books, 2024.

Murphy, Kevin C. Inside the Bataan March: Defeat, Travail, and Memory. McFarland, 2014.

Various Sources

# Did They Get Off?

**Introduction**

Douglas Munro, a Signalman First Class in the United States Coast Guard, is remembered as a true American hero for his extraordinary bravery during World War II. His selfless actions during the Battle of Guadalcanal not only saved the lives of many Marines but also earned him the distinction of being the only Coast Guardsman to receive the Medal of Honor. Munro's story is one of courage, sacrifice, and the deep bonds formed between service members in the heat of battle.

**Early Life**

Douglas Albert Munro was born on October 11, 1919, in Vancouver, British Columbia, Canada. His family moved to the United States when he was a child, eventually settling in Cle Elum, Washington. Growing up in a close-knit family, Munro was known for his strong work ethic and sense of duty. He was an active young man, participating in various sports and outdoor activities, which helped shape his character and leadership skills.

In 1939, as tensions in Europe escalated, Munro decided to enlist in the Coast Guard. He was motivated by a desire to serve his country and help those in need. After completing his training, he quickly rose through the ranks, demonstrating exceptional skill and dedication.

**The Guadalcanal Campaign**

By 1942, the United States was deeply involved in World War II, and the Pacific Theater was a focal point of the conflict. The Battle of Guadalcanal began on August 7, 1942, when American forces landed on the island in an effort to secure a strategic foothold against Japanese forces. Munro was assigned to the USS McCawley, a transport ship that played a crucial role in landing Marines on the island.

As the battle raged on, Munro's unit was tasked with transporting Marines to various locations along the coast. He quickly became known for his leadership and ability to navigate the treacherous waters of the Solomon Islands. His experience and training made him an invaluable asset to the Marine Corps, and he developed a strong bond with the Marines he served alongside.

## The Fateful Day

On September 27, 1942, Munro's courage would be put to the ultimate test. During a critical operation, a battalion of Marines found themselves trapped and under heavy fire from Japanese forces at Point Cruz. The situation was dire, and the Marines were in desperate need of evacuation. Munro, recognizing the urgency of the situation, volunteered to lead a group of landing craft back to the beach to rescue the beleaguered troops.

As Munro and his crew approached the beach, they came under intense enemy fire. Despite the danger, Munro remained focused on his mission. He directed the landing craft to provide cover for the Marines as they attempted to board. His bravery was evident as he maneuvered the boats into position, shielding the Marines from enemy fire while they scrambled to safety.

## The Ultimate Sacrifice

As the evacuation progressed, Munro's actions became increasingly heroic. He positioned his landing craft between the Marines and the enemy, drawing fire away from the soldiers as they boarded. His selflessness and determination to save his comrades were palpable. Tragically, as the last of the Marines boarded the craft, Munro was struck by enemy fire. He was mortally wounded but managed to regain consciousness long enough to ask, "Did they get off?".

Munro's sacrifice was not in vain; all of the Marines he had rescued made it to safety. His commanding officer later wrote to Munro's parents, praising their son's bravery and the impact he had on the lives of those he saved. Munro died on the beach, but his legacy would live on.

## Recognition and Legacy

In recognition of his extraordinary heroism, Douglas Munro was posthumously awarded the Medal of Honor. The citation highlighted his "extraordinary heroism and conspicuous gallantry in action above and beyond the call of duty" during the evacuation of the Marines at Point Cruz. The award was presented to his parents by President Franklin D. Roosevelt on May 24, 1943.

## Conclusion

Douglas Munro's story is a powerful reminder of the sacrifices made by those who serve in the military. His bravery during the Battle of Guadalcanal exemplifies the spirit of selflessness and duty that defines the best of the American armed forces.

## Sources

Williams, Gary L. Guardian of Guadalcanal: The World War II Story of Douglas A. Munro, United States Coast Guard. Lakota Press, 2014.

Frank, Richard B. Guadalcanal: The Definitive Account of the Landmark Battle. Penguin Books, 1992.

# The Pied Piper of Saipan

## Introduction

Guy Louis Gabaldon, born on March 22, 1926, in Los Angeles, California, is celebrated for his extraordinary heroics during World War II, particularly during the battles of Saipan and Tinian. His unique background and remarkable actions earned him the nickname "The Pied Piper of Saipan," and he became known for capturing or persuading over 1,300 Japanese soldiers and civilians to surrender. Gabaldon's story is one of bravery, cultural understanding, and the complexities of war.

## Early Life

Gabaldon was raised in a multi-ethnic environment in East Los Angeles. He was of Mexican descent and grew up in a large family, one of seven children. His early life was marked by hardship; at the age of ten, he helped support his family by shining shoes on Skid Row. During his youth, he became involved with a gang known as the "Moe Gang" but later found a sense of belonging with the Nakano family, a Japanese American family who took him in. He lived with them for several years, learning to speak Japanese and immersing himself in their culture.

When World War II broke out, the Nakano family was sent to a relocation camp, which deeply affected Gabaldon. He felt a strong sense of duty to serve his country and joined the United States Marine Corps on his 17th birthday, March 22, 1943. After completing basic training and language school, he was assigned to the 2nd Marine Regiment, 2nd Marine Division.

## The Battle of Saipan

The Battle of Saipan began on June 15, 1944, and was a crucial operation in the Pacific Theater. The capture of Saipan was essential for establishing airfields for the planned invasion of Japan. Gabaldon landed on Saipan with his unit and quickly recognized the dire situation faced by the Japanese forces, who were ordered to kill American soldiers or commit suicide rather than surrender.

Gabaldon's unique upbringing and language skills allowed him to communicate effectively with the Japanese soldiers. On the first night of the invasion, he ventured out alone, capturing two Japanese soldiers. Despite being reprimanded for leaving his post, he continued to take risks, returning the next

404

night with twelve more prisoners. His success led to him being allowed to operate independently, and he began to develop a reputation for his daring rescues.

### The Pied Piper of Saipan

Gabaldon's most notable achievement came when he convinced a Japanese officer to surrender, leading to the capitulation of over 800 Japanese soldiers and civilians. He would approach enemy positions, often under fire, and call out in Japanese, assuring the soldiers that they would be treated well if they surrendered. His ability to speak the language and his understanding of Japanese culture played a crucial role in his success. Gabaldon's exploits on Saipan resulted in him being credited with capturing approximately 1,500 Japanese soldiers and civilians, a feat that was unprecedented at the time.

However, Gabaldon's actions were not without controversy. Some accounts suggest that he exaggerated the number of prisoners he captured, and there were claims that many of those he brought in were civilians rather than soldiers. Despite this, his bravery and the intelligence he gathered from the prisoners significantly contributed to the American war effort.

### The Battle of Tinian

After the capture of Saipan, Gabaldon continued his service on Tinian, where he again demonstrated his skills in negotiation and persuasion. He was involved in further operations that led to the capture of additional Japanese soldiers. His actions during these battles earned him the respect of his fellow Marines and commanding officers.

Gabaldon was wounded during the fighting on Tinian, which ultimately led to his discharge from the Marine Corps. He was initially awarded the Silver Star for his bravery, but in 1960, this was upgraded to the Navy Cross, the second-highest military decoration for valor.

### Conclusion

Guy Gabaldon's story is a powerful testament to the courage and resilience of those who served in World War II. His ability to bridge cultural divides and his extraordinary bravery in the face of danger saved countless lives and exemplified the spirit of the Marine Corps. Gabaldon's legacy continues to inspire future generations, reminding us of the sacrifices made by those who fought for freedom and the importance of understanding and compassion in times of conflict.

### Sources

Gabaldon, Guy. Saipan: Suicide Island. Gabaldon, 1990.

Grehan, John. Saipan 1944: The Most Decisive Battle of the Pacific War. Frontline Books, 2021.

# The Youngest Recipient of the Medal of Honor

## Introduction

Jacklyn "Jack" Lucas was a remarkable figure in American military history, known for his extraordinary bravery during World War II. His actions during the Battle of Iwo Jima not only earned him the Medal of Honor but also made him the youngest recipient of this prestigious award since the Civil War. This story explores Lucas's early life, military service, and the heroic deeds that defined his legacy.

## Early Life

Jack Lucas was born on February 14, 1928, in Plymouth, North Carolina. Growing up in a modest household, he was always larger than his peers, which contributed to his desire to join the military at a young age. After the attack on Pearl Harbor in December 1941, Lucas felt a strong urge to serve his country. At just 14 years old, he forged his mother's signature to enlist in the United States Marine Corps, claiming to be 17.

Lucas's initial military experience was not what he had hoped for. After enlisting, he was assigned to a non-combat role, driving a truck in Hawaii. However, Lucas was determined to see action and stowed away on a transport ship bound for Iwo Jima, where he would soon find himself in the thick of battle.

## The Battle of Iwo Jima

On February 19, 1945, Lucas landed on Iwo Jima as a rifleman with the 1st Battalion, 26th Marines, 5th Marine Division. The battle was one of the fiercest of the Pacific campaign, marked by brutal fighting and heavy casualties on both sides. Lucas celebrated his 17th birthday at sea just days before the invasion, but the reality of war quickly overshadowed any celebrations.

On February 20, during a firefight in a trench, Lucas and three fellow Marines found themselves under attack from Japanese soldiers. Two grenades were thrown into their trench, and in a split-second decision that would define his legacy, Lucas acted without hesitation. He yelled "grenade!" and pushed one of his comrades out of the way before throwing himself on one grenade and pulling the other underneath him. The first grenade exploded, showering Lucas with shrapnel and causing severe injuries.

**Acts of Valor**

Despite the horrific injuries he sustained, Lucas did not lose consciousness. He was initially believed to be dead by his fellow Marines, who left the trench to continue their assault. However, Lucas remained alive and struggled to breathe amidst the chaos. A passing Marine discovered him and called for medical assistance. A Navy Corpsman arrived, treated Lucas's wounds, and defended him from an enemy soldier preparing to throw another grenade.

Lucas was evacuated to a hospital ship, where he underwent a series of surgeries to remove shrapnel from his body. In total, he would endure 26 operations to treat his injuries, which included wounds to his torso, arm, and face. Remarkably, Lucas made a significant recovery, although he faced a long road of physical therapy to regain the use of his arm.

**Recognition and Medal of Honor**

Jack Lucas's bravery did not go unnoticed. On October 5, 1945, he was awarded the Medal of Honor by President Harry S. Truman during a ceremony at the White House. Lucas was one of 27 servicemen to receive this honor for their actions during the Battle of Iwo Jima. At just 17 years old, he became the youngest recipient of the Medal of Honor in U.S. history.

Lucas's story did not end with the war. He continued to face challenges in his life, including a near-fatal parachuting accident while serving in the Army in 1961, where both of his parachutes malfunctioned. Miraculously, he survived the fall, attributing his survival to his stocky build and a last-minute roll upon landing.

**Later Life and Legacy:** After the war, Lucas struggled to adjust to civilian life. He briefly tried his hand at business but eventually found fulfillment in sharing his experiences with others. He wrote a memoir titled "Indestructible," detailing his life and the events of Iwo Jima. Lucas became a sought-after speaker, sharing his story with veterans and students across the country.

**Conclusion**

Jack Lucas's story is a powerful testament to the courage and sacrifice of those who served in World War II. His selfless act of heroism during the Battle of Iwo Jima exemplifies the spirit of the Marine Corps and the values of bravery and duty.

**Sources**

Thorne, Cassius. Little Known Heroes – Jacklyn Lucas. Kindle Publications, 2024.

Lucas, Jack H. Indestructible: The Unforgettable Memoir of a Marine Hero at the Battle of Iwo Jima. William Morrow Books, 2020.

# A German Officer's Courageous Defiance

## Introduction

In a time when humanity seemed to be losing its very soul, a quiet hero emerged from the ranks of the German Wehrmacht. His name was Karl Plagge, an officer who, against the backdrop of the Holocaust's unimaginable horrors, chose to act with remarkable courage and compassion. In a world where silence is often equated to complicity, Plagge's story stands out as a beacon of moral defiance. By risking his life to save hundreds of Jews, he demonstrated that even within the machinery of death, there was room for humanity. This is the true story of how Karl Plagge, through his extraordinary acts of bravery, defied the Nazi regime and became a savior to those he was supposed to oppress.

## Early Life

The rise of Adolf Hitler and the Nazi regime in Germany in 1933 marked the beginning of a dark chapter in human history. The regime's virulent anti-Semitism quickly manifested in policies aimed at isolating, persecuting, and ultimately exterminating Europe's Jewish population. The invasion of Poland in 1939 and the subsequent occupation of much of Europe brought millions of Jews under Nazi control, leading to the establishment of ghettos, forced labor camps, and extermination centers designed to carry out the Final Solution.

Karl Plagge was born in Darmstadt, Germany, in 1897. A veteran of World War I, he returned to civilian life only to witness the rise of Nazism and its corrosive impact on German society. Although Plagge joined the Nazi Party, his motivations were largely pragmatic, aimed at protecting his career rather than endorsing the party's ideology. In 1939, as World War II broke out, Plagge was called back to military service. By 1941, he was stationed in Vilnius, Lithuania, where he was placed in charge of a forced labor camp, known as Heereskraftfahrpark 562 (HKP 562), which provided maintenance and repairs for military vehicles.

It was in this camp, located in the heart of occupied Eastern Europe, that Plagge would begin his quiet rebellion against the Nazi atrocities.

## The Establishment of HKP 562

HKP 562 was established in 1943 as a forced labor camp for Jews, primarily those from the Vilnius Ghetto. For the Nazis, the camp's purpose was purely utilitarian: to exploit Jewish labor for the war effort. However, under Plagge's command, HKP 562 became something far more than just a labor camp—it became a refuge. Plagge, deeply troubled by the Nazi policies of extermination, saw an opportunity to save lives by ensuring that as many Jews as possible were assigned to his camp. By declaring them essential to the war effort, he could protect them from the deportations to death camps that were becoming increasingly frequent.

Plagge's actions were deliberate and calculated. He falsified records, overestimated the number of workers needed, and accepted entire families, knowing that this would make it harder for the SS to separate and deport them. Despite the constant threat of discovery, Plagge continued to expand his efforts, quietly informing the Jews under his protection about the realities of the Nazi plans for their extermination.

## The Rescue Efforts

As the war dragged on, the Nazi leadership became increasingly determined to eliminate all remaining Jews. In the spring of 1944, the SS ordered the liquidation of the Vilnius Ghetto, sending its inhabitants to concentration camps like Auschwitz. The liquidation of the ghetto was followed by intensified efforts to round up the remaining Jews, including those in labor camps like HKP 562.

Aware of the imminent danger, Plagge took extraordinary risks to warn the Jews in his camp. In July 1944, as the Red Army approached Vilnius, the SS prepared to conduct one final roundup of the Jews in HKP 562. Plagge, knowing that resistance was futile, made a bold decision. He called a meeting with the Jewish workers and, speaking in veiled language, informed them of the impending danger. His message was clear: they needed to hide or escape if they wanted to survive.

Thanks to Plagge's warning, many Jews in the camp were able to hide in the walls, attics, and other concealed spaces that had been prepared in advance. When the SS arrived, they found fewer Jews than expected, leading to confusion and delays that allowed even more to escape or hide. While many were still caught and murdered, Plagge's actions directly saved the lives of about 250 people.

## The Risks Plagge Took

Plagge's defiance was not without personal risk. As a member of the Wehrmacht, he was under constant scrutiny by the SS and other Nazi authorities. Any suspicion of disloyalty or fraternization with Jews could have led to his execution. Despite this, Plagge continued his efforts to protect those under his care, driven by a moral conviction that transcended the dangers he faced.

His position as an officer provided some cover, but it also made him a target for the more fanatical elements of the Nazi regime who saw any deviation from the party line as treason. Plagge walked a tightrope between his official duties and his covert resistance, always aware that discovery would mean death.

## Conclusion

The Significance of Plagge's Actions: Karl Plagge's actions during World War II stand as a powerful example of moral courage in the face of evil. In a time when most people followed orders without question, Plagge chose to act according to his conscience, saving hundreds of lives in the process. His story challenges the narrative of universal complicity within the German military, showing that even within the ranks of the Wehrmacht, some resisted the atrocities of the Nazi regime.

After the war, Plagge returned to Germany, where he lived a quiet life, rarely speaking about his wartime actions. It wasn't until the 1990s, when survivors of HKP 562 began to share their stories, that Plagge's heroism became widely known. In 2000, he was posthumously recognized as Righteous Among the Nations by Yad Vashem, Israel's Holocaust memorial, an honor bestowed upon non-Jews who risked their lives to save Jews during the Holocaust.

## Sources

Good, Michael. The Search for Major Plagge: The Nazi Who Saved Jews. Fordham University Press, 2006.

Malkes, Simon. The Righteous of the Wehrmacht. Academic Studies Press, 2014.

Various Sources

# The Great Escape

### Introduction

In the stories of World War II, few capture the imagination quite like the Great Escape from Stalag Luft III. This daring breakout, executed on a cold March night in 1944, stands as a testament to the human spirit in the face of oppression. It is a tale of extraordinary planning, unwavering determination, and ultimately, tragic sacrifice. As we delve into the depths of this remarkable event, we uncover not just a daring prison break, but a complex narrative of human resilience, ingenuity, and the harsh realities of war.

### The Prison on Sandy Soil

Our story begins in the heart of Nazi-occupied Europe, near the town of Sagan in Lower Silesia, approximately 100 miles southeast of Berlin. Here, amidst the pine forests and sandy soil, stood Stalag Luft III, a prisoner-of-war camp specifically designed to hold captured Allied airmen. Established in March 1942, this camp was no ordinary prison. It was a calculated attempt by the Luftwaffe, the aerial warfare branch of the German military, to contain some of the most escape-prone prisoners of the war.

The camp's design was a testament to German efficiency and paranoia. Barracks were raised off the ground to make tunneling more detectable. The very earth beneath the prisoners' feet was chosen for its treachery - sandy soil that would make tunnel construction a near-impossible task. As an added precaution, seismographic microphones were installed around the perimeter, their electronic ears constantly listening for the telltale sounds of underground activity.

Yet, despite these measures, life in Stalag Luft III was not as grim as one might expect. The Luftwaffe, adhering to the Geneva Convention, provided a relatively humane environment. Prisoners had access to a library, participated in sports leagues, and even put on theatrical performances. Red Cross parcels supplemented their diet, providing a lifeline of nutrition and hope.

But for many of these men, trained in the art of escape and driven by a sense of duty, the relative comfort of their confinement was no consolation. From the moment they arrived, their minds

turned to thoughts of freedom, of returning to the fight against Nazi tyranny. It was in this atmosphere of restless energy that the seeds of the Great Escape were sown.

## The Mastermind and His Vision

At the heart of this audacious plan was Squadron Leader Roger Bushell, a Royal Air Force pilot with a reputation for daring and leadership. Captured after being shot down over France, Bushell brought to Stalag Luft III not just his experience from previous escape attempts, but a bold vision that would push the boundaries of what was thought possible.

Bushell's plan was daring in its scope and ambition. He proposed not just a breakout of a handful of men, but a mass escape of 200 prisoners. This, he argued, would create chaos in the German ranks, forcing them to divert precious resources to the manhunt. It was a plan that spoke not just to the desire for personal freedom, but to a strategic imperative to continue the fight against Nazi Germany by any means necessary.

Under Bushell's leadership, an escape committee was formed, bringing together a diverse group of skilled individuals. Each man had a role to play, from tunnel diggers to forgers, lookouts to tailors. The camp became a hive of clandestine activity, with hundreds of prisoners contributing to the effort in ways both large and small.

## The Tunnels: Tom, Dick, and Harry

The centerpiece of Bushell's plan was the construction of not one, but three tunnels, codenamed "Tom," "Dick," and "Harry." This redundancy was a stroke of genius, ensuring that if one tunnel was discovered, the others could continue. The tunnels were engineering marvels, dug 30 feet below the surface to avoid detection by the camp's microphones.

The conditions in these tunnels were claustrophobic and dangerous. Davy Jones, a decorated bomber pilot from Arizona who became a prisoner at Stalag Luft III, later recounted the harrowing experience: "Digging through 30 feet of sand was no easy task. The air was thin, and the constant fear of cave-ins weighed heavily on our minds. But we pressed on, driven by the hope of freedom".

The ingenuity of the prisoners was on full display in the construction of these tunnels. Bed boards were repurposed to shore up the sandy walls. A ventilation system was crafted from hockey sticks and knapsacks. Lamps were fashioned from pajama cords and mutton fat. Even the disposal of the excavated sand became an art form, with prisoners nicknamed "penguins" using pouches hidden in their trousers to discreetly scatter the telltale yellow sand across the campgrounds.

## Forging Freedom

While the tunnels were the most visible aspect of the escape plan, equally crucial was the work being done above ground. A team of skilled forgers worked tirelessly to create a small mountain of fake documents - identity papers, travel passes, and even replica stamps made from boot heels and shoe polish.

The attention to detail was extraordinary. Clothes were altered to resemble civilian attire. Maps were meticulously copied and hidden in playing cards or Monopoly boards. Every aspect of life outside the wire was studied and replicated, from train schedules to local customs.

Jack Lyon, another former prisoner, spoke of the tense atmosphere that permeated the camp during these preparations: "There was a constant game of cat and mouse with the German guards. We had to be vigilant at all times, knowing that discovery could mean not just the end of our plans, but severe punishment".

## The Night of Nights

As winter gave way to spring in 1944, the stage was set for what would become known as the Great Escape. The night of March 24-25 was chosen for its promise of cloud cover and a moonless sky - ideal conditions for a covert operation.

But as with all plans, reality proved more challenging than theory. The exit of tunnel "Harry" - the one ultimately used for the escape - emerged short of the forest's edge, in open ground visible from a sentry tower. To compound matters, the unusually cold winter had frozen the exit hatch shut, delaying the start of the escape by over an hour.

Despite these setbacks, at 10:30 PM, the first man emerged from the tunnel into the frigid night air. What followed was a tense and methodical procession of men, each carrying forged papers and civilian clothes, each harboring dreams of freedom and home.

The escape moved slower than planned, with only one man exiting every six minutes instead of the intended one or two per minute. As the night wore on, the tension in the air was thick. Every sound, every shadow, held the potential for discovery and disaster.

## The Alarm Sounds

By 5 AM, 76 men had made it out of the tunnel. But as the 77th man emerged, fate intervened. A German sentry, on a routine patrol, spotted the escaping prisoner. In an instant, the alarm was raised, and the Great Escape came to an abrupt and chaotic end.

The camp erupted into a frenzy of activity. Sirens wailed, searchlights crisscrossed the compound, and guards rushed to secure the area. Inside the tunnel, the remaining would-be escapees faced a heart-wrenching decision - to push on and risk certain capture, or to retreat and destroy the evidence of their work.

## The Aftermath: Triumph and Tragedy

In the days that followed, a massive manhunt swept across Nazi-occupied Europe. Of the 76 men who had tasted brief freedom, all but three were eventually recaptured. Two Norwegian airmen managed to make their way to Sweden, while a Dutch pilot successfully reached Gibraltar.

But the story of the Great Escape does not end with these tales of daring and near-misses. In a dark turn of events that shocked even the hardened sensibilities of wartime Europe, Hitler, enraged by the audacity of the escape, ordered the execution of 50 of the recaptured airmen. This act, in clear violation of the Geneva Convention, would later be prosecuted as a war crime.

The impact of the Great Escape reverberated far beyond the confines of Stalag Luft III. It forced the Germans to divert significant resources to tighten security at POW camps across Europe. Thousands of troops, police officers, and even Hitler Youth were mobilized in the manhunt, drawing them away from other critical wartime duties.

Moreover, the escape became a powerful symbol of Allied resistance and ingenuity. It boosted morale among Allied forces and civilians alike, a reminder that even in the darkest hours of the war, the spirit of freedom could not be extinguished.

## Conclusion

The Great Escape from Stalag Luft III stands as one of the most daring and complex prisoner of war breakouts in military history. It is a story that encompasses the full spectrum of human experience - courage and fear, ingenuity and brutality, triumph and tragedy.

The legacy of the Great Escape extends far beyond the events of that fateful night in March 1944. It serves as a testament to the indomitable human spirit, the power of teamwork, and the unyielding desire for freedom. The meticulous planning, the countless hours of backbreaking labor, the risks taken by hundreds of men - all speak to a collective will that refused to be broken by captivity.

In the end, the Great Escape is more than just a thrilling tale of wartime adventure. It is a profound human drama that continues to captivate and inspire, reminding us of the extraordinary potential that lies within ordinary individuals when united by a common cause and an unbreakable spirit.

## Sources

Brickhill, Paul. The Great Escape. W.W. Norton & Company, 2004.

Vance, Jonathan F. The True Story of the Great Escape: Stalag Luft III, March 1944. Greenhill Books, 2019.

# The Heroics of Léo Major

## Introduction

Léo Major was a remarkable Canadian soldier whose extraordinary bravery and resourcefulness during World War II earned him a place in history as one of the war's unsung heroes. His actions, particularly during the liberation of the Dutch town of Zwolle, exemplify the courage and determination of those who fought against tyranny. This story explores Major's early life, military service, and the heroic deeds that defined his legacy.

## Early Life

Léo Major was born on January 23, 1921, in New Bedford, Massachusetts, to French-Canadian parents. His family moved to Montréal, Quebec, when he was very young. Growing up in a working-class environment, Major developed a strong sense of duty and a desire to serve his country. At the age of 19, he enlisted in the Canadian Army in 1940, motivated by the need to contribute to the war effort against the Axis powers.

## Military Service

Major was assigned to the Régiment de la Chaudière, a unit that would see significant action during the war. He landed on Juno Beach during the D-Day invasion on June 6, 1944, where he quickly distinguished himself by capturing a German half-track vehicle, which contained valuable intelligence equipment. His bravery was evident from the start, but it was during the subsequent battles that his heroics truly shone.

In the weeks following D-Day, Major participated in fierce fighting in Normandy. He was injured by a phosphorus grenade during a skirmish with German SS troops, which resulted in the loss of vision in his left eye. Despite this injury, he refused evacuation, demonstrating his resilience and commitment to his comrades.

## The Battle of the Scheldt

One of Major's most notable achievements occurred during the Battle of the Scheldt in late 1944. Tasked with locating a missing patrol of fresh recruits, Major ventured into enemy territory alone after his

415

companion fell ill. In a remarkable display of bravery, he captured 93 German soldiers single-handedly. This feat was so extraordinary that he was initially recommended for the Distinguished Conduct Medal (DCM), the second-highest award for gallantry in the British Commonwealth.

However, Major famously declined the medal, reportedly due to his disdain for Field Marshal Bernard Montgomery, whom he considered incompetent. This refusal did not diminish his reputation among his peers, who recognized his exceptional courage and skill.

### The Liberation of Zwolle

Léo Major's most famous act of heroism occurred during the liberation of Zwolle, a city in the Netherlands. In April 1945, as Canadian forces approached the city, Major and his friend Corporal Wilfrid Arsenault volunteered for a reconnaissance mission to assess the German defenses. They hoped to gather intelligence that could spare the city from destruction by Allied artillery.

Upon entering Zwolle, Major and Arsenault encountered German troops. Tragically, Arsenault was killed during the engagement, leaving Major to continue the mission alone. Fueled by grief and anger, Major pressed on, using his knowledge of the area and his combat skills to outmaneuver the German forces. He engaged the enemy, creating the illusion of a much larger Canadian force attacking the city. His tactics included setting fire to the German headquarters, which further demoralized the defenders.

By the end of the day, Major had successfully liberated Zwolle, and his actions saved the city from extensive damage. His bravery and quick thinking earned him the respect and admiration of the local population, who celebrated him as a hero. Major's efforts were recognized with the Distinguished Conduct Medal, which he accepted after the liberation of Zwolle.

### Post-War Life and Legacy

After World War II, Léo Major returned to civilian life but continued to serve his country by volunteering for the Korean War in 1950. He once again demonstrated his exceptional skills and bravery, earning a bar to his DCM for his actions during the conflict. Following his military career, Major settled in Montreal, where he lived a quiet life, often returning to Zwolle to visit the friends he had made during the war.

Léo Major passed away on October 12, 2008, at the age of 87. His legacy as a hero endures, not only through the medals he earned but also through the stories of his bravery that continue to inspire future generations. In Zwolle, a street was named in his honor, and he is remembered as a symbol of courage and resilience.

### Conclusion

Léo Major's story is one of extraordinary bravery and selflessness in the face of adversity. His actions during World War II, particularly in the liberation of Zwolle, exemplified the spirit of those who fought for freedom and justice.

### Sources

Heaps, Leo. The Grey Goose of Arnhem: The Story of the Most Amazing Mass Escape of World War II. Sapere Books, 2020.

Lepine, Luc. Leo Major: The Resilient Hero. Hurtubise HMH, 2019.

# Japanese American 442nd Regimental Combat Team

### Introduction
This true story delves into the extraordinary journey of the Japanese American 442nd Regimental Combat Team, known as the Nisei. We explore their origins, their experiences of adversity and discrimination in the aftermath of Pearl Harbor, the formation of their combat unit, their remarkable achievements on the battlefield, and the recognition they received for their heroism.

### Born and Raised
The Nisei were second-generation Japanese Americans born and raised in the United States. Following the attack on Pearl Harbor in December 1941, suspicion and fear spread across the country, leading to the internment of Japanese Americans. Despite their loyalty, Japanese Americans faced prejudice and discrimination, considered potential threats due to their ancestry.

### Formation of 442$^{nd}$ Regimental Combat Team
The U.S. government formed an all-Japanese-American combat unit to respond to the prevailing prejudice and mitigate public concerns. In January 1943, the 442nd Regimental Combat Team was activated under the leadership of Colonel Charles W. Pence. The unit consisted of Nisei volunteers who demonstrated their patriotism and desire to prove their loyalty to the country.

The 442nd Regimental Combat Team achieved remarkable feats during their service in World War II. They fought in the European Theater, distinguishing themselves in several pivotal battles. One of their most notable accomplishments was rescuing the "Lost Battalion" of the 141st Infantry Regiment during the Battle of Bruyères in France.

### Go for Broke

The unit's motto, "Go for Broke," encapsulated their relentless spirit and willingness to risk everything for victory. Despite facing significant casualties, the 442nd became the most decorated unit for its size and duration of service in American military history, earning numerous awards, including 21 Medals of Honor, more than any other regiment in the U.S. Army.

The heroic actions of the Nisei soldiers did not go unnoticed. Their courage and sacrifices garnered admiration and respect from fellow soldiers and military commanders. However, it is essential to note that their recognition came with a bittersweet undertone, as it highlighted the irony of fighting for a country that had initially treated them as potential enemies due to their Japanese ancestry.

In the years following the war, the Nisei soldiers gradually received increased recognition for their contributions. However, it was not until several decades later that their heroism was indeed acknowledged and celebrated. In 2010, the surviving unit members were awarded the Congressional Gold Medal, the highest civilian honor bestowed by the U.S. Congress, in recognition of their extraordinary service and sacrifices.

## Conclusion

The story of the Japanese American 442nd Regimental Combat Team, the Nisei, stands as a testament to the resilience, courage, and unwavering patriotism of a group of Americans who overcame adversity, discrimination, and the internment of their families to serve their country with honor and distinction.

## Sources

Kiyonaga, John C. Uninvited Valor: The Forsaken Soldiers of WWII: Based on the Epic True Story of the 442$^{nd}$ Regimental Combat Team. Dartfrog Books, 2024.

Marsh, Carole. The 442$^{nd}$ Regimental Combat Team: Japanese American Heroes of World War II. Gallopade International, 2011.

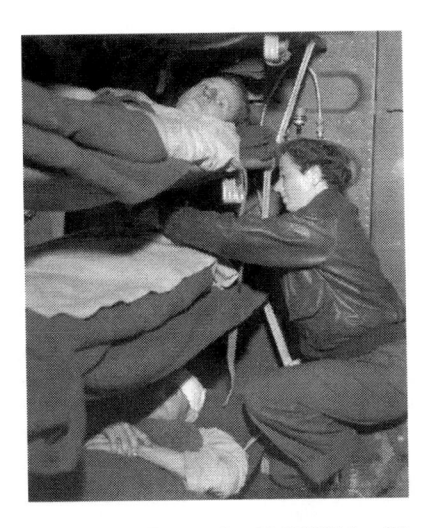

# The Journey of America's Only Female POW in Europe

## Introduction

In the vast tapestry of World War II history, some threads remain hidden, their stories untold or forgotten. One such thread is the remarkable life of Reba Zitella Whittle, a flight nurse whose courage and resilience in the face of adversity make her story one of the most compelling yet overlooked narratives of the war. As the only American female prisoner of war in the European Theater during World War II, Whittle's experiences offer a unique perspective on the conflict, the role of women in the military, and the challenges faced by those who served their country in unconventional ways. This is the story of a woman who soared through the skies, endured captivity, and fought for recognition long after the guns of war had fallen silent.

## A Texas Girl Takes Flight

Reba Zitella Whittle's story begins in the heart of Texas, where she was born on August 19, 1919, in the small town of Rocksprings, Edwards County. Growing up in the vast expanses of the Lone Star State, young Reba might never have imagined the heights she would reach or the challenges she would face. Her journey from a small-town girl to a pioneering military nurse is a testament to her determination and the changing role of women in American society.

Whittle's path to becoming a flight nurse began with her education at North Texas State College. It was here that she first felt the call to nursing, a profession that would not only define her career but also shape her destiny. Following her time at North Texas State, Whittle pursued her nursing education at the Medical and Surgical Memorial Hospital School of Nursing in San Antonio, Texas. This rigorous training laid the foundation for her future service and prepared her for the challenges that lay ahead.

## Answering the Call to Serve

As the storm clouds of war gathered over Europe and the Pacific, Reba Whittle felt compelled to serve her country. On June 10, 1941, she was commissioned into the United States Army Nurse Corps at Fort Sam Houston, Texas. As a second lieutenant, Whittle began her military career with an assignment to the

Station Hospital at Albuquerque Army Air Base in New Mexico, where she served as a general duty ward nurse. Her dedication and skill soon led to a transfer to Mather Field in Sacramento, California, where she continued to hone her nursing skills and adapt to military life.

But Whittle's ambitions reached beyond the confines of ground-based hospitals. The skies called to her, and on August 6, 1943, she took a significant step in her career by being accepted into the Army Air Forces School of Air Evacuation. This specialized training program, located at Bowman Field, Kentucky, was designed to prepare nurses for the unique challenges of providing medical care in the air.

The training was intense and comprehensive. Flight nurses were expected to be largely self-sufficient during flights, capable of handling a wide range of medical emergencies without the immediate support of a physician. They learned to manage pain, control bleeding, and treat shock in the challenging environment of a moving aircraft. Whittle excelled in this demanding program, graduating with excellent grades on November 26, 1943. Her performance during training foreshadowed the courage and competence she would display in the skies over Europe.

## Into the Skies of War

With her training complete, Reba Whittle took to the skies as a fully qualified flight nurse. Her role was critical in the war effort, providing essential medical care to wounded soldiers as they were evacuated from the front lines to medical facilities further from the combat zones. Whittle's dedication to her duty was evident in her impressive record: she logged over 500 hours of flight time and participated in 40 missions, each one fraught with danger and the ever-present risk of enemy action.

The life of a flight nurse was far from glamorous. It required a unique blend of nursing skills, courage, and the ability to work effectively in the cramped, noisy confines of a military aircraft. Whittle and her fellow nurses faced not only the medical challenges of caring for severely wounded patients but also the constant threat of enemy fire and the unpredictable dangers of wartime flying.

## A Fateful Flight

On September 27, 1944, Reba Whittle boarded a C-47 Skytrain aircraft, tail number 43-48395, nicknamed "Mary." The mission was routine: transport medical supplies from England to a U.S. Army field hospital in northeast France, then return with wounded American soldiers. Whittle was part of a crew that included 1st Lt. Ralph Parker as the pilot, 2nd Lt. David Forbes as co-pilot, Sergeant Harold Bonser as flight engineer, Corporal Chester Bright as radio operator, and Tech-3 Jonathan Hill as a surgical technician.

As the C-47 approached the Franco-German border near Aachen, Germany, fate intervened. Due to a navigational error, the aircraft strayed into German airspace. In the fog of war, with the plane unmarked by the Red Cross symbol due to its outbound cargo of military supplies, German anti-aircraft batteries opened fire. The C-47 was hit, and Whittle's world turned upside down as the aircraft plummeted from the sky.

The crash landing was violent, leaving Whittle with a concussion and lacerations to her face and back. As she regained consciousness amidst the wreckage, the gravity of the situation became clear. She and the surviving crew members were now in enemy territory, their fate uncertain.

## Captivity and Courage

German soldiers quickly surrounded the crash site, and Whittle found herself in a situation for which no training could have fully prepared her: she was now a prisoner of war. The Germans, unprepared for a female POW, were initially unsure how to handle her. Whittle was separated from her male counterparts and taken to the Luftwaffe interrogation center at Oberursel, near Frankfurt.

Despite her injuries and the shock of capture, Whittle's nursing instincts remained strong. She recalled the experience years later: "Even though I was a prisoner, I was still a nurse. I couldn't turn off that part of me, no matter the circumstances."

Her captivity took her to several locations, including Reserve Lazarett IX-C(a) at Obermaßfeld and later to IX-C(b) at Meiningen. In these POW hospitals, Whittle found herself in a unique position. Despite being a prisoner, she was allowed to use her nursing skills to care for other captives. She worked with burn patients and at a rehabilitation center for amputees, providing not just medical care but also a source of hope for her fellow prisoners.

The conditions were challenging, and the psychological strain of being the only American female POW in the European Theater weighed heavily on Whittle. She later described her initial cell as "extremely depressing," a stark contrast to the skies she had so recently navigated. Yet, through it all, Whittle maintained her dignity and her commitment to her fellow servicemen, earning the respect of both prisoners and captors.

## Freedom and the Fight for Recognition

As the war in Europe neared its end, Whittle's status as a POW was finally recognized by the International Committee of the Red Cross. This recognition set in motion the process for her release. On January 25, 1945, after four months of captivity, Reba Whittle was repatriated as part of a prisoner exchange. She was transported to Switzerland and then flown back to the United States on February 2, 1945.

Upon her return, Whittle was awarded the Purple Heart for the injuries she sustained during the crash and the Air Medal for her meritorious service in aerial flights. In March 1945, she was promoted to first lieutenant, a bittersweet advancement as her flying status was revoked due to recurrent headaches resulting from her wartime injuries.

Whittle's military career continued briefly after her return. She served as a ward nurse at the Army Air Forces Redistribution Station in Miami Beach, Florida, and later at the Air Debarkation Hospital in Hamilton Field, California. However, the physical and emotional toll of her experiences led to her discharge from active duty in January 1946 due to medical reasons.

In August 1945, Whittle married Lieutenant Colonel Stanley W. Tobiason, and they had two sons, one of whom would later serve as a naval aviator in Vietnam. Her personal life offered a new chapter, but the struggle for full recognition of her service was far from over.

Despite her significant contributions and unique status as a POW, Whittle faced a prolonged battle for official recognition. It wasn't until 1954, after several appeals, that the Army Physical Disability Appeal Board recognized her discharge as being due to physical disability, granting her retirement pay benefits.

The full acknowledgment of her status as a POW would take even longer. It wasn't until 1983, two years after Whittle's death, that she was officially recognized as a POW by the Department of the Army. This recognition came largely due to the tireless advocacy of her husband, Stanley Tobiason, who fought to ensure that Whittle's service and sacrifice were properly honored.

In a final act of recognition, Reba Whittle was posthumously awarded the Prisoner of War Medal in 1997, more than half a century after her capture and release. This long-delayed honor served as a poignant reminder of the challenges faced by women in military service during World War II and the often-overlooked contributions of female service members.

## Conclusion

The story of Reba Zitella Whittle is more than just a tale of wartime heroism; it is a testament to the resilience of the human spirit and a powerful reminder of the often-overlooked contributions of women in military service. From the skies over Europe to the confines of a POW camp, and through the long years of seeking recognition, Whittle's journey embodies the challenges and triumphs of women who served their country during World War II.

Her experiences as the only American female POW in the European Theater offer a unique perspective on the war, highlighting both the progress made in women's military roles and the obstacles that remained. Whittle's story serves as a bridge between the traditional narratives of World War II and the evolving understanding of women's contributions to the war effort.

The delayed recognition of Whittle's service and sacrifice underscores the broader struggles faced by women veterans in receiving acknowledgment and benefits for their military service. Her posthumous honors, while long overdue, represent a step towards a more inclusive and comprehensive understanding of military history.

## Sources

Frank, Mary E, The Forgotten POW: Second Lieutenant Reba Z. Whittle, AN. PN, 1990

Churchill, Sir Winston. The Second World War: A Complete History. Mariner Books, 1986.

Various Sources

# Desert Ghosts in Sicily

## Introduction

In the sweltering summer of 1943, as the tide of World War II began to turn in favor of the Allies, a group of elite soldiers prepared for one of the most daring and consequential operations of the conflict. Operation Husky, the Allied invasion of Sicily, would mark a turning point in the war, opening a new front in Europe and setting the stage for the eventual liberation of the continent from Axis control. At the forefront of this massive amphibious assault was a small but formidable unit: the Special Air Service (SAS), led by the legendary Colonel Blair "Paddy" Mayne.

This is the story of Mayne and his men, the "Desert Ghosts" who would play a crucial role in the success of Operation Husky. Their exploits during the invasion of Sicily not only contributed significantly to the Allied victory but also cemented the SAS's reputation as one of the most effective and daring special forces units in military history.

As the invasion fleet sailed towards the Sicilian coast on the night of July 9-10, 1943, Mayne and his team prepared for a mission that would test their skills, courage, and innovative tactics that had made the SAS such a formidable force. The success or failure of their operation would have far-reaching implications for the entire invasion and, by extension, the course of the war in the Mediterranean.

## The Man Behind the Legend

To understand the SAS operations in Sicily, one must first understand the extraordinary man who led them. Colonel Blair "Paddy" Mayne was no ordinary soldier. Born on January 11, 1915, in Newtownards, County Down, Ireland, Mayne's early life was marked by athletic prowess and academic achievement. A talented rugby player who represented Ireland and the British Lions, Mayne was also a skilled boxer and studied law at Queen's University of Belfast.

When World War II broke out, Mayne put his legal and sporting careers on hold, joining the Royal Ulster Rifles in 1940. It was here that his exceptional qualities caught the attention of David Stirling, the founder of the SAS. Mayne's combination of physical prowess, tactical acumen, and natural leadership made him an ideal candidate for the fledgling special forces unit.

Mayne quickly distinguished himself in the SAS, earning a reputation for daring raids and innovative tactics. His leadership style was characterized by relentless training and a close-knit camaraderie among his men. As one of his soldiers later recalled, "Paddy Mayne was a man you'd follow into hell itself. He never asked us to do anything he wouldn't do himself, and he had a knack for making the impossible seem possible."

By the time of the Sicily invasion, Mayne had already become a legendary figure within the SAS. His exploits in North Africa, where the SAS had cut its teeth conducting long-range desert raids against Axis airfields and supply lines, had earned him the Distinguished Service Order (DSO) and the respect of both his men and his superiors.

## The Stage is Set: Operation Husky

Operation Husky was one of the largest amphibious operations in military history, involving over 150,000 troops, 3,000 ships, and 4,000 aircraft. The invasion of Sicily was seen as a crucial step in the Allied strategy to knock Italy out of the war and gain a foothold in Europe.

As the massive invasion force prepared for the assault, Mayne and his SAS team were tasked with a critical mission that would help pave the way for the main landings. Their objective was the destruction of the Lamba Doria gun battery, a heavily fortified position on Cape Murro di Porco, south of Syracuse.

The Lamba Doria battery, with its three 6-inch guns, posed a significant threat to the Allied invasion fleet. Its strategic location on the southern tip of the Maddalena Peninsula gave it a clear line of sight to the invasion beaches. If left intact, it could wreak havoc on the approaching Allied ships and potentially jeopardize the entire operation.

Mayne's team, officially known as the Special Raiding Squadron (SRS), was handpicked for this crucial mission. Among them were some of his most trusted men, including Richard Lea, Captain John Tonkin, and Sergeant Ernest 'Buttercup Joe' Goldsmith. These men had fought alongside Mayne in the deserts of North Africa and had honed their skills in the art of covert operations and lightning raids.

## The Raid on Lamba Doria

In the pre-dawn hours of July 10, 1943, as the main invasion force approached the Sicilian coast, Mayne and his team prepared for their assault on the Lamba Doria battery. The conditions were far from ideal. A storm had whipped up the sea, making the approach treacherous. The rocky cliffs that protected the battery on the landward side presented a formidable obstacle.

Undeterred by these challenges, Mayne led his men as they scaled the cliffs under the cover of darkness. Each man carried heavy weaponry and explosives, their muscles straining as they inched their way up the sheer rock face. The team moved with the silent efficiency that had become their hallmark, their months of rigorous training paying off in this crucial moment.

As they crested the top of the cliffs, Mayne signaled for the assault to begin. The SAS team moved swiftly, catching the Italian defenders completely by surprise. The battle was fierce but brief. Mayne, leading from the front as always, personally took out several enemy positions.

One of Mayne's men, who witnessed his commander in action that night, later recounted: "It was like watching a force of nature. Paddy moved through the enemy defenses like a whirlwind, always seeming to be exactly where he was needed most. His courage inspired us all to push beyond our limits."

Within hours, the Lamba Doria battery had been neutralized. The gun emplacements were destroyed, their barrels pointed uselessly at the sky. As dawn broke over Sicily, Mayne and his team melted away into the countryside, leaving behind a scene of destruction that would baffle the Axis commanders and significantly ease the way for the main Allied landings.

**Beyond Lamba Doria: Continuing the Fight**

The destruction of the Lamba Doria battery was just the beginning of the SAS's involvement in Operation Husky. In the days that followed, Mayne led his team on a series of raids against other coastal defenses and strategic targets further inland.

These operations were characterized by the same blend of meticulous planning and audacious execution that had made the SAS so effective. Mayne's team would strike swiftly, causing maximum disruption to the enemy before disappearing into the Sicilian landscape.

One particularly daring raid saw Mayne's team infiltrate an Italian headquarters, capturing vital intelligence and sowing confusion among the enemy command. Another operation involved the destruction of a key bridge, severing an important Axis supply route.

Throughout these missions, Mayne's leadership was instrumental. His ability to think on his feet and adapt to rapidly changing situations kept his team one step ahead of the enemy. As one of his officers noted, "Paddy had an almost supernatural ability to sense danger and opportunity. He could read a battlefield like others read a book."

The success of these operations did not come without cost. The SAS team faced constant danger, operating deep behind enemy lines with little support. The physical and mental toll was immense, with the men often pushing themselves to the limits of human endurance. It was not uncommon for Mayne and his team to go days without sleep, relying on sheer willpower and, occasionally, Benzedrine tablets to keep going.

**The Broader Impact**

The SAS operations in Sicily, under Mayne's leadership, had a significant impact on the overall success of Operation Husky. By neutralizing key defensive positions and disrupting enemy communications and supply lines, Mayne and his men helped to create the conditions for the Allied advance across the island.

The psychological impact of these raids should not be underestimated. The seemingly random nature of the SAS strikes, coupled with their effectiveness, spread fear and confusion among the Axis forces. Italian and German commanders found themselves constantly looking over their shoulders, never knowing where the next attack might come from.

Moreover, the success of the SAS operations in Sicily further cemented the unit's reputation and demonstrated the value of special forces in modern warfare. The lessons learned and tactics developed during these missions would influence military doctrine for years to come.

## The Man Behind the Myth

While Mayne's exploits in Sicily added to his growing legend, it's important to separate the man from the myth. Some accounts have portrayed Mayne as a larger-than-life figure, prone to reckless behavior and excessive violence. However, those who served with him paint a more nuanced picture.

Mayne was undoubtedly a fierce warrior, capable of extraordinary acts of courage in battle. But he was also a thoughtful tactician and a leader who cared deeply for the welfare of his men. His unconventional methods were born not of recklessness but of a keen understanding of the unique demands of special operations warfare.

One of Mayne's officers, reflecting on his leadership years later, said: "Paddy was a complex man. He could be tough as nails when the situation demanded it, but he also had a softer side. He never asked us to take risks he wouldn't take himself, and he always made sure we understood the 'why' behind our missions. That's what made us willing to follow him anywhere."

## Aftermath and Legacy

The success of Operation Husky, including the crucial role played by Mayne and the SAS, marked a turning point in the war in the Mediterranean. Sicily fell to the Allies after 38 days of fighting, leading to the collapse of Mussolini's regime and Italy's eventual surrender.

For Mayne and the SAS, the Sicily campaign was another chapter in an already illustrious record. Mayne would go on to lead the SAS in further operations in Italy and later in France and Germany. By the end of the war, he had become one of the most decorated soldiers in the British Army, with four Distinguished Service Orders to his name.

Despite his remarkable war record, Mayne was controversially denied the Victoria Cross, the highest British military award for valor. The reasons for this remain a subject of debate, with some attributing it to his reputation as a maverick and others to the secretive nature of much of his work with the SAS.

## Conclusion

The story of Colonel Blair "Paddy" Mayne and the SAS during the Allied invasion of Sicily is one of courage, innovation, and the power of small, elite units to influence the course of major military operations. Their daring raids and strategic strikes played a crucial role in the success of Operation Husky, helping to pave the way for the Allied advance into Europe.

Mayne's leadership during this campaign exemplified the qualities that made the SAS such an effective force: adaptability, audacity, and an unwavering commitment to the mission. His ability to inspire and lead his men in the face of overwhelming odds set a standard for special operations forces that endures to this day.

## Sources

Mitcham, Samuel. The Battle of Sicily. How the Allies Lost Their Chance for Total Victory. Stackpole Books, 2007.

Ross, Hamish. Paddy Mayne: Lt. Col Blair "Paddy" Mayne, 1 SAS Regiment. The History Press, 2023.

# The Heroism of Edward "Butch" O'Hare

### Introduction

In the archives of naval aviation history, few stories shine as brightly as that of Edward "Butch" O'Hare. His extraordinary courage and skill in the face of overwhelming odds not only saved countless lives but also earned him a place among America's greatest war heroes. This narrative explores O'Hare's journey from a young man with a talent for marksmanship to a celebrated naval aviator whose actions would help shape the course of World War II in the Pacific. Through his story, we gain insight into the broader context of America's early involvement in the war and the pivotal role played by naval aviation in turning the tide against Japanese aggression.

### A Destiny Forged in Turbulent Times

Edward Henry "Butch" O'Hare was born on March 13, 1914, in St. Louis, Missouri, to Edward Joseph O'Hare and Selma Anna Lauth. His early life was marked by a curious blend of privilege and controversy. O'Hare's father, a lawyer with connections to the infamous gangster Al Capone, would later play a crucial role in Capone's downfall by providing evidence that led to his conviction for tax evasion. This decision, while cementing the elder O'Hare's place on the right side of the law, likely cost him his life when he was murdered in 1939.

Despite the tumultuous backdrop of his family life, young Butch showed early promise. At the Western Military Academy in Alton, Illinois, he distinguished himself as a marksman, becoming president of the rifle club. This early aptitude for precision and calm under pressure would serve him well in the cockpit of a fighter plane.

In 1932, O'Hare entered the United States Naval Academy at Annapolis, Maryland. It was here that he earned the nickname "Butch," a moniker that would stick with him throughout his naval career. His friendly demeanor and natural leadership abilities made him popular among his peers, foreshadowing the respect he would command as a naval aviator.

## From Ensign to Ace

After graduating from the Naval Academy in 1937, O'Hare was commissioned as an ensign and began his naval career aboard the battleship USS New Mexico. However, it was in the air that O'Hare would truly find his calling. In 1939, he began flight training at Naval Air Station Pensacola in Florida, where he honed his skills on various aircraft, including the Boeing F4B-4A and the SBU Corsair.

O'Hare's exceptional flying abilities quickly caught the attention of his superiors, particularly Lieutenant Commander John Thach, who became his mentor. Thach, himself a brilliant tactician who would later develop the famous "Thach Weave" combat maneuver, recognized in O'Hare, a rare combination of natural talent and unwavering courage.

As tensions in the Pacific escalated, O'Hare found himself assigned to Fighter Squadron Three (VF-3) aboard the USS Saratoga. The skills he had developed under Thach's tutelage would soon be put to the ultimate test.

## A Date with Destiny

On February 20, 1942, just over two months after the devastating attack on Pearl Harbor, O'Hare was serving aboard the aircraft carrier USS Lexington. The carrier was part of Task Force 11, operating in the South Pacific with the aim of disrupting Japanese operations at Rabaul. The wounds of Pearl Harbor were still fresh, and the United States Navy was eager to strike back against Japanese aggression.

As the task force sailed through the Coral Sea, radar operators aboard the Lexington detected an incoming formation of nine Japanese Mitsubishi G4M "Betty" bombers. These long-range bombers posed a serious threat to the carrier and the entire task force. O'Hare and his wingman, Lieutenant (junior grade) Marion Dufilho, were scrambled to intercept the incoming threat.

As they climbed to meet the enemy, disaster struck. Dufilho's guns jammed, leaving O'Hare as the sole defender between the Japanese bombers and the vulnerable Lexington. In that moment, facing overwhelming odds, O'Hare's true mettle would be tested.

## Valor in the Face of Overwhelming Odds

With a calmness that belied the gravity of the situation, O'Hare pushed his F4F Wildcat to its limits. He closed in on the enemy formation, carefully conserving his limited ammunition. In a series of daring attacks, O'Hare demonstrated not just courage, but extraordinary skill and precision.

His first pass through the enemy formation was devastatingly effective. O'Hare's well-aimed bursts of fire tore into two of the bombers, sending them plummeting into the sea. But the young pilot knew his work was far from done. Banking hard, he came around for another attack.

Time and again, O'Hare braved the defensive fire from the bombers, each pass bringing down another enemy aircraft. By the time he had expended the last of his ammunition, five Japanese bombers had fallen to his guns, with a sixth severely damaged.

O'Hare's actions were nothing short of miraculous. In the span of a few minutes, he had single-handedly broken up the Japanese attack, saving the Lexington and potentially hundreds of American lives. As he returned to the carrier, low on fuel and out of ammunition, the magnitude of his achievement began to sink in.

## Recognition and Legacy

News of O'Hare's extraordinary feat spread quickly. His actions were hailed as one of the most daring single-handed combat missions in aviation history. For his "conspicuous gallantry and intrepidity" in action, O'Hare was awarded the Medal of Honor, becoming the first naval aviator to receive this highest military decoration during World War II.

President Franklin D. Roosevelt, in presenting the medal, praised O'Hare's "gallant action and selfless devotion to duty" which were "in keeping with the highest traditions of the United States Naval Service." O'Hare was also promoted to Lieutenant Commander, a testament to both his heroism and his leadership abilities.

O'Hare's story captured the imagination of a nation still reeling from the shock of Pearl Harbor. Here was a young American hero who had stood alone against the enemy and emerged victorious. His actions not only saved lives but also provided a much-needed morale boost to a country finding its footing in a global conflict.

## The Final Mission

Tragically, O'Hare's brilliant career was cut short on November 26, 1943. Leading the U.S. Navy's first-ever nighttime fighter attack launched from an aircraft carrier, O'Hare's plane was lost in action near the Gilbert Islands. Despite extensive search efforts, neither O'Hare nor his aircraft were ever found.

The loss of such a skilled and courageous pilot was a blow to the Navy and the nation. However, O'Hare's legacy lived on. In 1949, Chicago's Orchard Field Airport was renamed O'Hare International Airport in his honor, ensuring that his name would be remembered for generations to come.

## Conclusion

The story of Edward "Butch" O'Hare is more than just a tale of individual heroism. It is a testament to the courage, skill, and sacrifice of the men and women who served in the United States military during World War II. O'Hare's actions on February 20, 1942, stand as a shining example of the difference one person can make in the face of overwhelming odds.

## Sources

Backlund, Herman. Setting the Record Straight About O'Hare, the Hero. H. Backlund. 1993

Gordon, John S. Pearl Harbor: A History. New York: Simon & Schuster, 2001.

Various Sources

# Resistance Heroes

# The Formation and Impact of Resistance Groups

World War II was not only a battle fought on the front lines but also a struggle for survival and dignity among those oppressed by Nazi tyranny and Axis occupation. While conventional warfare dominated the headlines, a parallel struggle unfolded behind enemy lines, marked by the formation of European resistance groups. These groups, composed of ordinary citizens, soldiers, and defectors, played a crucial role in undermining the Axis powers and ultimately contributed significantly to the war's outcome.

**The Context of Resistance:** The rise of resistance movements during World War II can be traced back to the rapid expansion of Axis powers throughout Europe in the late 1930s and early 1940s. Countries such as France, Poland, Belgium, Norway, and the Netherlands fell under Nazi occupation, leading to widespread discontent and despair among their populations. The brutal methods employed by the Nazis—mass arrests, executions, forced labor, and the Holocaust—fueled anger and a desire for retribution among those who were oppressed.

As the war progressed, the initial shock of occupation transformed into organized resistance efforts. The initial small-scale acts of defiance—such as distributing anti-Nazi pamphlets, sabotaging German supply lines, or hiding individuals targeted by the regime—gradually evolved into more coordinated and sophisticated networks. These resistance groups were often formed out of necessity, drawing on a mix of political activists, former military personnel, and ordinary citizens united by a common goal: to free their nations from oppression.

**Early Resistance Efforts:** Resistance efforts began taking shape even before the full-scale occupation of countries. In France, for instance, the fall of Paris in June 1940 prompted a surge of underground movements. The most notable of these was the **French Resistance**, which comprised various groups with differing ideologies, including communists, socialists, and nationalists. Key figures like Jean Moulin worked tirelessly to unify these factions, leading to the formation of the **Conseil National de la Résistance** (CNR) in 1943. This organization coordinated efforts across France, providing a framework for sabotage, intelligence gathering, and the dissemination of information.

In Poland, the **Home Army (Armia Krajowa)** was established to oppose both Nazi and Soviet occupations. The Home Army operated under the Polish government-in-exile and was responsible for significant operations, including the **Warsaw Uprising** in 1944, which sought to liberate the capital as the Soviet army approached. Similarly, in Norway, the **Norwegian Resistance** grew in response to German occupation, with its members participating in high-profile sabotage operations, such as the destruction of the heavy water plant at Vemork, which was critical to Nazi Germany's nuclear weapons program.

**The Role of External Support:** The effectiveness of resistance movements was often bolstered by external support from Allied nations. The **Office of Strategic Services (OSS)** in the United States and the **Special Operations Executive (SOE)** in Britain played pivotal roles in strengthening these groups. The SOE, in particular, was tasked with "setting Europe ablaze," providing training, weapons, and financial support to various resistance movements across the continent.

For instance, agents were parachuted into occupied territories to assist local groups in their operations. This external backing was crucial, especially in early resistance efforts that struggled with limited resources. The connections built through these alliances facilitated the exchange of information and strategies, enhancing the effectiveness of the resistance.

**Acts of Sabotage and Intelligence Gathering:** One of the primary activities of resistance groups was sabotage. These actions ranged from disrupting supply lines to damaging critical infrastructure. For example, in France, resistance fighters engaged in railway sabotage, derailing trains carrying German troops and supplies. This not only hindered the enemy's logistical capabilities but also boosted the morale of the local population, demonstrating that the occupiers were not invulnerable.

Intelligence gathering was another crucial function of resistance movements. Local operatives provided valuable information about German troop movements, fortifications, and plans, which were relayed to Allied command. The D-Day landings on June 6, 1944, were significantly aided by reports from the French Resistance, which helped the Allies understand the layout of defenses along the coast.

In Poland, the Home Army's intelligence network was responsible for gathering crucial information about Nazi atrocities, including the systematic extermination of Jews. This information was essential in raising awareness among the Allies and pushing for action against the Holocaust.

**The Human Cost of Resistance:** While resistance groups played a vital role in undermining the Axis powers, their activities came at a tremendous cost. Members of these groups faced severe reprisals, including torture, execution, and mass arrests. In France, for example, the Gestapo conducted widespread crackdowns on suspected resistance members, leading to the execution of thousands. The resistance was often forced to operate in secrecy, and betrayal from within could lead to devastating consequences.

Despite these dangers, the resolve of resistance fighters remained unwavering. Their commitment to the cause of freedom and justice inspired many to join their ranks, creating a network of solidarity among those who opposed the occupiers.

**The Impact on the War's Outcome:** The contributions of resistance movements were felt across Europe and played a significant role in the overall outcome of the war. As the tide began to turn in favor of the Allies, the actions of resistance groups intensified. Their sabotage operations disrupted German operations at critical moments, while their intelligence efforts provided vital information that enabled successful military campaigns.

The liberation of France in 1944 highlighted the importance of the resistance. French fighters played a significant role in the liberation of Paris, coordinating with Allied forces to ensure a successful operation. The successful uprisings and coordinated efforts in occupied territories demonstrated that the Axis powers could be challenged from within.

Moreover, the ideological ramifications of the resistance movements had a lasting impact on post-war Europe. The experiences of those who fought against fascism contributed to the establishment of democratic governments and the promotion of human rights in the aftermath of the war. **Conclusion**

The formation of resistance groups during World War II was a testament to the human spirit's resilience in the face of tyranny. These groups, often composed of ordinary citizens, played a crucial role in the fight against Axis powers, contributing significantly to the war's outcome. Through acts of sabotage, intelligence gathering, and unwavering commitment, they undermined the occupiers and inspired hope among their fellow countrymen.

# Sisters from the Dutch Resistance

## Introduction

World War II saw countless acts of bravery by ordinary citizens who rose up against the brutal occupation of their countries by Nazi forces. Among these resistance fighters were two Dutch sisters, Truus and Freddie Oversteegen, whose courage, determination, and resourcefulness made them critical to the Dutch Resistance. Together with their friend and fellow resistance fighter Hannie Schaft, the Oversteegen sisters played a pivotal role in sabotaging Nazi operations, assassinating collaborators, and rescuing Jewish children from persecution.

Truus and Freddie Oversteegen were only teenagers when they joined the resistance movement, but their youth did not prevent them from participating in highly dangerous missions. They became adept at deception, ambushes, and sabotage, using their perceived innocence to lull their targets into a false sense of security. The story of Truus and Freddie is one of remarkable bravery and a testament to the power of ordinary people standing up against tyranny.

This is the true story of Truus and Freddie Oversteegen, their fight against the Nazi occupation of the Netherlands, and their legacy as symbols of resistance.

## Early Life

Truus Oversteegen was born in 1923, followed by her younger sister Freddie in 1925. They grew up in a working-class family in Haarlem, a city in the Netherlands. Raised by their single mother, Trijn Oversteegen, the sisters were taught from an early age to be independent, self-reliant, and socially conscious. Their mother was a strong-willed woman who instilled in her daughters a deep sense of justice and a commitment to helping those in need.

Before the war, the Oversteegen family lived in a modest houseboat, where their mother sheltered refugees fleeing Nazi Germany. This early exposure to the plight of refugees, combined with their mother's anti-fascist beliefs, shaped the sisters' views on injustice and oppression. When Nazi Germany invaded the Netherlands in May 1940, life for the Oversteegen family, like many others, was turned upside down.

The German occupation brought with it the horrors of Nazi ideology—persecution of Jews, forced labor, and the brutal suppression of any form of resistance. Truus and Freddie, barely out of childhood, were soon drawn into the fight against the occupiers. Despite their youth, their desire to resist the Nazis was fierce, and it wasn't long before the Dutch Resistance recruited them.

## Joining the Resistance

In 1941, when Truus was just 16 years old and Freddie was 14, the two sisters were approached by a member of the Dutch Resistance who saw potential in their boldness and determination. At first, their mother hesitated to let her daughters get involved in such dangerous work, but ultimately, she gave her blessing. The sisters were eager to do their part to help rid their country of the Nazi oppressors.

The Sisters were first approached by Haarlem Council of Resistance commander Frans van der Wiel after they were seen passing out anti-Nazi pamphlets. The Oversteegen sisters were assigned to a resistance group specializing in sabotage, assassinations, and intelligence gathering. They were so valuable to the resistance because of their youth and appearance. As teenage girls, Truus and Freddie were often underestimated by the Nazis and their collaborators. They were able to travel without drawing much suspicion, which allowed them to carry out covert missions with relative ease.

Their initial tasks involved distributing underground newspapers, pamphlets, and anti-Nazi propaganda, which helped to bolster morale and inform the public about resistance activities. However, as the war intensified, the sisters took on far more dangerous roles. They began sabotaging railway lines used by the Germans, blowing up bridges, and participating in ambushes of Nazi troops and collaborators.

## Assassinations and Sabotage

One of the most harrowing aspects of the Oversteegen sisters' work in the resistance was their involvement in assassinations. Alongside their close friend Hannie Schaft, known as "the Girl with the Red Hair," Truus and Freddie were tasked with eliminating Nazi collaborators and high-ranking German officers. These missions were fraught with danger, as they required careful planning and execution.

One of their most successful tactics involved using their youthful innocence to lure their targets into a trap. The sisters would approach Nazi officers in public places, such as bars or cafes, and flirt with them, leading the unsuspecting men into secluded areas where they would be ambushed by other resistance fighters. In some cases, Truus and Freddie carried out the assassinations themselves, shooting the collaborators at close range.

Despite the danger and moral complexity of their work, the sisters understood that eliminating key Nazi figures and collaborators was necessary to protect the resistance and save lives. Truus later recounted that while the missions were difficult, she believed that their actions were justified in the context of the war. She once said, "I didn't feel like killing people, but we had to stop them."

## Rescuing Jewish Children

In addition to their work in sabotage and assassinations, Truus and Freddie Oversteegen were also involved in rescuing Jewish children from the Nazis. As the persecution of Jews intensified, the sisters helped to smuggle Jewish children out of the Netherlands, finding them safe hiding places with sympathetic families. These operations were incredibly dangerous, as anyone caught aiding Jews faced severe punishment, including death.

The Oversteegen sisters worked closely with other resistance members to create escape routes and false identification papers for the children. Freddie, in particular, was adept at forging documents that allowed the children to pass as non-Jews, helping them avoid detection by the Gestapo. The sisters' efforts saved the lives of many Jewish children who would have otherwise been sent to concentration camps.

Their involvement in rescuing Jewish children was one of the most emotionally taxing aspects of their resistance work. The sisters had to maintain their composure in the face of constant danger, knowing that the lives of innocent children depended on their actions.

**Hannie Schaft and the Resistance**

The Oversteegen sisters were particularly close to Hannie Schaft, another young woman who became a key figure in the Dutch Resistance. Schaft, who was studying law at the University of Amsterdam before joining the resistance, shared the sisters' fierce dedication to fighting the Nazis. The three young women became inseparable, carrying out missions together and supporting one another through the psychological toll of their work.

Hannie Schaft's distinctive red hair made her easily recognizable, and as her notoriety grew, she became one of the most wanted resistance fighters in the Netherlands. In 1945, just weeks before the end of the war, Schaft was captured by the Nazis. Despite being tortured, she refused to give up any information about the resistance. On April 17, 1945, Hannie Schaft was executed by the Nazis. Her death was a devastating blow to Truus and Freddie, who had considered her not only a comrade but a sister in arms.

**Repercussions and Legacy**

The efforts of Truus and Freddie Oversteegen, alongside their fellow resistance fighters, had a significant impact on the Dutch resistance movement during World War II. Though the occupation of the Netherlands lasted until the end of the war in 1945, the activities of resistance groups like theirs helped to disrupt Nazi control, sabotage German operations, and save the lives of many Jewish people and others targeted by the Nazis.

The sisters' bravery in carrying out dangerous missions—including assassinations of collaborators, sabotage of infrastructure, and the rescue of Jewish children—came with a heavy emotional toll. Both Truus and Freddie spoke later in life about the trauma they experienced during the war. Taking lives, even in the name of resistance, was not something either of them took lightly. Freddie, in particular, reflected on how difficult it was for her to process the violence they had to enact in their fight against Nazi collaborators.

After the war, the Oversteegen sisters continued to live in the Netherlands, though they pursued different paths. Truus Oversteegen became an activist, artist, and public speaker. She dedicated much of her post-war life to advocating for the recognition of resistance fighters, including their friend Hannie Schaft, who had been executed by the Nazis in 1945. Truus' efforts ensured that Schaft became a national hero in the Netherlands, with annual memorial services held in her honor.

Freddie, on the other hand, led a quieter life. She rarely spoke publicly about her wartime experiences, preferring to stay out of the spotlight. Both sisters, however, remained committed to preserving the memory of the Dutch resistance and the sacrifices made by their comrades. Over the years, they received numerous honors for their bravery, including the Mobilization War Cross, a Dutch military decoration awarded for service during World War II.

In 2014, Truus and Freddie were awarded the Willem Arondéus Medal, a Dutch honor given to individuals who demonstrated extraordinary courage during the war. This recognition was a testament to their contributions to the resistance movement and their lifelong dedication to fighting for justice.

Freddie Oversteegen passed away in 2018 at the age of 92, and Truus had passed away two years earlier in 2016. Their legacy, however, endures. The story of the Oversteegen sisters has become emblematic of the many unsung heroes of World War II—ordinary people who took extraordinary risks to fight against tyranny and injustice. Their commitment to the cause of freedom and their refusal to back down, even in the face of incredible danger, continues to inspire new generations.

## Conclusion

Truus and Freddie Oversteegen's story is a powerful reminder of the courage displayed by resistance fighters during World War II. As young women, they risked their lives to fight against Nazi occupation, using their skills in sabotage, deception, and combat to strike back at the forces of oppression. Their determination to resist, even when the odds seemed insurmountable, underscores the impact that ordinary individuals can have in the face of extraordinary evil.

## Sources

Brady, Tim. Three Ordinary Girls: The Remarkable Story of Three Dutch Teenagers Who Became Spies, Saboteurs, Nazi Assassins – and WWII Heroes. Citadel, 2021.

Castelein, Klaas. The Dutch Resistance 1940-1945: World War II Resistance and Collaboration in the Netherlands. Osprey Publishing, 2022.

## Courage and Resistance in Naples

**Introduction**

World War II was marked by countless acts of heroism and resistance against tyranny, especially in occupied territories where ordinary citizens rose to confront the horrors of fascism. One such hero was Maddalena "Lenuccia" Cerasuolo, a resident of Naples, Italy, who played a pivotal role in organizing local resistance against Nazi soldiers. Cerasuolo, along with her fellow Neapolitans, bravely faced down Nazi troops, attacking barracks to free captives and surrounding a group of soldiers in a factory. Her daring actions demonstrated remarkable courage and contributed significantly to the Allied war effort. This story explores Cerasuolo's background, the context of her resistance in Naples, and her subsequent contributions to the Special Operations Executive (SOE).

**Roots of Resistance: Lenuccia's Early Life**

Maddalena Cerasuolo, affectionately known as "Lenuccia," was born on February 2, 1922, in the Stella Quarter of Naples, Italy. Her childhood unfolded against the backdrop of a nation grappling with the rise of fascism and the looming specter of war. Lenuccia's father, Carlo Cerasuolo, was more than just a cook; he was a man whose experiences in World War I had forged him into a staunch monarchist and anti-fascist. This political awareness would prove to be a defining influence on young Lenuccia's life.

The Cerasuolo family, like many in Naples, faced economic hardships. After losing his job as a cafeteria manager, Carlo, along with his wife Annunziata Capuozzo, turned to street food vending, selling fried pizzas to make ends meet. This entrepreneurial spirit in the face of adversity was a trait that Lenuccia would inherit and later channel into her resistance activities.

Growing up in a politically conscious household, Lenuccia was exposed to anti-fascist ideals from an early age. The streets of Naples, with their vibrant culture and close-knit communities, became her classroom, teaching her the value of solidarity and the importance of standing up for one's beliefs. As a young woman, Lenuccia found work in a shoe factory, a job that would later play an unexpected role in her resistance activities.

## The Gathering Storm: Naples Under Occupation

As the 1930s gave way to the 1940s, the political climate in Italy grew increasingly tense. The alliance between Mussolini's fascist regime and Nazi Germany plunged the country into World War II, bringing untold suffering to its people. Naples, with its strategic port and industrial significance, became a target for Allied bombing and, later, German occupation.

The situation in Naples deteriorated rapidly following Italy's armistice with the Allies on September 8, 1943. As the Italian government's control crumbled, German forces moved swiftly to occupy key positions in the city. The Neapolitans found themselves caught between the retreating Italian forces, the advancing Allies, and the occupying Germans.

It was in this chaotic environment that Lenuccia's journey from factory worker to resistance fighter began. The catalyst for her involvement came when the German occupiers introduced compulsory labor services for young males. Lenuccia's primary motivation was to protect her brother, John, from being captured and forced into labor. This personal stake in the resistance movement would soon evolve into a broader commitment to her city's liberation.

## The Four Days of Naples: Lenuccia's Finest Hour

The turning point in Lenuccia's life, and indeed in the history of Naples, came with the eruption of "Le Quattro Giornate di Napoli" (The Four Days of Naples) from September 27 to September 30, 1943. This spontaneous uprising against the German occupation forces marked a defining moment in the Italian Resistance movement.

Lenuccia's role in this uprising was nothing short of heroic. Alongside her father and other partisans from the Materdei and Stella neighborhoods, she took part in the defense of the Ponte della Sanità, a crucial bridge that served as a vital entrance to the city. The strategic importance of this position cannot be overstated – it not only controlled access to the city but also protected a critical branch of the aqueduct supplying water to central Naples.

The scene at the Ponte della Sanità was one of intense drama and danger. Lenuccia, armed with courage and determination, stood shoulder-to-shoulder with seasoned fighters. Her presence was not merely symbolic; she actively engaged in combat, participating in gunfights to repel German troops attempting to loot a nearby shoe factory – perhaps the very one where she had once worked.

One of the most remarkable aspects of Lenuccia's involvement was her willingness to put herself in harm's way by volunteering to negotiate directly with Nazi officials. This was an extraordinarily risky endeavor, as she did not have the protection of the Geneva Convention. Her bravery in these face-to-face encounters with the enemy showcased not only her courage but also her quick thinking and diplomatic skills.

## Beyond the Four Days: Continued Resistance

The liberation of Naples on October 1, 1943, by Allied forces did not mark the end of Lenuccia's involvement in the resistance. Her commitment to the cause led her to collaborate with the British Special Operations Executive (SOE), where she operated under the alias "Maria Esposito." In this capacity, she participated in missions codenamed "Hillside II" and "Kelvin," which aimed to sabotage German military installations.

While these later missions did not achieve their intended objectives, they demonstrated Lenuccia's unwavering dedication to the resistance cause. Her willingness to continue the fight, even after her city's liberation, speaks volumes about her character and her belief in the broader struggle against fascism and oppression.

## Recognition and Legacy

Lenuccia's extraordinary contributions to the Neapolitan Resistance did not go unnoticed. In recognition of her bravery during the Four Days of Naples, she was awarded the Bronze Medal of Military Valor, a prestigious honor that acknowledged her significant role in the city's liberation.

The impact of Lenuccia's actions extended far beyond the immediate aftermath of the war. Her story became an integral part of Naples' collective memory, a symbol of the city's resilience and fighting spirit. A commemorative plaque installed in her honor serves as a tangible reminder of her bravery and the sacrifices made by the people of Naples during those tumultuous days.

## The Aftermath: A Life Shaped by Resistance

The years following the war brought new challenges and opportunities for Lenuccia and her fellow resistance fighters. Like many who had participated in the liberation struggle, she faced the task of reintegrating into civilian life in a nation that was rebuilding itself politically and socially. The transition from resistance fighter to civilian was not always easy, as the experiences of war and occupation left deep scars on both individuals and communities.

While specific details about Lenuccia's post-war life are scarce, it is likely that she, like many of her contemporaries, continued to advocate for the ideals she had fought for during the resistance. The Italian Republic, founded in 1946, was built on the principles of democracy and anti-fascism championed by resistance fighters like Lenuccia.

## Conclusion

The story of Maddalena "Lenuccia" Cerasuolo is more than just a tale of individual heroism; it is a window into a pivotal moment in Italian history. Through her actions during the Four Days of Naples and beyond, Lenuccia embodied the spirit of resistance that would ultimately lead to Italy's liberation and its post-war rebirth as a democratic nation.

Lenuccia's journey from a shoe factory worker to a decorated resistance fighter illustrates the extraordinary circumstances that can transform ordinary individuals into heroes. Her willingness to risk her life, whether in armed combat or tense negotiations with enemy officials, speaks to a courage that transcends gender and age.

In the end, Maddalena "Lenuccia" Cerasuolo's legacy is not just about her wartime exploits, but about the enduring power of resistance, the importance of standing up for one's beliefs, and the vital role that ordinary citizens play in shaping the destiny of their communities and nations. As long as her story continues to be told, the spirit of the Neapolitan Resistance – and the courage of those who fought for freedom – will live on, inspiring future generations to stand firm in the face of tyranny and injustice.

**Sources**

Behan, Tom. The Italian Resistance: Fascists, Guerillas and the Allies. Pluto Press, 2009.

Luzzatto, Sergio, Promo Levi's Resistance: Rebels and Collaborators in Occupied Italy. Metropolitan Books, 2016.

Cotugno, Olga. Maddalena Cerasuolo, the heroine of Naples. Movery.it. 2021.

# The Girl with Red Hair

### Introduction

In the dark days of World War II, when the shadow of Nazi occupation loomed over the Netherlands, a young woman with fiery red hair emerged as a beacon of hope and resistance. Hannie Schaft, known to many as "the girl with the red hair," became one of the most iconic figures of the Dutch Resistance. Her story is one of unwavering courage, fierce determination, and ultimate sacrifice in the face of tyranny. From her early days as a law student to her daring exploits as a resistance fighter, Hannie Schaft's life exemplifies the extraordinary lengths to which ordinary people will go to defend freedom and justice. This is the tale of a woman who chose to fight against overwhelming odds, leaving an indelible mark on the history of the Netherlands and inspiring generations to come.

### A Childhood Shaped by Justice

Jannetje Johanna Schaft, known to history as Hannie Schaft, was born on September 16, 1920, in the city of Haarlem, Netherlands. From her earliest years, Hannie was immersed in an environment that valued education and social justice. Her father, Pieter Schaft, was a teacher, and her mother, Aafje Talea Vrijer, was a homemaker who instilled in her daughter a strong sense of moral responsibility. The Schaft household was a place of intellectual curiosity and ethical discussions, laying the foundation for Hannie's future commitment to fighting injustice.

Growing up in the interwar period, Hannie witnessed the rise of fascism in Europe with growing concern. Her parents' emphasis on education and critical thinking encouraged her to question the world around her and to stand up for what she believed was right. This upbringing would prove crucial in shaping the choices Hannie would make when her country faced its darkest hour.

### From Law Student to Resistance Fighter

Hannie's academic prowess led her to the University of Amsterdam, where she pursued a law degree. Her dream was to become a human rights lawyer, a career that aligned perfectly with her deep-seated sense of justice. However, the outbreak of World War II and the subsequent Nazi occupation of the Netherlands in May 1940 would dramatically alter the course of her life.

The harsh realities of occupation quickly became apparent. The Nazis imposed severe restrictions on Dutch society, particularly targeting the Jewish population. For Hannie, who had Jewish friends and classmates, the injustice was intolerable. She could not stand idly by while people she knew and cared about were persecuted and deported.

Hannie's transition from law student to resistance fighter was gradual but resolute. It began with small acts of defiance – helping Jewish friends hide, distributing illegal newspapers, and forging identity documents. As the occupation intensified, so did Hannie's involvement in the resistance. She joined the Raad van Verzet (Council of Resistance), a group known for its more militant approach to fighting the Nazis.

## The Girl with Red Hair in Action

Hannie's striking red hair, which would later become her trademark, initially posed a security risk. To avoid detection, she often dyed it black or wore wigs. Despite these precautions, her courage and skill soon made her one of the most effective – and most wanted – resistance fighters in the Netherlands.

Hannie's activities in the resistance were diverse and daring. She became part of a famous trio with sisters Truus and Freddie Oversteegen, undertaking some of the most dangerous missions against the Nazi occupiers. Her law background proved invaluable in gathering intelligence and planning operations.

One of Hannie's most crucial roles was in sabotage operations. She participated in missions to blow up railway lines and disrupt communication systems, severely hampering the German war effort. These actions required not only bravery but also meticulous planning and execution.

Perhaps the most perilous of Hannie's activities were the assassination missions targeting high-ranking Nazi officers and Dutch collaborators. Working closely with fellow resistance member Jan Bonekamp, Hannie carried out several successful operations. These missions were fraught with danger, requiring nerves of steel and split-second decision-making.

Hannie's work as a courier was equally vital to the resistance effort. She transported weapons, illegal newspapers, and other crucial materials across Nazi-occupied territory. This role demanded quick thinking and composure under pressure, qualities that Hannie possessed in abundance.

## A Voice for the Voiceless

Throughout her time in the resistance, Hannie never lost sight of her original motivation – protecting the vulnerable, especially the Jewish community. She was deeply involved in efforts to rescue Jewish children, finding them safe houses and forging the necessary documents to protect them from deportation. These actions saved countless lives and demonstrated Hannie's unwavering commitment to human rights.

Truus Oversteegen, one of Hannie's closest allies in the resistance, later spoke of the emotional toll their work took. "It was tragic and very difficult and we cried about it afterwards," Truus recalled, highlighting the immense psychological burden carried by these young resistance fighters. Yet, despite the hardships and dangers, Hannie's determination never wavered.

## The Final Mission

As the war entered its final stages, the Nazis intensified their efforts to crush the Dutch Resistance. On March 21, 1945, while distributing the illegal communist newspaper "De Waarheid" (The Truth), Hannie was arrested at a military checkpoint in Haarlem. Even in captivity, her spirit remained unbroken.

Despite the war's imminent end, the Nazis were determined to make an example of the infamous "girl with the red hair." On April 17, 1945, just three weeks before the Netherlands was liberated, Hannie Schaft was executed in the dunes near Bloemendaal.

## Legacy of Courage

Hannie Schaft's death, so close to the war's end, was a tragic loss for the resistance movement and the Netherlands as a whole. However, her courage and sacrifice quickly became a symbol of Dutch resilience and defiance against oppression.

In the years following the war, Hannie's story spread throughout the Netherlands and beyond. She was posthumously awarded several honors, including the Resistance Memorial Cross. The Dutch government recognized her contributions, and her story became an integral part of the nation's collective memory of the war years.

Today, Hannie Schaft's legacy lives on in numerous ways. Streets and schools bear her name, ensuring that new generations learn of her bravery. The Hannie Schaft Foundation, established to honor her memory, works to promote the values she fought for – freedom, justice, and human rights.

Annual commemorations, particularly on National Remembrance Day, pay tribute to Hannie and other resistance fighters. Her grave in the Erebegraafplaats in Overveen has become a place of pilgrimage for those seeking to honor her memory.

Hannie's story has inspired numerous books, films, and documentaries, each seeking to capture the essence of her courage and commitment. These works ensure that the "girl with the red hair" continues to inspire and educate, long after her passing.

## Conclusion

The story of Hannie Schaft is more than just a tale of wartime heroism; it is a testament to the power of individual conviction in the face of overwhelming evil. From her early days as a law student dreaming of defending human rights to her final moments facing Nazi executioners, Hannie's life was defined by an unwavering commitment to justice and freedom.

Her journey from an idealistic young woman to a skilled and daring resistance fighter illustrates the transformative power of moral courage. In choosing to fight against the Nazi occupation, Hannie not only risked her life but also sacrificed her personal dreams and aspirations for a greater cause.

The legacy of "the girl with red hair" extends far beyond the Netherlands. It serves as a powerful reminder that even in the darkest of times, individuals can make a difference. Hannie's story challenges us to consider our moral courage and what we might be willing to sacrifice in the defense of our principles.

**Sources**

Atwood, Kathryn. Women Heroes of World War II. Chicago Review Press, 2011.

Brady, Tim. Three Ordinary Girls. The Remarkable Story of Three Dutch Teenagers Who Became Spies, Saboteurs, Nazi Assassins and World War II Heroes. Highbridge, 2021.

Other Sources

# The Brave Saboteur

### Introduction

World War II was characterized by acts of incredible bravery and resilience among those who resisted Nazi oppression. Among these heroes was Hélène Podlasky, a French Resistance member who faced the horrors of being a prisoner of war (POW) and subsequently found herself forced into slave labor in a German factory. Despite the dire conditions, Podlasky demonstrated extraordinary courage by sabotaging the production of Panzerfausts, the infamous single-shot anti-tank weapons used by the Nazis. Her story is one of defiance against tyranny and an unwavering commitment to the fight for freedom. This story delves into Podlasky's background, her experiences as a POW, and her acts of sabotage that contributed to the resistance against the Nazi war machine.

### Early Life and Involvement in the Resistance

Hélène Podlasky was born in 1920 in France, where she grew up in a politically active environment that fostered her sense of justice and civic duty. As a young woman, she became increasingly aware of the injustices brought about by the Nazi occupation of France following the German invasion in 1940. The harsh realities of war and occupation motivated her to join the French Resistance, where she contributed to various anti-Nazi activities, including distributing leaflets and gathering intelligence.

Podlasky's commitment to the Resistance put her at great risk, and she eventually became a target for the Nazis. In 1943, she was arrested by the Gestapo and subsequently imprisoned. Her capture did not deter her spirit; instead, it strengthened her resolve to continue resisting Nazi oppression.

### Life as a POW and Slave Laborer

Following her arrest, Podlasky was transported to Germany, where she was held as a POW. Many captured members of the French Resistance were subjected to harsh treatment and forced labor, and Podlasky was no exception. She was sent to a factory in Germany where she was forced to work on the production of Panzerfausts, a crucial weapon for the German military.

The conditions in the factory were grueling. Workers, many of whom were POWs or forced laborers, endured long hours, inadequate food, and brutal oversight by German guards. Despite the oppressive environment, Podlasky sought ways to undermine the Nazi war effort from within.

## Working at the Factory

Upon arrival at the factory, Hélène Podlasky quickly realized the importance of the Panzerfaust in German military strategy. The weapon was designed to be a simple, effective anti-tank weapon that could be operated by a single soldier. Production ramped up significantly as the war progressed, which meant that the factory was under intense pressure to meet production quotas.

Podlasky was assigned to work in the temperature garage, a critical area where the metal castings for the Panzerfausts were treated to ensure they hardened properly. The success of the weapon depended on the precise temperature and timing of the metal casting process. Hélène understood that if she could sabotage this process, it could lead to catastrophic failures in the weapons produced.

## The Sabotage Plan

Drawing on her experience in the Resistance, Podlasky devised a plan to disrupt the production of the Panzerfausts. She began to discreetly sabotage the temperature regulation system in the garage. This involved manipulating the settings and equipment so that the castings would not reach the necessary temperatures for proper hardening.

Hélène worked carefully, knowing that discovery would mean severe punishment or even execution. She took advantage of the chaotic environment within the factory, where the production demands often led to oversights by the guards and supervisors. Her position allowed her to move around with some degree of freedom, which she used to her advantage.

## Executing the Sabotage

As the days turned into weeks, Hélène continued her sabotage efforts. She meticulously adjusted the temperature settings, ensuring that the metal castings would remain soft and malleable instead of hardening into the resilient material required for the Panzerfausts. The metal would need to glow red hot for appearances but did not reach the optimal temperature for hardening.

The results were soon evident. The first batch of sabotaged Panzerfausts was sent out to the front lines. Reports began to emerge of failures in the weapons during training exercises. Soldiers found that the castings often exploded or malfunctioned when fired, leading to injuries and confusion among the ranks. This was precisely the outcome Hélène had aimed for—she was disrupting the enemy's capabilities through her cunning and bravery.

## The Consequences of Her Actions

Podlasky's sabotage efforts did not go unnoticed. As failures in the Panzerfausts began to rise, the German military launched an investigation into the production process. Hélène understood that the increased scrutiny could lead to her exposure. When confronted, she acted simple-minded and confused with the interrogation questions. She was monitored but was not found to be deviating from the hardening standards she was trained on. However, she remained resolute, believing that her actions were contributing to the larger goal of defeating the Nazis.

Despite the risks, her determination to undermine the Nazi war effort never wavered. Hélène continued her work, knowing that each sabotaged weapon represented a small victory against her oppressors. Her courage inspired other laborers around her, some of whom were also members of the Resistance or had been involved in anti-Nazi activities.

**Liberation and Legacy**

As the war progressed and Allied forces began to advance into Germany, the conditions for POWs and forced laborers began to change. In early 1945, as the situation became increasingly precarious for the Nazis, the factory was on high alert, fearing sabotage from within.

Eventually, Allied troops liberated the area, freeing Podlasky and her fellow laborers. Although she had endured tremendous hardship, Hélène emerged from her experiences with a sense of purpose and determination to continue the fight for freedom.

Hélène Podlasky's actions during her time as a slave laborer in Germany have been included in various historical accounts of the French Resistance. Her unique contributions highlight the role of women in the resistance movement and the creative ways in which individuals could undermine the Nazi war effort.

Podlasky's story has been featured in documentaries and books focused on the experiences of women during World War II, emphasizing the importance of their roles in resistance movements. Her acts of sabotage are celebrated as examples of courage in the face of overwhelming odds.

**Conclusion:**

Hélène Podlasky's remarkable actions during World War II exemplify the extraordinary courage and resilience of those who resisted Nazi oppression. Her sabotage of the Panzerfaust production process not only contributed to the weakening of the German military but also highlighted the vital role of individuals in the broader struggle for freedom.

**Sources**

Gildea, Robert. Fighters in the Shadows: A New History of the French Revolution. Belknap Press, 2015.

Cobb, Matthew. The Resistance: The French Fight Against the Nazis. Simon & Schuster, 2013.

# The Young Heroine of the Soviet Resistance

## Introduction

Zinaida Portnova is a poignant symbol of youthful heroism and resistance during World War II. Born in Leningrad in 1926, she became a member of the Young Communist League (Komsomol) and later a courageous fighter in the Soviet partisan movement against Nazi Germany. Her story is one of bravery, ingenuity, and tragic sacrifice, embodying the spirit of resistance among Soviet youth during the war. As the world faced one of its darkest hours, Zinaida's actions illuminated the resilience of ordinary people who stood up against tyranny.

## Early Life and the War's Onset

Zinaida Portnova grew up in a working-class family in Leningrad (now Saint Petersburg), a vibrant city known for its rich cultural heritage and revolutionary history. Her early life was typical of many Soviet teenagers, involving school and participation in youth organizations like the Komsomol, which fostered a sense of community and political engagement among the youth. Zinaida was an active participant in these organizations, where she learned about the ideals of communism and the importance of collective action.

However, her life dramatically changed in 1941 when Nazi Germany invaded the Soviet Union on June 22, marking the beginning of the Eastern Front of World War II. The invasion brought chaos and destruction to the Soviet homeland. In the aftermath of the invasion, Zinaida's family, like many others, faced the harrowing decision to flee their home in search of safety. Shortly after the German occupation began, her family evacuated to the village of Vasilishki in Belarus, a region that would soon become a major center of partisan resistance against the occupying forces.

In Vasilishki, Zinaida witnessed the brutal realities of war firsthand. The village was filled with fear and uncertainty as the German army established control. Families were torn apart, and the lives of ordinary citizens were upended. Yet, amid the despair, Zinaida became increasingly aware of the potential for resistance. The stories of bravery from adults and other young people around her sparked a fire within her to fight back against the oppressors. This desire for freedom and justice would soon lead her to take up arms.

## Joining the Partisans

In 1942, at the age of 16, Zinaida made a life-changing decision to join the underground Komsomol organization, which was actively involved in the Soviet partisan resistance movement. This group consisted of young people who were determined to fight against the Nazi occupation and support the Soviet war effort. Zinaida's enthusiasm and commitment quickly caught the attention of her peers and leaders within the movement.

Her initial tasks involved intelligence gathering and distributing anti-Nazi leaflets to raise awareness among the local population about the resistance effort. Zinaida quickly demonstrated an aptitude for these tasks, using her charm and intelligence to gather vital information about German troop movements and supply lines. However, her role soon expanded as the partisans recognized her determination and capabilities. She was eager to take on more significant responsibilities that would directly confront the enemy.

As she became more involved in the partisan activities, Zinaida honed her skills in sabotage and guerrilla warfare. The partisans operated in small, mobile groups, relying on the cover of forests and rural landscapes to launch surprise attacks against German forces. The danger was ever-present, but Zinaida's youthful spirit and unwavering resolve drove her to take part in increasingly daring operations.

## Sabotage and Acts of Resistance

Zinaida's involvement in active resistance began with her work at a German food warehouse in the Vasilishki area, where she obtained a job through her partisan connections. This position allowed her to gather critical intelligence about German supply chains and the everyday lives of enemy soldiers. Using her position, she managed to poison the food stores, causing severe illness among the German soldiers stationed there. This act of sabotage not only disrupted the enemy's operations but also boosted the morale of her fellow partisans and the local population.

Following this successful act of sabotage, Zinaida continued to engage in more direct combat activities. She participated in ambushes against German patrols, showcasing her ability to handle firearms and navigate dangerous situations. The thrill of resistance fueled her spirit, and she quickly became known among her comrades for her bravery and ingenuity.

During one particularly daring operation, Zinaida and her unit planned an ambush on a supply convoy that was known to travel a specific route through the forest. As the convoy approached, the partisans lay in wait, camouflaged by the dense underbrush. When the time was right, they launched their attack, utilizing rifles and homemade explosives to devastating effect. Zinaida played a crucial role in the ambush, demonstrating her tactical skills and fearlessness in the face of danger.

Despite the success of such operations, the constant threat of German retaliation loomed large. The Nazis were notorious for their brutal reprisals against local populations suspected of aiding partisans. Zinaida's resolve only grew stronger as she witnessed the suffering of her fellow citizens. She knew that every act of resistance was not just a blow against the enemy but also a message of hope for those living under oppression.

## Capture and Imprisonment

However, in late 1943, Zinaida's activities eventually led to her capture by the Nazis. It is believed that local informants, possibly coerced by the Germans, provided information about her involvement in the partisan movement. The moment she was apprehended marked a turning point in her life. She was subjected to three months of brutal interrogation and torture, as the Germans tried to extract information about partisan networks and future plans.

During her imprisonment, Zinaida endured unimaginable hardships. The Nazis employed various methods of torture to break her spirit and force her to betray her comrades. Despite the severe treatment, she remained defiant, showcasing an extraordinary level of mental strength and resilience. Her unwavering commitment to the cause was evident; she refused to betray her comrades or reveal any significant information, even under the most harrowing conditions.

The psychological and physical torment she faced in captivity only strengthened her resolve. Zinaida's bravery during this time became a source of inspiration for her fellow prisoners, who admired her courage in the face of such brutality. Stories of her defiance spread among the prisoners, and she became a symbol of hope and resistance, demonstrating that even in the darkest moments, one could stand firm against tyranny.

## Escape and Final Act of Defiance

Zinaida's courage shone even during captivity. In a daring moment during one of her interrogations, she managed to seize the opportunity to escape. Using her quick thinking, she shot a German officer with his own pistol during an interrogation session. This act of defiance exemplified her determination to fight back even in the face of death.

Unfortunately, Zinaida's brief escape was short-lived. She was recaptured shortly after she attempted to flee, and the consequences of her actions were severe. The Nazis, enraged by her defiance, sought to make an example of her. They intensified their efforts to extract information from her, but Zinaida remained resolute, refusing to give in.

According to some accounts, during her final confrontation with the Germans, she fought fiercely. Zinaida's spirit and determination were evident as she resisted her captors with all her might. Tragically, she was ultimately killed by her captors in January 1944, at the tender age of 17. Her death marked the loss of a young hero who had already made significant contributions to the fight against fascism.

## Legacy and Recognition

Zinaida Portnova's bravery and sacrifice did not go unnoticed. Following the war, her story became a poignant reminder of the courage and resilience that characterized the Soviet resistance. In recognition of her extraordinary contributions, Zinaida was posthumously awarded the title of Hero of the Soviet Union in 1958, the highest honorary title bestowed by the Soviet state for acts of heroism.

Numerous monuments and memorials have been erected in her honor across Belarus and Russia, ensuring that her legacy endures in the collective memory of the nation. Schools and youth organizations have been named after her, celebrating her spirit of resistance and dedication to the cause of freedom.

Zinaida's story is particularly significant as it highlights the role of women and young people in the Soviet resistance against Nazi Germany—a testament to the widespread involvement of ordinary citizens in the war effort. Portnova became an iconic figure representing the fierce patriotism and resilience of the Soviet people during one of the darkest periods in their history.

**Conclusion**

Zinaida Portnova's life and heroics during World War II reflect the extraordinary contributions of youth to the Soviet war effort. Her story is a powerful reminder of the personal sacrifices made by individuals in the larger context of global conflict. It underscores the impact that one determined person can have, even against the backdrop of a devastating war. Zinaida remains a symbol of bravery and resistance, inspiring future generations to remember the cost and heroes of the past.

**Sources**

Zander, Patrick G. Hidden Armies of the Second World War: World War II Resistance Movements. Praeger, 2017.

Ishak, Natasha. Zinaida Portnova: The Teenage Partisan Who Became a Soviet Hero During World War II. AllThatsInteresting.com, 2020.

# From Resistance Fighter to War Hero

## Introduction

During World War II, the French Resistance played a critical role in disrupting Nazi operations in occupied France. Among the courageous individuals who joined the fight was Andrée Borrel, a young Frenchwoman who became a key figure in the clandestine operations of the British Special Operations Executive (SOE). Borrel, known for her bravery, resourcefulness, and dedication to the cause of freedom, was instrumental in organizing sabotage missions and aiding Allied forces. Tragically, her service came to a brutal end when she was captured by the Gestapo and executed at the Nazi concentration camp at Natzweiler-Struthof in 1944.

This is the story of Andrée Borrel, a French Resistance fighter and SOE agent whose fearless actions helped pave the way for the liberation of France. Through her life and death, Borrel remains a symbol of resistance and sacrifice in the face of tyranny.

## Patriotism and Duty

Andrée Raymonde Borrel was born on November 18, 1919, in Bécon-les-Bruyères, a suburb of Paris. Raised in a working-class family, Borrel was known for her intelligence, determination, and adventurous spirit. As a young woman, she trained as a nurse, a skill that later proved invaluable in her resistance activities. At the outbreak of World War II, Borrel was living in Paris and, like many young French people, was deeply affected by the German invasion of France in 1940.

In the aftermath of the French defeat, Borrel, driven by a sense of patriotism and duty, became involved in resistance activities. Along with her close friend and fellow nurse Denise Bloch, Borrel joined the French Resistance and began assisting in the clandestine efforts to sabotage the Nazi occupation. Her role in the resistance would quickly evolve from distributing underground newspapers to taking part in more dangerous missions involving sabotage and espionage.

## Joining the French Resistance

Borrel's involvement in the French Resistance began in 1941, shortly after the German occupation of France. She joined a group of young resistance fighters led by Georges Lamarque. The group was focused on harassing German forces through acts of sabotage, including the destruction of railways, military installations, and communication lines. Borrel's primary responsibilities were helping Allied soldiers and downed pilots escape to neutral Spain and caring for wounded members of the Resistance.

Her nursing background made her an invaluable asset to the Resistance, but it was her courage and quick thinking that set her apart. In one instance, Borrel helped guide an Allied airman through Nazi-occupied territory, risking her life to ensure his safe passage. These early experiences solidified Borrel's commitment to the Resistance, and she quickly became one of its most trusted members.

By 1942, Borrel's skills and reputation had caught the attention of the British Special Operations Executive (SOE), an organization created by Winston Churchill to conduct espionage, sabotage, and reconnaissance in occupied Europe. The SOE was actively recruiting French nationals who could work behind enemy lines, and Borrel's resistance work made her an ideal candidate.

## Recruited by the Special Operations Executive (SOE)

In 1942, Andrée Borrel was recruited by the SOE to work as a field agent in France. After undergoing extensive training in sabotage, parachuting, and radio operations in Britain, Borrel was assigned to the Prosper network, a key SOE circuit operating in and around Paris. The Prosper network, named after its leader Francis Suttill (code-named "Prosper"), was tasked with organizing and coordinating resistance groups, distributing weapons and supplies, and carrying out acts of sabotage against German forces.

On the night of September 24, 1942, Borrel became one of the first female SOE agents to parachute into occupied France. Alongside Lise de Baissac, another female agent, Borrel landed in a field near the town of Mer in the Loire Valley. From there, she made her way to Paris, where she immediately began working with the Prosper network to expand resistance operations.

As an SOE agent, Borrel took on the code name "Denise" and was responsible for setting up safe houses, organizing sabotage missions, and facilitating the delivery of weapons and explosives to resistance fighters. She worked closely with Francis Suttill and other SOE agents, coordinating efforts to weaken the German occupation through targeted attacks on military installations, railway lines, and supply depots.

## The Betrayal of the Prosper Network

For several months, the Prosper network flourished under Borrel's and Suttill's leadership, carrying out a series of successful sabotage operations that disrupted German military logistics. However, the growing success of the network attracted the attention of the German secret police, the Gestapo. Unbeknownst to Borrel and her colleagues, the network had been infiltrated by a German double agent, Henri Déricourt, who had been passing information to the Gestapo.

In June 1943, the Gestapo launched a massive crackdown on the Prosper network. On June 23, 1943, Francis Suttill was arrested by the Gestapo in Paris, and over the following weeks, dozens of other agents, including Andrée Borrel, were captured. Borrel was betrayed by Déricourt and arrested by the Gestapo on June 23, 1943, just days after Suttill's capture. She was immediately taken to Gestapo headquarters for interrogation.

## Interrogation and Imprisonment

Following her arrest, Andrée Borrel was subjected to brutal interrogation by the Gestapo, but despite being tortured, she refused to betray her fellow resistance fighters or reveal any valuable information.

Borrel's courage and stoic refusal to cooperate with the Nazis earned her the admiration of her fellow prisoners. Her resilience in the face of torture was a testament to her unwavering commitment to the cause of the French Resistance.

After months of imprisonment in Paris, Borrel was transferred to Fresnes Prison and later deported to Ravensbrück concentration camp, a notorious camp for women. Along with other SOE agents, Borrel was singled out for execution by the Nazis due to her involvement in resistance activities. In July 1944, Borrel and three other female SOE agents, Denise Bloch, Vera Leigh, and Diana Rowden, were transferred to the Natzweiler-Struthof concentration camp in Alsace.

**Execution at Natzweiler-Struthof**

On July 6, 1944, Andrée Borrel, along with the other SOE agents, was executed by lethal injection at Natzweiler-Struthof. After being injected, their bodies were cremated in the camp's ovens. Borrel was just 24 years old at the time of her death. The execution of Borrel and her fellow agents was part of the Nazis' effort to eliminate key members of the French Resistance and undermine SOE operations in occupied France.

The capture and execution of Andrée Borrel was a significant blow to the SOE's operations in France, but it did not spell the end of the French Resistance. The efforts of Borrel and her fellow agents helped inspire continued resistance against the German occupation, and their sacrifices were honored in the years following the war.

In the post-war years, Borrel and the other SOE agents who were executed at Natzweiler-Struthof were posthumously awarded some of the highest honors in France and Britain. **Conclusion**

Andrée Borrel's story is one of extraordinary bravery, resilience, and sacrifice. From her early days as a nurse and resistance fighter in France to her role as a key agent in the SOE, Borrel displayed an unwavering commitment to the fight against Nazi tyranny. **Sources**

Gildea, Robert. Fighters in the Shadows: A New History of the French Resistance. Belknap, 2015.

Janes, Keith, Hellier, Stella. Andree Borrel. Conscript Heroes. 2002.

# Unifier of the French Resistance

## Introduction

Jean Moulin, a name synonymous with courage and resilience, emerged as a key figure in the French Resistance during World War II. His efforts to unify disparate resistance groups under a single banner were instrumental in galvanizing France's fight against Nazi occupation. Despite facing unimaginable challenges, Moulin's leadership and sacrifices left a profound impact on the course of the war and on France's post-war history. This narrative explores Jean Moulin's pivotal role in the French Resistance, his enduring legacy, and the ultimate sacrifice he made for his country.

## From Civil Servant to French Resistance Hero

Jean Moulin was born on June 20, 1899, in Béziers, France. A highly talented and ambitious individual, Moulin began his career as a civil servant, eventually becoming a prefect—a significant administrative role within the French government. His career was marked by a deep commitment to public service and an adherence to democratic principles.

With the outbreak of World War II and the subsequent fall of France in 1940, Moulin's role shifted dramatically. The Vichy government, led by Marshal Philippe Pétain, collaborated with the Nazi regime, creating a climate of oppression and resistance. This period of occupation saw the emergence of various resistance groups, each with its own agenda and methods. Recognizing the need for a unified front against the occupiers, Moulin became a central figure in orchestrating this collaboration.

## The Call to Resistance

In the wake of the armistice signed with Germany in June 1940, France was divided into occupied and unoccupied zones. The Vichy government, led by Pétain, endorsed Nazi policies and enacted repressive measures against dissenters. It was during this tumultuous period that Jean Moulin, driven by his deep patriotism and sense of duty, became involved in the resistance movement.

Initially working behind the scenes, Moulin's activities were marked by clandestine efforts to support and coordinate resistance activities. His experience and administrative skills made him an ideal candidate to help unify the fragmented resistance groups operating across France.

## Unification Efforts

In 1942, Moulin was appointed by Charles de Gaulle, the leader of the Free French Forces, to bring together the various resistance factions under a single organizational structure. This task was monumental, given the diverse nature of the resistance groups, which ranged from communist factions to conservative elements and various local cells with differing strategies and goals.

Jean Moulin used his considerable administrative skills to negotiate and mediate between different factions, advocating for a unified resistance front. His efforts culminated in the creation of the National Council of the Resistance (CNR) in May 1943. This body brought together representatives from various resistance groups, including communists, socialists, and other political movements.

## Challenges and Betrayal

Jean Moulin's work was fraught with danger. The Gestapo, the Nazi secret police, was relentless in its pursuit of resistance leaders, employing sophisticated methods of surveillance and infiltration. Despite his precautions, Moulin was betrayed by a double agent within the resistance network.

In June 1943, Moulin was arrested by the Gestapo in Lyon. His capture marked the beginning of a harrowing ordeal. Despite intense torture and brutal interrogation, Moulin refused to divulge information about his fellow resistance members or the workings of the CNR. He was tortured by infamous Nazi interrogator and torturer Klaus Barbie, known as the Butcher of Lyon.

## Legacy and Recognition

Jean Moulin's ultimate sacrifice had a profound impact on the French Resistance and the Allied war effort. His ability to unify the resistance groups played a crucial role in strengthening the internal resistance against Nazi occupation and provided a more organized and effective opposition to the Germans.

After his death in July 1943, Moulin was posthumously recognized for his bravery and contributions. He was awarded the Grand Cross of the Legion of Honour, France's highest decoration, and remains a revered figure in French history.

## Conclusion

Jean Moulin's role in the French Resistance was pivotal in unifying disparate groups into a cohesive force against Nazi occupation. His strategic acumen, leadership, and unwavering commitment to the cause of liberation demonstrated extraordinary courage and dedication.

## Sources

Marnham, Patrick. Army of the Night: The Life and Death of Jean Moulin, Legend of the French Resistance. Bloomsbury, 2022.

Chemins de Memoire. In the Footsteps of the Resistance in Lyon. Ministere Des Armees,

# The Smiling Resistance Fighter

## Introduction

World War II was not only a battle between armies on open fronts but also a struggle in the shadows, where resistance fighters played a crucial role in the fight against Nazi oppression. Across Europe, underground networks worked tirelessly to sabotage German efforts, gather intelligence, and assist the Allied cause. Among these brave individuals was Georges Blind, a member of the French Resistance who became a symbol of defiance in the face of Nazi terror. Blind's story, particularly his legendary smile during a staged execution by German soldiers, has come to represent the unwavering courage of resistance fighters who, despite the danger and fear, refused to bow to their oppressors. This true story recounts the life of Georges Blind, his involvement in the Resistance, his arrest, and the moment that cemented his legacy.

## The Early Life of Georges Blind

Georges Blind was born on January 7, 1904, in Belfort, a small town in the northeastern part of France near the border with Germany. Belfort, with its strategic location, had been a point of contention between France and Germany for centuries, and it would play a pivotal role during both world wars. Like many in his generation, Blind grew up with a sense of national pride and a deep-seated resentment for the German occupation that had plagued his country during World War I and now again in World War II.

Before the war, Georges Blind led an ordinary life, working as a fireman for the city of Belfort. He was known by those around him as a calm, reliable man who showed a sense of responsibility toward his family and community. However, when the German occupation of France began in 1940, Blind, like many others, felt compelled to resist. He could not stand by and watch as his homeland was subjugated by the Nazis, and so he joined the French Resistance, risking his life for the freedom of his country.

## Joining the French Resistance

As part of the French Resistance, Blind became a member of an underground network dedicated to undermining the Nazi regime. Resistance groups across France were involved in a wide range of activities, from sabotaging railways and communication lines to gathering intelligence for the Allies and helping downed Allied pilots escape to safety. Although the Resistance was made up of ordinary citizens—students, farmers, factory workers, and the like—it proved to be a significant thorn in the side of the Nazi occupation.

The Resistance in the Alsace-Lorraine region, where Blind was active, was particularly important. This region, which bordered Germany, had been annexed by the Nazis and was heavily militarized. Resistance fighters like Blind played a crucial role in disrupting the German war effort in the area, gathering intelligence, and coordinating with the broader Resistance network across France.

The work of the Resistance was incredibly dangerous. The Gestapo, Nazi Germany's secret police, were relentless in their efforts to crush the Resistance. Anyone caught helping the movement faced severe punishment, including imprisonment, torture, and execution. Despite the ever-present threat of betrayal and capture, Georges Blind continued to work with his Resistance comrades, sabotaging German operations and gathering valuable intelligence to support the Allied war effort.

**Arrest and Imprisonment**

In October 1943, Georges Blind was arrested by the Gestapo. The circumstances surrounding his capture remain somewhat unclear, but it is believed that he was betrayed by an informant. Blind, like many members of the Resistance, knew the risks involved in his work, and he had prepared himself mentally for the possibility of arrest. However, the reality of being taken into Gestapo custody was far more brutal than any preparation could have made it.

After his arrest, Blind was taken to Montbéliard, where he was interrogated by the Gestapo. The Nazis were notorious for their brutal interrogation techniques, often resorting to torture to extract information from prisoners. It is almost certain that Blind was subjected to physical and psychological torture during his time in captivity, as the Gestapo sought to uncover details about his Resistance network and other members of the movement.

Despite the Gestapo's efforts, Georges Blind refused to cooperate. He gave no information about his comrades, choosing instead to remain silent in the face of overwhelming pressure. This defiance only heightened the Gestapo's frustration, and they decided to make an example of him. Blind's refusal to break, even under the most trying circumstances, epitomized the spirit of resistance that had come to define the movement across Europe.

**The Staged Execution**

One of the most famous moments in Georges Blind's life occurred during his imprisonment. After failing to extract any useful information from him, the Gestapo decided to stage a mock execution in an attempt to break his spirit. The plan was to lead him to believe that he was about to be executed by firing squad in the hopes that, in his final moments, he would divulge the information they sought.

On an October morning in 1943, Blind was led out of his cell by German soldiers. They took him to a courtyard, where they had arranged a firing squad. Blind was placed in front of a wall, and the soldiers raised their rifles, ready to fire on command. It was at this moment, when most people would have been gripped by fear, that Georges Blind did something remarkable—he smiled.

A photograph taken during this staged execution captured Blind standing calmly before the firing squad, with a smile on his face. The image has since become iconic, symbolizing the unbreakable resolve of the Resistance and the defiance of those who refused to bow to Nazi terror. Blind's smile was not one of arrogance or contempt but rather a demonstration of his inner strength and his refusal to give the Gestapo the satisfaction of seeing him break.

The staged execution did not succeed in extracting any information from Blind, and the photograph stands as a testament to his incredible courage in the face of death.

## The Final Days of Georges Blind

Unfortunately, Georges Blind's defiance was not enough to save him from the fate that awaited many Resistance fighters. After the failed mock execution, he was transferred to a concentration camp—likely one of the many labor camps established by the Nazis to imprison and exploit those who were considered enemies of the Reich.

Details of his final days are scarce, but it is widely believed that Georges Blind died in the concentration camp, likely from the harsh conditions, malnutrition, or disease that claimed the lives of so many who were imprisoned by the Nazis.

## Legacy and Impact

The story of Georges Blind, particularly the photograph of him smiling in the face of his would-be executioners, has become a symbol of the indomitable human spirit. His actions during his time with the French Resistance, and his unyielding defiance in the face of Nazi terror, continue to inspire those who hear his story. The photograph of Blind standing before the firing squad, with a calm and confident smile, has been published in history books, magazines, and memorials dedicated to the Resistance.

## Conclusion

The story of Georges Blind, the smiling Resistance fighter, is a powerful reminder of the courage ordinary people can display in the face of unimaginable adversity. Blind's unwavering defiance in the face of the Gestapo, and his calm smile during a staged execution, exemplify the spirit of the French Resistance and the determination of those who fought against Nazi tyranny.

## Sources

Gildea, Robert. Fighters in the Shadows: A New History of the French Resistance. Belknap Press, 2015.

Fraga, Kaleena. 11 Incredible Stories of Resistance Fighters Who Took on the Nazis. AllThatsIntesrting.com, 2023.

# The Life and Legacy of Dietrich Bonhoeffer

## Introduction

Dietrich Bonhoeffer stands as one of the most profound figures in the history of theology, ethics, and resistance against tyranny during World War II. A German Lutheran pastor, theologian, and anti-Nazi dissident, Bonhoeffer's life and work were marked by a deep commitment to his faith, a profound understanding of morality, and a willingness to take action against the injustices perpetrated by Adolf Hitler's regime. His involvement in the German resistance movement led to his execution by the Nazis in April 1945. Bonhoeffer's legacy endures as a symbol of moral courage, highlighting the importance of standing up against oppression and injustice, even at great personal cost.

## Early Life and Education

Dietrich Bonhoeffer was born on February 4, 1906, in Breslau, Germany (now Wrocław, Poland), into a prominent and educated family. His father, Karl Bonhoeffer, was a psychiatrist, and his mother, Paula, was a teacher. Growing up in a liberal and intellectual environment, Dietrich was exposed to a variety of philosophical and theological ideas that would shape his worldview.

In 1923, Bonhoeffer began studying theology at the University of Tübingen, where he quickly distinguished himself as a gifted student. He later transferred to the University of Berlin, where he studied under prominent theologians such as Adolf von Harnack and Emil Brunner. Bonhoeffer's theological perspective was deeply influenced by his interaction with other scholars and his experiences in the ecumenical movement.

## The Rise of Nazism

As Bonhoeffer was completing his studies, Germany was undergoing significant political turmoil. The rise of Adolf Hitler and the Nazi Party in the early 1930s posed a profound threat to the moral and ethical foundations of German society. The Nazis promoted an ideology rooted in anti-Semitism, nationalism, and totalitarianism, leading to the marginalization and persecution of various groups, particularly Jews.

Bonhoeffer, increasingly alarmed by the growing influence of the Nazi regime, began to articulate his opposition to its policies. His commitment to social justice and human dignity, deeply rooted in his Christian faith, compelled him to confront the moral implications of the Nazis' actions.

**Theological Opposition to Nazism**

In 1933, as Hitler came to power, Bonhoeffer became actively involved in the Confessing Church, a movement within German Protestantism that resisted the Nazi regime's attempts to control the church. The Confessing Church opposed the Nazi-sponsored "German Christian" movement, which sought to align Protestantism with Nazi ideology. Bonhoeffer's theological stance emphasized the importance of maintaining the integrity of the Christian faith in the face of political pressure.

Bonhoeffer's writings from this period reflect his deep conviction that Christians must act against injustice. He famously stated," Silence in the face of evil is itself evil." This belief would guide his actions as he sought to oppose the regime's policies and protect the victims of Nazi oppression.

**A Call to Action**

In 1939, as the threat of war loomed large, Bonhoeffer traveled to the United States for a brief period of study at Union Theological Seminary in New York City. While in America, he became increasingly troubled by the complacency of some Christians in the face of injustice and the rise of fascism in Europe. He returned to Germany in 1939, convinced that he could not remain silent or inactive while his country faced such moral decay.

Upon his return, Bonhoeffer became involved in various resistance efforts, including efforts to assist Jews in escaping the Nazis. He used his connections to help smuggle Jewish individuals out of Germany and into safer territories. His work placed him at significant personal risk, but his faith compelled him to act.

**Involvement in the Resistance**

As World War II progressed, Bonhoeffer's involvement in the resistance deepened. He was introduced to a group of conspirators plotting to assassinate Hitler, which included military officers and political dissidents. The group, known as the Kreisau Circle, sought to overthrow the Nazi regime and establish a new, democratic government.

Bonhoeffer's theological insights played a crucial role in shaping the ethical framework of the resistance. He believed that the Christian faith demanded active opposition to evil and that the moral imperative to act could justify violent resistance if necessary. This belief was not taken lightly, as it challenged traditional Christian teachings on pacifism and the sanctity of life.

In 1943, Bonhoeffer was appointed as a secret liaison between the resistance and the German military. His role involved facilitating communication and planning among various factions opposed to Hitler. He continued to advocate for a return to a just and ethical society, believing that the time had come for Christians to take a stand against tyranny.

## Arrest by the Gestapo

On April 5, 1943, Bonhoeffer was arrested by the Gestapo. His involvement in the resistance and his efforts to assist Jews had made him a target for the Nazi regime. Following his arrest, Bonhoeffer was imprisoned in various locations, including the notorious Tegel Prison in Berlin.

During his imprisonment, Bonhoeffer maintained his commitment to his faith and continued to write extensively. He penned letters, essays, and theological reflections that explored the moral and ethical implications of his actions. His writings during this period reveal a deep sense of hope and a profound understanding of the human condition, even in the face of despair.

Despite the harsh conditions of prison life, Bonhoeffer remained resilient. He continued to minister to fellow prisoners, offering support and guidance to those who were suffering. His commitment to his faith and his unwavering moral compass provided solace to those around him.

## Trial and Execution

As the war progressed and the tide turned against the Nazis, Bonhoeffer's fate became increasingly precarious. In February 1945, he was transferred to the concentration camp at Flossenbürg. As the Allies advanced into Germany, the Nazis sought to eliminate potential threats to their regime.

On April 8, 1945, just weeks before the end of the war in Europe, Bonhoeffer was executed by hanging. His death came as a devastating blow to his family, friends, and the broader resistance movement. He was only 39 years old.

## Impact on Theology and Ethics

Dietrich Bonhoeffer's legacy extends far beyond his martyrdom. His writings, particularly "The Cost of Discipleship" and "Letters and Papers from Prison." continue to influence Christian theology and ethics. His concept of "cheap grace"—the idea that grace should not be taken for granted without true commitment to the teachings of Christ—remains a profound challenge to Christians today.

Bonhoeffer's thoughts on the relationship between faith and action, particularly in the context of social justice, resonate with contemporary discussions on the role of religion in public life. His insistence on the necessity of taking a stand against evil has inspired countless individuals and movements advocating for human rights and social change.

## Commemoration and Recognition

In recognition of his bravery and moral courage, numerous memorials and institutions have been established in Bonhoeffer's honor. His legacy is celebrated in many ways, including events, lectures, and theological discussions that explore his impact on faith and ethics.

The Dietrich Bonhoeffer Society, founded in 1996, aims to promote his writings and ideas, fostering dialogue about the relevance of his thoughts in contemporary society. Additionally, many churches and organizations commemorate his life on April 9, the anniversary of his execution, as a day of reflection and remembrance.

Bonhoeffer's story has also been captured in literature and film, ensuring that his contributions to theology and resistance are not forgotten. Works such as Bonhoeffer: Pastor, Martyr, Prophet, Spy by Eric Metaxas, and various documentaries explore his life and legacy, bringing his story to new audiences.

## A Symbol of Resistance

Dietrich Bonhoeffer has become a symbol of moral courage in the face of tyranny. His life exemplifies the struggle to reconcile faith with action, particularly in times of crisis. In a world where moral dilemmas persist, Bonhoeffer's example encourages individuals to stand up against injustice, even when it comes at a great personal cost.

His writings on ethics, responsibility, and the nature of discipleship challenge individuals to consider their role in society and the impact of their actions. Bonhoeffer's life serves as a reminder that the fight against oppression is not only a political struggle but also a deeply spiritual one.

## Influence on Contemporary Movements

Bonhoeffer's legacy continues to inspire contemporary movements advocating for social justice, human rights, and religious freedom. His emphasis on the importance of community and solidarity resonates with those working to address systemic injustices and promote equality.

In many ways, Bonhoeffer's message is more relevant today than ever. As societies grapple with issues of oppression, discrimination, and violence, his call to act against injustice remains a powerful challenge to individuals and communities worldwide.

## Conclusion

Dietrich Bonhoeffer's life and legacy are a testament to the enduring power of faith, courage, and moral integrity. His commitment to resisting tyranny and standing up for justice, even at the cost of his own life, serves as an inspiration for generations to come.

## Sources

Metaxas, Eric. Bonhoeffer: Pastor, Martyr, Prophet, Spy. Thomas, Nelson, 2020.

Hull, Bill. Bonhoeffer in Prison. The Bonhoeffer Project.

# The Courageous Story of the White Rose Group

## Introduction

The story of the White Rose is one of remarkable bravery, moral conviction, and the indomitable spirit of youth in the face of tyranny. During the dark years of Nazi Germany, a group of students at the University of Munich formed a clandestine resistance movement that sought to expose the atrocities of the Third Reich and awaken the German people to the need for active opposition. Through their powerful written words and bold actions, the members of the White Rose left an indelible mark on the history of resistance against Nazi oppression.

## The Founding Members

The White Rose was founded in June 1942 by Hans Scholl, a 24-year-old medical student, and his 21-year-old sister Sophie, who studied biology and philosophy at the University of Munich. They were joined by Christoph Probst, Alexander Schmorell, and Willi Graf, all of whom were students at the university and shared a deep disgust towards the Nazi regime and its crimes against humanity.

The group's name, "The White Rose," was chosen as a symbol of purity and innocence in the face of the dark evil of Nazism. The members of the White Rose were inspired by their Christian faith and belief in the fundamental dignity and rights of all human beings, regardless of race, religion, or nationality.

## The Leaflet Campaign

The primary activity of the White Rose was the creation and distribution of a series of six leaflets that denounced the Nazi regime and called on the German people to resist. The leaflets, which Hans Scholl and Alexander Schmorell wrote, were printed on a hand-operated duplicating machine, distributed through the mail, left in telephone booths, and placed on parked cars.

The first four leaflets, published between June and July 1942, focused on exposing the atrocities committed by the Nazi regime, including the persecution and murder of Jews, the suppression of individual freedoms, and the corruption of German society. The leaflets also called on the German people to engage in passive resistance against the Nazi state, such as by refusing to donate to Nazi charitable organizations or to give the "Heil Hitler" salute.

The fifth and sixth leaflets, published in January and February 1943, were more explicitly political and called for the overthrow of the Nazi government. These leaflets were distributed in several German cities, including Hamburg, Stuttgart, and Vienna, with the help of other resistance groups.

**Expansion and Collaboration**

As the White Rose grew in size and influence, it began collaborating with other resistance groups within Germany and abroad. The group established contacts with the German resistance group the Kreisau Circle and fighters in France and Norway.

In addition to their leaflet campaign, the members of the White Rose engaged in other forms of resistance, such as painting anti-Nazi slogans on buildings and collecting donations for the families of political prisoners.

**Arrest, Trial, and Execution**

On February 18, 1943, Hans and Sophie Scholl were caught distributing leaflets at the University of Munich by a custodian who was a member of the Nazi party. They were arrested and interrogated by the Gestapo, along with Christoph Probst, who was implicated by a draft of a seventh leaflet found in Hans Scholl's pocket.

On February 22, 1943, the three were brought before the People's Court, a Nazi tribunal notorious for its ruthless treatment of political dissidents. In a trial lasting less than an hour, Hans, Sophie, and Christoph were found guilty of treason and sentenced to death. They were executed by guillotine the same day.

In the months that followed, other members of the White Rose, including Alexander Schmorell, Willi Graf, and Kurt Huber, a professor who had helped the group, were also arrested, tried, and executed.

**Conclusion**

Despite the tragic fate of its members, the White Rose has endured as a powerful symbol of resistance against tyranny and oppression. Hans Scholl wrote in one of the White Rose leaflets, "We will not be silent. We are your bad conscience. The White Rose will not leave you in peace!"

**Sources**

Spitzer, Tanja B. Sophie Scholl and the White Rose. The National WWII Museum. 2020.

Ray, Michael. White Rose. Britannica.com. 2003.

# Holocaust Heroes

# The Forger Who Saved Thousands

## Introduction

In the chronicles of World War II resistance movements, few stories are as compelling and impactful as that of Adolfo Kaminsky. Born into a world on the brink of chaos, Kaminsky's life would become inextricably linked with one of history's darkest periods. His journey from a young Jewish immigrant to a master forger for the French Resistance is a testament to the power of individual action in the face of overwhelming oppression. This story explores Kaminsky's extraordinary life, his ingenious techniques, and the profound impact his work had on saving thousands of lives during the Holocaust and beyond.

## Early Life and Background

Adolfo Kaminsky's story begins far from the European theater of World War II. Born on October 1, 1925, in Buenos Aires, Argentina, Kaminsky was the child of Russian Jewish parents who had fled the pogroms in their homeland. This early experience of displacement would foreshadow the role Kaminsky would later play in helping others escape persecution.

The Kaminsky family's search for safety and opportunity led them to France when Adolfo was still a child. Settling in Paris, they faced the challenges common to many immigrant families of the time – financial hardship and the struggle to assimilate into a new culture. Despite these difficulties, young Adolfo showed an early aptitude for chemistry, a skill that would prove crucial in his future clandestine activities.

Kaminsky's interest in chemistry blossomed during his work at a dye shop. Here, he gained invaluable knowledge about the properties of various chemicals and dyes, laying the foundation for his later expertise in document forgery. Little did he know that this seemingly mundane job would one day equip him with the skills to save thousands of lives.

## War Begins

The rise of Nazi power in Europe and the subsequent occupation of France in 1940 dramatically altered the course of Kaminsky's life. As a Jewish family, the Kaminskys found themselves directly threatened by the anti-Semitic laws and deportations initiated by the Vichy regime and the occupying German forces.

This environment of danger and persecution set the stage for Adolfo's involvement in the French Resistance.

Kaminsky's entry into the world of forgery was both serendipitous and born of necessity. His knowledge of chemistry, particularly his ability to remove permanent blue ink from official documents using lactic acid, caught the attention of resistance members. This skill was crucial for altering existing documents and creating new ones, a vital service in helping Jews and others escape persecution.

## The Master Forger at Work

Kaminsky's work as a forger during World War II was nothing short of extraordinary. Operating from a secret laboratory in Paris, he and his team worked tirelessly to produce high-quality forged documents that were virtually indistinguishable from the originals. His techniques were both innovative and meticulous, showcasing a level of skill that would save countless lives.

Kaminsky's forgery methods were diverse and sophisticated:

1. He used sewing machines to create perfect perforations in stamps.

2. He mastered the art of forging signatures to match official documents.

3. He developed techniques to reproduce watermarks, ensuring the authenticity of his creations.

4. His chemical expertise allowed him to alter existing documents seamlessly.

The scale of Kaminsky's operation was as impressive as its quality. He could produce up to 500 forged documents a week, working at a relentless pace. His famous quote, "If I sleep for an hour, 30 people will die," encapsulates the urgency and gravity of his work. This sense of responsibility drove Kaminsky to push himself to the limits of human endurance, often working for days without sleep.

## Impact on Saving Jewish Lives

The impact of Kaminsky's work during World War II cannot be overstated. His forged documents provided a lifeline for thousands of Jews facing deportation and almost certain death at the hands of the Nazi regime. Conservative estimates suggest that Kaminsky's efforts saved as many as 14,000 Jews from deportation to concentration camps.

The documents Kaminsky produced were not mere pieces of paper; they were, quite literally, the difference between life and death. A forged identity card could allow a Jewish person to pass as non-Jewish, avoiding the ever-present threat of arrest and deportation. Fake passports enabled families to flee to safer territories, escaping the tightening noose of Nazi occupation.

Kaminsky's work extended beyond just creating false identities. He also forged ration cards, which were essential for survival in the resource-starved wartime economy. These forgeries allowed people in hiding to obtain food and other necessities without arousing suspicion.

The quality of Kaminsky's work was so high that many of his forged documents were never detected. This level of craftsmanship was crucial in a time when a single mistake could lead to discovery and death. Kaminsky's attention to detail and commitment to perfection undoubtedly saved countless lives that might have been lost had his forgeries been less convincing.

## Beyond World War II

Kaminsky's commitment to fighting injustice did not end with the liberation of France in 1944. Recognizing that his skills could still be used to help those in need, he continued his work as a forger for various causes long after the war had ended.

In the immediate post-war period, Kaminsky assisted Jews attempting to immigrate to British Mandate Palestine, defying British immigration restrictions. His forged documents helped many Holocaust survivors find a new home in what would soon become the state of Israel.

During the Algerian War of Independence (1954-1962), Kaminsky put his skills to use for the Algerian National Liberation Front (FLN) and French draft dodgers. He set up another clandestine lab in Paris, continuing his tradition of working in the shadows to support those fighting against oppression.

Kaminsky's work also extended to other liberation movements across the globe. He provided support to anti-colonial struggles in Africa, including Angola and Guinea-Bissau. He aided dissidents fighting against dictatorships in Portugal and Spain, and even helped American draft dodgers during the Vietnam War.

Throughout these years, Kaminsky maintained the same principles that had guided him during World War II. He never accepted payment for his forgeries, viewing his work as a moral obligation rather than a commercial enterprise. This commitment to principle over profit underscores the depth of Kaminsky's dedication to justice and human rights.

## Legacy and Recognition

Adolfo Kaminsky's extraordinary life and work remained largely unknown to the public for many years after the war. It wasn't until much later that his story began to gain wider recognition, thanks in part to the efforts of his daughter, Sarah Kaminsky, who wrote a biography titled "Adolfo Kaminsky: A Forger's Life."

In recent years, Kaminsky's story has been featured in various media, including documentaries and television interviews. In a notable appearance on "60 Minutes," Kaminsky shared his experiences with Anderson Cooper, providing a first-hand account of his wartime activities and the techniques he used to save lives.

Kaminsky's legacy extends far beyond the documents he forged. He stands as a powerful example of how individual action, driven by moral conviction, can make a significant difference even in the face of overwhelming evil. His story challenges us to consider what we might be willing to risk for the sake of others in times of crisis.

## Conclusion

Adolfo Kaminsky's life story is a testament to the power of skill, courage, and unwavering moral conviction in the face of unimaginable adversity. From his early days as a young Jewish immigrant to his role as a master forger for the French Resistance, Kaminsky's journey embodies the best of human nature in the worst of times.

His work saved thousands of lives during World War II, providing hope and a chance at survival for Jews facing the horrors of the Holocaust. Beyond the war, Kaminsky's continued commitment to fighting injustice around the world showcases a lifelong dedication to the principles of human rights and freedom.

As we reflect on Kaminsky's extraordinary life, we are reminded of the impact that one individual can have in shaping history. His story serves as an inspiration, challenging us to consider how we might use our own skills and resources to stand up against injustice and oppression in our time.

Adolfo Kaminsky passed away on January 9, 2023, at the age of 97, leaving behind a legacy that will continue to inspire generations to come. His life's work stands as a powerful reminder that in the darkest of times, acts of courage and compassion can light the way toward a more just and humane world.

**Sources**

Reinhardt, Von Nora. The Hidden Life of the Humanitarian Forger. Spiegel International, 2011.

Rosenstein, Beryl MD. Adolf Kaminsky: A Forger's Life. WhereWhatWhen.com. 2023.

# A Diplomat's Courage

### Introduction

Hiram Bingham IV, an American diplomat, is often celebrated for his extraordinary bravery and moral courage during one of the darkest periods in history—World War II. As the Vice Consul in Marseilles, France, Bingham played a pivotal role in saving thousands of Jewish refugees from the clutches of the Nazi regime by issuing visas that allowed them to escape to safety. His actions exemplify the power of individual courage in the face of widespread persecution and highlight the moral responsibilities of those in positions of authority. This story delves into Bingham's early life, his diplomatic career, the harrowing circumstances faced by Jews in Europe, and his lasting legacy as a humanitarian hero.

### Setting and Early Life

Hiram Bingham IV was born on July 17, 1903, in Salem, Connecticut. He came from a distinguished family; his father, Hiram Bingham III, was a prominent explorer and politician who served as a U.S. Senator from Connecticut. The elder Bingham is best known for his discovery of the Incan city of Machu Picchu in 1911. Growing up in such an influential family instilled in Hiram a sense of adventure and a commitment to public service.

Bingham attended Yale University, where he studied history and graduated in 1924. He later pursued a career in diplomacy, joining the U.S. Foreign Service in 1927. His early postings took him to various locations, including South America and Europe, where he developed a reputation for diligence and competence.

By the late 1930s, Bingham had settled into his role as Vice Consul at the U.S. Consulate in Marseilles, France. This position would place him at the heart of a humanitarian crisis as World War II unfolded and the Nazis began their systematic persecution of Jews across Europe.

### The Rise of the Nazi Regime

As Hitler's regime gained power in Germany, anti-Semitic policies intensified, culminating in the widespread persecution of Jewish people. Following the Anschluss in 1938 and the subsequent outbreak of World War II in September 1939, thousands of Jews fled to France, seeking refuge from the horrors of the Holocaust. By 1940, France itself was occupied by German forces, complicating the situation for refugees who were already in the country.

The fall of France in June 1940 brought about a new wave of fear and desperation among Jewish populations. Many were trapped in a rapidly deteriorating situation, with borders closing and opportunities for escape dwindling. In this perilous context, Hiram Bingham IV began to take action that would ultimately save countless lives.

## Humanitarian Efforts in Marseilles

In 1940, Bingham became acutely aware of the plight of Jewish refugees seeking visas to escape to the United States and other countries. The bureaucratic hurdles and restrictive immigration policies made obtaining these visas increasingly difficult. However, Bingham recognized that these policies could not justify the suffering he witnessed around him.

Working in an environment rife with fear and uncertainty, Bingham began to issue visas to Jewish refugees, often against the directives of the State Department. He forged documents and provided other means of escape, including transit visas that allowed refugees to travel to third countries. His actions were motivated by a deep sense of morality and the belief that it was his duty to assist those in desperate need.

Bingham's colleagues at the consulate and local Jewish organizations were often in awe of his bravery. He worked tirelessly, often late into the night, to process visas for as many refugees as possible. His efforts were not without risk; by defying government orders, he placed himself in a precarious position. Nevertheless, he remained undeterred, driven by compassion and a commitment to saving lives.

## The Visa Campaign

Bingham's most significant contribution came through a visa campaign that allowed thousands of refugees to escape Nazi-occupied Europe. He worked closely with organizations such as the American Jewish Joint Distribution Committee and local Jewish leaders to identify individuals and families in need of assistance. His willingness to go above and beyond bureaucratic protocols made a tangible difference in many lives.

In total, Bingham is credited with helping to save approximately 2,500 Jewish lives by issuing visas. His actions provided a lifeline for those seeking to escape the horrors of the Holocaust and reach safety in the United States or other nations. Many of those he helped maintained contact with him long after the war, expressing their gratitude for his bravery and compassion.

## The Risks and Consequences

Despite his noble efforts, Bingham faced significant risks. The Vichy government, which collaborated with the Nazis, closely monitored consular activities, and Bingham's actions could have easily led to his arrest or worse. He was aware of the dangers but chose to prioritize human life over his safety.

In late 1941, Bingham's superiors in the State Department began to take notice of his activities. Concerned about potential repercussions, they ordered him to cease issuing visas and adhere strictly to government protocols. However, Bingham remained resolute in his commitment to helping refugees, continuing to issue visas in secret.

Eventually, his defiance caught up with him. In 1943, after several warnings, Bingham was recalled to Washington, D.C. His removal from Marseilles marked the end of his direct involvement in visa issuance, but not the end of his commitment to humanitarian efforts.

**Post-War Life and Recognition**

After the war, Bingham served in various diplomatic roles, including postings in South America and Europe. However, the impact of his humanitarian work during the war began to receive recognition much later. The stories of the lives he saved started to come to light as survivors began sharing their experiences.

In 1980, Bingham was recognized by Yad Vashem, Israel's official memorial to the victims of the Holocaust, as one of the Righteous Among the Nations. This honor is bestowed upon non-Jews who risked their lives to save Jews during the Holocaust. Bingham's legacy as a humanitarian and a hero began to take shape, and his contributions were celebrated by those whose lives he had touched.

**Conclusion**

Hiram Bingham IV's story serves as a powerful reminder of the impact that individual actions can have in times of crisis. His bravery and moral courage exemplify what it means to stand up against oppression and injustice. The lessons learned from his life continue to resonate, especially in discussions surrounding human rights and the moral responsibilities of individuals in positions of authority.

**Sources**

Kahn, Sam. History Ponders the Heroism of Bingham. Yale Daily News, 2005.

Eisner, Peter. Saving the Jews of France. Smithsonian Magazine, 2009.

# The Dutch Hero Who Defied the Nazis

## Introduction

In the dark days of World War II, when the Nazi regime's terror reached its apex, there were those whose courage shone as a beacon of hope amidst the devastation. Johan van Hulst, a Dutch educator and resistance fighter, is remembered for his extraordinary bravery in rescuing Jewish children from the Hollandsche Schouwburg, a deportation center in Amsterdam. Van Hulst's actions saved over 600 children from certain death, illustrating the profound impact of individual courage and moral conviction during one of history's most brutal periods.

## Joining the Futch Resistance

The Hollandsche Schouwburg, a former theater in Amsterdam, was repurposed by the Nazis as a collection and transit center for Jews being deported to concentration camps. By 1943, the Nazis had intensified their efforts to deport Jews from the Netherlands, a process that involved rounding up Jewish families and sending them to extermination camps, primarily Auschwitz and Sobibor.

Johan van Hulst was born in 1911 in Amsterdam. By the time World War II erupted, he was a prominent educator and principal at a teacher training college. His role in education and his personal convictions would later place him at the heart of a resistance network that worked tirelessly to save lives from the Holocaust.

The Dutch Resistance, a network of clandestine groups and individuals, played a critical role in defying Nazi occupation and aiding Jews and other persecuted groups. The resistance's efforts included sabotage, espionage, and direct acts of bravery such as smuggling people to safety. Van Hulst's involvement in this resistance was marked by a commitment to humanitarian principles and a willingness to confront overwhelming danger.

## Van Hulst's Role and the Rescue Operation

In 1943, as the Nazis continued their systematic round-up of Jews, the Hollandsche Schouwburg became a focal point of the deportation process. Jewish families, including children, were gathered there before being transported to concentration camps. The plight of these children, many of whom were separated from their parents and facing imminent death, deeply moved Johan van Hulst.

Van Hulst, who was already involved in underground activities, recognized the opportunity to act when he learned about the dire situation at the Schouwburg. He planned to use his position and network to rescue as many children as possible. With the help of his colleagues in the resistance, he devised a plan to smuggle children out of the deportation center and into hiding.

Van Hulst's approach involved several key strategies. He exploited his connections with local Jewish and non-Jewish networks to find safe houses and escape routes. His role was not just that of a planner but also an active participant in the logistics of the rescue operation. He used his authority and trust within his community to facilitate the safe transfer of children from the Schouwburg to these hidden locations.

## The Challenges and Risks

The operation was fraught with peril. The Nazi authorities maintained strict security around the Schouwburg, and any attempt to rescue prisoners involved significant risk of exposure. Van Hulst and his network had to navigate a complex web of surveillance and repression. Additionally, the emotional toll of dealing with the children's plight and the constant threat of arrest added to the pressure.

## The Impact and Legacy

Johan van Hulst's efforts culminated in the successful rescue of over 600 children, who were saved from deportation and likely death in Nazi concentration camps. The impact of his actions was profound, not only in terms of the lives saved but also in the morale and hope they provided to the Jewish community and the broader Dutch population.

After the war, Van Hulst's heroism was recognized by many, although he remained modest about his role. His contributions were later honored by various organizations and institutions, including being named Righteous Among the Nations by Yad Vashem, Israel's Holocaust memorial authority. His story serves as a powerful reminder of the capacity for individual bravery and moral courage in the face of tyranny.

## Conclusion

Johan van Hulst's courageous efforts to rescue Jewish children during World War II stand as a testament to the strength of the human spirit in the darkest of times. His actions saved hundreds of lives and offered a glimmer of hope amidst the horror of the Holocaust. Van Hulst's story is a poignant example of how one person's determination and compassion can make a profound difference.

## Sources

Blakemore, Erin. Dutch Teacher Who Saved 600 Jewish Children from Nazis Dies at 107. History.com, 2018.

Miller, Dr. Yvette Alt. Johan van Hulst Risked his Life to Save Jewish Children. Aish.

# Saving Hundreds of Jewish Children

## Introduction

During World War II, Europe witnessed the horrific persecution of Jews by Nazi Germany, resulting in the death of six million Jews in the Holocaust. In the face of this unimaginable horror, some individuals risked everything to save lives. One such person was Irena Sendler, a Polish social worker who, through immense courage, resourcefulness, and compassion, managed to save around 2,500 Jewish children from the Warsaw Ghetto. With the help of a clandestine network and her incredible bravery, Sendler's efforts allowed these children to escape certain death at the hands of the Nazis. This story of Irena Sendler shines as an enduring beacon of hope in the darkest of times.

## Early Life and Career

Irena Sendler (née Krzyżanowska) was born on February 15, 1910, in Warsaw, Poland, into a family of strong humanitarian values. Her father, a doctor who treated many impoverished Jewish patients, taught her the importance of compassion and helping those in need regardless of their background or religion. When Sendler was just seven years old, her father died of typhus, contracted while treating patients during an epidemic. Despite this personal loss, her father's dedication to others left a lasting impression on Sendler, shaping her outlook on life.

After completing her studies in social work at the University of Warsaw, Sendler worked as a social worker, focusing on the poorest areas of the city. Her work brought her into close contact with marginalized communities, and she developed a strong commitment to social justice and equality. These values would later guide her during the darkest days of the Holocaust.

When the Nazis invaded Poland in September 1939, life for Jews in Warsaw became increasingly unbearable. The establishment of the Warsaw Ghetto in 1940, which confined over 400,000 Jews in a small, overcrowded area of the city, marked the beginning of the systematic persecution and eventual extermination of the Jewish population. As a social worker, Sendler witnessed the growing oppression and resolved to take action, even as doing so could lead to her own death.

## The Warsaw Ghetto and the Jewish Persecution

The Warsaw Ghetto was the largest of all Jewish ghettos in Nazi-occupied Europe, and conditions there were abysmal. Disease, starvation, and violence were rampant, and residents faced constant threats of deportation to concentration camps. The situation became even more dire in July 1942, when the Nazis began mass deportations from the ghetto to the Treblinka extermination camp.

Irena Sendler, deeply moved by the suffering around her, knew that something had to be done. She became involved with the Żegota, or the Council for Aid to Jews, a Polish underground resistance organization formed to help Jews during the Holocaust. Under the leadership of Żegota, Sendler took on a crucial and dangerous role: rescuing Jewish children from the ghetto and smuggling them to safety.

Sendler had already gained access to the ghetto through her work as a social worker with the Warsaw municipality's Department of Social Welfare. Officially, she was allowed to enter the ghetto to inspect sanitary conditions and prevent the spread of disease, which allowed her to establish contact with Jewish families and organize escape plans for their children.

## The Rescue Operation

In late 1942, Irena Sendler became the head of Żegota's children's section, responsible for organizing the rescue of Jewish children from the Warsaw Ghetto. With the help of a network of brave individuals, including other social workers, nuns, and Polish families, Sendler devised ingenious ways to smuggle children out of the ghetto, sometimes one at a time, and sometimes in groups.

The escape methods varied depending on the situation, but all were fraught with danger. Some children were smuggled out through secret passageways, such as the sewers or underground tunnels. Others were hidden in ambulances or coffins, while still more were carried out in sacks or boxes as part of regular garbage collections. Babies and very young children were sometimes sedated to keep them from crying during the escape. Each method required careful planning, quick thinking, and a great deal of courage.

Once the children were out of the ghetto, Sendler and her network placed them with sympathetic Polish families, convents, or orphanages, where they were given new identities and taught to blend in as Catholic children. They were provided with false documents, including birth certificates and baptismal certificates, to help disguise their Jewish origins. Some children were even taught Catholic prayers and rituals to avoid suspicion if they were questioned by the Nazis.

One of the most remarkable aspects of Sendler's operation was her meticulous record-keeping. She believed that it was not enough just to save the children from immediate danger—she wanted to ensure that they could be reunited with their families after the war, if possible. To this end, Sendler kept detailed lists of the children's real names and their new identities, carefully recording each child's journey to safety. These lists were written on small pieces of tissue paper and hidden in glass jars, which were then buried under a tree in a friend's garden.

## Betrayal and Arrest

Despite the secrecy and care with which Sendler carried out her work, the danger of discovery was always present. In October 1943, after more than a year of successfully smuggling children out of the Warsaw Ghetto, Sendler was betrayed by a fellow worker who informed the Gestapo of her activities. She was arrested by the Nazis and taken to Pawiak Prison, a notorious detention center in Warsaw where many members of the resistance were tortured and executed.

The Gestapo interrogated Sendler for days, demanding that she reveal the names of her collaborators and the locations of the rescued children. Despite being brutally tortured, Sendler refused to divulge any information. Her courage and resolve in the face of extreme suffering saved the lives of countless children and members of the resistance. The Nazis sentenced her to death, but, incredibly, she was saved at the last moment.

Żegota, aware of Sendler's arrest, bribed a guard at Pawiak Prison to secure her release. On the day of her scheduled execution, Sendler was secretly freed and her name was added to the list of those who had been executed. This allowed her to go into hiding and continue her work with the resistance under a new identity.

## The End of the War and Sendler's Legacy

When the war ended in 1945, Irena Sendler emerged from hiding and began the heartbreaking task of trying to reunite the rescued children with their surviving family members. Tragically, many of the children's parents had perished in the Holocaust, and the children had to remain with the Polish families, convents, or orphanages where they had been placed. However, because of Sendler's careful record-keeping, hundreds of children were able to reconnect with relatives or learn about their true identities.

Sendler's heroic efforts during the war went largely unrecognized for decades. In the immediate aftermath of the war, Poland fell under Soviet control, and the new communist government downplayed the contributions of many resistance fighters, particularly those like Sendler who had worked with underground organizations like Żegota. For many years, her story remained unknown outside of Poland.

However, in the late 1990s, Irena Sendler's story began to receive international attention, thanks in part to a group of American high school students from Kansas who created a play called 'Life in a Jar', based on her life. The play brought Sendler's story to a wider audience, and she began to receive recognition for her incredible bravery. In 1965, she was named a Righteous Among the Nations by Yad Vashem, Israel's official memorial to the victims of the Holocaust. She was also nominated for the Nobel Peace Prize in 2007, though she did not win.

Sendler lived to see the world acknowledge her heroism. She passed away on May 12, 2008, at the age of 98, having saved approximately 2,500 Jewish children during the Holocaust. Despite the immense risk she faced, Sendler remained humble about her actions, often stating that she wished she could have saved more.

## Conclusion

Irena Sendler's story is one of extraordinary courage, compassion, and selflessness. In the face of unimaginable danger, she risked her life again and again to save Jewish children from the horrors of the

Holocaust. Her actions, guided by a deep sense of moral responsibility and empathy, saved not only lives but also the future of countless families. Sendler's meticulous record-keeping ensured that many of the children she rescued could one day learn of their true identities, even when their parents had been lost to the Holocaust. Today, Irena Sendler stands as a symbol of the power of individual action in the face of evil, and her legacy continues to inspire people around the world.

**Sources**

Sheltering the Jews: Stories of Holocaust Rescuers, Fortress Press, 1996.

Mazzeo, Tilar J. Irena's Children: A True Story of Courage. Gallery Books, 2017.

# The British Passport Officer Who Saved Thousands

## Introduction

In the shadow of the Third Reich, where oppression and cruelty reigned supreme, acts of quiet heroism often went unnoticed. One such hero was Francis "Frank" Foley, a British passport officer stationed in Berlin during the rise of Nazi Germany. Foley's story is one of remarkable courage and humanity, as he risked his life to save thousands of Jews from the Holocaust, operating in the heart of the Nazi regime while using nothing more than a diplomatic cover and an unyielding moral compass.

## Head of Berlin MI6 Station

Born on November 24, 1884, in Highbridge, Somerset, Frank Foley led a life that, on the surface, seemed unremarkable. After serving in World War I, he joined the British intelligence service, MI6, where he operated undercover as a passport control officer in Berlin during the 1920s and 1930s. As Adolf Hitler rose to power and the Nazis began their systematic persecution of Jews, Foley found himself in a position of quiet yet profound influence.

Despite his official title as a passport officer, Foley was, in reality, the head of MI6's Berlin station. His work involved gathering intelligence on Nazi Germany, but as the persecution of Jews escalated, Foley's mission took on a new, far more personal dimension. He recognized the growing danger faced by Jewish families and resolved to use his position to help them escape the impending genocide.

## The Beginnings of Foley's Rescue Efforts

As the Nazi regime tightened its grip on Germany, Jewish citizens found it increasingly difficult to flee the country. Emigration required extensive documentation, including visas for entry into other nations, which many countries were reluctant to issue. For Jews, obtaining these documents often meant the difference between life and death. Foley, understanding the gravity of the situation, began to use his position to circumvent the bureaucracy and provide Jews with the papers they needed to escape.

Foley operated with extraordinary bravery and resourcefulness. Although his office was under constant scrutiny by the Gestapo, he found ways to issue visas to Jews without the strict requirements normally enforced by the British government. He often bent or ignored the rules, going so far as to forge documents, hide Jews in his home, and even visit concentration camps to secure the release of those held there.

## Saving Thousands from the Holocaust

One of Foley's most significant contributions was his role in helping Jewish refugees obtain visas to Palestine, which was then under British control. The British government had imposed strict immigration quotas, but Foley recognized the dire need and worked tirelessly to maximize the number of Jews who could be saved. He provided visas to families who would otherwise have been turned away, sometimes personally escorting them to safety.

Foley's actions were not without risk. He was technically violating British immigration law, and his work put him in constant danger from the Nazi authorities. Despite these dangers, Foley remained undeterred. He knew that every visa he issued represented a life saved from the horrors of the concentration camps.

Among those Foley helped was the family of Dr. Hermann Simon, a prominent Jewish lawyer. Foley not only arranged for the Simon family to escape to Palestine but also ensured they had the necessary documents to secure their future. Stories like these were not isolated incidents; Foley's interventions were responsible for saving an estimated 10,000 Jews from the Holocaust.

## A Quiet Hero in a Dangerous Time

Foley's heroism extended beyond the issuance of visas. He often sheltered Jews in his own home, offering them a safe haven from the Gestapo. He helped smuggle people out of Germany, using his diplomatic status to protect those he could. Foley's actions were driven not by a sense of duty as an intelligence officer but by his deep moral conviction that he had to do what was right, regardless of the personal cost.

Despite the enormous risks he took, Foley remained modest about his actions. After the war, he returned to England and lived a quiet life, never seeking recognition for his efforts. It was only decades later, after his death in 1958, that the full extent of his heroism became widely known.

## Conclusion

Frank Foley's story is a testament to the power of individual courage in the face of overwhelming evil. Operating in the heart of Nazi Germany, Foley used his position not to gather intelligence or advance his career but to save lives. Foley's legacy is now honored in both the United Kingdom and Israel. In 1999, he was posthumously recognized as Righteous Among the Nations by Yad Vashem, Israel's official memorial to the victims of the Holocaust. This honor is reserved for non-Jews who risked their lives to save Jews during the Holocaust, and Foley's name now stands among those who exemplified the best of humanity during one of history's darkest chapters.

## Sources

Joiner, Preston. A Spy's Nazi Germany Resistance: The True Story of Frank Foley. Independently published, 2024.

Smith, Michael. Foley: The Spy Who Saved 10,000 Jews. Hodder Stoughton, 1999.

# Dancing Ballerina of Auschwitz

## Introduction

Among the countless tragic and horrifying stories that emerged from the Nazi concentration camps, one stands out for its defiance, bravery, and the final act of resistance carried out by a woman who used her grace and cunning to fight back against her captors. Franceska Mann, a talented Polish-Jewish ballerina, is remembered for a moment of astonishing courage at the Auschwitz concentration camp, where she turned the tables on her oppressors in a final, desperate act. Although her life, like so many others, ended tragically in the Holocaust, Franceska Mann's story resonates as an example of how even in the face of imminent death, an individual can strike back against tyranny and leave a legacy of courage. This is the story of Franceska Mann, the "Dancing Ballerina of Auschwitz."

## Early Life and Career

Franceska Mann was born on February 4, 1917, in Warsaw, Poland. She was raised in a well-off Jewish family that recognized and nurtured her artistic talents from a young age. Mann developed a passion for dance early in her life and pursued it with dedication. Her beauty, grace, and extraordinary skill in ballet earned her a place among Poland's most promising young dancers.

Mann attended one of the most prestigious ballet schools in Warsaw, where she was trained in classical ballet and modern dance. She quickly rose through the ranks of the dance world, performing at prominent theaters in Warsaw and other European cities. By the late 1930s, she was known as one of the most talented dancers in Poland, and many believed she was on the verge of an international breakthrough.

However, Mann's promising career and the life she had built were shattered when Nazi Germany invaded Poland in September 1939. The invasion marked the beginning of World War II and the systematic persecution of Jews, including Mann and her family. Poland fell under German occupation, and like millions of other Jews, Mann's life was soon consumed by the horrors of the Holocaust.

## Nazi Occupation and Deportation

As the German occupation of Poland intensified, the situation for the country's Jewish population became increasingly desperate. The Nazis quickly implemented a series of anti-Semitic laws that stripped Jews of their rights and forced them into ghettos. Mann, like many other Jewish residents of Warsaw, was confined to the Warsaw Ghetto, where conditions were harsh and survival was a daily struggle.

Despite the dire circumstances, Mann continued to dance in underground performances and shows within the ghetto, providing a brief escape from the misery that surrounded her. Her grace and poise in such a brutal environment made her a symbol of resilience. But as the Nazis began deporting Jews from the ghettos to concentration and extermination camps, Mann's fate took a terrifying turn.

In 1943, Mann was arrested by the Gestapo and deported to the infamous Auschwitz-Birkenau concentration camp. Located in occupied Poland, Auschwitz was the largest and deadliest of the Nazi camps, where millions of Jews, Roma, and others were systematically murdered in gas chambers. Mann's arrival at Auschwitz marked the beginning of the most horrifying chapter of her life.

**The Final Journey to Auschwitz**

In late October 1943, Franceska Mann was among a group of Jews who were transported to Auschwitz-Birkenau. However, unlike many who were immediately sent to the gas chambers upon arrival, the people in Mann's group were led to a section of the camp known as the "Sauna," which was used as a disinfection center. Here, prisoners were told to undress under the pretense that they were being prepared for showers—a lie that the Nazis often told to disguise the true purpose of the gas chambers.

Mann, however, quickly realized the truth. She, like many others, had heard rumors about what awaited those who were forced into the so-called showers. The Nazis had perfected the process of deception, creating a façade that lulled their victims into compliance until it was too late. Yet Franceska Mann decided that if she was going to die, she would not go quietly.

**The Ballerina's Defiant Last Stand**

According to multiple survivor accounts, Franceska Mann's final moments were filled with bravery and defiance. As the SS guards ordered the prisoners to undress, Mann reportedly used her beauty and charm to distract the guards. Slowly removing her clothing, she captivated the attention of the SS men watching over the prisoners. Mann's grace as a dancer had not left her, even in this horrifying moment. She was said to have danced and moved seductively, catching the eye of one particular guard.

Then, in an instant, Mann struck. Using one of her high-heeled shoes, she attacked the SS officer nearest to her. In some accounts, she managed to strike the guard in the face with her heel, blinding him. Mann seized his weapon and, in a flash of courage, shot him. Chaos erupted as Mann's defiance sparked a brief but intense rebellion among the other prisoners. Several other women in the room joined her in attacking the guards, using whatever makeshift weapons they could find.

The rebellion, however, was short-lived. The SS quickly regained control of the situation, and Mann, along with the other women who had joined in the uprising, was executed on the spot. Despite the brevity of the resistance, Franceska Mann's courageous act left a lasting impression on the survivors who witnessed it. She had chosen to fight back in the face of certain death, a final act of defiance that would echo through the memories of those who survived Auschwitz.

**Survivor Accounts and Legacy**

The story of Franceska Mann's final act of resistance has been recounted in various testimonies from survivors of Auschwitz, although the details vary slightly depending on the source. Some accounts suggest that Mann killed two SS officers, while others recall her wounding one. What remains consistent, however, is the bravery and defiance she displayed in her final moments.

Mann's story stands out as a rare example of physical resistance within the Nazi death camps, where most prisoners were too weakened or terrorized to fight back. Her courage in the face of overwhelming odds made her a symbol of resistance and dignity.

After the war, as the full extent of the Holocaust became known, the story of Franceska Mann was passed down through the oral histories of survivors. Her defiance at Auschwitz became part of the larger narrative of Jewish resistance during the Holocaust, alongside stories of other uprisings, such as the Warsaw Ghetto Uprising and the revolts at Treblinka and Sobibor.

## The Myth and Reality of Franceska Mann

Over time, Franceska Mann's story has become the subject of myth and legend, as is often the case with extraordinary tales of heroism. The lack of detailed historical records from within the death camps has made it difficult to verify every aspect of her story, and some historians have expressed caution about the exact details of the event. Nevertheless, the core elements of Mann's defiance—her attack on the SS guard and the brief uprising that followed—are widely accepted as true.

## Conclusion

Franceska Mann's life was tragically cut short by the Holocaust, but her final act of defiance in Auschwitz has ensured that her story endures. A talented ballerina whose grace and beauty were once celebrated on the stages of Europe, Mann used her skills in one last, desperate performance—this time, to strike back at her oppressors.

## Sources

Southern, Cynthia. The Vixen Who Shot a Nazi: The story of Franceska Mann, who shot SS Guard Josef Schillinger, in Auschwitz-Birkenau. Amazon Publications. 2014.

Southern, Cynthia. The Auschwitz Trilogy: Three Unique Biographies from Auschwitz-Birkenau. Amazon Publications, 2017.

# The Catholic Seminarian Who Saved 3,000 Hungarian Jews

## Introduction

Tibor Baranski's extraordinary journey during World War II is a compelling tale of courage, ingenuity, and unwavering determination to save lives. As a young Hungarian seminarian/diplomat, Baranski was instrumental in rescuing thousands of Jews in Nazi-occupied Hungary from the Holocaust, showcasing the profound impact one individual can have even amidst the darkest of times.

## Strong Sense of Moral Responsibility

Born on June 11, 1922, in Budapest, Tibor Baranski grew up in a devout Catholic family in Hungary. His early life was marked by religious education and a strong sense of moral responsibility, which was deeply ingrained in him by his parents. Baranski entered seminary school in 1943, a turbulent time in Hungary as the country found itself increasingly under the influence of Nazi Germany.

Hungary, initially an ally of Nazi Germany, had maintained a relatively independent stance during much of World War II. However, by March 1944, as Germany's fortunes on the Eastern Front waned, Adolf Hitler lost trust in Hungary's leader, Admiral Miklós Horthy, and the Nazis occupied the country. This occupation marked the beginning of a systematic campaign against Hungary's Jewish population, which numbered more than 800,000 at the time.

In the summer of 1944, the Nazis, with the collaboration of the Hungarian Arrow Cross Party, began the mass deportation of Jews to concentration camps. The pace of deportations accelerated after Horthy was removed from power in October 1944, and hundreds of thousands of Jews were sent to Auschwitz. As the death toll mounted, Hungary became one of the last theaters of the Holocaust, with the Jewish population of Budapest, Hungary's capital, increasingly targeted.

It was during this period of terror that Tibor Baranski, still a seminary student, became an unlikely yet effective rescuer of Jews. Working in collaboration with Angelo Rotta, the Vatican's Apostolic Nuncio (ambassador) to Hungary, Baranski became deeply involved in a network of individuals and organizations dedicated to saving as many Jews as possible from Nazi extermination.

## Joining the Vatican's Efforts

In 1944, as the Holocaust unfolded in Hungary, the Vatican was among the international institutions trying to intervene. Pope Pius XII had instructed Catholic clergy across Europe to do whatever they could to help protect Jews. In Hungary, Angelo Rotta took this directive seriously and began issuing letters of protection, known as Sckutzpasses, to Jewish families, designating them as under the protection of the Vatican. This status, while often ignored by the Hungarian government and Nazi forces, did offer some measure of protection, particularly if backed by the presence of diplomatic or church officials.

Rotta recruited Tibor Baranski to help with the enormous task of issuing these protective letters. As a seminary student with connections to the Church, Baranski was seen as trustworthy and dedicated. He was appointed by the Papal Nuncio, Angelo Rotta, to head a special Vatican protective mission for Jews. His role quickly expanded from simply helping with paperwork to organizing and leading rescue efforts on the ground.

Baranski, just 22 years old at the time, took on a pivotal and dangerous mission: he was responsible for delivering protective letters directly to Jewish families, negotiating with Hungarian officials and Nazi officers, and securing safe houses for those at immediate risk of deportation. His work required quick thinking, a deep understanding of the bureaucratic system, and a willingness to confront danger head-on.

## Saving Lives Amid Chaos

One of Baranski's most remarkable qualities was his ability to improvise and navigate the chaos of Nazi-occupied Budapest. With the Arrow Cross militia patrolling the streets and regularly rounding up Jews for deportation or execution, Baranski's daily activities placed him in extreme danger. Armed with nothing but his protective letters and a determination to save lives, Baranski would approach Jewish families, inform them of their protective status under the Vatican, and in many cases, physically lead them to safe houses or Vatican-protected buildings.

The protective letters, issued under the authority of the Vatican, were often Baranski's only weapon. These letters provided Jewish families with temporary immunity from deportation, as the recipients were technically under the protection of a neutral state—the Vatican. However, the protection offered by these letters was tenuous at best, as both the Arrow Cross and Nazi officials often disregarded them. In such cases, Baranski's courage and resourcefulness were put to the test. On more than one occasion, he confronted Arrow Cross officers, arguing forcefully for the lives of Jews and even bribing guards to secure their release.

In one of his most daring rescues, Baranski learned that a group of Jewish families, including women and children, were being held in a building set to be raided by the Arrow Cross. Knowing that time was running out, Baranski rushed to the scene, confronted the armed guards, and demanded the release of the families, waving his Vatican-issued documents. In the confusion and under the weight of his authority as a Vatican representative, the guards allowed him to take the Jews to safety. These families were then hidden in Vatican-protected buildings, where they remained until the end of the war.

## The Role of the Vatican and Diplomatic Immunity

The Vatican's role in Hungary during the Holocaust was complex, and Tibor Baranski operated at the intersection of diplomacy, religion, and resistance. Diplomatic immunity allowed Vatican representatives to act with a certain degree of impunity, though this protection was often more theoretical than real. The Arrow Cross government and the Gestapo viewed the Vatican's humanitarian efforts with suspicion, and anyone involved in aiding Jews risked execution. Yet, Baranski's position as a seminary student and his association with the Vatican provided him with a critical cover that he used to maximum effect.

Baranski's ability to navigate this perilous terrain was crucial to his success. He often invoked the authority of the Vatican, knowing that many Arrow Cross officials feared international repercussions if they openly defied the Church. This diplomatic tightrope walk allowed Baranski to save thousands of lives, as he leveraged the Vatican's diplomatic status to protect Jews in ways that others could not.

In addition to issuing protective letters, Baranski and his colleagues worked tirelessly to set up safe houses across Budapest. These buildings, marked with Vatican flags or symbols, became sanctuaries for Jews fleeing deportation. Baranski personally oversaw the transfer of hundreds of Jewish families into these safe houses, where they were provided with food, shelter, and, most importantly, protection from the Nazi death squads. Many of these safe houses survived until the Soviet liberation of Budapest in early 1945, by which time thousands of Jews had been saved.

**Risking His Life for Others**

Baranski's work often placed him in direct confrontation with the most dangerous forces in Nazi-occupied Hungary. In one harrowing incident, Baranski was arrested by Arrow Cross officers while trying to escort Jewish families to safety. He was interrogated and threatened with execution but managed to talk his way out of the situation by invoking his connection to the Vatican and emphasizing the potential diplomatic fallout if they harmed him. His quick thinking and the fear of international consequences led to his release, allowing him to continue his rescue efforts.

Despite the daily risks, Baranski remained undeterred. His deep Catholic faith and moral conviction drove him to act, even when it meant putting his own life on the line. For Baranski, the idea of standing by while innocent people were sent to their deaths was inconceivable, and he saw his mission as a form of spiritual duty. This sense of purpose, combined with his remarkable courage, allowed him to accomplish what few others could during one of the darkest periods of the war.

**Repercussions and Legacy**

By the time Soviet forces liberated Budapest in February 1945, Baranski had helped save over 3,000 Jews. Some reports claim the number saved from deportation is closer to 12,000 – 15,000 Jews. His efforts, along with those of other rescuers such as Raoul Wallenberg and Carl Lutz, made a significant impact on the survival of Hungary's Jewish population.

Baranski's post-war life was marked by further trials. In 1950, after Hungary fell under Soviet influence, Baranski was imprisoned by the Communist regime for his opposition to the government and his association with the Vatican. After spending time in prison, he eventually immigrated to the United States, where he continued his work as an educator and advocate for Holocaust remembrance. His story remained largely untold until later in life, when he was honored for his contributions to saving lives during the Holocaust.

In 1979, Baranski was recognized by Yad Vashem, Israel's Holocaust memorial, as one of the "Righteous Among the Nations," a title awarded to non-Jews who risked their lives to save Jews during the Holocaust. This recognition solidified his legacy as a humanitarian and a hero.

Baranski's defiance of the Arrow Cross and his direct confrontations with Nazi and Hungarian officials also had symbolic value. His actions demonstrated that moral courage and steadfastness could challenge the inhumanity of the Nazi regime. While the physical impact of his rescues was immediate—saving thousands of Jews from deportation and death—the symbolic value of his resistance contributed to the broader narrative of defiance against the forces of evil that characterized the war.

Lastly, the legacy of Baranski's work became part of the post-war reconciliation and remembrance efforts that focused on honoring those who risked their lives to save others during the Holocaust. His recognition by Yad Vashem as one of the "Righteous Among the Nations" helped to underscore the importance of individual action in resisting tyranny. Baranski's story became an example of how one person, motivated by faith and a sense of duty, could make a profound difference in the lives of thousands.

**Conclusion**

Tibor Baranski's life and work during World War II remain a testament to the power of individual courage in the face of overwhelming evil. As a young Catholic seminary student, Baranski took it upon himself to risk his life daily to save thousands of Hungarian Jews from the Holocaust. His actions, supported by the Vatican and carried out through a network of safe houses and protective letters, saved over 3,000 lives and prevented countless families from being torn apart by the Nazis' genocidal campaign.

**Sources**

Yad Vashem. The Jews of Hungary During the Holocaust

Kirst, Sean. He Saved 3,000 Jews in World War II, and now lives quietly in Buffalo. Buffalo News, 2019.

# The Diplomat Who Saved Thousands of Jewish Lives

### Introduction

Raoul Wallenberg is one of the most extraordinary figures of World War II and the Holocaust, a man who, despite the immense personal risk, helped save tens of thousands of Hungarian Jews from almost certain death at the hands of the Nazis. As a Swedish diplomat stationed in Budapest during the war's final months, Wallenberg used his diplomatic immunity, ingenuity, and an unwavering sense of morality to defy Adolf Eichmann's Final Solution. His actions were nothing short of heroic, and despite his mysterious disappearance after the war, Wallenberg's legacy endures as one of the most profound stories of courage, human decency, and moral conviction.

### Early Life and Career

Raoul Wallenberg was born on August 4, 1912, into one of Sweden's most prominent and wealthy families. The Wallenberg family was renowned for its banking and business empire, which gave young Raoul a life of privilege. His father, Raoul Oscar Wallenberg, was an officer in the Swedish Navy, but he died just three months before Raoul's birth. Raised primarily by his mother, Maj Wising Wallenberg, Raoul grew up in a family known for its humanitarian efforts and diplomatic connections.

Wallenberg showed an early interest in international affairs. After completing his military service in Sweden, he studied architecture at the University of Michigan in the United States. Following his graduation in 1935, Wallenberg traveled extensively, working in a variety of positions, including in South Africa and Israel. These experiences broadened his understanding of different cultures and political climates, shaping the man who would later stand against Nazi atrocities.

In 1941, Wallenberg joined a trading company in Sweden that was partly owned by a Hungarian Jew, Kálmán Lauer. Through this position, Wallenberg frequently traveled to Hungary, where he saw firsthand the increasing persecution of Jews under the pro-Nazi government. His time in Hungary and his association with Lauer would eventually lead to his involvement in the most daring humanitarian mission of the Holocaust.

## The Situation in Hungary

By 1944, the Holocaust was at its most brutal stage. Adolf Eichmann, one of the chief architects of the Final Solution, had been sent to Hungary to oversee the deportation and extermination of the country's Jewish population. Hungary had a large and vibrant Jewish community, with over 800,000 Jews living there at the start of the war. However, after the Nazi occupation in March 1944, the Hungarian government, under Miklós Horthy, capitulated to Nazi demands, and mass deportations to Auschwitz began almost immediately.

In just a few months, more than 400,000 Hungarian Jews were deported to Auschwitz, where most were immediately murdered in the gas chambers. By the summer of 1944, as the war entered its final phase, the remaining Jews in Budapest were facing annihilation. The international community, particularly neutral countries like Sweden, Switzerland, and Spain, became increasingly concerned about the fate of Hungarian Jews, leading to a series of diplomatic efforts aimed at saving as many lives as possible.

## Wallenberg's Mission in Budapest

In response to the crisis, the U.S. War Refugee Board, with funding from Jewish organizations, sought to deploy a Swedish diplomat to Budapest to rescue Hungarian Jews. Raoul Wallenberg, known for his intelligence, resourcefulness, and fluency in several languages, was chosen for the task. He arrived in Budapest in July 1944, armed with limited diplomatic authority but driven by an unshakeable moral imperative to save lives.

Wallenberg's strategy was multifaceted, involving the use of diplomacy, bribery, and sheer audacity. His primary tool in the effort to save Jews was the creation of Swedish "protective passports" or "Schutz-Passes." These documents, though not officially recognized by the Nazis, declared the bearers to be under Swedish protection and allowed them to be exempt from deportation. With the help of local collaborators, Wallenberg printed thousands of these passports, distributing them to Jewish families at great personal risk.

Additionally, Wallenberg established more than 30 "safe houses" throughout Budapest. These buildings, marked with the Swedish flag, were declared part of Swedish diplomatic property, meaning that Jews who lived in them were under the protection of Sweden and theoretically immune from Nazi persecution. Thousands of Jews found refuge in these houses, and Wallenberg worked tirelessly to ensure they remained under Swedish protection.

## Defying Eichmann and the Nazis

Wallenberg's actions placed him in direct opposition to Adolf Eichmann, who was determined to see the Jewish population of Hungary exterminated. Despite the enormous pressure from the Nazis and the pro-Nazi Hungarian government, Wallenberg showed remarkable courage. He regularly intervened in deportations, often personally pulling Jews off death marches or out of train cars bound for Auschwitz, armed only with his diplomatic credentials and an unrelenting determination to save lives.

In one famous instance, Wallenberg intercepted a group of Jews being forced onto a train at the Budapest train station. Standing in front of the train, he demanded that all individuals holding Swedish protective passports be released. When the Nazi officer in charge refused, Wallenberg, undeterred, threatened to have him arrested for violating international law. His bluff worked, and dozens of Jews were freed that day.

Wallenberg's boldness extended to bribing Nazi officials, securing the release of countless Jews by offering money or goods in exchange for their lives. He did this with the understanding that while he could not stop the Holocaust, he could at least slow it down, saving as many people as possible.

## Saving the Jews of Budapest

Wallenberg's efforts were nothing short of extraordinary. His combination of legal maneuvering, personal bravery, and strategic thinking resulted in the survival of tens of thousands of Jews. Estimates suggest that Wallenberg directly saved around 20,000 Jews by issuing protective passports and providing safe houses. Indirectly, his actions contributed to the survival of approximately 100,000 Jews in Budapest by delaying deportations and protecting Jewish ghettos.

As the Soviet Red Army advanced on Budapest in late 1944, the situation grew even more precarious. Eichmann, realizing that the war was lost, sought to accelerate the extermination of the remaining Jews. Wallenberg, however, redoubled his efforts, negotiating with both Nazi and Hungarian officials to prevent further atrocities. When the Soviet Army finally entered Budapest in January 1945, Wallenberg had helped save more than half of the city's Jewish population.

## Mysterious Disappearance

Raoul Wallenberg's story takes a dark and mysterious turn after the liberation of Budapest. On January 17, 1945, Wallenberg was taken into custody by Soviet forces under the pretext of needing to travel to their headquarters for a debriefing. He was never seen again.

For decades, Wallenberg's fate remained one of the great mysteries of World War II. The Soviet government claimed that he died of a heart attack in a Moscow prison in 1947, but no credible evidence was ever provided to support this claim.

## Conclusion

Despite his tragic and mysterious fate, Raoul Wallenberg's legacy as a hero of the Holocaust is undeniable. He has been honored posthumously by numerous countries and organizations, including being named one of the "Righteous Among the Nations" by Israel's Yad Vashem in 1963, an honor given to non-Jews who risked their lives to save Jews during the Holocaust.

## Sources

Carlberg, Ingrid. Raoul Wallenberg: The Heroic Life and Mysterious Disappearance of the Man Who Saved Thousands of Hungarian Jews from the Holocaust. MacLehose Press, 2017.

Marton, Kati. Wallenberg: The Incredible Story of the Man Who Saved the Jews of Budapest. Arcade, 2011.

# The Polish Doctors Who Created a Fake Disease

## Introduction

Amid the horrors of World War II and the Holocaust, acts of courage and ingenuity emerged from unlikely places. One such story comes from Poland, where two doctors, Eugeniusz Łazowski and Stanislaw Matulewicz, devised a clever and dangerous ruse to protect Jews and Polish citizens from Nazi persecution. They created the illusion of an outbreak of a deadly infectious disease, which scared the Nazis into quarantining entire villages, thus sparing many lives. This story reveals how these two doctors used their medical knowledge and creativity to defy the Nazi occupiers and save hundreds of Jews and Poles from deportation and execution.

## Nazi Occupation of Poland

When Nazi Germany invaded Poland in September 1939, life for the Polish people changed overnight. The Nazis imposed harsh occupation policies, systematically targeting Jews, political dissidents, and anyone suspected of resistance. Under Adolf Hitler's brutal regime, millions of Jews were rounded up, forced into ghettos, or deported to concentration camps, where most would face execution.

In the town of Rozwadów, located in southeastern Poland, two doctors were working under the constant threat of Nazi oversight: Eugeniusz Łazowski, a young physician, and his colleague and mentor, Stanislaw Matulewicz. Both men were acutely aware of the Nazi's racial policies and the growing violence against Jews. It was during this time that the doctors conceived of a daring plan to protect the people of Rozwadów and nearby villages from being sent to labor camps or worse.

## The Creation of a Fake Epidemic

Łazowski and Matulewicz understood that the Nazis were terrified of contagious diseases, especially typhus, a deadly illness spread by lice that had devastated populations throughout history. Nazi propaganda painted Jews and other "undesirables" as carriers of disease, and any outbreak of infectious disease would lead to strict quarantine measures by the Germans, often including cordoning off entire areas to prevent the spread.

In 1942, the doctors discovered that a harmless bacterium, Proteus OX19, could be used to simulate the symptoms of typhus in medical tests. When injected into a patient's bloodstream, the bacterium would trigger a positive result for typhus in blood tests, even though the person was perfectly healthy. Łazowski and Matulewicz realized that by injecting this bacterium into healthy people, they could create the appearance of a typhus epidemic, thus causing the Germans to quarantine the area and halt deportations.

The plan was risky. If the Nazis discovered the deception, the doctors and their patients would be executed. Nevertheless, Łazowski and Matulewicz believed it was worth the risk to save lives. They began injecting the harmless bacteria into the bloodstreams of villagers, ensuring that when blood tests were sent to German laboratories, they would test positive for typhus. The goal was to create a large-scale "epidemic" that would make the Nazis avoid the area out of fear of contagion.

**Saving Lives Through Deception**

As news of the supposed typhus outbreak spread, the Germans reacted just as Łazowski and Matulewicz had hoped. Nazi officials, terrified of the disease, placed the villages of Rozwadów and the surrounding areas under quarantine. They halted deportations of the Jewish population, fearing that the "infected" villagers would spread the disease to German soldiers and labor camps. This quarantine effectively saved the lives of hundreds of Jews who had been hiding in the area, as well as many non-Jewish Poles who would have been sent to labor camps or executed.

The success of the ruse quickly became apparent. German soldiers and SS officers, normally eager to patrol Polish towns and enforce Nazi laws, now avoided the quarantined area altogether. This allowed Jews in hiding to move more freely, and it bought time for many to escape to safer locations or find better hiding places. For more than two years, the fake epidemic continued, with Łazowski and Matulewicz carefully managing the spread of "cases" to avoid raising suspicion.

The doctors were careful to inject only those villagers who were not in immediate danger from the Nazis, as any direct contact with German soldiers could lead to medical examinations that might expose the fraud. They also took care to maintain the appearance of a growing epidemic without overplaying their hand. The deception worked so well that German authorities even sent medical teams to investigate the outbreak. However, the visiting doctors relied primarily on the positive blood tests provided by Łazowski and Matulewicz and did not conduct their thorough investigations, allowing the ruse to continue unchallenged.

**The Risks and Dangers**

While the ruse was largely successful, the danger was ever-present. Łazowski and Matulewicz knew that if the Germans discovered the truth, the entire village—and especially the doctors—would face brutal reprisals. German authorities were known to execute anyone found guilty of harboring Jews or undermining Nazi policies, and the penalties for falsifying medical records would have been severe.

The doctors had to be exceptionally careful not to overextend the deception. If too many cases of typhus were reported, it might arouse suspicion. On the other hand, if too few cases were reported, the Germans might send soldiers into the area, increasing the risk of detection. Despite these dangers, the doctors managed to maintain the illusion of a widespread typhus outbreak without drawing too much attention to their activities.

At one point, Nazi authorities sent a team of German doctors to investigate the "epidemic" more closely. Łazowski and Matulewicz were able to manipulate the investigation by providing just enough evidence to satisfy the inspectors, while still keeping the true nature of their operation hidden. The German doctors were convinced that the outbreak was real and recommended that the quarantine remain in place, further protecting the villagers.

## The Legacy of Courage and Deception

By the time the war ended in 1945, Łazowski and Matulewicz's fake typhus epidemic had saved an estimated 8,000 people, including hundreds of Jews. Their courage and ingenuity in the face of overwhelming odds made a significant difference in the lives of the people in Rozwadów and the surrounding areas. Though their actions put them at great personal risk, they never wavered in their commitment to saving as many lives as possible.

After the war, both doctors continued their medical careers. Eugeniusz Łazowski emigrated to the United States, where he became a respected professor of pediatrics at the University of Illinois. He lived out his life quietly, rarely speaking of the incredible risks he had taken during the war. It wasn't until later in life that Łazowski's story became more widely known, thanks to historians and journalists who uncovered the details of his and Matulewicz's deception.

The actions of Łazowski and Matulewicz are a powerful reminder of the impact that individuals can have in the face of evil. Using their medical knowledge and resourcefulness, they outwitted one of the most fearsome regimes in history and saved thousands of lives.

## Conclusion

The story of Eugeniusz Łazowski and Stanislaw Matulewicz exemplifies the extraordinary courage and ingenuity that arose in response to the horrors of Nazi occupation. Through their creation of a fake typhus epidemic, these two doctors saved thousands of lives, using their medical expertise to manipulate the Nazi obsession with disease. In doing so, they defied the brutal regime and offered hope to those who faced unimaginable persecution. Their actions remind us of the power of human decency and creativity in the face of great evil.

## Sources

Bretan, Juliette. The Faked Epidemic that Saved Hundreds of Lives. Culture.PL. 2020.

Facing History and Ourselves. The Holocaust in Poland. 2016

# The Polish Nurse Who Defied the Nazis

**Introduction:**

In the brutal landscape of World War II, where fear and cruelty dominated, acts of compassion were both rare and immensely dangerous. Irene Gut Opdyke, a young Polish nurse, emerged as a beacon of courage during this dark period. Her story is not just one of survival but of defiance, as she risked everything to protect and shelter Jewish people from the horrors of the Nazi regime. Amidst the widespread terror, Irene's actions were a testament to the profound impact one individual can have when they choose to stand up against evil.

**Faith and Her Moral Compass**

Irene Gut was born in 1918 in Kozienice, Poland, into a Catholic family. Her early life was marked by a strong sense of faith and an unwavering moral compass. She pursued a career in nursing, a profession that would soon place her in the heart of the conflict. When Nazi Germany invaded Poland in September 1939, Irene was 21 years old. The invasion unleashed a wave of violence and oppression, particularly against the Jewish population, who were subjected to systemic persecution, forced into ghettos, and eventually deported to concentration camps.

The occupation of Poland was brutal, with the Nazis imposing draconian laws and committing countless atrocities. Irene witnessed these horrors firsthand, and the experiences would forever change her. Initially, Irene served as a nurse for the Polish underground resistance, but after being captured by the Germans, she was forced into labor in a munitions factory. Her courage, however, remained undiminished, and she seized every opportunity to resist the Nazi regime.

## Irene's Employment Under Major Rugemer

In 1942, Irene was assigned to work in the household of a high-ranking German officer, Major Eduard Rugemer, in the city of Tarnopol (now in Ukraine). This position, while perilous, presented her with a unique opportunity to help those in need. Rugemer, like many Nazis, took advantage of his position, living in relative luxury while others suffered. However, he was largely unaware of the true nature of the young nurse working under his roof.

Irene's duties included managing the household staff, overseeing meals, and ensuring the villa ran smoothly. But beneath this facade of compliance, Irene was secretly aiding Jewish people, providing them with food, medical supplies, and information about Nazi activities. The situation grew more urgent as deportations increased, and ghettos were liquidated.

## The Secret Shelter

Driven by a sense of moral duty, Irene made the extraordinary decision to hide 12 Jews in the cellar of Rugemer's villa. These were individuals she had known from the local ghetto, people she could not abandon to their fate. The cellar, cold and dark, became a refuge from the relentless hunt by the Gestapo and the German military. However, the risk was enormous. If discovered, Irene and those she sheltered would face certain death.

The days were fraught with tension. Irene had to carefully balance her duties to avoid arousing suspicion while secretly tending to her hidden charges. She devised intricate plans to keep them safe, such as sending the staff away on errands during inspections and using coded signals to communicate. The fear of discovery was a constant shadow, but Irene's resolve never wavered.

## Acts of Defiance

Irene's bravery extended beyond simply hiding the Jews. She secured food and medicine for them, often stealing supplies from the German stores under Rugemer's command. She also managed to obtain false identity papers, which allowed some of her hidden charges to escape the city and find safer refuge in the countryside. Each act of defiance was a calculated risk, but Irene knew the stakes and refused to be paralyzed by fear.

One of the most harrowing moments came when Major Rugemer nearly discovered the hidden Jews. Suspicious of Irene's behavior, he began to investigate the household more closely. In a desperate bid to protect those she sheltered, Irene took the extraordinary step of becoming Rugemer's mistress, using the relationship to distract him and keep his attention away from the cellar. It was a sacrifice she made without hesitation, driven by her determination to save lives.

## Liberation and Aftermath

As the war dragged on, the situation in Tarnopol grew increasingly dangerous. Soviet forces were advancing, and the German grip on the region was weakening. In 1944, as the Red Army approached, the area was liberated. Irene's actions ensured that all 12 of the Jews she sheltered survived the war. Their survival was a direct result of her extraordinary courage and ingenuity.

After the war, Irene faced the difficult task of rebuilding her life in a world that had been torn apart by conflict. She eventually emigrated to the United States, where she settled in California. It was not until decades later that she began to speak publicly about her wartime experiences. Her story was met with admiration and respect, and in 1982, Yad Vashem, the World Holocaust Remembrance Center in Israel, honored her as one of the Righteous Among the Nations.

**Conclusion**

Irene Gut Opdyke's story is a powerful reminder of the difference one can make in the face of overwhelming evil. Her actions during World War II saved lives and her legacy inspired generations. The recognition she received later in life was a testament to the enduring impact of her moral choices. In a time when many turned a blind eye to the suffering around them, Irene stood up, demonstrating that compassion and courage can prevail even in the darkest of times.

**Sources**

Opdyke, Irene Gut. In My Hands: Memories of a Holocaust Rescuer. Ember, 2016.

Opdyke, Irene Gut. Into the Flames: The Life Story of a Righteous Gentile. Borgo Press, 1992.

# Kindertransport and the Lifeline for Jewish Children

## Introduction

The Kindertransport, or "Children's Transport," was one of the most remarkable humanitarian efforts in the months leading up to World War II. It involved the evacuation of approximately 10,000 Jewish children from Nazi-occupied territories to safety in the United Kingdom between 1938 and 1940. These children, most of whom never saw their parents again, were saved from the horrors of the Holocaust by a network of individuals and organizations who took bold action in a time of growing danger. The Kindertransport remains a powerful symbol of the compassion and courage displayed in the face of overwhelming adversity.

The operation was made possible by a combination of political pressure, grassroots activism, and the tireless work of ordinary citizens who refused to stand by as Jewish children faced the threat of annihilation. Heroes such as Nicholas Winton, Norbert Wollheim, and others were instrumental in organizing these transports, securing visas, and finding foster homes for the children in Britain. This story tells of their bravery and dedication, and the extraordinary rescue mission that gave thousands of children a chance at life.

## Kindertransport is Born

By 1938, Nazi persecution of Jews in Germany and Austria had reached terrifying new levels. The Nuremberg Laws of 1935 had already stripped Jews of their civil rights, and Jewish businesses, homes, and synagogues were increasingly targeted by violent mobs. The situation escalated dramatically on November 9-10, 1938, during Kristallnacht, or the "Night of Broken Glass," when Nazis attacked Jewish communities across Germany and Austria. Thousands of Jewish businesses were looted, synagogues were set ablaze, and nearly 100 Jews were murdered. Over 30,000 Jewish men were arrested and sent to concentration camps, signaling a new phase of state-sponsored terror.

Kristallnacht shocked the world, and international pressure mounted on Western governments to respond to the plight of Jewish refugees. However, most countries, including the United States, maintained strict immigration quotas, making it difficult for Jews to flee Nazi persecution. The United Kingdom, though also hesitant to accept large numbers of adult refugees, opened its doors to Jewish children, spurred by the efforts of British and Jewish activists who lobbied for the creation of the Kindertransport program.

The Kindertransport was formally approved by the British government in late 1938. The government agreed to allow Jewish children under the age of 17 to enter the country without visas, provided that private citizens or organizations guaranteed their care and financial support. This set in motion a race against time, as individuals and organizations across Europe worked to identify children at risk and arrange their safe passage to Britain.

### Nicholas Winton and the Prague Rescue Effort

One of the most famous figures associated with the Kindertransport is Nicholas Winton, a young British stockbroker who played a crucial role in organizing the evacuation of children from Nazi-occupied Czechoslovakia. In December 1938, Winton was planning a skiing holiday in Switzerland when he received a call from a friend involved in refugee work in Prague, imploring him to come to Czechoslovakia to help Jewish families facing imminent danger.

Upon arriving in Prague, Winton was horrified by the desperate situation of Jewish families trying to flee the country. He quickly took action, setting up an office in a hotel room and working tirelessly to organize the evacuation of Jewish children. Winton faced numerous obstacles, including obtaining travel permits, raising funds, and securing foster families in Britain willing to take in the children. Despite these challenges, Winton managed to arrange eight transports from Prague to Britain between March and August 1939, saving 669 children.

Winton's work remained largely unknown for decades. He never sought recognition for his efforts, and it wasn't until the 1980s that his heroism was publicly acknowledged. Today, Winton is remembered as one of the great humanitarians of the 20th century, a man whose quiet determination saved hundreds of lives.

### Norbert Wollheim and the Berlin Effort

While Nicholas Winton is perhaps the best-known hero of the Kindertransport, many others played pivotal roles in organizing the evacuation of Jewish children from different parts of Europe. Norbert Wollheim, a German Jewish social worker and activist, was instrumental in coordinating the transport of children from Berlin. As an active member of the Jewish community, Wollheim had been involved in efforts to assist Jewish refugees even before the outbreak of war.

After Kristallnacht, Wollheim became a leading figure in the Kindertransport effort in Berlin, working closely with the Reichsvertretung der Juden in Deutschland, the official Jewish community organization in Nazi Germany. He helped identify Jewish children who were at risk of deportation to concentration camps and worked to secure their places on the Kindertransport. Despite the dangers he faced as a Jew in Nazi Germany, Wollheim continued his work until 1941, when the last Kindertransport left Berlin.

Wollheim's own story took a tragic turn during the war. In 1943, he was deported to Auschwitz, where his wife and young son were murdered. Remarkably, Wollheim survived the war and later became a key figure in the post-war effort to seek compensation for Holocaust survivors. His work during the Kindertransport, however, ensured that hundreds of children were spared the fate that befell so many others.

## The Journey to Safety

The logistics of the Kindertransport were complex and fraught with danger. Most of the children had to leave their families behind, often with little more than a suitcase and a label pinned to their clothing. Parents, desperate to save their children from the escalating violence, made the heart-wrenching decision to send them away, knowing they might never see them again. The children were taken to railway stations in cities such as Vienna, Berlin, and Prague, where they boarded trains bound for the Netherlands or Belgium. From there, they crossed the English Channel by ferry and arrived at the port of Harwich in southern England.

Upon arrival in Britain, the children were placed with foster families, many of whom were strangers who had volunteered to take in refugee children. Others were housed in hostels or schools set up by Jewish and Quaker organizations. The British Jewish community played a significant role in organizing the reception of the children, providing financial support and coordinating their care. Despite the overwhelming generosity of the British people, the experience of being uprooted from their families and thrust into a new and unfamiliar country was traumatic for many of the children.

For some, life in Britain brought safety and stability. However, others faced difficult adjustments, including language barriers, homesickness, and the uncertainty of their family's fate in Nazi-occupied Europe. As the war progressed, news of the Holocaust began to reach Britain, and many Kindertransport children learned that their parents had been deported to concentration camps, never to return.

## The Heroes Behind the Kindertransport

While figures like Nicholas Winton and Norbert Wollheim played central roles in the Kindertransport, the success of the operation depended on a vast network of individuals and organizations working together. In addition to Jewish and Quaker groups, other religious and humanitarian organizations, such as the Movement for the Care of Children from Germany, were heavily involved in coordinating the rescue effort.

One of the most significant organizations was the Central British Fund for German Jewry (CBF), which later became known as World Jewish Relief. The CBF worked tirelessly to raise funds, negotiate with the British government, and secure foster homes for the children. They were aided by figures like Sir Samuel Hoare, a British politician who pushed for the Kindertransport within the British government, and Rabbi Solomon Schonfeld, who personally arranged the rescue of hundreds of Orthodox Jewish children.

The Kindertransport also relied on the courage and sacrifice of countless parents who made the impossible decision to send their children away, knowing they might never see them again. Their bravery in the face of unimaginable danger is a testament to the lengths parents will go to protect their children, even at great personal cost.

## Repercussions and Legacy

The Kindertransport saved approximately 10,000 Jewish children from the horrors of the Holocaust, but it was not without its limitations. The program ended abruptly when Britain declared war on Germany in September 1939, cutting off further transports. Sadly, many of the children's parents who remained behind perished in the Nazi death camps, leaving thousands of Kindertransport survivors as orphans.

For the children who were rescued, the Kindertransport had a profound impact on their lives. Many of the children went on to make significant contributions to British society, excelling in fields such as science, medicine, and the arts. Others became vocal advocates for Holocaust remembrance and education, ensuring that the memory of the Kindertransport and the lessons of the Holocaust would not be forgotten.

The legacy of the Kindertransport endures as a powerful example of what can be achieved when ordinary people come together to confront injustice and save lives. The operation showed that even in the darkest times, compassion and bravery can triumph over hatred and indifference. The efforts of individuals like Nicholas Winton, Norbert Wollheim, and countless others ensured that thousands of children were given a chance to survive, thrive, and remember.

**Repercussions on the Wider War Effort**

While the Kindertransport was primarily a humanitarian mission, it had notable repercussions on the broader war effort, both in terms of morale and geopolitics. The British government's decision to accept 10,000 Jewish children not only saved lives but also sent a powerful message about Britain's opposition to Nazi persecution and its commitment to human rights. This was particularly significant at a time when many Western nations, including the United States, maintained restrictive immigration policies, leaving countless refugees trapped under Nazi rule.

The Kindertransport helped strengthen Britain's moral standing on the global stage, distinguishing the country as a refuge for the persecuted. As the horrors of the Nazi regime became more widely known, the decision to take in these vulnerable children became a point of pride for the British public and a reminder of the nation's role in standing up against tyranny. This moral leadership would later help to galvanize international support for the Allied cause and provide justification for Britain's wartime policies aimed at defeating Nazi Germany.

In addition to its symbolic value, the Kindertransport had practical implications for the war effort. Many of the children who were rescued went on to contribute to the Allied war effort in various ways. Some joined the British military, working as translators, intelligence officers, or in other capacities. Others played key roles in post-war reconstruction, helping to rebuild Europe and promote peace. Many Kindertransport survivors remained in Britain after the war, integrating into British society and contributing to the nation's recovery.

The success of the Kindertransport also highlighted the potential for international cooperation in the face of humanitarian crises. Though it was a British-led effort, the Kindertransport involved collaboration between numerous countries and organizations, from Jewish relief groups in Germany and Austria to Quaker and Christian aid organizations in Britain. This spirit of cooperation laid the groundwork for post-war efforts to assist displaced persons and refugees across Europe.

However, the Kindertransport also exposed the limitations of Western governments in addressing the refugee crisis more broadly. While the operation saved 10,000 children, millions of Jews and other persecuted groups remained trapped in Nazi-occupied Europe, many of whom were later murdered in the Holocaust. The Kindertransport, though heroic in its scope, underscored the failure of international diplomacy to prevent or mitigate the horrors of the Holocaust.

In the years that followed the war, the Kindertransport became a symbol of the importance of acting swiftly and decisively in response to humanitarian emergencies. It served as a reminder that, in times of crisis, the international community has a responsibility to protect the most vulnerable—particularly children—and that even in the darkest times, compassion can make a difference.

## Conclusion

The Kindertransport remains one of the most remarkable humanitarian efforts of World War II. The operation, which saved 10,000 Jewish children from the clutches of the Nazi regime, was a testament to the courage and compassion of the individuals and organizations that made it possible. Heroes like Nicholas Winton, Norbert Wollheim, and countless others risked their safety and reputations to ensure that these children were given a chance at life.

While the Kindertransport could not save everyone, it offered hope in a time of despair and demonstrated that, even in the face of overwhelming evil, acts of goodness and humanity can prevail. The children who survived went on to live full lives, many contributing greatly to the countries that took them in, including the United Kingdom. Their legacy is not only one of survival but also of resilience, showing how a generation displaced by war can rise from tragedy and contribute to a better world.

## Sources

Harris, Mark Jonathon. Into the Arms of Strangers: Stories of the Kindertransport. Bloomsbury USA. 2000.

Hammel, Andrea. The Kindertransport: What Really Happened. Polity, 2024.

# Spies

# From Housewife and Mother to Master Spy

## Introduction

During World War II, countless men and women risked their lives to fight against Nazi Germany's oppressive regime. One of the most remarkable stories of bravery and sacrifice is that of Odette Hallowes, a British-French spy who played a critical role in supporting the Allied cause. As an agent of the Special Operations Executive (SOE), Odette infiltrated Nazi-occupied France, gathered vital intelligence, and worked with the French Resistance to sabotage German operations. Despite being captured and brutally tortured by the Gestapo, Odette remained defiant, never revealing crucial information that could compromise the war effort. This story explores Odette Hallowes' journey from a quiet life in England to becoming one of the most decorated female agents of World War II, and her unwavering courage in the face of unimaginable adversity.

## From France to England

Odette Hallowes was born Odette Marie Céline Brailly on April 28, 1912, in Amiens, France. Her father, who had served in the French army during World War I, was killed in combat just a few months before Odette's birth. His death left a lasting impact on her, instilling a strong sense of patriotism and resilience in her from a young age. Odette grew up in France but eventually moved to England after marrying an Englishman, Roy Sansom, in 1931. The couple had three daughters, and Odette settled into a quiet life in the English countryside.

When World War II broke out in 1939, Odette was determined to contribute to the war effort, despite having a family to care for. Her deep sense of duty, combined with her fluency in French, made her an ideal candidate for intelligence work. In 1942, after responding to a request for photographs of the French coastline for the war effort, Odette caught the attention of the Special Operations Executive (SOE)—a secret British organization created by Winston Churchill to carry out espionage, sabotage, and reconnaissance missions in Nazi-occupied Europe.

## Joining the SOE and Training as a Spy

The SOE's mission was to "set Europe ablaze" by supporting resistance movements and undermining the German war machine. Given her French background and fluency in the language, Odette was a perfect candidate for clandestine operations in France. After being recruited by the SOE, Odette underwent rigorous training in Scotland, where she learned essential espionage skills such as wireless communication, cryptography, and how to evade capture.

Odette's training also included weapons handling, hand-to-hand combat, and sabotage techniques, all of which were necessary for her survival in Nazi-occupied territory. While the SOE had many female agents, the risks were immense—if captured by the Germans, agents faced certain torture and likely death. Despite these dangers, Odette was resolute in her desire to contribute to the fight against the Nazis.

In 1942, Odette was assigned to work in the French section of the SOE, under the codename "Lise." Her mission was to support the Resistance and gather intelligence that could be used to undermine German operations in France. In October of that year, Odette left her family behind and parachuted into Nazi-occupied France to begin her dangerous mission.

**Operating in Nazi-Occupied France**

Once in France, Odette joined forces with Captain Peter Churchill, another SOE agent who was not related to Winston Churchill, despite sharing the same surname. Together, they worked in the southern region of France, setting up safe houses, organizing sabotage missions, and establishing communication lines between the Resistance and SOE headquarters in London. The information they gathered was vital to the Allied war effort, as it helped the British and American forces plan their operations in France, leading up to the D-Day invasion in 1944.

Odette and her team were instrumental in coordinating sabotage efforts that disrupted German supply lines, communications, and transportation networks. They also helped deliver supplies and weapons to the French Resistance fighters, who carried out attacks on German forces and collaborators. Operating under constant threat of discovery, Odette lived in a world of danger, where one wrong move could lead to capture, torture, and death.

Despite the perilous nature of her work, Odette was known for her bravery and resourcefulness. She often had to outwit German soldiers and collaborators to avoid arrest, relying on her training and quick thinking to evade detection. However, her luck ran out in April 1943, when she and Peter Churchill were betrayed by a double agent named Hugo Bleicher.

**Capture and Torture by the Gestapo**

On April 16, 1943, Odette and Peter Churchill were arrested by the Gestapo, the Nazi secret police, in the town of St. Jorioz in the French Alps. The Gestapo had been tipped off to their activities by Bleicher, a German intelligence officer posing as a member of the French Resistance. After their capture, Odette and Peter were taken to Fresnes Prison near Paris, where they were interrogated and tortured.

Odette endured unimaginable suffering at the hands of the Gestapo, who were determined to extract information about the SOE's operations and the French Resistance. She was subjected to beatings, starvation, and electric shock torture, but she refused to betray her comrades or reveal any details about her mission. To protect Peter Churchill, Odette told her captors that she was his wife and that he was the nephew of Winston Churchill, hoping this false connection would spare them both from execution. The Gestapo believed her story, and while they continued to torture her, they did not immediately execute her.

Odette's resilience in the face of torture earned her the respect of her captors, but it did not spare her from further suffering. In 1944, she was transferred to the infamous Ravensbrück concentration camp, a brutal facility primarily for women, where many prisoners died from disease, starvation, and executions. Odette was kept in solitary confinement for much of her time at Ravensbrück and was frequently subjected to further interrogations and abuse.

**Survival and Liberation**

Despite the horrific conditions at Ravensbrück, Odette managed to survive. Her unwavering spirit and determination to protect her fellow agents and the Resistance helped her endure the unimaginable horrors of the camp. In early 1945, as the war drew to a close, the camp's commandant, Fritz Suhren, fearing capture by the advancing Allies, decided to use Odette as a bargaining chip. Believing that she was related to Winston Churchill, Suhren took Odette with him as he attempted to surrender to American forces.

On May 1, 1945, just days before the official German surrender, Odette was liberated by American troops. She had survived nearly two years of imprisonment and torture at the hands of the Nazis, emerging as one of the few SOE agents to endure the full brutality of the Gestapo and concentration camps.

**Post-War Recognition and Legacy**

After the war, Odette Hallowes returned to Britain, where she was celebrated as a war hero. In 1946, she was awarded the George Cross, the highest civilian decoration for bravery in the United Kingdom, for her courage and resilience during her time in Nazi captivity. She was the first woman to receive this honor. She also received the Legion d'Honneur, France's highest military honor, in recognition of her contributions to the Resistance.

**Conclusion**

Odette Hallowes' contribution to the Allied cause during World War II is a remarkable story of courage, resilience, and sacrifice. As an SOE agent, she risked her life to support the French Resistance and gather intelligence critical to the success of the Allied war effort. Despite being captured and enduring horrific torture at the hands of the Gestapo, she never wavered in her commitment to protecting her comrades and her country.

**Sources**

Sergeant, Kit. The Spark of Resistance: Women Spies in WWII. Independently published, 2020.

Pedace, Donna. Women Warriors: The Hidden Spies of WWII. RMK Publications. 2024.

# Homegrown Nazi and Japanese Spies in America

## Introduction

During World War II, the United States faced not only external threats but also internal subversion as Nazi Germany and Imperial Japan deployed espionage networks across America. These networks included American citizens and residents who, driven by ideology, coercion, or profit, provided vital intelligence to the Axis powers. This story delves into the activities of these spies, the methods by which they operated, and the counterintelligence efforts to thwart their operations.

## The Espionage Landscape

The threat of espionage on American soil became a significant concern for the U.S. government as relations with Germany and Japan deteriorated in the 1930s. Both Axis powers sought to gather military, political, and economic intelligence to bolster their war efforts and disrupt American capabilities. Spies were recruited from diverse backgrounds, including expatriates, sympathizers, and even American citizens.

## Recruitment

Nazi Espionage Efforts German intelligence operations were primarily orchestrated by the Abwehr, the German military intelligence office, under Admiral Wilhelm Canaris. The Abwehr recruited spies from the German-American community and used returning American citizens who had lived in Germany to gather intelligence. One of the most notorious cases was that of Fritz Duquesne, a South African-born German spy who led a network that sought to sabotage American industrial production and relay information back to Germany.

## The Duquesne Spy Ring

Formed by Fritz Duquesne in the late 1930s, this spy ring was composed of over 30 men and women tasked with collecting information on American munitions production and troop movements. The ring operated by infiltrating key industries and military facilities. However, the ring was infiltrated by the FBI, which conducted a lengthy surveillance operation culminating in the arrests of the ring members in 1941, in what was then the largest espionage case in U.S. history.

Duquesne himself was a veteran spy who had been active since World War I, and his network was able to recruit German-Americans and sympathetic individuals to gather key military and industrial information. Their activities included photographing defense sites and ships, smuggling blueprints of defense facilities, and even plotting sabotage operations. Ultimately, 33 members of the Duquesne Spy Ring were convicted in 1942, thanks to the FBI's covert operation led by double agent William Sebold, who played a crucial role in bringing down the network.

**Japanese Espionage Efforts**

Japan's espionage activities were coordinated by the Japanese Imperial Navy and the Kempeitai, the military police arm of the Imperial Japanese Army. Japanese spies often operated under diplomatic cover in locations such as New York and Washington, D.C., gathering intelligence on naval movements and defense preparations.

**The Doll Woman**

Velvalee Dickinson, known as the "Doll Woman," was an American-born spy for Japan. Operating a doll shop in New York City as a cover, Dickinson used her business to send coded messages about U.S. naval operations in the Pacific. She corresponded with Japanese officials and sent letters written in code that appeared to discuss doll sales, but in reality, contained detailed information about the positions and movements of American naval ships.

The FBI grew suspicious of Dickinson when they intercepted letters containing coded messages disguised as inquiries about doll shipments. When they cross-referenced these letters with reports on the movement of naval ships, it became clear that Dickinson was passing critical military information to the Japanese. She was arrested in 1944, charged with espionage, and sentenced to 10 years in prison.

**A Spy Under Diplomatic Cover**

Kanegoro Nakamura was a Japanese diplomat in the United States, tasked with collecting intelligence on U.S. defense installations and political movements in Washington, D.C. Nakamura used his diplomatic immunity to send detailed reports to Tokyo regarding military production, ship movements, and political developments that could impact Japan's strategy in the Pacific. Though his diplomatic status protected him from immediate arrest, Nakamura was quietly expelled from the U.S. shortly after the attack on Pearl Harbor. His network, however, continued to operate through other covert agents.

**Other Notable Espionage Cases**

The Double Dealing Diplomat: Saburo Kurusu, a Japanese diplomat, played a pivotal role in Japanese espionage efforts before and during World War II. Although his primary role was to negotiate peace between Japan and the United States (a cover for Japan's final preparations for the attack on Pearl Harbor), Kurusu had also facilitated intelligence gathering in the United States. Using his diplomatic connections, Kurusu passed along critical information to the Japanese military.

**Max Stephan**

The Nazi Sympathizer: Max Stephan, a German-born restaurant owner in Detroit, was a passionate Nazi sympathizer. In 1942, Stephan harbored a German Luftwaffe pilot, Hans Peter Krug, who had escaped from a Canadian prisoner of war camp. Stephan helped Krug cross into the United States and provided him with shelter and money. His actions amounted to aiding the enemy, and Stephan became the first person in the U.S. to be convicted of treason during World War II. He was sentenced to death but later had his sentence commuted to life in prison.

**Counterintelligence Efforts**

The U.S. response to internal espionage threats was multifaceted, involving the FBI, the Office of Naval Intelligence (ONI), and later the Office of Strategic Services (OSS). Counterintelligence efforts were ramped up significantly after the attack on Pearl Harbor, leading to increased surveillance, tighter security around sensitive installations, and stricter control of information.

The FBI, led by J. Edgar Hoover, became the primary agency tasked with neutralizing Axis espionage threats within the United States. One of its most successful operations involved the infiltration of the Duquesne Spy Ring, where the Bureau used double agents like William Sebold to gather intelligence on the network's activities and eventually bring down its members.

Another notable success was the unraveling of Velvalee Dickinson's spy operation. Through careful analysis of intercepted correspondence and the use of cryptography, the FBI was able to decode the seemingly benign letters and expose the true nature of her espionage activities. These operations helped the FBI build its reputation as a formidable counterintelligence agency during the war.

**Conclusion:**

The efforts of Nazi Germany and Imperial Japan to infiltrate America through espionage during World War II were largely foiled by effective U.S. counterintelligence. The cases of Fritz Duquesne and his spy ring, Velvalee Dickinson, and others illustrate the Axis' persistent attempts to gather crucial military information from within the United States. However, the rapid and efficient response of the FBI, ONI, and other agencies helped neutralize these threats before they could significantly harm American interests.

**Sources**

Casey, Barbara. Velvalee Dickinson: The "Doll Woman" Spy. Strategic Media Press. 2019.

Gimpel, Erich. Agent 146: The True Story of a Nazi Spy in America. Thomas Dunne Books, 2003.

Various Sources

# How the SOE Derailed Nazi Nuclear Ambitions

## Introduction

One of the most vital of covert operations was the sabotage of the Nazi heavy water plant at Vemork, Norway. This daring mission, orchestrated by the British Special Operations Executive (SOE) and executed by Norwegian commandos, stands as a testament to the power of strategic sabotage and the indomitable human spirit in the face of tyranny. The operation not only dealt a significant blow to Nazi Germany's nuclear ambitions but also demonstrated the effectiveness of unconventional warfare tactics in turning the tide of the war.

## The Nazi Nuclear Threat

As the world plunged into the chaos of World War II, a silent race was underway – one that could have altered the course of history. Nazi Germany, under the guidance of Werner Heisenberg and other brilliant scientists, had embarked on an ambitious nuclear program known as the Uranverein or "Uranium Club". Their goal was clear: to harness the power of nuclear fission and develop the world's first atomic bomb.

Central to this endeavor was the production of heavy water (deuterium oxide), a crucial component for sustaining nuclear chain reactions. The Vemork hydroelectric plant, nestled in the rugged terrain of Telemark, Norway, became the focal point of this effort. As the only facility in Nazi-controlled Europe capable of producing heavy water in significant quantities, Vemork was both a crown jewel and an Achilles' heel of the German nuclear program.

## The SOE: Churchill's Secret Army

Recognizing the existential threat posed by potential Nazi nuclear weapons, the Allied powers knew they had to act. Enter the Special Operations Executive (SOE), a clandestine organization formed in July 1940 at the behest of British Prime Minister Winston Churchill. Tasked with the mission to "set Europe ablaze," the SOE became the vanguard of unconventional warfare against the Axis powers.

Under the leadership of Sir Frank Nelson and later Brigadier Colin Gubbins, the SOE developed a reputation for daring operations and innovative tactics. Their agents, drawn from diverse backgrounds and nationalities, were trained in the art of sabotage, espionage, and guerrilla warfare. The SOE's reach extended across occupied Europe and beyond, but few missions would prove as critical as the one targeting the Vemork plant.

## Operation Freshman: A Costly Lesson

The first attempt to sabotage the Vemork plant, codenamed Operation Freshman, was launched in November 1942. This ambitious plan involved British Royal Engineers who were to be flown into Norway using gliders. However, the harsh Norwegian winter and the challenging terrain proved to be formidable adversaries. Poor weather conditions and navigation errors led to a disastrous outcome – the gliders crashed, and the surviving soldiers were captured and executed by the Gestapo under Hitler's infamous Commando Order.

The failure of Operation Freshman was a sobering reminder of the risks involved and the need for a more nuanced approach. It also highlighted the importance of local knowledge and expertise in navigating the treacherous Norwegian landscape.

## Operation Gunnerside: The Perfect Storm

Learning from the tragic outcome of Operation Freshman, the SOE devised a new plan that would leverage the skills and local knowledge of Norwegian resistance fighters. This operation, codenamed Gunnerside, would become one of the most celebrated acts of sabotage in World War II.

The team selected for this mission was composed of Norwegian commandos from Company Linge, specially trained by the SOE in Scotland. Led by the young but determined Joachim Rønneberg, these men were not only skilled in sabotage and survival techniques but also intimately familiar with the harsh Norwegian terrain.

On February 16, 1943, the Gunnerside team parachuted into the snow-covered mountains of Norway. After rendezvousing with the advance team (Operation Grouse) that had been gathering intelligence, they began their perilous journey to Vemork.

The commandos chose a daring approach, descending into a steep gorge that the Germans had deemed impassable. This decision, while incredibly risky, allowed them to bypass most of the German defenses. Crossing an icy river and scaling a 500-foot cliff, the team reached the plant under the cover of darkness on February 27, 1943.

In a display of meticulous planning and flawless execution, the commandos infiltrated the heavily guarded facility through a cable tunnel. They quickly located the heavy water production room and planted their explosives. The entire operation was carried out in near silence, without a single shot fired.

As the team made their escape, the explosions rocked the Vemork plant, destroying the vital electrolysis chambers and with them, Nazi Germany's immediate hopes for heavy water production. The saboteurs then embarked on an epic ski journey to evade capture, with some making it to neutral Sweden while others remained in Norway to continue resistance activities.

## The Aftermath: Ripples Through History

The success of Operation Gunnerside reverberated far beyond the mountains of Telemark. The destruction of the heavy water production facilities at Vemork dealt a severe blow to the German nuclear program, causing significant delays and forcing a reevaluation of their approach to nuclear research.

While the Germans attempted to rebuild their heavy water capabilities, the Allied forces remained vigilant. In 1944, Norwegian resistance fighters sank the ferry SF Hydro, which was attempting to transport the remaining heavy water stocks to Germany, further cementing the operation's success.

The impact of the Vemork sabotage extended beyond the immediate strategic gains. It provided a tremendous morale boost to resistance movements across occupied Europe, demonstrating that the Nazi war machine was not invincible. For the SOE, it was a vindication of their unconventional approach to warfare and a testament to the effectiveness of well-trained and highly motivated operatives.

## Conclusion: A Legacy of Courage

The operation to destroy the Nazi heavy water plant at Vemork stands as one of the most successful acts of sabotage in military history. It showcases the critical role played by the SOE and the Norwegian resistance in altering the course of World War II. The courage, ingenuity, and determination displayed by the commandos of Operation Gunnerside continue to inspire to this day.

As we reflect on this extraordinary mission, we are reminded of the power of individual actions in the face of overwhelming odds. The saboteurs of Vemork not only disrupted Nazi Germany's nuclear ambitions but also struck a blow for freedom that resonated throughout occupied Europe and beyond.

In the words of Joachim Rønneberg, who led the Gunnerside team: "We were a gang of friends doing a job, not a bunch of heroes. We just planned for everything, and it worked out." This humble statement belies the enormous impact of their actions – actions that may well have changed the course of history and helped secure the peace we enjoy today.

## Sources

Charles River Editors. Operation Gunnerside: The History and Legacy of the Allied Mission to Sabotage Nazi Germany's Nuclear Weapons Program during World War II. Independently published, 2021.

Bascomb, Neal. The Winter Fortress: The Epic Mission to Sabotage Hitler's Atomic Bomb. Head of Zeus, 2017.

# The British Man Who Betrayed His Country

### Introduction

World War II, a time of intense struggle and heroism, also bore witness to acts of treachery that defied the moral code of nations at war. Among the most infamous of these betrayals was that of Harold Cole, a British man who, under the guise of loyalty, committed one of the most egregious acts of treason against his own country. Cole's actions during the war led to the deaths of countless resistance fighters and Allied agents, marking him as one of the most notorious traitors in British history.

### Conman and Thief

Harold Cole was born on January 24, 1906, in London, into a working-class family. His early life was marked by petty crime and a series of minor legal infractions, which foreshadowed the deceitful and treacherous path he would later take. By the time World War II broke out, Cole had already established a reputation as a conman and thief, having been involved in various schemes that took advantage of the vulnerable.

In 1939, as the world plunged into war, Cole saw an opportunity to reinvent himself. He enlisted in the British Army, presenting himself as a patriotic soldier eager to serve his country. However, his true nature soon surfaced, and he was discharged from the army for theft. Despite this, he managed to re-enlist under a different name, eventually finding himself stationed in France with the British Expeditionary Force. It was here that his journey into treachery truly began.

### From Soldier to Traitor

In the chaos following the fall of France in 1940, Cole found himself cut off from the British forces during the Dunkirk evacuation. Rather than attempt to return to Britain, he chose to stay behind in France, where he quickly adapted to the new reality of Nazi occupation. Using his charm and cunning, Cole presented himself to the French Resistance as a British officer and an escaped prisoner of war. The Resistance, desperate for experienced soldiers and Allied support, accepted Cole into their ranks, unaware that they were welcoming a wolf in sheep's clothing.

Cole ingratiated himself with the Resistance, learning their secrets and gaining their trust. He worked closely with key figures in the network, gathering information on their operations, safe houses, and the identities of members. All the while, he was secretly communicating with the German Gestapo, feeding them critical intelligence that would lead to the capture and execution of countless Resistance fighters and Allied agents.

**Betraying the Resistance**

Cole's betrayal had devastating consequences. Armed with the information he provided, the Gestapo launched a series of raids across France, rounding up Resistance members and dismantling entire networks. Many of those captured were tortured and executed, their deaths a direct result of Cole's treachery. The full extent of the damage he caused is difficult to quantify, but it is estimated that hundreds, if not thousands, of lives were lost because of his actions.

Cole's ability to deceive both the Resistance and the Gestapo was a testament to his manipulative skill. He played both sides expertly, all the while ensuring his own safety and financial gain. The Gestapo rewarded him handsomely for his services, providing him with money and protection as he continued to pose as a British officer working with the Resistance.

**The Downfall and Final Capture**

In late 1943, Cole was finally exposed. The French Resistance, suspicious of the increasing number of arrests within their ranks, began to investigate and soon uncovered the truth about Cole's duplicity. His betrayal sent shockwaves through the Resistance, but by the time they realized the extent of his treachery, it was too late for many of their comrades.

Cole fled from France, using his stolen money to evade capture. He made his way back to England, where he attempted to disappear into the chaos of wartime London. However, British intelligence was now aware of his actions, and a manhunt was launched to bring him to justice. Cole proved elusive, moving frequently and using his skills as a conman to avoid detection.

His capture finally came in January 1945, in a dramatic confrontation in the Montmartre district of Paris. Cole had been tracked down by French police working with British intelligence. When the police closed in, Cole attempted to shoot his way out, but was fatally wounded in the ensuing gunfight. He died from his injuries before he could be brought to trial.

**Conclusion**

Harold Cole's story is a dark chapter in the history of World War II, a tale of greed, deception, and ultimate betrayal. His actions not only led to the deaths of countless brave men and women but also highlighted the devastating impact that one traitor could have on a cause as vital as the fight against Nazi tyranny.

**Sources**

Murphy, Brendan. Turncoat: The Strange Case of British Sergeant Harold Cole, the Worst Traitor of the War. Harcourt, 1987

Ireland, Josh. The Traitors: A True Story of Blood, Betrayal and Deceit. John Murray, 2018.

# The German Double Agent Who Betrayed the SOE

## Introduction

In the complex and shadowy world of World War II espionage, few figures are as controversial and enigmatic as Henri Déricourt. A former French airman turned double agent, Déricourt's role in the British Special Operations Executive (SOE) would become one of the most damaging betrayals of the war. While posing as an SOE agent tasked with organizing clandestine flights in and out of Nazi-occupied France, Déricourt was secretly working for the Abwehr (German military intelligence) and later for the Gestapo. His treachery resulted in the capture and death of many SOE agents, yet he would escape post-war justice in a web of intrigue that has puzzled historians for decades.

This is the true story of Henri Déricourt—his rise within the SOE, his betrayal, and the ultimate consequences of his double-dealing that led to one of the most infamous chapters in the history of World War II espionage.

## Playing Both Sides

Henri Alfred Eugène Déricourt was born on September 2, 1909, in the small town of Coulonges-sur-Sarthe, France. By the time World War II erupted in 1939, Déricourt had already lived a life filled with adventure. A skilled pilot, he had flown with the French Air Force and worked as a bush pilot in French Indochina before the war. After the fall of France in 1940, Déricourt found himself in occupied Paris, where he used his aviation skills to work as a civilian pilot under German occupation.

It was during these years that Déricourt began making contacts within both the French Resistance and the German intelligence community. He would later claim that his involvement with German intelligence was a necessary evil, allowing him to maintain his freedom in occupied France. However, it soon became clear that Déricourt was more than a passive participant—he was about to play both sides in one of the most dangerous games of the war.

## Joining the Special Operations Executive (SOE)

The SOE, known as Churchill's "secret army," was tasked with conducting sabotage, espionage, and reconnaissance in Nazi-occupied Europe. Its mission was to "set Europe ablaze" by organizing and supporting resistance groups behind enemy lines. In 1942, Déricourt was recruited into the SOE, likely due to his piloting skills, knowledge of France, and connections within the Resistance. He was trained in sabotage and espionage by the British, who believed he would be an invaluable asset for their operations in France.

Déricourt was given the code name Gilbert and tasked with serving as an air-operations officer for the Prosper network, one of the largest and most important SOE circuits operating in France. His job was to coordinate the landing of Allied aircraft that were delivering supplies and agents to the Resistance and, in turn, evacuating key figures back to Britain.

At first, Déricourt proved effective in this role. He coordinated numerous successful landings of SOE aircraft, establishing himself as a trusted figure within the organization. His charm and seemingly deep commitment to the cause made him a popular figure among his British colleagues and the French Resistance. However, unbeknownst to the SOE, Déricourt had already been compromised.

## The Betrayal Begins

Déricourt's ties to German intelligence began as early as 1941, when he was first approached by Karl Boemelburg, the head of the Gestapo's counter-intelligence operations in France. Déricourt, always a pragmatist, agreed to collaborate with the Germans, likely viewing it as a way to protect himself and his future.

By the time he joined the SOE in 1942, Déricourt had become a double agent, passing information to the Abwehr and later the Gestapo about SOE operations. His role as an air-operations officer gave him access to critical information, including the identities of SOE agents, their landing zones, and the details of their missions. Déricourt passed much of this information directly to the Gestapo, setting the stage for one of the most devastating betrayals of the war.

The most notorious consequence of Déricourt's treachery came in 1943, when the Prosper network, led by Francis Suttill (code name "Prosper"), was infiltrated and destroyed by the Germans. Suttill and dozens of other SOE agents were arrested by the Gestapo, many of whom were later tortured and executed. It is widely believed that Déricourt was instrumental in this betrayal, providing the Germans with the intelligence they needed to dismantle the network.

## The Fall of the Prosper Network

The collapse of the Prosper network in June and July 1943 was one of the greatest disasters in SOE history. The network, which had been vital in supporting the French Resistance and conducting sabotage missions, was methodically dismantled by the Gestapo. Suttill was arrested in Paris on June 23, 1943, and was later executed at Sachsenhausen concentration camp. Many other agents, including Andrée Borrel, Vera Leigh, and Denise Bloch, were also arrested and later executed at the Natzweiler-Struthof concentration camp.

The precise role Déricourt played in the fall of the Prosper network remains a subject of debate. Some historians argue that he was directly responsible for providing the Gestapo with the intelligence needed to infiltrate the network. Others suggest that he may have been more of a passive accomplice, turning a blind eye to the activities of his German handlers while continuing to serve the SOE. What is clear, however, is that Déricourt's duplicity contributed to the deaths of many brave men and women who had risked their lives for the Resistance.

**Revelations and Investigation**

Déricourt's double-dealing remained hidden for much of the war, and even after the fall of the Prosper network, the SOE was slow to realize the extent of the betrayal. In 1944, suspicions began to grow within the SOE that Déricourt might have been working for the Germans. An internal investigation was launched, but the SOE leadership, eager to avoid a scandal, was reluctant to take definitive action.

After the war, more evidence came to light implicating Déricourt in the betrayal of the Prosper network. Survivors of the network, as well as former Gestapo officers, testified that Déricourt had been in regular contact with German intelligence and had passed information about SOE operations to the enemy. Despite this, Déricourt was never officially charged with treason, and he maintained his innocence until his death.

One of the most puzzling aspects of Déricourt's story is why he was never prosecuted. Some historians believe that the British government, embarrassed by the failure to detect his treachery, chose to cover up his activities rather than risk a public scandal. Others speculate that Déricourt may have been acting as a triple agent, providing some information to the Germans while feeding disinformation back to the SOE. Whatever the case, Déricourt's true motivations remain shrouded in mystery.

**Post-War Life and Legacy**

After the war, Henri Déricourt returned to civilian life, working as a pilot and attempting to distance himself from his wartime activities. In 1948, he was briefly arrested by French authorities and charged with collaborating with the enemy, but the case was dismissed due to a lack of evidence. Déricourt continued to live in France, largely avoiding the spotlight.

Déricourt's death in a plane crash in Laos in 1962 added another layer of intrigue to his life. Some have speculated that his death was not accidental, suggesting that he may have been silenced by former colleagues or intelligence agencies to prevent him from revealing sensitive information about his wartime activities. However, no concrete evidence has ever emerged to support these claims.

The legacy of Henri Déricourt remains one of the most controversial in the history of World War II espionage. His betrayal of the SOE and his role in the destruction of the Prosper network left a stain on the reputation of the British intelligence services and led to the deaths of many courageous agents. To this day, historians continue to debate the full extent of his treachery and whether he was acting out of self-preservation, greed, or some more complex motivation.

**Repercussions and Legacy**

The repercussions of Déricourt's actions were felt long after the war. The collapse of the Prosper network not only weakened the French Resistance at a critical time but also forced the SOE to reassess its security protocols. The betrayal shook the confidence of many within the SOE and led to greater scrutiny of agents working behind enemy lines.

Déricourt's story also serves as a cautionary tale about the complexities of espionage. The world of intelligence is one where loyalties can be fluid, and agents like Déricourt exploited the murky lines between ally and enemy for their own advantage. His ability to operate undetected for so long, despite growing suspicions, highlights the difficulties intelligence agencies face in vetting their operatives and ensuring their loyalty.

For the families of the SOE agents who were betrayed, Déricourt's name is a symbol of treachery and betrayal. The sacrifices of those agents—many of whom were tortured and executed in Nazi camps—stand in stark contrast to the self-serving actions of Déricourt, who evaded justice for his role in their deaths.

**Conclusion**

Henri Déricourt remains one of the most enigmatic and controversial figures of World War II espionage. His betrayal of the SOE and his role as a German double agent led to the destruction of one of the most important Resistance networks in occupied France and resulted in the deaths of many brave men and women who had risked their lives to fight Nazi oppression. Despite his actions, Déricourt largely escaped post-war justice, leaving unanswered questions about the extent of his cooperation with the Germans and why he was never fully prosecuted.

**Sources**

Rymills, Bunny. Henri Dericourt: Double or Triple Agent. Lulu.com, 2013.

Fuller, Jean Overton. Dericourt: The Chequered Spy. Sapere Books, 2023.

# The Nazi Plan to Infiltrate America with Spies

## Introduction

During World War II, the struggle between the Allied and Axis powers extended beyond the battlefields of Europe and the Pacific. One of the more secretive and audacious attempts by Nazi Germany to bring the war to American shores was Operation Pastorius, a covert mission designed to infiltrate the United States with saboteurs. Named after Francis Daniel Pastorius, a German-American settler, the operation aimed to destroy key American infrastructure, cripple the U.S. war effort, and sow panic among the civilian population. However, this plan, despite its bold conception, failed due to a combination of poor execution, personal betrayal, and the vigilance of U.S. intelligence. This is the story of Operation Pastorius, a German espionage mission that ended in scandal and betrayal rather than success.

## The Origins of Operation Pastorius

As the United States ramped up its industrial and military production following its entry into the war in December 1941, Nazi Germany recognized the growing threat posed by American involvement. Adolf Hitler and his military advisors understood that the U.S. industrial base, particularly its manufacturing and transportation infrastructure, was critical to the Allied war effort. Disrupting this infrastructure would not only slow down production but also demoralize the American public.

In 1942, Hitler approved a plan for a sabotage mission to be carried out on U.S. soil, with the goal of crippling American production and creating widespread panic. The mission was code-named Operation Pastorius, after the German founder of Germantown, Pennsylvania, in an attempt to link the operation to Germany's historical ties to America. The plan called for the deployment of a group of German saboteurs, trained in sabotage techniques, to carry out a series of coordinated attacks on key targets in the U.S.

The operation was overseen by Admiral Wilhelm Canaris, the head of the Abwehr, Nazi Germany's military intelligence service. Canaris, who was known for his ambivalence toward Hitler and the Nazi regime, was nonetheless tasked with ensuring that the operation would be a success. The men selected for the mission were German agents who had lived in the United States and were familiar with the language, culture, and geography, making them well-suited for covert operations on American soil.

## Training the Saboteurs

The saboteurs chosen for Operation Pastorius were carefully selected for their knowledge of the United States and their ability to blend in with the local population. Many of them had previously lived and worked in the U.S. before returning to Germany during the early years of the war. This familiarity with American society was considered a crucial asset, as it would allow the saboteurs to operate under the radar without arousing suspicion.

A group of eight men was assembled for the mission. The leader of the group was George John Dasch, a German national who had spent time in the U.S. as a waiter before returning to Germany in 1941. Dasch was joined by Ernest Peter Burger, Herbert Haupt, Richard Quirin, Heinrich Heinck, Edward Kerling, Werner Thiel, and Hermann Neubauer. Most of these men were in their twenties or thirties, and several had experience in the U.S., working as laborers or professionals in various cities.

The saboteurs underwent intensive training at a secret sabotage school located near Berlin. The training program, which lasted several weeks, included instruction in bomb-making, the use of explosives, and other sabotage techniques. The men were taught how to handle various types of explosives, including timed incendiary devices, which could be used to destroy factories, railways, and bridges. They also received training in covert operations, including how to avoid detection by American authorities and how to blend into civilian life once they arrived in the U.S.

Despite the thoroughness of their training, the saboteurs were not professional soldiers or spies. Most had no prior experience in intelligence work or covert operations, and their motivations for joining the mission varied. Some were ideologically committed to the Nazi cause, while others were driven by financial incentives or personal ambition. This lack of cohesion and professionalism would ultimately contribute to the failure of the mission.

## The Mission: Infiltrating the United States

The plan for Operation Pastorius called for the saboteurs to be divided into two teams of four men each. Both teams would be transported to the United States via German U-boats, which would drop them off on the east coast. Once ashore, the teams would split up and begin their sabotage missions, targeting factories, railroads, power plants, and water facilities. The ultimate goal was to disrupt the American war effort by crippling the country's industrial infrastructure.

The first team, led by George Dasch, was dropped off by U-202 on June 13, 1942, near Amagansett, a small town on Long Island, New York. The team's primary targets included railroads, aluminum plants, and bridges in the New York area. However, shortly after landing, the operation ran into trouble. The team was spotted by a Coast Guard patrolman, John Cullen, who became suspicious of their behavior. Dasch, thinking quickly, pretended to be a fisherman and attempted to bribe Cullen with $260 to forget the encounter. Cullen played along but reported the incident to his superiors as soon as possible.

Meanwhile, the second team, led by Edward Kerling, landed in Ponte Vedra Beach, Florida, on June 17, 1942, after being dropped off by U-584. Their targets included critical infrastructure in the Midwest, such as hydroelectric plants and railroads. Both teams were expected to rendezvous in Cincinnati before splitting up again to carry out their respective sabotage missions across the country.

## Betrayal and Capture

Despite the extensive planning and training that went into Operation Pastorius, the mission quickly unraveled due to the incompetence and indecision of the saboteurs, as well as Dasch's internal conflict about the mission. Soon after arriving in New York, Dasch began to have second thoughts about the operation. He was not fully committed to the Nazi cause and had doubts about the mission's chances of success. Rather than following through with the sabotage plan, Dasch decided to turn himself into U.S. authorities.

On June 19, 1942, Dasch contacted the FBI in Washington, D.C., and offered to reveal the entire operation in exchange for leniency. At first, the FBI did not take him seriously, but when he arrived in Washington with a suitcase full of cash intended for the mission, he was able to convince them of the authenticity of his story. Dasch provided the FBI with detailed information about the operation, including the identities of the other saboteurs and their mission objectives.

Over the next few days, the FBI, led by J. Edgar Hoover, quickly rounded up the remaining saboteurs. Dasch's team members were arrested in New York, while the second team, which had landed in Florida, was captured in Chicago. The entire group was in custody by the end of June, less than two weeks after the operation had begun.

## The Trial and Execution of the Saboteurs

The failure of Operation Pastorius was a major embarrassment for Nazi Germany, and the U.S. government was determined to make an example of the captured saboteurs. President Franklin D. Roosevelt authorized the use of a military tribunal to try the men, rather than a civilian court, as the saboteurs were considered unlawful combatants engaged in espionage and sabotage.

The trial began on July 8, 1942, in Washington, D.C., and was presided over by six military officers. The prosecution argued that the men had come to the United States to carry out acts of sabotage against American military and civilian targets and that they were agents of a hostile foreign power. The defense, meanwhile, attempted to argue that the men had been coerced into participating in the mission and had no intention of actually carrying out the sabotage.

After a brief trial, all eight saboteurs were found guilty. Six of them—Burger, Heinck, Haupt, Kerling, Quirin, and Neubauer—were sentenced to death. George Dasch, who had voluntarily turned himself in, was spared execution and sentenced to 30 years in prison. Ernest Burger, who had also cooperated with authorities, was sentenced to life in prison.

On August 8, 1942, just over two months after the mission began, the six condemned saboteurs were executed in the electric chair at the District of Columbia Jail. It was the largest mass execution in the United States in the 20th century. Dasch and Burger were eventually released from prison after the war, though they were deported to Germany.

## The Legacy

Operation Pastorius was a complete failure, but its legacy lives on as one of the most significant examples of Nazi espionage on American soil during World War II. The operation demonstrated the difficulties Nazi

Germany faced in conducting covert operations in the United States, where the FBI and other law enforcement agencies were highly effective in countering espionage efforts.

The failed mission also had broader implications for U.S. policy. The use of a military tribunal to try the saboteurs set a precedent for how the U.S. government would handle cases of espionage and terrorism in the future. The case has been cited in legal discussions surrounding the treatment of unlawful combatants and the use of military courts in the post-9/11 era.

In the end, Operation Pastorius was a stark reminder of the importance of vigilance and intelligence in times of war. While the saboteurs' plan to sabotage American infrastructure never came to fruition, their capture and the subsequent trial showcased the effectiveness of American counterintelligence efforts during World War II. The operation also highlighted the challenges of conducting covert operations on foreign soil, especially when relying on individuals with varying levels of commitment to the cause. Operation Pastorius, though a failed mission, left a lasting mark on both the legal and intelligence landscapes of the United States.

## Conclusion

Operation Pastorius was one of Nazi Germany's boldest attempts to strike directly at the United States during World War II. By infiltrating the country with trained saboteurs, the Nazis hoped to disrupt American industry and infrastructure, undermining the Allied war effort. However, the mission quickly fell apart due to poor planning, weak leadership, and the personal betrayal of George Dasch. The swift response of the FBI and the trial and execution of the saboteurs demonstrated the United States' determination to root out enemy agents on its soil. Operation Pastorius serves as a cautionary tale of how even the most well-planned espionage missions can be undone by human error and disloyalty. While the operation ultimately failed, its impact on U.S. legal and intelligence practices continues to be felt today.

## Sources

Charles River Editors. Operation Pastorious: The History of the Nazi Intelligence Operation to Commit Sabotage in the United States During World War II. Independently published, 2020.

Dobbs, Michael, Saboteurs: The Nazi Raid on America. Knopf, 2004.

# The Double Agents of the Allies and Axis

## Introduction:

World War II was not only fought on the battlefields but also in the shadows, where intelligence and counterintelligence played a critical role. Among the most intriguing figures in the war's espionage campaigns were double agents, individuals who appeared to serve one side while secretly working for the other. These agents, many of whom played dangerous and complex roles, were crucial in deceiving their enemies and providing vital information that shaped the outcomes of key battles. Both the Allies and the Axis powers relied on these operatives to gain an edge in the war, with several double agents achieving legendary status for their daring exploits.

Double agents such as Juan Pujol García (code-named "Garbo"), Eddie Chapman (code-named "Zigzag"), and Duško Popov (code-named "Tricycle") became central figures in Allied and Axis intelligence operations. These individuals helped mislead the enemy and secure victories in some of the most significant campaigns of the war, including the Normandy invasion. Their actions were critical in turning the tide of the war, but their work often came at great personal risk.

This is the true story of the most famous double agents of World War II, their roles in intelligence operations, and the lasting impact of their dangerous games of deception.

## Playing Both Sides

The use of double agents dates to the early days of espionage, but it was during World War II that the practice reached new levels of sophistication. Both the Allies and the Axis powers sought to gather intelligence about each other's plans and movements, and counterintelligence agencies on both sides worked tirelessly to identify and turn enemy agents into double agents. This was especially true for MI5, Britain's domestic intelligence agency, which ran one of the most successful double agent programs in history, known as the Double-Cross System (or XX System).

The XX System was designed to capture German spies operating in Britain and either turn them into double agents or feed them false information that would be passed back to German intelligence. The success of this system depended on the skill and loyalty of the double agents, who walked a fine line between providing just enough accurate information to maintain the trust of their German handlers while misleading them about critical Allied operations.

On the Axis side, the Abwehr, Germany's military intelligence agency, also sought to employ double agents to infiltrate Allied operations and gather information. However, many of these agents were either captured or turned by the Allies, leading to a devastating collapse of German intelligence networks in Britain and beyond.

## Juan Pujol García: Garbo, the Master Deceiver

Perhaps the most famous double agent of World War II was Juan Pujol García, a Spanish national who operated under the code name "Garbo." Pujol, initially motivated by a deep hatred of fascism, approached the British to offer his services as a spy but was initially rejected. Undeterred, Pujol began working for the Germans on his own initiative, convincing the Abwehr that he had established a vast network of agents in Britain. In reality, Pujol was fabricating reports from Lisbon, using nothing more than his creativity and an old guidebook to Britain.

After gaining the trust of the Germans, Pujol eventually succeeded in contacting British intelligence, and MI5 realized his potential as a double agent. They brought him to London, where he became a key figure in the XX System. Over the course of the war, Pujol fed the Germans a steady stream of disinformation, helping to deceive them about Allied plans and movements.

Pujol's most significant contribution came in the lead-up to D-Day, the Allied invasion of Normandy in June 1944. As part of Operation Fortitude, a massive deception campaign designed to convince the Germans that the invasion would take place at Pas-de-Calais rather than Normandy, Pujol provided the Abwehr with false information about the location and timing of the invasion. His carefully crafted reports convinced the Germans that the Normandy landings were a feint, and they kept critical divisions away from the actual invasion site for several days after D-Day, allowing the Allies to establish a beachhead.

For his service, Pujol was awarded both the Iron Cross by Germany and the MBE (Member of the Order of the British Empire) by Britain, a testament to his unparalleled success as a double agent.

## Eddie Chapman: Zigzag, the Rogue-Turned Hero

Eddie Chapman was an unlikely hero. A British career criminal and safecracker, Chapman was serving time in a Jersey prison when the island was occupied by German forces in 1940. Seizing the opportunity to get out of prison, Chapman offered his services to the Germans as a spy. The Germans accepted and sent him to France for training, after which Chapman was parachuted into Britain with orders to sabotage key military targets.

Upon landing in Britain, Chapman immediately turned himself in to MI5 and offered to work as a double agent. MI5, recognizing the value of having an agent inside the German intelligence network, accepted his offer and gave him the code name "Zigzag." Chapman's first mission as a double agent involved convincing the Germans that he had successfully sabotaged a British aircraft factory, when in reality, no damage had been done. Chapman's handlers in the **Abwehr** were so impressed with his supposed success that they awarded him the Iron Cross, making him one of the few Britons to receive the honor.

Throughout the war, Chapman played a key role in feeding disinformation to the Germans, including details about British defenses and the progress of the war. His exploits, including faking bombings and conducting phony sabotage operations, earned him a reputation as one of the most daring and unpredictable double agents of the war.

## Duško Popov: Tricycle, the Inspiration for James Bond

Duško Popov, a Yugoslav-born playboy and businessman, became one of Britain's most valuable double agents during the war. Known by the code name "Tricycle," Popov worked for the Germans as an agent but secretly served MI6, Britain's foreign intelligence service. Fluent in several languages and moving easily between high society circles in Europe, Popov was an ideal agent, able to gather intelligence and feed false information to the Germans without arousing suspicion.

One of Popov's most critical contributions came in 1941 when he alerted the FBI to German interest in U.S. naval installations, including Pearl Harbor. Though the warning was not heeded by the Americans, Popov's intelligence suggested that the Germans were aware of Japanese plans for a potential attack.

Throughout the war, Popov played a crucial role in deceiving the Germans about Allied plans, including participating in Operation Fortitude, the same deception campaign that Pujol was involved in, which successfully misled the Germans about the location of the D-Day landings.

Popov's daring exploits and his lavish lifestyle—he was known for his love of gambling and women—are said to have inspired Ian Fleming's creation of James Bond, making him one of the most famous real-life figures behind the iconic fictional spy.

## The XX System: A Web of Deception

The success of the XX System was not just due to individual agents like Garbo, Zigzag, and Tricycle, but to the entire network of double agents that MI5 managed to recruit and run. By the end of the war, MI5 had turned nearly all of the German spies operating in Britain into double agents, feeding false information back to the Abwehr. This success was largely due to the skill of Thomas Argyll Robertson, known as Tar Robertson, the MI5 officer who oversaw the XX System.

One of the system's greatest triumphs was its role in the deception leading up to D-Day. Through a series of carefully coordinated reports, the network of double agents convinced the Germans that the Allies would invade at Calais rather than Normandy, leading the Germans to misallocate their forces and allowing the Allies to gain a critical foothold in France.

On the Axis side, the Abwehr struggled to maintain effective double agents. Many of their operatives, including agents sent to Britain and the United States, were captured or turned by Allied intelligence services. The Germans often relied on these compromised agents for vital information, which ultimately contributed to their downfall.

## Repercussions and Legacy

The use of double agents during World War II had a profound impact on the course of the war, particularly in shaping the outcome of critical campaigns like the Normandy invasion. The ability of Allied intelligence to mislead the Axis powers through the use of double agents helped tilt the balance of the war in favor of the Allies. The success of the XX System demonstrated the importance of counterintelligence and the potential for double agents to influence the outcome of large-scale military operations.

For the Germans, the failure to effectively manage their double agents was one of the reasons for the collapse of their intelligence efforts. The reliance on compromised agents and the inability to detect deception contributed to the misallocation of resources and the ultimate failure of the German war effort.

In the post-war years, the exploits of double agents like Pujol, Chapman, and Popov became the stuff of legend. Their daring, ingenuity, and willingness to operate in the most dangerous environments have made them enduring figures in the history of espionage. Their stories continue to inspire films, books, and television series, highlighting the critical role of intelligence in modern warfare.

**Conclusion**

The double agents of World War II played a pivotal role in the shadowy world of espionage, where deception and counterintelligence were just as important as battles fought on the ground. Figures like Juan Pujol García, Eddie Chapman, and Duško Popov demonstrated extraordinary courage and cunning as they manipulated their enemies and helped shape the course of the war. These double agents not only saved lives but also played a key role in securing Allied victories by misleading the Axis powers, particularly in crucial operations such as the D-Day landings. Their actions exposed the fragility of intelligence networks and showcased the strategic importance of deception in modern warfare.

**Sources**

Garcia, Juan Pujol. Operation Garbo: The Personal Story of the Most Successful Spy of World War II. Biteback Publishing, 2011.

Burton, Penelope. Agent GARBO: The Story of Juan Pujol Garcia (Secret Agents of D-Day). Hindle Publishing 2024.

# The Betrayal of British MI5 Officer Kim Philby

**Introduction**

The story of Kim Philby, a senior officer in MI5 and MI6, who became one of the most notorious spies in history, is a chilling tale of loyalty, betrayal, and espionage during one of the most dangerous times in world history. Born into a privileged British family, Philby rose to prominence in British intelligence during World War II, all the while secretly working as a double agent for the Soviet Union. His espionage career, which spanned decades, caused untold damage to British and Allied security, not only during the war but throughout the Cold War. Philby's actions led to the exposure of countless agents, the sabotage of crucial operations, and a deep crisis of trust within the British intelligence community.

This story delves into Kim Philby's covert betrayal, the secrets he revealed to the Soviets during World War II, and the long-lasting repercussions of his treachery.

**Early Life and Recruitment**

Harold Adrian Russell "Kim" Philby was born on January 1, 1912, in Ambala, India, where his father, St. John Philby, served as a British colonial officer. His father was a renowned Arabist and explorer who held controversial views, including sympathies toward the cause of Arab nationalism, which may have influenced his son's anti-imperialist sentiments.

Kim Philby was educated at Westminster School and later attended Trinity College, Cambridge, where he first became exposed to radical leftist ideologies. It was during his time at Cambridge that Philby developed communist sympathies, which would eventually lead him down the path of treachery. Cambridge, during the 1930s, was a hotbed of political discourse, and several key figures within the Cambridge Five—a notorious ring of Soviet spies—were recruited during this period. Philby's closest associates included Guy Burgess, Donald Maclean, Anthony Blunt, and John Cairncross, all of whom would become Soviet agents.

Philby was recruited into Soviet intelligence by Arnold Deutsch, a NKVD (the Soviet intelligence agency before the KGB) officer who was in charge of recruiting British students with leftist inclinations. Philby's role as a Soviet agent would remain hidden for years, even as he rose through the ranks of British intelligence.

**Joining British Intelligence**

In 1940, as World War II raged across Europe, Kim Philby was recruited into the British Secret Intelligence Service (SIS), known as MI6, due to his connections and apparent loyalty to the British cause. His position within MI6 provided him with access to some of the most sensitive wartime information, particularly regarding British and Allied intelligence efforts.

One of Philby's early roles was in the MI6 Section D, which focused on sabotage, subversion, and covert operations behind enemy lines. His work in this division allowed him access to highly classified information, including covert operations against Nazi Germany. Philby's charm, intelligence, and aristocratic background made him a rising star within British intelligence, and he was soon placed in charge of Section V, the division responsible for counterespionage against the Soviets.

Despite his growing influence in MI6, Philby remained a dedicated Soviet agent. His loyalty was never to Britain, but to the Soviet Union, and he used his position to funnel vast amounts of critical information to his Soviet handlers. Philby's betrayal during World War II was devastating for British intelligence, but at the time, no one suspected that he was working for the enemy.

**Secrets Revealed to the Soviets**

Throughout World War II, Kim Philby provided the NKVD with valuable intelligence that significantly undermined British and Allied operations. Some of the most damaging information he passed on included:

**Allied Plans and Strategies:** Philby had access to top-secret intelligence regarding the Allied invasion plans for Europe, including operations in North Africa and the D-Day landings. Although he did not singlehandedly reveal the details of these operations, his information allowed the Soviets to have a comprehensive understanding of the Allies' strategic intentions. The Soviets, although allied with Britain and the United States against Nazi Germany, used this information to position themselves more advantageously for the post-war order.

**Counterintelligence Operations:** One of Philby's most harmful contributions to Soviet intelligence was his role in compromising British counterintelligence efforts against Soviet spies. In his position within MI6, Philby was responsible for identifying Soviet espionage activities in Britain. Instead of exposing Soviet agents, he protected them, allowing many to continue their operations unhindered. This led to a situation in which Soviet spy rings in Britain and across Europe operated with relative impunity during the war.

**The Fate of Anti-Soviet Agents:** Perhaps the most devastating consequence of Philby's betrayal was his role in exposing anti-Soviet agents to the NKVD. Many Eastern European agents who were recruited by MI6 and tasked with infiltrating Soviet-occupied territories were betrayed by Philby. These individuals were often captured, tortured, and executed by Soviet forces. The fate of these agents remains one of the darkest aspects of Philby's espionage activities during the war.

**Anglo-American Intelligence Sharing**: As MI6 developed close ties with American intelligence agencies, particularly the Office of Strategic Services (OSS) (the forerunner of the CIA), Philby was able to pass on American secrets to the Soviets as well. This included intelligence related to U.S. covert operations in Europe and Asia. Philby's actions compromised numerous joint intelligence efforts between Britain and the U.S., which had long-term consequences for trust between the two allies.

**Operation Venona:** One of the most significant pieces of intelligence Philby betrayed was the existence of Operation Venona, a top-secret Allied effort to decrypt Soviet communications. Although Venona's full impact would not be realized until after the war, Philby's revelations allowed the Soviets to take countermeasures to protect their communications networks.

## The Cambridge Spy Ring

Philby's wartime activities were only part of the larger picture of Soviet espionage within Britain. He was a key member of the Cambridge Five, a group of British spies who worked for the Soviet Union throughout the 1930s, 1940s, and 1950s. The other members of the group, including Guy Burgess and Donald Maclean, also held positions of influence within the British government and provided valuable intelligence to the Soviets.

The network operated under the radar for many years, thanks in part to the class privileges and connections that allowed its members to avoid suspicion. Philby's reputation as a loyal British patriot and his aristocratic background helped shield him from scrutiny, even as he was actively betraying his country.

By the end of World War II, the Cambridge Spy Ring had compromised a significant portion of British intelligence operations. The full extent of their treachery would not be revealed until much later, but their activities during the war had already caused irreversible damage.

## Post-War Activities and Increasing Suspicion

After World War II, Kim Philby continued to rise within British intelligence. In 1949, he was appointed the MI6 liaison to the CIA in Washington, D.C., a position that gave him access to some of the most sensitive American intelligence operations. During this time, he also continued to pass information to the Soviets, further undermining Allied efforts during the early stages of the Cold War.

However, as Soviet defections began to increase in the early 1950s, suspicion began to fall on Philby. In 1951, two of his closest associates, Guy Burgess and Donald Maclean, were tipped off about impending arrests and defected to the Soviet Union. Their escape raised serious questions within MI5 and MI6, and Philby's connection to them made him a prime suspect.

Despite mounting evidence, Philby managed to evade arrest for several more years, largely due to his powerful connections and his ability to deflect suspicion. However, by 1963, after years of investigation, MI5 finally confronted Philby with undeniable evidence of his espionage activities. Rather than face arrest, Philby fled to the Soviet Union, where he would spend the rest of his life.

## The Consequences of Philby's Betrayal

The damage caused by Kim Philby's betrayal was immeasurable. During World War II, his actions directly led to the deaths of numerous anti-Soviet agents and compromised critical Allied operations. His post-war espionage continued to undermine British and American intelligence efforts during the early years of the Cold War, and his defection to the Soviet Union was a profound embarrassment for British intelligence.

Philby's betrayal also had lasting consequences for the Special Relationship between Britain and the United States. The CIA, in particular, was deeply shaken by the realization that their trusted MI6 liaison had been a Soviet spy for decades. The revelation of Philby's activities led to a significant deterioration of trust between British and American intelligence agencies, which took years to rebuild.

## Conclusion

Kim Philby's betrayal during World War II and the early Cold War remains one of the most significant intelligence breaches in history. His ability to operate as a Soviet agent while rising through the ranks of British intelligence allowed him to pass critical secrets to the Soviet Union, undermining Allied efforts and shaping the post-war geopolitical landscape. The full extent of the damage caused by Philby's espionage may never be known, but his story serves as a chilling reminder of the potential for betrayal even among the highest echelons of government and intelligence.

## Sources

Macintyre, Ben. A Spy Among Friends: Kim Philby and the Great Betrayal. Crown, 2015.

Holzman, Michael. Spies and Traitors: Kim Philby, James Angleton and the Friendship and Betrayal that Would Shape MI6, the CIA and Cold War. Pegasus Books, 2021.

# Traitors and Spies within the Vatican

## Introduction:

During World War II, the Vatican was positioned at the heart of Europe, both geographically and politically. As the epicenter of the Catholic Church, it was a unique institution caught in the complex web of diplomacy, intrigue, and wartime politics. Although Pope Pius XII maintained a policy of official neutrality, seeking to preserve the Church's independence amid the warring powers, there were individuals within the Vatican who quietly sympathized with, and in some cases actively aided the Nazi regime. These traitors within the Vatican—cardinals, priests, guards, and other officials—acted against the Allies by leaking information, collaborating with Axis powers, or even aiding in the escape of Nazi war criminals after the war. This story reveals the tangled web of allegiances within the Vatican during one of the most tumultuous periods in modern history.

## The Vatican's Position During the War

When World War II began in 1939, the Vatican, under the leadership of Pope Pius XII, declared itself neutral. The Pope believed that maintaining neutrality was essential for preserving the Church's independence and its ability to provide humanitarian assistance to war victims on both sides. Despite his stance, Pius XII faced criticism for his alleged silence in the face of the Holocaust and the atrocities committed by Nazi Germany. The Vatican's archives from the wartime period have only recently been opened to scholars, revealing a more complex picture of the Vatican's role during the war.

While the Pope sought to maintain neutrality, the Vatican was not immune to internal divisions. Some within its ranks were sympathetic to the Nazi cause, either for ideological reasons or because they believed that the rise of fascism in Europe could serve as a bulwark against communism, which the Catholic Church viewed as a greater threat. Others saw the potential for personal gain or influence by collaborating with the Nazis or betraying the Allies. These individuals operated in secret, often undermining the Vatican's official position of neutrality.

## Cardinals and Priests with Nazi Sympathies

Several high-ranking Church officials were known to harbor sympathies for the Nazi regime, either due to ideological alignment or opportunism. One of the most notorious figures was Cardinal Alois Hudal, an Austrian cleric who held considerable influence within the Vatican. Hudal was a fierce opponent of communism and a strong supporter of the fascist regimes in Italy and Germany. He was the author of 'The Foundations of National Socialism', a book that praised Adolf Hitler and defended the principles of Nazism.

Hudal saw Nazism as a force that could help restore traditional values in Europe and defend Christianity from the perceived threat of communism. Although he held a senior position within the Church, Hudal's pro-Nazi views put him at odds with many of his fellow clergy members. Nevertheless, he used his position to support Nazi collaborators and sympathizers, both during and after the war. After Germany's defeat, Hudal became notorious for his involvement in the so-called 'Ratlines', the clandestine networks that helped Nazi war criminals escape to South America. Hudal used his connections within the Church to secure false documents and safe passage for figures like Adolf Eichmann and Josef Mengele, some of the most notorious architects of the Holocaust.

While Hudal was the most prominent example of a pro-Nazi cleric, he was not alone. Other priests and cardinals also expressed sympathy for the Nazi regime. Some saw the rise of fascism as a means to protect the Church's interests in Europe, particularly in countries like Spain and Italy, where fascist regimes were closely aligned with Catholicism. These individuals provided various forms of assistance to the Nazis, ranging from moral support to logistical aid in their efforts to evade justice after the war.

## Vatican Officials Involved in Espionage

The Vatican's position as an independent state and a center for diplomacy made it a prime target for espionage during the war. Both the Axis and the Allies sought to infiltrate the Vatican and gather intelligence on each other's activities. Within the Vatican, certain officials actively collaborated with the Nazis, providing them with valuable intelligence and compromising the Vatican's stance of neutrality. These individuals, motivated by various personal, ideological, or political reasons, played a dangerous game of espionage in one of the world's most secretive institutions.

One of the most notable cases involved Monsignor Ludwig Kaas, a German cleric and a close advisor to Pope Pius XII. Although Kaas had previously opposed the Nazis during the rise of Hitler, his later actions raised suspicions of collaboration. While there is no direct evidence that Kaas was a Nazi sympathizer, his connections to the German government and his influence within the Vatican made him a person of interest for Allied intelligence agencies. It was believed that he may have acted as a conduit for secret communications between the Nazi regime and certain factions within the Vatican.

In addition to high-ranking clergy, lower-level Vatican officials, including Swiss Guards and administrative staff, were also implicated in espionage activities. These individuals had access to sensitive information, and some were suspected of passing it to Axis intelligence services. The Vatican's position as a neutral state allowed it to receive diplomats and emissaries from both the Allied and Axis powers, making it a hotbed of diplomatic intrigue. Several Vatican insiders were believed to have used their positions to gather intelligence and funnel it to Nazi agents, particularly as the war reached its final stages.

## The Ratlines and Vatican Assistance to Nazi War Criminals

One of the most troubling aspects of Vatican involvement with the Nazis was the post-war role played by certain clergy members in aiding the escape of war criminals. The Ratlines were covert networks that helped former Nazis and fascists flee Europe to evade prosecution for war crimes. Many of these escape routes led to South America, where countries like Argentina, under the leadership of Juan Perón, offered sanctuary to fleeing Nazis.

Cardinal Alois Hudal, as previously mentioned, was a key figure in facilitating these escapes. He used his position within the Church to provide false identity papers and travel documents to high-ranking Nazi officials, including SS officers and war criminals. With the help of Hudal and other sympathetic priests, these individuals were able to avoid the Nuremberg Trials and live out their lives in relative obscurity in countries like Argentina, Brazil, and Paraguay.

In addition to Hudal, other priests and Vatican officials played similar roles. Father Krunoslav Draganović, a Croatian priest, was heavily involved in helping members of the Ustaše, a fascist organization responsible for horrific crimes in Croatia during the war, to escape to South America. Draganović worked closely with the Vatican to provide safe passage for these individuals, using Church resources and diplomatic channels to shield them from Allied authorities.

The Vatican's involvement in the Ratlines has been the subject of much controversy. While some argue that the Church was simply providing humanitarian assistance to displaced individuals after the war, others believe that certain members of the clergy were fully aware of the war crimes committed by those they were helping. The full extent of Vatican's complicity in these operations is still being uncovered, but the role of figures like Hudal and Draganović is well-documented.

## Vatican Neutrality and the Allegiances Within

Despite the actions of individuals like Hudal and Draganović, it is important to note that the Vatican as an institution maintained its official stance of neutrality throughout the war. Pope Pius XII's primary concern was the survival of the Church and its ability to continue its spiritual mission in a war-torn world. The Pope and many high-ranking Church officials were deeply concerned about the rise of both Nazism and communism, viewing both as threats to the Church's authority and to Christian values.

However, this policy of neutrality created a fertile ground for intrigue and betrayal within the Vatican. The Holy See was home to a wide range of views, and while some within its ranks were sympathetic to the Nazi regime, others were staunchly opposed. Figures like Bishop Konrad von Preysing and Monsignor Giovanni Montini (the future Pope Paul VI) were known for their opposition to fascism and their efforts to assist Jews and other persecuted groups during the war. Montini, in particular, played a key role in organizing efforts to provide aid to refugees and worked to facilitate secret negotiations aimed at ending the war.

The divisions within the Vatican reflected the broader divisions within Europe at the time. As the war progressed and the atrocities of the Nazi regime became more widely known, many within the Church began to distance themselves from the fascist regimes they had once tolerated or even supported. However, for some, the fear of communism remained a more pressing concern than the threat posed by the Nazis, leading them to continue their collaboration with Axis powers even as the war drew to a close.

## The Aftermath and the Church's Reckoning

In the years following World War II, the Vatican faced increasing scrutiny over its wartime actions, particularly its role in helping Nazi war criminals escape justice. While the Church has made efforts to address this dark chapter in its history, including the opening of Vatican archives to researchers, questions remain about the extent of its involvement in the Ratlines and its relationships with Axis powers.

In 2020, the Vatican announced that it would make its archives from the pontificate of Pope Pius XII available to scholars, allowing historians to examine the role of the Church during the war more thoroughly. Early research has revealed a complex picture of the Vatican's involvement in wartime politics, with some members of the clergy working to resist the Nazis while others aided them. The release of these documents has led to renewed calls for accountability and transparency from the Church regarding its wartime actions.

## Conclusion

The story of traitors within the Vatican during World War II is one of moral complexity, intrigue, and betrayal. While the Vatican officially maintained a stance of neutrality, individuals within its ranks, such as Cardinal Alois Hudal and other sympathetic clergy, used their positions to collaborate with the Nazi regime and assist in the escape of war criminals after the war. These actions stand in stark contrast to those of other clergy members who risked their lives to resist fascism and protect the victims of Nazi persecution.

## Sources

Alvarez, David. Spies in the Vatican: Espionage and Intrigue from Napoleon to the Holocaust. University of Kansas Press, 2002.

Bokun, Branko. Spy in the Vatican, 1941-1945. Tom Stacey LTD., 1973.

# Codebreakers

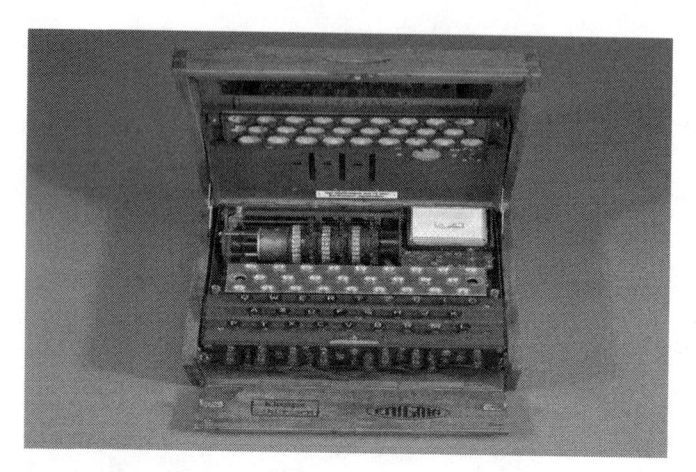

# Cracking the Enigma Machine and the Nazi Response

## Introduction

The Enigma machine, a cipher device used by Nazi Germany during World War II, was a pivotal tool in their military communications. The ability to decipher these encrypted messages was crucial for the Allies in their fight against the Axis powers. The efforts to crack the Enigma code not only showcased human ingenuity and determination but also significantly impacted the course of the war. This story explores the development of the Enigma machine, the groundbreaking work of codebreakers at Bletchley Park, and the subsequent adjustments made by the Nazis in response to Allied successes.

## The Enigma Machine

The Enigma machine was invented in the early 1920s by German engineer Arthur Scherbius. Initially developed for commercial use, it was later adopted by the German military for secure communication. The machine used a series of rotating wheels, or rotors, each with 26 letters, to encrypt messages. By changing the settings of these rotors, the machine could create a virtually infinite number of possible configurations, making it extremely difficult for anyone without the correct settings to decipher the messages.

By the late 1930s, the Enigma machine was extensively used by the German military, including the Army, Navy, and Air Force. The complexity of the machine and the constant evolution of its settings made it a formidable tool for secure communications. However, the Allies soon recognized that cracking the Enigma code could provide critical intelligence that could alter the course of the war.

## The Need for Codebreakers

As World War II escalated, the need for effective intelligence gathering became paramount. The Allies were aware of the significance of the Enigma machine but faced significant challenges in understanding its inner workings. Each military branch used different versions of the machine, and the configuration settings changed daily, making it increasingly difficult to intercept and decipher communications.

The British government, recognizing the importance of codebreaking, established the Government Code and Cypher School at Bletchley Park in 1939. This facility became the hub of Allied cryptanalysis efforts, bringing together some of the brightest minds in mathematics, linguistics, and engineering to tackle the Enigma challenge.

## The Early Codebreaking Efforts

In the early stages of the war, the efforts to crack Enigma codes were hampered by limited resources and a lack of understanding of the machine's mechanics. However, the initial breakthrough came from the work of Polish mathematicians Marian Rejewski, Jerzy Różycki, and Henryk Zygalski. In the 1930s, they had successfully managed to reverse-engineer the Enigma machine and develop methods to decipher its codes.

The Polish codebreakers were able to construct a device known as the "Bombe" which was designed to test various combinations of Enigma settings. They shared their findings with the British and French intelligence services in 1939, just before the outbreak of World War II. This collaboration laid the groundwork for the subsequent efforts at Bletchley Park.

## The Work at Bletchley Park

Upon receiving the Poles' information, the British codebreakers, led by figures like Alan Turing, Gordon Welchman, and Dilly Knox, began to refine and expand upon the existing techniques for breaking Enigma codes. Bletchley Park became a melting pot of talent and innovation. The diverse group included mathematicians, chess champions, linguists, and even crossword puzzle enthusiasts, all working toward a common goal.

Alan Turing, a brilliant mathematician and logician, played a crucial role in the development of techniques to decipher Enigma communications. He designed a more advanced machine called the "Bombe" which automated the process of testing different rotor settings and speeds. Turing's bombe could analyze large volumes of encrypted messages much faster than human analysts could. This technological advancement greatly increased the chances of breaking the Enigma codes.

In addition to the Bombe, codebreakers at Bletchley Park developed a systematic approach to understanding the patterns in intercepted messages. They analyzed the frequency of letters and common phrases, identifying weaknesses in the German encryption methods. By exploiting these weaknesses, they were able to uncover the daily key settings used by the Enigma machines.

## The Breaking of the Enigma Code

By late 1940, the codebreakers at Bletchley Park had achieved significant successes in breaking Enigma codes used by the German Navy. This was particularly important because the Navy's communications included critical information about U-boat movements and their attacks on Allied shipping. The intelligence gained from deciphering these messages, known as "Ultra" intelligence, played a crucial role in the Battle of the Atlantic.

The breaking of the Enigma code was not without its challenges. The Germans continually updated their encryption procedures, increasing the complexity of the codes. In 1941, they introduced a new version of the Enigma machine, known as the "Kriegsmarine" Enigma, which featured additional rotors and settings. This adjustment posed a significant challenge to the codebreakers at Bletchley Park, as they had to adapt their methods to keep pace with the evolving technology.

## The Role of Ultra Intelligence

The intelligence gleaned from breaking the Enigma codes had significant implications for military operations throughout the war. The Allies were able to intercept and decode vital communications, providing them with foresight into German troop movements, naval operations, and strategic plans.

One of the most notable examples of the impact of Ultra intelligence was during the Battle of El Alamein in 1942. By decoding German communications, the Allies were able to anticipate Rommel's movements and formulate effective counter-strategies. This decisive victory in North Africa marked a turning point in the war and demonstrated the critical role played by codebreaking efforts.

**The German Response**

As the Allies continued to break the Enigma code, the Germans became increasingly aware of the need to secure their communications. In 1942, they began to implement changes to their encryption methods in response to the growing threat posed by Allied intelligence efforts. These adjustments included changing the daily keys more frequently and increasing the complexity of the Enigma machine.

The Germans also sought to improve the security of their communications by using additional layers of encryption. They implemented a system known as "Schlüssel" (key), in which they combined Enigma encryption with other cryptographic methods to create a more secure communication system. However, these adjustments did not fully mitigate the effectiveness of the Allied codebreakers.

**Challenges Faced by Bletchley Park**

The codebreakers at Bletchley Park faced ongoing challenges as the Germans adapted their strategies. Introducing new machines and encryption methods required constant innovation and flexibility on the part of the codebreakers. Despite these challenges, the team at Bletchley Park remained determined to crack the codes.

In addition to the technical challenges, the secrecy surrounding their work posed difficulties. The codebreakers operated under strict security protocols, and their achievements were often not recognized outside of Bletchley Park. The pressure to deliver results while working in relative obscurity added to the challenges faced by the team.

**Continued Success**

Despite the obstacles, the codebreakers at Bletchley Park continued to make significant strides. By early 1943, they had developed new techniques and improved their bombes to keep pace with the evolving Enigma codes. The combination of technical expertise, mathematical ingenuity, and relentless determination allowed them to maintain a foothold in the battle for intelligence supremacy.

The successful breaking of Enigma codes continued to provide the Allies with critical information throughout the war. The intelligence gained from Ultra played a vital role in various campaigns, including the D-Day invasion in 1944. By understanding German communications, the Allies could formulate strategies that would ultimately lead to victory in Europe.

**The End of the War**

The relentless efforts of the codebreakers at Bletchley Park, along with the intelligence derived from breaking the Enigma code, contributed significantly to the Allied victory in World War II. By the war's end in 1945, the work done at Bletchley Park was regarded as one of the most important contributions to the Allied war effort.

The success of the codebreakers not only altered the course of the war but also left a lasting impact on the fields of cryptography and information security. The techniques developed during this time laid the groundwork for modern cryptographic practices and the understanding of secure communication.

**Recognition and Secrecy:** For many years after the war, the work done at Bletchley Park remained shrouded in secrecy. The significance of breaking the Enigma code was not fully acknowledged until decades later. It was only in the 1970s that the contributions of the codebreakers began to receive broader recognition.

In 1994, the British government officially acknowledged the work done at Bletchley Park, honoring the contributions of the codebreakers and providing them with the recognition they deserved. The legacy of their work continues to be celebrated today, with Bletchley Park now functioning as a museum and heritage center dedicated to the history of codebreaking and its impact on the war.

**Conclusion:**

The story of cracking the Enigma machine and the subsequent adjustments made by Nazi Germany is a testament to human ingenuity, determination, and the critical importance of intelligence in warfare. The successful efforts at Bletchley Park altered the course of World War II and laid the foundation for modern cryptography and information security.

**Sources**

Lachman, Charles. Codename Nemo: The Hunt for the Nazi U-Boat and the Elusive Enigma Machine. Diversion Books.

Hodges, Andrew: The Enigma: The Book that Inspired the film 'The Imitation Game'. Simon & Schuster, 1983.

# British Linguists and the Battle of Britain

## Introduction

The Battle of Britain, fought between July and October 1940, stands as one of the most pivotal air campaigns in history. As the Royal Air Force (RAF) defended the skies against the German Luftwaffe, a lesser-known battle was being waged on the airwaves. This is the story of the British linguists who played a crucial role in deceiving Luftwaffe pilots, contributing significantly to the defense of Britain. Their work, shrouded in secrecy for decades, exemplifies the power of linguistic prowess and intelligence operations in shaping the outcome of war. This story explores the context of their operations, the methods they employed, and the lasting impact of their ingenious deceptions on the course of World War II.

## The Battle of Britain: A Fight for Survival

The Battle of Britain emerged as a critical conflict following the fall of France in June 1940. With Britain standing as the last major European power resisting Nazi Germany, Adolf Hitler set his sights on securing air superiority over the island nation as a precursor to a planned invasion, codenamed Operation Sea Lion. The Luftwaffe's objective was clear: to destroy Britain's air defenses and pave the way for a successful amphibious assault across the English Channel.

The battle officially began on July 10, 1940, with the Luftwaffe launching attacks on British shipping convoys in the English Channel. As the conflict intensified, key dates such as August 13 (Eagle Day), August 15 (The Greatest Day), and September 15 (Battle of Britain Day) saw some of the most intense aerial combat in history. The RAF, outnumbered but fighting with determination, faced the daunting task of repelling wave after wave of German aircraft.

## British Intelligence: The Unseen Front

While the heroic efforts of RAF pilots, immortalized as "The Few" by Winston Churchill, are well-documented, the role of British intelligence in this victory has often been overlooked. Behind the scenes, a network of brilliant minds worked tirelessly to give the defenders an edge. Among these unsung heroes were the linguists and intelligence officers who engaged in a sophisticated campaign of deception and misinformation.

The British intelligence apparatus, including MI5 and MI6, had been preparing for this moment long before the first Luftwaffe plane crossed the Channel. They had developed a multifaceted approach to intelligence gathering and deception, which included the interception and analysis of enemy communications, the use of double agents, and the manipulation of radio transmissions.

## The Linguists' Arsenal: Methods of Deception

At the heart of this intelligence effort were the linguists, whose skills in German language and culture made them invaluable assets. These individuals, often recruited from academic backgrounds or from among those who had lived in Germany before the war, brought a nuanced understanding of German military jargon and communication patterns.

The linguists employed several sophisticated techniques to deceive Luftwaffe pilots:

**1. Linguistic Mimicry:** By carefully studying intercepted German communications, British linguists could mimic the speech patterns, accents, and idiomatic expressions used by Luftwaffe pilots and ground controllers. This allowed them to create convincing false transmissions that could be seamlessly integrated into German radio traffic.

**2. False Information Dissemination**: Linguists crafted messages containing misleading information about weather conditions, the location of RAF squadrons, and the status of potential targets. This false intelligence was designed to confuse German pilots and lead them away from their intended objectives.

**3. Psychological Operations** (PsyOps): Leveraging their understanding of German culture and psychology, linguists created messages designed to demoralize enemy pilots. These could include exaggerated reports of Luftwaffe losses or false information about the effectiveness of British defenses.

**4. Interception and Manipulation**: Working closely with signals intelligence units, linguists helped intercept genuine German communications. They could then use this information to craft more convincing deceptive messages, often responding to real German transmissions with false information.

**5. Creation of Phantom Squadrons**: In some cases, linguists helped create entire fictional RAF squadrons, complete with false radio chatter. This tactic was designed to make the Luftwaffe overestimate the strength of British air defenses.

## The Battle of the Beams: A Linguistic Triumph

One of the most significant contributions of British linguists came in the form of the "Battle of the Beams." This operation involved British efforts to identify, locate, and develop countermeasures against German radio navigation systems. Linguists played a key role in intercepting and deciphering the communications related to these systems, allowing British forces to jam German signals and provide false navigation information.

By manipulating these navigation beams, British forces could mislead German bombers about their positions and targets. This deception was instrumental in disrupting bombing raids and protecting key British military and civilian targets.

## Impact and Immediate Aftermath

The impact of these linguistic deceptions was profound. By sowing confusion and doubt among Luftwaffe pilots, the British were able to disrupt German bombing patterns, reduce the effectiveness of their attacks, and ultimately contribute to the RAF's ability to maintain air superiority over Britain.

The success of these operations had an immediate effect on the course of the battle. German pilots, faced with seemingly contradictory information and unexpected challenges, found their missions increasingly difficult to execute effectively. This confusion, combined with the bravery of RAF pilots and the effectiveness of British radar and ground defenses, played a crucial role in thwarting the Luftwaffe's attempts to gain air supremacy.

By September 17, 1940, Hitler was forced to postpone Operation Sea Lion indefinitely, acknowledging the failure to gain the necessary air superiority for an invasion. The Battle of Britain officially ended on October 31, 1940, with the Luftwaffe having failed to achieve its objectives.

**Legacy and Long-term Impact**

The legacy of the linguistic deception operations during the Battle of Britain extends far beyond the immediate military success. These operations highlighted the critical importance of intelligence and deception in modern warfare, influencing military strategies for decades to come.

The techniques developed and refined by British linguists during this period laid the groundwork for subsequent operations in World War II, such as Operation Mincemeat and Operation Fortitude. These later operations used similar principles of deception to mislead the enemy about Allied intentions, most notably in the lead-up to the D-Day landings.

**Conclusion**

The story of the British linguists who fooled Luftwaffe pilots during the Battle of Britain is a testament to the power of intellect and innovation in warfare. Their ability to understand, mimic, and manipulate enemy communications played a crucial role in defending Britain against seemingly insurmountable odds.

**Sources**

Holland, James. The Battle of Britain: Five Months that Changed History, May – October 1940. St. Martin's Griffin, 2012.

Sarkar, Dilip. Battle of Britain Attack of the Eagles: 13 August 1940 – 18 August 1940. Air World, 2024.

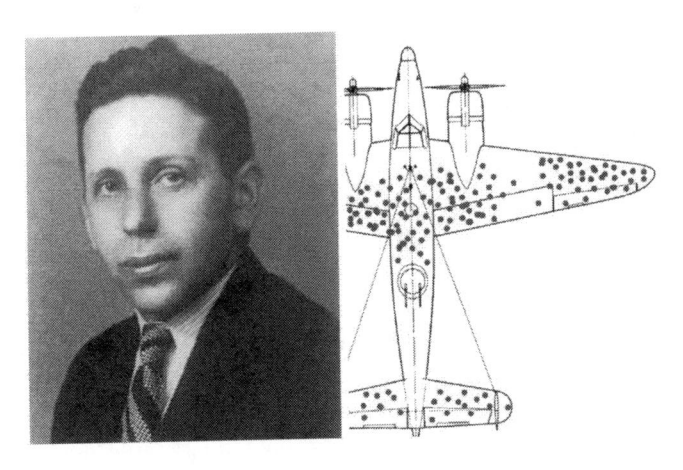

# Abraham Wald and the Armor Enigma

## Introduction

Few stories exemplify the power of innovative thinking quite like that of Abraham Wald and his revolutionary approach to aircraft armor design. Set against the backdrop of a global conflict that pushed the boundaries of technology and human ingenuity, Wald's tale is one of mathematical brilliance, counterintuitive reasoning, and the profound impact of statistical analysis on military strategy. This story explores the life of Abraham Wald, from his early days as a brilliant young mathematician in Europe to his crucial role in the Statistical Research Group during World War II, where his insights into survivorship bias would save countless lives and change the course of aerial warfare.

## A Mind Forged in Adversity

Abraham Wald's journey began far from the war rooms and aircraft hangars of World War II. Born on October 31, 1902, in Kolozsvár, Transylvania, then part of the Austro-Hungarian Empire, Wald entered the world as part of a Jewish family that valued education but faced significant societal limitations due to their faith. The young Wald's early education was unconventional by necessity; unable to attend school on Saturdays due to religious observance, he was homeschooled by his parents, laying the foundation for a brilliant academic career.

Despite the challenges posed by anti-Semitic discrimination, Wald's mathematical prowess shone through. He graduated from the University of Cluj in 1928 with a degree in mathematics, before pursuing further studies at the University of Vienna. It was here, under the tutelage of the renowned Karl Menger, that Wald earned his Ph.D. in mathematics in 1931, establishing himself as a rising star in the field.

However, the political climate of 1930s Europe cast a long shadow over Wald's career prospects. Despite his academic brilliance, he found himself unable to secure a university position due to prevalent anti-Semitism. This setback led him to the Austrian Institute for Economic Research, where he began applying his mathematical skills to economics, a twist of fate that would later prove crucial to his wartime contributions.

## Escape to a New World

As the specter of Nazism loomed larger over Europe, Wald's situation became increasingly precarious. The annexation of Austria by Nazi Germany in 1938 made it clear that he could no longer remain in his homeland. Fortune smiled upon him in the form of an invitation from the Cowles Commission for Research in Economics to come to the United States. Wald seized this lifeline, embarking on a journey that would not only save his life but also place him at the center of one of the war's most critical statistical challenges.

In the United States, Wald found a new home at Columbia University, where his unique blend of mathematical genius and economic insight quickly caught the attention of military planners grappling with the complexities of modern warfare. As the United States entered World War II, Wald was recruited into the Statistical Research Group (SRG), a classified program that brought together some of the finest minds in applied mathematics and statistics to tackle pressing military problems.

## The Armor Enigma

By 1943, the air war had reached a critical juncture. Allied bombers were suffering catastrophic losses on missions over Nazi-occupied Europe, and military commanders were desperate for solutions. The problem seemed straightforward: how to better protect aircraft from enemy fire. The initial approach was to analyze the bullet hole patterns on returning planes and reinforce the areas that showed the most damage.

It was here that Wald's unique perspective would prove invaluable. While others saw a simple matter of reinforcing damaged areas, Wald saw a classic case of survivorship bias. He realized that the military was only considering the planes that had survived to return home. The bullet holes in these aircraft represented damage that a plane could sustain and still fly. The truly vulnerable areas, Wald deduced, were those that showed no damage on returning planes – because aircraft hit in these areas simply didn't make it back.

## A Counterintuitive Solution

Wald's recommendation flew in the face of conventional wisdom: instead of armoring the areas showing the most damage, he advised reinforcing the areas that showed little or no damage on returning aircraft. His reasoning was elegant in its simplicity – the undamaged areas on returning planes were likely the points where a single hit would be catastrophic, preventing the aircraft from returning at all.

This insight was a classic application of survivorship bias, a logical error of concentrating on the people or things that made it past some selection process and overlooking those that did not, typically because of their lack of visibility. In this case, the selection process was survival, and the invisible data points were the downed aircraft that never returned.

Wald's approach was met with initial skepticism. It seemed counterintuitive to ignore the visible evidence of damage and focus on areas that appeared unscathed. However, the logic of his argument was undeniable, and military leaders, desperate for any advantage in the brutal air war, decided to implement his recommendations.

## Impact and Implementation

The impact of Wald's insight was profound and immediate. By focusing armor on the truly critical areas – engines, cockpits, and control systems – rather than on the more resilient sections of the airframe, aircraft survivability increased dramatically. Bomber losses decreased, more crews returned from their missions, and the effectiveness of Allied air power grew significantly.

This success was not just a triumph of mathematics over intuition; it represented a fundamental shift in how military planners approached problem-solving. Wald's work demonstrated the power of statistical analysis in military strategy and highlighted the importance of considering unseen data in decision-making processes.

## Beyond the War

Wald's contributions extended far beyond his work on aircraft survivability. His development of sequential analysis, a statistical method allowing for real-time decision-making as data is collected, revolutionized fields ranging from quality control to clinical trials. His work in decision theory, formalizing the process of making decisions under uncertainty, laid the groundwork for advances in economics, operations research, and even modern machine learning.

Tragically, Wald's life was cut short in 1950 when he died in a plane crash while traveling to India. The irony of his death in an aircraft accident was not lost on those who knew of his crucial work in improving aircraft survivability during the war.

## Conclusion

Abraham Wald's story is more than just a tale of mathematical brilliance; it is a testament to the power of innovative thinking in the face of complex challenges. His journey from a young Jewish mathematician facing discrimination in Europe to a key figure in the Allied war effort exemplifies the often unexpected paths that lead to world-changing innovations.

Wald's work on aircraft survivability not only saved countless lives during World War II but also left a lasting legacy in the fields of statistics, operations research, and decision theory. His ability to see beyond the obvious, to consider the unseen and the unrepresented, continues to influence how we approach problem-solving in various fields today.

## Sources

Wald, Abraham, Sequential Analysis. Dover Publications, 2013.

Mangel, Marc, Samaniego, Francisco J. Abraham Wald's Work on Aircraft Survivability. Journal of the American Statistical Association, 1984.

# The Navajo Code Talkers

**Introduction:**

During World War II, the United States faced unprecedented challenges in communication and intelligence, particularly in the Pacific Theater against Japan. To combat these challenges, the U.S. Marine Corps enlisted the help of a group of Native American soldiers known as the Navajo Code Talkers. This unique unit developed an unbreakable code based on the Navajo language, which played a crucial role in securing vital communications and contributing to the Allied victory. The story of the Navajo Code Talkers is one of bravery, ingenuity, and cultural pride, highlighting their significant yet often overlooked contributions to military history.

**The Navajo Nation**

The Navajo Nation, located in the southwestern United States, is one of the largest Native American tribes, with a rich cultural heritage and a complex social structure. The Navajo people, or Diné, have a deep spiritual connection to their land and a strong tradition of oral storytelling. Their language, a complex and nuanced tongue, was primarily spoken and had no written form, making it a unique asset for secure communication.

The Navajo language was not widely known outside their community, which made it an ideal choice for military encryption. When World War II erupted, many Navajo men were eager to enlist and serve their country, motivated by patriotism and a desire to prove their worth in a society that had often marginalized them.

**Recruitment of the Code Talkers**

In 1942, the U.S. Marine Corps began looking for ways to improve secure communications in the Pacific Theater, where the Japanese had proven adept at intercepting and decoding messages. Inspired by the success of the Choctaw code talkers in World War I, military officials sought to create a similar program using the Navajo language.

The recruitment of Navajo men for this initiative began in May 1942. Philip Johnston, a World War I veteran and son of a missionary who had lived among the Navajo people, played a crucial role in advocating for the use of the language as a military code. Johnston was fluent in Navajo and understood the potential of the language for secure communication. He proposed the idea to Marine Corps officials, who quickly recognized its value.

The Marine Corps enlisted 29 Navajo men to serve as the first group of code talkers. These individuals were trained in military operations and communications, and they developed a code that would serve as a vital asset in the war.

**Development of the Code**

The Navajo Code Talkers created a complex system that transformed words and military terms into a code based on the Navajo language. The code was developed on the principle of using existing Navajo words to represent military terms, geographical locations, and various phrases. For example, the Navajo word for "tortoise" was used to represent "tank," while "tiger" was used for "bomb."

Additionally, the Navajo language itself was inherently difficult for non-Navajo speakers to learn or understand. This complexity, combined with the unique code they developed, made their communications unbreakable.

The code talkers practiced their new system rigorously, ensuring that they could convey messages quickly and accurately in the heat of battle. They also developed a phonetic alphabet, allowing them to spell out names and unfamiliar terms. Their training emphasized speed and accuracy, as effective communication was critical for military operations.

**Deployment in the Pacific Theater**

The Navajo Code Talkers made their combat debut during the Battle of Guadalcanal in 1942. As the Marines faced fierce resistance from Japanese forces, the code talkers provided crucial support by transmitting messages securely and swiftly. Their ability to communicate in real-time allowed commanders to coordinate operations effectively and respond to changing battlefield conditions.

Throughout the war, the code talkers served in several key battles, including the battles of Tarawa, Saipan, Iwo Jima, and Okinawa. Their contributions were instrumental in the success of these operations. In the Battle of Iwo Jima, for instance, the code talkers transmitted over eight hundred messages in a matter of days, all without a single error.

Their presence on the front lines not only enhanced military communications but also fostered a sense of pride among the Navajo community. Many code talkers viewed their service as an opportunity to demonstrate the value and capabilities of their culture, countering stereotypes and prejudices that had persisted against Native Americans.

**Recognition and Challenges**

Despite their significant contributions, the Navajo Code Talkers faced challenges during their service. They often encountered prejudice and discrimination, both from within the military and society at large. However, their unwavering commitment to their country and their fellow soldiers helped them overcome these obstacles.

The code talkers operated under strict secrecy, and their contributions were not widely recognized during the war. The military kept their role confidential to maintain the effectiveness of the code. As a result, many code talkers returned home after the war without any formal acknowledgment of their service.

In 1945, the war ended, and the code talkers returned to civilian life. While they had played a crucial role in securing victory in the Pacific, their contributions remained unrecognized for decades.

## Post-War Recognition

It was not until the 1960s and 1970s that the contributions of the Navajo Code Talkers began to gain recognition. In 1968, the United States Congress passed a resolution honoring the code talkers for their service during World War II. The acknowledgment of their bravery and sacrifice marked a significant turning point in how Native American contributions to the war were viewed.

In 1982, the U.S. government officially recognized the Navajo Code Talkers by awarding them the Congressional Gold Medal, one of the highest honors bestowed by Congress. The ceremony was attended by many surviving code talkers and their families, symbolizing a long-overdue acknowledgment of their service and sacrifice.

In 2001, the last remaining code talkers were awarded the Congressional Silver Medal, further solidifying their legacy in American history. The recognition of their contributions helped to bring awareness to the broader struggles faced by Native Americans, highlighting their resilience and contributions to the nation.

## Cultural Impact

The story of the Navajo Code Talkers has inspired numerous books, documentaries, and films, ensuring that their legacy endures. Their experiences serve as a powerful reminder of the importance of diversity and the unique contributions that diverse cultures can bring to the fabric of society.

The Navajo Nation has also embraced their story, working to preserve their history and language. Efforts to educate younger generations about the significance of the code talkers and the Navajo language underscore the importance of cultural heritage and the need to honor those who served.

## Conclusion

The story of the Navajo Code Talkers is a powerful testament to the bravery and ingenuity of individuals who played a crucial role in securing victory during World War II. Their ability to create and implement an unbreakable code based on their native language highlights the resilience of the human spirit and the strength found in cultural heritage.

## Sources

Nez, Chester. Code Talker: The First and Only Memoir by One of the Navajo Code Talkers of WWII. Dutton Caliber, 2012.

Hoena, Blake. Navajo Code Talkers: Top Secret Messengers of World War II. Capstone Press, 2019.

# The Secret Capture: U-Boat U-110 and the Enigma Prize

## Introduction

Few events had as profound an impact on the course of the conflict as the capture of the German submarine U-110 and the seizure of its Enigma machine. This daring operation, which unfolded in the frigid waters of the North Atlantic on May 9, 1941, would prove to be a pivotal moment in the Battle of the Atlantic and, indeed, the entire war effort. The story of U-110's capture is one of bravery, quick thinking, and extraordinary luck – a tale that would remain shrouded in secrecy for decades after the war's end. This story explores the events leading up to the capture, the operation itself, and its far-reaching consequences, shedding light on a critical chapter in the Allied struggle against Nazi Germany's formidable U-boat fleet.

## The Enigma Machine: Germany's Unbreakable Code

At the heart of this story lies the Enigma machine, a device that had become the cornerstone of German military communications. Developed initially for commercial use, the Enigma was adopted and refined by the German military during World War II. Its complexity was staggering; with a system of rotors and plugboard, it offered billions of possible encryption combinations, making it seem virtually unbreakable.

The machine's operation was ingenious in its simplicity yet profound in its implications. Each keystroke triggered the rotation of the machine's rotors, changing the encryption scheme with every letter. This meant that even if the same letter appeared multiple times in a message, it would be encoded differently each time. The addition of a plugboard further scrambled the letters, exponentially increasing the number of possible configurations.

For the German military, particularly the Kriegsmarine (navy), the Enigma represented the pinnacle of secure communication. It allowed for the coordination of complex operations, including the dreaded U-boat wolfpack tactics that were wreaking havoc on Allied shipping in the Atlantic. The Germans believed their communications were impenetrable, a confidence that would prove to be their undoing.

## U-110: A Wolf of the Atlantic

U-110 was a Type IXB submarine, one of the larger and more formidable U-boats in the Kriegsmarine's arsenal. Commissioned on November 21, 1940, under the command of the experienced Kapitänleutnant

549

Fritz-Julius Lemp, U-110 was part of the 2nd U-boat Flotilla. In its brief operational career, the submarine had already proven its mettle, sinking three ships and damaging two others.

On what would be its final patrol, U-110 set out as part of a wolfpack, targeting Allied convoys in the treacherous waters of the North Atlantic. The submarine's crew, like their counterparts across the U-boat fleet, were buoyed by their recent successes and the seeming invulnerability provided by their Enigma-encrypted communications.

## The Hunt Begins

On May 9, 1941, U-110 found itself engaged in an attack on Convoy OB 318 south of Iceland. Unknown to Lemp and his crew, they were about to become the quarry rather than the hunters. The British convoy escort group, led by Commander Joe Baker-Cresswell aboard HMS Bulldog, included the destroyer HMS Broadway and the corvette HMS Aubretia.

As U-110 maneuvered to attack the convoy, it was detected by HMS Aubretia using ASDIC, an early form of sonar. What followed was a tense cat-and-mouse game beneath the waves, as the British ships sought to pinpoint and neutralize the threat lurking in the depths.

## The Fateful Depth Charge Attack

The British escort ships launched a series of depth charge attacks, the underwater explosions rocking U-110 and causing significant damage. Kapitänleutnant Lemp, faced with a rapidly deteriorating situation, made the difficult decision to surface the submarine. It was a move born of desperation, as the alternative was certain death for his entire crew.

As U-110 broke the surface, Lemp believed that the British ships were moving to ram his vessel. In the heat of the moment, he gave the order to abandon ship, a decision that would have far-reaching consequences. In their haste to escape what they thought was imminent destruction, the German crew left behind a treasure trove of intelligence, including the intact Enigma machine and its codebooks.

## The Boarding Party's Daring Mission

Commander Baker-Cresswell, displaying a remarkable presence of mind, quickly recognized the opportunity before him. Instead of sinking the U-boat, he ordered a boarding party to be assembled. Led by Sub-Lieutenant David Balme, a small team from HMS Bulldog prepared to board the abandoned submarine.

The boarding operation was fraught with danger. As Balme and his men approached U-110 in a small boat, they were acutely aware of the risks. The submarine could still be booby-trapped, or German sailors might be lying in wait to ambush them. Balme later described the experience as terrifying, his heart pounding as he descended into the silent, alien world of the enemy vessel.

## The Prize: Enigma Captured

What Balme and his team discovered aboard U-110 exceeded their wildest expectations. In the submarine's radio room, they found an Enigma machine, seemingly abandoned during operation. Alongside it were codebooks, charts, and other vital documents that would prove invaluable to Allied intelligence efforts.

The significance of this find cannot be overstated. For years, Allied cryptanalysts, including the brilliant minds at Bletchley Park, had been working tirelessly to crack the Enigma code. The capture of an intact machine, complete with its operational settings and codebooks, represented a quantum leap in their efforts.

## The Secret Kept

Recognizing the immense value of their prize, the British forces acted quickly to preserve the secrecy of their capture. U-110 was taken under tow, but it sank before reaching port, taking with it any evidence of the boarding operation. The Enigma machine and associated materials were spirited away to Bletchley Park, where they would play a crucial role in the ongoing efforts to break German codes.

The entire operation was shrouded in secrecy. A cover story was concocted, claiming that U-110 had sunk before it could be boarded. The German high command, unaware that their prized Enigma had fallen into enemy hands, continued to use the machine, confident in the security of their communications.

## The Impact: Turning the Tide of War

The capture of U-110's Enigma machine and codebooks had an immediate and profound impact on the war effort. At Bletchley Park, the new materials provided crucial insights that accelerated the process of breaking German naval codes. This intelligence breakthrough, codenamed "Ultra," allowed the Allies to anticipate and counter German naval operations with unprecedented effectiveness.

The results were dramatic. In the months following the capture, Allied shipping losses plummeted. From a staggering 432,000 tons lost in June 1941, losses dropped to less than 80,000 tons by August. This turnaround in the Battle of the Atlantic was critical, ensuring the vital supply lines between North America and Britain remained open.

The intelligence gained from decrypting Enigma messages influenced numerous aspects of the war effort. It allowed for more effective routing of convoys, avoiding U-boat concentrations. It provided insights into German military planning, influencing Allied strategy across multiple theaters of war. Some historians estimate that the breaking of the Enigma code shortened the war by as much as two years, potentially saving millions of lives.

## Recognition and Legacy

Due to the highly classified nature of the operation, the heroes of U-110's capture did not receive immediate recognition for their actions. It was only decades later, as the full story of the Enigma breakthrough came to light, that the significance of their achievement was publicly acknowledged.

Sub-Lieutenant David Balme, who led the boarding party, was eventually honored for his role in the operation. Commander Joe Baker-Cresswell's decision to capture rather than sink U-110 was recognized as a moment of strategic brilliance. The entire episode came to be seen as a testament to the bravery, quick thinking, and professionalism of the Royal Navy personnel involved.

## Conclusion

The capture of U-110 and its Enigma machine stands as one of the most significant intelligence coups of World War II. It exemplifies the often-overlooked role that individual acts of bravery and split-second decisions can play in shaping the course of history. The operation's success was a product of skill, daring, and no small amount of luck – a combination that would prove decisive in the Allied victory over Nazi Germany.

The story of U-110 also highlights the critical importance of intelligence in modern warfare. The ability to intercept and decrypt enemy communications proved to be a game-changer, demonstrating that in war, knowledge truly is power. The legacy of this operation extends far beyond World War II, influencing the development of cryptography, computer science, and intelligence gathering in the decades that followed.

**Sources**

Roskill, Stephen. The Secret Capture: U-110 and the Enigma Story. Naval Institute Press, 2011.

Loomis, Greg. U-110. Pawtuxet Editions, 2012.

# The Genius Who Broke Enigma

## Introduction

Alan Turing, a brilliant British mathematician and logician, made one of the most pivotal contributions to the Allied victory in World War II. His work in deciphering the Enigma machine, a complex German coding system, saved countless lives and shortened the war by an estimated two years. Despite his critical role, Turing's post-war life was marred by persecution due to his homosexuality, leading to tragic consequences. This story traces Turing's remarkable achievements at Bletchley Park, his contribution to breaking the Enigma code, and his heartbreaking treatment by the very government he helped save.

## Early Life and Education

Alan Turing was born on June 23, 1912, in London, England. From an early age, it was clear that Turing had an exceptional mind. His passion for mathematics, science, and logic set him apart from his peers, and by the time he attended King's College, Cambridge, his brilliance was undeniable. Turing quickly became known for his groundbreaking work in mathematical logic, and in 1936, at the age of 24, he published a paper that introduced the concept of the "Turing machine," a theoretical device that could simulate the logic of any computer algorithm. This work laid the foundation for modern computer science.

## The Enigma Machine and the Outbreak of World War II

As World War II broke out in 1939, the British government faced a significant challenge: how to break the German military's encrypted communications. The Germans used the Enigma machine, a sophisticated encryption device that allowed them to transmit messages securely. The machine had billions of possible settings and each day, the code settings changed, making it nearly impossible for the Allies to decode their communications.

The Germans believed that Enigma was unbreakable. However, the British government's cryptography team at Bletchley Park, a secret codebreaking center located about 50 miles north of London, was tasked with cracking it. Alan Turing was among the first to be recruited by the Government Code and Cypher School to work at Bletchley Park. His work would prove to be instrumental in turning the tide of the war.

## Turing's Work at Bletchley Park

At Bletchley Park, Turing joined a team of cryptanalysts who worked tirelessly to break the Enigma code. Previous work had been done by Polish mathematicians, who had made significant progress in understanding the machine before the war, but the Germans continually upgraded the Enigma's complexity, rendering previous efforts insufficient.

Turing approached the problem in a novel way. He theorized that, rather than trying to decipher every possible Enigma setting, they could focus on the "cribs"—common or predictable phrases the Germans used in their messages, such as weather reports or salutations like "Heil Hitler." Turing designed an electromechanical machine, known as the Bombe, to automate the process of testing these cribs against the daily Enigma settings. The Bombe sped up the decryption process, allowing the codebreakers to break Enigma more consistently.

The success of Turing's Bombe machine, along with his innovative use of probabilistic techniques, eventually led to the decryption of vast amounts of German communications. These decrypted messages, known as "Ultra" intelligence, provided critical information about German military operations, including U-boat movements in the Atlantic and the planning of key offensives.

## Impact on the War

The intelligence gathered from breaking Enigma had a profound effect on the outcome of the war. One of the most significant victories attributed to Turing's work was the Battle of the Atlantic. German U-boats had been wreaking havoc on Allied shipping, sinking vital supply convoys bound for Britain. By decrypting the U-boats' communications, Turing and his team provided the British Navy with the information needed to avoid or ambush the submarines, ensuring that supplies and troops could reach their destinations.

Ultra intelligence also played a pivotal role in the success of Operation Overlord, the D-Day landings in Normandy. By knowing the location and movements of German forces, the Allies could plan their invasion with greater precision, leading to the successful liberation of Western Europe.

Historians estimate that Turing's work at Bletchley Park shortened the war by at least two years and saved millions of lives. His contribution was so critical that Winston Churchill reportedly said that Turing made the single biggest contribution to the Allied victory in the war.

## Post-War Contributions:

After the war, Turing continued his work in mathematics and computer science. He was involved in the development of the first modern computers and wrote several papers that are now considered foundational to the field of artificial intelligence. Turing's vision of creating machines that could "think" would later become the basis for the development of artificial intelligence, and his famous "Turing Test" remains a benchmark for measuring a machine's ability to exhibit intelligent behavior.

## The Tragic Treatment by the British Government

In 1952, Turing's life took a devastating turn. Turing was a homosexual, and during this period in Britain, homosexuality was illegal. After reporting a burglary at his home, Turing inadvertently revealed his relationship with a man named Arnold Murray, which led to his arrest and prosecution for "gross indecency."

Rather than serve a prison sentence, Turing agreed to undergo chemical castration, a treatment involving hormone injections designed to reduce libido. The treatment had debilitating physical and psychological effects, and Turing's career was effectively ruined. He lost his security clearance and was barred from continuing his work with government agencies.

In 1954, at the age of 41, Turing died of cyanide poisoning. His death was ruled a suicide, though some have speculated that it may have been accidental. Regardless of the circumstances, Turing's death marked the tragic end of a life that had contributed immeasurably to science and the survival of the free world.

## Posthumous Recognition and Legacy

Decades after his death, Turing's achievements finally received the recognition they deserved. In 1966, the Turing Award was established by the Association for Computing Machinery, and it remains one of the most prestigious awards in the field of computer science. His work at Bletchley Park was declassified in the 1970s, and his role in breaking Enigma became widely known.

In 2009, after a public campaign led by historians and scientists, then-Prime Minister Gordon Brown issued a formal apology on behalf of the British government for Turing's treatment. In 2013, Turing was granted a royal pardon by Queen Elizabeth II. **Conclusion**

Alan Turing's work during World War II not only helped win the war but also laid the foundations for modern computing and artificial intelligence. His extraordinary intellect and relentless determination enabled the Allies to break the Enigma code, saving millions of lives and altering the course of history. However, the post-war treatment of Turing remains a tragic stain on his legacy, as the government he had helped protect turned on him for his sexuality.

## Sources

Turing Dermot. Alan Turing Decoded: The Man They Called Prof. The History Press, 2022.

Turing, Sir John Dermot. The Codebreakers of Bletchley Park: The Secret Intelligence Station that Helped Defeat the Nazis. Arcturus, 2020.

# Polish Mathematicians and the Enigma Code

## Introduction

The breaking of the Enigma code stands as one of the most significant achievements in the history of cryptography, playing a crucial role in the Allied victory during World War II. While the efforts of British codebreakers at Bletchley Park, particularly Alan Turing, are widely celebrated, the foundational work of a group of brilliant Polish mathematicians often remains in the shadows of history. This narrative explores the remarkable contributions of Marian Rejewski, Jerzy Różycki, and Henryk Zygalski, whose early breakthroughs in the 1930s laid the groundwork for the eventual decryption of the Enigma machine. Their story is one of ingenuity, perseverance, and international collaboration that changed the course of history.

## The Rise of the Enigma Machine

In the aftermath of World War I, as nations sought to protect their military communications, the Enigma machine emerged as a formidable tool of encryption. Initially developed for commercial purposes, the device was adopted and refined by the German military, becoming the cornerstone of their secure communications. The Enigma's complexity was staggering; with its system of rotors and plugboard, it offered billions of possible encryption combinations, making it seem virtually unbreakable.

The machine's operation was ingenious in its simplicity yet profound in its implications. Each keystroke would trigger the rotation of the machine's rotors, changing the encryption scheme with every letter. This meant that even if the same letter appeared multiple times in a message, it would be encoded differently each time. The addition of a plugboard further scrambled the letters, exponentially increasing the number of possible configurations.

As Germany began to rearm and expand its military capabilities in the 1930s, the threat posed by the Enigma machine became increasingly apparent to its neighbors, particularly Poland, which found itself in a precarious geopolitical position.

## Poland's Cryptographic Awakening

In the interwar period, Poland was acutely aware of its vulnerable position between Germany and the Soviet Union. The Polish government, recognizing the importance of intelligence in maintaining national security, established the Cipher Bureau, a specialized unit within the Polish General Staff's Second

Department. This bureau was tasked with both creating secure communication systems and breaking enemy codes, a mission that would prove crucial in the years to come.

The formation of the Cipher Bureau in 1931 marked a turning point in Poland's approach to cryptography. The bureau's leadership made a strategic decision to recruit mathematicians, recognizing that their analytical skills and understanding of complex systems could be invaluable in the field of cryptanalysis. This decision would prove to be prescient, leading to the selection of three brilliant young mathematicians who would change the course of history: Marian Rejewski, Jerzy Różycki, and Henryk Zygalski.

## The Polish Codebreakers: Early Lives and Education

Marian Rejewski, born on August 16, 1905, in Bydgoszcz, Poland, showed an early aptitude for mathematics. His education at the University of Poznań not only honed his mathematical skills but also introduced him to the emerging field of cryptography through a specialized course organized by the Polish General Staff's Cipher Bureau.

Jerzy Różycki, born on July 24, 1909, in Olszana, and Henryk Zygalski, born on July 15, 1908, in Poznań, followed similar paths. Both studied mathematics at the University of Poznań and, like Rejewski, participated in the cryptology course that would shape their future careers.

The education and early experiences of these three mathematicians were crucial in preparing them for the monumental task that lay ahead. Their training in mathematics, combined with their introduction to cryptography, provided them with the unique skill set necessary to tackle the complexities of the Enigma machine.

## The Breakthrough: Cracking the Enigma

In 1932, Marian Rejewski achieved what many had thought impossible: he reconstructed the internal wiring of the German military Enigma machine without ever having seen the device. This remarkable feat was accomplished through a combination of mathematical brilliance, innovative thinking, and a stroke of luck in the form of leaked Enigma operating manuals.

Rejewski's approach was groundbreaking. He applied permutation group theory to analyze the structure of Enigma messages, deducing the machine's internal workings through pure mathematical reasoning. This achievement laid the foundation for all subsequent efforts to break Enigma codes throughout the war.

Building on Rejewski's work, the Polish team developed several innovative techniques and tools to aid in their cryptanalysis. One of their key inventions was the "bomba," an electromechanical device designed to test various rotor settings of the Enigma machine. This machine significantly sped up the process of finding the correct settings, allowing the Poles to decrypt German messages with increasing efficiency.

Zygalski contributed to the effort with his invention of perforated sheets, known as "Zygalski sheets," which were used to determine the rotor settings of the Enigma machine. These sheets, when overlaid correctly, would reveal the day's Enigma settings, allowing for the decryption of intercepted messages.

The Polish codebreakers' success was remarkable. By 1938, they were able to read a significant portion of German Enigma traffic, providing valuable intelligence to the Polish government. However, as war loomed on the horizon, the Germans introduced additional complexities to the Enigma machine, making the Polish methods increasingly difficult to apply.

## Sharing the Secret: Collaboration with the Allies

As the threat of war grew more imminent, the Polish Cipher Bureau made a crucial decision that would have far-reaching consequences for the Allied war effort. Recognizing that their work might soon be lost if Poland were to fall, they decided to share their findings with their British and French allies.

In July 1939, just weeks before the outbreak of World War II, a secret meeting was held near Warsaw. Here, the Polish mathematicians revealed their Enigma decryption techniques and provided replicas of the Enigma machine to stunned British and French intelligence officers. This transfer of knowledge was a pivotal moment in the history of World War II cryptography.

The impact of this sharing cannot be overstated. It provided the British codebreakers at Bletchley Park with a crucial head start in their efforts to crack the wartime Enigma codes. Alan Turing and his team were able to build upon the Polish work, developing the more advanced "bombe" machines that would prove instrumental in keeping pace with the evolving German encryption methods.

## The Legacy of the Polish Contribution

The work of Rejewski, Różycki, and Zygalski had a profound impact on the Allied war effort. Their early breakthroughs and the subsequent sharing of knowledge with the British and French significantly accelerated the Allied ability to read German communications. This intelligence, codenamed "Ultra," provided crucial insights into German military plans and operations throughout the war.

The ability to decrypt Enigma messages played a vital role in numerous Allied victories. It was particularly crucial in the Battle of the Atlantic, where it helped protect Allied shipping from German U-boat attacks. The intelligence gained from decrypted messages also influenced key decisions in other theaters of war, including the preparations for the D-Day landings.

Historians estimate that the breaking of the Enigma code shortened the war by at least two years, saving countless lives in the process. Sir Dermot Turing, Alan Turing's nephew, has acknowledged that without the Polish contributions, the British might have taken much longer to achieve the same results, potentially altering the course of the war.

## Post-War Recognition and Legacy

Despite their crucial role, the contributions of the Polish mathematicians were not widely recognized until many years after the war. The secrecy surrounding the Enigma project and the political climate of the Cold War contributed to this oversight. Rejewski, who survived the war, returned to Poland and worked as an accountant, unable to speak about his wartime achievements for decades.

In recent years, efforts have been made to honor the work of the Polish codebreakers. Commemorative plaques, exhibitions, and academic studies have helped to bring their story to light. Their legacy serves as a powerful reminder of the importance of international collaboration in the face of global threats and the critical role that mathematics and cryptography play in national security.

## Conclusion

The story of the Polish mathematicians and their role in cracking the Enigma code is a testament to the power of human ingenuity, perseverance, and collaboration. Marian Rejewski, Jerzy Różycki, and Henryk

Zygalski, through their brilliant application of mathematics to cryptography, laid the foundation for one of the most significant intelligence operations of World War II.

Their work not only provided the Allies with a crucial advantage in the war but also revolutionized the field of cryptography. The techniques they developed and the machines they created paved the way for modern computer science and cryptanalysis.

**Sources**

Gawlowski, Robert. The First Enigma Codebreaker: Marian Rejewski Who Passed the Baton to Alan Turing. Naval Institute Press, 2023.

Perry, BP. The Polish Cryptographers Who Cracked the Enigma Code. History.co.uk.

Various Sources

# The Codebreaker Who Changed the Course of World War II

## Introduction

Few figures have played as pivotal a role in shaping the outcome of the Pacific Theater as Joseph John Rochefort. A brilliant cryptanalyst, linguist, and naval officer, Rochefort's work in breaking Japanese codes proved instrumental in the United States' victory at the Battle of Midway, a turning point that altered the course of the war. This story explores Rochefort's remarkable life, from his early naval career to his crucial contributions during World War II, and the belated recognition of his invaluable service to his country.

## Early Life and Naval Career

Joseph John Rochefort's journey began on May 12, 1900, in Dayton, Ohio. Raised in Los Angeles, California, young Rochefort displayed an early aptitude for problem-solving and complex games, foreshadowing his future career in cryptanalysis. In 1918, while still in high school, Rochefort made a decision that would shape the course of his life: he enlisted in the United States Navy, creatively adjusting his birth year to meet the age requirement.

Rochefort's naval career began with his enlistment as an electrician third class. Initially aspiring to join the Naval Reserve Flying Corps, he instead found himself transferred to the Naval Auxiliary Reserve in New York. There, he attended the Navy Steam-Engineering Training School at Stevens Institute of Technology in Hoboken, New Jersey, graduating in June 1919. This education led to his commission as a temporary ensign and his first significant naval role as the engineering officer on the tanker USS Cuyama.

It was during these early years that Rochefort's unique talents began to surface. His superiors noticed his skill in solving puzzles and playing complex card games like auction bridge. This aptitude led to a recommendation that would change the course of his career: Rochefort was selected to attend a Navy cryptanalysis class in Washington, D.C.

## The Path to Cryptanalysis

Rochefort's introduction to the world of codebreaking came under the tutelage of Captain Laurance Safford, and he had the opportunity to work alongside Agnes Meyer Driscoll, a renowned codebreaker of the time. This experience marked the beginning of Rochefort's journey into the secretive and crucial world of naval intelligence.

From 1926 to 1929, Rochefort served as the second chief of the Division of Naval Communications' newly created cryptanalytic organization, OP-20-G. This role further honed his skills in cryptanalysis and deepened his understanding of the critical role intelligence plays in naval operations.

Recognizing the growing importance of Japan in global affairs, the U.S. Navy made a strategic decision in 1929 that would prove crucial in the years to come. They sent Rochefort to Japan to study the Japanese language, a three-year immersion that lasted until 1932. This experience not only provided Rochefort with fluency in Japanese but also gave him invaluable insights into Japanese culture and mindset, assets that would prove critical during World War II.

Upon his return to the United States, Rochefort was assigned to the Office of Naval Intelligence in Washington, D.C. Throughout the 1930s, he alternated between intelligence work and sea duties, building a diverse skill set that combined practical naval experience with deep expertise in cryptanalysis and Japanese language and culture.

**World War II and the Battle of Midway**

As tensions in the Pacific escalated, Rochefort's unique combination of skills placed him at the center of U.S. naval intelligence efforts. In June 1941, he was appointed as officer in charge of Station HYPO, the Combat Intelligence Unit at Pearl Harbor. This assignment would lead to his most significant contribution to the war effort.

Following the devastating attack on Pearl Harbor on December 7, 1941, Rochefort and his team at Station HYPO intensified their efforts to break Japanese naval codes. Their primary focus was on JN-25, a complex "book" cipher system used by the Japanese Navy for operational communications.

Rochefort's approach to codebreaking was multifaceted and innovative. He and his team employed a combination of techniques, including:

1. Frequency analysis, examining the occurrence of letters or groups of letters to deduce underlying patterns in the code.

2. The use of IBM punch-card sorting machines to manage and analyze vast amounts of intercepted data, allowing for the identification of patterns and inferences about code groups.

3. Cross-referencing and contextual inference, comparing intercepted messages and using contextual clues to infer the meanings of specific code groups.

Perhaps Rochefort's most famous and impactful contribution came in the lead-up to the Battle of Midway. In May 1942, his team intercepted Japanese communications indicating a major operation targeting a location referred to as "AF." Rochefort deduced that "AF" likely referred to Midway Atoll, but he needed to confirm this hypothesis.

In a stroke of brilliance, Rochefort devised a clever ruse. He suggested sending a false message from Midway reporting a shortage of fresh water. When Japanese communications subsequently mentioned that

"AF" was experiencing a water shortage, it confirmed Rochefort's theory. This critical piece of intelligence allowed Admiral Chester W. Nimitz to prepare for the impending attack on Midway.

Rochefort's work faced skepticism from some quarters in Washington, who doubted his conclusions about the Japanese target. However, his direct communication with Admiral Nimitz, facilitated by Lieutenant Commander Edwin T. Layton, ensured that this vital intelligence reached the decision-makers who could act on it.

Armed with Rochefort's intelligence, Nimitz was able to position U.S. forces strategically, setting up an ambush for the Japanese fleet. The resulting Battle of Midway, fought from June 4 to June 7, 1942, was a decisive victory for the United States. The U.S. Navy sank four Japanese aircraft carriers and dealt a crippling blow to Japan's naval aviation capabilities, marking a turning point in the Pacific War.

**Aftermath and Controversy**

Despite the crucial role Rochefort played in the victory at Midway, his immediate post-battle career took an unexpected and disappointing turn. In a move that shocked many, Rochefort was reassigned from his cryptanalysis duties to command the floating dry dock ABSD-2 in San Francisco. This reassignment, widely viewed as a demotion, was influenced by internal Navy politics and personal vendettas, particularly from Admiral Ernest King, who reportedly had a personal dislike for Rochefort.

The reasons for this controversial decision were complex. Complaints from Commander John Redman about the operations at the Hawaii cryptologic station played a part, as did the influence of Redman's brother, Rear Admiral Joseph Redman. Rochefort found himself caught in the crossfire of internal Navy rivalries and became a scapegoat for the embarrassment of OP-20-G, the Navy's cryptologic organization.

Adding insult to injury, despite Admiral Chester W. Nimitz's recommendation for Rochefort to receive the Navy Distinguished Service Medal, the recommendation was rejected by Admiral King. King's objection was reportedly based on his perception of Rochefort as "one of the most unmilitary-looking officers he had ever encountered".

**Legacy and Belated Recognition**

While Rochefort's contributions went largely unrecognized during his lifetime, his legacy has since been firmly established. At the end of World War II, he was awarded the Legion of Merit, though this too came over Admiral King's objections.

It wasn't until long after his death that Rochefort received the full recognition he deserved. In 1985, he was posthumously awarded the Navy Distinguished Service Medal, and in 1986, he received the Presidential Medal of Freedom. These awards served as a testament to Rochefort's significant contributions to the U.S. Navy's success during World War II, particularly at the Battle of Midway.

Rochefort's legacy continues to be honored in various ways. In 2000, he was inducted into the National Security Agency's Central Security Service Hall of Fame. In 2012, the CAPT Joseph J. Rochefort Building was dedicated at the NSA facility within a Joint Base Pearl Harbor Hickam Annex, Hawaii, further cementing his status as a pivotal figure in naval cryptology.

## Conclusion

Joseph J. Rochefort's life story is one of brilliance, dedication, and perseverance in the face of adversity. His unique combination of skills – engineering expertise, cryptanalytic brilliance, and deep understanding of Japanese language and culture – made him an invaluable asset to the U.S. Navy during one of the most critical periods in American history.

Rochefort's work, particularly his role in the lead-up to the Battle of Midway, demonstrates the crucial importance of intelligence in modern warfare. His ability to piece together disparate bits of information, devise innovative strategies for confirming hypotheses, and communicate effectively with military leadership played a pivotal role in changing the course of the Pacific War.

## Sources

Carlson, Elliot W. Joe Rochefort's War: The Odyssey of the Codebreaker Who Outwitted Yamamoto at Midway. Naval Institute Press, 2013.

Kitchen, Commander Etta-Belle. The Reminiscences of Capt. Joseph J. Rochefort, USN (Ret): 1989-1976. Naval Institute Press, 2016.

# The Fall of Axis Ambitions: Analyzing the Failures of Hitler, Mussolini, and Japan

## Introduction

The ambitions of the Axis powers during World War II were grand and far-reaching, aiming for world domination through military conquest and ideological supremacy. Adolf Hitler's Nazi Germany sought to establish a totalitarian regime across Europe, Benito Mussolini's Italy aimed to recreate a Roman Empire, and Imperial Japan pursued dominance in East Asia and the Pacific. However, despite their initial successes, each of these powers ultimately failed in their quests. This story explores the multifaceted reasons behind these failures, examining strategic miscalculations, logistical challenges, and the resilience of their opponents.

## Background

The rise of the Axis powers was rooted in the socio-political turmoil following World War I and the Great Depression. Germany, humiliated by the Treaty of Versailles, experienced economic chaos and political instability. Hitler capitalized on these grievances, promoting a vision of German expansion and racial superiority. Mussolini, similarly, exploited Italy's post-war discontent, portraying fascism as a path to national rejuvenation. Meanwhile, Japan, driven by imperial ambitions and a desire for resources, embarked on military conquests in China and the Pacific.

By the late 1930s, these three nations had formed an alliance, believing that their combined strength could reshape the world order. However, their ambitions would soon collide with the realities of warfare, diplomacy, and the resilience of their adversaries.

## Hitler's Failure in Europe

Adolf Hitler's failure to achieve world domination can be traced to several critical miscalculations and strategic blunders. Initially, his rapid military successes during the early years of World War II, including the invasions of Poland, France, and the Low Countries, created an illusion of invincibility. However, these victories came at a cost, as they overstretched German resources and military capabilities.

One of Hitler's most significant errors was his decision to invade the Soviet Union in June 1941 in Operation Barbarossa. Driven by a mix of ideological zeal and strategic calculation, Hitler underestimated the Soviet Union's vastness, industrial capacity, and the resilience of its people. The harsh Russian winter caught the German forces unprepared, leading to catastrophic losses. The Battle of Stalingrad (1942-1943) marked a turning point, as the Soviet Red Army encircled and defeated the German Sixth Army, inflicting a devastating blow to Hitler's ambitions.

Additionally, Hitler's insistence on direct control over military strategy led to poor decision-making. His disregard for the advice of experienced military leaders resulted in a series of tactical blunders that contributed to Germany's eventual defeat. The failure to secure a quick victory in the East drained resources that could have been used to defend against the Allied counteroffensives in the West.

Furthermore, Hitler's ideology fueled his downfall. His racial policies alienated potential allies and incited fierce resistance among occupied populations. The brutality of the Nazi regime galvanized resistance movements in occupied territories, further draining German resources. The invasion of Allied forces in Normandy (D-Day) in June 1944 marked the beginning of the liberation of Western Europe, but by then, Germany was already on the defensive.

## Mussolini's Downfall

Benito Mussolini's quest for a new Roman Empire was equally fraught with challenges. His ambitions were evident in the invasion of Ethiopia in 1935 and military interventions in the Balkans. However, Mussolini's military strategies were often plagued by incompetence and underestimation of his adversaries.

One major factor in Mussolini's failure was Italy's lack of military preparedness compared to the other major powers. The Italian armed forces were poorly equipped, and their invasion of Greece in 1940 quickly turned into a debacle. The Greeks mounted a fierce resistance, pushing Italian forces back into Albania. This failure necessitated German intervention to stabilize the situation, further illustrating Italy's reliance on Nazi support.

Mussolini's alliance with Hitler also proved to be a double-edged sword. While it initially provided Italy with a sense of strength, it ultimately exposed the weaknesses of the Italian military. The Germans increasingly overshadowed Italian efforts in North Africa and the Balkans, leading to a loss of prestige for Mussolini. The failure of the Axis powers in North Africa culminated in the defeat at El Alamein in late 1942, marking a significant turning point in the North African campaign.

As the war progressed, Mussolini's grip on power weakened. The Allied invasion of Sicily in 1943 and the subsequent Italian armistice led to Mussolini's ousting and arrest. Although he was rescued by German forces, his regime was effectively over. Mussolini's failure to secure a decisive victory and to maintain the loyalty of the Italian populace ultimately led to his downfall, culminating in his execution by Italian partisans in 1945.

## Japan's Quest for Dominance in the East

Japan's quest for dominance in East Asia was driven by a desire for resources and territorial expansion. The invasion of Manchuria in 1931 and subsequent aggression in China demonstrated Japan's imperial ambitions. However, Japan's expansionist policies led to fierce resistance and conflict with other powers, particularly the United States.

One critical miscalculation by Japanese leaders was the attack on Pearl Harbor in December 1941. While the attack aimed to cripple the U.S. Pacific Fleet and secure Japanese dominance in the Pacific, it galvanized American resolve and led to a full-scale war against Japan. The United States possessed vast industrial resources and manpower, which Japan could not match in the long run.

Japan's initial successes in the Pacific—including the capture of the Philippines and Malaya—were soon met with counteroffensives from the U.S. The Battle of Midway in June 1942 marked a decisive turning point, as American forces inflicted significant losses on the Japanese navy, shifting the balance of power in the Pacific. The subsequent island-hopping campaign by the Allies further eroded Japanese territorial gains.

Additionally, Japan's military strategy was hampered by logistical challenges and overextension. The vast distances of the Pacific theater made supply lines vulnerable, and as the Allies recaptured key islands,

Japan found itself increasingly isolated. The inability to secure resources from conquered territories further weakened Japan's war effort.

Moreover, Japan's harsh occupation policies alienated local populations in occupied territories, fostering resistance movements. The brutal treatment of prisoners of war and civilians led to widespread resentment, complicating Japan's efforts to maintain control over its empire. The eventual use of atomic bombs on Hiroshima and Nagasaki in August 1945 forced Japan to surrender unconditionally, marking the end of its imperial ambitions.

**Conclusion**

The failures of Hitler, Mussolini, and Japan in their quests for domination during World War II can be attributed to a combination of strategic miscalculations, logistical challenges, and the resilience of their adversaries. Hitler's overreach in the Soviet Union, Mussolini's military incompetence, and Japan's underestimation of American resolve all contributed to their ultimate defeat.

The consequences of their failures were profound, reshaping the global order and leading to the establishment of international institutions aimed at preventing future conflicts. The lessons learned from the Axis powers' ambitions continue to resonate, serving as a reminder of the dangers of totalitarianism, militarism, and imperialism. As the world reflects on this dark chapter in history, it is essential to remember the sacrifices made by those who resisted tyranny and fought for freedom, ensuring that the horrors of the past are not repeated.

# The "What If" Game and Alternate Historical Outcomes of WWII

## Introduction:
Alternate history scenarios can serve as intriguing exercises to understand the impact of historical events. By speculating on what might have happened if Japan had not bombed Pearl Harbor, if the United States had remained neutral, and if Nazi Germany had won WWII, we can explore how different wartime outcomes could have reshaped the world.

## Scenario 1: Japan Does Not Bomb Pearl Harbor
If Japan had chosen not to attack Pearl Harbor, the United States might have delayed its entry into World War II. Without the direct provocation, American isolationist sentiment, which was significant then, could have prevailed for a more extended period. This delay in U.S. involvement could have allowed the Axis powers to consolidate their gains in Europe and Asia, potentially leading to a prolonged war or different diplomatic outcomes.

## Scenario 2: The United States Remains Neutral
A United States that maintained neutrality would have significantly affected the Allied logistical support. The Lend-Lease program, which provided critical support to the Allies, mainly to Britain and the Soviet Union, may never have been implemented to its full extent. This could have weakened the Allied resistance against the Axis powers, potentially altering the outcome of battles or campaigns.

## Scenario 3: Nazi Germany Wins WWII
A victorious Nazi Germany would have implemented its vision of a New Order, profoundly affecting the political, social, and economic landscape of Europe. The continuation of the Holocaust and the further implementation of genocidal policies would have resulted in an even more tragic loss of life. Europe might have become a continent dominated by totalitarian regimes, with the German Reich exerting control over vast territories.

## Implications for the Post-War World:
In a world where these alternate scenarios played out, the global geopolitical landscape would be vastly different:

**European and Asian Geopolitics:** Without U.S. intervention, the map of Europe and Asia could have been redrawn according to the territorial ambitions of the Axis powers. This could have resulted in a German-dominated Europe and a Japanese imperial sphere of influence in Asia.

**The Cold War:** The dynamic of the Cold War, assuming it would still occur, could have been vastly different, with the U.S. and the weakened Soviet Union potentially facing stronger Axis powers rather than each other.

**Decolonization:** The process of decolonization might have been delayed or taken a different course, as European colonial powers would have been weakened or absent, potentially leaving a power vacuum in their former colonies.

**Technological and Economic Development:** The United States, having focused on domestic affairs, might have had a delayed technological boom without a wartime economy and the innovations it spurred. Conversely, Germany's focus on advanced weaponry and engineering might have continued to advance, potentially leading to a different pace and direction of global technological progress.

**Global Institutions:** The formation of the United Nations and other international bodies might have been prevented or delayed, potentially resulting in a world with less emphasis on international cooperation and human rights.

**Conclusion:**
The scenarios described above represent just a glimpse into the vast possibilities that could have arisen from different outcomes in World War II. It is essential to recognize that these speculations are based on historical knowledge but are not definitive portrayals of what would have occurred. History results from complex and often contingent events and small changes could have produced disproportionately large and unpredictable effects. The value in exploring these "What if" scenarios lies in the opportunity to reflect on the fragility of historical outcomes and the profound impact that key events have had on shaping our world.

**Sources:**

Young, James. Acts of War: A World War II Alternative History. Independently published, 2021.

Bresnahan, Jim, Refighting the Pacific War: An Alternative History of World War II. Naval Institute Press, 2011.

Made in the USA
Columbia, SC
06 February 2025